THE SOFTWARE PUBLISHERS ASSOCIATION

LEGAL GUIDE TO MULTIMEDIA

Thomas J. Smedinghoff

Addison-Wesley Publishing Company
Reading, Massachusetts • Menlo Park, California • New York
Don Mills, Ontario • Wokingham, England • Amsterdam
Bonn • Sydney • Singapore • Tokyo • Madrid • San Juan
Paris • Seoul • Milan • Mexico City • Taipei

Many of the designations used by manufacturers and sellers to distinguish their products are claimed as trademarks. Where those designations appear in this book, and Addison-Wesley was aware of a trademark claim, the designations have been printed in initial capital letters or all capital letters.

The authors and publishers have taken care in preparation of this book, but make no expressed or implied warranty of any kind and assume no responsibility for errors or omissions. No liability is assumed for incidental or consequential damages in connection with or arising out of the use of the information or programs contained herein.

The publication is sold with understanding that the author and the publisher are not engaged in rendering legal, accounting, or other professional service. Changes occur in legal matters and in the interpretation of law. Some legal matters are subject to opinion and judgment rather than hard and fast rules. Therefore no written material on the law can render a warranty of the completeness or accuracy of its contents. If you require legal, accounting, or other expert assistance, you should consult a professional advisor.

Library of Congress Cataloging-in-Publication Data

Smedinghoff, Thomas J., 1951–
    The Software Publishers Association legal guide to multimedia /
    Thomas J. Smedinghoff.
        p.   cm.
    Includes index.
    ISBN 0-201-40931-3
    1. Multimedia systems—Law and legislation—United States.
    2. Software protection—Law and legislation—United States.
    3. Multimedia systems industry—Law and legislation—United States.
    I. Software Publishers Association.   II. Title.
    KF390.5.C6S59   1994
    346.7304'8—dc20
    [347.30648]   94-12959
                                                                                      CIP

Sponsoring Editor: Philip Sutherland
Project Manager: Eleanor McCarthy
Production Coordinator: Lora L. Ryan
Cover design: Barbara T. Atkinson
Set in 11 point Palatino by Miracle Type

1 2 3 4 5 6 7 8 9 -MA- 987969594
First printing, October 1994

Addison-Wesley books are available for bulk purchases by corporations, institutions, and other organizations. For more information please contact the Corporate, Government and Special Sales Department at (800) 238-9682.

To my wife, Mary Beth,
and our children
Mark, Anne, Regina, and Joan

ABOUT THE AUTHOR

Thomas J. Smedinghoff is a partner in the Chicago law firm of McBride, Baker & Coles where he co-chairs the firm's Information/Technology Law Department. A former computer systems analyst, Mr. Smedinghoff has concentrated in technology-related law since 1978, representing software firms, multimedia developers, and publisher's, electronics firms, and other businesses in dealing with the unique legal issues involved in the development, protection, marketing, and use of new technologies, and the issues of electronic commerce. He also serves as intellectual property counsel to the Software Publishers Association.

Mr. Smedinghoff is vice-chairman of the EDI and Information Technology Division of the Section of Science and Technology of the American Bar Association, and is the author of two other books: the *SPA Guide to Contracts and the Legal Protection of Software* (Software Publishers Association, 1993), and *The Legal Guide to Developing, Protecting and Marketing Software* (John Wiley & Sons, Inc., 1986). He is also a member of the editorial Advisory Panel of *The John Marshall Journal of Computer and Information Law* (published by the Center for Computer/Law and The John Marshall Law School) and the Board of Editors of *The DataLaw Report* (published by Clark, Boardman Callaghan). He is an adjunct professor of computer law at The John Marshall Law School.

He can be reached at McBride Baker & Coles, 500 West Madison Street, 40th Floor, Chicago, Illinois 60661-2511. Phone: 312-715-5700. Fax: 312-993-9350. America Online: TJSmed; AT&T Mail: !Smedinghofft; Compuserve: 70403,1300.

CONTENTS

PART 1

THE LAW OF MULTIMEDIA

PART 5

CHECKLISTS AND SAMPLE AGREEMENTS

PART 6

APPENDICES

FOREWORD

The multimedia revolution is not only here; it is flourishing. The recent introduction of powerful new personal computers with triple or quadruple speed CD-ROMs has spawned new software that touches virtually every human endeavor, from interactive entertainment to medical and surgical procedures. The startling capacity of CDs is making it possible for computer users to have access to vast amounts of information in digital form. This information, commonly called "content," comes from nearly a dozen industries with myriad acquisition and licensing practices. The procedures for including photographs is different from that involved in obtaining video, recorded music, or animation.

The SPA's Legal Guide to Multimedia is the first truly comprehensive guide to the legal issues involved in development, protection, and distribution of multimedia products. The SPA supported the development of this work because our members have struggled through new legal minefields in an effort to bring multimedia products to market. This book is not intended to become shelfware—a nice looking reference book that is rarely consulted. Instead, Tom Smedinghoff has successfully blended important legal principles with sage practical advice for developers of multimedia software intended for any market or discipline. Don't let this book wander too far. If you are serious about the issues involved in merging code and content, you will want this guide to be nearby.

On behalf of the SPA's staff and 1,100 member companies, we would like to congratulate Tom Smedinghoff for a fine job at making complex issues easier for the non-lawyer to understand. Now let's get to work and learn how to clear content, protect it, and build software products that bring the power of the information age home to everyone.

Ken Wasch
Executive Director
Software Publishers Association

ACKNOWLEDGMENTS

I would like to gratefully acknowledge the assistance of my partners and colleagues who have so generously given of their time to help in the preparation of this book. In particular, I would like to thank Elizabeth S. Perdue for her assistance in the preparation of the trademark, publicity, privacy, and defamation material; Lorijean Oei, for her assistance in the preparation of the motion picture licensing and entertainment material; Susan Alexander, for her assistance in the preparation of the music licensing material; Sara Pace, for her assistance in the preparation of the defamation material; and Lela Crockett, for the many hours she spent typing and editing the manuscript.

GUIDE TO USING THIS BOOK

The purpose of this book is to provide practical, understandable, and useful information on the current state of the law as it relates to multimedia. It is designed to help you to recognize and deal with the legal issues you will inevitably face when developing and marketing multimedia, and to help you ensure that your interests are adequately protected.

This book is written for multimedia developers, publishers, and their attorneys, and seeks to provide a single, comprehensive explanation of the basic legal concepts and issues relevant to the development, protection, and distribution of multimedia products. It is my intent that it will serve as a guide to making business decisions by helping readers to recognize the legal issues they face in a given situation, and to more fully understand their options and the consequences of their actions. The text is written for the nonlawyer, but extensive citations to authorities are provided for attorneys or other readers who would like to obtain further information.

This book is designed to be used in two ways: first, to be read cover-to-cover in order to gain a general understanding of the law that applies to multimedia; and second, to be used as a reference book to provide answers to specific questions. This will help you select a particular course of action, and will provide a background in the legal issues that will be invaluable when you deal with your attorney.

Each substantive area of the law has been set forth in one or two self-contained chapters, but there is often a significant interrelationship among what may appear to be separate distinct legal issues. Copyright law, for example, is critical to both content licensing and to protecting the multimedia works you create. In addition, it plays an important role in employee agreements and multimedia distribution contracts. Appropriate cross-references are provided to assist in understanding these relationships.

When reading any chapter, you should keep in mind that, although it may set forth a number of seemingly simple and straightforward rules, there are always exceptions and special circumstances that could change the result. It is somewhat like saying that it is against the law to kill someone. This is certainly true in most cases, but there are exceptions for self-defense, insanity, mistake, execution of a convicted criminal, and so forth. This book tries to indicate the main exceptions to any rule, but there are always other unique factual situations that will change the result. This is where the advice of an attorney familiar with the law applicable to multimedia can be invaluable.

You should also be aware that a number of the issues discussed in this book are governed by state rather than federal laws. In particular, the law relating to the rights of privacy and publicity, trade secret law, the law governing employer-employee relationships, and general contract law are all governed by state rather than federal law. This means, of course, that the rules differ somewhat from state to state. This presents something of a problem, since it is impossible in a book of this nature to thoroughly analyze the differences in the laws of all fifty states. Moreover, because the applicability of the law to multimedia products is so new, a number of the issues raised in this book are yet unresolved.

Accordingly, you should be aware that discussions of issues governed by state law frequently draw on whatever limited materials (that is, statutes and court decisions) are available, and thus may not completely cover all of the unique rules in any given state. Where the text refers to a California case for a particular proposition, for example, that may be the only case in the nation having been decided on that particular subject, or may be just an example of how one court of many has handled the problem. Therefore, it is entirely possible that a court in another state will reach (or perhaps already has reached) a different conclusion when faced with the same issue. It should be noted, however, that it is common for courts in one state to look to the decisions made in another state for guidance when an issue comes up for the first time. Thus, for example, it is entirely possible that a court in the state of Illinois will rely upon a California court's opinion in reaching a decision on a particular issue that has not previously been decided in Illinois. However, there is no assurance that this will occur.

This book presents the general legal principles as they have evolved to date. However, if you are contemplating taking particular action in reliance on those principles, you should consult with legal counsel in your state to determine whether the law varies in the state involved, whether the law has changed, or whether the unique facts of the transaction will alter the outcome.

It is assumed that you are familiar with the multimedia concepts and terms used throughout the book, so these are not explained in much detail. Because you are probably not familiar with all of the legal terms that have been used, however, a glossary has been included to provide definitions of those terms.

Many of the statements made throughout the book are annotated by endnotes following each chapter. They are included to indicate the authority for the referenced statement, or to provide additional information. They usually refer to the statute, government regulation, court opinion, or other authority on which the statement is based, in order to allow you or your lawyer to locate further information. The referenced material is available in most law school and county court libraries, and at a number of larger public libraries. This is of assistance to attorneys and anyone else researching a particular issue.

The endnotes are not necessary to an understanding of the text and can be totally ignored. However, because application of this law to multimedia is so new, it is important to provide citations to the material that is available. Explanations for most of the terms used in the citations can be found in the Glossary.

CHAPTER 1

Introduction: The Subject and the Legal Issues

1. Defining Multimedia

   1.1 What Is It?

      1.1.1 Software Plus Content

      1.1.2 In Digital Form

      1.1.3 Stored and Delivered Via Computer Technology

      1.1.4 Interactive and Nonlinear

   1.2 What Is It Used For?

2. What Law Applies to Multimedia?

   2.1 Legal Issues Relating to Multimedia Content

      2.1.1 Copyright Law

      2.1.2 Trademark and Unfair Competition Law

      2.1.3 Right of Publicity

      2.1.4 Right of Privacy

      2.1.5 Defamation Law

      2.1.6 Guilds and Unions

   2.2 Legal Issues Relating to Multimedia Technology

      2.2.1 Copyright Law

      2.2.2 Trade Secret Law

      2.2.3 Patent Law

Introduction: The Subject and the Legal Issues

The ability to store, transmit, and access text, data, sound, images, and other types of information in digital form has led to an explosion in the development of multimedia products. As a consequence, we are beginning to see the convergence of the computer, communications, entertainment, music, and publishing industries.

Just as multimedia relies on the combination of content and technology from a variety of industries, the legal issues raised by the development, protection, and distribution of multimedia products touch many different areas of the law. Moreover, because multimedia is such a new technology, the rules that govern the development, protection, and distribution of multimedia products will undoubtedly strain the capabilities of existing law to its limits. This book provides a practical guide to the legal issues that arise with respect to the development, protection, and distribution of this emerging digital medium known as multimedia.

1. Defining Multimedia

Understanding the legal issues relating to multimedia begins with a basic definition of the subject matter and the way it is used.

1.1 What Is It?

A **multimedia** product typically includes text, sounds, and images combined into an integrated product that is accessed interactively by a user via a computer or television screen. The user typically navigates through the multimedia title by pressing a key, clicking a mouse, or pressing a touch screen. The content for the multimedia product is typically created, copied, and adapted via a variety of software tools, sewed together using a software product known as an authoring tool, presented to the user via a user interface, and navigated by the user through the use of a software search engine or other software tool. Moreover, as the content is put together into the product, it is frequently altered, edited, enhanced, sampled, morphed, and otherwise revised or adapted using special software tools designed for this purpose. And as the content is stored within the multimedia title, additional technical requirements become important, such as links between content (e.g., hypertext), and compression techniques used to reduce the amount of storage required for the content.

From a legal perspective, the definition of multimedia includes four components: (1) a combination of software and multiple forms of content, (2) in digital form, (3) that are stored and delivered via computer technology, and (4) that are used in an interactive and nonlinear manner.

1.1.1 Software Plus Content.   Multimedia includes some combination of two or more of the following types of **content**: text, sound (such as spoken words, music, or sound effects), and visual images (such as still photographs, graphics, motion pictures, or animation), along with the **software** necessary to access, interact with, and navigate through the content.

The combination of software and multiple forms of content typically involves several different industries, such as the book publishing, music, motion picture, and computer software industries. This is particularly true where the multimedia developer uses a large variety of preexisting content and software instead of independently developing all of the content and software needed for the multimedia product. Each industry has developed its own set of rules, procedures, and practices with respect to the licensing and use of its material. As a consequence, putting together a multimedia product that involves the use of content from several different industries requires dealing with a wide variety of different rules.

Moreover, the problem of dealing with copyright owners in multiple industries is further compounded by the fact that a multimedia product typically involves the use of small segments of a very large number of different copyrightable works. It is not uncommon, for example, for a multimedia product to incorporate portions of over 1,000 different (and separately owned) copyrightable works. As a consequence, the difficulties of dealing with a number of different industry approaches to licensing are significantly compounded by the shear volume of licenses that may be required for a typical multimedia product.

The use of multiple forms of content is typically emphasized in definitions of multimedia. For example, popular books on the subject have defined multimedia as "any combination of text, graphic art, sound, animation, and video that is delivered by computer,"[1] "anything that uses more than one way to present information,"[2] or "the combination of two or more media."[3] However, this is not the sole defining characteristic of multimedia. If it were, then traditional movies (which combine sound and visual images) would be considered multimedia. Something more is required.

1.1.2 In Digital Form. All of the content and software that comprise a multimedia product exists in a digital machine-readable form. As a consequence, it is all the same. That is, unlike traditional text, photographs, motion pictures, and sound recordings, which represent distinctly different types of works to a casual observer and from a legal perspective, the digital representation of each of these types of works is identical —that is, it is a series of 1s and 0s recorded in a machine-readable format.

The digital nature of a multimedia work (and the content and software included within it) means that it can be easily copied, manipulated, edited, sampled,[4] adapted, morphed,[5] combined and distributed easily, quickly, and without the loss of any quality or resolution, and without any evidence of any changes or modifications. Since most of the digital information in a multimedia work is protected by copyright, storing it in a form that enhances and further facilitates the copying, adaptation, and distribution of this information necessarily creates new potential problems (or at least amplifies existing problems) for content owners and multimedia developers trying to protect their proprietary rights. This, of course, will present significant legal challenges for the future.

1.1.3 Stored and Delivered Via Computer Technology. Because of its digital format, a multimedia work is typically stored on either a magnetic or optical machine-readable medium (such as magnetic disks or optical compact disc read-only memory [CD-ROM] discs). While there is nothing magical about the form in which a multimedia work is stored, the immense storage requirements of digitized sound recordings, still images, and motion pictures often dictate that a high-capacity storage medium such as CD-ROM be used. However, for larger computer systems with access to voluminous on-line magnetic storage, there is no reason why disk or other randomly accessible magnetic media cannot be used.

Delivery of multimedia works typically takes two forms. The most common form of delivery for a single multimedia title is to use a tangible medium, such as a CD-ROM disc. A copy of both the multimedia work and the medium—the CD-ROM disc —on which it is stored is delivered to users, who then insert it in their own computer systems in order to access the multimedia work.

Alternatively, multimedia works can be delivered via a computer network or the land and wireless telephone, cable television, broadcasting, satellite, or other communications systems that have the capacity to deliver digital voice, data, image and video traffic to telephones, televisions, and computers. Transactions of this type typically do not involve the delivery of any tangible media (such as CD-ROMs), generally do not leave the user with a copy of the multimedia product, and are typically characterized by a pay-per-view or a subscription-based transaction. A good example is interactive television. The proposed National Information Infrastructure will presumably provide for the on-line delivery of multimedia works.[6]

A hybrid form of delivery, involving aspects of the two methods mentioned above, involves delivery of multimedia products via a local area network. In that case, a **copy** of the multimedia work is initially delivered to the owner of the local area network on a tangible media (typically a CD-ROM disc), and then made available over the network to users who will be able to access the product on demand, but will not retain a physical copy of it.

1.1.4 Interactive and Nonlinear.   In addition, two other attributes of multimedia are worth noting. First, most multimedia works are interactive—that is, the work typically requires some sort of input from the user, such as search queries, menu selections, answers, and so on, unlike traditional works such as movies and sound recordings where the user assumes a much more passive role. Second, multimedia works generally allow for what is called "nonlinear" access—that is, the user can jump around within the work, accessing those portions of the work that he or she desires to use, often linking directly to parts relevant to the section being viewed (e.g., as in hypertext), unlike traditional works, such as books, movies, and sound recordings, where the user is typically expected to read, view, or listen to the work from beginning to end.

1.2 What Is It Used For?

The uses for multimedia are endless. Numerous applications can be found in professional, business, educational, home computer, and consumer markets.

Professional applications for multimedia include creative design, advertising, graphic art design, music composing, desktop video production and publishing, simulation and modeling, diagnosis, and special effects creation.

Business applications for multimedia include retail point of sale merchandising, public access information, corporate communications and corporate presentations, interactive corporate publications, sales and marketing, trade show presentations, corporate training, electronic data interchange, cataloging, and archiving.

Educational uses for multimedia include computer-aided instruction, various educational products, interactive reference works, directories and encyclopedia, research and reference products, and electronic books.

Home computer applications include entertainment, home shopping, virtual reality, movies on demand, television on demand, catalog shopping, and games. Consumer multimedia products include various forms of multimedia games, television, sports, and video on demand, electronic photo albums, video home movies, interactive books, adult self-improvement, music appreciation, and travel information.

In short, the uses and applications for multimedia are virtually endless—limited only by the imagination of multimedia developers.

2. What Law Applies to Multimedia?

There is no single body of multimedia law. Instead the law applicable to the development, protection and distribution of multimedia works is found in a variety of traditional legal sources. These include copyright law (which has perhaps the biggest impact), trademark and unfair competition law, the law protecting one's right of publicity and privacy, defamation law, trade secret law, and patent law.[7] To understand the relevance of each of these areas of the law to the development of a multimedia work requires looking at the various components of the work and determining the nature of the component (i.e., is it software or content, and if content, what is the nature of the content?), and the identity of the person(s) creating the component and owning the rights to it.

The components of a multimedia work consist of a combination of content—the text, sound recordings, and visual images that the user reads, hears, and sees when using the product—and the software and other technology necessary to create and facilitate the use of the multimedia product (such as the authoring tools required to sew together the content that makes the multimedia work, the software that drives the user interface and supports the interactivity of a multimedia work, and the software search engines that allow users to move around within the multimedia title). Different areas of the law are involved, depending on whether you are dealing with the software and technology part of a multimedia title or the content that makes up the title itself. Moreover, different rules apply depending on the type of content you are dealing with, such as text, databases, musical works, sound recordings, photographs, or motion pictures.

You can personally create all of the content and software that comprise a multimedia title, you can employ other persons to do the work, or you can use preexisting materials created by someone else. In each case there are important issues of ownership and rights. For example, who owns the right in the work product created by you or by persons you hire? What rights do you have to use what you have created? What rights to copy, adapt, and distribute it, and what potential legal liability will result from your proposed course of action? Since you will frequently be using materials created by others, you need to understand how the law applies to multimedia so that you can obtain appropriate permissions, licenses, and releases in order to avoid liability for infringing upon the rights of others.

Whether you create your own content or use content created by others, similar questions arise with respect to the completed product. What rights do you have in the resulting product, and how do you protect those rights? You will want to use the legal means available to you to protect your rights in the product you have created, and to pursue those who have infringed or misappropriated your product. To do that, you need to ensure that you own (or at least have appropriate rights) to the product that you create.

In virtually every case, the law is a two-edged sword. Copyright law, for example, is the primary means of protecting your multimedia works (including the software and content comprising those works). On the other hand, it is important that you take great care to ensure that you do not infringe the copyrights of any other parties when developing your multimedia titles. The same is true of the other areas of law previously mentioned. That is, to the extent that the law helps you protect the multimedia works you create, you will also need to take care that in the creation process you do not infringe upon or misappropriate the rights of any other parties.

To help put into context the legal issues surrounding the development of a multimedia work, let us begin with an example. Suppose that you want to develop an interactive multimedia encyclopedia covering a wide variety of subjects. All topics to be covered would, of course, include text describing and explaining the subject. In addition, photographs and illustrations would be included where appropriate, and in some cases motion picture clips, television clips, and animation would also be included to show a historical event, illustrate a point, or further enhance the reader's understanding of the subject matter. Finally, sound recordings would be included, where appropriate. These might be statements or speeches made by individuals who are the subject of features in the encyclopedia, recordings of sounds made by various animals discussed in the title, performances of songs by artists featured in the work, or performances of music designed to illustrate the various periods of classical music.

In addition to the content that makes up the encyclopedia, it is necessary to include an appropriate user interface that allows users to easily access and navigate the various subjects of the encyclopedia, and a search engine to allow them to search for various topics.

What are the legal issues that you are likely to face in putting together a project of this type? To answer this question, we divide the issues into two categories: those relating to the content included in the multimedia title (i.e., the text, sound recordings, and visual images); and those relating to the software and other technology used to make the multimedia title "work" for the user.

2.1 Legal Issues Relating to Multimedia Content

2.1.1 Copyright Law.   All multimedia works, as well as the content incorporated within those works—for example, text, sound, and images—are automatically protected by federal **copyright** from the moment of their creation. Thus, copyright provides a valuable form of protection for the multimedia encyclopedia you create. At the same time, however, it can present a significant and serious obstacle to using content created by others, especially in the absence of permission from the owner of the copyright of the content.

Most of the content for the multimedia encyclopedia is copyrightable subject matter. This includes the text written to explain each of the subjects included, a collection of data about a particular topic, the pictures, drawings, photographs, and designs used for illustrative purposes, the motion picture film clips and videotape footage included in the work, and all of the sound recordings, including President Nixon's resignation speech, Martin Luther King's "I Have a Dream" speech, a recording of "The Star Spangled Banner," and sound recordings of things like bird calls, crowd noises, or the roar of an airplane engine. Accordingly, whoever owns the copyright to each of the multiple segments of content included in the encyclopedia controls the right to copy, adapt, distribute, display, and perform that particular content.

Although multimedia products can be (and in many cases are) originally created, a multimedia encyclopedia is likely to use at least some preexisting copyrighted content, such as text, pictures, film clips, animation, music, and sound recordings, as the building blocks of the product. A segment designed for children might, for example, use drawings or photographic images of *Sesame Street* characters, along with, perhaps, a short clip of a segment of one of the *Sesame Street* television broadcasts. A segment on movie production might incorporate a clip from a popular film (such as *Jurassic Park*). And a segment on music might include a recording from a recently released popular song.

Unless this content is in the public domain, or is available via the doctrine of fair use, copyright issues become very important. Copying preexisting content into a multimedia work, combining, editing, revising, sampling, morphing, and otherwise adapting the content, and distributing or publicly displaying the resulting product, constitute copyright infringement unless the content has been properly licensed from the copyright owner.

Some content is in the public domain. For example, you can use a copy of the words that make up the Declaration of Independence without obtaining anyone's permission. But public domain is not as simple as it looks. A photograph of the original Declaration of Independence, for example, is copyrighted, and use of the photograph would be prohibited without permission. Similarly, while the Bible is in the public domain, a new translation is copyrightable. And while Shakespeare's plays are in the public domain, a movie depicting a scene from one of those plays is clearly copyrightable.

Sometimes portions of copyrightable content can be used without permission in circumstances where the use constitutes a "fair use." But fair use is also a difficult and ill-defined concept, and not likely to apply if the encyclopedia is being developed for commercial distribution.

Normally, it will be necessary to obtain appropriate permissions from the copyright owners of any preexisting copyrightable content to be incorporated in the encyclopedia. And the permissions must cover the particular use that you contemplate. Thus, for example, if you want to edit some text on a particular subject to shorten it so that it will fit on the screen, or you would like to alter a picture or modify a sound recording, permission to make these adaptations is required. Permission to use and/or distribute the original content is not sufficient.

In addition, it is important to understand that in most cases, much of the preexisting content you want to use contains several overlapping copyrights, and permissions will need to be obtained from all of the copyright owners involved. A sound recording of a popular song, for example, includes a copyright in both the musical composition and the sound recording itself, and each of these copyrights is likely to be owned by different persons.

If you decide to create your own content, there are other copyright implications to consider. For example, if you hire someone to write text on a particular subject, you need to examine the rules relating to who owns the copyright in the resulting text, and if the result is not acceptable to you, you need to modify that result contractually. And, of course, you always need to be sure that the process of creating your own content does not infringe the copyrights of others. For example, while you can hire your own singer to perform a popular song (thereby eliminating the need to obtain permission to use a sound recording created by another artist), you will still need permission from the owner of the copyright in the song itself, or the performance you have created will also be considered infringing.

You also need to consider taking appropriate steps to protect the copyrightable works that you create. These include not only the multimedia product itself, but any content that you create for use in the multimedia product. Protecting those copyrights involve not only ensuring that you are the owner, but also involve the use of a proper copyright notice and registration with the Copyright Office.

2.1.2 Trademark and Unfair Competition Law.   **Trademark** law will impact the multimedia encyclopedia in a number of ways. The animated characters displayed in a segment on cartoons (such as Mickey Mouse, Bugs Bunny, and the Pink Panther) are all protected by federal trademark law (as well as copyright law). Similarly, the sound recording of the commercial jingle that you may want to use in a segment on advertising may also be a registered trademark.

If you use someone's trademark in the content that you develop or license, you need to consider whether it is likely to constitute trademark infringement or unfair competition. For example, you may have a problem if you use the trademark in a manner that implies that your multimedia product is created by, associated with, or endorsed by the owner of the trademark. This is particularly true if you use the trademarks of others as part of the title of your multimedia work, as this might cause the public to somehow relate the multimedia work to the owner of the trademark or its products (such as by assuming that both works were created by the same person or entity, the creator of the first work has endorsed the second work, or the second work is a substitute for the first work).

And, of course, there is the issue of what name do you give to your product. While calling it "Encarta" may sound like a good idea, that's one that is probably best avoided, in light of the use of this name by Microsoft Corporation. Ideally, you should come up with an original trademark to use when marketing your multimedia encyclopedia. In that case, you will want to take appropriate steps to ensure that the trademark you choose is protectible and that you have properly registered and perfected your rights to the trademark.

Related to trademark law is the law of unfair competition, which can have a significant impact on the way in which the content is displayed within your multimedia work, or the way in which the work itself is marketed. For example, it has been suggested that sampling a portion of a song by a popular recording artist without appropriate permission, and including the sample within a multimedia work, constitutes unfair competition to the extent that it implies that the recording artist is affiliated with or has somehow endorsed the multimedia product in which the sample is used.

2.1.3 Right of Publicity.   Does the content include the image, likeness, or voice of any celebrities, public figures, or other well-known persons? Whenever the name, image, or voice of a person is included in the multimedia encyclopedia, this raises potential issues relating to that person's rights of publicity and privacy, as well as the right to be free from defamation.

In creating multimedia works, you need to be aware of, and avoid infringing, other people's **rights of publicity.** These are rights people have in their persona and identity, such as their name, image, likeness and voice. Thus, the right of publicity may become important whenever you use a photograph, movie clip, or other image or likeness of an identifiable public person, the voice of an identifiable public person, or the name of a public person.

2.1.4 Right of Privacy.

Does the content used in the encyclopedia incorporate the image, likeness, or voice of, or make reference to, any living person or allegedly fictional person that is readily comparable to a living person? If so, it is important to take particular care that its use does not place such person in a false light, not misappropriate the person's name or likeness for a commercial purpose, not disclose embarrassing private facts about the person, and not intrude upon the person's solitude, as this may give rise to an action for infringement of the right of privacy. This is so even though the information may be completely true and accurate.

Whenever a multimedia work incorporates a name, photograph, or other reference to a person, you need to ensure that there is no infringement of that person's **right of privacy.** The right of privacy protects against personal embarrassment and intrusion. It can arise in a variety of ways. Using a stock photograph of a woman to illustrate an article about mothers who abandon their children, for example, has been found to infringe her right of privacy.

2.1.5 Defamation Law.

If the content used in the encyclopedia incorporates the image, likeness, or voice of, or makes reference to, any living person or allegedly fictional person that is readily comparable to a living person, it is also important to take particular care that it does not include false and defamatory statements about the person, as they may give rise to an action for defamation.

A **defamatory** communication is one that is false and injurious to the reputation of another, if made with the requisite intent. It can arise not only when you make a false statement about a person, but also in a variety of other ways, such as when you juxtapose a photograph with certain text that is defamatory in relationship to the photograph.

2.1.6 Guilds and Unions.

If any of the preexisting content that will be incorporated in a multimedia product was created using union talent, the union contract may have reserved the right to certain payments as a condition of using the content in a market other than that for which it was originally developed. In many cases, this may involve payments to several unions.

2.2 Legal Issues Relating to Multimedia Technology

The second set of legal issues relates to the multimedia technology—that is, the software used in multimedia products. It includes not only copyright law, but also trade secret and patent law.

2.2.1 Copyright Law.   All software used to develop a multimedia product (authoring tools, editing tools, etc.), as well as the software incorporated within the completed product (the run-time software, software controlling the user interface, search engine, etc.) is copyrightable. As such, you face many of the same copyright issues as you do regarding copyrightable content. In addition, copyright issues may also arise with respect to the format in which the data is represented, and the structure, sequence, and organization of the multimedia title itself.

2.2.2 Trade Secret Law.   The process of developing a multimedia work may result in the creation of valuable **trade secrets** that you would like to protect. In addition, it may require the use of trade secrets owned by others. Any confidential business or technical information that gives its owner an economic advantage over those who do not have the information can constitute a trade secret. Such trade secrets typically relate to the technology used in the development of the multimedia title. They may also relate to the nature of an unreleased title itself, or the technology behind the authoring tools used to create it, the search and retrieval engine developed for user interaction, or compression techniques used to reduce storage requirements.

Like copyright, trade secret rights are automatically obtained and can prove highly valuable if properly protected. On the other hand, you will need to take care that you do not misappropriate trade secrets lawfully belonging to other parties in the development process.

2.2.3 Patent Law.   As of November 1993, **patent** law became a potentially important consideration for multimedia producers. The announcement by Compton's NewMedia of its patent for a multimedia search process highlighted the fact that multimedia developers need to concern themselves with whether the processes incorporated within their multimedia works infringe the patents of any third party.[8] See chapter 9, section 2.

Patents are most likely to apply to the manner in which a multimedia product functions, or the underlying technology that supports its operation. As with other legal areas, you will need to concern yourself both with ensuring that you do not infringe the patents of any third party, and also with considering whether you have developed any patentable inventions for which filing may be appropriate.

ENDNOTES

1   TAY BAUGHAN, MULTIMEDIA: MAKING IT WORK (1993).

2   LINDA E. TWAY, WELCOME TO MULTIMEDIA (1992).

3   JEFF BURGER, THE DESKTOP MULTIMEDIA BIBLE (1993).

4   Digital **sampling** (of music) has been described as "the conversion of analog sound waves into a digital code. The digital code that describes the sampled music . . . can then be re-used, manipulated or combined with other digitalized or recorded sounds using a machine with digital data processing capabilities, such as a . . . computerized synthesizer." *Jarvis v. A & M Records*, 27 U.S.P.Q.2d 1812, 1813 (D.N.J. 1993). Sampling also refers to the process of copying a portion of a sound recording in a digital form for subsequent editing and/or incorporation in a new work.

5   **Morphing** (short for metamorphosis) is a process that involves a transition of two documents (such as pictures) into a third; a dynamic blending of two still images creating a sequence of in-between images that, when played back rapidly, metamorphoses the first image into the last.

6   The current efforts to promote the development of an integrated and affordable "infrastructure" of data networks and highways known as the National Information Infrastructure (NII) will allow ready access to digitized voice, data, image, and video information. By using telecommunications networks, cable television, broadcasting, satellite, and computers, the NII will provide such services as video-on-demand, high-speed data transfer, and video-conferencing.

7   A summary of each of these areas of the law is provided in chapters 3 through 9.

8   The grant of this patent was subsequently reversed by the Patent Office on the basis of prior art. But that decision has been contested by the patent holders. As of August 1994, the issue has not been finally resolved. However, regardless of the final outcome, it demonstrates the type of multimedia processes that can be patentable (assuming they represent new inventions).

CHAPTER 2

Roadmap to the Law of Multimedia

1. The Law Applicable To Components of Multimedia
   - **1.1** Text
   - **1.2** Databases
   - **1.3** Characters
   - **1.4** Musical Works
   - **1.5** Sound Recordings
   - **1.6** Pictures and Still Images
   - **1.7** Motion Pictures and Other Audiovisual Works
   - **1.8** Software and Other Technology
   - **1.9** Completed Multimedia Products
2. Obtaining the Content
   - **2.1** Copyright
   - **2.2** Trademark
   - **2.3** Right of Publicity
   - **2.4** Right of Privacy
   - **2.5** Defamation
   - **2.6** Unions
3. Obtaining the Technology
   - **3.1** Copyright
   - **3.2** Trade Secret
   - **3.3** Patent

Roadmap to the Law of Multimedia

There is no single body of "multimedia law." Instead, the law applicable to the development, protection, and distribution of multimedia products is found in a variety of traditional legal sources. These include copyright law, trademark and unfair competition law, the law regarding the right of publicity, the law regarding the right of privacy, defamation law, trade secret law, and patent law. The specific legal issues important to any particular situation depend on a variety of factors, including:

- the element of a multimedia product that you are working with (for example, a specific form of content, software, or the complete multimedia work itself),

- the manner in which you propose to acquire the element (for example, develop it yourself, license it from a third party, or in some cases, use a preexisting work without permission from the original developer), and

- the reason for your interest in the legal issue (for example, are you attempting to develop a multimedia product without infringing the rights of others, are you seeking to protect your rights in the multimedia product you have created, or are you seeking to distribute your multimedia products in a manner designed to maximize the value of your asset and minimize the likelihood of piracy?).

To help you understand the law applicable to multimedia, and its impact on your efforts to develop multimedia products, this book approaches the subject from four perspectives. Part 1 provides an overview of the substance of the law in each of the seven primary areas of law impacting multimedia (copyright, trademark and unfair competition law, right of publicity, right of privacy, defamation, trade secret law, and patent law). Part 2 addresses the impact of those general areas of the law on the various activities that you will engage in during the process of developing your multimedia products. Part 3 reviews the various steps that you can take to protect the valuable intellectual property rights that you create in the process of developing a multimedia product. Part 4 examines the issues that you need to address when distributing your multimedia product to the public.

To begin this process, and to help you to put the legal issues in perspective, this chapter provides an overview, or a roadmap, to the various legal issues that you should take into consideration when developing, protecting, and distributing multimedia products. To do this, this chapter provides an overview of:

- the law applicable to each of the components of a multimedia product—that is, the content (e.g., text, data, music, sounds, pictures, and motion pictures) that goes into a multimedia product, and the technology (e.g., software and other technology) that goes into a multimedia product; and

- the legal issues raised by the multimedia development process.

1. The Law Applicable to Components of Multimedia

A review of multimedia legal issues begins with an understanding of the areas of the law that are applicable to the various components of a multimedia work. This depends, to a certain extent, on whether you are dealing with the content or the technology that comprises a multimedia product, and the specific element within each of these categories. Accordingly, we review the law applicable to multimedia with reference to the specific form of content or technology involved.

Developing a multimedia product involves the creation, collection, adaptation, combination, coordination, and synchronization of multiple and varying types of content. For purposes of this book, the varying types of content have been grouped into the following seven categories: text, databases, characters, musical works, sound recordings, pictures and still images, and motion pictures and other audiovisual works. Each of these types of content presents several unique legal issues that need to be considered and resolved before incorporation of the content into a multimedia work.

1.1 Text

Text is one of the most common forms of multimedia content. It is the form you can most easily create yourself, although there may also be instances where you will want to use text previously written by someone else. Whether you create your own text or use text previously created by others, several areas of the law are potentially implicated, including copyright, trademark and unfair competition, the right of privacy, defamation, and trade secret law.

- **Copyright Law.** Virtually all text, both fiction and non-fiction, is automatically protected by copyright upon its creation. As a consequence, copyright protection is available for most of the text you create, and your right to use text created by others will be restricted by the provisions of the copyright law. Therefore, the copyright law is a factor to be considered with respect to virtually all of the text to be incorporated in your multimedia products. Copyright law is discussed generally in chapters 3, 23, and 24. Text and the copyright law are also specifically discussed in chapter 14, section 1.1.

- **Trademark Law.** If the text that you use in a multimedia product includes the trademarks of others, it may be necessary to consider the impact of trademark law. This might occur, for example, if you mention the trademarks of others, such as Ford, Paramount, Mickey Mouse, Apple, or Microsoft, or if the title of your multimedia product is the same as, or includes, a registered trademark (such as a title that refers to Mickey Mouse, Bugs Bunny, or Superman). Trademark law is discussed generally in chapters 4 and 25. Text and the trademark law are also specifically discussed in chapter 14, section 1.2.

- **Right of Privacy.** To the extent that the text you propose to use makes reference to an actual person or a fictional person that is readily comparable to an actual person, you need to be concerned about violating that person's right of privacy. The law relating to the right of privacy is discussed generally in chapter 6.

- **Defamation.** To the extent that the text you propose to use makes reference to an actual person or a fictional person that is readily comparable to an actual person, you also need to be concerned about the law of defamation. The law relating to defamation is discussed generally in chapter 7.

- **Trade Secret Law.** The use of text generally does not involve the law of trade secrets. However, it is certainly possible that the text you are contemplating using may disclose your trade secrets or the trade secrets of a third party. For example, if a story on the development of Coca-Cola included the secret formula for Coke, and such formula was included without authorization of the owner of the trade secret, this could constitute trade secret misappropriation. Trade secret law is discussed generally in chapters 8 and 26.

1.2 Databases

A **database** can be a compilation or collection of just about anything. Examples include databases of names, addresses, and telephone numbers, databases of copyrighted articles (such as NEXIS or DIALOG), and databases of court opinions (such as LEXIS and WestLaw). A multimedia product may include all or a portion of a database, or may simply include elements taken from a database. Whether you create a database or use all or a part of a database previously created by others, your conduct will likely be impacted by the copyright law. Trademark law and the right of privacy may also be impacted by your use of a database.

- **Copyright Law.** A database is typically considered to be copyrightable compilation. This is true regardless of whether the contents of the database are copyrightable (such as a database of copyrightable articles) or noncopyrightable (such as a database of uncopyrightable facts). As a consequence, copyright protection will probably be available for databases you create, and your right to use databases created by others (or information from such databases) will be restricted by the provisions of the copyright law. Copyright law is discussed generally in chapters 3, 23, and 24. Databases and the copyright law are also specifically discussed in chapter 15, section 1.1.

- **Trademark Law.** If you use a database that involves numerous trademarks (such as a database of copyrighted articles that includes the trademark under which the articles were published), you will have to consider the restrictions on your use of those marks imposed by the trademark law. Trademark law is discussed generally in chapters 4 and 25.

- **Right of Privacy.** If you are dealing with a database that contains personal information about a number of individuals, right of privacy concerns may also become important. The law relating to the right of privacy is discussed generally in chapter 6.

1.3 Characters

Characters can be represented pictorially, such as the cartoon characters Mickey Mouse and Bugs Bunny, or they can exist only in the words of a book or play, such as the characters Columbo or the Hardy Boys. In either case, the use of characters in a multimedia product can raise a variety of legal issues, including copyright and trademark.

- **Copyright Law.** Characters represented in a pictorial form are clearly copyrightable. Classic examples are the Disney cartoon characters such as Mickey Mouse and Donald Duck. Characters that exist only in the words of a book or a play can also be copyrightable, although that depends upon the degree to which they are developed in the story. Therefore, whether you create your own characters or use characters previously created by someone else, copyright law will most likely be a factor. Copyright law is discussed generally in chapters 3, 23, and 24. Characters and the copyright law are also discussed in chapter 16, section 1.1.

- **Trademark and Unfair Competition Law.** Characters may also be protected by trademark law. As a consequence, trademark protection may be available for any characters that you create, and your right to use characters created by others may very well be restricted by the provisions of the trademark law, as well as those of the copyright law. Trademark law is discussed generally in chapters 4 and 25.

1.4 Musical Works

Musical works include both the music written by the composer and the accompanying words (if any) written by the lyricist. Whether you create your own musical works or use musical works previously created by others, your conduct will be impacted by the copyright law.

■ **Copyright Law.** The Copyright Act specifically protects musical works, including any accompanying words. Copyright protection for musical works extends to both the words and the music. As a consequence, copyright protection will be available for any musical works you create, and your right to use musical works created by others will be restricted by the provisions of the Copyright Act. Accordingly, the copyright law will be an important factor with respect to your creation and/or use of any musical works. Copyright law is discussed generally in chapters 3, 23, and 24. Musical works and the copyright law are also discussed in chapter 17, section 1.

1.5 Sound Recordings

A **sound recording** is the fixation (that is, a recording) of a series of musical, spoken, or other sounds. Examples include sound recordings of musical works, sound recordings of human speech, such as speeches, lectures, and dramatic readings, sound recordings of the sounds of nature, such as animal sounds, thunderstorms, and waves, and sound recordings of special effects, such as crashes, explosions, and other noises. Whether you create your own sound recordings or use all or a part of a sound recording previously created by others, several areas of the law are potentially implicated, including copyright, trademark and the right of publicity.

■ **Copyright Law.** Sound recordings are copyrightable only if they were created after February 15, 1972. As a consequence, copyright protection will be available for any sound recordings that you create, and your right to use sound recordings created by others after February 15, 1972 will be restricted by the provisions of the Copyright Act. Copyright law is discussed generally in chapters 3, 23, and 24. Sound recordings and the copyright law are also discussed in chapter 17, section 1.2 and chapter 18, section 1.1.

In addition, sound recordings created prior to February 15, 1972, may be protected by common law and local state laws relating to record piracy. Legal theories used to protect pre-February 15, 1972, sound recordings include unfair competition, common law copyright, and state statutes relating to record piracy.

- **Trademark and Unfair Competition Law.** In some cases, sound recordings may be protected by trademark law. The examples include commercial songs and television program themes. In such a case, your right to use the sound recording is restricted by the provisions of the trademark law. Trademark law is discussed generally in chapters 4 and 25.

- **Right of Publicity.** Sound recordings can implicate the right of publicity, especially where the sound recording of a famous person is used without permission, or a soundalike of such a person is used in a manner that creates the impression that the celebrity either created the recording or somehow endorsed or is associated with the recording. The law relating to the right of publicity is discussed generally in chapter 5. Sound recordings and the right of publicity are also discussed in chapter 18, section 1.2.

- **Contract Rights of Third Parties.** In addition to obtaining permission from the owner of the copyright, it may also be necessary to obtain permission (and pay appropriate reuse fees) to the union and/or guilds who have retained contractual rights to the performance of the sound recording, even though they may have assigned their copyrights to the producer of the sound recording. These contract rights are discussed in chapter 18, section 1.3, and chapter 21, sections 1.2, 5.2, and 6.2.

1.6 Pictures and Still Images

Pictures and still images include photographs, advertisements, commercial prints, labels, cartoons, comic strips, drawings, paintings, murals, floor and wall covering designs, games, puzzles, greeting cards, holograms, computer and laser artwork, logo artwork, maps, cartographic works, masks, models, mosaics, patterns, photographs, photomontages, reproductions, technical drawings, architectural drawings or plans, blueprints, diagrams, and mechanical drawings. Pictures, photographs, and other still images are a standard component of virtually all multimedia works.

Whether you create your own pictures or other still images, or use pictures, photographs, and still images previously created by others, there are several areas of the law that you will need to consider, including copyright, trademark and unfair competition law, the right of publicity, the right of privacy, and defamation.

■ **Copyright Law.** Virtually all pictures and still images are copyrightable. As a consequence, copyright protection is available for the pictures, photographs, and other still images that you create, and your right to use pictures, photographs, and other still images created by others will be restricted by the provisions of the copyright law. Therefore, the copyright law is a factor that you must consider with respect to all of the pictures, photographs, and other still images that you incorporate within your multimedia work. Moreover, copyright applies not only to the act of capturing and digitizing an image, but also to the acts of adapting or otherwise manipulating or morphing images, as well as the acts of reproducing and distributing images. Copyright law is discussed generally in chapters 3, 23, and 24. Photographs and the copyright law are discussed in chapter 19, section 1.1.

■ **Trademark and Unfair Competition Law.** Pictures and graphic images can also include trademarks. To the extent they do, your use of the image in a multimedia product must be done with due consideration of the trademark laws. Trademark law is discussed generally in chapters 4 and 25.

■ **Right of Publicity.** The use of the image of a person can implicate the person's right of publicity. Specifically, if you use the image of a person in a manner designed to capitalize on the person's reputation or imply endorsement, you may infringe the celebrity's right of publicity. The law relating to the right of publicity is discussed generally in chapter 5. Photographs and the right of publicity are also discussed in chapter 19, section 1.2.

■ **Right of Privacy.** The use of a picture or other image of a person may violate that person's right of privacy. This is particularly true if the picture places a person in a false light, misappropriates a person's name or likeness for commercial purposes, discloses embarrassing private facts about the person, or otherwise intrudes upon the person's solitude. The law relating to the right of privacy is discussed generally in chapter 6. Photographs and the right of privacy are also discussed in chapter 19, section 1.3.

■ **Defamation.** The use of a picture or other image of a person may constitute defamation. This is particularly true if the picture makes a false or misleading statement about the person or casts them in a false light. Examples include photographs that are displayed in a context (e.g., in conjunction with other photographs, captions, or text) that suggests a defamatory "fact" about the person in the photograph. The law relating to defamation is discussed generally in chapter 7. Photographs and defamation are also discussed in chapter 19, section 1.4.

1.7 Motion Pictures and Other Audiovisual Works

Audiovisual works are works that consist of a series of related images that are intended to be shown by the use of machines such as projectors, viewers, computers, or other electronic equipment, together with accompanying sounds, if any, regardless of the medium such as films or tapes, in which the work is embodied. **Motion pictures** are audiovisual works consisting of a series of related images that, when shown in succession, impart an impression of motion.

Thus, audiovisual works include a film strip, a set of slides, a film, a videotape, a videodisc, or a CD-i. Audiovisual works also include television news broadcasts and video games. Motion pictures and other audiovisual works can be recorded on videotape, videodisc, CD-ROM, or any other tangible form. A computer program may equally embody an audiovisual work. Whether you create your own motion pictures or other audiovisual works for use in your multimedia products, or whether you use motion pictures or other audiovisual works previously created by others, there are several areas of the law that you should consider, including copyright, trademark and unfair competition law, right of publicity, right of privacy, and defamation.

- **Copyright Law.** All motion pictures and other audiovisual works are copyrightable subject matter. As a consequence, copyright protection is available for any motion pictures or other audiovisual works that you create, and your right to use portions of motion pictures and other audiovisual works created by others will be restricted by the provisions of the copyright law. Thus, the copyright law will be a factor with respect to any use that you make of motion pictures or other audiovisual works. Copyright law is discussed generally in chapters 3, 23, and 24. Motion pictures and the copyright law are also discussed in chapter 20, sections 1.1 and 3.

- **Right of Publicity.** Each of the performers in any motion picture or other audiovisual work that you create or use have a proprietary right in their personas, which includes their names, visual images of their likenesses, and audio sounds of their voices. This right derives from the right of publicity.

Consequently, whether you create your own audiovisual work or use previously existing works created by others, it will be necessary to obtain appropriate releases from all of the performers who appeared in the audiovisual work. The law relating to the right of publicity is discussed generally in chapter 5.

■ **Right of Privacy.** Any person shown in a television clip also has a right of privacy that must be respected. This may limit the ways in which you can use the clip, or the other content with which it may be juxtaposed. The law relating to the right of privacy is discussed generally in chapter 6.

■ **Defamation.** It is possible that your use of motion picture or television clips of actual persons can also constitute defamation, depending upon the way the clip is used. Accordingly, you should consider the implications of the law of defamation with respect to your proposed use of this form of content. The law of defamation is discussed generally in chapter 7.

■ **Contract Rights of Third Parties.** When motion pictures, television programs, and other audiovisual works are created using union talent, it is common for the union to contractually reserve (in its collective bargaining agreement) certain rights in the event that the work is reused in a market other than that for which it was originally developed. Thus, for example, if you will be incorporating preexisting motion pictures, television programs, or other audiovisual works in your multimedia products, it may be necessary to pay additional compensation to the performers and other talent who participated in the original creation of the work, as well as additional compensation to the health and pension funds of the applicable unions. The role of unions and the contractual rights they reserve in their collective bargaining agreements are discussed generally in chapter 21. Motion pictures and the contract rights reserved by unions and performers are also discussed in chapter 20, section 1.3, and chapter 21, sections 1.2, 2.2, 3.2, 4.2, 5.2, and 6.2.

1.8 Software and Other Technology

The technology that goes into the creation of a multimedia product is used to create, adapt, combine, and coordinate the content of the multimedia product, present that content to the user, and allow the user to interact with, search, and otherwise use the multimedia product.

Computer programs are used both to prepare content for use in a multimedia work (to sample sounds, capture and digitize images, modify and adapt digitize content, and so on) and as part of the multimedia product itself (in order to allow users to access, interact with, search, and navigate through the content of a multimedia product). In addition to software, multimedia technology includes the many techniques, processes, and algorithms used to make a multimedia product "work," many of which are ultimately implemented in a computer program. Examples include compression techniques for the storage and retrieval of video images and audio recordings, index and search techniques to facilitate user-directed retrieval of information, and the like. Whether you create such software or technology, or use software or other technology previously created by others, three main areas of the law are implicated: copyright, trade secret, and patent law.

- **Copyright Law.** All software is automatically protected copyright upon its creation. As a consequence, copyright protection is available for the software you create, and your right to use software created by others will be restricted by the provisions of the copyright law. Copyright law is discussed generally in chapters 3, 23, and 24.

- **Trade Secret Law.** Courts have routinely recognized that computer programs and technical processes and algorithms can qualify for trade secret protection if, and to the extent, that they embody trade secrets. Thus, trade secret protection may be available for the software and other technology that you develop. In addition, to the extent that software and other technology that you obtain from third parties is held by them as a trade secret, you will be required to observe the restrictions and limitations on your use of it. Trade secret law is discussed generally in chapters 8 and 26.

- **Patent Law.** In some cases, some software products have also qualified for patent protection. Perhaps the best-known example is the Compton's New-Media patent issued in 1993 (discussed in chapter 9, section 2). The grant of this patent was subsequently reversed by the Patent Office in March 1994, following a reexamination instituted by the Patent Office and as of August 1994, is under further reconsideration following a response from the patent holders. However, regardless of the outcome, it provides a good example of the type of multimedia technology that may qualify for patent protection.

In addition, other forms of technology may also qualify for patent protection. While patent protection is not available for all technology, and can be rather expensive to obtain, it is something that should be considered with respect to new and novel technology that you might develop. Conversely, to the extent that you develop a new technology or product you need to be sure that it does not infringe the patent rights of any third party. Patent law is discussed generally in chapters 9 and 27.

1.9 Completed Multimedia Products

The content and the software that form the components of the multimedia products you develop may be protectable under a variety of legal theories, as noted above. In addition, however, the completed multimedia product itself represents yet another asset protectable under a variety of legal theories, because this is a product that you have created (regardless of whether you created the content and software of which it is composed, or licensed some or all of those components from other parties). Accordingly there are a number of legal issues relevant to the ownership, protection, and distribution of the asset comprised of the multimedia product itself.

- **Copyright Law.** All of the multimedia products that you create will be protected by federal copyright. Accordingly, to preserve and protect the value of the assets you have developed, it is important that you take steps to ensure that you are the owner of all of the rights in the copyright to the multimedia product, and that you take the necessary steps to further preserve and perfect the copyright, such as using an appropriate copyright notice and registering the copyright with the copyright office. Copyright laws discussed generally in chapters 3, 23, and 24. Perfecting your copyright is also discussed in chapter 24.

- **Trademark and Unfair Competition Law.** There may be legal issues raised by the title that you use for your multimedia product. Use of someone else's trademark or name can constitute infringement, unfair competition, or an infringement of their right of publicity. For example, the use of preexisting trademarks in the title of your multimedia product, such as "Superman," "Mickey Mouse," or "Batman" can expose you to liability. Similarly, references to celebrities may constitute an infringement of their right of publicity. Thus, for example, a title that includes a reference to a celebrity, such as

"Madonna's World" or "David Letterman's Top 10 Lists" is undoubtedly objectionable. The right of publicity is discussed generally in chapter 5.

In addition to issues related to the title, the brand name under which you market any multimedia products can constitute a trademark. Accordingly, it is necessary to ensure that you do not select a name that is already owned by someone else. Moreover, it is important that you take steps to preserve and protect the trademark that you do select, such as by federal registration, in order to protect the value of the trademark associated with your product. Selecting and protecting a trademark is discussed in chapter 25.

2. Obtaining the Content

The content to be incorporated in a multimedia work includes text, databases, musical works, sound recordings, photographs and still images, and motion pictures and other audiovisual works. Obtaining content raises numerous copyright issues, as well as, in certain situations, issues relating to rights of publicity, rights of privacy, defamation, and trademark law.

The legal consequences of developing a multimedia product vary widely, depending on a variety of factors, such as whether you create the content yourself or obtain it from third parties, whether recognizable persons appear in the content, and the extent to which preexisting content is adapted or altered.

The key issue, in the first instance, however, is the question of copyright. As noted in chapter 3, section 3.1, all content is automatically protected by federal copyright upon its creation. Thus, you will need to address the issue of copyright with respect to all of the content that you incorporate into a multimedia work.

2.1 Copyright

Generally, you have three choices with respect to the content that goes into a multimedia work:

1. you can create your own content;
2. in certain limited cases you can use preexisting content without the need for obtaining permission from the author; or

3. you can obtain permission to use preexisting content from the owners of the rights in that content.

Each of the foregoing approaches raises its own set of legal issues that can be summarized in the following sections.

● **Copyright in Content that You Develop.** If you develop your own content (either through your employees or by retaining an independent contractor), it is important that you understand the nature of the copyright rights that are automatically created in this process, and their impact on your proposed use of what you have created. (These rights are discussed in chapter 3, section 4.) This involves consideration of a number of important issues.

First, do you own the copyright to the content that you created? Merely paying someone to create it is often not sufficient to ensure that you own the resulting copyright. In many cases, appropriate copyright assignments or work for hire agreements will be required. Copyright ownership is discussed in chapter 10, sections 2.1 and 3.1, and chapter 23. If you will not own the copyright to the content that results from your development efforts, you need to ensure that you have the right to use the content to the extent necessary for the multimedia titles you propose to develop.

Second, if you do own the copyright, have you taken steps to adequately protect your rights and to preserve the value of the new asset that you have created? This includes using a proper copyright notice, registering your copyright claim, and recording of any assignment agreements? See discussion in chapter 24.

Third, if you do not own the copyright, have you secured a license from the copyright owner that grants you rights that are adequate to meet your particular needs? Basic licensing issues are discussed in chapter 13.

Fourth, has the process of developing the content resulted in an infringement of the copyright of anyone else? Even when work is ostensibly originally created, you need to ensure that the persons creating it do not either intentionally or inadvertently infringe the copyright of any third party.

● **Copyright Protection in Preexisting Content.** If you use preexisting content created by others, it is important that you understand the restrictions that the Copyright Act imposes on your use of the content, and the extent to which you need to obtain permission from the copyright owner. These issues are discussed in chapter 3, sections 4 and 8.

In some cases, you may be able to use the content without permission. This requires determining whether the content that you propose to use is protected by copyright or is in the public domain. (Public domain is discussed in detail in chapter 11, section 1). But even if the content is protected by copyright, it may be possible, in some cases, to copy a limited portion of the work under the doctrine of fair use. (Fair use is discussed in detail in chapter 11, section 2). To use most preexisting content, however, it is necessary to obtain a license from the owner of the copyright. (Content licensing is discussed in chapters 12 through 21.)

2.2 Trademark and Unfair Competition

If you use someone's trademark in the content that you develop or license, have you done so in a manner that is likely to constitute trademark infringement or unfair competition? For example, did you use it in a manner that implies that your multimedia product is created by, associated with, or endorsed by the owner of the trademark? If so, you may have potential problems. This is particularly true if you use the trademarks of others as part of the title of your multimedia work, as this might cause the public to somehow relate your multimedia work to the owner of the trademark or its products (such as by assuming that both works were created by the same person or entity, the creator of the first work has endorsed the second work, or that your work is a substitute for the first work). Trademark and unfair competition law is discussed in chapters 4 and 25.

2.3 Right of Publicity

Does the content that you develop or license incorporate the image, likeness, or voice of any performers, public figures, or other well-known persons? If so, you need to consider whether it may constitute an infringement of such persons' right of publicity. It may be necessary to get a release from such persons (or their estates if they are deceased) in order to avoid infringing their right of publicity. The law relating to the right of publicity is discussed in chapter 5.

2.4 Right of Privacy

Does the content that you develop or license incorporate the image, likeness, or voice of, or make reference to, any living person or allegedly fictional person that is readily comparable to a living person? If so, it is important to take particular care that you not place such person in a false light, not misappropriate the person's name or likeness for a commercial purpose, not disclose embarrassing private facts about the person, and not intrude upon the person's solitude, as this may give rise to an action for infringement of the right of privacy. This is so even though the foregoing information may be completely true and accurate. Privacy law is discussed in chapter 6.

2.5 Defamation

Does the content that you develop or license incorporate the image, likeness, or voice of, or make reference to, any living person or allegedly fictional person that is readily comparable to a living person? If so, it is important to take particular care that you not include false and defamatory statements about the person, as they may give rise to an action for defamation. Defamation law is discussed in chapter 7.

2.6 Unions

If any of the preexisting content that will be incorporated in your multimedia product was created using union talent, the union contract may have reserved the right to certain payments as a condition of using the content in a market other than that for which it was originally developed. In many cases, this may involve payments to several unions. The contract rights reserved by the various entertainment unions are discussed in chapter 21.

3. Obtaining the Technology

The software, algorithms, designs, structures, data compression techniques, and the like that are used in the creation of a multimedia product are typically protected by copyright, trade secret law, and in some cases by patents. Thus, to the extent that you develop this technology yourself, you must take care to ensure that you maximize the scope of the protection available to you for this technology. Alternatively (and perhaps most often), you will be licensing this technology (or at least portions of it) from other persons who own the copyrights and/or trade secret rights (and in some cases patent rights) to the technology. In such cases, it is important that you understand and respect the rights of these third parties, that the license under which you obtain the technology grants to you the rights necessary to use the technology to the extent that you require it for the development of your multimedia title, and that the resulting product, or the process by which it is created, does not infringe upon or misappropriate any of the rights belonging to third parties.

3.1 Copyright

• **Copyright in Technology that You Develop.** If you develop your own software for multimedia products (either through your employees or by retaining an independent contractor), it is important that you understand the nature of the copyright rights that are automatically created in this process, and their impact on your proposed use of what you have created. This involves consideration of a number of important issues.

First, do you own the copyright to the software that you created? Is it a work for hire, or have you obtained the appropriate assignment documents? Is it jointly owned with someone else? Generally, it is important to ensure that you are the owner of (or at least have appropriate rights to use) the technology that you create. Thus, if the content is created by anyone other than your employees, appropriate copyright assignments or work-for-hire agreements will be required. (Copyright ownership is discussed in chapter 10, sections 2.1 and 3.1, and in chapter 23). If you will not own the copyright in the software that results from your development efforts, you need to ensure that you have the right to use the technology to the extent necessary for the multimedia titles you propose to develop.

Second, if you do own the copyright, have you taken steps to adequately protect your rights and to preserve the value of the new asset that you have created? This includes using a proper copyright notice, registering your copyright claim, and recording any assignment agreements. These issues are discussed in chapter 24.

Third, if you do not own the copyright, have you secured a license from the copyright owner that grants you rights that are adequate to meet your particular needs? Basic licensing issues are discussed in chapter 13.

Fourth, has the process of developing the software resulted in an infringement of the copyright of anyone else? Even when work is ostensibly originally created, you need to ensure that the persons creating it do not either intentionally or inadvertently infringe the copyright of any third party.

• **Copyright in Preexisting Technology.** Virtually all preexisting software will be protected by federal copyright. Accordingly, in most cases it will be necessary to obtain an appropriate license from the owner of the copyright to authorize the proposed use that you seek to make of the copyrighted work. In that process, it is important that you understand the restrictions that the Copyright Act imposes on your use of the software, and the extent to which you need to obtain permission from the copyright owner. These issues are discussed in chapter 3, sections 4 and 8.

The software and other technology used in connection with the development of a multimedia title fall into two general categories. The first category is the development tools that are used in the development process, but not included in the final product. Examples include software designed for creating and editing text, such as word processing software, software for sampling and editing sounds, scanning, digitizing, adapting, and morphing images, and software designed to sew together the various types of content to form a multimedia title, such as authoring software.

The second category is software tools and other technology that will be incorporated in the resulting multimedia product. Examples include software designed to display a user interface on the user's computer screen and respond to input from the user, search and retrieval software engines, software designed to compress and decompress data as it is stored and/or retrieved by the user, and so on.

The scope of the rights that you need with respect to these two categories of technology vary greatly. With respect to development tools, for example, you typically need the right to "use" a single copy. For example, if you will be editing, manipulating, and/or morphing digital images, you may need the right to use a single copy of software capable of performing these processes. On the other hand, for the software products and other technology that will be incorporated in each copy of your multimedia title you will need a license to copy such software, incorporate it within the multimedia title you are creating, and to distribute it along with your multimedia title as so incorporated. The license to use a development tool may be a one-time fixed-fee paid-up license. The license to copy, incorporate, and distribute a search and retrieval engine with your multimedia title is much broader, raises a much larger group of issues, and presumably will require the payment of royalties based on sales or licenses of your multimedia title.

The bottom line, however, is that it is important to ensure that you obtain the rights necessary for your intended use of the software and technology being licensed.

3.2 Trade Secret

Software often qualifies for trade secret protection. If you are developing your own software, you need to consider taking appropriate steps to preserve and protect any trade secrets that may arise from this development process. See discussion of trade secret law in chapters 8 and 26.

If you are using preexisting software that someone else claims as their trade secret, you need to ensure that you have obtained a license that grants appropriate permission for the use that you intend to make of the software. If that license imposes any obligations to preserve and protect the trade secrets, or any restrictions on your use of the trade secret material, you need to ensure that they do not unduly interfere with your anticipated use of the software.

3.3 Patent

In some cases, software qualifies for patent protection. If you are developing your own software, you should be alert to the possibility that you may have created a patentable invention, in which case you should at least consider whether filing for a patent is a desirable course of action.

Whether you are developing your own software or using software developed by others, you also need to be concerned about possible infringement of the patent rights of others. Patent law is discussed in chapters 9 and 27.

PART 1

The Law of Multimedia

Copyright Law

Copyright Law

Copyright law applies to all aspects of a multimedia product. As such, it is the primary source of most of the legal issues affecting the development, protection, and distribution of multimedia works.

A multimedia product, the content incorporated within it, and the software that makes it work are automatically protected by federal copyright law from the moment they are created. The author is not required to use a copyright notice, register with the U.S. Copyright Office, spend any money, wait any specified amount of time, or, for that matter, take any other action whatsoever. The protection applies automatically.

But this is only the beginning. Because copyright protection is automatic, it is important to understand who is entitled to claim ownership of the copyright, the nature of the protection it provides, and its limitations. What is the scope of the rights you have created by virtue of the development of a multimedia product? Are you the rightful owner of the content you develop? Have you ensured that your use of content owned by others is lawful? Do you understand the limitations on your right to use content that you have licensed from others?

This chapter will explain the nature of copyright and its implications for the development of a multimedia product. Determining who owns the copyright is discussed in chapter 23, and the steps necessary to perfect a copyright (notice and registration) are discussed in chapter 24.

1. Relationship of Copyright to Multimedia

Copyright protection is the most easily obtained and probably the most commonly used legal form of protection for multimedia works, multimedia content, and multimedia software. As such, it is a two-edged sword. It provides a valuable form of protection for the works you create. At the same time, however, it presents an obstacle to your use of content and software created by others. Because virtually all such content and software is automatically protected by federal copyright, any use of content or software owned by another without appropriate permission constitutes copyright infringement. Thus, to effectively take advantage of the protection that copyright affords to multimedia works, and to ensure that the content incorporated within your multimedia works does not infringe the rights of another, you must understand what copyright does and what it does not protect and how it provides that protection.

2. What Works Are Protected by Copyright?

The Copyright Act[1] protects virtually everything that goes into a multimedia product, as well as the multimedia product itself. Thus, to understand the impact of copyright on a multimedia work, we need to look at it from three perspectives: copyright protection for the content (for example, the text, sound recordings, and visual images) that goes into a multimedia product; copyright protection for the technology (the software) that is used to develop a multimedia product and/or incorporated within a completed multimedia product; and the completed integrated multimedia product itself.

2.1 Multimedia Content

Virtually all of the content that goes into a multimedia work is eligible for copyright protection. This includes literary works, such as text and databases; musical works, including any accompanying words; sound recordings, including recordings of musical, spoken or other sounds; pictorial and graphic works, including works of fine, graphic, and applied art, photographs, prints, and art reproductions, maps, charts, diagrams, models, technical drawings, and architectural plans; and motion pictures and other audiovisual works.[2]

- **Text**. Text is protected by copyright. This includes literary works such as books, plays, poems, articles and the like, as well as other works expressed in words, numbers, or other symbols.[3] Both fiction and nonfiction, such as newspapers, history books, and biographies are copyrightable. (Text is discussed in more detail in chapter 14.)

- **Databases**. Databases are normally copyrightable as compilations.[4] (Compilations are discussed in chapter 23, section 2.2). This is true for databases comprised of copyrightable components (such as a database of news articles), as well as for databases comprised of uncopyrightable facts (such as a database of names and addresses or part numbers). However, the scope of protection provided by copyright law for databases of uncopyrightable facts is much less than that provided for databases of copyrighted materials. (Databases are discussed in more detail in chapter 15.)

- **Characters**. Fictional characters can exist in a visual form (e.g., Mickey Mouse, Superman), in a literary form, such as in the text of a story (e.g., Sherlock Holmes, The Hardy Boys, or James Bond), or as represented by actors in a motion picture or television program (e.g., James Bond, E.T., Darth Vader, or Superman). In each of these cases they *can* be entitled to copyright protection.[5]

  Characters are most readily protectable when they exist in some sort of pictorial or graphic form in both the original work and the work in which they are copied. Classic examples are cartoon characters such as Mickey Mouse, Donald Duck, Superman, and Charlie Brown.[6]

  Characters that exist only in the words of a book or play can also be copyrightable, separate and apart from the text containing the story in which they appear. In this case, however, whether or not they are protected by copyright depends on the degree to which they are developed in the story. The less developed the characters, the less likely it is that they are be copyrightable.[7] (Characters are discussed in more detail in chapter 16.)

- **Musical Works**. Musical works are protected by copyright.[8] Copyright protection for musical works extends to both the words and the music.[9] Even if the music alone or the lyrics alone are in the public domain or not sufficiently original and expressive to qualify for copyright, the combination may be original enough to qualify.[10] (Musical works are discussed in more detail in chapter 17.)

- **Sound Recordings**. A sound recording is a work that results from the recording of a series of musical, spoken, or other sounds, regardless of the nature of the physical medium, such as discs or tapes, in which they are embodied.[11] However, a sound recording does not include any sounds accompanying a motion picture or other audiovisual work. In that case, the sound is treated as part of the motion picture or audiovisual work that it accompanies.[12]

  Sound recordings are copyrightable regardless of the nature of the sounds recorded.[13] Common examples of a copyrightable sound recording include a recording of a performance of a copyrighted or public domain musical work, a recording of spoken words, such as a drama or a speech (whether or not copyrighted), a recording of sounds of nature (e.g., birds chirping, waves crashing onto the shore, etc.), special sound effects (e.g., a door slamming, cars crashing together, etc.), or virtually any other sound that can be recorded.[14] (Sound recordings are discussed in more detail in chapter 18.)

- **Photographs and Still Images**. Pictorial, graphic and sculptural works are copyrightable.[15] They include two-dimensional and three-dimensional works of fine, graphic, and applied art, photographs, prints and art reproductions, maps, globes, charts, diagrams, models, and technical drawings, including architectural drawings.[16] Also included are illustrations, plans and drawings, and works in any of the foregoing categories intended for use in advertising and commerce.[17] There is no implied criterion of artistic taste, aesthetic value, or intrinsic quality necessary for copyrightability.[18]

  Examples of works that qualify for copyright protection as "pictorial, graphic and sculptural works" include advertisements, commercial prints, labels, cartoons, comic strips, drawings, paintings, murals, floor and wall covering designs, games, puzzles, greeting cards, holograms, computer and laser artwork, logo artwork, maps, cartographic works, masks, models, mosaics, patterns, photographs, photomontages, reproductions, technical drawings, architectural drawings or plans, blueprints, diagrams, and mechanical drawings.[19] (Pictures and still images are discussed in more detail in chapter 19.)

- **Motion Pictures and Other Audiovisual Works.** The Copyright Act specifically states that motion pictures and other audiovisual works are copyrightable subject matter.[20]

Audiovisual works are works that consist of a series of related images that are intrinsically intended to be shown by the use of machines or devices such as projectors, viewers, VCRs, televisions, computers, or other electronic equipment, together with accompanying sounds, if any.[21] Thus, audiovisual works include film, a videotape, a videodisc, a television news broadcast,[22] and a videogame.[23]

Motion pictures are a subset of audiovisual works. Specifically, they are audiovisual works consisting of a series of related images that, when shown in succession, impart an impression of motion.[24] The impression of motion is the essence of a motion picture. A series of slides shown sequentially, although an audiovisual work, is not a motion picture, because it does not when shown impart an impression of motion.[25] Motion pictures, like other audiovisual works, can be embodied on film, videotape, videodisc, CD-ROM, CD-i, disk, or any other tangible form.

The copyright in a motion picture, by definition, includes the accompanying sounds, if any.[26] Thus, the sound track of a motion picture is also protected by the motion picture copyright. It is not considered a sound recording.[27] (Motion pictures and other audiovisual works are discussed in more detail in chapter 20.)

2.2 Multimedia Technology

All of the software used in a multimedia work, such as software that allows a user to navigate, search, and otherwise interact with the content comprising the multimedia product, as well as the software used to create or edit the content for a multimedia product, is protected by copyright.[28] Software used to create, edit, or otherwise adapt content for use in multimedia products includes general-purpose software such as word processors, spreadsheets, desktop publishing programs, and database programs; graphics software, animation software, sound software, video software, presentation software, and authoring software. Software included within a completed multimedia product (and distributed with the product) includes the run time or playback portions of authoring software products designed for distribution with the multimedia product, search engines, and other products designed to interact with the user.

2.3 Multimedia Products

In addition to protecting the content and the software that comprises the multimedia product (i.e., the component parts of the multimedia product), copyright also protects the multimedia product itself. In other words, even though a multimedia product may be composed of several different preexisting copyrighted elements comprising both content and software, there is an additional independent copyright in the completed multimedia work itself. Because the completed multimedia work is often composed of numerous works copyrighted by other parties and used with permission, it frequently falls into a special category of copyrighted works, such as a **compilation, collective work**, or **derivative work.** Compilations, collective works, and derivative works are discussed in chapter 23.

In some cases, there is a single copyright in a completed multimedia product. In most cases, however, a completed multimedia product involves several different copyrights, often owned by several different persons. Thus, there is a copyright in the completed multimedia product as a whole, as well as copyrights in each of the component elements of content and software incorporated within the work.

3. How Do You Get a Copyright?

3.1 Automatic Protection

Copyright protection applies *automatically* to any work of authorship that qualifies.[29] As soon as the work is created, it is protected by federal copyright, even if the author has not included a copyright notice, registered with the U.S. Copyright Office, or taken any other steps to assert a copyright claim.[30] For that matter, authors may initially be unaware of the applicability of copyright protection for their work. But so long as the work is one of the types protected by copyright, and meets the requirements to qualify for copyright protection, the protection applies automatically. (The requirements that must be met to qualify for copyrights protection are explained in this chapter, section 3.2).

As a consequence, when developing a multimedia product, virtually all preexisting content or software that you desire to use will be the subject of copyright protection. You cannot rely on the absence of a copyright notice or the failure of the copyright owner to register his or her work as indicators that it is safe to copy the work.[31] Accordingly, before using it, you will need to either verify that it is in the public domain or obtain permission from the copyright owner (see chapter 11, section 1).

On the other hand, the automatic nature of copyright protection means that the multimedia work you create will also be protected, automatically, upon its creation. As such, you will have an asset that, if properly perfected and protected, can become rather valuable (see chapter 24).

3.2 Requirements to Qualify

The Copyright Act sets forth only two minimal requirements that must be met in order for a work to qualify for copyright protection. The work must be *original* and it must be *fixed in a tangible form*.[32]

With respect to the first requirement, the quantum of originality required to support a copyright is minimal. *Original* means only (1) that the work was independently created by the author (as opposed to copied from other works), and (2) that it possesses at least some minimal degree of creativity.[33]

The level of independent creation necessary to support a copyright does not require either uniqueness or novelty.[34] What is required is only that the work originate with the author—that the author not directly copy another work. Thus, for example, a painting of a U.S. flag on the side of a motorcycle is sufficiently original to meet the requirement for copyrightability.[35]

The second aspect of originality—creativity—has nothing to do with the skill, training, knowledge, or effort required to create the work. Expending a great deal of time and effort does not, by itself, satisfy the originality requirement. Thus, for example, the mere fact that a person conducted extensive research to gather information for a map does not suffice to make the map copyrightable.[36] What is required is an original creative contribution in the expression of the information.[37]

Although the standard is very low, there are works that fail to meet the minimal standard of originality, and thus do not qualify for copyright protection. Examples of works that do not evidence the requisite quantum of originality include the white pages of a phone book;[38] words and short phrases such as names, titles, and slogans; familiar symbols or designs; mere variations of typographic ornamentation, lettering or coloring; mere listing of ingredients or contents; blank forms, such as time cards, graph paper, account books, diaries, bank checks, scorecards, address books, report forms, order forms and the like, which are designed for recording information and do not in themselves convey information; and works consisting entirely of information that is common property containing no original authorship, such as standard calendars, height and weight charts, tape measures and rulers, schedules of sporting events, and lists or tables taken from public documents or other common sources.[39]

Originality, however, is not enough. In order for an "original work of authorship" to be copyrightable, it must also be fixed in a tangible medium of expression, now known or later developed, from which it can be perceived, reproduced, or otherwise communicated, either directly or with the aid of a machine or device.[40] It makes no difference what the form, manner, or medium of fixation may be— whether it is in words, numbers, notes, sounds, pictures, or any other graphic or symbolic indicia, whether embodied in a physical object in written, printed, photographic, sculptural, punched, magnetic, optical, or any other stable form, and whether it is capable of perception directly or only through the use of a machine or device such as a computer, videocassette recorder (VCR), or compact disc (CD) player.[41] Thus, for example, there is no doubt that pictures and sound recorded on magnetic or optical media in digital form are sufficiently "fixed" to meet the requirement for copyrightability.

A work is *fixed* in a tangible medium of expression when it is sufficiently permanent or stable to permit it to be perceived, reproduced, or otherwise communicated for a period of more than transitory duration. Thus, a work fixed on paper, film, videotape, computer disk or tape, CD-ROM, or CD, meets the fixation requirement necessary for copyrightability. A computer program or other digital content loaded from a storage medium (such as a hard disk, floppy disk, or CD-ROM) into the memory of the central processing unit of a computer also meets the fixation requirement.[42] Even if a computer program resides in the RAM of a computer for only a millisecond, it is sufficiently fixed to meet the requirement of the Copyright Act.[43] By contrast, something that exists only in your mind, or statements that you make to other people, are not fixed in a tangible medium of expression, and thus are not copyrightable unless and until they are written down on paper, recorded in some fashion, and otherwise fixed in a form that allows the thoughts or words to be reproduced or otherwise communicated.

4. What Rights Do Copyright Owners Get?

The Copyright Act grants the owner of the copyright in a work[44] what is, in effect, a limited monopoly on the use of the work. To accomplish this, the copyright owner is given the exclusive rights to do the following:[45]

1. make copies of the work (the reproduction right);

2. prepare derivative works based upon the work (the adaptation right);

3. distribute copies of the work publicly by sale, rental, lease, or lending (the distribution right);

4. perform the work publicly (the public performance right)[46] ; and

5. display the work publicly (the public display right).[47]

When someone other than the copyright owner, or a person acting with the owner's permission performs one of those acts, it is an infringement of the copyright unless it comes within an exception provided by the law.[48] (These exceptions include the first sale doctrine discussed in chapter 3, section 4.3 and the doctrine of fair use discussed in chapter 11, section 2.) The following sections will explain each of these rights in detail.

4.1 Reproduction Right

The Copyright Act gives the copyright owner the exclusive right to reproduce, and to authorize others to reproduce, the copyrighted work in copies or **phonorecords**.[49] These terms—copies and phonorecords—refer to the material objects (or "media") containing the work.

A *copy* is any material object (other than a phonorecord) that contains the work and from which it can be perceived, reproduced, or otherwise communicated, either directly or with the aid of a machine.[50] A *phonorecord* is any material object that contains sounds, other than those accompanying a motion picture or other audiovisual work, and from which the sounds can be perceived, reproduced, or otherwise communicated, either directly or with the aid of a machine or device.[51]

Thus, for example, a CD-ROM containing copyrighted text or pictures stored in digital form is considered a copy, as is a magazine containing the same text and pictures. Similarly, a CD-ROM containing only sound recordings of songs in digital form is considered a phonorecord.

Consequently, because the owner of the copyright is the only one granted the right to reproduce a copyrighted work in copies or phonorecords, the process of digitally scanning or capturing a copyrighted photograph from a magazine and storing it on a disk constitutes making a copy, which, if not authorized by the copyright owner, constitutes copyright infringement.[52] Similarly, sampling a copyrighted sound recording and storing it on a disk constitutes making a phonorecord, which, if not authorized by the copyright owner, also constitutes copyright infringement.[53] (See further discussion of sampling in chapter 11, section 3.1.1.)

Thus, regardless of the name attached to these material objects—copies or phonorecords—there is no question that the right to reproduce them belongs to the copyright owner. Although the right is sometimes called an "exclusive" one, some limitations on the right exist. The primary limitation on the reproduction right of the copyright owner is the doctrine of fair use. That is, someone who is not the copyright owner may reproduce a copy or a phonorecord of a portion of a copyrighted work in certain limited situations that are considered to constitute "fair use." The doctrine of fair use is discussed in detail in chapter 11, section 2.

The exclusive right of the copyright owner to make copies has an impact at several stages in the multimedia process. When a multimedia work is first developed, content is copied as it is incorporated in the product itself. Second, when the multimedia work is being manufactured or replicated (such as on a CD-ROM disc), the content and associated software comprising the product is again being copied. Third, each time the multimedia work is used by a user, the content and the software is again being "copied" as it is loaded into the memory of the user's machine (even though such use is temporary).[54] And finally, if the multimedia product allows the user to make a hard copy or printout of the content, this constitutes yet another form of "copying." Thus, for content and software that you do not own, you need to obtain a license not only to copy the content yourself, but also (if necessary) to grant your customers the right to copy the content in connection with their "use" of your multimedia works.

4.2 Adaptation Right

The Copyright Act gives the copyright owner the exclusive right to prepare a derivative version of his or her work.[55] A *derivative version* is a new work that is based on the preexisting work. It could be a revision of the original version, a translation from one language to another, or any other way in which the original work can be recast, transformed, or adapted.[56] A French translation of an English novel, a movie based on a book, a book that tells the story of copyrighted choreography (for example, a ballet) in photographs,[57] "colorized" black and white motion pictures,[58] and digitally altered photographs are all examples of derivative works. In many cases, a multimedia work may be considered to be a derivative of the content on which it is based. (See chapter 23 for a discussion of when a multimedia product is a derivative work, and the impact of such a characterization.)

The adaptation right—the right to create derivative works—becomes especially important in those situations where you want to license the right to use a preexisting copyrighted work for incorporation in a multimedia title you are developing, and in the process would like to modify, enhance, transform, or otherwise adapt the licensed content. This might include, for example, editing the content, morphing two or more pictures, splitting or combining sound recordings or images, translating text into another language, or otherwise rewriting, revising, or modifying the content for use in a multimedia title.

Because the adaptation right is reserved to the copyright owner, if you intend to create a derivative work from content licensed for inclusion in your multimedia title, you need to obtain specific permission from the copyright owner to do so. As with the reproduction right, the only major exception to the content owner's adaptation right is found in the doctrine of fair use. Fair use is discussed in chapter 11, section 2.

4.3 Distribution Right

The Copyright Act gives the copyright owner the exclusive right to distribute the copyrighted work.[59] The concept of "distribution" includes the right to sell copies of the copyrighted work, but it also goes beyond sale. It includes such other forms of "transfer of ownership" as rental, lease, and lending. In once recent case, a court found that making copyrighted photographs available in digital form on a computer bulletin board for downloading by subscribers constituted infringement of the copyright owner's exclusive right to distribute the work.[60]

Although this right is also called an "exclusive" right, it is subject to an important limitation. After the copyright owner has sold a particular copy of the work (i.e., made the "first sale" of that copy), it has no right to control further disposition of that copy by the purchaser.[61] Thus, for example, when you buy a copy of a book in a bookstore or a CD in a music store, it is not a copyright infringement to sell[62] your copy to someone else (as long as you do not make any additional copies as well). This is known as the *first sale doctrine*. Under this doctrine, the copyright owner's right to distribute a particular copy or phonorecord is limited to the first time he or she sells or otherwise disposes of that specific copy.[63] Thus, the distribution right is limited to the exclusive right to sell a copy or phonorecord *once*, because once the owner parts with a particular copy or phonorecord, the new owner then has the right to sell or otherwise transfer it.

If the owner of the copyright wants to prohibit subsequent transfer of that copy of the work, it must license rather than sell copies of the work and insert appropriate restrictive language in the license agreement.

A narrow exception to the first sale doctrine applies to phonorecords and copies of computer programs. Owners of phonorecords and copies of computer programs may not rent, lease, or lend a copy or phonorecord to others without getting permission to do so from the copyright owner.[64]

4.4 Public Performance Right

Owners of most copyrighted works also have the exclusive right to perform their works publicly.[65] This right is limited, however, to public performances. It does not apply to private (e.g., in-home) performances. Thus, understanding the scope of the public performance right requires consideration of what it means to perform a work, and when such performance is done publicly.

To *perform* a work means to recite, render, play, dance, or act it, either directly or by means of any device or process or, in the case of a motion picture or other audiovisual work, to show its images in any sequence or to make the sounds accompanying it audible.[66] A performance may be accomplished either directly (e.g., a live performance on a stage) or by means of any device or process, including all kinds of equipment for reproducing or amplifying sounds or visual images, any sort of transmitting apparatus, any type of electronic retrieval system, and any other techniques and systems not yet in use or even invented.[67]

Thus, for example, a singer is performing when he or she sings a song; a broadcasting network is performing when it transmits the singer's performance (whether simultaneously or from records); a local broadcaster is performing when it transmits the network broadcast; a cable television system is performing when it retransmits the broadcast to its subscribers; and an individual is performing whenever he or she plays a phonorecord embodying the performance or communicates the performance by turning on a receiving set. All of these acts constitute copyright infringement if they are done "publicly" and without permission.[68]

The performance of a work is done *publicly* in two types of situations.[69] First, a performance is considered to be "public" if it occurs at a place open to the public or in any place where a substantial number of persons outside of a normal circle of a family and its social acquaintances is gathered. This includes performances in semi-public places such as clubs, lodges, factories, summer camps, and schools. However, routine meetings of businesses and government personnel would be excluded because they do not represent the gathering of a substantial number of persons.[70]

Second, the concept of a public performance includes not only performances that occur in a public place, but also acts that transmit or communicate a performance of the work to the public by means of any device or process. This includes all conceivable forms and combinations of wired or wireless communications media, including radio and television broadcasting as we know them.[71] It is also worth noting that a performance made available by transmission to the public at large is considered public even though the recipients are not gathered in a single place, and even if there is no proof that any of the potential recipients was operating a receiving apparatus at the time of the transmission.[72]

Most performances of the musical works, motion pictures, and other copyrighted elements of a multimedia work will be done privately (e.g., at a user's home), rather than publicly. As a consequence, they will not infringe the copyright owner's public performance right. However, in those situations where a public performance is contemplated (e.g., showing a multimedia work at a seminar or conference, making a multimedia work available to the public "on-demand" via a computer network or cable system, and via a kiosk in a museum or shopping center), the public performance right will be implicated.

An interesting public performance issue was raised in a December 1993 class action lawsuit filed on behalf of more than 140 owners of musical compositions against CompuServe. The suit alleged that the uploading to, storage by, and downloading from CompuServe of musical instrument digital interface (MIDI) files constitutes an infringement of the right of public performance granted to the owners of the copyright in the underlying musical composition.[73] MIDI files are computer files that contain instructions controlling how and when devices like digital synthesizers produce sound. They can be stored in a digital form on computer-readable media such as disks and CD-ROM discs and later recalled to play back the musical work that is the subject of the MIDI recording. The suit alleged that CompuServe, by allowing its users to upload and download MIDI files, has permitted, facilitated, and participated in the recording and distribution of performances of several copyrighted musical compositions. This is the first case to allege infringement of the public performance right in a musical composition by the transmission and storage of digital MIDI files.

4.5 Public Display Right

Owners of most copyrighted works also have an exclusive right to **display**, and to authorize others to display, the copyrighted work publicly.[74] This right relates to works that can be seen, as opposed to works containing only sounds that can be heard. Like the public performance right, this right is limited to public displays. The copyright owner has no right to prohibit private (e.g., in-home) display of the copyrighted work. Thus, understanding the public display right involves consideration of both what it means to display a copyrighted work, and when such display is done publicly.

The concept of *display* covers any showing of a copy of the work, either directly or by means of a film, slide, television image, or any other device or process. The right of public display applies to original works of art as well as to reproductions of them. With respect to motion pictures and other audiovisual works, it is a display (rather than a performance) to show their "individual images nonsequentially." In addition to the direct showings of a copy of a work, the term *display* would include the projection of an image on a screen or other surface by any method, the transmission of an image by electronic or other means, and the showing of an image on a cathode ray tube, or similar viewing apparatus connected with any sort of information storage and retrieval system.[75]

As with the performance right, the right to display a copyrighted work is limited to public displays. It does not apply to private (e.g., in-home) display.

The display of a work is done *publicly* in two type of situations.[76] First, a display is considered to be public if it takes place at a place open to the public or in any place where a substantial number of persons outside of a normal circle of a family and its social acquaintances is gathered. This includes performances in semipublic places such as clubs, lodges, factories, summer camps, and schools. However, routine meetings of businesses and government personnel would be excluded because they do not represent the gathering of a "substantial number of persons."[77]

Second, the concept of a public display includes not only displays that occur in a public place, but also acts that transmit or otherwise communicate a display of the work to the public by means of any device or process. This includes all conceivable forms and combinations of wired or wireless communications media, including but not limited to radio and television broadcasting as we know them.[78] It is also worth noting that a display made available by transmission to the public at large is considered "public" even though the recipients are not gathered in a single place, and even if there is no proof that any of the potential recipients was operating his or her receiving apparatus at the time of the transmission.[79] Thus, for example, making digital versions of copyrighted pictures available on a computer bulletin board systems for viewing by subscribers without authorization of the copyright owner constitutes infringement of the public display right, where the subscribers to the board consisted of a substantial number of persons outside of the normal circle of family and its social acquaintances.[80]

Most displays of the images contained in a multimedia work are done privately (such as at a user's home) rather than publicly. As a consequence, they do not infringe the copyright owner's public display right. However, in those situations where a public display is contemplated (e.g., showing a multimedia work at a seminar or conference, making a multimedia work available to the public "on demand" via a computer network or cable system, or via a kiosk in a museum or shopping center), the public display right will be implicated.

4.6 Moral Rights

The exclusive rights of reproduction, adaptation, distribution, performance, and display granted to the copyright owner are frequently referred to as **economic rights**. In addition, copyright law also provides a level of protection for what are known as an author's **moral rights**.

Unlike economic rights, which are owned by whoever owns the copyright, moral rights are reserved exclusively for the original author of the copyrighted work. They are intended primarily to protect the author's reputation. Thus, moral rights deal with the general issue of artistic control by the original author of the work. That is, the author of a copyrighted work may feel that in order to protect the quality of the work, and thus the author's reputation, the author must have some say in the manner in which the work is subsequently used.

With multimedia works, the initial combination of the content, as well as the potential for subsequent editing, may raise concerns for the authors of the content. For example, an author of content included in a multimedia work may object that the multimedia work does not properly reflect the author's contribution or that use of the author's name in connection with the multimedia work prejudices the author's professional standing. The author may also object that the author's work has been distorted by being joined with the other component works. Similarly, any alteration of an author's work, such as the use of only a snippet of a work, may also cause the author to object. But whether an author has standing to object to the use of his or her work in a multimedia product (assuming you have a valid license from the copyright owner) depends on the extent of moral rights protection available.

The moral rights of the author of a copyrighted work fall into four general categories, not all of which are recognized in the United States:[81]

1. *the right of attribution*[82] —the author's right to attribution and against misattribution, and to prevent others from using the work or the author's name in such a way as to prejudice the author's professional standing;

2. *the right of integrity*—the author's right to object to certain acts, such as the distortion, mutilation or destruction of the work, that affect the integrity of the work or the reputation of the author;

3. *the right of disclosure*—the author's right to control the work's publication; and

4. *the right of withdrawal*—the author's right to withdraw, modify or disavow a work after it has been published.

The doctrine of moral rights originated in France. However, it is important to note that not all countries subscribe to the moral rights doctrine, and of those that do, many do not embrace all four component rights.[83]

With one exception, U.S. copyright law does not explicitly recognize moral rights or provide a cause of action for their violation.[84] However, moral rights are, to a limited extent, available via the common law and various state[85] and federal statutes. For example, U.S. courts have long granted relief for misrepresentation of an artist's work by relying on theories outside the statutory law of copyright, such as contract law.[86] Other courts protect an author's rights via the tort of unfair competition.[87]

The first, and only, explicit statutory recognition of moral rights in the U.S. Copyright Act came in the Visual Artists Rights Act of 1990 (VARA).[88] However, VARA only provides moral rights protection for "works of visual art."

A "work of visual art" is narrowly defined as a "painting, drawing, print, or sculpture" that exists in a unique original or in a limited edition of two hundred copies or fewer.[89] A still photographic image is also protected, but only if produced for exhibition purposes. A work for hire does not qualify as a "work of visual art." In addition, certain other works are expressly ineligible. These include: (1) any poster, map, globe, chart, technical drawing, diagram, model, applied art, motion picture, or other audiovisual work, book, magazine, newspaper, periodical, data base, electronic information service, electronic publication, or similar publication; and (2) any merchandising item or advertising, promotional, descriptive, covering, or packaging material or container.[90] In addition, the right of attribution does not apply to any reproduction or use of the work in audiovisual and certain other works.

VARA confers upon artists attribution and integrity rights. The attribution right includes the right (1) to claim authorship,—for example, to demand that the artist's name be used in conjunction with a display of the work, (2) to prevent use of the artist's name in connection with a work the artist did not create, and (3) to prevent use of the artist's name in connection with a work the artist created, but that has been subject to a "distortion, mutilation, or other modification" that would be prejudicial to the artist's honor or reputation.[91] The integrity right includes the right (1) to prevent any intentional distortion, mutilation, or other modification of the work that is prejudicial to the artist's reputation, and (2) to prevent any destruction of a work of recognized stature.[92]

While VARA is not expected to have much of an impact on multimedia, it does signal a growing willingness to recognize moral rights in the United States. And the development of multimedia works can have significant moral rights implications. In the entertainment industry, many authors obtain the equivalent of moral rights protection for their works by entering into contractual commitments whereby they retain the right to control certain aspects of the use subsequently made of their works, even though the economic rights in the copyright have been assigned to someone else.[93]

Thus, your proposed use of preexisting content may have significant "moral rights" implications, regardless of whether the source of those rights is the copyright law or a private contract between the author and the person to whom he or she has assigned the copyright.

The moral rights of the authors of content, to the extent they exist by statute or contract, pose several potential problems for you in connection with the multimedia development process. The author's right of integrity, for example, is not always clearly defined, and as a consequence, it is difficult to know what amounts to derogatory treatment of an author's work in violation of the right of integrity. This may be a particular problem with multimedia products that arguably facilitate infringement of the author's right of integrity by allowing users to manipulate or distort content as part of their interaction with the multimedia work itself.

Similarly, the right of attribution may present a practical problem for a multimedia work (such as a multimedia encyclopedia) that consists of literally thousands of different works of authorship. Identifying all of the individual authors may be rather difficult from a logistical perspective.

Even though the author of a particular work may have assigned his or her copyright to someone else, the moral rights or their equivalent may be retained, often by express contractual provision. As a consequence, obtaining permission from the new copyright owner to significantly alter a copyrighted work will have no impact on the moral rights of the original author of the work, to the extent they exist. Consequently, you may also need to obtain permission from the original author.

5. Transferring Rights

The rights granted to the owner of a copyright may be transferred from one party to another. Such a transaction typically takes the form of either an assignment or a license. If the transaction is an assignment, the owner of the copyrighted work relinquishes all rights of ownership and control over the particular copyright rights that are assigned. If the transaction is a license, the owner of the copyrighted work merely grants permission to use the work in accordance with the terms of the license.

In either case, it is important to understand that the rights that comprise a copyright are infinitely divisible. That is, any subset of the rights granted to the copyright owner may be licensed or assigned and owned separately.[94] (See this chapter, section 6).

5.1 Assignments

The ownership of a copyright (or any part of it) may be transferred by any means of conveyance or by operation of law, and may be bequeathed by will or pass as personal property by the applicable law of intestate succession.[95] Regardless of whether all or only some of the copyright rights are assigned, the transfer of copyright ownership is not valid unless the assignment is in writing and signed by the owner of the rights conveyed or the owner's duly authorized agent.[96] A sample assignment is included in chapter 29.

Documents evidencing assignments of copyright rights may be recorded in the Copyright Office.[97] There are advantages to recording assignments with the Copyright Office. For example, in the event there are two conflicting transfers of the same copyright, the one executed first will prevail if it is recorded in the Copyright Office within one month after its execution in the United States or within two months after its execution outside the United States, or at any time before the second transfer is recorded. Otherwise, the later transfer will prevail if it was recorded first and if it was taken in good faith for consideration and without notice of the earlier transfer.[98]

With respect to the preexisting content that you might want to incorporate in a multimedia product, it will typically be the case that the original author will have assigned his or her copyright to another person or entity. Accordingly, it may take some work to determine the identity of the current owner of the copyright. Searches of the copyright office may be helpful if the assignment has been recorded. Copyright office searches are discussed in chapter 12, section 3.3.

When one or more of the copyright rights to a work are assigned, the term of that assignment may be limited by the assignment document. For example, the document of assignment itself may provide for a termination of the assignment as of a specified date (e.g., fifteen years after the date of the assignment), and a reversion of the copyright to the original author at that time. Otherwise, an assignment of a copyright in a work created after January 1, 1978, will normally continue for the entire remaining life of the copyright.

Regardless of the terms of the assignment document, however, the Copyright Act gives the author the right to terminate the transfer during a five-year period beginning at the end of thirty-five years from the date of the assignment, or if the grant covers the right of publication, thirty-five years from the date of publication or forty years from the date of the grant, whichever is shorter.[99] To terminate the assignment, the original author must serve a written notice on the transferee within the time limits specified by the copyright law.[100]

5.2 Licenses

A **license** to use a copyrightable work is the most basic, the most common, and one of the most important of all transactions involving copyrightable works. The vast majority of all copyrightable content available in the market today is licensed rather than assigned.

Strictly speaking, a "license" is a grant of permission to do something that would not otherwise be allowed, or to exercise rights the licensee does not own. A license to use copyrightable content is a contract by which the owner of the copyright to the content grants to the licensee (such as a multimedia developer) the permission or right to use a particular copy of the copyrightable content, and defines the scope of the permission granted. Licenses are discussed in detail in chapters 13 through 20.

It is important to distinguish the concept of a license from that of an assignment (or sale) discussed above. In the case of a license, the licensee does not become the owner of any rights in the copyrightable content. It merely obtains the right to use it, subject to all the restrictions imposed by the license agreement. In the case of an assignment (or sale) however, title to the copyright rights is transferred to the buyer, who is then able to exercise those rights to the copyrightable content in any manner he or she desires—free from any restrictions.

Like assignments, *exclusive* licenses of copyright rights must be in writing. However, *nonexclusive* licenses to use copyrighted works do not have to be in writing. A nonexclusive license to a copyrightable work can arise by virtue of an oral agreement or can be implied by law or the conduct of the parties, much the same as any other contract can arise in those situations. Nonetheless, it is generally best for all parties if a nonexclusive license to copyrightable content is in writing. This allows the parties to define the exact scope of the rights granted, and to avoid disputes at a later date.

Copyright licenses are typically limited with respect to the scope of the rights that the licensee is authorized to exercise. For example, a license might authorize reproduction and distribution of a copyrighted work but prohibit adaptation of the work or the public performance or public display of the work. Moreover, even as to the rights granted in the license, a number of restrictions may be imposed as to the manner in which those rights may be exercised. For example, the use of the copyrighted work might be limited to a particular project (for example, a specified multimedia title), a particular medium (for example, CD-ROM), and a particular platform (for example, the Apple/Macintosh platform). In addition, distribution may be limited to a particular territory (for example, the United States). These and other restrictions often imposed in copyright licenses are discussed in chapter 13, section 2.

The term of a copyright license is frequently specified in the license agreement itself. For example, a license may have a stated term of five years, in which case the license will terminate at the end of the five years. In addition, the license may provide for earlier termination in the event of default by the licensee, or in the event that such certain other conditions or events occur.

Regardless of the term set forth in a license agreement, any license granted by the original author of a work is terminable by the author at any time during a five-year period beginning thirty-five years after the date of execution of the license by the author.[101] This is the same termination right that applies to assignments of copyright discussed above. Obviously, however, if the license agreement itself provides for a shorter term, the license agreement will prevail.

If you obtain a license to use copyrightable content and incorporate the content within a multimedia title, and the license to such content is terminated pursuant to the thirty-five-year termination rule noted above, the Copyright Act specifically provides that the derivative work you prepared under authority of the license before it was terminated (i.e., the multimedia title containing the content) may continue to be utilized under the terms of the license after its termination, but you will be deprived of the right to use the content to prepare any other derivative works.[102] On the other hand, if the license expires earlier as a result of a shorter license term appearing in the contract, your right to use the content, even in the original multimedia work in which it was incorporated, will expire when the license expires.

A unique variation on the license termination issue is the so-called *Rear Window* problem. This issue is a potential problem only when licensing works created prior to January 1, 1978, that are currently in their first term of copyright protection.

Under the Copyright Act in effect prior to January 1, 1978, copyright protection was available for two twenty-eight-year terms. If the copyright owner licensed someone to use a work during the first twenty-eight-year term of copyright protection, the copyright in the work reverted back to the copyright owner at the end of that initial twenty-eight-year term. At that point, the copyright had to be renewed (or it would enter the public domain), and the licensee needed to obtain a license to use the work in the second twenty-eight-year term of the copyright.

Although licensees typically require the copyright owner to grant rights in both the first and the second term of copyright protection, a major problem can arise if the copyright owner dies before the end of the first copyright term. In that case, the copyright reverts back to the owner's heirs, who may renew the copyright without any obligation to grant any rights to the original licensee. In those circumstances, the original licensee may find that it has created a derivative work based on the license it originally obtained that it can no longer exploit in the marketplace.

This very factual scenario played itself out with regard to the Hitchcock classic, *Rear Window*, starring James Stewart. After the initial term of copyright expired in the underlying work, *It Had To Be Murder*, Sheldon Abend, who had acquired the renewal rights in *It Had To Be Murder*, sued the film company that owned *Rear Window* when it continued to exhibit the film during the period of the renewal rights. Mr. Abend charged that the film company had infringed his rights in *It Had To Be Murder*, and the Supreme Court agreed.[103] In other words, because the movie *Rear Window* was a derivative work based on the story *It Had To Be Murder*, and because the license to that story was obtained during the first term of copyright protection, the right to show the movie terminated at the end of the first term of copyright protection, notwithstanding a clause in the license agreement obligating the copyright owner to continue the license during the second term of copyright protection. That was because the copyright owner died before the end of the first term of copyright protection and his heirs renewed the copyright themselves and assigned it to Mr. Abend. As a consequence, the owners of the movie *Rear Window* had to negotiate a license with the new owner of the rights in *It Had to Be Murder* in order to continue showing the movie.

As of 1995, this issue is of practical concern only when you want to license content that was in its first term of copyright protection between January 1, 1967, and December 31, 1977. However, to the extent you obtain a license to any works in their first term of protection during this time frame, beware that your rights may terminate prematurely if the *Rear Window* scenario repeats itself.

6. Separation of Rights

The rights in a copyright can be assigned in whole or in part.[104] Each of the five economic rights discussed above may be subdivided indefinitely, and each such subdivision of an exclusive right may be owned and enforced separately.[105]

This ability to grant and restrict the exercise of the rights inherent in a copyright has led to a phenomenon sometimes referred to as *separation of rights*. Separation of rights is heavily used in the entertainment industries, and involves the use of assignments or exclusive licenses or other contractual commitments to carve up the rights inherent in a copyright in a myriad of different ways.

In the publishing industry, for example, the rights to a book may be divided by the geographic area of distribution. Thus, one publisher may obtain the exclusive rights to publish the work in North America or in all English-speaking countries, whereas another may obtain rights for Europe or some other geographic area.

Similarly, the rights may be divided by the medium of publication. Thus one publisher may obtain the right to publish the work in hard copy form, another publisher may obtain the right to publish the work in paperback form, and yet a third publisher may obtain the right to publish the work in electronic form. The manner in which rights may be divided depends, to a certain extent, on the industry involved.

As a consequence, the issue of separation of rights can be a serious potential problem when you are attempting to license the rights to use preexisting content in a multimedia product that you are developing. Quite simply, the copyright owner with whom you are dealing may not possess the specific rights that you require for your intended use of the content. For example, if you were negotiating with a book publisher for a license to use portions of a book, but the publisher only has North American distribution rights, you will not be able to obtain a license to distribute the text worldwide. Similarly, if the publisher only has rights to publish the work in the print media, it would not be in a position to grant you electronic rights to the same work.

7. The Problem of Overlapping Copyrights

When you use content created by others for your multimedia products, it is important that you understand the nature of all of the various rights of the copyright owner discussed above, and the many ways in which those rights can be separated. In addition, it is important to understand that the content you want to use may also be the subject of *overlapping copyrights*. That is, the work may be composed of more than one copyright, and in order to obtain adequate rights to use the content in a multimedia work, it will be necessary to obtain permission from each of the copyright owners.[106]

Unless you obtain permission from the owners of *all* of the copyrights, your use of the content will constitute infringement of the copyrights with respect to which you have not obtained permission. Likewise, the multimedia product that you create will itself be a copyrightable work consisting of overlapping copyrights (if you license content from other persons), and your continued reproduction and distribution of your own multimedia work will constitute infringement of the copyrights in any content incorporated in your work if and when your license to that content expires.

The problem of overlapping copyrights can best be illustrated by an example. If someone would like to make a movie based on a book, and include in the movie a recording of a popular copyrighted song, the resulting movie will contain a number of overlapping copyrights. First, as a derivative work based on the underlying book, the movie will contain material from the book. Second, the movie will contain a recording of a copyrighted song. But the movie itself is also a copyrightable work. Thus, anyone who copies the movie without permission will be infringing at least three copyrights: the copyright that the movie producer has in the movie itself, the copyright that the author of the underlying book has in his or her story (because copyrightable aspects of the book will be copied when the movie is copied), and the copyright that the composer has in his or her song (because copying the movie also results in making another copy of the song). In other words, the act of copying the movie includes the act of copying aspects of three separate copyrightable works. Conversely, obtaining permission to use the movie requires obtaining permission to make copies of portions of three separately copyrightable works—something that frequently requires obtaining permission from three separate copyright owners.

The same is true, of course, of any multimedia work that you create using content licensed from any other person. Thus, for example, if you create a multimedia title for which you license 72 copyrighted photographs and 28 copyrighted songs (in addition to text you write yourself), the resulting multimedia title will include at least 101 copyrights. That is, there is a copyright in the multimedia title itself, the 72 photograph copyrights, and the 28 song copyrights (see discussion in chapter 23). And if you licensed sound recordings of those 28 songs, you will have an additional 28 copyrights as part of your work, since there are 2 copyrights in each sound recording of a popular song (the copyright in the song itself and the copyright in the sound recording of the song—see discussion in chapter 17, section 1.2 and chapter 18, section 1.1.2). Consequently, if the term of your license to use any one of those 128 copyrightable works expires, your continued reproduction or distribution of your multimedia work will constitute copyright infringement with respect to the copyright to which the license has expired.

8. What Constitutes Infringement?

Anyone who exercises any of the exclusive rights that are reserved to the owner of a copyright without the permission of the owner, unless excused by one of the exceptions, such as fair use, is guilty of copyright infringement. The following sections summarize the more common methods by which a copyright may be infringed.

8.1 Copying

The most obvious of all forms of copyright infringement is the act of copying. Every time copyrightable content is copied by someone other than the copyright owner and is done without his or her permission, the owner's copyright has been infringed, unless the copying is fair use or otherwise excused. Exact copying is not required for infringement. If someone takes copyrighted content, for example, and alters it in order to disguise the copying, it will still be a copyright infringement. A plagiarist will not be allowed to escape punishment by making immaterial variations.

In one case, for example, the defendants rerecorded popular songs but made a number of changes to them, such as increasing and decreasing the speeds of the songs and adding new synthesizer-generated sounds. Despite the changes in rhythm or speed, however, the court concluded that so long as the work was produced by rerecording the original sounds, or recapturing those sounds, the work constitutes copyright infringement, notwithstanding the fact that, by electronically altering the sounds, the defendants had not made an exact copy of the original sound recording.[107]

Scanning and digitizing a photograph, or sampling a sound recording of a musical work, are examples of copying that can constitute copyright infringement. At present, however, there is a major debate over whether sampling is, or should be, copyright infringement. By definition, sampling is copying. Thus, if copyrightable material is "sampled" from another work, it is highly likely that the sampling will constitute copyright infringement. In fact, according to one court "there can be no more brazen stealing of music than digital sampling."[108]

The few cases that have considered sampling have generally found the practice to constitute infringement. In one case, for example, the court found that the copyright for the master recording of a song, as well as its underlying musical composition, had been violated by the unauthorized use of a three-word sample.[109] In another case, the court held that sampling the attention-grabbing parts from another's recording could be copyright infringement.[110] In a third case, the court found that sampling of the sounds "Brrr" and "Hugga Hugga" could constitute copyright infringement.[111]

8.2 Adaptations and Modifications

Modifying, adapting, and revising content, like copying, constitutes copyright infringement, unless authorized by the copyright owner or one of the statutory exceptions, such as fair use. Remember, one of the exclusive rights reserved to the owner of the software copyright is the right to prepare derivative works, that is, the right to adapt the work. This includes translations. Thus, colorizing a black and white film or morphing two pictures is just as much a copyright infringement as translating a book from English to French or making a movie based on a book.

8.3 Distribution

The distribution of unauthorized copies of a copyrighted work is also an infringement of the copyright owners exclusive right of distribution. Except for the rights the owner of a copy has under the first sale doctrine (see this chapter, section 3.4), no one is allowed to sell, license, or in any other way distribute a copyrighted work without permission of the copyright owner.

8.4 Public Performance or Display

Publicly performing or displaying a copyrighted work without permission, such as playing a CD recording of a popular song at a convention, showing a film clip at a seminar, transmitting content to cable television subscribers, or making a photograph available for viewing on a computer bulletin board system, all constitute copyright infringement.[112]

8.5 Use of Work in Excess of License Rights

Whenever a licensee utilizes a copyrighted work in a manner or to an extent not authorized by the terms of the license agreement, the licensee's conduct constitutes copyright infringement.[113]

9. Remedies for Infringement

A variety of remedies are available to a copyright owner who can prove that the copyright has been infringed. A court may allow the owner, in appropriate circumstances, to stop (or enjoin) the infringement, to impound and destroy all infringing copies, to obtain compensation for damages, and, in certain cases, to obtain reimbursement for its attorneys' fees. In addition, criminal penalties may be involved. Thus, at least in theory, the copyright owner may bring an impressive array of sanctions to bear upon a copyright infringer.

9.1 Injunction

The first goal of the copyright owner is to stop the infringement. This is accomplished by obtaining a court-ordered injunction prohibiting the **defendant** from continuing to copy, and (where appropriate) from continuing to market the infringing copies of the plaintiff's work. If the owner of the copyright—that is, the **plaintiff**—can demonstrate that he is likely to prevail on his claim of infringement, the court has the power to issue a temporary injunction at the beginning of the lawsuit that will remain in effect while the case is being decided.[114] At the conclusion of the lawsuit, if it is determined that the defendant has infringed the copyright in the plaintiff's work, the court has the authority to make the injunction permanent[115] and to provide the other relief discussed in the following sections. (For a more detailed discussion of injunctions see chapter 8, section 7.1.)

9.2 Impoundment of Infringing Copies

The Copyright Act authorizes the court to order the impoundment of all allegedly infringing copies of the copyrighted work at any time during the pendency of a copyright infringement lawsuit.[116] This is done to ensure that all infringing copies of the work can be destroyed at the conclusion of the lawsuit if the plaintiff prevails.

9.3 Destruction of Infringing Copies

At the conclusion of the lawsuit, if the court determines that the defendant has infringed the plaintiff's copyright in its work, it may, as part of the final judgment or decree, order the destruction or other reasonable disposition of all copies of the work found to have been made or used in violation of the copyright owner's exclusive rights, as well as all discs, tapes, masters, or other articles by means of which such copies may be reproduced.[117]

9.4 Damages

A plaintiff whose work has been infringed is also entitled to an award of money damages as compensation for the financial injury caused by the misappropriation. Generally, two alternative damage measures are available to the plaintiff: **actual damages** measured by the sum of the plaintiff's actual losses and the defendant's profits, or **statutory damages.**

The plaintiff has the right to recover any damages that it suffered as a result of the infringement, plus any profits made by the infringer.[118] Actual damages may include lost profits as well as the reduced market value of the work caused by the unauthorized distribution of infringing copies. In addition, the plaintiff may recover the profits made by the defendant on the marketing of the infringing work to the extent they are not taken into account in calculating the plaintiff's actual damages.[119]

If it is difficult for the plaintiff to prove the exact dollar amount of its losses resulting from the defendant's infringement, the plaintiff may elect, at any time during the lawsuit, to recover "statutory damages." Then there is no need to prove the actual loss. Under the Copyright Act, the court may award statutory damages to the plaintiff of $500 to $20,000.[120] And, if the court finds that the defendant acted willfully, it may increase the award of statutory damages to as much as $100,000.[121] Remember, however, that the option to take statutory damages is not available unless the work has been registered within the time period required by the statute (see chapter 24, section 2.3).

9.5 Costs and Attorneys' Fees

The Copyright Act specifically allows the court to award the costs of the litigation, including reasonable attorneys' fees, to the prevailing party.[122] It is important to note, however, that attorneys' fees are available to the prevailing party only if the work has been registered within the time period required by the statute (see chapter 24, section 2.3).

9.6 Criminal Penalties

In certain cases, persons who infringe a copyright may be liable for criminal as well as civil penalties. Specifically, the copyright law makes it a criminal offense to infringe a copyright "willfully and for purposes of commercial advantage or private financial gain."[123] The penalty can be up to five years in prison and a fine of up to $250,000.[124] Thus anyone who is infringing a copyright for purposes of marketing the infringing copies may be guilty of criminal copyright infringement.

In addition to infringement, the Copyright Act also makes it a criminal offense to place a false copyright notice on any article, or to publicly distribute an article bearing such a notice with fraudulent intent.[125] Similarly, it is a crime to remove a copyright notice with a fraudulent intent.[126] Finally, it is also a criminal offense to knowingly make a false representation of a material fact in the application for a copyright registration.[127] The penalty for all of these activities is a fine of up to $2,500.

Endnotes

1   All references to the "Copyright Act" refer to the Copyright Act of 1976 (17 U.S.C. §§ 101-810 unless otherwise indicated. This statute became effective on January 1, 1978.

2   17 U.S.C. §§ 101, 102(a).

3   17 U.S.C. § 102(a)(1); 17 U.S.C. § 101 (definition of "literary works").

4   17 U.S.C. §§ 101 (definition of "literary works") and 103(a).

5   See *Walt Disney Prods. v. Air Pirates*, 581 F.2d 751 (9th Cir. 1978) ("Mickey Mouse", "Donald Duck", and several other Disney characters); *Detective Comics, Inc. v. Bruns Publications, Inc.*, 111 F.2d 432, 433-34 (2d Cir. 1940) ("Superman" character); *United Feature Syndicate, Inc. v. SunRise Mold Co.*, 569 F. Supp. 1475, 1480 (S.D. Fla. 1983) ("Peanuts" characters); *Eden Toys, Inc. v. Florelee Undergarment Co.*, 697 F.2d 27 (2d Cir. 1982) ("Paddington Bear", a character in a series of children's books); *Nichols v. Universal Pictures Corp.*, 45 F.2d 119, 121 (2d Cir. 1930) (discussing copyrightability of literary characters), *cert. denied*, 282 U.S. 902 (1931); *Filmvideo Releasing Corp. v. Hastings*, 509 F. Supp. 60, 66. (S.D.N.Y. 1981) (Hopalong Cassidy character developed in a series of books was sufficiently delineated, developed and well-known to the public to be copyrightable"), *aff'd*, 668 F.2d 91 (2d Cir. 1981).

6   See *Walt Disney Prods. v. Air Pirates*, 581 F.2d 751, 755 (9th Cir. 1978) ("while many literary characters may embody little more than an unprotected idea . . . , a comic book character, which has physical as well as conceptual qualities, is more likely to contain some unique elements of expression").

7   *Nichols v. Universal Pictures Corp.*, 45 F.2d 119, 121 (2d Cir. 1930), *cert. denied*, 282 U.S. 902 (1931).

8   17 U.S.C. § 102(a)(2).

9   See *Mills Music, Inc. v. Arizona*, 187 U.S.P.Q. 22, 31 (D. Ariz. 1975), *aff'd*, 591 F.2d 1278 (9th Cir. 1979).

10   *Plymouth Music Co. v. Magnus Organ Corp.*, 456 F. Supp. 676, 679 (S.D.N.Y. 1978).

11   17 U.S.C. § 101 (definition of "sound recordings").

12   17 U.S.C. § 101 (definition of "sound recordings").

13   17 U.S.C. § 102(a)(7).

14   See, e.g., *Innovative Concepts in Entertainment, Inc. v. Entertainment Enters., Ltd.*, 576 F. Supp. 457, 461 (E.D.N.Y. 1983) (sound recording of crowd noises from an actual hockey game was copyrightable).

15   17 U.S.C. § 102(a)(5).

16   17 U.S.C. § 101.

17   H.R. Rep. No. 1476, 94th Cong., 2d Sess. 54 (1976), *reprinted in* 1976 U.S.C.C.A.N. 5659, 5667.

18   H.R. Rep. No. 1476, 94th Cong., 2d Sess. 54 (1976), *reprinted in* 1976 U.S.C.C.A.N. 5659, 5667.

19   Copyright Office Cir. 40, Copyright Registration for Works of the Visual Arts 2 (1990).

20   17 U.S.C. § 102(a)(6).

21   17 U.S.C. § 101 (definition of "audiovisual works").

22   See *WGN Continental Broadcasting Co. v. United Video, Inc.*, 693 F.2d 622, 626 (7th Cir. 1982).

23   See *Midway Mfg. Co. v. Artic Int'l, Inc.*, 704 F.2d 1009, 1011 (7th Cir.), *cert. denied*, 464 U.S. 823 (1983).

24   17 U.S.C. § 101 (definition of "motion pictures").

25   See H.R. Rep. No. 1476, 94th Cong., 2d Sess. 56 (1976), *reprinted in* 1976 U.S.C.C.A.N. 5659, 5669.

26   17 U.S.C. § 101 (definition of "motion pictures").

27   17 U.S.C. § 101 (definition of "sound recordings").

28   See, e.g., *Computer Assocs. Int'l, Inc. v. Altai, Inc.*, 23 U.S.P.Q. 2d 1241, 1249 (2d Cir. 1992) ("it is now well settled that the literal elements of computer programs, i.e., the source and object codes, are the subject of copyright protection").

29   17 U.S.C. § 102(a).

30   The rules are somewhat different for works created prior to January 1, 1978, the effective date of the current copyright law.

31   Under the Copyright Act of 1909, publication of a work without a copyright notice injected the work into the public domain. Under the Copyright Act of 1976, publication of a work without a notice also generally resulted in a loss of the copyright, but the law was not as unforgiving. There were a number of remedial provisions that the copyright owner could take to retain his or her copyright. Effective as of March 1, 1989, however, a copyright notice is no longer required on any copyrighted work first published after that date. Also, under the Copyright Act of 1976, registration of a copyright has always been optional (although it is required as a condition of bringing the lawsuit).

32   17 U.S.C. § 102(a).

33   *Feist Publications, Inc. v. Rural Tele. Serv. Co.*, 499 U.S. 340, 111 S. Ct. 1282, 1287 (1991). See also *Alfred Bell & Co. v. Catalda Fine Arts, Inc.*, 191 F.2d 99, 103 (2d Cir. 1951) (originality requirement is "little more than a prohibition of actual copying. No matter how poor the author's addition, it is enough if it be his own").

34   *Feist Publications, Inc. v. Rural Tele. Serv. Co.*, 499 U.S. 340, 111 S. Ct. 1282, 1287 (1991).

35   *INT-Elect Eng'g, Inc. v. Clinton Harley Corp.*, 27 U.S.P.Q. 2d 1631, 1633 (N.D. Cal. 1993).

36   See *Feist Publications, Inc. v. Rural Tele. Serv. Co.*, 499 U.S. 340, 111 S. Ct. 1282, 1291-93 (1991); *Rockford Map Publishers, Inc. v. Directory Serv. Co.*, 768 F.2d 145, 148 (7th Cir. 1985) (the input of time is irrelevant—copyright can inure in "the work of an instant," such as a photograph).

37   See *Tin Pan Apple, Inc. v. Miller Brewing Co.*, 1994 U.S. Dist. LEXIS 2178 at *9 (S.D.N.Y. Feb. 24, 1994) denying defendant's motion for summary judgment and holding that the jury could find that the "Brrr" and "Hugga-Hugga" sounds, used as lyrics in a copyrighted musical composition, were sufficiently creative to warrant copyright protection).

38   *Feist Publications, Inc. v. Rural Tele. Serv. Co.*, 499 U.S. 340, 111 S. Ct. 1282, 1291-93 (1991).

39   37 C.F.R. §§ 202.1(a), (c) and (d).

40   17 U.S.C. § 102(a).

41   H.R. Rep. No. 1476, 94th Cong., 2d Sess. 52 (1976), *reprinted in* 1976 U.S.C.C.A.N. 5659, 5665.

42   *MAI Sys. Corp. v. Peak Computer, Inc.,* 991 F.2d 511, 518 (9th Cir. 1993), *cert. dismissed,* 114 S. Ct. 671 (1994); *Advance Computer Servs., Inc. v. MAI Sys. Corp.,* 845 F. Supp. 356 (E.D. Va. 1994); *Triad Sys. Corp. v. Southeastern Express Co.,* 1994 U.S. Dist. LEXIS 5390 at *16-17 (N.D. Cal. Mar. 21, 1994).

43   *Triad Sys. Corp. v. Southeastern Express Co.,* 1994 U.S. Dist. LEXIS 5390 at *16-17 (N.D. Cal. Mar. 21, 1994) ("the Copyright Law is not so much concerned with the temporal 'duration' of a copy as it is with what that copy does, and what it is capable of doing, while it exists. 'Transitory duration' is a relative term that must be interpreted and applied in context. This concept is particularly important in cases involving computer technology where the speed and complexity of machines and software is rapidly advancing, and where the diversity of computer architecture and software design is expanding at an ever increasing rate.").

44   The identity of the "owner" of the copyright is a key issue. This is discussed in chapter 23.

45   17 U.S.C. § 106.

46   This right applies only to literary, musical, dramatic, and choreographic works, pantomimes, and motion pictures and other audiovisual works. It does not apply to sound recordings or to pictorial, graphic, or sculptural works.

47   This right applies only to literary, musical, dramatic, and choreographic works, pantomimes, and pictorial, graphic, or sculptural works, including the individual images of a motion picture or other audiovisual work. It does not apply to sound recordings.

48   17 U.S.C. § 501(a). These exceptions include the first sale doctrine discussed at chapter 3, section 4.3 and the doctrine of fair use discussed at chapter 11, section 2.

49   17 U.S.C. § 106(1).

50   17 U.S.C. § 101 (definition of "copies").

51   17 U.S.C. § 101 (definition of "phonorecords").

52   See, *e.g., Playboy Enters., Inc. v. Frena,* 839 F. Supp. 1552 (M.D. Fla. 1993).

53   *Grand Upright Music, Ltd. v. Warner Bros. Records, Inc.,* 780 F. Supp. 182 (S.D.N.Y. 1991); *Jarvis v. A & M Records,* 827 F. Supp. 282, 27 U.S.P.Q.2d 1812 (D.N.J. 1993); *Tin Pan Apple, Inc. v. Miller Brewing Co.,* 1994 U.S. Dist. LEXIS 2178 (S.D.N.Y. 1994).

54   *MAI Sys. Corp. v. Peak Computer, Inc.,* 991 F.2d 511, 518 (9th Cir. 1993); *Advanced Computer Servs., Inc. v. MAI Sys. Corp.,* 845 F. Supp. 356 (E.D. Va. 1994).

55   17 U.S.C. § 106(2).

56   17 U.S.C. § 101.

57   *Horgan v. MacMillan, Inc.,* 789 F.2d 157, 163 (2d Cir. 1986).

58   See *Copyright Registration for Colorized Versions of Black and White Motion Pictures. Notice of Proposed Rulemaking,* Docket No. RM86-1A (June 11, 1987); *Copyright Registration for Colorized Versions of Black and White Motion Pictures,* 52 Fed. Reg. 23443 (1987).

59   17 U.S.C. § 106(3).

60   *Playboy Enters., Inc. v. Frena,* 839 F. Supp. 1552 (M.D. Fla. 1993).

61 17 U.S.C. § 109.

62 However, this exception does not apply to the *rental* of sound recordings or computer programs. That is, although someone who purchases a copy of a phonorecord embodying a sound recording or a computer program has the right to resell that particular copy, the rental or leasing of that copy constitutes copyright infringement. 17 U.S.C. § 109(b).

63 17 U.S.C. § 109(a).

64 17 U.S.C. § 109(b). Note, however, that the prohibition on the rental of computer programs expires on October 1, 1997.

65 The performance right does not apply to sound recordings. See 17 U.S.C. § 114(a). By its nature, it also does not apply to pictorial, graphic, or sculptural works. 17 U.S.C. § 106(4).

66 17 U.S.C. § 101.

67 H.R. REP. No. 1476, 94th Cong., 2d Sess. 63-64 (1976), *reprinted in* 1976 U.S.C.C.A.N. 5659, 5677. Thus, for example, using a CD player and an amplifier to play a song recorded on a CD at a seminar or conference is just as much a "performance" as standing on a stage at a public auditorium and singing the same song "live" for the assembled audience.

68 H.R. REP. No. 1476, 94th Cong., 2d Sess. 63-64 (1976), *reprinted in* 1976 U.S.C.C.A.N. 5659, 5677.

69 17 U.S.C. § 101.

70 H.R. REP. No. 1476, 94th Cong., 2d Sess. 64 (1976), *reprinted in* 1976 U.S.C.C.A.N. 5659, 5677-78.

71 H.R. REP. No. 1476, 94th Cong., 2d Sess. 64 (1976), *reprinted in* 1976 U.S.C.C.A.N. 5659, 5677-78.

72 H.R. REP. No. 1476, 94th Cong., 2d Sess. 64-65 (1976), *reprinted in* 1976 U.S.C.C.A.N. 5659, 5678.

73 *Frank Music Corp. v. CompuServe, Inc.*, 93 N. Civ. 8153 (S.D.N.Y. filed Dec. 1993).

74 17 U.S.C. § 106(5). The display right does not apply to sound recordings. See 17 U.S.C. § 114(a). With respect to motion pictures and other audiovisual works, the public display right applies to individual images, as opposed to showing the motion picture itself, which would constitute a performance rather than a display. See 17 U.S.C. § 106(5).

75 H.R. REP. No. 1476, 94th Cong., 2d Sess. 64 (1976), *reprinted in* 1976 U.S.C.C.A.N. 5659, 5677-78. See also *Playboy Enters., v. Frena*, 839 F. Supp. 1552 (M.D. Fla. 1993) (holding that use of a computer bulletin board system that allowed subscribers to look at copyrighted pictures stored on the bulletin board system constituted an infringement of the copyright owner's public display right).

76 17 U.S.C. § 101.

77 H.R. REP. No. 1476, 94th Cong., 2d Sess. 64 (1976), *reprinted in* 1976 U.S.C.C.A.N. 5659, 5677-78.

78 H.R. REP. No. 1476, 94th Cong., 2d Sess. 64 (1976), *reprinted in* 1976 U.S.C.C.A.N. 5659, 5677-78.

79 H.R. REP. No. 1476, 94th Cong., 2d Sess. 64-65 (1976), *reprinted in* 1976 U.S.C.C.A.N. 5659, 5678.

80   *Playboy Enters., Inc. v. Frena*, 839 F. Supp. 155 (M.D. Fla. Dec. 9, 1993) See also *Thomas V. Pansy Ellen Prods., Inc.*, 672 F. Supp. 237, 240 (W.D. N.C. 1987) (display at a trade show was public even though limited to members); *Ackee Music, Inc. v. Williams*, 650 F. Supp. 653, 655-56 (D. Kan. 1986) (performance of copyrighted songs at defendant's private club constitute a public performance).

81   See generally 2 PAUL GOLDSTEIN, COPYRIGHT, § 15.23 (1989); 2 MELVILLE B. NIMMER & DAVID NIMMER, NIMMER ON COPYRIGHT, § 8.21 (1993).

82   The right of attribution is also referred to as the "right to paternity."

83   The Berne Convention, an international copyright treaty signed by 96 countries, including the United States, requires member states to recognize the moral rights of integrity and attribution. It provides: "independently of the author's economic rights, and even after the transfer of said rights, the author shall have the right to claim authorship of the work and to object to any distortion, mutilation, or other modification of, or other derogatory action in relation to, the said work, which shall be prejudicial to his honor or reputation." BERNE CONVENTION, Article *6bis*. However, there is not necessarily any consistency in the scope of protection provided for moral rights among the various countries that have signed the Berne Convention.

84   Thus, moral rights are not as important in the United States (where moral rights are not strongly recognized) as they are in other countries (such as France and Japan) where moral rights are considered very important.

85   At least eleven states have also enacted laws protecting, to varying extents, the rights of integrity and attribution for visual artists. See 2 MELVILLE B. NIMMER & DAVID NIMMER, NIMMER ON COPYRIGHT, § 8.21[B], at 8-282.5 & n.51 (1993).

86   See, e.g., *Gilliam v. American Broadcasting Cos.,* 538 F.2d 14, 24 (2d Cir. 1976); *Granz v. Harris*, 198 F.2d 585 (2d Cir. 1952) (substantial cutting of original work constitutes misrepresentation).

87   *Gilliam v. American Broadcasting Cos., 538 F. 2d 14, 24 (2d Cir. 1976); Prouty v. National Broadcasting Co.,* 26 F. Supp. 265 (D. Mass. 1939); *Stevens v. National Broadcasting Co.,* 148 U.S.P.Q. 755 (Cal. Super. Ct. 1966).

88   The VARA is codified at 17 U.S.C. §§ 101, 101 note, 106A, 106A note, 107, 113, 301, 411, 412, 501, and 506. The VARA was effective June 1, 1991.

89   17 U.S.C. § 101.

90   17 U.S.C. § 101.

91   17 U.S.C. §§ 106A(a)(1),(2).

92   17 U.S.C. § 106A(a)(3)(A),(B). The legislative history of the VARA can be found at H.R. REP. No. 514, 101 Cong., 2d Sess. 1 (1990), *reprinted in* 1990 U.S.C.C.A.N. 6802, 6915-34.

93   See, e.g., *Gilliam v. American Broadcasting Cos.,* 538 F.2d 14 (2d. Cir. 1976) (where owner of Monty Python television scripts retained right to control alterations in script, alteration of television programs that involved the insertion of commercials without permission likely to constitute copyright infringement); *In re Arbitration between Directors Guild of America, Inc., Warren Beatty, JRS Prods., Inc., Paramount Pictures Corp. and American Broadcasting Cos.,* 6 Ent. L. Rep. No. 12, at 8 (May 1985) (Warren Beatty, the producer, director and star of the film "Reds" asserted contract right to control editing of film to object to ABC's plan to cut

about 6 minutes and 25 seconds from the film for time format purposes).

94   17 U.S.C. § 201(d)(2).

95   17 U.S.C. § 201(d)(1).

96   17 U.S.C. § 204(a). This rule does not apply, however, in the case of transfers that occur by operation of law. See 17 U.S.C. § 204(a).

97   17 U.S.C. § 205(a). Documents of assignment may be recorded in the Copyright Office by sending the original copy of the assignment document to the Copyright Office, along with a fee of $20 for the first title covered by the transfer, along with a fee of $10 for each group of not more than 10 additional titles. 17 U.S.C. § 708(a)(4).

98   17 U.S.C. § 205(d).

99   See 17 U.S.C. § 203. It is also important to note that the author has the right to terminate the assignment notwithstanding any agreement to the contrary. 17 U.S.C. § 203(a)(5).

100   See 17 U.S.C. § 203(a)(3), (4).

101   17 U.S.C. § 203(a).

102   17 U.S.C. § 203(b)(1).

103   *Abend v. MCA, Inc.*, 863 F.2d 1465 (9th Cir. 1988), *aff'd. sub nom., Stewart v. Abend,* 495 U.S. 207, 110 S. Ct. 1750 (1990).

104   17 U.S.C. § 201(d)(1).

105   H.R. Rep. No. 1476, 94th Cong., 2d Sess. 61 (1976), *reprinted in* 1976 U.S.C.C.A.N. 5659, 5674-75; 17 U.S.C. § 201(d)(2).

106   In addition, each of these copyrights may have more than one owner. The issues that arise from a jointly owned copyright are discussed in section 23-31. However, the discussion at this point focuses on works that involve more than one copyright, regardless of the number of owners of each of the copyrights involved.

107   *United States v. Taxe*, 380 F. Supp. 1010, 1017 (C.D. Cal. 1974), *aff'd in part and vacated in part,* 540 F. 2d 961 (9th Cir.), *cert. denied,* 429 U.S. 1040 (1976).

108   *Jarvis v. A&M Records*, 27 U.S.P.Q.2d 1812, 1821 (D.N.J. 1993). See also *Tin Pan Apple, Inc. v. Miller Brewing Co.,* 1994 U.S. Dist. LEXIS 2178 at *14 (S.D.N.Y. Feb. 24, 1994) (noting that "it is common ground that if defendants did sample plaintiff's copyrighted sound recording, they infringe that copyright . . .").

109   *Grand Upright Music, Ltd. v. Warner Bros. Records, Inc.,* 780 F. Supp. 182 (S.D.N.Y. 1991).

110   *Jarvis v. A&M Records,* 827 F. Supp. 282, 27 U.S.P.Q.2d 1812 (D.N.J. 1993).

111   *Tin Pan Apple, Inc., v. Miller Brewing Co.,* 1994 U.S. Dist. LEXIS 2178 (S.D.N.Y. Feb. 24, 1994).

112   *Playboy Enters., Inc. v. Frena*, 839 F. Supp. 1552 (M.D. Fla. 1993).

113   *Marshall v. New Kids On The Block Partnership,* 780 F. Supp. 1005, 1009 (S.D.N.Y. 1991).

114   17 U.S.C. § 502.

115   17 U.S.C. § 502.

116   17 U.S.C. § 503.

117   17 U.S.C. § 503(b).

118   17 U.S.C. §§ 504(a) and (b).

119   17 U.S.C. § 504(b).

120   17 U.S.C. § 504(c)(1).

121   17 U.S.C. § 504(c)(2).

122   17 U.S.C. § 505. See also *Fogerty v. Fantasy, Inc.*, 1994 U.S. LEXIS 2042 (U.S. March 1, 1994)

123   17 U.S.C. § 506.

124   18 U.S.C. §§ 2319, 3571ff.

125   17 U.S.C. § 506(c).

126   17 U.S.C. § 506(d).

127   17 U.S.C. § 506(e).

Trademarks and Unfair Competition

Trademarks and Unfair Competition

In creating multimedia works, you should be aware of the potential for trademark infringement and unfair competition. The appeal and recognizability of famous trademarks often makes them attractive candidates for inclusion in a multimedia work, whether it be a product logo, a commercial song or slogan, or a parody of a well-known name. Use of such elements can, however, expose you to liability for trademark infringement in certain circumstances. Similarly, use of someone else's trade name or trade dress, or unfair competition such as false advertising, can expose you to liability.

In addition, you should be aware that your own name and logos can constitute trademarks and trade names, which can be protected or, if not properly chosen, can expose you to liability for infringement. The following sections will discuss basic principles of trademark and unfair competition law and how they affect multimedia development. Protecting your own trademarks is discussed in chapter 25.

1. What Is a Trademark?

A **trademark** can be any word, name, symbol, or slogan used by a person or company to identify its products and to distinguish them from products of others.[1] "Coke," "IBM," "Westinghouse," "MPC," and "Reebok" are all examples of trademarks.

When a mark is used to identify services instead of goods, it is called a *service mark*. "Radio Shack," "McDonald's," "Safeway," "American Express," and "Greyhound" are all examples of service marks. In this chapter, the term *trademark* will be used to refer to both trademarks and service marks, unless the context otherwise requires.

Trademarks are governed by state law, as well as by a federal statute known as the Lanham Act.[2]

1.1 Forms of Trademarks

Any number of items can constitute a trademark. The most commonly used forms of trademarks are:

- **Words and Phrases**. Examples include "Xerox," "Kodak," "Don't Leave Home Without It," and "You Deserve A Break Today."

- **Pictures and Symbols**. Examples include the rainbow-colored apple used by Apple Computer, the Playboy bunny, and the RCA figure of a dog listening to "his master's voice."

- **Numerals and Letters**. Examples include "IBM," "AT&T," "Lotus 1-2-3," and television and radio station call letters.

- **Abbreviations and Nicknames**. Examples include: "Coke" for Coca-Cola,[3] "Beatle" for a particular type of Volkswagen automobile,[4] "Pan-Am" for Pan-America Airways.[5]

- **Products and Packaging**. Distinctive product and package shapes and designs can be trademarks. Examples include the shape of the Coca-Cola bottle and the McDonald's golden arches.

- **Colors**. Some colors can be trademarks, if they become closely associated with a product. An example of a color trademark is the color pink for Owens Corning insulation.

- **Sounds and Music**. Examples include commercial songs and television program themes.

- **Characters**. Examples include cartoon and other characters, such as Mickey Mouse and Superman (see chapter 4, section 1.4).

- **Titles**. Some titles can qualify as trademarks in limited situations[6] (see chapter 4, section 1.5).

1.2 Trademark Distinctiveness or Strength

Trademarks may be strong or weak, depending on their degree of distinctiveness. The stronger the mark, the greater its scope of protection. The intrinsic "strength" of a mark may be rated (from strongest to weakest), as follows:

- **Fanciful or Coined.** Marks that are invented and have no inherent meaning whatsoever are categorized as *fanciful or coined marks*. They enjoy the strongest trademark protection. Examples of coined marks include "Exxon," "Xerox," and "Kodak." Their strength as trademarks is due to the fact that they have no meaning other than to identify and distinguish a particular product brand.

- **Arbitrary.** A word that has meaning in itself, but no connection to the product on which it is used, is an *arbitrary mark*. An arbitrary mark can be a very strong trademark. Examples include "Apple" as applied to computers, "Camels" as applied to cigarettes, and "Shell" as applied to gasoline.

- **Suggestive.** A *suggestive mark* is a mark that suggests something about the product but does not actually describe it. A mark is suggestive when imagination, thought, or perception is required to reach a conclusion about the nature of the goods or services. Examples of suggestive marks are "Ultrasuede," "Playboy," and "Roach Motel." Suggestive marks qualify for trademark protection, but they are considered to be weaker marks.

- **Descriptive.** A *descriptive mark* is one that describes the product or service itself or one or more of its functions, qualities, components, properties, or other attributes. Examples of descriptive marks are "Computerland" when applied to computer stores and "Quik-Print" when applied to printing services. Misspelling or varying the spelling of a descriptive term will not generally prevent it from being found descriptive.[7]

  Descriptive marks do not automatically qualify for trademark protection. This is because they are not considered distinctive enough in themselves to grant exclusive rights to one user. However, once the public has come to associate a descriptive mark with a particular company's product or service, it is considered to have acquired a "secondary meaning" and then it may be protected as a trademark. For example, "Hair color so natural only her hairdresser knows for sure" was a descriptive phrase that developed sufficient secondary meaning for trademark protection. By contrast, a court found that the mark "Computerland" was descriptive and had not yet acquired the level of consumer awareness required to establish a second meaning.[8]

- **Generic.** A term that is a common name for a product is considered *generic* and is not entitled to trademark protection at all. A generic term identifies a type of product to the public by answering the question "what is it?", rather than distinguishing one brand from another by answering the question "whose is it?" Thus, terms such as "software,"[9] "video,"[10] and "multimedia" will not qualify for trademark protection by themselves when used on products that they generically describe.[11] However, combinations of words that include generic terms can often be trademarks. Moreover, a word that is the common name for one class of products may qualify for protection as a trademark when it is used in connection with a product it does not describe. For example, the word "apple" cannot be a trademark for the fruit, but does qualify as a trademark for computers.

As stated before, the stronger or more distinctive the mark, the greater the trademark protection. Strength may be derived from the intrinsic quality of the mark as categorized above, or from external factors relating to public recognition of marks. Intrinsically weak marks may be made stronger by obtaining public recognition, and intrinsically strong marks may become weak if the same mark is used by others on other goods or services. The importance of trademark strength is described further in chapter 4, section 3.

1.3 Difference Between Trademarks and Trade Names

A *trade name* is the name of a business enterprise or organization. It symbolizes the reputation of the business as a whole, while a trademark or service mark is used to identify products and services sold by the business. As discussed in chapter 4, section 6, trade names are now afforded similar protection to trademarks under federal law.

1.4 Characters as Trademarks

Characters are frequently used in multimedia works. Accordingly, it is important to understand that characters can qualify as trademarks (and are frequently registered as trademarks) in a variety of forms.[12] Moreover, they are often protected under both copyright and trademark laws.

As one court has stated:

> Dual protection under copyright and trademark laws is particularly appropriate for graphic representations of characters. A

> character deemed an artistic creation deserving copyright protection . . . may also serve to identify the creator, thus meriting protection under theories of trademark or unfair competition. . . . Indeed, because of their special value in distinguishing goods and services, names and pictorial representations of characters are often registered as trademarks under the Lanham Act.[13]

Thus, for example, cartoon characters such as Mickey Mouse, Bugs Bunny, and Superman are all registered trademarks.

In addition to characters represented pictorially, trademark protection may also be appropriate for characters that are merely described through the text of the stories in which they appear. In one case involving the scripts for the *Amos 'n Andy* radio programs (which were in the public domain, and thus not protected by copyright), the court noted that the characters' names and other distinctive features of the *Amos 'n Andy* radio show may be protected by the law of trademark or unfair competition.[14]

1.5 Titles as Trademarks

The title of a single book, newspaper, magazine, movie, or play cannot be registered as a federal trademark.[15] However, the title of a series of creative works is eligible for trademark registration,[16] and if secondary meaning is shown, the title of a single work can be *protected* as a trademark, even if it cannot be registered.[17]

1.6 Designs, Shapes, and Symbols

Any picture, design, geometric shape, or symbol can qualify as a trademark.[18] Examples include the Rainbow-colored apple used by Apple Computer, and the familiar Chevrolet logo.

Geometric shapes, such as circles, squares and rectangles are generally not protectable unless secondary meaning has been established. However, unusual shapes or symbols can qualify for trademark protection.[19]

Pictures and other still images can also qualify for trademark protection. Thus, for example, a picture of a Volkswagen automobile has been protected as a trademark,[20] and the Planter's Peanut Company picture of a top-hatted man with a peanut body qualified for trademark protection.[21]

2. Who Owns the Trademark?

Unlike copyright ownership, which is based on authorship, trademark ownership is generally based on use.[22] The first one to use a mark to distinguish goods or services is deemed the owner of the mark, as applied to those goods and services and in the area where they are marketed.[23]

The trademark owner does not have exclusive rights to the mark for all purposes, however. The owner can only prevent others from using the same mark in a way that is likely to cause confusion as to source or sponsorship of goods and services. This means that the same mark may be used by different owners on a variety of goods; as long as there is no likelihood of confusion, they may coexist. For example, the mark "Apple" can be seen on a wide variety of unrelated goods and services without confusion: "Apple" computers, "Apple" bank, and "Apple" rent-a-car service. The tests for determining likelihood of confusion are discussed in chapter 4, section 3.

3. What Is Trademark Infringement?

Unlike copyright protection, which is concerned with protecting the owner's authorship rights, trademark law has the dual goal of protecting the owner from unfair competition and protecting the public from confusion. While copyright law prohibits any and all copying of the protected item, trademark law only protects against confusing or deceptive copying. Thus, the same or similar mark may be used by someone else, as long as there is no likelihood of confusion as to the source of the goods or services.

Trademark infringement occurs (1) when someone uses a mark that is the same as or similar to someone else's mark, (2) in connection with the sale or advertising of goods or services, and (3) when the use is likely to cause confusion as to source or sponsorship of goods or services.

3.1 Factors Relating to Likelihood of Confusion

Whether there is likelihood of confusion depends on the facts of each case. The following factors are usually considered:

1. the similarity of the goods or services on which the marks are used (including a comparison of price ranges);[24]

2. the similarity of the marks with respect to appearance, sound, connotation, and commercial impression[25];

3. the similarity of the markets being served (e.g., wholesale or retail, sophisticated or unsophisticated consumers);

4. the number and nature of similar marks in use on similar goods;

5. the nature and extent of any actual confusion that may already have arisen;

6. whether the marks have coexisted for a period of time without evidence of actual confusion;

7. the variety of goods on which a mark is used; and

8. the extent of potential confusion.[26]

For example, the following marks have been found to create a likelihood of confusion based on the above factors:

SOUNDBLASTER (computer sound card)	VOICE BLASTER (voice recogni tion, software to be used in conjunction with Sound Blaster cards)[27]
SUPERCUTS (hair salon)	SUPERCLIPS (hair salon)[28]
APPLE (computers)	PINEAPPLE (computers)[29]
BLACK LABEL (beer)	BLACK LABEL (cigarettes)[30]
GODIVA (chocolates)	DOGIVA (dog biscuits)[31]

By comparison, the following marks have been found not to create a likelihood of confusion:

WHEATIES (for cereal)	OATIES (for cereal)[32]
SWATCH (watches)	T-WATCH (watches)[33]
MIRACLE WHIP	YOGOWHIP[34]
FAMILY CIRCLE (magazine)	FAMILY CIRCLE (department store)[35]

In an infringement action, the strength of the marks, discussed in this chapter, section 1.2, may become important. This is because a weak mark is generally given a narrower scope of protection than a strong one. The owner of a weak mark thus may not be able to prevent its use on another product that is significantly different from its own, whereas if the mark were strong, the owner might be able to prevent its use on a variety of different products. For example, the owner of the strong arbitrary mark "K2" used on skis was able to stop the same mark from being used on a totally different product, cigarettes,[36] whereas the owner of the weaker mark "Mustang" for campers was unable to prevent its use on a similar product, automobiles.[37]

3.2 Remedies for Infringement

If the trademark owner can prove infringement, a court can order the infringer to stop using the mark by issuing an injunction.[38]

In addition, the owner may be awarded damages equal to the infringer's profits from the sale of goods using the infringing mark. The owner may also get treble the amount of damages it has suffered, that is, sales or profits lost because of the infringement. This type of recovery is available only if the owner has used the proper trademark notice or the infringer had actual notice of registration.[39]

The court may also order the destruction of all infringing labels, signs, prints, packages, wrappers, receptacles, and advertisements bearing the infringing mark, as well as all plates, molds, or other means of making copies of the infringing mark.[40]

Finally, the Trademark Act prohibits the unauthorized importation of any goods which bear a copy or simulation of a federally registered trademark.[41] The owner of a registration mark can have U.S. Customs stop such goods at the border.

3.3 "Fair Use" Concepts in Trademark Law

While trademark cases do not use the term "fair use" to describe defenses to infringement liability, there are some concepts in trademark law that are somewhat similar to "fair use" under copyright law.

● **Descriptive Uses.** If a word or phrase is not used as a trademark to distinguish goods or services, but is merely used to fairly describe the goods and services, there is no infringement of someone else's trademark.[42] For example, the owner of the trademark "FISH-FRI" could not prevent others from using the ordinary term "Fish Fry" to describe their goods or services.[43] This exception is based on the principle that trademark rights are essentially monopolies, and these rights should not be so broadly construed as to prohibit all use of ordinary descriptive language.

• **Personal Names.** A person may use his or her own name in a business, even though it may be the same as the trademark of another, as long as it is not being used as a trademark or service mark. For example, Joseph Gallo, the brother of Ernest and Julio Gallo, was stopped from using the mark ''Joseph Gallo'' as a trademark for cheese, since the public was likely to be confused.[44] But Pablo Gucci, grandson of the founder of the famous leather goods company was permitted to use his name to identify himself as a designer of goods marketed under a different name, with a disclaimer, so long as it was not used as a trademark.[45]

• **Parodies and Satire.** The First Amendment's protection for free speech can apply to certain trademark uses, such as parodies or satires. When legal rights under federal and state laws (such as trademark laws) come into conflict with the First Amendment's protection for free speech, the courts balance the rights to be protected. In situations involving *noncommercial* expression or political commentary, such as news stories, satires, and documentaries, the balance is often in favor of free speech. In situations involving *commercial* expression, however, the First Amendment protection is more limited.[46]

It is difficult to formulate a rule on when a satire or parody mark will be protected and when it will be an infringement, because the courts have not been consistent in their analysis.[47] It appears that if the parody involves a trademark for a literary or media work, the courts will more likely protect it under the First Amendment. For example, parodies of *Cliff's Notes* and the L. L. Bean catalog were protected, and not found infringing.[48]

On the other hand, when a parody is used to sell products or services, the courts have been less sympathetic to parodists. For example,

GARBAGE PAIL KIDS for stickers was an infringement.[49]

HERE'S JOHNNY on portable toilets was a violation of the right of publicity.[50]

MUTANT OF OMAHA on T-shirts was a infringement.[51]

But:

BAGZILLA was not an infringement of GODZILLA.[52]

LARDASCHE was not an infringement of JORDACHE.[53]

As one commentator indicated, a cynic might say that whether a court will find infringement by a parody mark may depend on whether or not the judge was amused.[54] Thus, if you want to use a trademark as a parody, you should carefully weigh the risks before proceeding, and should not assume that a court would allow the use of First Amendment protection.

4. How Do Trademark Issues Arise for Multimedia Developers?

You may encounter trademark issues in a number of different ways. First, you may wish to use the trademarks of others (or similar marks) as creative elements in a multimedia work, such as showing clips of product commercials, using advertising jingles, product slogans or logos, showing scenes with products in them, or using trademarked characters. These types of uses may be especially desirable from a creative point of view in multimedia works for corporate audiences, such as training films and sales presentations. As discussed below, these types of uses may or may not be permissible, depending on the situation and context.

Second, you may encounter trademark issues in connection with your own name or identity. When you use a name or logo to promote your own products and services (such as your production services or the multimedia works themselves), you are by definition using a trademark or service mark. This mark can be protected, thereby enhancing its business identity and goodwill. On the other hand, if the mark is not carefully chosen, it may not qualify for trademark protection, or worse, you can incur liability for infringing someone else's mark.

The following sections discuss some particular situations in which you are most likely to encounter trademark issues.

4.1 Use of Trademarks as Incidental Creative Elements

As noted above, the purpose of trademark law is primarily to protect the public against confusion, and to preserve the trademark owner's goodwill. Thus, trademark law does not prohibit all uses of others' trademarks. The nature and context of the use is extremely relevant to issues of infringement.

This distinction is particularly important if you want to incorporate the trademarks of others as creative elements in a multimedia work. If trademarks are used in a context where there is no connection with a product or service, and there is no likelihood of confusion as to source or sponsorship, such use is permitted under trademark law. This occurs most often in creative pieces that are not focused on or appearing to promote or endorse a particular product or service. For example, when the movie *E.T.* showed E.T. eating Reese's Pieces candies, it was not using the mark to promote a product or service, and there was no implication that the trademark owner had sponsored or endorsed the movie.[55] There should therefore be no trademark infringement due to this use. Of course, each situation will differ, and the totality and context of the presentation will be relevant in determining whether there is trademark infringement.

Of course, using trademark elements can still expose you to liability under other laws, such as copyright or right of publicity laws. For example, the E.T. character is protected by copyright (see chapter 16), and the face of Colonel Sanders may be protected under the right of publicity (see chapter 5).

When using another person's trademarks in a multimedia work, you should take care to use them in the proper form and spelling. Trade associations and manufacturers often provide informational services to media producers about proper trademark formats.[56]

4.2 Use of Trademarks in Connection with Promotion of Products or Services in a Multimedia Work

Another situation you may encounter is one in which the work promotes or may be seen to promote a specific product or service. For example, consider a situation where you are creating a promotional work for a client, such as a sales presentation or advertising piece. You may wish to use someone else's trademarks (or similar marks) in the work—these may be for purposes of product comparison or example. Such uses could constitute trademark infringement, if there is a likelihood of confusion among the viewers as to source or sponsorship. Using the example cited above, if a peanut butter or candy manufacturer used the Reese's Pieces trademark (or even a clip from the movie *E.T.*) in advertising or promotion for its own products, in a context where the viewers would likely be deceived into thinking that Hershey had endorsed or made the product, that could be trademark infringement. Using a clip from a movie could also constitute copyright infringement, as discussed in chapter 20.

Whether there is a likelihood of confusion will depend on a number of factors, discussed in this chapter, section 3. For example, if the work is intended only for presentation to a client's internal sales force, the salespeople might be considered a sophisticated audience that is less likely to be confused than the general public. By contrast, use of trademarks in multimedia advertisements for the public have a greater potential for confusion.[57]

Finally, in considering the use of others' trademarks in a promotional context, you should be aware of the need to avoid misrepresentations or misleading statements about products or services, whether those of the client or others. The issues relating to false advertising are discussed in this chapter, section 7.1.

4.3 Use of Trademarks to Identify a Multimedia Work

A multimedia work is itself a product, and you should be careful to avoid trademark infringement when choosing a title for or promoting the work. Even an ostensibly noncommercial work such as a training or educational film can encounter trademark problems if there is a likelihood of confusion as to source or sponsorship. For example, if a training film for auto mechanics were entitled *Mr. Goodwrench Goes to Work*, the audience might be deceived into believing that General Motors had endorsed the film. In choosing a name, logo, or other identifier, you should follow the trademark clearance and protection procedures described in chapter 25.

4.4 Use of Trademarks in Connection with Services

Finally, you should be aware that your business name and other identifiers are themselves trademarks, if used to distinguish your services from those of others. Thus, if you adopt a name such as "Paramount Multimedia Pictures," you might receive an infringement complaint from Paramount Pictures. Again, in choosing a name, logo, or other identifier, you should follow the trademark clearance and protection procedures described in chapter 25.

5. Trademark Licensing

The increased importance and value of brand identity has resulted in a growth of trademark licensing. Under a trademark license, the trademark owner gives someone else permission to use its trademark on goods or services manufactured, sold, or offered by the licensee. This can be as simple as a manufacturing agreement where the licensee contracts to manufacture the licensor's goods in accordance with the licensor's specifications and standards, or can be as complex as a national franchise where each franchisee is permitted to use the trademark owner's marks on its goods and services, such as restaurants, service stations, and the like.

Another growth area for licensing is the extension of a brand identity beyond the trademark owner's original product line, such as use of a clothing designer's name for other products such as perfumes and luggage, or the use of a cartoon or film character in connection with collateral merchandise such as clothing and games.

Trademark licenses are important to you for two reasons. First, when determining whether there is a likelihood of infringement, you should be aware that the scope of goods and services on which an existing mark is used may be broader than you might expect. For example, the owner of mark for fragrances may have licensed its use on a broad range of goods, such as clothing and handbags. Familiarity with the industry involved is therefore important when assessing the risks of an infringement claim.

Second, you should consider the possibility of obtaining licenses to permit you to use others' marks, or granting licenses to others to use your marks. Trademark licenses usually require the payment of royalties based on sales, and will always carry with them requirements that the licensor's specifications or quality standards be met. Quality control is an essential element of any trademark license, and no licensor should permit unfettered use of its mark without some degree of control or supervision over the quality of the goods and services.

6. Trade Names

A trade name is the name of a business organization or enterprise. Federal registration is not available for a trade name, unless it also serves as a trademark or servicemark. In many situations, this will be the case. For example, "IBM" is both a trademark and a trade name.

Even if not registrable as a trademark or servicemark, a trade name can be protected under the federal Lanham Act. The owner of a trade name can prevent a similar trademark from being federally registered by opposing an application for registration, if there is a likelihood of confusion as to source or sponsorship of goods or services. Similarly, the owner of a trade name may protect against infringements under Section 43(a) of the Lanham Act.[58] Essentially, trade name owners can sue for infringement under the same principles as trademark owners, even though they cannot get some of the procedural benefits that come with federal registration.[59]

7. Unfair Competition

The term "unfair competition" describes a wide range of federal and state law concepts prohibiting unfair business practices, including trade libel, misappropriation, false advertising, and trade dress infringement. Unfair competition laws are included under the federal Lanham Act, as well as under a variety of state laws.

Because the various laws have been applied in an extremely broad manner to redress various perceived unfair business practices, that may not be easily classifiable, a complete treatment of unfair competition is beyond the scope of this work.[60] This chapter will outline some of the more traditional types of unfair competition that you may encounter.

7.1 False Advertising and Related Issues

It is a violation of the federal Lanham Act when a person "in commercial advertising or promotion, misrepresents the nature, character, quality or geographic origin of his . . . goods, services or commercial activities."[61] This type of activity is commonly referred to as "false advertising" but it is not limited to advertising. State laws have similar or even broader provisions.[62]

Obviously, when a company makes false or misleading statements about its own product or service, it could be liable for false advertising. But the concept of "false advertising" is much broader than that, and includes:

- Putting a copyright notice on an infringing work, since this falsely implies the infringer owns the copyright.[63]

- Using a creative person's name on a work that was not authorized by him or her.[64]

- Severely editing a *Monty Python* film.[65]

- "False endorsements," such as by using unauthorized lookalikes and soundalikes.[66]

- Misrepresenting an artist's true participation in or contribution to a work.

- Misrepresenting the currency of a work, such as by selling an old recording with a current picture of the artist.[67]

- Using false credits, such as by deleting the correct name and substituting another, or giving credit to one artist as composer when there were multiple composers.[68]

Another context in which you may encounter false advertising issues is in comparative advertising. When comparing one person's products to another's, it is important to make sure that all claims are truthful and supported by reasonable evidence. Claims that a product meets certain standards, is endorsed by a certain body, or is the "only" product that performs in a certain way, must all be supported by objectively verifiable evidence, such as scientific studies or market surveys. It is noted, however, that many types of subjective claims (such as "best," "finest," "greatest") are considered mere "puffery" that are not actionable.

In addition to possible liability under the Lanham Act or state laws, the false advertiser could be subject to Federal Trade Commission enforcement action under the FTC Act.[69] A number of media associations, such as the Association of Advertising Agencies and the National Association of Broadcasters, also may subject their members to sanctions for violating industry standards relating to false advertising.

7.2 Trade Libel

Trade libel or product disparagement is similar to false advertising, except that it involves misrepresentations about *someone else's* product, services, or commercial activities. Basically, product disparagement is a statement about a competitor's goods that is untrue or misleading and that is made to influence others not to buy the competitor's goods.[70] Trade libel claims may be asserted under state law as well as Section 43(a) of the Lanham Act.

7.3 Passing Off; False Endorsements

Section 43(a) of the Lanham Act also prohibits the use of any designation, or false or misleading description or representation, that is likely to cause confusion as to source or sponsorship with another person's goods, services, or commercial activities.[71] This includes the historical concept of "passing off," where one person passed off its goods or services as those of another.

Most situations of passing off involve trademark infringements, where the infringer passes off its goods as those of another by using the plaintiff's trademark. However, this section of the federal law has been more broadly applied, including situations where someone's name, likeness, or character is used without permission to promote a work.

Passing off can occur under a variety of circumstances relevant to the development of multimedia products. One example involves false attribution of credit. For example, in one case, the makers of the movie *The Lawnmower Man* improperly implied in the movie credits that the author of the book, Stephen King, had been involved in making the movie.[72] The court found this to be improper passing off, and an attempt to deceive the public into thinking King had been involved in the movie.[73] Similarly, when a video store used a Woody Allen lookalike and soundalike to promote its services, Mr. Allen succeeded in enjoining the activity. The court required a very clear disclaimer of any endorsement by Mr. Allen.[74]

7.4 Trade Dress

"Trade dress" is a broad term covering the design of a product or the packaging or presentation of a product or service. When one person copies someone else's trade dress and it causes a likelihood of confusion, this can be an infringement under the Lanham Act and state law. Examples of trade dress that have been protected include:

- The decor, menu, and style of a Mexican restaurant[75]
- The package and bottle design of Chanel perfume[76]
- The distinctive design of the Dallas Cowboys cheerleaders costumes[77]
- *People Magazine*'s cover format[78]
- Rubik's Cube puzzle design[79]
- The appearance of a video game console[80]
- The distinctive design of the automobile used on the *Dukes of Hazzard* television show.[81]

It is difficult to speculate exactly how you might encounter trade dress issues in multimedia, but given the almost limitless creative potential of new technology, anything seems possible. For example, a multimedia game program might place a character in a setting that imitates someone else's trade dress, such as a well-known restaurant, amusement park setting, or television show setting. This could be a trade dress infringement.

7.5 Antidilution Laws

Another concept under the broad umbrella of unfair competition is known as "dilution." Since trademark infringement is based on the likelihood of confusion between goods or services, it does not protect against nonconfusing uses. Many states therefore have antidilution laws prohibiting the use of a trademark (or trade dress) when it would "dilute the distinctive quality" of another's mark, regardless of whether any confusion was likely.

Courts have described the rationale behind antidilution laws in a number of ways, including: protection against "a gradual whittling away" of the distinctiveness or unique character of a mark; protection of the "selling power" of a distinctive mark; or protection against "blurring" of a distinct mental image.[82]

A typical dilution case involves a nonconfusing use of a famous mark on unrelated goods or services, that is found to dilute the distinctive quality of the famous mark. For example, Polaroid succeeded in stopping use of the mark "Polaraid" on heating systems, and Hyatt Hotels succeeded in a suit against "Hyatt Legal Services," despite the lack of competition or confusion.[83] Other famous marks that have successfully prevailed in antidilution cases include "Trivial Pursuit," "Tiffany," and the shape of a Coke bottle.[84]

When you are tempted to use or parody a famous trademark in a multimedia work, you should be aware of the potential for violating antidilution laws. Remember that, unlike trademark infringement, a dilution action can be brought even if there is no competition or confusion. One court, however, held that if one of the marks is marketed to a sophisticated audience, there is little likelihood of dilution.[85]

You should note, however, that the remedy under current state antidilution laws is limited to injunctive relief—that is, the court can order the defendant to stop using the mark, but cannot award damages.[86]

Endnotes

1   15 U.S.C. § 1127.

2   15 U.S.C. §§ 1051 *et seq.*

3   *Coca-Cola Co. v. Busch*, 44 F. Supp. 405, 410 (E.D. Pa. 1942).

4   *Volkswagenwerk Aktiengesellschaft v. Wheeler*, 814 F.2d 812 (1st Cir. 1987).

5   *Pan American World Airways, Inc. v. Pan America School of Travel, Inc.*, 648 F. Supp. 1026 (S.D.N.Y.), *aff'd*, 810 F.2d 1160 (2d Cir. 1986).

6   See, e.g., *Hospital For Sick Children v. Melody Fare Dinner Theatre*, 516 F. Supp. 67, 209 U.S.P.Q. 749 (E.D. Va. 1980).

7   *In re Application of Quik-Print Copy Shops, Inc.*, 616 F.2d 523 (C.C.P.A. 1980) ("Quik" is descriptive).

8   *Computerland Corp. v. Microland Computer Corp.*, 586 F. Supp. 22 (N.D. Cal. 1984).

9   *Technical Publishing Co. v. Lebhar-Friedman, Inc.*, 729 F.2d 1136, 1140 (7th Cir. 1984)("Software" and "Software News" are generic terms).

10   *Reese Publishing Co. v. Hampton Int'l Communications, Inc.*, 620 F.2d 7 (2d Cir. 1980) ("Video Buyer's Guide" held to be generic).

11   Microsoft Corporation's application for registration of the trademark "Windows" was initially refused by the Trademark Office on the grounds that it was a generic term. However, at the time this book went to press, Microsoft had overcome the Trademark Office's objection, and it remains to be seen whether the industry will raise objections at the trademark opposition phase.

12   Cases involving characters as trademarks include *MGM-Pathe Communications Co. v. Pink Panther Patrol*, 774 F. Supp. 869 (S.D.N.Y. 1991) (Pink Panther); *In re Paramount Pictures*, 213 U.S.P.Q. 1111 (TTAB 1982) (Mork and Mindy); *Silverman v. CBS, Inc.*, 632 F. Supp. 1344 (S.D. N.Y. 1986) (Amos 'n' Andy); *Conan Properties, Inc. v. Conans Pizza, Inc.*, 752 F.2d 145 (5th Cir. 1985) (Conan the Barbarian); *In re D.C. Comics*, 689 F.2d 1042 (CCPA 1982) (Superman). *See also D.C. Comics, Inc. v. Filmation Assoc.s*, 486 F. Supp. 1273 (S.D.N.Y. 1980); *National Comics Publications, Inc. v. Fawcett Publications, Inc.*, 191 F.2d 594 (2d. Cir. 1951).

13   *Frederick Warne & Co. v. Book Sales, Inc.*, 481 F. Supp. 1191, 1196 (S.D. N.Y. 1979).

14   *Silverman v. CBS, Inc.*, 632 F. Supp. 1344, 1355-58 (S.D.N.Y. 1986). This case was subsequently reversed, however, because the Court of Appeals ruled that any trademark rights in the characters had been abandoned, and thus were also in the public domain. *Silverman v. CBS, Inc.*, 870 F.2d 40 (2d Cir. 1989).

15   *Application of Cooper*, 254 F.2d 611, 613 (CCPA 1958), *cert. denied*, 358 U.S. 840 (1958); *In re Hal Leonard Publishing Corp.*, 15 U.S.P.Q.2d 1574, 1576 (TTAB 1990).

16   *In re Scholastic, Inc.*, 23 U.S.P.Q.2d 1774 (TTAB 1992) ("The Magic School Bus" series of children's books); *Inc. Publishing Corp. v. Manhattan Magazine, Inc.*, 616 F.Supp. 370, 376-77 (D.C.N.Y. 1985), *aff'd*, 788 F.2d 3 (2d Cir. 1986) ("Inc. Magazine"); *Metro Publishing, Ltd. v. San Jose Mercury News*, 987 F.2d 637, 641 (9th Cir. 1993) ("Public Eye" column in weekly newspaper); *Walt Disney Co. v. Cable News Network, Inc.*, 231 U.S.P.Q. 235, 237 (C.D. Cal. 1986) (*Business Day* television series).

17   *Rogers v. Grimaldi*, 875 F.2d 994, 998 (2d Cir. 1989).

18   *In re Corning Glass Works*, 6 U.S.P.Q.2d 1032 (TTAB 1988) ("a design which has ornamental value may nevertheless be registered if it also functions as a trademark").

19   *In re Dairy Queen of Georgia, Inc.*, 134 U.S.P.Q. 136 (TTAB 1962) (Star-shaped figure with representation of face).

20   *Volkswagenwerk Aktiengesellschaft v. Rickard*, 175 U.S.P.Q. 563 (N.D. Tex. 1972), *modified*, 492 F.2d 474 (5th Cir. 1974).

21   *Planters Nut & Chocolate Co. v. Crown Nut Co.*, 305 F.2d 916 (C.C.P.A. 1962).

22   Under the 1989 amendments to the Lanham Act, however, a new system was introduced permitting some trademark rights to be created prior to actual use of a mark. Under this system, an applicant who files a trademark application claiming a bona fide intention to use a trademark can get trademark rights dating back to the date of filing. However, these retroactive rights only arise once the mark is in fact used. See chapter 25.

23   Exclusive rights for a mark that is not federally registered are limited to the specific geographic area in which the mark was used. For example, if an unregistered mark is used only in the Los Angeles area, the trademark rights extend only to that area. If someone else were to start using the same mark in another area of the country, that person would acquire trademark rights in the same mark for that separate area. To obtain trademark rights for the entire country without actually having to use a mark nationwide, it is necessary to obtain a federal registration. See chapter 25.

24   For example, the purchaser of a $1,500 snowmobile is not likely to be confused by a similar mark on a $40 automobile tire. *J. C. Penney Co. v. Arctic Enters., Inc.*, 375 F. Supp. 913 (D.C. Minn. 1974).

25   In making the comparison, misspellings or differences in spelling tend to be irrelevant. See *Citibank, N.A. v. City Bank of San Francisco*, 206 U.S.P.Q. 997 (N.D. Cal. 1980) ("City Bank" and "Citibank" confusingly similar).

26   *Digicom, Inc. v. Digicon, Inc.*, 328 F. Supp. 631, 635-36 (S.D. Tex. 1971).

27   *Creative Technology, Inc. v. SRT, Inc.*, 29 U.S.P.Q.2d 1474, 1477 (N.D. Cal. 1977).

28   *Supercuts, Inc. v. Super Clips*, 18 U.S.P.Q. 2d 1378 (D. Mass 1990).

29   *Apple Computer, Inc. v. Formula Int'l, Inc.*, 725 F.2d 521 (9th Cir. 1984) (preliminary injunction granted).

30   *Carling Brewing Co. v. Philip Morris, Inc.*, 277 F. Supp. 326 (N.D. Ga. 1967).

31   *Grey v. Campbell Soup Co.*, 650 F. Supp. 1166 (C.D. Cal. 1986).

32   *Quaker Oats Co. v. General Mills, Inc.*, 134 F.2d 429 (7th Cir. 1943).

33   *Swatch Watch S.A. v. Taxor, Inc.*, 785 F.2d 956 (11th Cir. 1986) (preliminary injunction denied).

34   *Henri's Food Products Co. v. Kraft, Inc.*, 717 F.2d 352 (7th Cir. 1983).

35   *Family Circle, Inc. v. Family Circle Assoc., Inc.*, 332 F.2d 534 (3d Cir. 1964).

36   *Philip Morris, Inc. v. K2 Corp.*, 555 F.2d 815, 816 (C.C.P.A. 1977).

37   *Westward Coach Mfg. Co. v. Ford Motor Co.*, 388 F.2d 627, 634-35 (7th Cir.), *cert. denied*, 392 U.S. 927 (1968). In this case, the "Mustang" mark was considered weak because it had already been used by different persons on a wide variety of items.

38   15 U.S.C. § 1116.

39   15 U.S.C. §§ 1111, 1117.

40   15 U.S.C. § 1118.

41   15 U.S.C. § 1124.

42   15 U.S.C. § 1115(b)(4).

43   *Zatarains, Inc. v. Oak Grove Smokehouse, Inc.*, 698 F.2d 786 (5th Cir. 1983).

44   *E. & J. Gallo Winery v. Gallo Cattle Co.*, 12 U.S.P.Q. 2d 1657 (E.D. Cal. 1989), *aff'd*, 955 F.2d 1327 (9th Cir. 1992).

45   *Gucci v. Gucci Shops, Inc.*, 688 F. Supp. 916 (S.D.N.Y. 1988).

46   See *Board of Trustees of State University of New York v. Fox*, 492 U.S. 469, 477-80 (1989).

47   For a good discussion of how courts should (but may not) balance trademark law and the First Amendment, see Arlen Langvardt, *Trademark Rights and First Amendment Wrongs: Protecting the Former Without Committing the Latter*, 83 THE TRADEMARK REPORTER 633 (Sept./Oct. 1993)

48   See *Cliffs Notes. Inc. v. Bantam Doubleday Dell Publishing Group, Inc.*, 886 F.2d 490 (2d Cir 1989); *L.L. Bean, Inc. v. Drake Publishers, Inc.*, 811 F.2d 26 (1st Cir. 1987). But see *Dallas Cowboys Cheerleaders, Inc. v. Pussycat Cinema, Ltd.*, 604 F.2d 200 (2d Cir. 1979) (cheerleader uniforms in a porno movie - infringement).

49   *Original Appalachian Art Works, Inc. v. Topps Chewing Gum, Inc.*, 642 F. Supp. 1031 (N.D. Ga. 1966) (preliminary injunction granted).

50   *Carson v. Here's Johnny Portable Toilets, Inc.* 698 F.2d 831 (6th Cir. 1983) (no infringement since no confusion; however, right of publicity was violated).

51   *Mutual of Omaha Ins. Co. v. Novak*, 836 F.2d 397 (8th Cir. 1987).

52   *Toho Co. v. Sears Roebuck & Co.*, 645 F.2d 788 (9th Cir. 1987) (garbage bags).

53   *Jordache Enters., Inc. v. Hogg Wyld Ltd.*, 828 F.2d 1482 (10th Cir. 1987) (jeans).

54   J. THOMAS MCCARTHY, TRADEMARKS AND UNFAIR COMPETITION § 31-38 [1][6] (1993).

55   In practice, product manufacturers may arrange for their products to be prominently featured in movies, in order to increase public exposure. However, if a producer decides to truthfully show a product in a movie or multimedia work, no permission is needed at least from a trademark law perspective, as long as there is no confusion or implied endorsement.

56   For example, the International Trademark Association, 1133 Avenue of the Americas, New York, New York (formerly known as the U. S. Trademark Association) provides such a service.

57   For this reason, if the multimedia work is intended for a certain sophisticated audience, you may wish in some cases to contractually limit its use to avoid potential trademark problems.

58   15 U.S.C. § 1125(a).

59   This has not historically been the case. However, the 1989 amendments to the Lanham Act have expanded the remedies available under Section 43(a) to be substantially equivalent to those available to federal trademark registrants.

60   Doctrines of unfair competition are by nature extremely inclusive and creative, and have been applied by courts to deal with situations that are not easily classified elsewhere under the law. The California Supreme Court has noted: "When a scheme is involved which on its face violates the fundamental rules of honesty and fair dealing, a court of equity is not impudent to frustrate its consummation because the scheme is an original one. There is a maxima as old as law that there could be no right without a remedy, and in searching for a precise precedent, an equity court must not lose sight, not only of its power, but of its duty to arrive at a just solution." *American Philatelic Society v. Claibourne,* 3 Cal. 2d 689, 46 P.2d 135 (1935).

61   Lanham Act Section 43(a); 15 U.S.C. § 1125(a)

62   The federal Lanham Act provision relating to "false advertising" is contained in Section 43(a); 15 U.S.C. § 1125(a). State unfair competition laws include the Uniform Deceptive Trade Practices Act, nonuniform acts, and a variety of consumer protection acts.

63   *F.E.L Publications, Ltd. v. Catholic Bishop of Chicago,* 214 U.S.P.Q. 409 (7th Cir. 1982); *Eden Toys, Inc. v. Florelee Undergarment Co.,* 697 F.2d 27, 37 (2d Cir. 1982) (putting false copyright notice on an infringing copy of a copyrighted work constitutes a "false designation of origin" or "false description" within the meaning of Section 43(a) of the Lanham Act. "This deception can mislead consumers into believing that the [product] they purchased is a unique novelty instead of a common copy").

64   *Williams v. Weisser,* 273 Cal. App. 3d 726, 16 U.S.P.Q. (2d Div. 1969).

65   *Gilliam v. American Broadcasting Cos.,* 538 F.2d 14, 24-25 (2d Cir. 1976) (ABC edited a Monty Python film in a way that "appalled" the Monty Python group with its "mutilation" and "discontinuity." The court held that the Monty Python group would likely succeed on its claim that the edited version impaired the integrity of the author's work and represented to the public as the product of the authors what was actually a "mere caricature" of their talents).

66   *Allen v. National Video, Inc.,* 610 F. Supp. 612 (S.D.N.Y. 1985) (Woody Allen lookalike).

67   *CBS, Inc. v. Springboard Int'l Records,* 429 F. Supp. 563 (S.D.N.Y. 1976).

68   *Smith v. Montoro,* 648 F.2d 602 (9th Cir. 1981); *Lamoth v. Atlantic Recording Corp.,* 847 F.2d 1403 (9th Cir. 1988). Note that the Lanham Act does not require that all artists be given credit on a work. It merely requires that any credits given must not be false or misleading. However, authors of certain types of fine artworks must be given proper credit under the VARA, discussed in section 3-4.6.

69   15 U.S.C. § 45.

70   *Aerosonic Corp. v Trodyne Corp.,* 402 F.2d 223, 231 (5th Cir. 1968).

71   15 U.S.C. § 1125(a). State statutes and common law contain similar prohibitions.

72   *King v. Innovation Books, Inc.,* 976 F.2d 874 (2d Cir. 1992).

73   See also, *Nice Man Merchandising, Inc. v. Logocraft, Ltd.,* 23 U.S.P.Q.2d 1290 (E.D. Pa. 1992); *Wyatt Earp Enters., Inc. v. Sackman, Inc.,* 157 F. Supp. 621 (E.D.N.Y. 1958).

74   *Allen v. National Video, Inc.,* 610 F. Supp. 612 (S.D.N.Y. 1985).

75   *Taco Cabanna Int'l, Inc. v. Two Pesos, Inc.,* 932 F.2d 1113, 19 U.S.P.Q.2d 1253 (5th Cir. 1991); *aff'd,* 112 S.Ct. 2753, 23 U.S.P.Q. 2d 1081 (1992) (the infringer, who had copied the design of

a competing restaurant, was ordered to pay damages of $1.9 million plus $900,000 in attorneys' fees).

76   *Chanel, Inc., v. Suttner*, 109 U.S.P.Q. 493 (S.D.N.Y. 1956).

77   *Dallas Cowboys Cheerleaders, Inc. v. Pussycat Cinema, Ltd.*, 604 F.2d 200 (2d Cir. 1979).

78   *Time Inc. Magazine Co. v. Globe Communications Corp.*, 712 F. Supp. 1103 (S.D.N.Y. 1989).

79   *Ideal Toy Corp. v. Plawner Toy Mfg. Corp.*, 685 F.2d 78 (3d Cir. 1982).

80   *M. Kramer Mfg. Co. v. Andrews*, 783 F.2d 421 (4th Cir. 1986).

81   *Warner Bros., Inc. v. Gay Toys, Inc.*, 658 F.2d 76 (2d Cir. 1981), *on remand* 553 F. Supp. 1018 (S.D.N.Y. 1983); *Processed Plastic Co. v. Warner Communications, Inc.*, 675 F.2d 852 (7th Cir. 1982).

82   See J. THOMAS MCCARTHY, TRADEMARKS AND UNFAIR COMPETITION (Clark, Boardman Callaghan 1993), § 24:13.

83   *Hyatt Corp. v. Hyatt Legal Servs., Inc.*, 736 F.2d 1153 (7th Cir. 1984), *on remand* 610 F. Supp. 381 (N.D. Ill. 1985) (case settled); *Polaroid Corp. v. Polaraid, Inc.*, 319 F.2d 830 (7th Cir. 1963).

84   *Coca-Cola Co. v. Alma-Leo USA, Inc.*, 719 F. Supp. 725 (N.D. Ill. 1989) (bottle shape diluted by bottle for bubble gum powder); *Horn Abbot, Ltd. v. Sarsaparilla, Ltd*, 601 F. Supp. 360 (N.D. Ill. 1984) ("Trivial Pursuit" diluted by use of mark on book); *Tiffany & Co. v. Boston Club, Inc.*, 231 F. Supp. 836 (D.C. Mass 1964) ("Tiffany" diluted by use on restaurants).

85   For example, when Toyota adopted the name "LEXUS" for a new car, Mead Data complained that this diluted its mark "LEXIS" for its computerized legal database services. The court found that since the LEXIS mark was only known to a sophisticated audience— attorneys — there was no likelihood of dilution. *Mead Data Central, Inc. v. Toyota Motor Sales, Inc.*, 875 F.2d 1026 (2d Cir. 1989). Whether other courts will follow this theory remains to be seen.

86   During consideration of the 1989 amendments to the Lanham Act, Congress considered adopting a federal antidilution law. Congress ultimately did not adopt this approach, and antidilution remains at present a creature of state law only.

CHAPTER 5

Right of Publicity

Right of Publicity

In creating multimedia works, you need to be aware of, and avoid infringing, other people's rights of publicity. Rights of publicity are separate and apart from other rights such as copyrights and trademarks, and arise when you use a person's identity, such as a name, image or voice. These rights, and their relation to multimedia development, are discussed in the following sections.

1. What Is the Right of Publicity?

Every person has the right to control and profit from the commercial value of his or her own identity. This is the right of publicity. As a practical matter, the right of publicity tends to be invoked primarily to protect celebrities, but technically all individuals have a right of publicity (see this chapter, section 3).

There are several rationales behind the right of publicity: (1) it protects the financial interests of those whose livelihoods are based on their fame, (2) it allows such persons to protect their reputations, by helping them prevent unauthorized endorsements and other misuses, and (3) it prevents unauthorized people from unfairly profiting from the efforts and reputations of others.

It is important to remember that the right of publicity arises under state law, which differs from state to state.[1] This chapter will discuss the general legal principles of the right of publicity, but reference should be made to the law of any specific state involved.

2. What Does the Right of Publicity Protect?

The right of publicity protects the right of every person to control the commercial use of his or her identity. It is a state-law created intellectual property right that is infringed by:

1. the unauthorized use of a person's identity or persona;
2. in a way that is likely to cause harm to the commercial value of that identity or persona;
3. unless such use is privileged under the First Amendment.

2.1 Use of Identity

First, for there to be an infringement of the right of publicity, there must be a use of a person's "identity." This can occur through the use of:

- Names (including nicknames, professional names or group names)
- Images (photographs, videos)
- Likenesses (portraits, drawings)
- Voices
- Imitations or impersonations (including soundalikes)
- Biographical facts

For example, courts have found right of publicity violations in the following cases:

- Printing baseball players' photographs on chewing gum cards[2]
- Using the phrase "Here's Johnny" as part of a name for a portable toilet[3]
- Using a Jackie Onassis lookalike in a Christian Dior ad[4]
- Using rock stars' names on T-shirts[5]
- Combining the head of Cary Grant with the body of a model, as part of a fashion article[6]
- Imitating Groucho Marx's "persona" in a play.[7]
- Using a soundalike of singer Tom Waits in a Frito-Lay commercial and a soundalike of Bette Midler in a car commercial[8]

The types of "identities" protected by the right of publicity may be expanding. In an interesting 1992 case, a court found that Vanna White's right of publicity could be violated by an ad showing a robot dressed in a wig and costume resembling Ms. White, posed next to a game board like that on the "Wheel of Fortune".[9] Thus, for right of publicity purposes, identity will not necessarily be limited to names and photographs.[10]

Remember, however, that the right of publicity only protects against *unauthorized* uses. Thus, you can (and should) avoid concerns about infringing the right of publicity by obtaining the proper permission.

2.2 Commercial Uses

The right of publicity protects against uses that cause damage to *commercial* interests. Unfortunately, almost every use of a person's name, likeness or person, other than for news purposes, can be found to affect their commercial interests so this element is not often useful as a defense.

One interesting case involved a movie titled *Ginger and Fred*, based on a true story of two dancers who were generally known by those names because their dancing style was similar to that of Fred Astaire and Ginger Rogers. The court found the rights of Fred Astaire and Ginger Rogers were not violated, since the title was related to the story and was not an attempt to commercially exploit the names of Ginger Rogers and Fred Astaire.[11]

2.3 First Amendment Exception

Finally, there is an exception to the right of publicity that permits use of a person's identity in some cases, even if technically for commercial purposes. This exception is based on the right of free expression under the First Amendment of the U.S. Constitution, which gives a "privileged" status to certain types of works dealing with news, political commentary, satire, and other communications of public interest.

To determine whether a work is "privileged" under the First Amendment, the courts apply a balancing test to the specific facts and circumstances, weighing the competing interests of the individual's right of publicity against the benefits to society of news dissemination and free expression.

The following types of works have been held to be privileged under the First Amendment, and therefore did not violate the right of publicity:

- Newspaper or magazine articles with news of current interest using celebrities' names and pictures to illustrate a story
- Factual biographies of public interest using celebrity names and likenesses
- A photo-biography of Marilyn Monroe by Norman Mailer[12]
- A fictionalized account of an event in the life of Agatha Christie[13]
- A videotape of a speech by Jesse Jackson[14]

It should be noted, however, that there are limits to the First Amendment rights, particularly in the area of "commercial" speech, which is generally accorded more limited First Amendment protection.

In the following situations, the use was held to be infringing, and not protected by the First Amendment:

- Use of a person's *entire* performance as a "human cannonball" in a news program[15]
- Publication of a "memorial" Elvis Presley poster, which defendant claimed was a celebration of a newsworthy event[16]

While there are not yet any cases applying a First Amendment analysis in the area of computer-generated multimedia works, the courts should certainly apply the same types of balancing tests. By analogy, then, it is fair to assume that using a person's name or image in a news article on an informational bulletin board or in a multimedia news documentary would be permitted, but not use of a person's name or image in a computer game or advertisement without permission.

3. Who Is Protected by the Right of Publicity?

As a practical matter, the right of publicity is asserted primarily in cases involving celebrities. This is because the right of publicity relates to the commercial value of a person's identity, and a noncelebrity will probably have little value associated with his or her name or likeness, or voice.

However, most courts follow the view that even a relatively unknown person's identity can have economic value and be protected by the right of publicity. For example, in a case involving the use of a noncelebrity's identity to advertise a real estate firm, a New Jersey court observed that:

> However little or much plaintiff's likeness and name may be worth, defendant, who has appropriated them for his commercial benefit, should be made to pay for what he has taken, whatever it may be worth. . . . Plaintiffs' names and likenesses belong to them. As such they are property. They are things of value. Defendant has made them so, for it has taken them for its own commercial benefit.[17]

In that case, the plaintiff was a father of eight children who had secured a home using the defendant's real estate services. When the real estate firm used the plaintiff's name and story in an ad without his permission he sued and won.

Even if monetary damages are minor, a plaintiff can still get an injunction against the activity.

Corporations or other entities generally do not have a right of publicity.[18] However, it is possible that an individual will transfer or license his or her right of publicity to a corporation, which will then be able to enforce that right.[19] Moreover, the right of publicity has been extended to musical groups that have a "persona."[20]

4. Does the Right of Publicity Continue After Death?

If the right of publicity ended with a celebrity's death, it would be easy for you to avoid right of publicity problems by only using name or pictures of people after their death. Unfortunately, the law in this area differs from state to state. In some states, the right survives death, whereas in others it does not. [21]

In the majority of states, the right of publicity continues after death. The length of time it survives differs from state to state; time periods range from ten years, to one hundred years, to forever. In at least one state, the right only survives if the celebrity exploited his or her identity while alive.[22]

The minority position is that a person's right of publicity does not survive his or her death.[23] In states applying that rule, once a celebrity dies, then others are free to use his or her identity without violating any right of publicity.

5. How Does the Right of Publicity Arise in Multimedia?

Given the above general legal principles, it is apparent that multimedia products have great potential for infringing the right of publicity. You may often want to incorporate names, photographs, and video footage or simulations of famous (and not-so-famous) people in a multimedia product. However, just because this type of material is easily available from public sources such as television, newspapers, and videos, and may be in the public domain for copyright purposes, does not mean it may be freely used under the right of publicity. This poses a burden on you to obtain a myriad of permissions for even short works.

Because of the collage-like nature of many multimedia works, where an image is seen only momentarily and sometimes as a part of a larger picture, a question arises as to whether a "fair use" exception should exist for such creations. If it did, a fleeting or momentary use of a person's image might be arguably permissible. Unfortunately, multimedia is too new an area to have yet developed substantial case law, and to date, no such "fair use" exception has been applied.[24]

● **Sound Recordings**. The right of publicity provides protection for the commercial value of the identity or persona of each of the performers who participated in the creation of a sound recording. This can have an important impact on the proposed use of a sound recording in two respects.

First, if you want to license the right to use a sound recording that includes the voice of a relatively well-known personality, obtaining a license from the copyright owner in the sound recording will not necessarily be sufficient. You will also need to obtain a release of the rights of publicity held by each of the performers to the sound recording.

Second, although the copyright protection for a sound recording protects only the actual sounds as recorded, and does not prohibit one from making another sound recording that imitates or simulates the copyrighted sound recording,[25] any attempt to imitate or simulate a sound recording by a particular artist, although not copyright infringement, may nonetheless infringe their right of publicity. Thus, for example, in a well-known case involving a Ford Motor Company commercial, a court found that using someone to imitate Bette Midler's voice while singing a particular song represented an infringement of her right of publicity.[26]

● **Still Images.** The use of photographs and other still images that include actual persons can result in an infringement of the right of publicity of the persons depicted, at least where the use amounts to a commercial exploitation of their image or likeness without their consent. This is particularly true if the photograph is of a well-known person. Use of the person's likenesses may infringe his or her right of publicity if done without permission, even for many years after their deaths. Thus, for example, courts have found that the use of photographs has resulted in an infringement of one's right of publicity where photographs of baseball players were used on chewing gum cards without permission,[27] and where a picture of the head of Cary Grant was combined with the body of a model, as part of a fashion article.[28]

Accordingly, you should consider not only who owns the copyright to the photograph, but also any rights attached to the people in the photo. Ideally, you should obtain releases from any of the recognizable persons (whether private persons or public figures) appearing in the picture.

• **Motion Pictures and Other Audiovisual Works**. When licensing film or TV clips, you will need to address the right of publicity of each of the performers that appears in the film or TV clip. Performers have a proprietary right in their personas, that includes their names, visual images of their likenesses, and audio sounds of their voices.

Thus, before using a film or video clip licensed from the copyright owner, it will be necessary to obtain a release of these rights—that is, the rights to use the name, likeness and voice of each recognizable person who appears in the motion picture clip being licensed. Note that obtaining clearance of this right is independent of obtaining a license from the copyright owner to use the film clip. Moreover, it is necessary regardless of whether or not the copyright to the film clip is in the public domain.[29]

6. The Need to Obtain Consent

In situations where the right of publicity is likely to exist, the solution is to obtain the consent or a release from the persons involved. See sample release in chapter 31. A word of caution is in order, however, when dealing with minors. In some states, minors are allowed to disaffirm contracts upon reaching majority.

Endnotes

1   Twenty-four states recognize a right of publicity. Eleven states protect it by common law: Connecticut, Georgia, Hawaii, Illinois, Michigan, Minnesota, Missouri, New Jersey, Ohio, Pennsylvania, Utah. Nine states protect it by statute: Kentucky, Massachusetts, Nebraska, Nevada, New York, Oklahoma, Rhode Island, Tennessee, Virginia. Four states have both statutes and common law: California, Florida, Texas, Wisconsin.

2   *Haelan Lab., Inc. v. Topps Chewing Gum, Inc.,* 202 F.2d 866 (2d Cir.), *cert. denied,* 346 U.S. 816 (1953).

3   *Carson v. Here's Johnny Portable Toilets, Inc.,* 498 F. Supp. 71 (E.D. Mich. 1980), *aff'd in part and rev'd in part,* 698 F.2d 831 (6th Cir. 1983).

4   *Onassis v. Christian Dior-New York, Inc.,* 472 N.Y.S.2d 254 (Sup. Ct. 1984), *aff'd,* 110 A.D.2d 1095 (N.Y. App. Div. 1985).

5   *Bi-Rite Enters., Inc. v. Button Master,* 555 F. Supp. 1188 (S.D.N.Y. 1983).

6   *Grant v. Esquire, Inc.,* 367 F. Supp. 876 (S.D.N.Y. 1973) (remanded for review of First Amendment issues).

7   *Groucho Marx Prods. v. Day & Night Co.,* 523 F. Supp. 485 (S.D.N.Y. 1981), *rev'd on other grounds,* 689 F.2d 317 (2d Cir. 1982). The case was dismissed on appeal because under California law, the right of publicity did not survive Groucho Marx's death. See section 5-5.

8   *Waits v. Frito Lay, Inc.,* 978 F.2d 1093 (C.D. Cal. 1990) ($2.5 million in damages); *Midler v. Ford Motor Co.,* 849 F.2d 460 (9th Cir. 1988). Until the *Midler* case, soundalikes were not traditionally protected under the right of publicity.

9   *White v. Samsung Elecs. America, Inc.,* 971 F.2d 1395 (9th Cir. 1992), *reh'g denied en banc,* F.2d 1512 (9th Cir.), *cert. denied,* 113 S. Ct. 2443 (1993).

10 It should be noted, however, that the types of "identities" protected will depend on the particular state law involved. For example, the New York statute only protects against uses of names and likenesses.

11 *Rogers v. Grimaldi,* 875 F.2d 994 (2d Cir. 1989).

12 *Frosch v. Grosset & Dunlap, Inc.,* 427 N.Y.S.2d 828 (N.Y. App. Div. 1980).

13 *Hicks v. Casablanca Records,* 464 F. Supp 426 (S.D.N.Y. 1978). If Agatha Christie had been alive, however, she might have had a cause of action for violation of her right of privacy under a "false light" theory. See chapter 6.

14 *Jackson v. MPI Home Video,* 694 F. Supp. 483 (N.D. Ill. 1988). However, a preliminary injunction was granted based on copyright infringement and Section 43(a) of the Lanham Act (the video package was likely to confuse the public into believing that Jackson had endorsed the videotape).

15 *Zacchini v. Scripps-Howard Broadcasting Co.,* 433 U.S. 562, 97 S. Ct. 2849 (1977) (the court held that because 100 percent of the defendant's performance was shown, it preempted the demand for the live performance, and the First Amendment rights did not outweigh his right of publicity. If only a clip had been shown, the outcome might have been different.)

16 *Factors Etc., Inc. v. Pro Arts, Inc.*, 579 F.2d 215 (2d Cir. 1978), *cert. denied*, 440 U.S. 908 (1979), *rev'd on other grounds*, 652 F.2d 278 (2d Cir. 1981).

17 *Canessa v. J. I. Kislak, Inc.*, 97 N.J. Super. 327, 235 A.2d 62, 75-76 (1967).

18 See *Rauch v. Hite*, 5 Media L. Rep. 2069 (N.Y. Sup. Ct. 1979); *Eagles Eye, Inc. v. Ambler Fashion Shop, Inc.*, 627 F. Supp. 856 (E.D. Pa. 1985).

19 See, e.g., *Bi-Rite Enters., Inc. v. Button Master*, 555 F. Supp. 1188 (S.D.N.Y. 1983); *Cepeda v. Swift & Co.*, 415 F.2d 1205 (8th Cir. 1969). In a recent case, a New York court held that one person's right of publicity may be marital property, subject to equitable distribution or divorce. *Elkurs v. Elkurs*, 572 N.Y.S.2d 901 (N.Y. App. Div. 1991) (Opera singer Fredericke von Stade).

20 See, e.g., *Bi-Rite Enters., Inc. v. Button Master*, 555 F. Supp. 1188 (S.D.N.Y. 1983).

21 See generally Bangman, *A Descendable Right of Publicity: Has the Time Finally Come For A National Standard?* 17 Pepperdine L. Rev. 933 (1990).

22 The "exploitation during life" requirement was applied at various times in a number of states, but was later rejected in most, by statute or case law. Utah appears to be the only state where the exploitation requirement remains in effect. *Nature's Way Prods., Inc. v. Nature-Pharma, Inc.*, 736 F. Supp. 245 (D. Utah 1990).

23 At this writing, Ohio and New York appear to be the only jurisdictions rejecting the survival of rights of publicity. *Reeves v. United Artists*, 572 F. Supp. 1231 (N.D. Ohio 1983), *aff'd*, 765 F.2d 79 (6th Cir. 1985) (federal court interpreting Ohio law); *Pirone v. MacMillan, Inc.*, 894 F.2d 579 (2d Cir. 1990). While there has been discussion in Tennessee and California cases that denied postmortem rights of privacy, these holdings appear to have been subsequently changed by statute.

24 However, even under copyright notions of fair use based on insubstantial takings, the test is how much of the *injured party's* work was taken, rather than how significant the taken portion is to the whole of the new work. 17 U.S.C. § 107. Thus, even if a fair use concept were applied to the right of publicity, it might not result in a defense for most multimedia works. It may be more useful to claim that a fleeting image in a multimedia work does not cause much damage to the plaintiff's reputation.

25 See chapter 18, section 1.1.4.

26 *Midler v. Ford Motor Co.*, 849 F.2d 460 (9th Cir. 1988).

27 *Haelan Lab., Inc. v. Topps Chewing Gum, Inc.*, 202 F.2d 866, 868-69 (2d Cir.), *cert. denied*, 346 U.S. 816 (1953).

28 *Grant v. Esquire, Inc.*, 367 F. Supp. 876, 878-80 (S.D.N.Y. 1973) (remanded for review of First Amendment issues).

29 For a discussion of the copyright issues that arise with regard to motion picture and film clips that are in the public domain, see chapter 11, section 1.2.

Right of Privacy

Right of Privacy

As a multimedia developer, you will often wish to include names, images, and in some cases information about individuals in your multimedia works. In doing so, you should be aware of the basic rules regarding rights of privacy, and should avoid infringing these rights. Every person, whether or not that person is a public figure or celebrity, has a right to privacy. Therefore, you cannot assume you are always free to use pictures or other information about people, even if they are available from public sources.

1. What Is the Right of Privacy?

The right of privacy is based on the general principle that each person has the "right to be left alone." Essentially, there are four types of right of privacy violations:

1. publicity that places a person in a *false light*;
2. *misappropriation* of a person's name or likeness for commercial purposes;
3. public disclosure of embarrassing *private facts*; and
4. *intrusion* upon a person's solitude.[1]

The right of privacy is in some ways similar to the right of publicity, but differs in one vital respect. The right of privacy generally protects against personal embarrassment and intrusion, while the right of publicity protects a person's commercial interests in his or her identity. The right of privacy also differs from defamation in that it may involve the publication of true information, while defamation typically involves false information. Truth is a defense to defamation, but not to a violation of rights of privacy or publicity. (See chapter 5 for a discussion of the right to publicity, and chapter 7 for a discussion of defamation.)

2. What Does the Right of Privacy Protect?

The right of privacy protects a person's right to control the dissemination of information about himself. The four basic types of privacy violations are discussed separately below. Like the right of publicity, the rules regarding privacy rights differ from state to state, and this discussion is a summary of the general approach taken in most states.

2.1 False Light

The first type of invasion of privacy involves publications that place a person in a "false light." This is the category you are most likely to encounter. This type of violation involves (1) publication of false or misleading material,[2] (2) that places a person in a false light, (3) in a manner that is highly offensive to a reasonable person, (4) with knowledge of, in reckless disregard as to, or negligence as to its falsity.[3]

There are a variety of ways to place a person in a false light. They include adding false material to a true report, distorting facts or images, omitting relevant details, and attempting to fictionalize a recognizable person. The following are examples of cases where courts have found right of privacy violations based on placing a person in a false light:

- Portraying a widow in a news article as not grieving—the widow was described as "wearing the same mask of nonexpression she wore at her husband's funeral," even though the reporter had not in fact interviewed her.[4]

- Illustrating a classical guitarist's album cover with a photo of a bearded half-clad man who was not the guitarist.[5]

- Using stock footage of a Mardi Gras parade, with recognizable people, as incidental background to an adult film.[6]

- Using union members' photos in a senator's campaign materials.[7]

- Publishing a book that contained a fictionalized (but recognizable) portrayal of a psychologist who conducted nude encounter sessions.[8]

- Using the photograph of a woman to illustrate an article about a mother who abandoned her child.[9]

- Using a photograph of a couple kissing to illustrate an article on the shallowness of love at first sight.[10]

- Using the photograph of a woman in conjunction with two newspaper articles on the subject of neighborhood prostitution, when in fact the woman had no connection with prostitution.[11]

- Televising a report on "arson for profit" that implicated an apartment building's manager by displaying his knowledge of arson schemes, but omitting the context of his remarks.[12]

News reports, documentaries, and other newsworthy portrayals may be protected to a certain extent by the First Amendment. In some cases, courts have found a person's interest in privacy can be outweighed by the public's interest in obtaining the news, *even if* the person is portrayed in a false light.[13]

Because of the nature of multimedia—which can combine different images, sounds and information in creative or unusual ways—there is great potential for creating works or images that place someone in a false light. For example, if you use a person's face with an offensive picture of another's body, or combine a person's picture with an offensive setting or with offensive sounds, these could be privacy violations. In combining or creating images, you should view your creations from the individual's point of view; if the person is placed in an offensive or false light, and the newsworthiness does not outweigh the individual's interests, you could be violating the right of privacy.

2.2 Misappropriation

Another type of right of privacy violation involves **misappropriation** of a person's name or likeness, usually for commercial purposes. This is similar to the right of publicity, but protects against injuries to a person's feelings or dignity, while the right of publicity protects the commercial value of a persons' identity. In particular, whereas the right to publicity protects an individuals' right to *profit from* commercial use of his or her name or likeness, the right of privacy protects an individual's interest in *avoiding* the public limelight. In some states, such as New York, there are specific statutes protecting against misappropriation for commercial purposes,[14] and in other states the right has developed under case law.

The following are examples of cases where misappropriation existed:

- A person's photograph used to advertise insurance[15]
- An advertisement for safes that included a news story about the plaintiff[16]
- A photograph of a Vietnam veteran used in connection with advertising a book[17]
- An actor's attempt to change his name to "Peter Lorrie," which was objected to by actor Peter Lorre[18]
- An advertisement for Christian Dior using a Jackie Onassis lookalike[19]

It is important to note that, unlike other types of privacy and publicity violations, neither falsity, offensiveness, nor intrusion is required for there to be a misappropriation. As cases in this category tend to involve commercial rather than news situations, the First Amendment defenses tend not to be applicable.[20]

2.3 Private Facts

A third way you could violate privacy rights is by disclosing private facts about a person, if that information would be highly offensive to a reasonable person. A violation can exist even if the information is truthful; truth is not a defense.[21]

It is unlikely that you will be involved in this type of privacy violation, if you use publicly available materials instead of private information. The courts generally find there is no invasion of privacy when the facts are publicly available, such as from a court file or other public records.[22]

First Amendment protection for free speech is also applied to cases in this category. As discussed above, the courts will balance the offensiveness of the activity against the newsworthiness of the facts revealed. If the public's interest in the news outweighs the damage to the individual, there is no privacy violation. For example:

- Details about the private life of a famous child prodigy were found newsworthy and therefore protected.[23]
- Identification of a county home resident who had been sterilized was considered newsworthy and therefore protected.[24]

One court boldly summarized the reason for overriding privacy rights by First Amendment interests as follows: "Truth may not be the subject of either civil or criminal sanctions where discussion of public affairs is concerned."[25] Indeed, one author has cynically expressed the view that most judges perform little balancing and "simply accept the press's judgment about what is and what is not newsworthy."[26] However, it is difficult to generalize, and not all private facts will be deemed a matter of legitimate public interest, even in the context of news.[27]

2.4 Intrusion

The right of privacy also includes the right not to have others intrude on one's solitude or private affairs, if the intrusion would be highly offensive to a reasonable person.[28] Generally, cases involving intrusion relate to improper news gathering practices, such as illegal surveillance or trespass. For example, a reporter who uses fraud to obtain access to someone's home to take photographs [29] or who violates federal or state laws against wiretapping[30] has committed an invasion of privacy. These situations are not usually relevant to the average multimedia developer, who is more likely to use readily available materials.

There is, however, one type of intrusive invasion of privacy that may be more relevant to multimedia developers. If you obtain someone's consent to use information or materials, and violate the conditions of the consent, there may be a privacy violation if there is an intrusion into the subject's private affairs. For example, if a person permits use of a photograph based on the condition that the image be shown only in a certain way, there could be an invasion of privacy if you do not comply with the conditions. In one case, an acquired immune deficiency syndrome (AIDS) patient gave permission to use his image in unidentifiable silhouette; violation of this condition was a privacy violation.[31] Similarly, in a case involving Jackie Onassis, invasion of privacy was found when a photographer violated a court ordered restriction on the distance from which he could photograph her.[32]

In an invasion of privacy based on intrusion, whether by overt means or by exceeding the conditions of consent, neither truth nor newsworthiness is a defense. The act of intrusion, and the harm to the individual from that act, are the essence of the wrong.

3. Who Is Protected by the Right of Privacy?

The right of privacy protects individuals, whether or not they are celebrities. In fact, as a practical matter, private individuals may have an even greater right of privacy than celebrities, since information about celebrities or public figures may in some cases be considered more newsworthy and protected under the First Amendment. Whether or not the newsworthiness of private information outweighs the interest of the individual (celebrity or otherwise) is a decision that the courts will make considering all the facts and circumstances of a case.

4. Does the Right of Privacy Continue After Death?

The right of privacy is considered an individual's personal right, and does not survive death.[33] Therefore, you will not violate the right of privacy if you use only material relating to deceased persons. However, you should be aware that other rights do survive death, such as copyright rights and rights of publicity.

5. The Right of Privacy and Multimedia

If any literary material that you want to use makes reference to any actual persons, or any fictional persons that are readily comparable to actual persons, you should consider whether there is any infringement of such person's right of privacy.

Similarly, if you use a database that contains private facts about individuals, you should consider whether the proposed use of the database constitutes an infringement of such individuals' right of privacy. A database containing payment and credit information, or a database of medical records, for example, may raise such an issue.

The use of photographs can also constitute an infringement of an individual's right of privacy. This frequently occurs when a photograph is used in relation to other content in a manner that creates an improper negative impression about the person in the photo.

In one case, for example, a court found an invasion of privacy occurred through the use of a photograph of a woman to illustrate an article about a mother who abandoned her child.[34] In another case, a photograph of a couple kissing to illustrate an article on the shallowness of love at first sight was found to constitute an infringe-ment of the right of privacy.[35] And in yet another case, a court found that using the photograph of a woman in conjunction with two newspaper articles on the subject of neighborhood prostitution, when in fact the woman had no connection with prostitution, could constitute an infringement of her right of privacy.[36]

Everyone has a privacy right that may be violated by the use of his or her photo-graph. Thus, you should be sure to get the necessary release from any person whose image appears in a photograph.

6. The Need to Obtain Consent

Right of privacy violations arise only from *unauthorized* activity. Although consent can in some cases be implied from the conduct of the person involved, it is best obtained by using a signed release. (See chapter 31 for sample release.)

You should obtain the release directly from the person involved, rather than relying on a third person (such as a photographer) to obtain the proper consent or release. In one case, for example, a publisher relied on a consent form provided by a photographer in publishing a picture of the model, only to learn later that the model had never signed the release. The court held that whether the publisher failed to scrutinize the release adequately was a question for the jury to decide; if the jury found the publisher had not exercised enough care, he should be liable.[37]

If you have to rely on consents or releases obtained by third parties, you should try to get the third party to warrant the validity of the release along with an indem-nification in the event the release is found to be invalid or ineffective.

Endnotes

1   Prosser, *Privacy*, 48 CAL. L. REV. 383 (1960).

2   Some commentators have taken the view that falsity is not required, but the overwhelming view of the courts is that it is. This can be accomplished by the use of false innuendo or false impressions created by the use of the facts. *Godbehere v. Phoenix Newspapers, Inc.*, 162 Ariz. 335, 783 P.2d 781, 787 (1989).

3   RESTATEMENT (SECOND) OF TORTS § 652E. The knowledge or disregard standard is usually applied to public figures, and the negligence standard to nonpublic figures. However, dif-ferent states apply different standards.

4   *Cantrell v. Forest City Publishing Co.*, 419 U.S. 245 (1974).

5   *Jumez v. ABC Records, Inc.,* 3 Media L. Rep. 2324 (S.D.N.Y. 1978).

6   *Easter Seal Soc'y for Crippled Children & Adults, Inc., v. Playboy Enters., Inc.,* 530 So. 2d 643 (La. Ct. App.), *cert. denied,* 532 So. 2d 1390 (La. 1988).

7   *Cox v. Hatch,* 761 P.2d 556 (Utah 1988).

8   *Bindrim v. Mitchell,* 92 Cal. App. 3d 61, 155 Cal. Rep. 29 (Cal. Ct. App.), *cert. denied,* 444 U.S. 984 (1979).

9   *Prystash v. Best Medium Publishing Co.,* 157 Conn. 507, 254 A.2d 872 (1969); see also RESTATEMENT (SECOND) OF TORTS § 652E, illustrations 6-9.

10   *Gill v. Curtis Publishing Co.,* 38 Cal. 2d 273, 239 P.2d 630 (1952).

11   *Parnell v. Booth Newspapers, Inc.,* 572 F. Supp. 909 (W.D. Mich. 1983).

12   *Cantrell v. American Broadcasting Cos.,* 529 F. Supp. 746, 8 Media L. Rep. 1239 (N.D. Ill. 1981).

13   See *Leopold v. Levin,* 45 Ill. 2d 434, 259 N.E.2d 250 (1970) (documentary novel and motion picture using a fictionalization of a famous murder were protected by the First Amendment).

14   N.Y. Civ. Rights. Law §§ 50-51.

15   *Pavesich v. New England Life Ins. Co.,* 122 Ga. 190, 50 S.E. 68 (1905).

16   *Flores v. Mosler Safe Co.,* 164 N.E.2d 853, 7 N.Y. 2d 276 (1959).

17   *Tellado v. Time Life Books, Inc.,* 643 F. Supp. 904 (D.N.J. 1986). When a newsworthy work is protected by the First Amendment, advertisements for the work using portions of the protected work are also protected. *See Guglielni v. Spelling-Goldberg Prods.,* 25 Cal. 3d 860, 603 P.2d 45 (1979). In the *Tellado* case, however, the photograph used in the advertisement was not from the book.

18   *In re Weingand,* 231 Cal. App. 2d 289 (1964).

19   *Onassis v. Christian Dior-New York, Inc.,* 472 N.Y.S.2d 254 (1984) (a public figure does not forfeit right of privacy).

20   For example, the news story about plaintiff and safes in *Flores v. Mosler Safe Co.,* noted above in note 16, was presumably protected under the First Amendment. Use of the story for advertising was not.

21   See *Cox Broadcasting Corp. v. Cohn,* 420 U.S. 469, (1975); *Time, Inc. v. Hill,* 385 U.S. 374 (1967).

22   See *Cox Broadcasting Corp. v. Cohn,* 420 U.S. 469 (1975) (rape victim's name available from court records).

23   *Sidis v. F-R Publishing Corp.,* 113 F.2d 806 (2d Cir.), *cert. denied,* 311 U.S. 711 (1940).

24   *Howard v. Des Moines Register & Tribune Co.,* 283 N.W.2d 289 (Iowa 1979), *cert. denied,* 445 U.S. 904 (1980).

25   *Garrison v. Louisiana,* 379 U.S. 64, 74 (1964). RESTATEMENT (SECOND) OF TORTS § 652D, comments g and j.

26   Zimmerman, *Requiem for Heavywright: A Farewell to Warren's and Brondeis Privacy Tort,* 68 CORNELL L. REV. 291, 353 (1983).

27   *Y.G. v. Jewish Hosp.,* 795 S.W.2d 488 (Mo. Ct. App. 1990) (no public interests in identifying parents of triplets as part of news item on fertilization program); *Fortich v. Lifetime Cable,* 19 Media L. Rep. 1795 (D.D.C. 1991) (in documentary about life of plaintiff, scenes about her being allegedly abused as a child may not be protected by First Amendment).

28   See RESTATEMENT (SECOND) OF TORTS § 652B.

29   *Dietemann v. Time, Inc.*, 449 F.2d 245 (9th Cir. 1971).

30   *Boddie v. American Broadcasting Cos., Inc.*, 731 F.2d 333 (6th Cir. 1984).

31   See *Anderson v. Strong Memorial Hosp.,* 140 Misc. 2d 770 (N.Y. Sup. Ct. 1988), *aff'd,* 542 N.Y.S2d 96 (1989).

32   *Galella v. Onassis,* 487 F.2d 986 (2d Cir. 1973).

33   SELZ AND SIMENSKY, 2 ENTERTAINMENT LAW § 19.02, at 19-10 (1983) and cases cited therein.

34   *Prystash v. Best Medium Publishing Co.,* 157 Conn. 507, 254 A.2d 872 (1969); see also RESTATE-MENT (SECOND) OF TORTS, § 652E, illustrations 6-9.

35   *Gill v. Curtis Publishing Co.,* 38 Cal.2d 273, 239 P.2d 630 (1952).

36   *Parnell v. Booth Newspapers, Inc.* 572 F. Supp. 909, 921-22 (W.D. Mich. 1983).

37   *McCabe v. Village Voice, Inc.,* 550 F. Supp. 525 (E.D. Pa. 1982).

CHAPTER 7

Defamation Law

Defamation Law

Multimedia technology involves the interactive communication of words, images, and sounds. Thus, like any other form of communication, it has the potential to defame. While there is currently no case law applying the principles of defamation law specifically to multimedia, the general rules should apply.

Defamation is a broad term for two specific torts: (1) **libel** (written and visual defamation), and (2) **slander** (oral and aural defamation). Defamation is governed by state common law and statute. This chapter outlines the basic principles of defamation law, but the law will differ from state to state.

1. What Is Defamation?

Because defamation is a complex area of the law, it is difficult to summarize simply without risking inaccuracy. Nonetheless, the following elements are generally required to bring an action for either libel or slander:

1. *false and defamatory* communication;
2. *of and concerning* the plaintiff;
3. that is *published* to a third party;
4. with some degree of *fault*;
5. that results in *injury* to the plaintiff.[1]

As the following discussion explains, each of these elements is complicated by a number of related considerations.

1.1. False and Defamatory Communication

A *defamatory communication* is one that is both false and injurious to the reputation of another. Put another way, defamation is

> that which tends to injure "reputation" in the popular sense; to diminish the esteem, respect, goodwill or confidence in which the plaintiff is held, or to excite adverse, derogatory or unpleasant feelings or opinions against him.[2]

Merely annoying, hurtful, embarrassing, or unflattering statements, however, will generally not be considered defamatory.[3] Defamation may occur directly or through inference, insinuation, sarcasm, and even statements made in jest (unless clearly not meant, or taken, seriously). The court, or the jury, will determine whether a statement, taken in context, would be reasonably understood to be defamatory when taken in context. For example, to say someone is a "scab" may or may not be defamatory depending upon whether it is meant (and understood) to communicate that the plaintiff is a "scoundrel" (defamatory) or unwilling to participate in a labor strike (nondefamatory).[4]

It is often thought that stating an opinion is not defamatory, if clearly denoted as such. Unfortunately, the law is not so clear-cut, and will depend on how the communication is reasonably interpreted.[5] For example, if a statement couched as an opinion gives rise to an *inference* that it is based on fact, whether because of the wording or the context, it can be defamatory.[6] Not surprisingly, it is not easy for a court to decide whether a statement is primarily one of "opinion" or "fact", and these decisions are generally made on a subjective, case by case basis.

Accurately quoting a statement made by someone should generally not be defamatory of that person if accurate and in context. Indeed, slight alterations may not be actionable unless they result in a material change in the meaning of the quoted statement.[7] With multimedia, since it is easy to alter or manipulate oral and written statements, you should be careful with quotations, their attributions and context.

In addition to words, a photograph or image can clearly be defamatory.[8] For example, in one case, a photograph of a female model was juxtaposed with a picture of an elderly man holding a book widely known to be vulgar and offensive, and used as an advertisement for bed sheets. The court found the combination was defamatory since it improperly implied that the model "was a call girl waiting to be used by a stranger whetting his sexual appetite."[9] In another case, a photograph was defamatory when published in connection with a magazine story about gangs, because the individuals in the photograph were not connected with gangs or with the story.[10] In another case, the *Saturday Evening Post* was liable for publishing a satirical article on taxicab drivers with a picture of a cab driver, because the combination incorrectly implied that she was one of the cab drivers described in the story.[11] Obviously, multimedia technology creates real potential for defamation liability based on altered images, sounds, or misleading combinations. This is especially true because digital technology makes it impossible to distinguish an altered image from the original.

1.2 Of and Concerning Plaintiff

The second element requires that the defamatory statement be about, or *of and concerning* the plaintiff.[12] Courts considering this issue look to what a reasonable person in the audience would conclude, rather than what was intended—"not who is *meant* but who is *hit*."[13]

Only individuals or entities, not groups, can sue for defamation. Thus, if a statement is made about a group, a question arises as to whether the statement is sufficiently "of and concerning" the individual members to justify a defamation action. No individual is defamed if the group is so large that "there is no likelihood that a reader would understand the article to refer to any particular member." As the size of the group increases, it becomes more and more difficult for the plaintiff to show he was the one at whom the article was directed. Thus, "the cases in which recovery has been allowed usually have involved numbers of twenty-five or fewer."[14]

Generally, any living person can be defamed, as can a corporation or other entity capable of having a reputation. Because a defamation action is personal to the plaintiff, however, neither the dead nor their survivors have a case unless the survivors are independently defamed.

1.3. Publication to a Third Party

A defamation action requires that the objectionable material be *published* to at least one third party. This means that someone other than the plaintiff and defendant must hear, read, or otherwise comprehend the communication.[15] Publication need not be intentional. Indeed, a defamatory communication could be negligently published.

For example, someone could leave a written document somewhere where a third party is likely to read it, or could speak so loudly that it is likely a third party will overhear.[16]

Publication does not usually occur when the *defamed person* repeats the statement to a third person. However, in some states, if (1) it was reasonably foreseeable that the defamed person would repeat the statement to a third party, and (2) the third party was aware of the statement's defamatory character, there may be publication.

What happens if you merely reprint defamatory material that was produced by someone else? Unfortunately, you are not insulated from a charge of defamation. "One who republishes a libel is subject to liability just as if he had published it originally, even though he attributes the libelous statement to the original publisher, and even though he expressly disavows the truth of the statement."[17] However, because defamation requires some level of fault (discussed below) your totally innocent and nonnegligent replication of someone else's libel or slander may be safe, assuming you have taken adequate steps to verify its truth.[18] You should also consider getting a warranty from the source that the content is not in any way defamatory, and an indemnification against possible liability.

1.4. Fault

The degree of *fault* a plaintiff must prove is one of the most complicated issues in defamation law, because it is so intertwined with First Amendment free speech considerations. Essentially, the degree of fault required depends on the status of the defamed person.

If the defamed person is a *public figure* or a *public official*, then a statement about him or her will be considered defamatory only if it was published with *actual malice*—that is, with knowledge that it was false or with reckless disregard as to whether or not it was false.[19] This rule is primarily intended to safeguard the freedom of speech and freedom of the press guaranteed by the First Amendment. Accordingly, there is greater freedom in reporting about and criticizing the activities of public figures and public officials. A person may be a public figure in either of two ways. First, the individual may achieve such pervasive fame or notoriety that he or she becomes a public figure for all purposes and in all contexts. More commonly, however, an individual voluntarily injects himself or herself or is drawn into a particular public controversy, and thereby becomes a public figure for a limited range of issues.[20]

Persons who are not public figures have an easier standard for proving defamation. Generally, each state's law will set the appropriate level of "fault" required, usually negligence.[21]

1.5. Injury and Damages

Injury to the defamed person is an essential element of the defamation claim. However, in some cases, injury will be presumed and need not be proved. This presumption arises in cases when a communication is within one of the four categories deemed to be "defamatory per se." Statements are considered "defamatory per se" if they impute to another person (1) a criminal offense, (2) a loathsome and communicable disease, (3) conduct tending to injury them in their business, trade, profession, or office, or (4) in some states, unchastity in a woman.[22] In these cases, no proof of injury is required because the subject matter is considered so clearly defamatory that injury is presumed. With other types of statements, the injurious effect on reputation would need to be specifically shown.

If the plaintiff succeeds on his or her claim, the court or jury may award damages. These can include (1) compensatory or actual damages caused by the defamation, such as loss of a contract or a job, and mental anguish or humiliation[23] (2) presumed damages and (3) punitive damages. Presumed damages and punitive damages usually require a showing of actual malice.[24]

2. Defenses to Defamation

There are a number of defenses to defamation, which may differ from state to state. Truth is in most cases an absolute defense to defamation, even if injurious or published with malicious intent.[25] Indeed, the Supreme Court has held that the plaintiff has the burden of proof to show falsity, rather than the defendant being required to prove truth.[26] Of course, if a statement is literally accurate but leaves a false impression, there may be defamation.[27]

Statements made in certain situations are privileged, and may not be the subject of a defamation action. For example, statements made in a judicial or legislative proceeding are privileged, at least if they have some reasonable relationship to the case.[28] Reporting these types of statements may also be privileged, in some states, but as noted above, care must be taken with accuracy, attributing and avoidance of defamatory inference or innuendo.

There is also a defense for communications considered "fair comment." The First Amendment protects comment on legitimate matters of public interest, as long as not made with actual malice.

Finally, parodies may also enjoy First Amendment protection, at least with respect to public figures. However, most parody cases have involved situations when the material was so clearly a parody that no one could reasonably believe it to be based on fact.

3. Multimedia: Slander Or Libel?

In some states, slander and libel are subject to different rules.[29] Thus, given the potential for oral, aural, visual, and written defamation to occur in combination via multimedia technology, the question sometimes arises whether multimedia defamation constitutes slander, libel or perhaps a new breed of tort altogether.

The closest analogous question that the courts have considered is whether defamatory radio or television broadcasts constitute libel or slander. Radio and television, like multimedia technology, combine oral, written, and visual modes of communication and "publish" those communications to large audiences. If the courts' response to the development of television is any indication of what to expect with multimedia the result can only be confusion.

Courts are currently divided four ways on how to classify broadcast defamation. The majority of courts to consider this question have held that defamatory statements broadcast by radio or television constitute libel when read from a prepared script.[30] Others have held that such statements constitute libel regardless of how they are prepared.[31] In contrast, a few courts have held that defamatory statements broadcast by radio or television constitute slander rather than libel.[32] Finally, a very small minority of courts have held either that the distinctions of libel and slander do not apply to broadcast defamation,[33] or that broadcast defamation should be considered a distinct tort altogether, referred to as "defamacast."[34]

Unfortunately, given these divergent views, there is no clear answer at this point as to where multimedia will fit in to the law of defamation.

Endnotes

1   See RESTATEMENT (SECOND) OF TORTS § 558 (1977).

2   PROSSER AND KEETON ON TORTS § 111, at 773 (5th ed. 1984), and cases cited therein. The RESTATEMENT (SECOND) OF TORTS § 559 (1977) defines a defamatory statement as one that "tends so to harm the reputation of another as to lower him in the estimation of the community or to deter third persons from associating or dealing with him."

3   *Gordon v. Lancaster Osteopathic Hosp. Ass'n,* 489 A.2d 1364, 1369 (Pa. Super. Ct. 1985); *Pierce v. Capital Cities Communications, Inc.,* 576 F.2d 495, 503-04 (3d Cir.), *cert. denied,* 439 U.S. 861 (1978).

4   *Wozniak v. United Elec. Radio & Mach. Workers,* 57 Wis. 2d 725, 205 N.W.2d 369 (1973). *See also Zinda v. Louisiana Pacific Corp.,* 149 Wis. 2d 913, 440 N.W.2d 548, 552 (1989)("If the statements are capable of a nondefamatory as well as a defamatory meaning, then a jury question is presented as to how the statement was understood by its recipients").

5   *Gertz v. Robert Welch, Inc.,* 418 U.S. 323, 94 S. Ct. 2997 (1974). See also *National Ass'n of Gov't Employees, Inc. v. Central Broadcasting Corp.,* 396 N.E.2d 996 (Mass. 1979).

6   *Milkovich v. Lorain Journal Co.,* 497 U.S. 1, 110 S. Ct. 2695, 2706 (1990).

7   See *Stitch v. Oakdale Dental Center,* 12 A.D.2d 794, 796, 501 N.Y.S.2d 529 (N.Y. App. Div. 1986); *Masson v. New Yorker Magazine, Inc.,* 501 U.S.496, 111 S. Ct. 2419, 2425-26 (1991).

8   *Regan v. Sullivan,* 557 F.2d 300, 308 (2d Cir. 1977) (showing plaintiff's picture as part of "rogues gallery" may be libel; it was a jury question as to whether such exhibition implied the person was a criminal).

9   *Russell v. Marboro Books,* 18 Misc. 2d 166, 183 N.Y.S.2d 8, 17 (1959).

10   *Metzger v. Dell Publishing,* 136 N.Y.S.2d 888 (1955).

11   *Peay v. Curtis Publishing Co.,* 78 F. Supp. 963 (D.D.C. 1948).

12   *Auvil v. CBS "60 Minutes",* 800 F. Supp. 928 (E.D. Wash. 1992).

13   *Camer v. Seattle Post-Intelligencer,* 45 Wash. App. 29, 723 P.2d 1195, 1201 (1986), *quoting* ASHLEY, SAY IT SAFELY 30 (3d ed. 1966) (emphasis added).

14   *Golden North Airways, Inc.* v. *Tanana Publishing Co.,* 218 F.2d 612, 618-20 (9th Cir. 1954); *Louisville Times Co. v. Stivers,* 252 Ky. 843, 846, 68 S.W.2d 411, 412 (1934); RESTATEMENT (SECOND) OF TORTS § 564A, Comment B (1977).

15   PROSSER AND KEETON ON TORTS § 111, at 797-98 (5th ed. 1984).

16   *Geraghty v. Suburban Trust Co.,* 238 Md. 197, 208 A.2d 606 (1965); *Great Atlantic & Pacific Tea Co. v. Paul,* 261 A.2d 731 (Md. Ct. Spec. App. 1970).

17   *Hoover v. Peerless Publications, Inc.,* 461 F. Supp. 1206, 1209 (E.D. Pa. 1978).

18   See *Cubby, Inc. v. CompuServe, Inc.,* 776 F. Supp. 135, 140 (S.D.N.Y. 1991) (where CompuServe was found not to be liable for republication of defamatory material uploaded to CompuServe by a third party without any knowledge on the part of CompuServe that the contents were defamatory).

19   *New York Times Co. v. Sullivan,* 376 U.S. 254, 84 S. Ct. 710, 726 (1964); *Curtis Publishing Co. v. Butts,* 388 U.S. 130, 87 S. Ct. 1975 (1967).

20   *Gertz v. Robert Welch, Inc.*, 418 U.S. 323, 353, 94 S. Ct. 2997, 3012-13 (1974).

21   *Gertz v. Robert Welch, Inc.*, 418 U. S. 323, 347, 94 S. Ct. 2997, 3010 (1974).

22   RESTATEMENT (SECOND) OF TORTS §§ 570, 574 (1977).

23   Generally, a plaintiff may recover for mental anguish only upon showing an injury to rep-
      utation. *Abofreka v. Alston Tobacco Co.*, 288 S.C. 122, 341 S.E.2d 622 (1986).

24   In *Dun & Bradstreet v. Greenmoss Builders, Inc.*, 472 U.S. 749 (1985), which involved a false
      credit report, the Supreme Court held that presumed damages and punitive damages were
      available to non-public figure plaintiffs despite lack of actual malice, when there was no
      "public concern" content in the defamation.

25   *Curtis Publishing Co. v. Butts*, 388 U.S. 130, 151, 87 S. Ct. 1975, 1989 (1967). In some states,
      however, truthful statements published with malicious intent may be actionable. For exam-
      ple, in West Virginia, good faith is required for publishing truthful statements in print,
      while truth is an absolute defense for oral defamation. *Burdette v. FMC Corp.*, 566 F. Supp.
      808 (S.D. W.Va. 1983).

26   *Philadelphia Newspapers, Inc. v. Hepps*, 475 U.S. 767, 106 S. Ct. 1558 (1986).

27   *Coughlin v. Westinghouse Broadcasting & Cable, Inc.*, 603 F. Supp. 377 (E.D. Pa.), *aff'd*, 780 F.2d
      340 (3d Cir. 1985), *Cert. denied*, 476 U.S. 1187 (1986).

28   See *Hagendorf v. Brown*, 699 F.2d 478 (9th Cir. 1983).

29   In some states, the scope of liability for libel (written) is broader than for slander (oral). In
      those states, all defamation by libel is actionable, unlike for slander, only slander per se or
      slander resulting in special damages would be actionable. *Gonzalez v. Avon Prods., Inc.*, 609
      F. Supp. 1555 (D.C. Del. 1985).

30   *Charles Parker Co. v. Silver City Crystal Co.*, 142 Conn. 605, 116 A.2d 440 (1955); *Gearhart v.
      WSAZ, Inc.*, 150 F. Supp. 98 (D. Ky. 1957), *aff'd*, 254 F.2d 242 (6th Cir. 1958); *Hryhorijiv (Grig-
      orieff) v. Winchell*, 180 Misc. 574, 45 N.Y.S.2d 31 (N.Y. Sup. Ct. 1943), *aff'd*, 267 A.D. 817, 47
      N.Y.S.2d 102 (N.Y. App. Div. 1944).

31   *First Independent Baptist Church v. Southerland*, 373 So. 2d 647 (Ala. 1979); *Gray v. WALA-TV*,
      384 So. 2d 1062 (Ala. 1980).

32   *White v. Valenta*, 234 Cal. App. 2d 243, 44 Cal. Rptr. 241 (1965); *Arno v. Stewart*, 245 Cal. App.
      2d 955, 54 Cal. Rptr. 392 (1966).

33   *Summit Hotel Co. v. National Broadcasting Co.*, 336 Pa. 182, 8 A.2d 302 (1939); *Purcell v. West-
      inghouse Broadcasting Co.*, 411 Pa. 167, 191 A.2d 662 (1963); *see also S & W Seafoods Co. v. Jacor
      Broadcasting*, 194 Ga. App. 233, 390 S.E.2d 228 (1990)("[d]efamation by broadcast includes
      elements of both libel . . . and slander").

34   *American Broadcasting-Paramount Theatres, Inc. v. Simpson*, 106 Ga. App. 230, 126 S.E.2d 873
      (1962); *Fuqua Tele., Inc. v. Fleming*, 134 Ga. App. 731, 215 S.E.2d 694 (1975); *Jamison v. First
      Georgia Bank*, 193 Ga. App. 252, 387 S.E.2d 375 (1989).

CHAPTER 8

Trade Secret Law

Trade Secret Law

The process of developing a multimedia work may result in the creation of valuable trade secrets. In addition, it may require the use of trade secrets owned by others.

In many cases, for example, one of the most valuable aspects of a multimedia product is the technology you develop to make it "work" for the user. The software that facilitates user interaction, the algorithms and the processes that implement its operations, its overall design and structure, or other of its technical characteristics, may allow it to achieve an effect never before accomplished, or to perform a routine task faster or in a more efficient manner. Protecting the secrecy of these elements can be as important as preventing the distribution of unauthorized copies of the multimedia product itself. But the copyright law only prohibits copying of expression, not ideas. The copyright law does not prohibit a competitor from using your ideas. Protecting this type of information falls within the realm of the law of trade secrets.

Conversely, when you use trade secrets owned by others in the development of a multimedia product, it is important to ensure that you have obtained permission to use the technology or information, and that your use does not exceed the scope of the permission granted to you.

Trade secret protection is governed by state law, not federal law. Consequently, the definition of a trade secret and the scope of its protection may vary from state to state. This chapter will explain the general principles of trade secret law, but you should be aware that the law in any particular state may be different in some respects.

1. Relationship of Trade Secrets to Multimedia

Trade secret law can play a significant role in the development of multimedia products. It determines what you can and cannot do with secret information that you obtain from another party in order to facilitate development of a multimedia product, and it helps protect the secrets that you may create in the course of your product development efforts.

Trade secret law primarily applies to the technology behind multimedia. That is because trade secret law only protects secret, not public information. Authoring tools, the software engine that drives a multimedia product (such as search and retrieval or hypertext software), and data compression techniques, may all be considered trade secrets by the parties from whom they are licensed. In such situations, you need to understand the protection that trade secret law provides to you or others who may own this technology.

In contrast to the technology, the actual content of a multimedia product is normally not a trade secret, since it usually has been disclosed to the public, such as by the publication of a movie, television broadcast, sound recording, etc. However, in those limited situations where you use content that has not yet been publicly disclosed, and such content is considered to be a trade secret by the owner (such as, for example, new and unique sound effects for a yet-to-be-released movie), trade secret law may play an important role, whether the content was created by you or someone else.

The multimedia products you create and your business plans for them may also be considered trade secrets prior to their public release. Until a multimedia product is published, for example, you may want to keep its content and your marketing plans secret, so that you can enjoy a lead time in the marketplace before competing products can be developed.

Whether you are trying to protect your own trade secrets, or are obligated to protect the trade secrets of others, it is important to understand the law relating to trade secrets.

2. What Is a Trade Secret?

Any formula, pattern, program, process, plan, device, tool, mechanism, compound, or compilation of information can qualify as a trade secret provided that (1) it is kept a secret, and (2) it gives the person who possesses it an advantage over those who do not.[1] One of the best known examples of a trade secret is the formula for Coca-Cola. Computer software, techniques, know-how, algorithms, customer lists, product designs, manufacturing processes, and business plans are also frequently kept as trade secrets. Basically any idea, algorithm, formula, process, and the like can qualify as a trade secret if it is not obvious, is valuable to its owner, is kept secret, and would require a substantial investment of time or money by another to produce the same result independently.

Theoretically, trade secret protection can last forever, but the protection can also be lost in an instant. This is because a trade secret is protected only as long as it is kept a secret and so long as no one else duplicates it by legitimate, independent research or reverse engineering.[2] But, as in the case of the Coca-Cola formula, if proper steps are taken to preserve secrecy, trade secret protection can last indefinitely.

3. When Does Information Qualify as a Trade Secret?

The trade secret laws will not protect all information. To qualify as a trade secret, information must have two basic characteristics: it must be secret, and it must provide its owner with economic value—that is, an advantage over competitors who do not have it.

3.1 Secrecy Requirement

The secrecy requirement may be somewhat obvious, but is also of critical importance. In the absence of secrecy, there is no trade secret protection. The concept of "secrecy" is really a term of art; it has two elements: (1) the information must *be* secret, that is, it must not be known generally to the industry, and (2) the information must be treated as and kept secret. The first element is generally not controllable by the owner, but the second element is.

Whether the information *is* secret is determined by whether experts in the industry also possess the same information. Basically, it must be secret from other competitors within the industry. Information that is general knowledge within an industry cannot be a trade secret even though it may not be known to most people, or even if customers are unable to figure out how it works. For example, a compression and decompression technique used for the storage and retrieval of digital motion picture data may be unknown to most people. However, if it is generally known to persons developing and using compression techniques within the industry, then it will not qualify as a trade secret.

To determine whether information is protectable as a trade secret, it is necessary to examine the extent to which it is known to anyone other than its owner, the extent to which it is known to the owner's employees, the extent of the measures taken by the owner to guard the secrecy of the information, and the ease or difficulty with which the information could properly be acquired or duplicated by others.[3] Absolute secrecy, however, is not required. When you develop information that you consider to be a secret, you may disclose it to persons legally obligated to keep it secret, such as employees, and to persons who expressly agree to keep it secret, such as customers, without compromising your trade secret protection. As long as the disclosure is made in confidence, and is so understood by both parties, the veil of secrecy will not be deemed to have been broken.

A disclosure of the secret is made "in confidence" when the person to whom the secret is disclosed signs a written agreement acknowledging that the material is secret and that he or she will not disclose it to others.[4] However, a written confidentiality agreement is not always necessary since the law will deem certain disclosures to have been made in confidence even without a written agreement. This is the case, for example, when the owner of a trade secret discloses it to his or her employees.[5]

Courts frequently evaluate the secrecy of information in terms of its novelty. With multimedia technology, for example, novelty can be found either in a new and unique function performed by the work, or in the method by which it performs a routine function. If a new multimedia work is developed that performs a function never before accomplished with a computer, it will certainly be considered novel. But even works of a routine nature can qualify. For example, a newly developed data compression technique can qualify for trade secret protection even though the function it performs (i.e., data compression) is certainly not novel. Moreover, this is true even if the new work makes use of some generally known techniques, algorithms, and information. Although the concept of data compression and many of the processes used to implement it are not themselves trade secrets (because they are not secret), a specific program using those generally known ideas can be, because of the unique logic and coherence by which it is designed and programmed.[6] In other words, while generally known concepts cannot be protected, a specific implementation involving a unique combination of general concepts may well amount to a trade secret.

This was recognized by a court in an early trade secret software case involving a time-sharing system, which the court held to embody a trade secret.[7] In doing so, it acknowledged the fact that all time-sharing software contains certain elements that perform similar functions and that utilize certain similar basic concepts. What is different (or novel) about each system is its specific engineering and its particular underlying technology and design, together with what has been referred to as its "logic and coherence," as well as its speed, accuracy, cost, and commercial feasibility. These qualities differ greatly from system to system, and inevitably reflect the peculiar and unique accomplishments and technical skills of the developers. Trade secret novelty (or secrecy) requires only that the particular architecture of a program is valuable and that it is not a matter of common knowledge or readily duplicated.[8]

In addition to the requirement that the information be secret within the industry, the law also requires that the trade secret owner take reasonable steps to maintain its secrecy. In essence, the law says that the information must not only be secret, but that the owner must also act as if it is a valuable secret and guard it accordingly. Otherwise, protection may be lost. In one case, for example, a court held that software used in the design and manufacture of class rings was not a trade secret because, among other things, the plaintiff never proved that it intended to keep the relevant information secret.[9] This conclusion was based in part on the fact that when the software was installed, no policy was established to keep it secret, and that the plaintiff had allowed one of its employees to write an article explaining the system to other experts in the field.

Depending on the circumstances, fulfilling this obligation to maintain secrecy may require the establishment of an affirmative course of action reasonably designed to ensure that the information will remain secret.[10] This may include steps such as restricting access to certain employees, using passwords and key codes, physical security measures such as locked file cabinets, and having employees and others sign confidentiality agreements. Steps that can be taken to ensure protection of your trade secrets are described in chapter 26, section 2.

In many cases, some disclosure of trade secrets is necessary in the course of business, such as disclosure to programmers, consultants, those involved in joint ventures, and in some cases customers. Information will still be protected if disclosed to someone legally obligated to keep it secret, such as an employee or someone who expressly agrees to keep it secret. As long as the disclosure is made in confidence, and is so understood by both parties, the veil of secrecy will not be deemed to have been broken.

3.2 Economic Value Requirement

In addition to being a secret, the information must provide its owner with economic value or an advantage over its competitors who do not have it. Otherwise, there really is not anything worth protecting. For example, if a software vendor were to develop computer program capable of printing documents backward it might represent an accomplishment of sorts, and the way in which it is done may be secret, but it is doubtful that it would provide its owner with any advantage over its competitors.[11]

Courts frequently analyze the competitive advantage of a trade secret by looking at the time and effort that has gone into its development. The time and money spent on developing multimedia technology frequently gives its owner a big head start over any competitor who is only beginning the process of developing similar technology. The essence of trade secret law is to protect the value of this head start by requiring competitors to spend their own time and money to create a competing product. In this way, the law protects the trade secret owner's investment in the product.

4. What Is the Scope of Trade Secret Protection?

Trade secret protection is in some ways broader, and in some ways more restrictive, than that afforded by copyright. In general, it will protect more aspects of multimedia technology than copyright, but will do so in fewer situations. To utilize the trade secret law effectively, it is important to understand its scope.

4.1 Idea and Expression

Trade secret law protects both ideas and the expressions of those ideas. Thus, it is much broader than copyright, which protects only the expression of an idea. For example, assume that you develop a new, better, and faster technique for indexing, linking, and allowing a user to interactively search the contents of a multimedia product. That technique may qualify as a trade secret, and the program in which it is implemented will also be protected by federal copyright. However, the copyright law only protects the way you wrote the code to implement the secret technique—it does not prevent others from reading your code, learning your technique, and writing their own computer program to implement it. This is where trade secret protection is important. In this example, the trade secret is the indexing and search technique (i.e., the idea), not the way it was coded (i.e., the way the idea was expressed). Trade secret law will protect that technique; anyone who reads the code and then uses or discloses it without authorization may be liable for trade secret misappropriation, if they do so in violation of a confidential relationship.

4.2 Confidential Relationship

Although the scope of trade secret protection is broader than the scope of copyright protection, its application is somewhat more limited. Whereas copyright prohibits any unauthorized copying of a work, trade secret law prohibits unauthorized use or disclosure of a trade secret only when it is done improperly, such as when it is done in violation of a confidential relationship.

A confidential relationship between an owner of trade secret information and someone else can arise in two ways: it can be implied by law, or it can be expressly agreed to in a contract. The best example of an implied obligation of confidentiality occurs in the employer-employee relationship. Employees are automatically bound not to disclose or use for their own benefit the trade secrets disclosed to them by their employer. No written contract is necessary to create this obligation.[12]

Conversely, when a trade secret is disclosed to a customer, joint venture partner, or other potential business partner, there is no obligation of confidentiality implied by law. Thus, to establish a relationship of confidentiality that will preclude the customer from exploiting a vendor's trade secret, it is normally necessary to enter into a written contract to this end.[13]

Imposing an obligation of confidentiality is very important. When there is no confidential relationship between the owner of a trade secret and someone who learns of it, the latter is free to use it in any way he or she desires. Thus, independent development of the same secret and reverse engineering of products purchased on the open market are perfectly proper.[14] If someone independently develops the secret, that person is, of course, under no obligation to anyone else who may also have the same secret. Similarly, if the owner discloses it to an outsider without any confidentiality restrictions, there is nothing wrong with using it. This frequently occurs when products are placed on the market and the trade secrets are disclosed by the product itself or are discernible through reverse engineering.

Establishing a confidential relationship with everyone who will receive the confidential information is critical to protecting the trade secrets. However, it should also be noted that an unauthorized user of a trade secret can also be held liable for misappropriation, even in the absence of a confidential relationship with the owner, if he knew that the trade secret had been obtained in violation of an obligation of confidentiality, or was subsequently informed of that fact.[15] The application of this principle is illustrated by a case involving a customer of a data processing service bureau.[16] The service bureau customer had requested a backup copy of the software being run on its behalf because it doubted the ability of the service bureau to remain in business. An employee of the service bureau provided such a copy, but, unbeknownst to the customer, this was done in violation of company policy. Before the customer could use the software, however, it was put on notice by the service bureau that the programs were its exclusive property. This notice, the court held, subjected the customer to trade secret liability for its subsequent use of the software for which it had paid no money. When the customer ignored the notice and used the software, it was held liable for trade secret misappropriation.

5. Bases of Liability for Misappropriation

Trade secret law does not prohibit the use or disclosure of another's trade secrets per se. Thus the mere fact that someone else uses or discloses trade secret multimedia technology or software does not necessarily mean that the owner of the trade secret can successfully bring a lawsuit for misappropriation. The law only prohibits the *unauthorized* use and disclosure of trade secrets obtained under an obligation of confidentiality, or by improper means.

If one's possession, use, and/or disclosure of another's trade secret does not fall into one of these categories, then he or she has done nothing wrong. For example, if an individual obtains a copy of your multimedia product without signing a **confidentiality agreement** (such as by purchase), he or she is free to try to reverse engineer that product in order to learn the secret of how it works, and then use that information or disclose it to others.[17] And, of course, anyone who discovers a trade secret on his or her own through independent work is free to do whatever they would like with it.

It is the improper conduct in obtaining, using, or disclosing a trade secret that gives rise to liability for misappropriation. In many cases, the improper conduct will relate to the way in which the trade secret was obtained. Theft of trade secret information is an obvious example. More often than not, however, the trade secret will have been obtained legitimately. For example, it may be disclosed to an employee on the job or to a customer who has signed a confidentiality agreement. In this case, liability for trade secret misappropriation occurs only if the employee or the customer use or disclose the trade secret in a way that breaches the obligation of confidentiality. This would occur, for example, if either of them used the trade secret to assist in starting a competing business, or gave it away to a third party.

If someone wrongfully obtains a trade secret, or uses or discloses a trade secret in violation of a confidential obligation, that person will be liable to the owner of the trade secret for damages regardless of the way in which the trade secret was used. Thus, for example, if someone improperly obtains information relating to a new trade secret digital data compression algorithm and then modifies or improves it for a use that is totally unrelated to the original product, that person will still be liable for misappropriation of the original trade secret. Improper "use" of a trade secret does not require precise duplication or copying. Modifications or improvements to the original trade secret will still subject one to liability if the secret of the original owner is substantially involved.[18]

Additionally, if a trade secret was obtained wrongfully, neither the fact that it could have been discovered by legitimate means, nor that it might have been independently developed, is a defense. It is the improper conduct that is the key to liability in a misappropriation case.[19]

The form in which the information is taken is also irrelevant. A trade secret can be appropriated not only by taking a physical disk, tape, source listing, or copy of a document, but also by memorizing it. Employees may be able to memorize algorithms, plans, techniques, formulae, and the like, but this does not mean that they can claim the information as their own knowledge. It is as much a breach of confidence for employees to reproduce their employer's trade secrets from memory as to copy them directly.

In one case, for example, the court found that a group of employees had over the years actually memorized their employer's plans and drawings, so that they actually had a mental picture of these trade secrets. This, the court held, was no different than having a copy or picture on paper. Since these "mental pictures" were obtained by the employees while working for their employer, the court concluded that "to carry them away in this manner was [as much] a violation of a confidence reposed in them by their employer, as if they had made copies or photographs and carried them away."[20]

In another case, involving misappropriation of on-line business software, the defendant, a former employee, claimed that he had not taken any documentation or other physical material away from his employer.[21] He contended that his software was independently developed, not copied. However, the court said that it made no difference whether or not he had taken the documentation since misappropriation by memory is also forbidden. Moreover, the court pointed out that it was not necessary that his software be an exact copy in order to impose liability.

6. Proving Trade Secret Misappropriation

In order to prove that a trade secret has been misappropriated, it is necessary to prove (1) that a trade secret exists, (2) that the trade secret was acquired by the defendant by improper means (such as by theft), or was subject to an obligation of confidentiality, and (3) that the defendant used or disclosed the trade secret in a manner not authorized by its owner (e.g., that the defendant violated the obligation of confidentiality). In many cases, the issue in dispute is whether the person who used the trade secret was free to do so, or whether the person was bound by an obligation of confidentiality prohibiting such conduct. In most cases, however, the issue is whether the defendant actually used or disclosed the plaintiff's trade secret.

6.1 Direct Evidence

Direct evidence of misappropriation is, of course, the best method of proof. Although situations in which such evidence is available are rare, it has occurred.

In one such case, the plaintiff was able to establish that the defendant obtained a copy of its software by bribing a customer's employee to deliver magnetic tapes of the software.[22] In another case, IBM was able to prove that one of its employees, who had been hired by the competitor, took a copy of the source code with him, which a competitor subsequently used in the development of its own product.[23]

Finding copies of stolen trade secret information in the defendant's possession also provides excellent evidence. In one criminal case, for example, the defendant copied his former employer's source code by accessing the computer through his home terminal. The phone call was traced, and the Federal Bureau of Investigation (FBI) obtained a search warrant. Upon searching his house, they found forty rolls of computer paper containing the stolen source code.[24]

6.2 Circumstantial Evidence

If direct evidence of misappropriation is not available, it may still be proved by circumstantial evidence. There are a number of ways to do this. One of the most common methods by which misappropriation is proved is by comparing of the time and expense of development incurred by both parties. Such a circumstantial case would consist of the following evidence:

1. the plaintiff spent large sums of money and/or a great deal of time and effort to develop a specific product;

2. the defendant, in some way, had access to the plaintiff's trade secret information; and

3. the defendant produced a functionally similar product in a fraction of the time and/or at a fraction of the cost.

In one case, the court concluded that Telex had misappropriated IBM's trade secrets in a disk storage system upon a showing that a former IBM employee familiar with the trade secret developed an equivalent device for Telex in eighteen months, although it had taken IBM five years.[25] In another case, the plaintiff spent more than $100,000 over an eighteen-month period to develop software that the defendant was able to develop in a few months for only $2,500.[26] The court had no trouble finding misappropriation.

In cases involving software, misappropriation may also be established by showing that the defendant's software duplicates some of the errors or arbitrary sequences of code contained in the plaintiff's software. In one case the court found misappropriation based on the testimony of plaintiff's experts who had "made a careful analysis of the two programs and found not only similarity in the overall structure and organization (some of which might be explainable on functional grounds) but they found identical segments of code that were solely arbitrary and, most significantly, deviations or quasi-mistakes that, in their judgment, could only be explained by copying."[27] In another case, the court found that the defendants had copied trade secret blueprints, noting that they "have even copied some of the plaintiff's mistakes."[28]

Misappropriation of software trade secrets may also be proved by a detailed comparison of the two programs, if such comparison establishes similarity of an unlikely number of program elements that would otherwise be arbitrarily decided.

Such elements might include input and output formats that would normally be arbitrarily decided, program call routines, the sequence of processing, error detection procedures, subprogram structures, optimization techniques, field and file sizes, and particular formulas. Thus, in one case, expert testimony that "it would be very unlikely that two computer programmers would be capable of drafting an accounts receivable program with as many similarities as are contained in the plaintiff's and defendant's programs," and testimony that the two programs had such "great similarity and likeness to the point where the programs are a copy, one of the other" was used to establish misappropriation.[29]

It should also be noted that the amount of the plaintiff's code that is appropriated by the defendant is not really important. The fact that only a small percentage of the plaintiff's routines may have been used by the defendant does not, in and of itself, provide a defense. A small portion of a program may make it unique.[30]

Frequently, all of the above factors are used, in combination, to establish trade secret misappropriation. A good example is a case filed by the owner of a jobber management system, called "JMS" against an employee of one of its customers.[31] The employee, along with another individual, had developed a comparable package called "FuelPak." The evidence at trial established that the two developers of Fuel-Pak had access to the JMS manual and used it; that JMS had taken twenty-two months to develop whereas FuelPak took only three to four weeks; that JMS cost $400,000 to develop whereas most of the money spent for FuelPak (the amount of which was never proved) went for marketing rather than development; that some of the design notes for FuelPak were remarkably similar to the JMS design; and that (as established by expert testimony), there were a great number of similarities between the two programs that were not accidental, and a certain number of cosmetic differences that were incorporated in FuelPak to disguise copying. On the basis of this evidence, the court concluded that the JMS trade secrets had been misappropriated.

7. Remedies for Misappropriation

Once misappropriation of trade secret information has been proven, the owner of the trade secret wants three things—to stop the misappropriation, to recover the losses sustained to date, and to deter future acts of misappropriation. Each of these remedies is available to the owner in an appropriate case.

7.1 *Injunction*

Putting a stop to the damages flowing from a misappropriation is usually accomplished by obtaining an injunction. An **injunction** is a court order prohibiting one party from doing a wrongful act that he or she is threatening to do, or to stop him or her from continuing to perform a wrongful act. For example, a court-ordered injunction could be used to prevent someone from marketing products utilizing misappropriated trade secrets.

There are essentially three types of injunctions that can be issued by a court. All three have exactly the same effect in terms of prohibiting certain conduct by the defendant, but they are issued at different stages of a lawsuit and have different durations.

The first type of injunction is called a **temporary restraining order (TRO).** A trade secret owner may seek a TRO at the very beginning of a lawsuit in order to prevent the occurrence of some imminent action by the defendant that is likely to cause immediate and irreparable harm to the plaintiff. A TRO, however, typically lasts for a very short time, usually no more than ten days. The purpose of such an injunction is to preserve the status quo and prevent additional injury to the plaintiff until the court can conduct a preliminary hearing into plaintiff's allegations.

After the preliminary hearing has been held, the court may be persuaded to issue a **preliminary injunction.** The purpose of such an injunction is to prevent the defendant from disclosing, marketing or continuing to market the allegedly misappropriated software until the issues are finally resolved at a trial. In order to obtain such an injunction, the following must be proved to the court's satisfaction:

1. the plaintiff will suffer "irreparable injury"[32] if the defendant is allowed to continue its activities or threatened activities while the case is waiting to go to trial; and

2. there is a strong likelihood that the plaintiff will win its case at trial.

Although in theory the court's disposition of a plaintiff's request for a preliminary injunction does not end the lawsuit, it frequently has that effect. This often occurs if the preliminary injunction has been granted because the judge will be viewed as having sent a strong signal to the defendant that the defendant is likely to lose the case for good when it comes to trial, and because the defendant will be prevented from continuing its challenged conduct during the interim. By the same token, if the court refuses to enter the preliminary injunction and the plaintiff is the losing party, the plaintiff often decides that the cost of continued litigation is not justified by the prospect of winning at trial years hence, by which time the trade secret may well have become obsolete. The preliminary injunction procedure thus can provide a very expeditious (and relatively inexpensive) resolution of a trade secret dispute.

If the case goes to trial, and if the defendant is successful in establishing that he or she did not misappropriate any of the trade secrets of the plaintiff, any preliminary injunction that was entered will be "dissolved" and the defendant will be free to continue doing business as before. However, whether or not a preliminary injunction was entered, if the plaintiff wins at the trial, the court will enter a **"permanent" injunction** prohibiting the defendant from doing whatever it is that was found to be wrongful. In trade secret cases, however, the use of the term "permanent" injunction is somewhat misleading. For the duration of such an injunction is generally limited to the amount of time that it would take the defendant to discover the trade secret independently, or to develop it by reverse engineering, rather than through misappropriation.[33] There are, however, some cases in which truly permanent injunctions have been entered in a trade secret misappropriation action.[34]

7.2 Damages and Profits

The courts have employed a variety of theories in calculating the measure of damages in a trade secret misappropriation case,[35] but they fall into two general categories: the first looks at how much the plaintiff lost as a result of defendant's wrongdoing (compensatory damages), and the second looks at how much the defendant gained (an "accounting").

The first approach represents an award of money "damages" to compensate plaintiff for its injury; the plaintiff must demonstrate how much money it lost because of the defendant's unlawful conduct. Thus, under this theory if the plaintiff cannot show any loss, it will recover nothing, even if the defendant has made money from the misappropriation.

However, courts can measure compensatory damages in a number of different ways. One way is by calculating what would amount to a reasonable royalty for the use of the plaintiff's trade secret by the defendant.[36] Another way to measure compensatory damages is to determine what an investor would pay for the projected return that would be realized by virtue of owning the trade secret, and to have the defendant reimburse the plaintiff for this amount.[37] A third approach is to compensate the plaintiff for the sales that it lost as a result of the misappropriation.[38] One final approach, applicable where the defendant has in some way destroyed the value of the trade secret, such as through publication, is to determine the value of the information to the plaintiff as a secret compared to its "value" after publication and to award the plaintiff the difference.[39]

Under the second approach, often referred to as an *accounting*, a court will determine the profits (not gross sales) made by the defendant by virtue of its misappropriation, and will then require the defendant to pay those profits to the plaintiff.[40] Alternatively, the development costs that were saved by the defendant as a result of the misappropriation are awarded to the plaintiff.[41]

In some cases, the plaintiff will be allowed to recover both its losses and the defendant's gains if it can establish that this will not result in a double recovery.[42]

In addition to actual damages suffered by the plaintiff, or actual gains made by the defendant, the plaintiff may also be entitled to punitive damages. When Telex was found to have misappropriated IBM's trade secrets, IBM was awarded $17.5 million in compensatory damages and $1 million in punitive damages.[43] Punitive damages are awarded, not to compensate the plaintiff for its injury (though they are paid to the plaintiff), but solely to punish the defendant for particularly outrageous wrongdoing.

7.3 Criminal Penalties

A number of states have enacted criminal statutes that expressly deal with trade secret theft. California, for example, has a comprehensive criminal statute for the wrongful appropriation of trade secrets,[44] with penalties up to one year in jail and a fine of up to $5,000. This statute has been applied to the theft of computer software.[45] In one case, an IBM employee was convicted of criminal theft of trade secrets from his employer.[46]

Endnotes

1   RESTATEMENT (FIRST) OF TORTS § 757, Comment b (1939). The Uniform Trade Secrets Act, which has now been adopted in thirty-two states, defines a trade secret as "information, including a formula, pattern, compilation, program, device, method, technique or process, that: (i) derives independent economic value, actual or potential, from not being generally known to, and not being readily ascertainable by proper means by other persons who can obtain economic value from its disclosure, and (ii) is the subject of efforts that are reasonable under the circumstance to maintain its secrecy." See Uniform Trade Secrets Act § 1(3).

2   *University Computing Co. v. Lykes-Youngstown Corp.*, 504 F.2d 518, 534 (5th Cir. 1974), *reh'g denied*, 505 F.2d 1304 (5th Cir. 1974).

3   RESTATEMENT (FIRST) OF TORTS § 757 comment b (1939).

4   See chapter 33 for sample confidentiality agreements.

5   See, e.g., *Integrated Cash Management Servs., Inc. v. Digital Transactions, Inc.*, 732 F. Supp. 370 (S.D.N.Y. 1989), *aff'd*, 920 F.2d 171 (2d Cir. 1990); *Engineered Mechanical Servs., Inc. v. Langlois*, 464 So. 2d. 329 (La. Ct. App. 1984), *cert. denied*, 467 So. 2d 531 (La. 1985).

6   *Cybertek Computer Prods., Inc. v. Whitfield*, 203 U.S.P.Q. 1020, 1024 (Cal. Super. Ct. 1977).

7   *Com-Share, Inc. v. Computer Complex, Inc.* 338 F. Supp. 1229, 1234 (E.D. Mich. 1971), *aff'd*, 458 F.2d 1341 (6th Cir. 1972).

8   *Dickerman Assocs., Inc. v. Tiverton Bottled Gas Co.*, 594 F. Supp. 30, 35 (D. Mass. 1984).

9   *Jostens, Inc. v. National Computer Sys., Inc.*, 318 N.W.2d 691, 700 (Minn. 1982).

10 *Amoco Prod. Co. v. Lindley*, 609 P.2d 733, 743 (Okla. 1980).

11 See also *Walker v. University Books, Inc.*, 602 F.2d 859, 865 (9th Cir. 1979) (plaintiff created a set of I Ching cards, using better colors and paper than the original, but court said that these "improvements" were not trade secrets, since they were minimal and gave her no competitive advantage).

12 See, e.g., *Integrated Cash Management Servs., Inc. v. Digital Transactions, Inc.*, 732 F. Supp 370 (S.D.N.Y. 1989), *aff'd*, 920 F.2d 171 (2d Cir. 1990); *Engineered Mechanical Servs., Inc. v. Langlois*, 464 So. 2d 329 (La. Ct. App. 1984), *cert. denied*, 467 So. 2d 531 (La. 1985).

13 See chapter 33 for sample confidentiality agreements.

14 Cal. Civ. Code § 3426; 765 ILCS § 1065/2.

15 RESTATEMENT (FIRST) OF TORTS §§ 757, 758 (1939).

16 *Computer Print Sys., Inc. v. Lewis*, 281 Pa. Super. 240, 422 A.2d 148, 155 (1980).

17 See *Atari Games Corp. v. Nintendo of America, Inc.*, 975 F.2d 832 (Fed. Cir. 1992); *Sega Enters., Ltd, v. Accolade, Inc.*, 977 F.2d 1510 (9th Cir. 1992).

18 RESTATEMENT OF (FIRST) TORTS § 757 comment b (1939); *M. Bryce & Assocs., Inc. v. Gladstone*, 215 U.S.P.Q. 81, 319 N.W.2d 907, 912 (Wis. App.), *cert. denied*, 459 U.S. 944 (1982); *Digital Dev. Corp. v. International Memory Sys.*, 185 U.S.P.Q. 136, 141 (S.D. Cal. 1973).

19 *Telex Corp. v. International Business Machs. Corp.*, 510 F.2d 894, 929-30 (10th Cir.), *cert. dismissed*, 423 U.S. 802 (1975).

20   *Schulenburg v. Signatrol, Inc.*, 33 Ill. 2d 379, 212 N.E.2d 865, 868 (1965), *cert. denied*, 383 U.S. 959 (1966).

21   *Cybertek Computer Prods., Inc. v. Whitfield*, 203 U.S.P.Q. 1020, 1024-25 (Cal. Super. Ct. 1977); see also *Jostens, Inc.* v. *National Computer Sys., Inc.*, 318 N.W.2d 691, 702 (Minn. 1982).

22   *University Computing Co. v. Lykes-Youngstown Corp.*, 504 F.2d 518, 529 (5th Cir. 1974).

23   *Telex Corp. v. International Business Machs. Corp.*, 510 F.2d 894, 911 (10th Cir.), *cert. dismissed*, 423 U.S. 802 (1975).

24   *United States v. Seidlitz*, 589 F.2d 152, 155 (4th Cir. 1978).

25   *Telex Corp. v. International Business Machs. Corp.*, 510 F.2d 894, 911 (10th Cir.), *cert. dismissed*, 423 U.S. 802 (1975).

26   *Analogic Corp. v. Data Translation, Inc.*, 371 Mass. 643, 358 N.E.2d 804, 806 (1976).

27   *Structural Dynamics Research Corp. v. Engineering Mechanics Research Corp.*, 401 F. Supp. 1102, 1117 (E.D. Mich. 1975).

28   *Schulenburg v. Signatrol, Inc.*, 33 Ill. App. 2d 379, 212 N.E.2d 865, 869 (1965), *cert. denied*, 383 U.S. 959 (1966).

29   *J & K Computer Sys., Inc. v. Parrish*, 642 P.2d 732, 735 (Utah 1982).

30   *Josten, Inc. v. National Computer Sys., Inc.*, 318 N.W.2d 691, 703 (Minn. 1982).

31   *Dikerman Assocs., Inc. v. Tiverton Bottled Gas Co.*, 594 F. Supp. 30 (D. Mass. 1984).

32   In legal parlance, an injury is "irreparable" if it cannot be remedied through the payment of money damages. This is frequently the case with the misappropriation of trade secrets since it is often difficult (if not impossible), to calculate the true extent of the plaintiff's loss.

33   See *Analogic Corp. v Data Translation, Inc.*, 371 Mass. 643, 358 N.E.2d 804, 807-08 (Mass. 1976); *K-2 Ski Co. v. Head Ski Co.*, 506 F.2d 471, 474 (9th Cir. 1974); *Anaconda Co. v. Metric Tool & Die Co.*, 485 F. Supp. 410, 431 (E.D. Pa. 1980); *C-E-I-R Inc. v. Computer Dynamics Corp.*, 183 A.2d 374, 381 (Md. 1962).

34   These include *Data General Corp. v. Digital Computer Controls, Inc.*, 357 A.2d 105, 114 (Del. Ch. 1975), and *BMC Software, Inc. v. Data-Base Technology Corp.*, No. 830-C-9026, slip op. (N.D. Ill. May 16, 1984) (consent judgment).

35   *Telex Corp. v. International Business Machs. Corp.*, 510 F.2d. 894, 930-31 (10th Cir.), *cert. dismissed*, 423 U.S. 802 (1975).

36   Cases using this approach have included *Structural Dynamics Research Corp. v. Engineering Mechanics Research Corp.*, 401 F. Supp. 1102, 1120 (E.D. Mich. 1975); *University Computing Co. v. Lykes-Youngstown Corp.*, 504 F.2d 518, 539 (5th Cir. 1974).

37   See *Precision Plating & Metal Finishing, Inc. v. Martin-Marietta Corp.*, 435 F.2d 1262, 1263-64 (5th Cir. 1970).

38   *See Telex Corp. v. International Business Machs. Corp.*, 510 F.2d 894, 931 (10th Cir.), *cert. dismissed*, 423 U.S. 802 (1975).

39   *See University Computing Co. v. Lykes-Youngstown Corp.*, 504 F.2d 518, 535 (5th Cir. 1974).

40   This sales approach was used in the case of *Telex Corp. v. International Business Machs. Corp.*, 510 F.2d 894, 931-32 (10th Cir.), *cert. dismissed*, 423 U.S. 802 (1975).

41   See *Koehring Co. v. National Automatic Tool Co.*, 257 F. Supp. 282, 291 (S.D. Ind. 1966), *aff'd*, 385 F.2d 414 (7th Cir. 1967).

42   This was allowed in *Telex Corp. v. International Business Machs. Corp.*, 510 F.2d 894, 930-33 (10th Cir.), *cert. dismissed*, 423 U.S. 802 (1975), and *Tri-Tron Int'l, v. Velto*, 525 F.2d 432, 437 (9th Cir. 1975). However, this approach was not allowed in the case of *Sperry Rand Corp. v. A-T-O, Inc.*, 447 F.2d 1387, 1393 (4th Cir. 1971), *cert. denied*, 405 U.S. 1017 (1972).

43   *Telex Corp. v. International Business Machs. Corp.*, 510 F.2d 894, 933 (10th Cir.), *cert. dismissed*, 423 U.S. 802 (1975); *see also Tri-Tron Int'l v. Velto*, 525 F.2d 432, 437-38 (9th Cir. 1975); *Sperry Rand Corp. v. A-T-O, Inc.*, 447 F.2d 1387, 1394-95 (4th Cir. 1971), *cert. denied*, 405 U.S. 1017 (1972).

44   Cal. Penal Code § 499C.

45   *Ward v. Superior Court*, 3 Computer L. Serv. Rep. 206 (Cal. Super. Ct. 1972).

46   *People v. Serrata*, 133 Cal. Rptr. 144; 62 Cal. App. 3d 9 (1976).

Patent Law

CHAPTER 9

Patent Law

Patent protection for multimedia technology offers the most comprehensive form of protection available. Patent protection is more expensive in the first instance than copyright or trade secret protection. It is time consuming to obtain and requires the assistance of a patent attorney. But a patent is the only form of protection that permits suit against innocent infringers. That is, no proof of copying or misappropriation is necessary. Unlike copyright and trade secret protection, however, patent protection is not always available. Only when multimedia technology meets certain requirements can it qualify.

Like the copyright and trade secret forms of protection, patent protection is important to you from two perspectives. First, it may provide a valuable form of protection for the technology that you create in the multimedia development process. (see chapter 27 regarding protecting the patent rights for the technology that you create). Second, you will need to take care to ensure that the technology that you incorporate in your multimedia works (both the technology you develop and the technology you obtain from other parties) does not infringe anyone else's patent.

It is very possible that technology you develop or license from others is claimed by someone else as being within the scope of a patent they have obtained. And while you may dispute the validity of such a patent in certain situations, you still need to consider whether you want to run the risk of defending an infringement law suit or pay the price of licensing the technology.

Patent protection normally applies to multimedia technology, not the content. The patentable technology is typically a system or process designed to accomplish a specific purpose, and is frequently implemented in a computer program.

1. What Is a Patent?

A *patent* is a grant by the federal government to an inventor that gives the inventor the right to exclude others from making, using, or selling his or her invention throughout the United States for a period of seventeen years.[2] During the life of a patent, no one is allowed to make, use, sell, or license the invention without the inventor's permission. It makes no difference whether they copy the inventor's invention or develop it independently.

When compared with the protection afforded by copyright and the law of trade secrets, patent protection is plainly the strongest of the three. Copyright prohibits only the actual copying of the author's expression of an idea. It does not protect the idea itself, nor does it protect an independent creation of the same expression, as long as there is no copying. Trade secret law goes a little further, providing protection for procedures, processes, systems, and methods of operation not protected by copyright, but such protection is only available as long as everything is kept secret. Once the secret is out everyone is free to use it. Moreover, reverse engineering of a trade secret is a legitimate form of competition, and trade secret law does not provide any protection against independent development. A patent precludes all forms of copying, all uses of the aspects of the invention covered by the patent, and all independent development of the same invention.

There is, however, a cost associated with obtaining the all-encompassing protection provided by a patent. In exchange for a patent, an inventor is required to make a complete and public disclosure of the invention with sufficient detail to enable one skilled in the art relating to the invention to practice the invention. Thus where a patent is granted for multimedia technology, the inventor is required to disclose enough detail about the invention so that another person of similar skill could reproduce the invention in accordance with the claims of the patent.

The reason for this disclosure requirement is rooted in the purposes of the patent laws. Basically, patent laws were set up to advance the arts and sciences. The theory is that inventors will be encouraged to disclose information concerning their inventions and their discoveries, and the sum of useful knowledge available to our society will be increased if, in exchange, they are given a limited control over the use of those inventions. In exchange for a disclosure of his or her invention, the inventor is given the right to prevent anyone else from creating the same invention for a period of seventeen years. At the end of those seventeen years, however, the patent expires.

Anyone is then free to reproduce the inventor's publicly disclosed invention with no liability to the original inventor.

2. What Multimedia Technology May Be Patented?

The Patent Act provides that "any new and useful process, machine, manufacture, or composition of matter, or any new and useful improvement thereof" may be patented.[3] The Patent Act does not expressly include computer software, but the Supreme Court has ruled that software is patentable,[4] and the Patent and Trademark Office (PTO) routinely grants patents on software.[5] In fact, it is estimated that 9,000-10,000 software patents have been granted to date.[6] That is not to say, however, that all software is patentable.

Most inventions, and most multimedia technology, will not qualify for patent protection. Under the patent law, an invention must meet a number of more or less strict criteria before it qualifies for patent protection.

Nonetheless, there is no doubt that patent protection can have a significant impact on multimedia technology. Perhaps the best example is the controversial Compton's NewMedia patent. On November 15, 1993, Compton's NewMedia, the largest publisher of CD-ROM multimedia titles, announced that it had been granted a patent on a multimedia search system. The system allowed the contents of a multimedia title stored on a CD-ROM to be searched by means of graphics as well as text.[1]

The Compton's patent, U.S. Patent 5,241,671 issued for a multimedia-implemented invention ("Multimedia Search System Using a Plurality of Entry Path Means Which Indicate Interrelatedness of Information"). This patent claimed a system for searching a multimedia database consisting of text, pictures, illustrations, sound, and motion pictures. Under the process covered by this patent, users are able to access and search a multimedia database using multiple textual and graphical "entry paths." The claims set forth in the patent cover elements such as a means for storing interrelated textual information and graphical information, a means for interrelating textual and graphical information, a means for accessing and searching textual and graphical information through a variety of methods, and so on.

The patent was developed in connection with Compton's Multimedia Encyclopedia, which was first released on CD-ROM in October 1989. This search system allows a user to click on a picture or graphics appearing on a screen in order to search the database for additional information. For example, the user can click on a map of the world to find information about a particular place, or click on a timeline to retrieve historical information about a particular time.

The patent created a great deal of controversy within the industry, and, in a rare move, was reexamined by the Patent Office and ultimately rejected due to prior art in March 1994. (However, as of August 1994, that rejection was under reconsideration.) If the patent had been upheld, it would have had an enormous impact on the thousands of CD-ROM titles currently on the market. Nonetheless, it provides a good example of the types of inventions one may claim as patentable and the potential risks of infringement faced by multimedia developers.

Other potentially important multimedia patents have also been issued. For example, in late 1993, TestDrive Corporation announced that it had received a patent in connection with its electronic software distribution CD-ROM products. According to TestDrive, the patent also covers systems for controlling electronic delivery of movies, music, and other data to the home. Numerous patents have also been issued with respect to technology related to the MPEG video compression standard.

3. Requirements to Obtain a Patent

In order to obtain a patent for multimedia technology, or for any other invention or discovery, the invention must meet the following five requirements:

1. the inventor must be the *first person* to invent or discover the invention;
2. the invention must be *patentable subject matter*;
3. the invention must be *novel*;
4. the invention must have *utility*; and
5. the invention must be *nonobvious*.

Each of the these requirements presents a hurdle on the road to obtaining a patent. Typically, the "nonobviousness" hurdle is the one of greatest consequence. These tests will be examined in detail in the following sections.

3.1. First Inventor

A patent may be issued only to the actual inventor (not that person's employer or assignee), and only if the inventor was the first person to create the invention.[7] Thus, if two persons independently create the same invention, the patent will not be issued to the first one who applies for it, but rather to the first one who actually created it.

To qualify as the first inventor, the invention must be both conceived and reduced to practice with diligence. An invention is *conceived* when the inventor has in his or her mind a definite and permanent idea of the complete invention, including all of the steps necessary to create it. The invention is *reduced to practice* when it is actually created and working. However, the date a patent application is filed is considered as constructive reduction to practice.[8]

If someone subsequently asserts that he or she made the invention first, it will become necessary to determine who was, in fact, first. Such determinations are normally made in a Patent and Trademark Office proceeding called an *interference,* which requires the assistance of a lawyer skilled in interference practice.

3.2. Patentable Subject Matter

Only certain types of inventions may be patented. The general categories of patentable inventions are described in the Patent Act as "any new and useful process, machine, manufacture, or composition of matter, or any new and useful improvement thereof."[9] Which inventions fall within these broad and general categories, and which do not, has been the subject of much controversy, particularly in the case of computer software. The problem arises from the fact that ideas, abstract principles, laws of nature, scientific truths, and algorithms are not patentable, whereas, as may be seen from the definition, concrete manifestations that utilize certain principles, ideas, laws of nature, and scientific truths are patentable. The difficulty lies in distinguishing between the two.

Most of the controversy over the patentability of computer software used to center around whether the particular software involved was merely an expression of an algorithm, which may not be patented, or whether it represents something more, which may be patentable. This controversy was essentially put to rest by a 1981 Supreme Court decision[10] and subsequent administrative rulings by the Patent and Trademark Office.

3.3. Novelty

To be patentable, the software or other multimedia technology must be *novel* as that term is defined in the Patent Act. This means that if the process steps performed by the software were known or used by others in this country, or were patented or described in a printed publication in this or a foreign country, the claimed invention is considered to have been "anticipated" by the prior art, and thus is not considered to be novel.[11] In essence, novelty requires that the software in question must be different from programs previously in existence.

Because "total" newness is rare in any technical field, the patent law recognizes the appropriateness of patenting "improvements" on existing processes. Hence, rejections of patent claims for lack of novelty is relatively rare and problems with this issue are often overcome during the examination process.

3.4. Utility

The requirement of *utility* refers to the usefulness of the invention. Essentially, the utility requirement is met if the invention works and is useful for any beneficial purpose. The utility requirement does not mean, however, that the invention must be a commercial success, or even that it be commercially practicable. Lack of utility is a very infrequent reason for the rejection of patent claims.

3.5. Nonobviousness

In addition to the requirements of novelty and utility, the invention must also be what the patent law terms *nonobvious*. If the invention is obvious, that is, if the differences between the subject matter sought to be patented and the prior art is such that the subject matter as a whole would have been obvious at the time the invention was made to a person having ordinary skill in the art to which said subject matter pertains, the invention may not be patented.[12]

This requirement is essentially a requirement that the invention be a contribution to the art sufficient to merit patent protection. There are four elements that go into making the nonobviousness determination:

1. the scope and content of the pertinent prior art;
2. the differences between the prior art and the claimed invention;

3. the level of ordinary skill in the pertinent art; and

4. the extent to which other factors indicative of nonobviousness are present
   These include:

   a. Commercial success of the patented invention

   b. Overwhelming acceptance, recognition, or adoption of the patented invention by the industry

   c. Copying or imitation of the patented invention

   d. Long-felt need in the industry for a solution to the problem solved by the patented invention and the failure of others to solve the problem[13]

The "other factors" category is considered by the courts to be as important as the first three factors in the nonobviousness equation.[14]

4. Infringement of Patents

Once a patent has been granted for an invention, if anyone other than the holder of the patent or his or her licensee develops and/or markets a product that performs the patented functions, they will be guilty of patent infringement.[15] Also guilty of infringement are those who contribute to or induce infringement.[16] It makes no difference whether the infringing product was developed independently and without knowledge of the patent, or whether the infringing product was stolen or copied from the patented product. In either case, the owner of the patent has the right to sue the infringer in order to obtain a court-ordered injunction prohibiting production, use, and marketing of the infringing product, and to recover any applicable damages.[17] In appropriate cases of willful infringement the damages may be trebled.[18] In "exceptional" cases, attorneys' fees may also be awarded.[19]

It is also important to note the patent infringement concept of *equivalency*, which provides protection against those who attempt to disguise patent infringement. As the Supreme Court has pointed out:

> One who seeks to pirate an invention, like one who seeks to pirate a copyrighted book or play, may be expected to introduce minor variations to conceal and shelter the piracy. Outright and

forthright duplication is a dull and very rare type of infringement. To prohibit no other would place the inventor at the mercy of verbalism and would be subordinating substance to form.[20]

The doctrine of equivalents evolved in response to this problem, and provides a penumbra around patent claims that will result in an infringement finding even if the accused multimedia is not precisely described by the patent claims. The rules surrounding the doctrine of equivalents are complex and have been in a state of flux. However, the rule is generally stated as follows: infringement by equivalency exists if the infringing device or process and the claimed device or process perform substantially the same function in substantially the same way to achieve substantially the same result.[21] The more of a breakthrough or pioneering an invention is, the greater the scope of the penumbra of equivalency around the patent claims for that invention.

5. Conclusion

Patents offer you a potentially powerful tool for defending your product and enhancing its value, but the protection is not available for all multimedia technology, and where available can be expensive to obtain. The cost of obtaining one or more patents for a multimedia product or process should be weighed against the value of exclusivity in the market place, of relief from the complexities and cost of maintaining trade secrets and confidentiality for the invention, and the enhancement of the value of your business which comes from owning exclusive rights.

Evaluation of the merits of patents for specific multimedia technology is best done in close consultation with a qualified patent lawyer.

On the other hand, patents held by others on technology or processes that you incorporate within your multimedia works (even if done without knowledge of the existence of such a patent) can expose you to potential liability for patent infringement. Accordingly, this enhances the importance of obtaining appropriate warranties of ownership and indemnifications against infringement with respect to technology licensed from others. In addition, you may want to consider a patent search with respect to technology that you develop yourself.

Endnotes

1   See U.S. Patent No. 5,241,671 "Multimedia Search System Using a Plurality of Entry Path Means Which Indicate Interrelatedness of Information."

2   35 U.S.C. § 154.

3   35 U.S.C. § 101.

4   *Diamond v. Diehr*, 450 U.S. 175, 178-79 (1981). The software in *Diehr* was part of a patent that covered an improved method for curing rubber, which used a computer to constantly recalculate the proper curing time based on a known formula. Thus, it is more accurate to say that the Supreme Court has decided that software that is part of a larger method or process is patentable. The Supreme Court has not ruled on the patentability of "pure software," that is, software alone that is not part of any larger method or process. Nevertheless, the Patent and Trademark Office routinely grants patents on "pure software."

5   Randall M. Whitmeyer, *A Plea for Due Processes: Defining the Proper Scope of Patent Protection for Computer Software*, 85 Nw. L. Rev. 1103, 1105 (1991).

6   More than 10,000 software patents have reportedly been issued since 1972. Garry Ray, *Are You Trading On Someone's Software Patent?* Computerworld 73 (Apr. 12, 1993); Gregory Aharonian, et al., *Setting the Record Straight on Patents*, 36 Communication of the ACM 17 (Jan. 1993) (estimating 9000 software patents have issued over the period of the late 1960s through 1992).

7   35 U.S.C. §§ 102(f), (g).

8   *Manual of Patent Examining Procedure* § 715.07 (1993).

9   35 U.S.C. § 101.

10   *Diamond v. Diehr*, 450 U.S. 175 (1981).

11   35 U.S.C. § 102(a).

12   35 U.S.C. § 103.

13   *Graham v. John Deere Co.*, 383 U.S. 1 (1966).

14   *Simmons Fastener Corp. v. Illinois Tool Works, Inc.*, 739 F.2d 1573 (Fed. Cir. 1984), *cert. denied*, 471 U.S. 1065 (1985).

15   35 U.S.C. § 271(a).

16   35 U.S.C. §§ 271(b), (c).

17   35 U.S.C. §§ 283, 284.

18   35 U.S.C. § 284.

19   35 U.S.C. § 285.

20   *Graver Tank & Mfg. Co. v. Linde Air Prods. Co.*, 339 U.S. 605, 607-08, 70 S. Ct. 854, 856 (1950).

21   *Graver Tank & Mfg. Co. v. Linde Air Prods. Co.*, 339 U.S. 605, 607-08, 70 S. Ct. 854, 856 (1950).

PART 2

Developing Multimedia Products

CHAPTER 10

Creating Your Own Content or Technology

Creating Your Own Content or Technology

When you hire creative and talented individuals to create the content or develop the software and other technology that will be part of your multimedia products, you should take appropriate steps to ensure that you own all of the rights in the work product they create, or that you at least have the rights that you need for your anticipated use of the work product they create. Just because you pay someone to develop something for you does not necessarily mean that you own the rights to what is created. In fact, in many situations you will not own the rights unless you take appropriate affirmative steps to obtain them. This may include executing a written contract with the individual or entity doing the work.

Taking the steps necessary to own the rights in the work product you hire someone to create begins with an understanding of the rights that you might be concerned about. For purposes of your dealings with the persons you hire, the issues can be divided into three categories.

First is the question of who owns the intellectual property rights that can arise when content and software are created. For content, the key right is the copyright that arises automatically when the work is created. For software, ownership of the copyright is also important. In addition, however, trade secret rights and patent rights may be involved. The rules regarding ownership of copyright are discussed in chapter 23; the rules regarding ownership of trade secret rights are discussed in chapter 26; and the rules regarding ownership of patent rights are discussed in chapter 27.)

Second, in addition to ownership of the rights created, you need to be concerned with taking the appropriate steps to secure your rights in trade secrets and other confidential information against disclosure or improper use. (This issue is discussed in chapter 26.)

Finally, it is important to ensure that your use of the content created for you will not infringe upon or otherwise interfere with the personal rights of the individuals who created it. These concerns relate primarily to the rights of privacy and publicity. (The right of publicity is discussed in chapter 5 and the right of privacy is discussed in chapter 6.)

1. Employee or Independent Contractor

Resolving the issue of proprietary rights ownership depends in part on which rights are involved and in part on the status of the person who created the work (i.e., whether that person is an employee or an independent contractor).

If patent rights are involved, the issue is relatively straightforward. Generally, the individual who discovers or creates a patentable invention is the owner of the patent rights, regardless of that individual's status as an employee or independent contractor. Thus, if you hire someone to develop software or other technology, you should obtain a written assignment of patent rights to ensure that you will own any patent rights in any resulting invention.

With respect to the copyright in any content or software being developed, as well as any trade secret rights in what is developed, the law generally treats employees and independent contractors differently. Accordingly, you should carefully examine whether the persons you are hiring are your employees or independent contractors. Unfortunately, the distinction often is not an easy one to make.

The Copyright Act does not define the terms "employee" and "independent contractor." Accordingly, the Supreme Court has indicated that the determination of whether someone is an employee or an independent contractor is to be made using principles of the general common law of agency.[1] To do this, the court said that you need to consider the following factors:

1. the source of the instrumentalities and tools used by the individual to perform the work—employees are more likely to get their tools from their employer, independent contractors are more likely to have their own tools;

2. the location of the work—employees are more likely to work at their employer's premises, independent contractors are more likely to work at their own office;

3. the duration of the relationship between the parties—the longer the relationship the more likely it is to be an employment relationship;

4. whether you have the right to assign additional projects to the hired party— this right is more likely to be present in employment relationships than independent contractor relationships;

5. the extent of the hired party's discretion over when and how long to work —independent contractors are more likely to be able to set their own hours;

6. the method of payment—employees are more likely to be paid via a regular payroll arrangement, whereas independent contractors typically invoice for services;

7. whether the work is part of your regular business—for example, if the production of sound recordings is not normally something you do as part of your business, it is more likely that you will use an independent contractor (rather than an employee) on the rare occasion when you do produce a sound recording;

8. whether you provide employee benefits—employee benefits are typically provided to employees, but not to independent contractors; and

9. how you treated the hired party for tax purposes—that is, withholding of income tax and FICA payments is typically done for employees, but not for independent contractors.

No one of these factors is determinative. However, certain of these factors, such as your right to control the manner in which the work is created, whether or not employee benefits are provided or Social Security taxes are withhold from the compensation paid, and your right to assign other projects to the persons performing the services, are considered to be some of the most important.[2]

2. Using Employees

If the persons that you hire to create content or software qualify as your employees under the list of factors outlined above, your job of acquiring ownership in the rights to what they create becomes much easier. However, it still cannot be totally ignored.

2.1 Ownership of Proprietary Rights

When employees are involved in the creation of content or software, you (as the employer) automatically own the copyright to the resulting product under the "work for hire" doctrine,[3] so long as the work was done within the scope of their employment. (The work for hire doctrine is explained in chapter 23, section 1.2). In other words, merely establishing an employment relationship is sufficient to vest you with ownership of the copyright in any works that your employees create. The only requirement is that the works be created within the scope of their employment as opposed to on their own time, with their own resources, and so on. This rule applies regardless of the nature of the work product being created—that is, content or software.

If you use employees to develop software, however, you also need to consider ownership of any trade secret and patent rights that may arise. Generally, you will own the rights in any trade secrets that your employees develop. However, this is a matter of state law, and in some states, employees may retain certain rights in trade secrets that they develop (as opposed to trade secrets disclosed to them by their employee).

With respect to any patent rights that may be created, the general rule is just the oppose of the copyright rule. That is, your employees will retain ownership of any patent rights that they develop (in most cases) (see chapter 27, section 1.)

In light of these possible problems, the best way to ensure that you will own all rights in the software developed by your employees is to require them to assign to you, in writing, all of their rights in any software that they develop. By using an assignment, you can obtain all rights in the work product that you would otherwise not automatically acquire under the work-for-hire doctrine. If this is clearly set forth in a written document, there can be no controversy at a later date.

It is important to note, however, that some states now have laws that prohibit an employer from requiring an assignment of ownership rights in any invention developed on an employee's own time and with his or her own resources, especially if the invention does not relate to the business of the employer.[4] Some of these statutes also require that employees be informed of the applicable law. In California and Illinois, for example, if an employment contract requires employees to assign their rights in any invention to the employer, the employer must also give the employee written notification, at the time the agreement is made, that it does not apply to inventions for which no equipment, supplies, facility, or trade secrets of the employer were used and that were developed entirely on the employees' own time.[5] Being mindful of these limitations will help you to draft fair and enforceable agreements.

2.2 Confidentiality

Much of the work that your employees are involved in may relate to information that you consider to be a trade secret, or otherwise confidential. (The law of trade secrets is discussed in chapters 8 and 26). You may, for example, want to keep secret certain information relating to imaging software or data compression techniques developed by your employees. There may also be nontechnical information that you want to keep secret, such as the very existence of a multimedia project currently under development, the details of the content and functionality of the product, or your business and marketing plans for its future release. While those latter categories of information will cease to be a protectible secret as soon as you begin distribution of the completed multimedia product, it may be very important, for competitive reasons, to keep the product (or at least its contents and functionality) a secret until its initial release.

Merely owning the rights to such trade secrets and confidential information is often not sufficient. It is also important that you take appropriate steps to protect this information and keep it secret. In other words, you need to ensure that everyone who has access to the information is subject to an obligation to keep it confidential (see chapter 26, section 2.2).

In most states, the law implies the existence of a confidential relationship between every employer and employee. In other words, the law implies an agreement that prohibits employees from disclosing any trade secrets *revealed to them* in the course of their employment, and from using those trade secrets for their own or someone else's benefit. However, in some states this implied obligation may not apply to trade secrets *developed by the employee*, or to confidential information of the employer that does not rise to the level of a trade secret.

In addition, an employee is entitled to fair notice of what material is considered to be the employer's trade secrets. Consequently, the implied obligation of confidentiality may only apply to information that (1) you have expressly informed the employee is a trade secret or otherwise confidential; or your employee should understand to be a trade secret or confidential information, such as from the context in which the information was disclosed, the measures you have taken to protect the secret, or from the knowledge that an employee can reasonably be expected to possess as to what provides one business with an advantage over its competitors.

To ensure that every employee is bound by an obligation of confidentiality with respect to *all* trade secrets and confidential information, and to ensure that all employees are aware of this obligation, it is often a good idea to enter into a written confidentiality (i.e., nondisclosure) agreement. (A sample employee confidentiality agreement is included in chapter 33). Through such an agreement, the employees expressly acknowledge that the information, technology and documentation with which they will be working and/or developing is considered to be your trade secret, and they agree not to improperly use or disclose it. Moreover, an employee confidentiality agreement serves to demonstrate that you consider your developments to be secret and valuable. It is the most persuasive possible evidence that employees were informed from the outset that they would not be permitted to use your trade secrets, except in your business.

If an employee leaves to work for a competitor, a confidentiality agreement gives you a sound legal basis for preventing the employee from taking or using secret information in that person's new job. The existence of a confidentiality agreement, if made known to the new employer, may also help to reduce its enthusiasm for exploiting your confidential knowledge.

2.3 Rights of Privacy and Publicity

In addition to the copyright in the content that your employees develop, you also need to consider the personal rights of your employees that may be infringed by your use of the content. In particular, if the name, image, likeness, or voice of an employee is incorporated into any of the content you are creating, they may, in some cases, retain rights of publicity and privacy with respect to the content that may inhibit your proposed use.

To address this concern, you should obtain an appropriate release of these rights from your employees (see sample release in chapter 31).

3. Using Independent Contractors

If the persons you use to develop content or software are independent contractors, the issues with respect to ownership of the rights involved become significantly more complicated. That is because, as a general rule, independent contractors will retain all rights in the work product that they develop, in the absence of an assignment to their client.

3.1 Ownership of Proprietary Rights

When you use an independent contractor to create content or develop software for your multimedia work, the issue of copyright ownership of the resulting product can become complex. Generally, because independent contractors are not employees, their work is *not* automatically considered as "work for hire," and consequently they will own the copyright in any content or software that they develop for you *unless*: (1) you enter into a work-for-hire agreement, or (2) you obtain an assignment of the copyright. Establishing a work-for-hire relationship with independent contractors is explained in chapter 23, section 1.2. Assignments are discussed in chapter 3, section 5.1.

There are a number of people in the process of developing content who, if working as an independent contractor, may claim copyright ownership. These include, for example, persons who write text, the performers in a sound recording and video recording, the photographer who takes a picture, movie, or video, the sound engineer who performs the task of capturing and electronically processing sounds, and the persons who actually compile and edit the recorded sounds. All of these persons are engaging in original acts of authorship, and thus, in the absence of a work-for-hire relationship, will own the copyrights in the resulting works. Accordingly, it may be necessary to obtain assignments from, or enter into work-for-hire relationships with, each of these persons.

Both an assignment and a work-for-hire relationship must be documented by a signed agreement. An assignment is perhaps the safest course of action, as there are some independent contractor relationships that cannot be governed by a work for hire relationship. (See chapter 23, section 1.2 for a list of those relationships that can be subject to a work for hire relationship.) However, an assignment can be terminated by the author between thirty-five and forty years after it was made. (See discussion in chapter 3, section 5 for information regarding this termination right.) In either case, however, it is important to clearly resolve the ownership issue in a written document so that there can be no controversy at a later date. (See chapter 33 for a sample agreement with an independent contractor.)

If you use independent contractors to develop software or other technology, they will most likely retain rights in any trade secrets and patentable inventions they create in absence of a written agreement. Accordingly, where independent contractors are used to develop software, a written agreement assigning all rights (copyrights, trade secret rights, and patent rights) to you is critical.

3.2 Confidentiality

As with employees, there is also a need to bind independent contractors to an obligation of confidentiality with respect to your trade secrets and other confidential information that they may participate in developing and/or have access to during the course of the relationship. However, there is a major difference between imposing an obligation of confidentiality on an employee and imposing an obligation of confidentiality on an independent contractor. Whereas employees are bound by law to keep confidential the trade secrets of their employer, there may not be an implied obligation on independent contractors. Accordingly, to the extent you have concerns about the protection of trade secret or other confidential information, you should have each independent contractor execute an appropriate confidentiality agreement (typically done, for example, as part of a work for hire agreement), in order to create an obligation of confidentiality. A sample confidentiality agreement (as part of a work-for-hire agreement) is included in chapter 33.

3.3 Rights of Privacy and Publicity

In addition to the copyright in the content developed for you by independent contractors, you also need to consider the personal rights of such independent contractors that may be infringed by your use of the content. In particular, if the name, image, likeness, or voice of any person is incorporated into any of the content you are creating, they retain the right of publicity and/or the right of privacy with respect to the content that may inhibit your proposed use.

   To address this concern, you should obtain an appropriate release of these rights from your independent contractors (see sample release in chapter 31).

4. Using Union Talent

If you want to use union talent in the process of developing content for your multimedia product, this may be done either via an employee or an independent contractor relationship. In either case, the ownership concerns relative to employees or independent contractors should be taken into consideration. However, a whole new set of issues become important when using union talent to develop multimedia content.

In many cases, some of the best available talent for your project can be found in the membership of the various entertainment industry unions. Writers, directors, actors and actresses, recording artists, musicians, voice-over artists, extras, and others may all be members of one of these unions. (Union issues are discussed generally in chapter 21.)

Generally, if you want to use union talent you must sign the collective bargaining agreement for the applicable union (frequently referred to as its "Basic Agreement"). In many cases, however, these agreements are intended for use in the production of movies or television programs, and may not be well suited for the production of a multimedia product. In response to these concerns, some unions are beginning to experiment with standard agreements specially designed for use with multimedia producers. See, for example, the Screen Actors Guild (SAG) Standard Interactive Media Agreement, discussed in chapter 21, section 4.1, and the American Federation of Television and Radio Artists (AFTRA) Interactive Media Agreement discussed in chapter 21, section 5.1.

Other unions allow multimedia producers to enter into a single production agreement that authorizes the hiring of union members for one project without requiring that you become a signatory to their Basic Agreement (see, for example, the Writers Guild of America (WGA) Interactive Program Contract discussed in chapter 21, section 2.1). These are frequently referred to as "one-production-only" or OPO agreements. In effect, they allow you to become a signatory to the union agreement for one production only.

With the proper union agreement in place, the ownership issues involved with the use of union talent are in many cases the same as those discussed above in this chapter at sections 2 and 3, depending upon whether the union member is an employee or an independent contractor. However, there are additional complications in some cases.

In many cases, union collective bargaining agreements either reserve certain rights to the union members involved in the creation of the work product, or contractually impose restrictions on your reuse of that content in markets or media that are different from those of which it was originally developed. A good example of this can be seen in the AFTRA Interactive Media Agreement that governs the use of

AFTRA performers in the development of interactive multimedia products. (This agreement is discussed in more detail in chapter 21, section 5.1.)

Under the Interactive Media Agreement, you are authorized to use AFTRA performers in the development of multimedia products. However, you also contractually agree to pay additional fees to the performers if you want to distribute your multimedia product via remote delivery systems (e.g., on-line services, cable television, telephone lines, wireless, etc.). In addition, your right to use the performer's performance is limited to a particular multimedia product. If you want to use the performance in another product, additional payments to the performer are also required. Thus, while you can obtain ownership of the copyright in any works they create (by entering into a work-for-hire relationship or requiring an assignment), you will still be subject to a number of contractual restrictions on your use of the content.

Endnotes

1   *Community For Creative Non-Violence v. Reid*, 490 U.S. 730, 109 S.Ct. 2166, 2172-73, 2178 (1989).
2   *Aymes v. Bonelli*, 980 F.2d 857 (2d Cir. 1992).
3   17 U.S.C. § 201.
4   See, e.g., Cal. Labor Code § 2780; 765 ILCS 1060/2; Minn. Stat. § 181.78; Wash. Rev. Code Ann. § 49.44.140.
5   765 ILCS 1060/2.

Using Preexisting Content Without Permission

Using Preexisting Content Without Permission

Although creating your own content may be desirable in many cases, there will undoubtedly be situations where you would like to use at least some preexisting content. This may be particularly true where the time and expense required to create your own content is simply not worth the effort.

When you use preexisting content, the first question that comes to mind is, of course, "Do I need to get permission to use it?" In most cases, the answer is a resounding "yes." The content is protected by federal copyright, and any use of the content without permission would constitute copyright infringement. Although you can use some preexisting content without permission, works that fall in this category are typically very limited.

Generally, you can use content without permission if (1) it is in the public domain, (2) the use that you are contemplating is considered a "fair use" under the copyright law, (3) the copying is considered *de minimis* such that it does not constitute infringement, or (4) what you propose to copy is not itself copyrightable, even though it comes from a copyrightable work. But you also need to be aware of the fact that there may still be other rights in the work for which permission is required, such as a release of the right of publicity of any persons depicted in the content you propose to use.

1. Content in the Public Domain

To the extent that the content you want to use is in the public domain, you may freely use, copy, adapt, distribute, and display it without fear of copyright infringement. But making this determination is frequently more difficult than it appears. Moreover, you may still have to consider whether the content violates someone's right of publicity (see chapter 5) or right of privacy (see chapter 6), constitutes defamation (see chapter 7), or constitutes trademark infringement or unfair competition (see chapter 4).

1.1 When Is a Work "Public Domain"?

Copyrightable content is in the public domain generally only in the following three situations: (1) the original copyright has expired, (2) the copyright has been abandoned by the copyright holder, or (3) the work was created by the federal government.

1.1.1 Copyright Has Expired.   Determining if a copyright has expired requires determining when the work was first created, and, in some cases, when it was first published.[1]

- **Works Created After January 1, 1978.** For works created after January 1, 1978, the rules are rather simple and straightforward. Copyright protection in a work created after January 1, 1978, begins as soon as the work is created. If the individual who created the work was also the original owner of the copyright, the copyright protection lasts for the life of the author plus fifty years.[2] If the individual who created the work did so under a work for hire relationship (e.g., as an employee) the copyright lasts for seventy-five years after the year of first publication, or one hundred years after the year of creation, whichever comes first.[3] (The concept of a "work for hire" is explained in chapter 23, section 1.2.) In the case of a **joint work** prepared by two or more authors who did not work for hire, the copyright endures for a term consisting of the life of the last surviving author plus fifty years after such last surviving author's death.[4] (The concept of a "joint work" is discussed in chapter 23, section 2.1). As a consequence, no work created under the current copyright law (i.e., created after January 1, 1978) can enter the public domain until 2029 at the earliest.

- **Works Created Before January 1, 1978—Generally.** Works created before January 1, 1978, were originally governed by the **Copyright Act of 1909**. Under that Act, copyright protection was granted for a term of twenty-eight years, with a one-time right to renew that protection for an additional twenty-eight-year term. When the Copyright Act of 1909 was superseded by the **Copyright Act of 1976**, certain adjustments were made to the remaining term of protection applicable to copyrighted works created prior to January 1, 1978 (the effective date of the Copyright Act of 1976). Those adjustments depend, however, on whether the work was copyrighted under the Copyright Act of 1909, and if so, whether the work is in its first or second twenty-eight-year term of copyright protection. Consequently, the rules for determining the term of copyright protection applicable to works created before January 1, 1978 (which are set forth in the following sections) can be somewhat complex and confusing. As a general rule, however, if the work was published prior to January 1, 1978, the maximum term of copyright protection allowed under the new copyright law was seventy-five years.[5]

- **Works Created But Not Published or Copyrighted Before January 1, 1978.** Prior to the enactment of the current copyright law, works that were created but *not published* were entitled to perpetual common law copyright protection, (so long as they remained unpublished and unregistered). When the current copyright law was passed, Congress abolished common law copyright protection and extended federal protection to all of these works. In doing so, it provided that the term of copyright protection for such works would be the same as the term of protection provided for works created after January 1, 1978, but with two important exceptions: (1) in no event would the copyright expire before December 31, 2002; and (2) if the work was subsequently published on or before December 31, 2002, in no event would the copyright expire before December 31, 2027.[6] Thus, if you are considering the use of content that was created before January 1, 1978, but was neither published nor was the copyright registered before January 1, 1978, it will not be in the public domain until 2003 at the earliest.

- **Works in Their First Term on January 1, 1978.** Works for which a copyright was secured[7] between January 1, 1950, and December 31, 1977, would have been in the first twenty-eight-year term of the available copyright protection (under the 1909 Copyright Act) as of January 1, 1978 (the date the current

Copyright Act became effective). Under the current Copyright Act, the term of copyright protection applicable to these works was modified to provide that they would be protected for twenty-eight years from the date the copyright was originally secured, with a right to renew that copyright for an additional forty-seven years, for a total term of seventy-five years.[8] Thus, if the content was created after January 1, 1950, the copyright will expire twenty-eight years after it was copyrighted, unless the copyright was renewed with the Copyright Office, in which case, the copyright will be extended for an additional forty-seven years. The oldest of such copyrights (assuming they were renewed) will not expire until the year 2025.

Prior to June 26, 1992, renewal of the copyright on works that were in their first twenty-eight-year term as of January 1, 1978, had to be made within the 1-year period immediately prior to the end of the first term of the copyright. If renewal was not made, the work entered the public domain. A good example of this can be seen with the copyright to the movie *It's a Wonderful Life*. Copyright for this movie was originally secured in 1946, and the first twenty-eight-year term expired in 1974. However, Republic Pictures, the owner of the copyright, failed to renew the copyright, thereby putting the movie into the public domain. (But, this does not mean that you are free to use portions of the movie. See discussion in this chapter, at section 1.2.)

Because of the serious consequences that could result from an inadvertent failure to renew a copyright, Congress passed the Copyright Renewal Act of 1992, which, effective June 26, 1992, automatically extended the copyright in all works that were in their first term as of January 1, 1978, for an additional forty-seven years, or a total combined term of seventy-five years. As a consequence, this provision applies to works that were first copyrighted between January 1, 1964, and December 31, 1977, since only works copyrighted during this period would still have been in the first term of copyright protection as of the effective date of the act.[9] Thus, any pre-1978 content that was copyrighted after January 1, 1964, will continue to enjoy copyright protection for a total of seventy-five years, with no need to renew. The first of these copyrights will not expire until 2039. On the other hand, any work copyrighted between 1950 and 1964 will now be in the public domain if the copyright was not renewed at the end of its first twenty-eight-year term.

■ **Works in Their Renewal Term on January 1, 1978.** Works for which a copyright was secured[10] between January 1, 1922, and December 31, 1949, would have been in the second twenty-eight-year term of the available copyright protection (under the 1909 Copyright Act) as of January 1, 1978, (the date the current Copyright Act became effective), assuming that the copyright was in fact renewed. If the copyright was not renewed, these works are now in the public domain. If the copyright was renewed, then the current Copyright Act automatically extended the term of copyright protection for such works to a total of seventy-five years.[11] As a consequence, the earliest of these copyrights will expire in 1997.

■ **Works Copyrighted Prior to 1922.** Works copyrighted prior to 1922 are now clearly in the public domain. Even assuming that the original term of the copyright was renewed, the fifty-six-year term of protection would have expired prior to January 1, 1978. However, note that this conclusion only applies to works that were published or copyrighted prior to 1922. As noted above, if the work was created prior to 1922, but was neither published nor registered for copyright before January 1, 1978, it will not enter the public domain until 2003 at the earliest.

1.1.2 Copyright Has Been Abandoned. A copyrighted work may enter the public domain before the copyright expires if it was first published before March 1, 1989, without a copyright notice. Works first published after this date, however, need not bear a copyright notice.[12]

If a work created prior to January 1, 1978 (i.e., a work governed by the Copyright Act of 1909) was published without a proper copyright notice, the work automatically entered the public domain.[13] However, for works created after January 1, 1978 (i.e., works governed by the Copyright Act of 1976) the law was not as unforgiving. For works in this category, there are three types of situations where publication without a notice would *not* invalidate the copyright: (1) where the notice was only omitted from a relatively small number of copies; (2) where registration of the work was made within five years after publication without notice and a reasonable effort to add the notice to all copies was made after the omission was discovered; and (3) where the notice was omitted in violation of an express requirement in writing as a condition of the copyright owner's authorization of the public distribution of the work.[14] Accordingly, any work created after January 1, 1978, and published without a notice prior to March 1, 1989, *might* be in the public domain. However, you cannot necessarily be sure of this conclusion, unless you can rule out the applicability of all three of these special cases.

Effective March 1, 1989, a copyright notice is not required at all on any copyrighted work. Accordingly, the omission of a copyright notice from any work first published after March 1, 1989, has no impact whatsoever on the copyright status of the work. As a consequence, you cannot rely on the lack of a copyright notice as indicating that the work is in the public domain. In other words, you run a risk in copying from a work published after March 1, 1989, that does not bear a copyright notice, as mere lack of a notice does not mean that the work is not copyrighted.

1.1.3 Work Was Created by the Federal Government.

If a work was created by the federal government or as "work for hire" for the federal government, the work is also treated as public domain material. By law, the federal government holds no copyright in works created by it or in works created for it as work for hire.[15] However, this rule applies only to the U.S. federal government. Works created by other governmental entities, such as state, municipal, and local governments, as well as foreign governments, may still be protected by copyright.[16] Moreover, the federal government is not precluded from receiving and holding copyrights transferred to it by assignment, bequest, or otherwise.[17] Thus, the fact that a document, map, survey, photograph, and so on is published by the government does not necessarily mean it is not protected by copyright. Only if the work was created by a government employee, or created by an independent contractor for the government pursuant to a work-for-hire arrangement, will the work be in the public domain.

Similarly, it is important to understand that works prepared by government officials or employees outside of the scope of their employment relationship are not subject to this rule, and thus may be copyrighted by the persons involved.[18] In one case, for example, public speeches by Admiral Rickover concerning naval matters with which he had dealt during the course of his career were held to be the Admiral's property and therefore eligible for copyright protection.[19] Likewise, works created for the federal government by independent contractors are copyrightable by the authors.[20]

A related problem also occurs with respect to works prepared under U.S. government contract or grant. The Copyright Act does not prohibit copyright protection in works prepared under government contract or grant. Instead, the terms of the grant or the contract in each case will determine whether the works created will be treated as government works not subject to copyright, or whether the creator of the works will be allowed to retain a federal copyright.[21]

Thus, as the foregoing makes clear, the mere fact that a work owes its origin to, or is otherwise related to, the federal government, does not necessarily mean that you can assume no copyright protection applies. Some further investigation may be necessary.

1.2 Risks in Using Public Domain Content

Determining that a copyrightable work is in the public domain does not end the inquiry. There are a number of other issues that may still prevent you from using the content without permission.

First, to the extent that the work is protected by copyright in more than one country, the duration of the copyright will frequently vary from country to country. For example, if a work is considered to be in the public domain because the term of copyright protection in the United States has expired, it is still very possible that the term of copyright protection in another country has not expired. Thus, use of the content in such other country will still constitute infringement in that particular country (although it will presumably not be infringement in the United States). Similarly, if the work was published without a copyright notice in the United States, this may result in the work being in the public domain in the United States, but will have no effect on its copyright status in another country that does not require such formalities. Accordingly, it may not be copyright infringement to copy and distribute the work in the United States, but foreign distribution may nonetheless be prohibited by the continuing foreign copyrights.

Second, it is important to understand that frequently a single work consists of a number of overlapping copyrights (see discussion of the problem of overlapping copyrights in chapter 3, section 7). Thus it is possible that a work now in the public domain may incorporate (with permission) copyrighted materials that are not in the public domain. A recording of a song, for example, includes a copyright in the underlying musical composition, and a separate copyright in the sound recording (see chapter 17, section 1.2 and chapter 18 section, 1.1.2). If the copyright in the sound recording enters the public domain, but the copyright in the musical composition does not, copying the sound recording will still result in infringement of the copyright in the underlying musical composition. In one case, for example, the court found that copying and distributing a sound recording of a *Lone Ranger* radio program that was not protected by copyright still constituted infringement of the underlying radio scripts on which the sound recording was based.[22]

Similarly, if a movie has entered the public domain,[23] you still have to consider the status of the story upon which the movie is based, or any musical compositions performed within the film. A movie may, for example, be based on a copyrighted book, and although the movie may enter the pubic domain for one of the reasons set forth above, that has no effect on the copyright in the underlying book on which the movie was based. Likewise, a movie may include a recording of a copyrighted song, and the fact that the movie is in the public domain does not invalidate the copyright in the underlying song, or give another party the right to copy that portion of the movie containing the song. In such a case, copying the public domain film may result in an infringement of the copyrights in the underlying story or musical compositions.

This is exactly the result that occurred in a case involving the motion picture *Pygmalion*, a movie based on the George Bernard Shaw play of the same name.[24] In that case, the motion picture had entered the public domain because the copyright owner had failed to renew the copyright. However, a valid copyright still existed in the play on which the movie was based. Accordingly, the distribution and exhibition of the motion picture was found to be copyright infringement, notwithstanding the fact that the movie was in the public domain, because the matter contained in the movie was a derivative of a work still covered by copyright.

Another example can be seen in the well-known movie *It's a Wonderful Life*. The copyright for this movie was secured in 1946, but the owner of the copyright, Republic Pictures, failed to renew the copyright in 1974, when the first twenty-eight-year term expired. Accordingly, the movie entered the public domain. As a consequence, the movie was shown repeatedly by most television stations every Christmas season, in part because no royalties were required. However, in June 1993, Republic Pictures took steps to reassert its control over the distribution and exhibition of this film by announcing that it was the owner of the copyright to the short story on which the movie was based, and, in addition, that it had acquired the copyrights to the music used in the film. Accordingly, Republic Pictures is asserting a right to royalties from anyone who wants to copy, sell, rent, distribute, or show the movie.

Finally, it is also important to note that a new work based on a public domain work may itself be the subject of copyright protection. Thus, a photograph of a public domain painting is protected by copyright, as is a movie based on a public domain work, such as one of Shakespeare's plays. While the underlying public domain work may be copied, the copy may not be made from the new work based on it (such as the photograph or the movie in the foregoing examples).

2. Fair Use of Copyrighted Content

Even if not in the public domain, portions of a copyrighted work may, in some situations, be copied, adapted, and distributed without permission of the copyright owner pursuant to the doctrine of *fair use*. But determining when the fair use doctrine applies to the copying of another's copyrighted work can be a rather difficult task. There is no bright line test; there are no hard and fast rules. Instead, each case must be decided on the basis of its unique facts and circumstances.[25]

The Copyright Act sets forth four factors to be considered in determining whether an act that would otherwise constitute an infringement is permitted by the doctrine of fair use:[26]

1. the purpose and character of the use, including whether the use is of a commercial nature or is for nonprofit educational purposes—that is, commercial uses are less likely to be fair use; nonprofit educational uses more likely qualify as fair use;

2. the nature of the copyrighted work—that is, copying from factual works is tolerated more than copying from more creative fictional works;

3. the amount and substantiality of the portion used in relation to the copyrighted work as a whole—that is, the more that is copied, or the more significant the portion that is copied (regardless of the quantity), the less likely that fair use will apply;

4. the effect of the use upon the potential market for or value of the copyrighted work—that is, if the use has an adverse impact on the market for the original work, it will not constitute fair use.

The Copyright Act itself does not specify how each of these factors is to be weighed. No single factor is dispositive, although one case has indicated that the fourth factor, the effect of the defendant's use on the market for the copyrighted work, is the most important factor to be considered.[27] Otherwise, the only guidance provided by the Copyright Act is a provision stating that fair use may apply when a preexisting copyrighted work is taken "for purposes such as criticism, comment, news reporting, teaching (including multiple copies for classroom use), scholarship, or research."[28]

Thus questions abound as to when, if ever, copying digital content, especially in small amounts, constitutes fair use. Cases have yet to consider the "digital" fair use issues that we are likely to see in the future, such as the practices of sampling, imaging, and morphing, as well as the many other ways in which a slice of digital content from one work can be adapted and incorporated within another work.

The process of sampling a small portion of a popular song or scanning and using a small section of a copyrighted picture is common, but is it "fair use"? Many people mistakenly believe that fair use applies so long as the resulting product is not marketed commercially, but this is not necessarily true. However, decisions suggest that courts will look unfavorably on any such copying, adaptation, and distribution of copyrighted content as part of a multimedia work, even when limited to internal business uses (such as in-house training or multimedia sales presentations).[29] While some people (e.g., teachers) may be able to engage in copying of a small portion of a copyrighted work for some purposes (e.g., educational classroom use), it is unlikely to constitute fair use in most commercial cases.

When courts consider whether a particular use of a copyrighted work is a "fair use" they typically analyze the use that is being made of the copyrighted work with respect to each of the four fair use factors set forth above. The gist of the fair use defense is reasonableness and good faith.[30] To date, no cases have applied the fair use analysis to the use of copyrighted content in a multimedia product. But the following summary of how the courts analyze each of the four fair use factors is likely to apply in the digital world as well.

2.1 The Purpose and Character of the Use

First, courts look at the purpose and character of your use of the copyrighted work. In doing so, they normally consider two factors: (1) whether the copying is for a non-commercial use, as opposed to a commercial purpose; and (2) whether the copying involves a transformative use of the original (i.e., whether the work in which the copied material is used involves a different purpose or different character than the original, such as by adding new expression, meaning, or message to the material copied from the original work), as opposed to the copying being merely an attempt to duplicate the original and multiply the number of copies.[31] If you can establish that your copying falls in either of these categories, the first fair use factor will likely be decided in your favor.

Generally, if you copy a portion of someone else's copyrighted work (without permission) for commercial or profit-making purposes there is a presumption that the copying is not fair use.[32] However, that presumption can be overcome if the use is considered to serve a broader public purpose, such as a transformative use. The more transformative the new work, the less will be the significance of any commercial use that may be involved.[33]

A *transformative use* of a copyrighted work is a secondary use that is productive in that it produces a new purpose or result, different from the original—in other words, a secondary use that transforms, rather than supersedes, the original.[34] It is a secondary use that does not merely copy and offer itself as a substitute for the original copyrighted material, but that uses the matter taken from the copyrighted material for some new objective or purpose.[35]

Where the copying is of a transformative nature, the presence of profit motivation will not be considered as important.[36] However, when the principal purpose of the proposed copying is to supersede the original and permit duplication, the presence of a commercial purpose will weigh heavily against a finding of fair use. This kind of copying contributes nothing new or different to the original copyrighted work. It simply multiplies the number of copies.

2.2 The Nature of the Copyrighted Work

The second factor in the fair use test is the "nature of the copyrighted work" from which the material was copied. Courts look at two issues when addressing this factor: (1) whether the copyrighted work is published or unpublished,[37] and (2) whether the copyrighted work is factual or creative.

In evaluating this factor, courts are less likely to find that the copying was fair use when the copyrighted work you seek to copy has not previously been published. "Publication of an author's expression before he has authorized its dissemination seriously infringes the author's right to decide when and whether it will be made public, a factor not present in fair use of published works."[38]

Similarly, there is a greater level of protection for works that are more creative in nature. Thus, courts look at whether a copyrighted work is *predominantly* factual or creative. In general, courts recognize a greater need to disseminate factual works than fictional works, and, therefore, are more likely to find fair use if what you copy is a factual work.[39] For example, copying from a news broadcast is more likely to be fair use than copying from a motion picture.[40]

Thus, in one case,[41] the court found that a partial reproduction of a *Consumer Reports* product evaluation was fair use, in part because the work was "primarily informational rather than creative." Notwithstanding that the material used by the defendant was the plaintiff's subjective evaluation of the product, rather than pure data, the court held that it was fair use for the defendant to quote the magazine's evaluation verbatim in its advertisement. The court noted that it served the goal of accurate reporting for the defendant to quote the portion precisely.

Where your proposed use relates entirely to published works, and the material at issue is essentially factual in nature, the second factor favors fair use, rather than the copyright owner.[42]

2.3 The Amount and Substantiality of the Portion Used

The third factor looks to "the amount and substantiality of the portion used in relation to the copyrighted work as a whole." Thus, as a general proposition, the greater the portion of a work that you copy, the less likely it is that the copying would be considered to be fair use. And in cases where you want to copy an entire copyrighted work, such as a complete musical work, sound recording, or photograph, your conduct is unlikely to qualify as fair use.[43] In fact, the reproduction of an entire copyrighted work ordinarily "militates against a finding of fair use."[44]

The quantity of material that you copy is not the only issue. Courts also examine the copied material from a qualitative perspective. In one case, for example, a magazine copied only approximately 300 words out of President Ford's memoirs, but in denying fair use, the court emphasized the significance of the quotations by noting that they amount to "the heart of the book," the part most likely to be newsworthy and important in licensing serialization rights.[45]

In addition, it is important to note that the courts look at issues of quantity and quality with respect to the work that you took the content from, not with respect to the multimedia work in which you will use the content. Thus, for example, if you copy a significant portion of a copyrighted song into your multimedia work, a court will likely find infringement even though the portion you copied represents a very small (and perhaps even insignificant) portion of the multimedia work into which it was incorporated.

However, the purpose and character of the multimedia work you are creating can have an impact on the extent of permissible copying.[46] For example, you may be able to copy more original work for use in a parody than you can for use in another type of work, since the parody must be able to conjure up at least enough of the original to make the object of its critical wit recognizable.[47] Likewise, substantial quotations from the original work might qualify as fair use in a review of a book or a news account of a speech, but not in a scoop of a soon to be published memoir.[48]

Notwithstanding the foregoing, however, it is possible for a court to find that copying of an entire copyrighted work constitutes fair use. In 1984, for example, the Supreme Court sanctioned the videotaping of television programs for home use. In that case, the court recognized that the copying was nonproductive and took the entirety of the copyrighted work, and acknowledged that these facts argued against a finding of fair use. However, the court justified a finding of fair use by the fact that the copying activity (1) was private, (2) was noncommercial, (3) was done to permit the consumer one viewing at a convenient hour of copyrighted material that was offered to him free of charge, and (4) caused no appreciable loss of revenue to the copyright owner.[49]

2.4 Effect of the Use on the Potential Market for the Copyrighted Work

The fourth fair use factor is often the most difficult to judge. However, it may also be the most important.[50] If your use of a portion of another's copyrighted work has no demonstrable effect on the potential market for, or the value of, the copyrighted work, it may be considered a fair use.[51] On the other hand, if your copying could have a potential impact on the market for the work from which the copy was taken, it is very likely that the copying will not be considered to be fair use. All that the copyright owner has to show is that if the challenged use should become widespread, it would adversely affect the *potential* market for the copyrighted work.[52]

Thus, in one case the court held that the market for the copyrighted work (the letters of J. D. Salinger) was impaired by the copying, despite the fact that Salinger had no immediate plans to publish the letters.[53] The court held that Salinger had the right to protect his *opportunity* to sell the letters.[54] Although the defendant's work would not displace the market for the published letters, the fact that the defendant had copied the "most interesting" parts made it likely that the market for the letters themselves would be impaired.

According to one recent court opinion, in most of the cases where the court found the fourth factor to favor fair use, the defendant's work filled a market niche that the plaintiff simply had no interest in occupying.[55] For example, copyright holders rarely write parodies or reviews of their own works, and are even less likely to write analyses of their underlying data from the opposite political perspective. On the other hand, it is a safe generalization that copyright holders, as a class, wish to continue to sell the copyrighted work and may also wish to prepare or license such derivative works as book versions or films.[56]

As you can see from the foregoing analysis, determining whether a particular act of copying from the copyrighted content of another is fair use is not necessary a simple analysis. Moreover, for most multimedia works it is probably best if you do not attempt to rely on the doctrine of fair use—at least with respect to works that you plan to publicly market and distribute. Products created by educational institutions solely for in-house use stand a better chance of qualifying under the fair use doctrine than do products created by profit-seeking business entities solely for in-house use. In either case, whenever use of the product is expanded to public distribution, the availability of the fair use defense becomes even less likely.

3. De Minimis Copying of Copyrighted Content

Image processing and digital audio sampling technology make it relatively easy to copy very small fragments of sound recordings, motion pictures and other audio-visual works, as well as still images. This raises a question as to whether it is possible to copy a small portion of a work without infringing the copyright in that work.

In theory, the answer is yes. That is, a de minimis rule has been applied to allow the literal copying of a small and usually insignificant portion of a copyrighted work.[57] However, determining whether the portion that you want to copy qualifies as de minimis requires considerations of both the quantity and quality of the portion used in relation to the whole of the copyrighted work. That is, how much of the copyrighted work has been copied and how important is the copied portion to the work as a whole.[58]

The first issue is whether what you have copied is a substantial portion of the copyrighted work from which it was taken.[59] If the portion you have taken is a quantitatively large portion of the entire work, a court is likely to find that you improperly appropriated the copyrighted work. It makes no difference that what you have copied comprises only a small portion of *your* multimedia work. Courts look only at how much of the copyrighted work you have taken.

However, even if the portion you have copied is quantitatively small, the analysis does not end here. The second issue a court will consider is the qualitative relationship of the portion you have copied to the whole of the work from which you copied it.

To constitute infringement it is not necessary that you copy all, or even a large portion, of a copyrighted work. It is only necessary that you copy a material and substantial part of it. Thus, you may be liable for infringement if a *quantitatively* small portion of a copyrighted work is *qualitatively* important to the work as a whole.[60] In other words, if you were to copy a small amount of qualitatively nonessential material, a court may find no infringement. However, if the material you copy is qualitatively essential, then a court is likely to find copyright infringement.

Thus, the fact that you only copy an expressive fragment does not necessarily prevent a finding of appropriation.[61] The practical problem is determining when material is "qualitatively essential." Unfortunately there is no easy rule such as using six notes of a song or one minute of a motion picture or five sentences from a literary work is noninfringing. The qualitative importance of a given quantity of material varies depending upon the type of work in question and in its relation to the rest of the plaintiff's work. Some specific examples may be more helpful.

3.1 Musical Works

In the case of music, courts often look to see whether the small portion that has been copied is the distinctive or "catchy" musical phrase or lyric that gives a song its appeal,[62] the part that "is pleasing to the ears of lay listeners,"[63] or the part that makes "it popular and valuable."[64] In one case, for example, the defendant copied four notes of a 100-measure jingle and the words "I Love" from the lyric "I Love New York." The court held that while on its face the taking was relatively slight, on closer examination "the musical phrase that the lyrics 'I Love New York' accompany, is the heart of the composition."[65]

Copying a portion of the chorus of a musical work is likely to constitute copyright infringement, as the chorus is typically considered to be one of the most commercially valuable portion of the musical work.[70] In one case, for example, involving two songs that were "considerably different, both in theme and execution," the court found infringement based on copying of the words "I hear you calling me" and the accompanying music. It concluded that such copying was infringement, notwithstanding that it was a very short phrase, because it had "the kind of sentiment in both cases that causes the audiences to listen, applaud, and buy copies in the quarter on the way out of the theater."[71] In other words, if the portion copied is commercially important to the original work, the copying will must likely constitute copyright infringement.

The courts have rejected an approach strictly based on the quantity of music that can be protected, and have held that as few as two to four bars of music constitute protectible expression.[66] However, a court has also held that the taking of six bars of music did not constitute an infringement.[67]

In a 1991 case involving digital sampling, the court concluded that the use of three words was enough to constitute a violation of the copyright law.[68] In that case, a rap artist named Biz Markie had used a three-word phrase and its accompanying music from the song "Alone Again (Naturally)." However, the court simply assumed that the copying was infringement, and did not specifically address issues relating to either the quantity or the quality of what was copied.

Two years later, in 1993, a court was called upon to decide a second sampling case involving the use of portions of a recorded song called "The Music Got Me" that were sampled and inserted without authorization into the defendant's song "Get Dumb? Free Your Body."[69] There was no question that portions of the original song were digitally copied, but the court did wrestle with the issue of whether the parts that were copied were "of great qualitative importance to the work as a whole." It concluded that because the portions copied were distinct and attention-grabbing, it could not rule that no infringement occurred, and instead decided to let the question go to a jury. In other words, sampling small but distinct and "attention-grabbing" portions of a copyrighted song can be copyright infringement.

3.2 Motion Pictures

In the case of motion pictures, "borrowing" bits and pieces of a film or television clip may also be copyright infringement. In one case, for example, the defendant used various clips of a number of Charlie Chaplin films averaging less than one minute in length. Despite the fact that the portions used were quantitatively small, the court held that the use infringed the copyright because the use was "qualitatively great" in that "each of the scenes [defendant] used was among Chaplin's best . . . and . . . each such excerpt was central to the film in which it appeared.[72]

Similarly in another case, the court found that a defendant who had used approximately 20 percent of a film had infringed the copyright because the excerpt was "qualitatively substantial" since the portion used was intimately tied to the story and was a main source of comedy for the motion picture as a whole.[73]

3.3 Photographs

Analogous to the practice of copying small portions of a sound recording by sampling, is the practice of using image processing to copy small fragments of a photograph. For example, one might take a tree, a patch of grass, or a portion of the sky from a copyrighted photograph for use in another product.

When will such copying constitute copyright infringement? Is copying of one or two pixels sufficient for infringement or is more required? To date, however, no case has considered the issue of digital infringement of a small fragment of a photograph.

Court decisions in similar situations provide some indications about how courts may treat image processing cases. Photographic reproductions of portions of a copyrighted work, as can be performed by computer cut and paste, have been held to constitute infringement.[74] "In mail order catalog copyright infringement actions, the court must look not to the substantial similarity of the entire catalog, but at the substantial similarity of the very small amount of protectable parts."[75]

4. Copying Noncopyrightable Aspects of a Work

Regardless of the copyright status of a work, the law is clear that anyone is free to copy "noncopyrightable" elements of that work. Determining what constitutes a noncopyrightable aspect of a work is often easier in theory than in fact, and in any event may be of little value to the multimedia development process. However, it should not be overlooked.

As a general proposition, copyright protection in any work does not extend to any idea, procedure, process, system, method of operation, concept, principle, or discovery that is described, explained, illustrated, or embodied in the work.[76] From this list, the noncopyrightable elements most important to multimedia works probably include discoveries (i.e., facts), and ideas.

Facts by themselves can never be copyrightable.[77] This is true of all facts—scientific, historical, biographical, and news of the day. They are part of the public domain available to every person.[78] Thus, for example, the names, towns, and telephone numbers of the persons living in a certain geographic area and listed in a phone book are uncopyrightable facts.[79]

In other words, notwithstanding a valid copyright, you are free to use the facts contained in another's publication, so long as you take only facts, and not the expression used by the author to communicate those facts.[80] No matter how much original authorship the work displays, the facts and ideas it exposes are free for the taking. The very same facts and ideas may be divorced from the context imposed by the author, and restated and reshuffled by second comers, even if the author was the first to discover the facts or to propose the ideas.[81]

The bottom line is that just because a work is copyrighted does not mean that every element of the work may be protected. Copyright protection may extend only to those components of a work that are original to the author. Thus, if the author clothes facts with an original collection of words, he or she may be able to claim a copyright in this written expression. Others may copy the underlying facts from the publication, but not the precise words used to present them.[82]

Similarly, "ideas" cannot be protected by copyright.[83] Protection is available only for the "expression" of an "idea".[84] Accordingly, if a given idea is reduced to a tangible form of expression (which any work must be in order to be eligible for copyright), only the form of expression will be protected; the underlying idea may be freely adopted and copied by others. Thus, for example, although a particular version of the "map" conveying "a New Yorker's view of the country" is copyrightable, the "idea" of creating such a distorted map is not.

Endnotes

1   *Publication* is a term of art under the Copyright Act. Generally, publication occurs when a copy of a copyrighted work is distributed to the public by sale or other transfer of ownership, or by rental, lease, or lending. Publication also occurs when the copyright owner offers to distribute copies of the work to a group of persons for further distribution. 17 U.S.C. § 101.

2   17 U.S.C. § 302(a).

3   17 U.S.C. § 302(c).

4   17 U.S.C. § 302(b).

5   17 U.S.C. § 304.

6   17 U.S.C. § 303.

7   Under the Copyright Act of 1909, a copyright was "secured" when the work was published with a proper copyright notice (regardless of when the work was actually created), 17 U.S.C. § 10 (1909). In addition, a copyright could be secured for works that were not published by registering the work with the U.S. Copyright Office. 17 U.S.C. § 12 (1909).

8   17 U.S.C. § 304(a).

9   17 U.S.C. § 304(a); Copyright Renewal Act of 1992, Pub. L. 102-307, 106 Stat. 264 (codified as amended in scattered sections of 17 U.S.C.).

10   Under the Copyright Act of 1909, a copyright was "secured" when the work was published with a proper copyright notice (regardless of when the work was actually created), 17 U.S.C. § 10 (1909). In addition, a copyright could be secured for works that were not published by registering the work with the U.S. Copyright Office. 17 U.S.C. § 12 (1909).

11   17 U.S.C. § 304(b).

12   17 U.S.C. § 401.

13   *Stewart v. Abend*, 495 U.S. 207, 110 S. Ct. 1750, 1766 (1990).

14   17 U.S.C. § 405.

15   17 U.S.C. § 105.

16   However, certain works by state and local governments may be found not copyrightable for public policy reasons. See, e.g., *Building Officials & Code Adm. v. Code Technology, Inc.*, 628 F.2d 730, 733-35 (1st Cir. 1980).

17   17 U.S.C. § 105.

18   H.R. REP. No. 1476, 94th Cong., 2d Sess. 58 (1976), *reprinted in* 1976 U.S.C.C.A.N. 5659, 5671-72.

19   *Public Affairs Assocs., Inc. v. Rickover*, 268 F. Supp. 444, 450 (D.D.C. 1967).

20   H.R. REP. No. 94-1476, 94th Cong., 2d Sess. 59 (1976), *reprinted in* 1976 U.S.C.C.A.N. 5659, 5672-73; *Schnapper v. Foley*, 667 F.2d 102, 108-09 (D.C. Cir. 1981), *cert. denied*, 455 U.S. 948, 102 S. Ct. 1448 (1982).

21   H.R. REP. No. 1476, 94th Cong., 2d Sess. 59 (1976), *reprinted in* 1976 U.S.C.C.A.N. 5659, 5672-73.

22   *Lone Ranger Tele., Inc. v. Program Radio Corp.*, 740 F.2d 718, 722 (9th Cir. 1984).

23   Three valuable compilations exist for locating films in the public domain: WALTER E. HURST & WILLIAM M. HALE, FILM SUPERLIST: 20,000 MOTION PICTURES IN THE U.S. PUBLIC DOMAIN (1978); WALTER E. HURST & WILLIAM M. HALE, FILM SUPERLIST FOR 1940-49 MOTION PICTURES IN THE PUBLIC DOMAIN (1979); WALTER E. HURST & WILLIAM M. HALE, FILM SUPERLIST FOR 1950-59 MOTION PICTURES IN THE PUBLIC DOMAIN (1989).

24   *Russell v. Price*, 448 F. Supp. 303 (C.D. Cal. 1977), *aff'd*, 612 F.2d 1123 (9th Cir. 1979), *cert. denied*, 446 U.S. 952 (1980).

25   *Campbell v. Acuff-Rose Music, Inc.*, 114 S. Ct. 1164, 1170; *Harper & Row Publishers, Inc. v. Nation Enters.*, 471 U.S. 539, 549, 105 S. Ct. 2218, 2225 (1985); see also *American Geophysical Union v. Texaco, Inc.*, 802 F. Supp. 1 (S.D.N.Y. 1992), *appeal docketed*, No. 92-9341 (2d Cir. Nov. 4, 1992), for an excellent discussion of the law relating to fair use.

26   17 U.S.C. § 107.

27   *Harper & Row Publishers, Inc. v. Nation Enters.*, 471 U.S. 539, 566, 105 S. Ct. 2218, 2233 (1985).

28   17 U.S.C. § 107. However, this list is not exhaustive and is not formally a part of the test for whether a particular use is fair use. *Pacific & Southern Co. v. Duncan*, 744 F.2d 1490, 1495 (11th Cir. 1984), *cert. denied*, 471 U.S. 1004 (1985) ("The preamble merely illustrates the sorts of uses likely to qualify as fair uses under the four listed factors.").

29   See *American Geophysical Union v. Texaco, Inc.*, 802 F. Supp. 1 (S.D.N.Y. 1992), *appeal docketed*, No. 92-9341 (2d Cir. Nov. 4, 1992).

30   *Television Digest, Inc. v. United States Tele. Ass'n*, 841 F. Supp. 5, 10 (D.D.C. 1993).

31   *Campbell v. Acuff-Rose Music, Inc.*, 114 S. Ct. 1164, 1171 (1994); *American Geophysical Union v. Texaco, Inc.*, 802 F. Supp. 1, 12 (S.D.N.Y. 1992), *appeal docketed*, No. 92-9341 (2d Cir. Nov. 4, 1992).

32   *Sony Corp. v. Universal City Studios*, 464 U.S. 417, 449, 104 S. Ct. 774, 793 (1984). The key issue is not whether the copier's sole motive for the use of the copyrighted material is monetary gain, but whether it stands to profit from exploitation of the copyrighted material without paying the customary price. *Harper & Row Publishers, Inc. v. Nation Enters.*, 471 U.S. 539, 562, 105 S.Ct. 2218, 2231 (1985). Thus, even if one does not directly profit in the sense of a monetary gain, a profit-making purpose can be found in cases where money is saved by copying rather than buying or licensing the required copies. See *Television Digest, Inc. v. United States Tele. Ass'n*, 841 F.Supp. 5, 9 (D.D.C. 1993). Moreover, the fact that you are a nonprofit organization does not compel a finding of fair use. *Marcus v. Rowley*, 695 F.2d 1171, 1175 (9th Cir. 1983).

33   *Campbell v. Acuff-Rose Music, Inc.*, 114 S. Ct. 1164, 1171 (1994); *Twin Peaks Prods., Inc. v. Publications Int'l, Ltd.*, 996 F.2d 1366, 1374 (2d Cir. 1993); *American Geophysical Union v. Texaco, Inc.*, 802 F. Supp. 1, 13 (S.D.N.Y. 1992), *appeal docketed*, No. 92-9341 (2d Cir. Nov. 4, 1992).

34   *American Geophysical Union v. Texaco, Inc.*, 802 F. Supp. 1, 11 (S.D.N.Y. 1992), *appeal docketed*, No. 92-9341 (2d Cir. Nov. 4, 1992).

35   *American Geophysical Union v. Texaco, Inc.*, 802 F. Supp. 1, 11 (S.D.N.Y. 1992), *appeal docketed*, No. 92-9341 (2d Cir. Nov. 4, 1992).

36   See, e.g., *Campbell v. Acuff-Rose Music, Inc.*, 114 S. Ct. 1164, 1171 (1994) (2 Live Crew rap song that parodied Roy Orbison's "Pretty Woman" qualified as fair use notwithstanding its commercial nature); *Salinger v. Random House, Inc.*, 811 F.2d 90, 96 (2d Cir.) (a biographer's use of copyrighted letters written by J. D. Salinger to enrich his biography of Salinger was fair use even though he expected to earn profits on the biography), *cert. denied*, 484 U.S. 890 (1987); *New Era Publications Int'l ApS v. Carol Publishing Group*, 904 F.2d 152 (2d Cir.) (author's use of quoted material "to enrich" his highly critical biography of the founder of the Church of Scientology is a protected fair use, "notwithstanding that he and his publisher anticipate profits"), *cert. denied*, 498 U.S. 921, 111 S. Ct. 297 (1990); *Consumers Union of United States, Inc. v. General Signal Corp.*, 724 F.2d 1044, 1049 (2d Cir. 1983) ("although the purpose of [the] use undoubtedly is commercial, this fact alone does not defeat a fair use defense . . . almost all newspapers, books and magazines are published by commercial enterprises that seek a profit"), *cert. denied*, 469 U.S. 23 (1984); *Rosemont Enters., Inc. v. Random House, Inc.*, 366 F.2d 303, 307 (2d Cir. 1966) ("whether an author or publisher reaps economic benefits

from the sale of a biographical work, or whether its publication is motivated in part by a desire for commercial gain . . . has no bearing on whether a public benefit may be derived from such a work. Moreover, the District Court in emphasizing the commercial aspects of the Hughes biography failed to recognize that "all publications presumably are operated for a profit"), *cert. denied*, 385 U.S. 1009 (1967). *American Geophysical Union v. Texaco, Inc.*, 802 F. Supp. 1, 12-13 (S.D.N.Y. 1992), *appeal docketed*, No. 92-9341 (2d Cir. Nov. 4, 1992).

37   *Harper & Row Publishers, Inc. v. Nation Enters.*, 471 U.S. 539, 553, 105 S. Ct. 2218, 2226-27 (1985).

38   *Harper & Row, Publishers, Inc. v. Nation Enters.*, 471 U.S. 539, 551, 105 S. Ct. 2218, 2226 (1985).

39   *Harper & Row, Publishers, Inc. v. Nation Enters.*, 471 U.S. 539, 563, 105 S. Ct. 2218, 2232 (1985).

40   See *Sony Corp. v. Universal City Studios*, 464 U.S. 417, 455 n. 40, 104 S. Ct. 774, 795 n. 40 (1984).

41   *Consumers Union of United States, Inc. v. General Signal Corp.*, 724 F.2d 1044, 1049 (2d Cir. 1983).

42   *American Geophysical Union v. Texaco, Inc.*, 802 F. Supp. 1, 17, (S.D.N.Y. 1992), *appeal docketed*, No. 92-9341 (2d Cir. Nov. 4, 1992).

43   *American Geophysical Union v. Texaco, Inc.*, 802 F. Supp. 1, 17, (S.D.N.Y. 1992), *appeal docketed*, No. 92-9341 (2d Cir. Nov. 4, 1992).

44   *Sony Corp. v. Universal City Studios*, 464 U.S. 417, 450, 104 S. Ct. 774, 792 (1984).

45   *Harper & Row Publishers, Inc. v. Nation Enters.*, 471 U.S. 539, 564-66, 568, 105 S. Ct. 2218, 2232-33, 2234-35 (1985).

46   *Campbell v. Acuff-Rose Music, Inc.*, 114 S. Ct. 1164, 1175 (1994) ("the extent of permissible copying varies with the purpose and character of the use").

47   *Campbell v. Acuff-Rose Music, Inc.*, 114 S. Ct. 1164, 1176 (1994) (reversing appellate court holding that 2 Live Crew rap song that parodied Roy Orbison's "Pretty Woman" was not fair use).

48   See *Harper & Row Publishers, Inc. v. Nation Enters.*, 471 U.S. 534, 564-66, 105 S. Ct. 2218, 2232-33 (taking some 300 words of President Ford's memoirs was not fair use where it constituted "the heart of the book," and "its dramatic focal points").

49   *American Geophysical Union v. Texaco, Inc.*, 802 F. Supp. 1, 22 (S.D.N.Y. 1992), *appeal docketed*, No. 92-9341 (2d Cir. Nov. 4, 1992).

50   *Harper & Row Publishers, Inc. v. Nation Enters.*, 471 U.S. 539, 566, 105 S. Ct. 2218, 2233 (the fourth factor, effect on the market, is "undoubtedly the single most important element of fair use"). Not all courts agree, however, that this is the effect of the Supreme Court's language. See *American Geophysical Union v. Texaco, Inc.*, 802 F. Supp. 1, 21 (S.D.N.Y. 1992), *appeal docketed*, No. 92-9341 (2d Cir. Nov. 4, 1992). Moreover, in *Sony* the Court noted that if the use by the defendant of the copyrighted work is for commercial gain, the likelihood of harm to the market for the copyrighted work may be presumed. *Sony Corp. v. Universal City Studios*, 464 U.S. 417, 451, 104 S. Ct. 774, 793 (1984).

51   *Sony Corp. v. Universal City Studios*, 464 U.S. 417, 450, 104 S. Ct. 774, 792-93 (1984).

52   *Campbell v. Acuff-Rose Music, Inc.* 114 S.Ct. 1164, 1177 (1994). (the fourth fair use factor "requires courts to consider not only the extent of market harm caused by the particular actions of the alleged infringer, but also whether unrestricted and widespread conduct of the sort engaged in by the defendant . . . would result in a substantially adverse impact on the potential market for the original").

53   *Salinger v. Random House, Inc.*, 811 F.2d 90 (2d Cir.), *cert. denied,* 484 U.S. 890 (1987).

54   Diminution of market value in plaintiff's works "is not lessened by the fact that their author has disavowed the intention to publish them during his lifetime. . . . He is entitled to
protect his *opportunity* to sell his letters." *Salinger v. Random House, Inc.,* 811 F.2d 90, 99 (2d
Cir. 1987) (emphasis in original); see also *Pacific & Southern Co. v. Duncan,* 744 F.2d 1490,
1496-97 (11th Cir. 1984) (where defendant copied news stories broadcast on plaintiff television station, court found injury to the plaintiff's potential market even though plaintiff had
not yet sold videos of its broadcasts), *cert. denied,* 471 U.S. 1004 (1985); *Meeropol v. Nizer,* 560
F.2d 1061, 1070 (2d Cir. 1977) (fact that copyrighted letters have been out of print for 20
years does not necessarily mean that they have no future market which can be injured).

55   *Twin Peaks Prods., Inc. v. Publications Int'l, Ltd.,* 996 F.2d 1366, 1377 (2d Cir. 1993).

56   *Twin Peaks Prods., Inc. v. Publications Int'l, Ltd.,* 996 F.2d 1366, 1377 (2d Cir. 1993).

57   *Warner Bros., Inc. v. American Broadcasting Cos., Inc.,* 720 F.2d 231, 242 (2d Cir. 1983); *G.R.
Leonard & Co. v. Stack,* 386 F.2d 38 (7th Cir. 1967); *Werlin v. Reader's Digest Ass'n, Inc.,* 528 F.
Supp. 451, 463-64 (S.D.N.Y. 1981).

58   *Smith v. Little, Brown & Co.,* 245 F. Supp. 451, 458 (S.D.N.Y. 1965).

59   *Atari, Inc. v. North Am. Philips Consumer Elec. Corp.,* 672 F.2d 607, 619 (7th Cir.) ("it is enough
that substantial parts were lifted"), *cert. denied,* 459 U.S. 880 (1982); see also *Vault Corp. v.
Quaid Software, Ltd.,* 847 F.2d 255, 267 (5th Cir. 1988) (copying 30 characters out of 50 pages
of source code is de minimis).

60   *Henry Holt & Co. v. Liggett & Myers Tobacco Co.,* 23 F. Supp. 302, 304 (E.D. Pa. 1938) (copying
three sentences from a book is not de minimis); *Iowa State Univ. Research Found., Inc. v. American Broadcasting Cos.,* 463 F. Supp. 902, 904-05 (S.D.N.Y. 1978), *aff'd,* 621 F.2d 57 (2d Cir. 1980)
(defendant's broadcast of one 12-second segment and one 2½-minute segment of plaintiff's film held to infringe); *Roy Export Co. Establishment, etc. v. Columbia Broadcasting Sys., Inc.,*
503 F. Supp. 1137 (S.D.N.Y. 1980), *aff'd,* 672 F.2d 1095 (2d Cir.) (segment of film lasting 1
minute and 15 seconds infringed), *cert. denied,* 459 U.S. 826 (1982); *Nikanov v. Simon & Schuster,
Inc.,* 246 F.2d 501, 503-04 (2d Cir. 1957) (while material copied was relatively small portion
of total text, it was an integral part and of real importance to the book as a whole).

61   See, e.g., *Harper & Row Publishers, Inc. v. Nation Enters.,* 471 U.S. 539, 564-66, 105 S. Ct. 2218,
2233 (1985) (finding that 300 words taken from plaintiff's 200,000 word manuscript was
infringing); *Henry Holt & Co. v. Liggett & Myers Tobacco Co.,* 23 F. Supp. 302, 304 (E.D. Pa.
1938) (copying three sentences from a book can constitute infringement); *Dawn Assocs. v.
Links,* 203 U.S.P.Q. 831, 835 (N.D. Ill. 1978) (defendant that copied one sentence from advertisement appropriated protected expression).

62   *Bright Tunes Music Corp. v. Harrisongs Music, Ltd.,* 420 F. Supp. 177 (S.D.N.Y. 1976), *modified,*
722 F.2d 988 (2d Cir. 1983); see also *Baxter v. MCA, Inc.,* 812 F.2d 421, 425 (9th Cir. 1987) (finding that taking as few as six notes can constitute copyright infringement).

63   *Arnstein v. Porter,* 154 F.2d 464, 473 (2d Cir.), *aff'd on reh'g,* 158 F.2d 795 (2d Cir. 1946).

64   *Johns & Johns Printing Co. v. Paull-Pioneer Music Corp.,* 102 F.2d 282, 283 (8th Cir. 1939).

65   *Elsmere Music, Inc. v. National Broadcasting Co.,* 482 F. Supp. 741, 744 (S.D.N.Y.), *aff'd,* 623 F.2d
252 (2d Cir. 1980). However, the court concluded that the parody of the song was entitled
to the fair use defense.

66   See, e.g., *Robertson v. Batten, Barton, Durstine & Osborn, Inc.*, 146 F. Supp. 795, 798 (S.D. Cal. 1956).

67   *Marks v. Leo Feist, Inc.*, 290 F. 959 (2d Cir. 1923).

68   *Grand Upright Music, Ltd. v. Warner Bros. Records, Inc.*, 780 F. Supp. 182 (S.D.N.Y. 1991).

69   *Jarvis v. A & M Records*, 827 F. Supp. 282 (D.N.J. 1993).

70   See *Johns & Johns Printing Co. v. Paull-Pioneer Music Corp.*, 102 F.2d 282, 283 (8th Cir. 1939).

71   *Boosey v. Empire Music Co.*, 224 F. 646, 647 (S.D.N.Y. 1915).

72   *Roy Export Co. Establishment, etc. v. Columbia Broadcasting Sys., Inc.*, 503 F. Supp. 1137, 1145 (S.D.N.Y. 1980), *aff'd*, 672 F.2d 1095 (2d Cir.), *cert. denied*, 459 U.S. 826 (1982).

73   *Universal Pictures Co. v. Harold Lloyd Corp.*, 162 F.2d 354, 360 (9th Cir. 1947).

74   *Sub-Contractors Register, Inc. v. McGovern's Contractors & Builders Manual, Inc.*, 69 F. Supp. 507, 510 (S.D.N.Y. 1946).

75   *Haan Crafts Corp. v. Craft Masters, Inc.*, 683 F. Supp. 1234, 1243 (N.D. Ind. 1988).

76   17 U.S.C. § 102(b).

77   *Feist Publications, Inc. v. Rural Tele. Serv. Co.*, 499 U.S. 340, 111 S. Ct. 1282, 1287, 1288, 1289, 1290, 1293 (1991); *Harper & Row Publishers, Inc. v. Nation Enters.*, 471 U.S. 539, 547, 105 S. Ct. 2218, 2224 (1985) ("no author may copyright facts or ideas").

78   *Feist Publications, Inc. v. Rural Tele. Serv. Co.*, 499 U.S. 340, 111 S. Ct. 1282, 1288-89 (1991).

79   But even though facts are not, by themselves, copyrightable, it is important to understand that a compilation (e.g., a database) of such non-copyrightable elements may itself be copyrightable. 17 U.S.C. § 103(a). A **compilation** is defined as "a work formed by the *collection and assembling of* preexisting materials or of data that are *selected, coordinated, or arranged* in such a way that the resulting work as a whole constitutes an original work of authorship" 17 U.S.C. § 101 (emphasis added). Thus, for example, notwithstanding that facts (such as the names of cities and streets) are not copyrightable, compilations of facts (such as a list of the 50 "most livable" cities in the United States) *may* be copyrightable. *Feist Publications, Inc. v. Rural Tele. Serv. Co.*, 499 U.S. 340, 111 S. Ct. 1282, 1289 (1991).

80   *Feist Publications, Inc. v. Rural Tele. Serv. Co.*, 499 U.S. 340, 111 S. Ct. 1282, 1289, 1295 (1991).

81   *Feist Publications, Inc. v. Rural Tele. Serv. Co.*, 499 U.S. 340, 111 S. Ct. 1282, 1289 (1991).

82   *Feist Publications, Inc. v. Rural Tele. Serv. Co.*, 499 U.S. 340, 111 S.Ct. 1282, 1289 (1991). In *Harper & Row Publishers, Inc. v. Nation Enterprises*, 471 U.S. 539, 105 S. Ct. 2218 (1985), for example, the Supreme Court held that President Ford could not prevent others from copying bare historical facts from his autobiography, although he could prevent others from copying his subjective descriptions and portraits of public figures.

83   17 U.S.C. § 102(b); *Harper & Row Publishers, Inc. v. Nation Enters.*, 471 U.S. 539, 547, 105 S. Ct. 2218, 2224 (1985) ("no author may copyright facts or ideas").

84   Specifically, the Copyright Act provides: "In no case does copyright protection for an original work of authorship extend to any idea, procedure, process, system, method of operation, concept, principal, or discovery, regardless of the form in which it is described, explained, illustrated, or embodied in such a work." 17 U.S.C. § 102(b). See also 37 C.F.R. § 202.1(b).

Obtaining Permission to Use Preexisting Content

Obtaining Permission to Use Preexisting Content

The process of obtaining permission to use preexisting content owned by another party—that is, clearing the rights to the content—involves several steps. In some cases, it may be a relatively simple process. In other cases it can be thoroughly complex, exceedingly difficult, time-consuming, and costly. Moreover, in each case the rights to be cleared, the procedures to be used, and the so-called "standard" license terms will vary significantly depending upon the industry involved (e.g., motion picture, music, book publishing, etc.).

In each case, however, the basic steps involved in the process of clearing the rights to content are essentially the same. They can be summarized as follows:

1. identify the content that you want to use;

2. identify the separate rights for which permission must be obtained;

3. identify and locate the owner of each right for which permission is required; and

4. negotiate and obtain the requisite form of permission.

In many cases, addressing these issues is best done by using a rights and permission professional. However, whether you do it on your own or use the assistance of another party, it is important that you understand the nature of the process.

1. Identifying the Content You Want to Use

The process of obtaining permissions begins with what is perhaps a self-evident proposition: you must know what it is that you want to use. In other words, what is the name of the song you want to use, what specific segment or clip from which movie do you want to incorporate in your multimedia product, which particular photograph do you want to publish, and so forth?

In most cases, you will only need to use a portion of the copyrighted content (e.g., a few paragraphs from a book, a few seconds of a sound recording, or a few seconds of a film clip). Thus, it is important that you accurately identify both the work and the specific portion of it that you want to use. This is not only necessary for purposes of defining the content covered by the **license** agreement, but may also have a significant impact on the scope of the rights the content owner is willing to grant to you, and the price to be charged.

In the music industry, for example, it may make a big difference whether you want to license the portion of a song constituting the well-known chorus, or whether you want to take a less recognizable portion. Similarly, the portion of a film clip that you would like to use will determine whether you need to license rights to a musical work included in the film, and the number of performers from whom it will be necessary to obtain releases.

2. Identifying the Rights for Which Permission is Required

Once you have identified the content you want to use, it is important to identify all of the rights in the work for which permission must be obtained. The rights to a work are analogous to the structure of a Russian nesting doll: that is, although it may look like a single object from a distance, it is actually composed of several layers, each of which is an integral part (or a foundation) of the whole work, and consequently, must be considered in order to make everything work together.

Thus, it is important to understand that any given work may contain several overlapping copyrights (discussed in chapter 3, section 7), may include (or comprise) a trademark (discussed in chapters 4 and 25), may implicate the rights of publicity and privacy of the persons depicted in or referred to by the work (the right of publicity is explained in chapter 5, and the right of privacy is explained in chapter 6), and may be subject to certain contract rights (such as royalty rights of star performers or recording artists, or **reuse fees** due to applicable unions or union members as discussed in chapter 21).

A sound recording of a musical work, for example, involves at least two copyrights: the copyright in the underlying musical work, and the copyright in the sound recording. These copyrights are typically owned by separate persons, and permission must be obtained from both of them if the sound recording is to be copied. Similarly, a film clip may include several copyrights. There is not only the copyright in the motion picture itself, but also the copyright in the underlying literary work on which the film is based, the copyrights in any separate songs or musical works used in the film, copyrights in any still photographs used in the film, copyrights in any animated characters used in the film, and perhaps others. Again, each of these copyrights may be owned by a different person, and the use of any clip involving them will require permission of each of the copyright holders.

In some cases, the text, sound recording, or photograph that you want to license will include the trademark of another (or may itself be the trademark). Depending upon the nature of your proposed use of the content, it may be necessary to obtain permission from the owner of the trademark.

In addition, if the film clip depicts any persons, or if the sound recording contains the voice of any famous celebrities, the rights of publicity and/or the rights of privacy may also be implicated by use of the content. As a consequence, even if you obtain a license from the copyright holder, the actors, musicians, and composers may still retain rights that could prevent use of the film or sound recording in a multimedia application without their permission as well.

Finally, certain persons or groups may have retained contract rights that must be dealt with before you can use the content. For example, some of the performers in a film or recording artists of a sound recording may have retained certain rights to approve the reuse or repurposing of the work in other media and/or to receive royalties for such reuse or repurposing. In addition, if union talent was involved in the creation of the content, the collective bargaining agreements between the union and the producer of the content (such as a film or recording studio) will typically require the payment of certain reuse fees, and payments to its pension and retirement fund.

The bottom line is that you should carefully analyze and evaluate any content that you want to use in order to identify the component parts of the work for which permission will be required. In this context, it is important to determine, in advance, the particular rights that you will require. For example, if you want to use a movie clip, but have no need for the accompanying music, there is no need to spend time acquiring permission to use the accompanying music.

A summary of the rights in each of the various types of content for which permission must be obtained is included in the discussion of the licensing of each form of content, as set forth in chapters 14 through 21.

3. Identifying the Owners of the Rights

The next step is to identify and locate the owners of the copyrights and other rights for which a license is required. This often requires a fair amount of detective work, as well as an understanding of the separation of rights that frequently occur with copyrighted content (separation of rights is explained in chapter 3, section 6).

3.1 Examining the Work Itself

The identity of the copyright holder can often be obtained by an examination of a published copy of the content itself. If available, the copy frequently includes information such as a copyright notice, the place and date of publication, the author, the publisher, and credits that identify incorporated works, actors, actresses, recording artists, musicians. Often the name of the artist, publisher, or production company will appear on a copy of the work (such as a book, CD, or video tape). These persons may or may not own the rights to the content, but their names will at least provide a starting point in the search to identify the owner. In many cases, however, it can be very difficult to even come up with a name or a lead to start the identification process.

3.2 Trade and Licensing Organizations

Professional trade organizations, unions, and licensing organizations can often provide invaluable assistance in identifying and locating the owner of a copyright to the content being sought. With respect to music, for example, a good place to begin is the **Harry Fox Agency** in New York[1] which represents over 60 percent of all music publishers. The **American Society of Composers, Authors and Publishers (ASCAP)**,[2] **Broadcast Music, Inc. (BMI)**,[3] or **SESAC, Inc.**[4] may also be able to assist in this process as these organizations represent and protect the performing rights of their members (primarily composers and publishers). (See chapter 17, sections 3 and 4 for a more detailed discussion of these organizations.)

Photographers are often represented by photo stock agencies. Many photo stock agencies belong to the Picture Agency Council of America (PACA). The PACA publishes a directory that includes information about each member agency, with a description of their collections.

Motion picture unions and trade associations may also be of assistance. These include the **Writers Guild of America (WGA)**, **Directors Guild of America (DGA)**, **Screen Actors Guild (SAG)**, **American Federation of Radio and Television Artists (AFTRA)**, and **American Federation of Musicians (AF of M)**. These organizations are discussed in chapter 21.

3.3 Copyright Searches

Another alternative that is frequently helpful is to do a search of the records of the Copyright Office of the U.S. Library of Congress to see if the copyright to the content has been registered. If it has, this will allow you to obtain the name and address of the copyright holder, or at least the name and address of the owner as of the date of the registration.

The Copyright Office is primarily an office of record where claims to copyright are registered[5] and documents pertaining to copyrights are recorded.[6] (Registration is explained in chapter 24). Registrations are indexed by the title of the work, the name of its author, and the name of the copyright claimant if it is not the same as the author. The Copyright Office does not maintain any listings of works that are in the public domain.[7]

The Copyright Office cannot advise you on questions of possible copyright infringement, draft or interpret contract terms, or grant you permission to use a copyrighted work.[8] However, a search of its records may give you the following information (if the work is registered):

1. title of the work
2. author of the work
3. year in which the work was completed
4. date the work was first published
5. owner of the copyright
6. whether the work incorporates other copyrightable works.

You can search the Copyright Office records yourself, have the Copyright Office conduct the search for you, or hire a commercial search service to perform the search.

• **Conducting Your Own Search**. A copyright search begins with a review of the *Catalog of Copyright Entries* (CCE), which is published by the Copyright Office and lists all registrations made.[9] The CCE is divided into parts according to the classes of works registered,[10] such as Nondramatic Literary Works, Motion Pictures and Film-strips, and Sound Recordings. The Library of Congress as well as a number of libraries throughout the United States maintain copies of the CCE.

The CCE has three primary limitations. First, it does not include entries for assignments or other recorded documents, and consequently cannot be used for searches involving the transfer of ownership of rights. Second, there is a lag time of at least one year between the time when a work is registered and the time when the registration is included in the CCE. Third, the CCE is not a verbatim transcript of the registration records, but is merely a summary of the essential facts about a particular registration.[11]

Because the CCE has these limitations, it is usually necessary to examine the actual records of the Copyright Office.[12] Most records are open to the public and include an extensive card catalog, an automated catalog containing records from 1978 to the present, and microfilm records of assignments and related documents.[13] However, not all records may be searched directly by the public.[14] For some records, such as correspondence files and deposit copies, the Copyright Office, upon request, will search its files for a search fee, and make any information located available for inspection.

In addition, records of the Copyright Office beginning January 1978 are online and can be searched through the *U.S. Copyrights* database that is produced by Dialog Information Services, Inc., an on-line database service.[15] This online database of 6,000,000 records provides access to registration details for all active copyright registrations on file at the Copyright Office. The database consists of two types of records: monograph records and legal document records. Monograph records contain information on the initial registration and renewal of a work. Legal document records contain information on the assignments and other information pertaining to the ownership status. The database also covers registered works that have been renewed.

• **Searches by the Copyright Office**. The Copyright Office will conduct a search of its records for you for a fee. The fee is set by statute and is currently $20 per hour or fraction of an hour for time spent locating Copyright Office records; similarly, the Copyright Office charges $20 per hour for the preparation of a search report summarizing the contents of these records.[16] Based upon the information you are able to provide, the Copyright Office will provide an estimate of the total search fee before any work begins.[17] Of course, the more information you are able to provide, the more quickly the Copyright Office will be able to search its records, and the less the search will cost.

If you want to have the Copyright Office conduct a search of its records, you should provide as much of the following information as possible:[18]

1. the title of the work, with any possible variations[19]

2. the names of the authors, including possible pseudonyms

3. the name of the probable copyright holder

4. the approximate year when the work was published or registered

5. the type of work involved, such as a motion picture, book, sound recording, and so forth

6. for a work originally published as part of a periodical or collection, the title of that publication and any other information to help identify it, such as the volume or issue number

7. the registration number or any other copyright data

The search request, and any other correspondence, should be sent to: Reference and Bibliography Section, LM-450, Copyright Office, Library of Congress, Washington, D.C. 20559-6000.[20]

It is also possible to request a search by telephone, by calling the Reference and Bibliography Section at (202) 707-6850 and asking to speak to a bibliographer. The Copyright Office will also accept search requests sent by facsimile (fax) transmission to (202) 707-6859. Upon receipt of your request, a Library of Congress bibliographer will contact you with an estimate of the fee for the search requested. The bibliographer will begin the search upon receipt of a check, sent to the address listed above, in the amount of the estimated fee. The search will take at least two weeks. A bibliographer may be able to give you a more precise estimate upon receipt of your request.

• **Commercial Search Services**. An easier and quicker alternative to conducting a search yourself or using the Copyright Office to perform the search is to hire a commercial search service to search the Copyright Office records for you. The customary charges are assessed by the hour and vary by service. Some services may have a minimum charge.

Reports provided by commercial services[21] are usually very comprehensive. The cost for such services typically ranges from $150 to $600 depending upon the breadth of the search and the amount of information you are able to provide.

Turnaround time for these commercial services is quick. Some are able to complete a full copyright search in twenty-four hours, at a premium, of course. Standard service is still faster than a personal or Copyright Office search. A list of some of the firms that provide copyright search services is included in chapter 36.

• **Limitations on Copyright Searches**. No copyright search, regardless of who performs it, is foolproof. This is because the search, while based on all information that the Copyright Office possesses, may be affected by information beyond that which the Copyright Office is obligated to maintain or to which it has access.

Searches of the Copyright Office catalogs and records are useful in determining the copyright status of a work, but they are not conclusive.[22] They will only disclose a limited set of information, and only if it was filed with the Copyright Office. If a search does not disclose any information about a particular work, this does not mean that the work is in the public domain. There are several reasons for this:[23]

1. Registration is generally not required as a precondition of copyright protection for all works created after 1978, and for works created before 1978 that were unpublished as of January 1, 1978. These works may be registered at any time during the term of protection

2. Works published before 1978 may be registered at any time within the first twenty-eight-year term of copyright protection which runs from the date of publication

3. A search report may not include registrations that have not yet been included in the CCE and other catalog records

4. The information in the search request may not have been specific enough to identify the work

5. The work may have been registered under a different title or as part of a larger work.

In addition, it is important to note that even if a work is in the public domain in the United States, it may be protected under the copyright laws of another country. The Copyright Office does not keep track of foreign registrations.

3.4 Trademark Searches

If the content to be used can also function as a trademark, a trademark search may also be advisable. There are several methods available for conducting or obtaining a trademark search.

First, publications are available that compile and list all registered trademarks as of a specified date. These include *Trademark Register of the United States 1881-1983*,[24] *Trade names Dictionary: Company Index*,[25] and *The Compu-Mark Directory of U.S. Trademarks*.[26]

In addition to published materials (which by their nature will not be completely current), it is also possible to search a computerized database of state and federal trademark registrations. One such database, known as "TrademarkScan," is compiled by Thomson & Thomson, and can be accessed through the Dialogue Information Service. This allows individuals to conduct a quick trademark search that is relatively current. However, some proficiency in the use of this database is required, as improperly conducted searches may miss relevant registrations.

A third alternative is to retain a commercial search service to conduct a trademark search. These services will conduct a thorough review of both federal and state trademark registrations, pending federal registrations, as well as other sources that might identify common law uses of trademarks.

A list of firms that provide trademark search services is included in chapter 36.

3.5 Rights and Permissions Professionals

A number of individuals and organizations provide services designed to assist in the process of obtaining clearance of content licenses. Sometimes referred to as rights and permissions professionals, they provide rights clearance services for virtually all types of content, including text, music, sound recordings, film and television clips, photographs, art, and the like.

Generally, the services provided by rights and permissions professionals include help in identifying the rights that need to be cleared to accommodate your proposed use of a particular work, identifying the owner of the rights, developing a strategy for locating and contacting the owner of the rights, and negotiating for the appropriate license, permission, or release. Moreover, because clearance is their business, they frequently have developed relationships with copyright owners, such as music publishers, record companies, movie and television production companies, book publishers, and photographers that can facilitate the clearance process.

These organizations charge a fee (either a flat fee or an hourly rate) for the service of locating and contacting the copyright holders and negotiating the appropriate copyright license. Some of the organizations providing this assistance are listed in chapter 36.

3.6 Verifying Ownership

Identifying the owner is not necessarily the end of your search. You also need to ensure that the person with whom you are dealing owns the specific rights you require. This involves dealing with the problem of the separation of rights that frequently occurs with copyrights in the entertainment industry. (Separation of rights is explained in chapter 3, section 6).

If you are seeking to license text from a book, for example, you might logically identify the publisher of the book as the owner of the copyright in the book. But it may turn out that the publisher owns only the right to publish the book in print form in North America. The print rights to the rest of the world may be owned by another publisher, and so-called "electronic rights" to publish the book in a computer-readable form may be owned by yet a third person. Thus, it is always important to look behind the rights allegedly owned by the person who claims to be the copyright holder.

A good example of this problem occurred when the BBC licensed several *Monty Python* television shows to Time-Life and the American Broadcasting Corporation (ABC) for broadcast in the United States.[27] In that case, although the BBC owned the copyright to the recorded television programs, they were based on copyrighted scripts licensed by the British Broadcasting Corporation (BBC) from Monty Python. The license did not grant the BBC the right to alter the program once it had been recorded, and therefore, the BBC could not license anyone else to do so. Nonetheless, the BBC granted Time-Life and ABC a license that allowed ABC to edit the programs for a variety of specific purposes such as inserting commercials. Monty Python then filed suit against ABC, and the court prohibited ABC from broadcasting the programs because the alternations made by ABC exceeded the scope of the license that the BBC was entitled to grant. As the court pointed out, even though the BBC may be the owner of the copyright in the recorded programs, its use of those programs is "limited by the license granted to BBC by Monty Python for use of the underlined scripts."[28]

Reviewing the contracts by which the content owner accrued its rights can go a long way toward resolving this issue, assuming the content owner is willing to disclose those contracts to you. Having a copyright search conducted may also provide additional information. And finally, including appropriate warranties and representations in the licensing agreement can be of critical importance in these types of situations. (Warranty provisions are discussed in chapter 13, section 9).

4. Forms of Permission

Before incorporating a copyrighted work or performer's persona into a multimedia work, you must secure permission to use the work or persona. Permission may take several forms, including an assignment, license, or release. Which type of permission you should or will be able to obtain depends upon what it is that you are incorporating into the multimedia product, your objectives, and the relative bargaining power of the two parties.

4.1 Assignment

An *assignment* is a transfer of ownership by a copyright holder of one or more of the exclusive rights in a copyrighted work.[29] The owner of the copyright loses all rights of ownership and control over the copyright rights that are assigned. Accordingly, if you obtain rights to use content by virtue of an assignment, you become the exclusive owner of those rights.

Assignments are frequently used in situations where you hire an independent contractor to develop content for you (see discussion in chapter 10, section 3). However, in most situations where the content you want to use has previously been created by someone else, you will merely seek to obtain a license to use the content, rather than complete and total ownership over the copyright rights to the content itself.

4.2 License

A *license* is permission to do an act that would infringe a copyright (or other right owned by the person granting permission) if the permission were not given.[30] It is a grant of permission to use the work to the limited extent provided in the license agreement. Unlike an assignment, a license does not transfer ownership of the copyright.

A license may be exclusive or nonexclusive. If you obtain a nonexclusive license, the copyright holder may grant permission to other persons to exploit the same right, to the same extent, or to a greater or lesser extent, than the permission granted to you.

The license may grant you permission to exploit all of the rights the copyright holder has to the content, or, more likely, will be limited to a specific portion of the copyright holder's rights. For example, a copyright holder might grant you a license to copy and make a derivative work based on a motion picture clip for distribution in North America, but not worldwide. Such a license involves less than all of the exclusive rights in the copyright—that is, it includes the reproduction right, the adaptation right, and the distribution right, but does not include the public performance or the public display right. In addition, the rights granted are restricted—that is, they are limited to the right to exploit those rights in the limited territory of North America.

4.3 Release

A *release* is the relinquishment or giving up of a right or claim by the owner of the right against someone using a copyrighted work or another's persona.[31] A release is usually given in response to an express request for permission to use a work or another's persona. A release does not transfer any rights or grant permission, but is the owner's promise not to assert a claim of infringement.

Generally, you should obtain a release from everyone who appears in a recognizable form in the content that you are licensing, in order to avoid claims based on an infringement of the right of publicity or invasion of privacy. (The right of publicity is discussed in chapter 5; the right of privacy is discussed in chapter 6.) In addition, if you are licensing content from someone who represents that he or she has obtained all of the necessary releases, you should review those releases, if possible.

4.4 Which Form Should You Obtain?

Which form of permission you should or will be able to obtain depends upon what it is that you are incorporating into your product, your objectives, and the relative bargaining power of the parties.

If you want to use a copyrighted work in your multimedia product, an assignment, license or a release might each be appropriate in differing circumstances. If you want to use a person's persona in a multimedia product, a release would be appropriate. Such a situation would arise where, for example, an identifiable performer appears in a television or motion picture clip that is incorporated into the multimedia product. (For a discussion of the rights of a performer in his or her persona, see chapters 5, 6 and 20.)

Where more than one type of permission is appropriate, cost is likely to be a primary consideration. As a general rule, an assignment confers more rights than an exclusive license, an exclusive license more than a nonexclusive license, and a nonexclusive license more than a release. Correspondingly, an assignment is likely to be the most costly, and a release the least costly, with the licenses falling somewhere in between.

Another consideration is whether you want to be the only one to exploit the content. If the economic viability of your multimedia product will be negatively impacted if the content were used by someone else, then an assignment or exclusive license will be necessary to prevent others from using the work. In this context, you should also consider whether it is important that all others be precluded from using the work or whether it is important that only other multimedia developers be precluded from using the work. If it is important that all others be excluded, either an assignment or exclusive license can accomplish this. If you seek a license in such a situation, you must be sure that the terms of the license agreement provide you with exclusive rights to use with regard to platform, market, media, territory, and term. If it is important that only other multimedia developers not be able to use the work, then an exclusive license to use the work on the particular platform and media you have chosen, and perhaps in closely related, competing platforms and media, is all that you need secure.

Similarly, if you anticipate that your multimedia product's useful life or the popularity of the underlying work is time-limited, a license for some period less than the full term of the copyright may suit your needs, making an assignment unnecessary, and a license more appropriate.

Other considerations include the territory in which you intend to market the product. If the product is intended for worldwide distribution or for some lesser geographic market, a license may be negotiated to reflect this.

Any assignment or exclusive license must be in writing.[32] If an assignment or exclusive license is not made in a written document, it will not be enforceable. Also, although there is no longer a requirement that an assignment or exclusive license be recorded with the Copyright Office, it is still a good idea to do so because the Copyright Act gives a recorded assignment or exclusive license priority over a conflicting assignment or license of the same rights.[33]

5. Negotiating for Permission

The process of obtaining a license to use content in a multimedia work is complicated by a variety of factors, including the following:

● You will be dealing with a variety of different creative industries (such as book publishing, music, motion picture, art, and so forth), each of which has developed its own practices and procedures with respect to the licensing of content. Thus, what is true of licensing in one industry will not necessarily be true of licensing in another.

● While each industry has developed a set of standard practices and procedures with respect to licensing content for traditional uses, there are virtually no accepted standards or procedures for licensing content for use in a multimedia work. As a consequence, you may find there is no consistency in licensing practices even within the same industry. In addition, you may find many content providers simply unwilling to license their content until more generally accepted practices have developed.

● No one really knows how to charge for a license to use content in a multimedia work. Thus, there will not necessarily be any consistency in license fees demanded, and many content licensors have refused to license their content out of a fear that they will not be properly compensated. There is a general lack of understanding of the nature of multimedia and its impact on the value of the content that you seek to license.

● There exists a rather significant fear among content owners that converting content to digital form, and distributing content in that form, will significantly enhance the opportunities for piracy of such content through unauthorized copying, adaptation, and/or distribution.

• The rights of content holders themselves are frequently in doubt—that is, it is often unclear whether a music publisher, motion picture producer, or book publisher (which has frequently acquired its rights by license and/or assignment), has the rights necessary to grant to you the right to use the content in a multimedia and/or electronic form.

• Although some of the foregoing factors may make licensing difficult in certain situations, it is important that you carefully determine the rights that you need to obtain before you begin the process of negotiating for permission.

While many industries have standard approaches to certain types of traditional licensing, they may not fit your requirements for use of content in a multimedia product. Accordingly, determine the specific rights you need, and make sure you get those rights before committing to entering into a license agreement.

Endnotes

1   Harry Fox Agency, Inc., 711 3rd Avenue, 8th Floor, New York, New York 10017; phone: (212) 370-5330.

2   ASCAP, One Lincoln Plaza, New York, New York 10023; phone: (212) 595-3050; fax: (212) 724-9064.

3   BMI, 320 W. 57th Street, New York, New York 10019; phone: (212) 586-2000; fax: (212) 246-2163.

4   SESAC, Inc., 156 W. 56th Street, New York, New York 10019; phone: (212) 586-3450; fax: (212) 397-4682.

5   17 U.S.C. §§ 408, 409; 37 C.F.R. § 202.3 (1993).

6   17 U.S.C. § 205; COPYRIGHT OFFICE CIR. 1B, LIMITATIONS ON THE INFORMATION FURNISHED BY THE COPYRIGHT OFFICE (1990); COPYRIGHT OFFICE CIR. 6, OBTAINING COPIES OF COPYRIGHT OFFICE RECORDS AND DEPOSITS 2, 3 (1990); COMPENDIUM OF COPYRIGHT OFFICE PRACTICES II, ch. 100, ¶ 106-107, at 100-2 to 100-3 (1984).

7   COPYRIGHT OFFICE CIR. 22, HOW TO INVESTIGATE THE COPYRIGHT STATUS OF A WORK 4-5 (1993).

8   37 C.F.R. § 201.2(a) (1993). The Copyright Office also cannot compare a work with other works deposited for registration to evaluate their similarities, draft or interpret contract terms or give any legal advice, enforce contracts, help to get a work published, recorded, or performed. COPYRIGHT OFFICE CIR. 1B, LIMITATIONS ON THE INFORMATION FURNISHED BY THE COPYRIGHT OFFICE (1990).

9   COPYRIGHT OFFICE CIR. 22, HOW TO INVESTIGATE THE COPYRIGHT STATUS OF A WORK 3 (1993).

10   COPYRIGHT OFFICE CIR. 22, HOW TO INVESTIGATE THE COPYRIGHT STATUS OF A WORK 3 (1993). Effective with the Fourth Series, Vol. 2, 1979 Catalogs, the CCE is published in microfiche form only. The CCE was previously published in book form.

11   Copyright Office Cir. 22, How to Investigate the Copyright Status of a Work 3 (1973).

12   The Copyright Office is located in the Library of Congress James Madison Memorial Building, 101 Independence Avenue S.E., Washington, D.C. For a discussion of the card catalog, on-line files, and suggestions for search strategies, see Copyright Office Cir. 23, The Copyright Card Catalog and the Online Files of the Copyright Office (1988).

13   Copyright Office Cir. 23, The Copyright Card Catalog and the Online Files of the Copyright Office 3 (1988); 37 C.F.R. § 201.2(b)(1).

14   37 C.F.R. § 201.2(b)(2). "It is the general policy of the Copyright Office to deny direct public access to in-process files and to any work (or other) areas where they are kept." This information is available for inspection upon request. 37 C.F.R. § 201.2(b)(3).

15   Dialog is accessible through a computer or terminal, modem, telephone line, communications software, and Dialog password.

16   Copyright Office Cir., Copyright Fees Increase (1990).

17   Copyright Office Cir. 22, How to Investigate the Copyright Status of a Work 4 (1993).

18   Copyright Office Cir. 22, How to Investigate the Copyright Status of a Work 4 (1993).

19   Some works, such as motion pictures, are often based on other works such as books or serialized contributions to periodicals or other composite works. If you want a search for an underlying work or for music from a motion picture, you must specifically request such a search. You must also identify the underlying works and music and furnish the specific titles, authors, and approximate dates of these works.

20   37 C.F.R. § 201.1(d).

21   Thomson & Thomson's copyright and title research services can be reached at 1750 K Street N.W., Suite 200, Washington D.C. 20006; phone: (800) 356-8630 or (202) 835-0240; fax: (800) 822-8823 or (202) 728-0744.

22   Copyright Office Cir. 22, How to Investigate the Copyright Status of a Work 5 (1993).

23   Copyright Office Cir. 22, How to Investigate the Copyright Status of a Work 5 (1993).

24   Trademark Register of the United States: 1881-1983, Cyril W. Sernak, rev. ed. (1983).

25   Trade Names Dictionary: Company Index, (Donna Wood ed. 1982).

26   *The Compu-Mark Directory of U.S. Trademarks* (1994).

27   See *Gilliam v. American Broadcasting Cos.*, 538 F.2d 14 (2d Cir. 1976).

28   *Gilliam v. American Broadcasting Cos.*, 538 F.2d 14 (2d Cir. 1976).

29   17 U.S.C. § 201(d)(2).

30   See Black's Law Dictionary 829 (5th ed. 1979).

31   Black's Law Dictionary 1159 (5th ed. 1979).

32   The Copyright Act requires that any transfer of ownership be made in writing and signed by the owner of the rights conveyed. 17 U.S.C. § 204(a).

33   17 U.S.C. §§ 205(d) and (e).

Licensing Content— Basic Issues

CHECKLIST OF BASIC ISSUES

ANALYSIS OF BASIC ISSUES

1. Subject Matter of License

2. Scope of Rights Granted

2.1. What Activities Are Authorized?

2.1.1 Reproduction Right

2.1.2 Adaptation Right

2.1.3 Distribution Right

2.1.4 Public Performance Right

2.1.5 Public Display Right

2.2. What Limitations are Imposed on the Rights Granted?

2.2.1 Specific Title

2.2.2 Media

2.2.3 Territories

2.2.4 Hardware and Software Platforms

2.2.5 Exclusive or Nonexclusive

2.3 The Problem of New Uses and Old Licenses

3. Term

4. Credits

5. Ownership of Content
6. Rights of Other Parties
7. Delivery
8. License Fees and Royalties
9. Warranties
10. Limitations of Liability
11. Indemnification
12. Default
13. Right to Assign

Licensing Content— Basic Issues

Unless you are the owner of the content that you plan to use in a multimedia title, the content is in the public domain, or its use constitutes "fair use," you will have to obtain a license from the copyright holder authorizing use of the content.

Although multimedia content license transactions frequently involve a unique combination of facts, circumstances, and issues, and are often driven by the practices and procedures of the industry involved (e.g., motion picture industry, music industry, book publishing industry, and so forth), there are a number of basic issues that are common to most content licensing transactions. While this book cannot evaluate all of the unique problems and circumstances that arise in the wide variety of multimedia content license deals being made today, it will attempt to provide a general overview of the basic issues that can be expected to arise most frequently.

Keep in mind, however, that it may not be necessary for a given content license to address all of the issues raised here. Alternatively, other issues may be relevant. Every license must be structured to meet the needs of the particular transaction, and should accurately reflect the agreement of the parties. However, in negotiating a multimedia content license, you should at least consider the issues raised in this chapter, although the extent to which they are relevant, and the way in which they are handled, will vary depending upon the particular situation and the type of contract involved.

To introduce these contract issues, we begin with a generic checklist of basic questions: an overview of the types of questions you should be asking when preparing or reviewing a multimedia content license.

CHECKLIST OF BASIC ISSUES

1. Subject Matter of License. What is the subject matter of the contract? Text? A musical composition? A sound recording? Still images? Video? Have you adequately identified the specific work to be licensed? If only a portion of the work will be licensed, have you accurately defined the portion to be licensed? (See this chapter, section 1.)

2. Scope of Rights Granted. What is the scope of your right to use the content? What activities are you authorized to engage in with respect to the content (e.g., reproduce it, adapt it, distribute it, perform it publicly, or display it publicly), and what limitations are imposed on your right to engage in those activities (e.g., do you get unlimited rights, or are your rights limited with respect to media, mode of distribution, territory, platform, operating system, and so forth)? (See this chapter, section 2.)

3. Term. For what period of time can you exercise the rights granted in the license? (See this chapter, section 3.)

4. Credits. Are you obligated to give credit to the copyright holder and/or the artists who created or appear in the content? (See this chapter, section 4.)

5. Ownership of Content. Have you verified that the copyright holder does, in fact, own the appropriate rights in the content being licensed? (See this chapter, section 5.)

6. Rights of Other Parties. Are there any parties (other than the copyright holder) who have a legal or contractual right to payment for your proposed use of the content and/or whose permission is required as a precondition to your proposed use of the content? (See this chapter, section 6.)

7. Delivery. Does the copyright holder have any obligations to deliver a master copy of the licensed content to you? If so, in what format or medium? (See this chapter, section 7.)

8. License Fees and Royalties. How much do you have to pay for the rights granted? What form of payment is required (e.g., a one-time paid-up license fee or royalties based on unit sales or gross revenues)? When is payment due? Are there any recordkeeping and reporting requirements to determine the royalties due to the copyright holder or any other third parties? (See this chapter, section 8.)

9. Warranties. What does the copyright holder warrant regarding the nature of the rights granted to you? (See this chapter, section 9.)

10. Limitations of Liability. To what extent is the copyright holder responsible for damages that you might suffer as a result of using the licensed content? Is there a limit on the nature or the extent of the copyright holder's liability? (See this chapter, section 10.)

11. Indemnification. Will the copyright holder defend you and pay any damages you incur in the event that you are sued on a claim that the licensed content infringes any copyrights, trademark rights, rights of publicity or privacy, or any other rights of any third parties? (See this chapter, section 11.)

12. Default. What are each party's rights in case of a default by the other? (See this chapter, section 12.)

13. Right to Assign. Does either party have the right to transfer its rights under the license to someone else? (See this chapter, section 13.)

ANALYSIS OF BASIC ISSUES

The questions raised by the preceding checklist will be examined in the chapter, sections that follow. Examples of contract terms that address the issues discussed in this chapter can be found in the sample content license agreements contained in chapter 30.

1. Subject Matter of License

What is the subject matter of the license? What is it about? Is it a license of text, a musical work, a sound recording, a still picture, a motion picture, animation, a character? What is its title? How else might it be identified? And what specific segment of text, sound, or video is covered?

It is important to clearly define the subject matter of the agreement. If you are licensing a two-minute movie clip, for example, you need to identify the movie the clip is taken from, as well as the specific two-minute segment that you will be authorized to use. The definition should be sufficiently specific so that an objective observer (such as a judge in a future dispute) can determine which specific portions of a book, film, sound recording, and so forth, are the subject of the agreement, and what form they will take.

Failing to adequately describe the content to be incorporated can be fatal to the enforceability of your license agreement. In one recent case, for example, the court held that an agreement authorizing a publisher to publish a collection of the copyright holder's short stories was unenforceable because the relevant language of the agreement lacked "definite and certain essential terms" and failed to "provide the court with a means of determining the intent of the parties." In particular, the agreement did not provide a minimum or maximum number of stories or pages to be included, nor did it indicate who would decide which stories would be included in the collection.[1]

2. Scope of Rights Granted

One of the most important chapter, sections in a content license agreement is the one in which the copyright holder (or its authorized agent) grants you selected rights to use the content, and imposes restrictions on the exercise of those rights. In analyzing this chapter, section of the license, you must consider both the activities that you will be authorized to engage in, and the limitations imposed on your right to engage in those activities.

Specifically, it is important to ensure that you obtain the right to engage in the activities necessary to accomplish your proposed use of the content (e.g., reproduce, adapt, distribute, perform, and display the licensed content as part of your multimedia product). You must also ensure that any limitations imposed on those rights (e.g., restrictions relating to media, distribution channel, platform, operating system, countries, languages, term, and so forth) do not unduly hamper or interfere with the multimedia product you propose to produce.

If you exceed the scope of the rights granted to you, you run the risk of being liable for copyright infringement and the issuance of an injunction prohibiting the further distribution of your multimedia product, as well as liability for damages.[2]

2.1 What Activities Are Authorized?

The owner of the copyright in the content you are licensing normally possesses the exclusive right to engage in five basic activities: to reproduce the content, to adapt the content (i.e., prepare derivative works based on the content), to distribute the content, to display the content publicly, and to perform the content publicly.[3] Thus, the first issue you should consider is which of the foregoing activities you will need permission to engage in.

Generally, the process of producing a multimedia title will require, at a minimum, that you obtain reproduction rights, adaption rights, and distribution rights. In addition, you may also need the right to publicly display the content, at least for marketing and promotional purposes, and, in some cases, the right to publicly perform the content. Each of these rights, to the extent they are necessary, should be clearly set forth in the license grant from the copyright holder.

2.1.1 Reproduction Right. The reproduction right (i.e., the right to copy the licensed content) is the most fundamental right that you must have with respect to the content being licensed. (The reproduction right is explained in chapter 3, section 4.1.) Even creating a single copy of a multimedia title that includes the licensed content requires that you make a copy of the licensed content. And, of course, if you will be making additional copies of the multimedia title for distribution (either for use on a limited basis, such as internally within your organization, or for distribution on a massive scale to the public), you will need to secure the right to copy the licensed content.

It is important to understand that several forms of "copying" take place in the process of developing, marketing, and using a multimedia product. All such forms of copying must be covered by the rights granted under the license.

First, copying of content occurs in the process of producing a multimedia work, in that the content is "copied" into the work itself. Scanning and digitizing a photograph, sampling a sound recording, and retyping text are all acts of copying that are frequently required for development of a multimedia product. Second, when the multimedia work is manufactured for distribution (such as on a CD-ROM disc), this constitutes additional acts of copying. Third, each time the multimedia work is used by an end user, loading the content into the memory of a computer for display on the user's video screen constitutes yet another form of copying.[4] Finally, to the extent that the multimedia work allows the user to print out a hard copy of the content (regardless of whether that content is text, photos, images, or sound), this constitutes yet another form of copying. It is important that the license authorize all of these forms of copying so that there is no ambiguity or misunderstanding.

There are also related forms of copying that you may want to consider. For example, you may want to include text, photographs, or other graphic art both in your multimedia product and in accompanying documentation, promotional literature, or advertising materials. If you intend to use the content for any of these purposes, it is important to ensure that the license authorizes the contemplated forms of copying.

2.1.2 Adaptation Right. In any situation where licensed content will be modified in any respect, it is important that the license authorize you to so adapt the content—that is, to prepare a derivative work based on the content. This right, which is frequently referred to as an adaptation right, is essential if you will be making any change in the licensed content. (The adaptation right is explained in chapter 3, section 4.2).

Taking content originally prepared for one market or medium (e.g., theatrical motion pictures), and using that content in another market and medium (e.g., multimedia delivered on CD-ROM or via interactive television) often requires certain adaptations to the content as part of the process of incorporating it into the multimedia product. At a minimum, you must have the right to digitize content that is not provided in digital form.

In addition, the multimedia development process frequently involves more than simply incorporating or copying content into a multimedia title. In many cases, the content is further adapted, modified, or altered. Thus, for example, the pitch or tone of a digitally sampled song may be altered; the appearance of a still image may be modified or morphed; text may be edited, rewritten, or revised; and content in general may be further altered, divided, modified, and/or enhanced as part of the multimedia product development. And if the content is to be translated into a foreign language, this also constitutes an adaptation (i.e., the preparation of a derivative work), for which permission is also required. Accordingly, in such cases, it is typically necessary to secure adaptation rights.

Ideally, the license should grant you adaptation rights without imposing any restrictions on the type or number of changes or modifications that you can make in the licensed content. However, many writers, musicians, actors, and other creative persons who are concerned with their image and reputation in the industry may object to allowing any adaptation of their work.[5] They may feel that, in order to protect the quality of their artistic expression, or their own reputation, it is necessary that they control certain aspects of the manner in which the content they created is used in a multimedia work, or at least that they have the right to review and veto any proposed uses that they feel diminish the quality of the work or injure their reputation. As one court has noted: "it is the writer or performer . . . who suffers the consequences of the mutilation, for the public will have only the final product by which to evaluate the work."[6]

Consequently, it is common in content licenses to find provisions whereby authors assert control over the use made of their work. In other words, the author will seek to obtain the equivalent of moral rights (i.e., the right to protect the work's integrity and to be identified as its creator) by a contractual arrangement. (Moral rights are explained in chapter 3, section 4.6).

There are a variety of ways in which artists may want to control the use of their work. These may include limitations or prohibitions on any adaptations or alterations of the work, a requirement that the author's name be displayed in a certain manner in connection with the use of the work, limitations or prohibitions on the use of less than the entire work, and restrictions relating to the modification or destruction of the work. In some cases, the copyright holder insists on a right to review and approve the adaptations before they are used.

In any case where limits are imposed on the adaptation right, (and this is common), you need to ensure that they are consistent with your planned used of the content.

In those cases where you obtain the right to adapt content for use in a multimedia product, you should also obtain a waiver of any moral rights held by the original author. While the moral rights issue is not resolved in the United States, future developments may bring moral rights law in the United States more in line with its European counterpart. It is therefore better to address the issue by obtaining a waiver than to take a chance on uncertain future developments. An example of such a waiver is

> Author hereby waives any and all moral rights or any similar rights with respect to the Work and agrees not to institute, support, maintain, or permit any action or lawsuit on the ground that any multimedia product produced hereunder constitutes an infringement of any moral right or any similar right, or is in any way a defamation or mutilation of the Work or a part thereof or of the reputation of the Author, or contains unauthorized variations, alterations, modifications, changes or translations.

Moreover, such a waiver can be critical if you intend to distribute your multimedia product outside the United States, in jurisdictions where moral rights are particularly important. Accordingly, any multimedia product destined for European markets where moral rights are recognized and enforced should, to the extent possible, anticipate and address moral rights claims that could be raised by foreign artists or by American artists in an international forum. Note, however, that in some countries a waiver of an author's moral rights is not allowed.

2.1.3 Distribution Right.   If you will be distributing copies of your multimedia title outside of your organization, it will be necessary to obtain the right to distribute the licensed content (as part of the multimedia title you develop). The distribution right is separate and distinct from the right to copy. (The distribution right is explained in chapter 3, section 4.3). If you merely obtain the right to copy the licensed content, you will not be authorized to distribute the copies that you make. Accordingly, for virtually all content licenses, the right to distribute will be another right you must obtain.

An example of the consequences of failing to obtain the right of distribution occurred in a case involving a license to synchronize a musical composition for use in the film *Medium Cool*.[7] The license in that case gave the **licensee** the right to record "in any manner, medium, form or language" the words and music of the musical composition involved, and it granted the right to make copies of these recordings and to perform the music everywhere. But there was no express language authorizing distribution of the copies to the public by sale or rental. The question arose whether this license included the right to distribute videocassettes of the film. The court held that it did not.

Normally the right to distribute content includes the right to distribute it by sale or by rental, lease, or lending. However, if the content you are licensing is a sound recording or a **computer program**, you should be aware that the Copyright Act specifically prohibits any rental of works of this type without the permission of the copyright owner.[8] If you merely obtain the right to distribute a sound recording or computer program as part of your multimedia product, you may find that you are unable to rent your multimedia product. If the right to rent your multimedia product is likely to be important, you need to secure from the content owner a specific grant of the right to rent the sound recording or computer program involved.

2.1.4 Public Performance Right.   The public performance right is normally not important for multimedia products that will be sold or licensed on CD-ROM for in-home use.[9] (The public performance right is explained in chapter 3, section 4.4). However, if you contemplate developing a product that will be transmitted via a cable television system to its subscribers (e.g., interactive television), or operated in a public setting (such as a kiosk or information center at a tourist attraction or museum, or for use at a seminar, conference, or public meeting) where it can be seen and/or heard by the public, obtaining the right to perform the content publicly will be important. The only exception is situations where the licensed content is a sound recording. The Copyright Act does not include any right of performance in sound recordings.[10] (See chapter 18, section 1.1.4).

2.1.5 Public Display Right.　If the licensed content consists of still photographs or images, or motion picture or animation in which any individual images will be displayed publicly in a nonsequential manner (e.g., a single image displayed on a screen in a conference hall), it will be necessary to obtain the right to display the content publicly. (The public display right is explained in chapter 3, section 4.5). As with the public performance right, however, the right is not applicable to sound recordings.[11] (See chapter 18, section 1.1.4).

2.2 What Limitations are Imposed on the Rights Granted?

In addition to specifying the activities authorized by the license (e.g., copy, adapt, distribute, and so forth), you must also consider the limitations that the copyright holder seeks to impose on your rights to engage in each of those activities. As owner of the copyright, the **licensor** can prescribe whatever conditions or restrictions it desires on the grant of rights that it makes.[12] For example, if the copyright holder limits your right to use the content in your multimedia work to a given medium (e.g., CD-ROM), then you cannot distribute your multimedia work in a different medium (e.g., interactive television) so long as it incorporates the content subject to the restrictions. As one court has noted: "A copyright proprietor must be allowed substantial freedom to limit licenses to perform his work in public to defined periods and areas or audiences".[13]

The copyright holder can impose a virtually unlimited number of different types of restrictions on your use of the content. These include restricting use of the content to a specific multimedia work, limitations regarding the nature of the media in which the content may be incorporated (e.g., CD-ROM, diskette, videodisc, television, cable broadcast, and so forth), limitations as to the platform on which the multimedia product incorporating the content can operate (e.g., Windows, Apple, Macintosh, Unix, and so forth), limitations as to the market in which the product can be distributed (e.g., educational market, consumer market, business market, legal market, and so forth), and limitations as to the territory in which the multimedia product containing the content can be distributed (e.g., United States, North America, Europe, and so forth).

This issue is sometimes referred to by the use of the shorthand terms **limited rights** and **unlimited rights.** That is, when there are no limits imposed on the scope of your right to engage in the activities authorized by the license (e.g., copy, adopt, distribute), the license is said to be an unlimited rights license. In that case, you can use the content licensed to you without any restrictions as to media, distribution channel, territory, hardware or software platform, and so on. On the other hand, a limited rights license will typically restrict your use of the content in a variety of ways, such as purpose, media, distribution channel, territory, market, term, and so on. However, the license fee for a limited rights license is normally lower than the fee for an unlimited rights license.

This is a major issue for both parties. Generally, the copyright holder will seek to limit the scope of the rights granted to you to the minimum possible, whereas you will usually want to obtain the most expansive grant that you can. The broader the scope of your rights, the greater your flexibility to leverage your investment in as many products, platforms, media, and territories as possible.

Accordingly, when you are contemplating entering into a limited rights license, you should evaluate the scope of each of the relevant rights that you require in order to ensure that you acquire a license broad enough to encompass the full scope of your anticipated use. This requires consideration of issues such as whether you need an exclusive or nonexclusive license, the media on which the content will be distributed (e.g., CD-ROM, CD-I, videodisc, diskette, broadcast television, and cable television), the platform on which the multimedia product will operate (e.g., PC, Apple, CD-I, 3DO, and so forth), the operating system under which your multimedia product will operate (such as MS-DOS, Windows, OS/2, Macintosh, and Unix), the language in which the content will appear, the countries in which your multimedia product will be marketed, the term for which the license is required, and so forth.[14]

If obtaining a broad license is impossible or too costly, try to negotiate as many options for additional uses as you can so you can avoid having to get additional licenses at a later time. First, however, carefully review the specific limited rights you require. In many cases, a license granting only such limited rights will be obtainable at a much lower cost than an unlimited rights license. Accordingly, it is appropriate to look at some of these limitations for further detail.

2.2.1 Specific Title. Frequently, content is licensed for use only in a particular specified work. Use of the content in any other work would exceed the scope of the license, and constitute copyright infringement. Accordingly, it is important to determine whether you would like to use the content in works other than the work currently in production, and if so, to obtain an expanded grant of rights.

As a corollary issue, you should consider whether there is a possibility of publishing sequels or subsequent editions or versions of your multimedia title. If so, it is important that the license authorize the use of the content in such subsequent versions.

2.2.2 Media. Content is frequently licensed only for use in a particular medium, such as print, phonorecord, film, videotape, compact disc, CD-ROM, diskette, cassette tape, computer tape, videodisc, broadcast television, and cable television. It is important that you obtain rights to use the content on the media contemplated for your project, and if appropriate, on such additional media as may possibly be used in the future.

Restrictions as to the media on which content may be used frequently cause problems when you want to use the content in a medium that is different from that originally licensed, even if closely related to it. This frequently occurs when a newly developed media, not contemplated by either of the parties at the time of the license, becomes available.[15]

From your perspective, the solution to this problem is to incorporate very broad and expansive language into the contract authorizing you to exploit the content "by any present or future method now known or hereafter developed." Although only a handful of courts have analyzed language of this type, most have held that it authorizes the licensee to use the content on later-developed technology not contemplated by the parties at the time the license was issued.[16] However, as you might imagine, it is often difficult to obtain such a broad license.

Even in cases where you are willing to accept a license that restricts use of the content to a very specific medium (e.g., CD-ROM), you should consider the issue carefully. You may need rights to use the content in another medium associated with the CD-ROM. For example, you may want to reproduce text or photographs in a printed manual that accompanies the product, or on the packaging material. Similarly, you may want to reproduce some of the content on both printed and audiovisual advertisements for your multimedia product. If any of these cases are possibilities, be sure to acquire the appropriate rights.

2.2.3 Territories.   It is important to consider where distribution will take place. Content licenses frequently limit use and distribution to a specific geographical area, such as the United States and/or selected other countries. Rights should be obtained for the territory in which the multimedia work will be marketed (such as the United States, the United States and Canada, worldwide, and so forth). Although a worldwide right is generally preferable, you should at least ensure that the scope of rights obtained is sufficient to match the contemplated distribution of your multimedia product.

2.2.4 Hardware and Software Platforms.   Content licenses frequently restrict the hardware and/or software platform on which the multimedia product incorporating the content can operate. For example, the scope of the license may limit use of the content to an IBM-compatible PC platform, an Apple/Macintosh platform, a 3DO platform, a Nintendo or Sega platform, and so forth. Likewise, content licenses also frequently restrict the operating system under which the multimedia product will operate. Examples include the DOS or Windows operating system platforms, the Apple operating system, the Unix operating system, the 3DO, Sega, and Nintendo systems, and so forth.

2.2.5 Exclusive or Nonexclusive.   Most multimedia content licenses are nonexclusive, thereby leaving the copyright holder free to license the same content to others. However, in certain situations it may be appropriate to seek an exclusive license. Because this will deprive the copyright holder of the right to relicense the same content to anyone else, and thus of the right to make additional revenue from the licensing of the content, the copyright holder will typically charge a higher license fee and require additional protection. Such protection may include larger royalty payments, specified marketing commitments, guaranteed minimum royalties, and automatic conversion to a nonexclusive license if certain royalty projections are not met.

In most cases, an exclusive license will not be necessary. However, if you are trying to be the first to develop a multimedia title with respect to a specific issue for specific content (e.g., the films of a particular director or artist), you may need some sort of exclusivity to ensure that your market is not undermined by competitors. But even in this case, you typically only need exclusivity in a limited area (e.g., digital reproduction in a multimedia title), thus leaving the content owner free to license the content to others for use in other media.

2.3 The Problem of New Uses and Old Licenses

As noted above, content licenses frequently limit use of the content to a work embodied in a particular medium, such as motion picture, television, CD, CD-ROM, videocassette, or cable broadcast. As new technologies continue to develop, however, questions frequently arise as to whether a license limited to one medium (e.g., television) includes the right to use the copyrighted content in a different (but similar or related) medium (such as cable television, videocassette, or videodisc).

In one recent case, for example, a licensee who had the exclusive perpetual right to exhibit the cartoon series *Rocky and His Friends* on television and in theaters without limitation" sought to exhibit the cartoons on cable television and to market them for use with home videocassette and videodisc players.[17] When this use was challenged by the owner of the copyright in the cartoon series, the court held that the license did not extend to videocassettes or videodiscs for home use "because these media comprise an entirely different device involving an entirely different concept and technology from that involved in a television broadcast." On the other hand, the court was unable to decide whether the right to exhibit the cartoons on television included "cable television" without obtaining more evidence to help it ascertain the intent of the parties when they entered into the agreements in 1959 and 1960. At that time, cable television existed but "had not yet been commercially exploited as a system for the mass distribution of paid television programming."

This issue can be a very important one for you in two ways. First, in many situations you will have to evaluate whether or not the person from whom you are seeking a license has the right to grant it to you. For example, if you wanted to license rights to use a portion of a cartoon series from someone who (as in the case noted above) had the right to exhibit the cartoons "on television and in theaters without limitation," you may have to make a judgment call as to whether the licensor has the necessary rights to grant you a license to use the cartoon series in a CD-ROM or interactive television multimedia product.

Second, with respect to the rights you obtain in a content license agreement, you may in the future need to decide whether you can distribute the multimedia product in a new medium not expressly contemplated by the license agreement.

As a general rule, when courts are asked to construe copyright licenses, they apply general contract law principles, and attempt to determine the intent of the parties. However, that is often rather difficult, especially in situations where you want to use the content on media not in existence (and thus not contemplated) at the time the license was created. It also becomes a problem when you want to use the content on media very similar to the media described in the license, but not literally identical with it (e.g., where the license refers to "television" and you want to distribute the content on "videocassette").[18]

When courts attempt to resolve disputes relating to the scope of the license grant regarding media, they consider a variety of factors including:

1. whether the technology was known or anticipated at the time of the license grant;[19]

2. whether the license specifically contemplated use of the content on media or with technology not yet known or developed;[20]

3. the experience and sophistication of the parties to the agreement;[21]

4. whether the licensor reserved any other rights or uses; and[22]

5. whether the court follows the rule that all rights not specifically granted are reserved to the licensor, or alternatively, the rule that all rights not specifically withheld are considered granted to the licensee.[23]

Generally, where the grant of rights is very broad and sweeping with respect to the media on which the content can be used, courts have no trouble concluding that the license includes media not necessarily contemplated by the parties at the time they entered into the license. In one case, for example, licenses executed in the 1930s and 1940s granted the right to exhibit certain films "by any present or future methods or means," and by "any other means now known or unknown."[24] The court concluded that this language made clear that the rights to distribute and exhibit the films "would be without limitation unless otherwise specified and further indicat[ed] that future technological advances in methods of reproduction, transmission, and exhibition would inure to the benefit of" the parties to whom the rights were granted. Thus, the court concluded that the licensee had the right to sell videocassettes of the films.

In another case, the issue was whether a license that granted to a film company the right to use certain songs on the soundtrack of the film *American Graffiti* also gave the film company the right to distribute that film on videodiscs and videocassettes.[25] Here again, the contract's language was very broad, including the right to "exhibit, distribute, [and] exploit . . . [the film] perpetually throughout the world by any means or methods now or hereafter known." The court decided that this language was "extremely broad and completely unambiguous, and precludes any need . . . for an exhaustive list of specific potential uses of the film." It was "obvious" that the contract could "fairly be read" as "including newly developed media, and the absence of any specific mention . . . of videotapes and videocassettes [was] thus insignificant."[26] In fact, the court went on to say that it would not look behind the written contract to determine whether the parties actually intended it to encompass this area. Instead, it stated that it was "immaterial whether the copyright holder anticipated all potential future developments in the manner of exhibiting motion pictures," in light of the expansive terms of the contract itself.[27]

Similarly, in a 1992 case, entertainer James Brown sued the defendants for using a clip from his television performance in their film *The Commitments*, arguing that an agreement he signed in 1964, shortly before performing on the television show, did not grant the right to use his performance in films, film promotions, and videocassettes.[28] The court considered Brown's argument that the grant of rights could not be read "to encompass the right to the videocassette market, since it was not specified nor was it even in existence" in 1964. However, it concluded that, "in this case, the sweeping contractual language—which grants the right to reproduce the performance 'perpetually and throughout the world . . . in and by all media and means whatever'—may 'fairly be read' to include release on videocassettes despite their nonexistence at the time the agreement was made."[29]

By contrast, where the language used in the contract is not so broad, the court may take a different approach. For example, in a case involving a license to synchronize music for use in the film *Medium Cool*, including the right to "exhibit" the film "by means of television," the court held that the license did not include the right to distribute videocassettes of the film.[30]

The language of the license gave the licensee the right to *record* "in any manner, medium, form or language" the words and music of the musical composition involved, and it granted the right to *make copies* of these recordings and to *perform* the music everywhere. But there was no express language authorizing *distribution* of the copies to the public by sale or rental. The question then became whether the distribution of videocassettes through sale and rental to the public for viewing in their homes fit within the paragraph of the contract that permitted performance.

The court decided that the distribution of videocassettes did not fit within that paragraph because the paragraph limited the right to perform to (1) exhibition of the film to audiences in motion picture theaters and other places of public entertainment where movies are customarily exhibited (this kind of exhibition was clearly not involved) and (2) exhibition by means of television. The licensee argued that the distribution of videocassettes for showing in private homes was the same as exhibition by means of television, but the court disagreed, stating that exhibition of a film on television "differs fundamentally" from exhibition by means of a VCR.

The court noted the differences between television exhibitions of a film and those using a VCR: Television requires an intermediary, such as a network, to send the television signal into the home. Further, the consumer has no way to capture any part of it; "when the program is over it vanishes, and the consumer is powerless to replay it" because television signals are "ephemeral." Videocassettes, on the other hand, are "markedly different" because viewers control the time and nature of what they see; they are liberated from any intermediary and the other constraints of television. Thus, these two media "have very little in common besides the fact that a [television monitor] may be used both to receive television signals and to exhibit a videocassette."[31]

Thus, the court viewed the two media as inherently different. But the court added that perhaps "the primary reason" for construing the contract to limit the right granted was that VCRs for home use were not invented nor known in 1969, when the license was executed, and the copyright holder "could not have assumed that the public would have free and virtually unlimited access to the film in which the composition was played."[32] Instead, he must have assumed that the film would be shown only in theaters and by television networks. "By the same token, the original licensee could not have bargained for, or paid for, the rights associated with videocassette reproduction."[33]

Unlike the other cases mentioned, where the language of the license was extremely broad and evidenced an intention to *include* future technological advances, in this case the license not only lacked such broad language but also expressly reserved to the copyright holder all rights not expressly granted. For that reason, the license did not grant the right to use the composition in connection with videocassette production and distribution of the film.

The courts have not been entirely consistent in interpreting licenses that are silent as to the licensee's rights to use the content in a particular medium. Some courts interpret the language of a license in an expansive manner, favorable to the licensee. As one court has noted: "If the words are broad enough to cover the new use, it seems fairer that the burden of framing and negotiating an exception should fall on the grantor; if [the grantor] or his assignors had desired to limit . . . [the scope of the license] . . . they could have said so."[34] Other courts, however, take a very narrow view of the license, finding that if the particular media in issue was not specifically mentioned, then no rights were granted with respect to it.[35]

There is no doubt, however, that the more sweeping the language, the greater the likelihood that the license will later be viewed by a court as including media and technologies that have not yet been developed. If you cannot obtain such sweeping language, however, you should try to get the most expansive language possible because some courts are likely to construe anything other than broad language in a way that narrows the scope of the rights granted.

You may also encounter a situation where a license or other grant of rights is already in existence because it was negotiated at an earlier time by others. If this situation arises, and you are forced to deal with the ambiguous terms agreed to by others at a previous time, the likelihood of getting an expansive interpretation of the license by a court is much lower.

3. Term

In any agreement in which the copyright holder grants rights to use or distribute its content to others, it may seek to specify the length of time for which those rights are granted. The licensor may want to limit the term of the license to a few years (e.g., three to five years), whereas you will normally want to obtain a perpetual license to use the content, at least with respect to the multimedia product in which it is to be initially incorporated.

It is important to understand that upon the expiration of the term of any license to use any content incorporated within your multimedia title, your right to continue to copy and distribute that title with the included content will also cease. That is, even though you may be the owner of the copyright to the multimedia title,[36] so long as your work includes the content owned by others and used with permission, you will not be able to continue to copy and distribute your own work if your right to copy and distribute the incorporated content expires.

There are many ways in which the term of the agreement can be structured. Typically, the term is perpetual, for a specified period of years or until a certain date, but it can also be indefinite and subject to being terminated by either party upon a specified number of days' or months' advance notice.

When a content license does not specifically state the terms or duration of the rights granted, courts will generally find that the license will remain in effect for the duration of the then-existing copyright term of the work.[37] However, it is important to note that term limitations may be implied from the scope of the rights granted in the license. For example, if the license is limited to use of the content in a multimedia work consisting of a series of titles (e.g., "Newsweek Interactive"), then if publication of that particular series ceases, the license will presumably terminate.[38]

If you obtained the license directly from the original author of the work, the author has a statutory right to terminate the license between thirty-five and forty years after the date of execution of the license, as well as a contract right to terminate the license earlier, if the license agreement so provides.[39] (Termination rights are explained in chapter 3, section 5.2).

If you want to get a license to use content that was first published before January 1, 1978, it may be important to determine whether the copyright is in its original or renewal term.[40] (The original and renewal terms of copyrights in works created before 1978 are explained in chapter 3, section 5.2). If the copyright is in its original term and the author dies before the time for renewal of the copyright, the heirs of the author have the right to recapture the copyright at the end of the original copyright term, and at that point terminate any license granted to a multimedia developer. This is sometimes referred to as the *Rear Window* problem, derived from the Alfred Hitchcock movie of the same name that became caught up in this issue. The *Rear Window* problem is discussed in chapter 3, section 5.2. This issue is of practical significance only for works first published during the years 1966 through 1977.

4. Credits

The copyright holder may want to be given credit in the work in which the content will be used. Consequently, many licenses will specify the wording of the credit, and in some cases, the location of the credit, the size and prominence of the display of the credit, and other similar information.

Displaying credits in a multimedia work composed of hundreds or thousands of separate copyrightable works may present serious logistical difficulties. Moreover, unless the credits are all displayed in one place (e.g., on one of the opening screens, in a sign-off sequence, or in the printed matter that accompanies the work), the nonlinear nature of multimedia works may otherwise make display of credits rather cumbersome. For example, displaying a credit each time the user selects a particular picture or causes the work to play a particular sound recording may be cumbersome at best. It may not be very desirable from an aesthetic point of view either.

5. Ownership of Content

The issue of ownership should be dealt with in every license agreement. Specifically, you should make certain that the licensor actually owns the content or is authorized by the owner to license to you the specific rights you need. Thus, you may want to insist that the agreement contain a warranty of ownership and/or authority to license the content. In some cases, you may want to go further, and review the contracts by which the licensor obtained the rights you seek to license, and/or by conducting your own search of the copyright office records.

It is extremely important to verify that the licensor owns, or at least has the right to license, all of the component elements of the content being licensed. For example, when licensing a movie clip containing a musical performance, the owner of the copyright in the movie may have obtained only a license from the author of the book on which the movie is based, for which license is limited to creating a derivative work in film, and to which does not extend to further licensing for use in electronic media. Likewise, the music performed within the movie may be the subject of at least two separate copyrights, one in the musical composition and one in the recording. The owner of the copyright in the film may or may not have rights in the copyrights to the musical composition and the recording of the song.

In a case like that one, it is important to document the ownership (or at least the right to license) with respect to each of the copyrightable components of the content being licensed, and to obtain warranties of title and indemnification from the licensor.

A good illustration of this problem can be seen in a case involving "Monty Python Flying Circus" television programs created by the BBC pursuant to a license granted by Monty Python, the owner of the copyright in the scripts on which the television programs were based.[41] The license granted Monty Python optimum control over proposed changes to the scripts, and did not grant the BBC any rights to alter a program once it had been recorded. Nonetheless, the BBC granted a license to Time-Life to distribute the programs in the United States, and granted Time-Life the right to edit the programs for "insertion of commercials, applicable censorship or governmental . . . rules and regulations, and National Association of Broadcasters and time segment requirements." But exercising this right, the court held, would constitute copyright infringement. That is, even though the BBC may have been the copyright owner in these television programs that it produced under license from Monty Python, its use of those television programs (e.g., its license to Time-Life) was limited by the terms of the license granted to the BBC by Monty Python for use of the underlying script.[42] Consequently, the court prohibited ABC (Time-Life's licensee) from broadcasting the edited program, because such alteration exceeded the scope of the license that the BBC was entitled to grant.[43]

The net result was that ABC could not rely on the fact that editing was permitted in the agreement between the BBC and Time-Life, or the agreement between Time-Life and ABC. Because the BBC was not entitled to alter the recordings once made, the "BBC's permission to allow Time-Life, and hence ABC, to edit the programs appears to have been a nullity."[44]

A similar problem occurred when Paramount Pictures licensed ABC television to broadcast the motion picture *Reds*.[45] Paramount granted ABC a license to broadcast the movie three times over a period of 4-1/2 years for a fee of $6.5 million. The agreement also granted ABC the right to edit the film "for purposes of time segment requirements. . . ." However, the financing and licensing agreements for the original production of the movie granted Warren Beatty final cutting rights on the movie, including "the right to prevent Paramount from allowing a television network to abridge the picture for any reason other than censorship reasons." Thus, ABC's intention to cut approximately 6 minutes and 25 seconds from the film was held to violate Beatty's contractual right of final cut on the film. In other words, when Paramount granted a license to ABC that authorized ABC to edit the movie for time cuts, Paramount exceeded the rights granted to it by Beatty, and thus the grant was invalid.

When addressing the issue of ownership, you also need to consider the issue of separation of rights. (Separation of rights is explained in chapter 3, section 6). Under separation of rights provisions contained in contracts governing the creation, license, or assignment of content, it is possible that the copyright in the work has been split up among a number of people in a variety of ways. For example, the publisher of a book may have only the right to publish the book in print in North America, with a second publisher having the right to publish the book in print in foreign countries, and the original author retaining the right to publish the book in electronic form. In such a case, negotiating with the publisher who holds the North American print publication rights would be of little value, since that publisher would not be in a position to grant you the multimedia rights that you require.

It is important to understand that the question of ownership of rights in content can be a very complicated subject. Consequently, the issue of who controls the rights to license specific content may not always be clear. In fact, in many cases, you cannot assume that someone actually owns the rights they believe they own. This is because many of the contracts under which they claim rights in content do not specifically address multimedia. This problem arises quite frequently when you are dealing with content owners who obtained their rights pursuant to older license agreements that did not specifically contemplate the technology in which you proposed to use the content. This matter is discussed in this chapter, section 2.3. As a consequence, it may be unclear whether the person with whom you are dealing has the right to grant you the license you need for your multimedia project.

Dealing with this problem may require a thorough review of the contracts by which the person with whom you are dealing claims to have rights in the content. In addition, it may be appropriate to conduct your own independent copyright office search, or other forms of due diligence, in order to determine who else might claim rights in the content you seek to license.

6. Rights of Other Parties

In some situations, obtaining a license to use content from the copyright holder may not be sufficient. Additional permissions may also be required from persons who have contractually reserved certain rights in the content. For example, well-known actors, actresses, and recording artists may have reserved certain rights to control the use of the film and/or sound recordings of their performances. In such cases, even though they do not retain the copyright, it will be necessary to secure their permission. Similarly, it is generally necessary to obtain releases from all recognizable persons appearing in photographs and film clips being licensed. Moreover, with television, film, and sound recordings, payments may be required by union or guild agreements in addition to the payments made to the copyright holder. These issues are discussed in detail in chapter 21.

Where such third-party rights are a factor, the license agreement should address them, and determine who is responsible for obtaining the appropriate permission or release and who is responsible for paying any relevant fees. If the copyright holder is to undertake this task, the license should obtain an appropriate warranty and indemnity with respect to the issue. On the other hand, if you are charged with the responsibility of undertaking the task, keep in mind that many license agreements will provide that they do not become effective until you have obtained all the appropriate releases and consents. The bottom line, however, is that these issues must be addressed and adequately dealt with. You cannot simply assume that the copyright holder will handle these issues.

7. Delivery

In many cases you may already possess a copy of the content (hopefully lawfully) and simply need permission to use it. This is likely to be the case, for example, with text taken from a readily available book. In other cases, however, you may not have a copy of what you want, or the quality of the copy you have is not good enough to meet your needs. In these situations, you need to obtain the material from someone.

The copyright holder of the content may not be in the business of providing copies, or may not even have a usable copy. In this case, you will look to the copyright holder for permission, but will have to look elsewhere for a usable copy. But if the copyright holder will be delivering a copy, you should address two basic issues.

First, what deliverables, if any, has the content owner agreed to provide? It is frequently important that you obtain a copy of the content in a particular form or format, and/or on a particular media. Thus, for example, it might be appropriate to specify that a recording of a song be delivered in digital form on a master tape or disc.

Second, when will the content be delivered? You need to work out an arrangement that will give you some assurance of getting the content within the timetable you require, while at the same time ensuring that the licensor is not expected to meet an unrealistic schedule.

8. License Fees and Royalties

The cost of the rights licensed is of primary concern to the parties in every license transaction. How much will a copyright holder charge you for the right to use or market its content? There is no limit to the number of ways in which the fee provision of a content license can be structured. The license fees, royalties, or other charges used in a content license vary greatly, depending on such factors as the type of content involved, its popularity, the amount being used, the nature and scope of the rights granted, industry custom, and so forth. Thus, it is important to examine some of the factors that should be considered in structuring the fee provision within a content license agreement. In addition, the payment terms, whatever they are, should be spelled out clearly and completely so that there are no disputes or disagreements between the parties.

The method of payment for a content license typically takes the form of a single fixed up-front license fee (i.e., a paid-up license, sometimes referred to as a *buyout*), or a royalty for each copy of the resulting multimedia product sold, or a combination of the two.

The *paid-up license* or *buyout* typically involves a single one-time license fee paid to the copyright holder in advance, in exchange for the specific rights granted in the license. Typically this fee is paid at the time the license is granted, although sometimes it may be paid in installments over a fixed period of time. The paid-up license bears no relationship to the number of copies of the multimedia work that you distribute, or the income that you receive.

Royalties, on the other hand are calculated on the basis of the number of copies of the multimedia work containing the content that you distribute, the income that you receive, or some other sales-related calculation. Two types of royalty structures are generally used. The first is an arrangement under which you pay a percentage of the income you receive from the distribution of the multimedia work containing the licensed content. Under this arrangement, the copyright holder's income will depend upon both the price you charge to your customers and on your success in the distribution of the multimedia work containing the licensed content. With the second type of royalty, you pay a fixed fee for each copy of the multimedia work containing the licensed content that you distribute. In this case, the copyright holder is assured of receiving a set fee for each copy of the content that is distributed, regardless of the price you charge.

Sometimes, the paid-up license fee and the royalty form of payment are combined. Such a payment structure typically involves a lower up-front fee (in many cases designed to cover administrative costs and to provide a minimal return to the content copyright holder), combined with a somewhat lower royalty rate for sales of the ultimate product. Obviously, the number of possible combinations and permutations of fixed-fee and royalty-rate licensing schemes is limited only by the imagination of the parties involved. Variations can include fees that increase or decrease based on the number of copies sold, the time frame in which they are sold, the markets to which they are sold, and other variables.

In situations involving both up-front fees and per-copy royalties, it is to your advantage to specify (if applicable) that the up-front fee is considered as an advance against future royalties.

Regardless of the payment form, it is also important to address the question of when payment is due. Generally, payment can be required on a specified date (such as March 15), at specified periodic intervals (such as monthly or quarterly), or upon the occurrence of specified events. Events that are often used to trigger payment obligations include the execution of the contract, the distribution of copies of the multimedia product containing the content, on an installment basis, at predefined intervals (as in a distribution or publishing arrangement), and so forth.

If the contract obligates you to pay a royalty for each copy of the multimedia work you distribute, it will also require you to keep complete records of all of your sales and to give the owner the right to audit those records to ensure that royalty payments are being promptly made.

9. Warranties

Ideally, you should obtain warranties from the content owner that (1) it is the owner of all applicable rights to the content, (2) it has the right to grant the license granted, (3) the grant is free and clear of all liens and encumbrances, (4) the work does not infringe any copyright, trademark, trade secret or other proprietary right of any third party, (5) the rights granted do not violate the rights of publicity or privacy of any third party, and do not constitute a libel or slander of any third party, and (6) they do not violate any other third-party rights. The following is a sample warranty clause:

> Copyright holder represents and warrants that it is the sole and exclusive owner of the copyright to the Work; that it has the power and authority to enter into this agreement; that the Work does not contain any libelous material; that the Work does not infringe any copyright, trade name, trademark, trade secret or other property right of any third party; and that the Work does not invade or violate any right of privacy, personal or proprietary right, or other common law or statutory right of any third party.

It is also important to understand that requesting warranties and representations from the copyright holder (whether or not they are agreed to) frequently encourages the copyright holder to disclose relevant information concerning the content being licensed.

In many situations, the licensor of the content may refuse to make any warranties whatsoever. Instead, the content may be licensed "as is," "with all faults," or otherwise, with no representations or warranties regarding title or otherwise. This is sometimes referred to as a *quitclaim* license. This may frequently be the case when the content involves potentially overlapping copyrights or rights of privacy and publicity. In such a case, if you decide to proceed with use of the content, you should consider conducting your own due diligence search to ensure that you have obtained all of the necessary rights and permissions.

10. Limitation of Liability

Content owners may seek to establish a limit on the scope of their liability for any damages you may suffer through the use of the content or their breach of contract. There are two key ways they can do this: (1) limit the total damages you are entitled to recover, and (2) exclude all liability for consequential damages.

Generally, the amount of a content owner's liability to you for damages can be limited to a dollar amount specified in the contract. Damage limitations are frequently tied to the license fee paid for the content. If the amount chosen is reasonable, the worst that can happen (from the content owner's point of view) is that it will have to refund your money. However, note that after investing heavily in the development and marketing of a multimedia title, merely having the right to a refund of the license fee you paid for one item of content may not be an adequate remedy.

In addition to limiting the dollar amount of any potential liability, content owners can also limit the type of **damages** for which they can be held liable. In particular, they may seek to exclude liability for consequential damages.

Consequential damages, sometimes called **indirect damages** or **special damages,** generally refer to losses that are not directly caused by the copyright holder's breach of contract, but rather as a consequence of the breach. For example, if the content is found to infringe another's copyright, your direct damages might be the cost of obtaining substitute content. But if, as a consequence of the breach you lose a major profitable business deal, your lost profit is considered as consequential damage. Because they can include such lost profits, consequential damages typically represent the licensor's largest potential exposure.

11. Indemnification

In addition to obtaining appropriate warranties, you should seek an indemnification from the copyright holder.

An **indemnification** clause attempts to deal with a situation where a licensor supplies content that infringes the copyright of a third party, violates the publicity rights or privacy rights of a third party, or is otherwise defamatory. It provides you with some protection in the case where you have no way of knowing whether the licensor has a legal right to license the content.

The typical indemnification clause provides that the licensor will defend you and pay any expenses you incur or damages you suffer in the event that you are sued under a certain enumerated list of theories, provided that you meet certain requirements set forth in the clause. One word of caution is in order: The protection provided by an indemnification clause is only as good as the financial strength of the indemnifier.

12. Default

A default section is often included in licenses in order to specify the procedures by which the copyright holder can terminate the license or pursue its other remedies. Specifying what constitutes a breach of the agreement is normally not necessary, since any act contrary to the terms of the contract, or any failure to do what is required by the contract, will be a breach of the agreement. Some breaches are more serious than others, however, and you may wish to limit those that will give the copyright holder the right to terminate the agreement or to invoke other specific types of remedies.

Generally, breach of a license agreement gives rise to a right of rescission that allows the non-breaching party to terminate the agreement.[46] After the agreement is terminated, any further distribution of the licensed content would constitute copyright infringement. However, a breach will justify rescission of a license agreement only when it is of so material and substantial a nature that it affects the very essence of the contract and serves to defeat the object of the parties. In other words, it must constitute a total failure in the performance of the contract.[47]

Another key purpose of a contract section dealing with default is to specify the procedures that must be followed in the event of a default. Ideally, the contract should provide that in the event the copyright holder wants to terminate the license for breach of the agreement, you must be given the written notice of the breach, and a specified number of days to cure the breach. If the breach has not been cured at the expiration of that time period, only then may it terminate the agreement and pursue its other remedies. However, if the breach is cured during that time period, the license should continue in full force.

As a general rule, if you commit a material breach of a license agreement, this gives the licensor a right of rescission that allows it to terminate the agreement. After such a termination, any further use or distribution of the licensed content would constitute infringement.[48] However, a breach will justify termination of a license agreement only when it is so material and substantial that it affects the very essence of the agreement and serves to defeat the party's intentions; the breach must constitute a total failure in the performance of the contract.[49]

13. Right to Assign

An assignment is a transaction in which one party to a contract transfers all of its rights and obligations to someone else. For example, if you have licensed content from a copyright holder, and you wish to transfer your right to use that content to a third party, you would accomplish this by assigning your license agreement to the third party. The third party then steps into your shoes with respect to the license. Note that because all of your rights under the license are transferred by an assignment, you can make this transfer only once.

Do you have the right to assign your license agreement to someone else without the copyright holder's consent? As a general rule, unless the contract states otherwise, a party may assign its rights under a contract.

For that reason, copyright holders frequently seek to insert a clause in the contract prohibiting assignment without its consent. In such a case, you should consider revising the clause to meet your need to assign the license in the event that you decide to sell your entire business, or in the event that you desire to transfer the content to another division or affiliate corporation. In addition, you should try to get a commitment that the copyright holder will not unreasonably withhold its permission for an assignment.

Endnotes

1   *Academy Chicago Publishers v. Cheever*, 578 144 Ill.2d 24, N.E.2d 981, 983-84 (1991).

2   See, e.g., *Marshall v. New Kids On The Block Partnership*, 780 F. Supp 1005, 1009 (S.D.N.Y. 1991).

3   These rights are explained in chapter 3, section 4.

4   *MAI Sys. Corp. v. Peak Computer, Inc.*, 991 F.2d 511 (9th Cir. 1993), *cert. dismissed*, 114 S. Ct. 671 (1994); *Advanced Computer Servs. of Michigan, Inc. v. MAI Sys. Corp.*, 845 F.Supp. 356 (E.D. Va. 1994).

5   See, e.g., *Gilliam v. American Broadcasting Cos.*, 538 F.2d 14 (2d. Cir. 1976) (owner of Monty Python television scripts objected to alteration of television programs that involved the insertion of commercials); *In the Matter of Arbitration between Directors Guild of America, Inc., Warren Beatty, JRS Prods., Inc., Paramount Pictures Corp. and American Broadcasting Cos.*, 6 Ent. L. Rep. No. 12, at 8 (May 1985) (Warren Beatty, the producer, director, and star of the film *Reds* objected to ABC's plan to cut 6 minutes and 25 seconds from the film for time-format purposes).

6   *Gilliam v. American Broadcasting Cos.*, 538 F.2d 14, 24 (2d. Cir. 1976); see also *Preminger v. Columbia Pictures Corp.*, 267 N.Y.S.2d 594 (N.Y. Sup. Ct.), *aff'd*, 269 N.Y.S.2d 913 (N.Y. App. Div.), *aff'd*, 18 N.Y.2d 659, 219 N.E.2d 431, 273 N.Y.S.2d 80 (N.Y. 1966) (director Otto Preminger sued to enjoin cuts in his film *Anatomy of a Murder* for television viewing, asserting that such cuts were "mutilation" that would both destroy the film's commercial value and damage his own reputation).

7   *Cohen v. Paramount Pictures Corp.*, 845 F.2d 851, 853 (9th Cir. 1988).

8   17 U.S.C. § 109(b).

9   If the purchaser of a multimedia title on a CD-ROM disc subsequently wants to publicly perform the multimedia work, it will be necessary for the purchaser to obtain a public performance license with respect to all of the content appearing on the multimedia product. The same, of course, is true for movies on videotape and musical works on CDs that are initially purchased by individuals for home use. They do not come with a public performance right.

10   17 U.S.C. § 114(a).

11   17 U.S.C. § 114(a).

12   "One who obtains permission to use a copyrighted script in the production of a derivative work . . . may not exceed the specific purpose for which permission was granted." *Gilliam v. American Broadcasting Cos.*, 538 F.2d 14, 20 (2d Cir. 1976).

13   *United Artists Tele. Inc. v. Fortnightly Corp.*, 377 F.2d 872, 882 (2d Cir. 1967), *rev'd on other grounds*, 392 U.S. 390, 88 S.Ct. 2084 (1968).

14   For a discussion of the potential problems that can result if the scope of the rights granted is not sufficient for certain contemplated uses, see the discussion regarding the problem of new uses and old licenses in chapter 13, section 2.3.

15   This issue of new uses and old licenses is discussed in chapter 13, section 2.3.

16   See, e.g., *Rooney v. Columbia Pictures Indus., Inc.*, 538 F. Supp. 211, 228-29 (S.D.N.Y.), *aff'd*, 714 F.2d 117 (2d Cir. 1982), *cert. denied*, 460 U.S. 1084 (1983); *Platinum Record Co. v. Lucasfilm, Ltd.*, 566 F. Supp. 226, 228 (D.N.J. 1983).

17   *General Mills, Inc., v. Filmtel Int'l Corp.*, 27 U.S.P.Q. 2d 1638 (N.Y. App. Div. 1993).

18   See e.g., *Cohen v. Paramount Pictures Corp.*, 845 F.2d 851 (9th Cir. 1988) (a license to synchronize music for use in the film *Medium Cool* included the right to "exhibit" the film "by means of television." Court held that this license did *not* include the right to distribute videocassettes of the film).

19   See *Ettore v. Philco Tele. Broadcasting Corp.*, 229 F.2d 481, 488 (3d Cir.), *cert. denied*, 351 U.S. 926 (1956); *Bartsch v. Metro-Goldwyn-Mayer, Inc.*, 391 F.2d 150, 154 (2d Cir.), *cert. denied*, 393 U.S. 826 (1968); *Cohen v. Paramount Pictures Corp.*, 845 F.2d 851, 853-54 (9th Cir. 1988).

20   *Wexley v. KTTV, Inc.*, 108 F. Supp. 558, 559 (S.D. Cal. 1952), *aff'd*, 220 F.2d 438 (9th Cir. 1955) (licensor granted the right to exhibit motion pictures "in any manner and method now or any time hereafter ever known or made available"); *Bartsch v. Metro-Goldwyn-Mayer, Inc.*, 391 F.2d 150, 152-53 (2d Cir.), *cert. denied*, 393 U.S. 826 (1968) (license to reproduce a "musical play or any adaptation or version thereof visually or audibly by the art of cinematography or any process analogous thereto"); *Hellman v. Samuel Goldwyn Prods.*, 26 N.Y.2d 175, 257 N.E.2d 634, 635 (1970) (licensee granted right to exhibit motion pictures "using any methods or devices for such purposes which are now or hereafter known or used"); *Rooney v. Columbia Pictures Indus., Inc.*, 538 F. Supp. 211, 228-29 (S.D.N.Y.) (licensee granted right to use films for various devices "and all other improvements and devices which are now or may hereafter be used in connection with the production and/or exhibition and/or transmission of any present or future kind or motion picture production"), *aff'd*, 714 F.2d 117 (2d Cir. 1982), *cert. denied*, 460 U.S. 1084 (1983).

21   *Warner Bros. Pictures, Inc. v. Columbia Broadcasting Sys.*, 216 F.2d 945, 949 (9th Cir. 1954) (noting that "Warner Bros. Corporation is a large, experienced moving picture producer," and therefore, licenses should be construed "under the assumption that [it] knew what it wanted and that in defining items in the instruments which it desired and intended to take, it included all of the items it was contracting to take"); *Ettore v. Philco Tele. Broadcasting Corp.*, 229 F.2d 481, 491 n.14 (3d Cir.) (court concluded that it was unfair to require a professional prize fighter to have known about the value of television rights in 1936 when he granted a license for movie rights), *cert. denied*, 351 U.S. 926 (1956); *Bartsch v. Metro-Goldwyn-Mayer, Inc.*, 391 F.2d 150, 154 (2d Cir.) (court notes that plaintiff was an "experienced businessman" and therefore, that he is bound by the natural implications of the language he accepted when he had reason to know of the new medium's potential), *cert. denied*, 393 U.S. 826 (1968); *Rey v. Lafferty*, 990 F.2d 1379, 1391 (1st Cir. 1993) (holding that license to distribute *Curious George* film episodes "for television viewing" did not encompass the right to distribute the films in videocassette form and citing the fact that the license was drafted by the licensee, a professional investment firm accustomed to licensing agreements, and signed by the licensor, an elderly woman who did not appear to have participated in its drafting or to have been represented by counsel during the larger part of the transaction).

22   See *Warner Bros. Pictures, Inc., v. Columbia Broadcasting Sys.*, 216 F.2d 945, 949 (9th Cir. 1954).

23　See *Rey v. Lafferty*, 990 F.2d 1379, 1387-88 (1st Cir.), *cert. denied*, 114 S.Ct. 94 (1993); *Bartsch v. Metro-Goldwyn-Mayer, Inc.*, 391 F.2d 150, 155 (2d Cir.), *cert. denied*, 393 U.S. 826 (1968); *Platinum Record Co. v. Lucasfilm, Ltd.*, 566 F. Supp. 226, 227 (D.N.J. 1983); *S.O.S., Inc. v. Payday, Inc.*, 886 F.2d 1081 (9th Cir. 1989).

24　*Rooney v. Columbia Pictures Indus., Inc.*, 538 F. Supp. 211 (S.D.N.Y.), *aff'd*, 714 F.2d 117 (2d Cir. 1982), *cert. denied*, 460 U.S. 1084 (1983).

25　*Platinum Record Co. v. Lucasfilm, Ltd.*, 566 F. Supp. 226 (D.N.J. 1983).

26　*Platinum Record Co. v. Lucasfilm, Ltd.*, 566 F. Supp. 226, 227 (D.N.J. 1983).

27　*Platinum Record Co. v. Lucasfilm, Ltd.*, 566 F. Supp. 226, 228 (D.N.J.1983).

28　*Brown v. Twentieth Century Fox Film Corp.*, 799 F. Supp. 166 (D.D.C. 1992), *aff'd*, 15 F.3d 1159 (D.C. Cir. 1994).

29　*Brown v. Twentieth Century Fox Film Corp.*, 799 F. Supp. 166, 171 (D.D.C. 1992), *aff'd*, 15 F.3d 1159 (D.C. Cir. 1994).

30　*Cohen v. Paramount Pictures Corp.*, 845 F.2d 851 (9th Cir. 1988).

31　*Cohen v. Paramount Pictures Corp.*, 845 F.2d 851 (9th Cir. 1988).

32　*Cohen v. Paramount Pictures Corp.*, 845 F.2d 851 (9th Cir. 1988).

33　*Cohen v. Paramount Pictures Corp.*, 845 F.2d 851 (9th Cir. 1988).

34　*Bartsch v. Metro-Goldwyn-Mayer, Inc.*, 391 F.2d 150, 155 (2d Cir.), *cert. denied*, 393 U.S. 826 (1968).

35　See *S.O.S. v. Payday, Inc.*, 885 F.2d 1081 (9th Cir. 1989).

36　See Chapter 23 for a discussion of ownership issues.

37　See *Viacom Int'l. Inc. v. Tandem Prods., Inc.*, 368 F. Supp. 1264, 1275 (S.D.N.Y. 1974), *aff'd*, 526 F.2d 593 (2d Cir. 1975).

38　See *Eliot v. Geare-Marston, Inc.*, 30 F. Supp. 301, 305 (E.D. Pa. 1939).

39　17 U.S.C. § 203(a).

40　The original and renewal terms of copyrights in works created before 1978 are explained in chapter 3, section 5.2.

41　*Gilliam v. American Broadcasting Cos.*, 538 F.2d 14 (2d Cir. 1976).

42　*Gilliam v. American Broadcasting Cos.*, 538 F.2d 14, 19-21 (2d Cir. 1976); See also *Davis v. E.I. DuPont de Nemours & Co.*, 240 F. Supp. 612 (S.D.N.Y. 1965).

43　*Gilliam v. American Broadcasting Cos.*, 538 F.2d 14 (2d Cir. 1976).

44　*Gilliam v. American Broadcasting Cos.*, 538 F.2d 14, 21 (2d Cir. 1976).

45　*In re matter of The Arbitration Between Directors Guild of America, Inc., Warren Beatty, JRS Prods., Paramount Pictures Corp. and American Broadcasting Cos.*, 6 Ent. L. Rep. No. 12, at 8 (May 1985).

46　*Rano v. Sipa Press, Inc.*, 987 F.2d 580, 586 (9th Cir. 1993); *Costello Publishing Co. v. Rotelle*, 670 F.2d 1035, 1045 (D.C. Cir. 1981).

47　*Rano v. Sipa Press, Inc.*, 987 F.2d 580, 586 (9th Cir. 1993); *Affiliated Hospital Products, Inc. v. Merdel Game Mfg. Co.*, 513 F.2d 1183, 1186 (2d Cir. 1975).

48　*Rano v. Sipa Press, Inc.*, 987 F.2d 580, 586 (9th Cir. 1993).

49　*Rano v. Sipa Press, Inc.*, 987 F.2d 580, 586 (9th Cir. 1993).

Licensing Text

Licensing Text

Text is one of the most commonly used forms of multimedia content. Although it is the form most easily created, there may be many instances where you will want to use text previously written by someone else. In such a case, you will be required to clear all of the necessary rights.

1. Rights to Be Cleared

Clearing the rights to text normally requires consideration of three forms of property rights: copyrights, trademark rights, and rights of privacy.

1.1 Copyright

Literary works and most other forms of text are protected by copyright.[1] This includes books, plays, poems, articles, and the like, as well as other works expressed in words, numbers, or other symbols.[2] Both fiction and nonfiction, such as newspapers, history books, and biographies are copyrightable. It makes no difference whether the literary work is embodied on paper, film, tape, disk, or CD-ROM.

Certain limited aspects of the text that comprises a literary work are not copyrightable. Specifically, individual words and short phrases, such as names, titles, and slogans are not copyrightable.[3] Even if a name, title, or short phrase is novel, distinctive, or lends itself to a play on words, it cannot be protected by copyright.[4] Likewise, the title of a book, movie, play, poem, or other work of authorship is generally not entitled to copyright protection.[5]

But the mere fact that words and short phrases are not protectable by copyright does not necessarily mean that they are free for the taking. In certain situations, names and short phrases may be protectable as trademarks, or under the law of unfair competition.[6] (This is discussed in chapter 4, section 1.5, and chapter 14, section 1.2).

To the extent that you want to use all or a part of a preexisting literary work, it will be necessary to obtain permission from the owner of the copyright. However, be aware of two key issues that may complicate your search for permission. First, the literary work that you want to license may contain several overlapping copyrights. Second, the person from whom you are seeking permission may not be the owner of the specific rights that you require.

The problem of overlapping copyrights frequently occurs with the pictures, illustrations, and other material (including text) incorporated within a book, magazine or other literary work. It is quite common, for example, that the author of a book, article, or other textual work will use (with permission) copyrighted pictures or illustrations owned by a third party to enhance the value of the work. Permission to use such material, however, is typically given only for that specific work. In other words, the owner of the copyright in the book may not have the right to grant you permission to use text, photographs, or other copyrighted material incorporated in the book.

Accordingly, you should not assume that a license from the copyright owner of a book necessarily includes the right to use the pictures and other illustrations appearing in the work. If you want to use these elements, you should separately verify who owns them and obtain permission from the owner.

The other key problem you may face is that the person with whom you are negotiating for permission may not have received or retained the particular rights that you require. For example, it is very possible that the author assigned the right to publish the book in printed form to the publisher, but retained (or assigned to someone else) the right to publish the book in electronic form. More likely, however, a determination of who has what rights with respect to a particular literary work will be less than clear.

For example, in one recent case, the author of a novel titled *Lonesome Dove* assigned the "electronic rights" to the book to the publisher (Simon & Schuster). The contract defined "electronic rights" as the right to use or adapt the work "as a basis for photographic, video, audio, digital, or any other form or method of copying, recording or transmission now known or hereafter devised. . . ." However, he reserved to himself the "motion picture rights," "educational picture rights," and "television rights."

The author then exercised the television rights that he retained for himself, and licensed Qintex Entertainment, Inc. to produce a television miniseries. Thereafter, a company called Dove Books on Tape, Inc. sought to distribute audiocassette versions of the sound track from the television miniseries, and obtained a license to do so from Qintix.

The book publisher, Simon & Schuster, sued to prevent distribution of the audiotapes. Although Simon & Schuster had presumably obtained the audio rights in the novel itself by virtue of the electronic rights clause in the contract, it was not clear that this included the soundtrack to the television miniseries. Thus, a major dispute developed over whether Qintex controlled the rights to the soundtrack to the television miniseries by virtue of the grant of television rights it received from the author, or whether Simon & Schuster owned the right to use that soundtrack in an audio-only form by virtue of its electronic rights clause it received from the author. This case clearly points out some of the risks in licensing content.[7]

1.2 Trademark and Unfair Competition

The textual material that you want to use may incorporate trademarks either in the body of the text or in the title. To the extent that a trademark is mentioned in the body of the text (e.g., a reference to a Ford truck or an Apple computer) it is generally not a problem so long as you are not using the mark as a trademark on your multimedia product. The use of a trademark in a title, however, generally presents more significant potential problems.

The title of a single book, newspaper, magazine, movie, or play cannot be registered as a federal trademark.[8] However, the title of a series of creative works can be eligible for trademark registration.[9] In addition, the title of even a single work may also be protectable via unfair competition causes of action known as "passing off" and "false designation of origin."[10] (Unfair competition is discussed in chapter 4, section 7.) Thus, using a well-recognized title (such as *Gone With The Wind*, *Casablanca*, or *The Wizard of Oz*) raises a risk of some legal liability if done without permission. This is especially true if the public might somehow relate the multimedia work in which the title is used to the prior work (such as by assuming that both works are created by the same person or entity, that the creator of the first work has endorsed the second work, or that the second work is a substitute for the first work).

Using registered trademarks in titles can also be particularly risky, especially if the trademark is used in a manner that might imply that the work is associated with the owner of the trademark. Thus, for example, using trademarks such as "Mickey Mouse," "Bugs Bunny," or "Superman" as part of a title without permission is likely to give rise to a claim for infringement.

1.3 Defamation and Right of Privacy

To the extent that the literary material you seek to license makes reference to any actual persons, or any fictional persons that are readily comparable to actual persons, you also need to be concerned about defamation and infringing such person's right of privacy. While obtaining a release from the persons depicted is the ideal solution, this is usually not practical. Defamation is discussed in chapter 7, and the right of privacy is discussed in chapter 6.

As an alternative, you should seek warranties and representations from the licensor to the effect that the material is not defamatory, and that it does not infringe anyone's right of privacy. In addition, if possible, you should seek to obtain an indemnification from the licensor in the event that you are sued for defamation or infringement of anyone's right of privacy as a result of your use of that material.

Finally, you should carefully review the material itself in an attempt to ascertain the risks of using it. This, however, is often less than satisfactory, as what may sound innocuous to you may in fact be defamatory or infringe someone's right of privacy.

2. Identifying and Finding the Owners of the Rights

The licensing of fictional works typically requires negotiation with the copyright holder through a literary agent and/or publisher. In the case of nonfiction works, the authors are less likely to have agents, and the publisher may control the rights.

There are a number of approaches you can use to identify and locate the publisher, author, or other person who owns the copyright in a literary work. They include the following:

• **Check the Work Itself.** If you have a copy of a literary work, or know the name of the work and can locate a copy such as through a library, the copyright owner will typically be identified on the work itself. However, if the work contains no information about where to contact the copyright owner, or does not identify the copyright owner at all, it will typically identify the publisher.

Generally, the publisher of the textual work you want to use will control the copyrights, or at least the exploitation of those copyrights through licensing. If not, the publisher should be able to direct you to the author or other copyright holder. If the author is dead, the publishing company may also be able to identify the heirs or executor of the author's estate.

• **Copyright Office Search.** Another alternative is to perform a search of the records of the Copyright Office in an attempt to locate the copyright registration for the literary work involved. This registration will disclose the name and address of the copyright owner. The process of performing a Copyright Office search is discussed in chapter 12, section 3.3.

• **Other Sources of Information**. Some literary writers may also be located by contacting various writers' guilds and unions, such as the Writer's Guild of America. Another source is *Literary Market Place*, a yearly survey and information guide to publishers, agents, and others working for and with the book publishing industry, that is published by R. R. Bowker Co.

3. Special Licensing Issues

When licensing text, it is important to decide exactly which rights you need to acquire. This will vary, however, based on the type of text being licensed (e.g., factual works or fiction, explanatory or educational material, etc.) and the amount being licensed.

If you are simply using a few paragraphs or pages of text, you may only need to get permission from the copyright owner—normally the publisher, although sometimes it will be the author. But if you are basing your entire multimedia work on a book and its plot, theme or characters, you may need to obtain a variety of rights in addition to the right to use the text, including the story rights, title rights, character rights, sequel rights, foreign language rights, and so forth.

In many situations, for example, you may want to create a multimedia title based on a particular book, but will not plan to use much of the text from the story itself.

Rather, your focus may be to use the characters, setting, theme, and general plot of the story to create a related multimedia work. For such a project, it is important that you acquire rights to (1) the story, including any unique plot or theme aspects of it, (2) the characters involved in the story, (3) the title of the story, and (4) the right to adapt or modify the story for use in the multimedia product. In connection with this last right, it is also important to secure a waiver of the author's moral rights. In addition, it may be important to secure **sequel rights** and/or foreign language rights if those are applicable.

Finally, if any of the copyrighted textual material will be printed, such as in a user's manual, accompanying text, or promotional material for the multimedia work, it will be necessary to obtain print rights. That is, if you want to display or reprint any of the text on paper accompanying the multimedia product (such as a user's manual, a book designed to accompany a CD-ROM disc, advertising material, brochures, and so forth), or otherwise use it to advertise or promote the multimedia work, it will be important to secure the rights necessary to do so.

Endnotes

1   17 U.S.C. § 102(a)(1).

2   17 U.S.C. § 101.

3   37 C.F.R. § 202.1.

4   COPYRIGHT OFFICE CIR. NO. 34, COPYRIGHT PROTECTION NOT AVAILABLE FOR NAMES, TITLES, OR SHORT PHRASES (1990).

5   See 37 C.F.R. § 202.1(a); *Duff v. Kansas City Star Co.*, 299 F.2d 320, 323 (8th Cir. 1962); *Becker v. Loews, Inc.*, 133 F.2d 889, 891 (7th Cir.) ("the copyright of a book or play does not give the copyright owner the exclusive right to the use of the title"), *cert. denied*, 319 U.S. 772 (1943); *Warner Bros. Pictures, Inc. v. Majestic Pictures Corp.*, 70 F.2d 310, 311 (2d Cir. 1934); *Arthur Retlaw & Assocs., Inc. v. Travenol Lab., Inc.*, 582 F. Supp. 1010, 1014 (N.D. Ill. 1984) ("one cannot claim copyright in a title").

6   See, e.g., *Leeds Music, Ltd. v. Robin*, 358 F. Supp. 650, 660 (S.D. Ohio 1973) (title of the rock opera *Jesus Christ Superstar* could not be used for a motion picture or television production).

7   See Johnathon L. Kirsch, *"Lonesome Dove" and the Electronic Rights Revolution in Book Publishing*, LOS ANGELES LAWYER (APR. 27, 1990); see also *Simon & Schuster, Inc. v. Qintex*, 1990 U.S. Dist. LEXIS 1997 (Feb. 14, 1990); *Simon & Schuster, Inc. v. Qintex*, 1991 U. S. Dist. LEXIS 20330 (Apr. 9, 1991).

8   *In re Cooper*, 254 F.2d 611, 613 (CCPA), *cert. denied*, 358 U.S. 840 (1958); *In re Hal Leonard Publishing Corp.*, 15 U.S.P.Q.2d 1574, 1576 (TTAB 1990).

9   *In re Scholastic, Inc.*, 23 U.S.P.Q.2d 1774, 1777 (TTAB 1992) (The *Magic School Bus* series of children's books); *Inc. Publishing Corp. v. Manhattan Magazine, Inc.*, 616 F. Supp. 370, 376-77 (S.D.N.Y. 1985), *aff'd*, 788 F.2d 3 (2d Cir. 1986) (*Inc. Magazine*); *Metro Publishing, Ltd. v. San Jose Mercury News*, 987 F.2d 637, 641 (9th Cir. 1993) ("Public Eye" column in weekly newspaper); *Walt Disney Co. v. Cable News Network, Inc.*, 231 U.S.P.Q. 235, 237 (C.D. Cal. 1986) (*Business Day* television series).

10   See *Brandon v. Regents of University of California*, 441 F. Supp. 1086, 1091 (D. Mass. 1977) (a file title is entitled to judicial protection under the doctrine of unfair competition when it has obtained a secondary meaning); *Hospital for Sick Children v. Melody Fare Dinner Theatre*, 516 F. Supp. 67, 73 (E.D. Va. 1980).

Licensing Databases

Licensing Databases

A database can be a compilation or collection of just about anything. Examples include databases of names, addresses, and telephone numbers (such as a phone directory), databases of copyrighted articles (such as NEXIS and Dialog), and databases of court opinions (such as LEXIS and WestLaw). A multimedia product may include all or a portion of a database, or simply include elements taken from a database.

1. Rights to Be Cleared

Clearing the rights to use all or a portion of a database primarily requires clearance of the copyright rights involved. In some cases, however, trademark and unfair competition issues, and individual rights of privacy may also be implicated.

1.1 Copyright

Databases are normally copyrightable as compilations.[1] (Compilations are explained in chapter 23, section 2.2). This is true for databases comprised of copyrightable components (such as a database of news articles), as well as for databases comprised of uncopyrightable facts (such as a database of names and addresses or part numbers). However, there is an important distinction between the scope of protection provided by copyright law for databases of uncopyrightable facts as opposed to databases of copyrighted materials. It is important to understand that distinction when licensing rights to databases.

1.1.1 Databases of Facts.   Facts by themselves can never be copyrightable. This is true of all facts —scientific, historical, biographical, and news of the day. They may not be copyrighted and are part of the public domain available to every person.[2] Thus, for example, the names, towns, and telephone numbers of the persons living in a certain geographic area and listed in a phone book are uncopyrightable facts, as are the birth dates of famous persons and the populations of each of the cities and towns in the United States.

But even though facts are not, by themselves, copyrightable, it is important to understand that a compilation (such as a database) of such noncopyrightable elements may itself be copyrightable.[3] Thus, for example, notwithstanding that facts (such as the names of cities and streets) are not copyrightable, compilations of facts (such as in a list of the fifty "most livable" cities in the United States) *may* be copyrightable.[4]

The key to understanding how a collection of uncopyrightable facts can achieve copyrightable status lies in the copyright requirement of originality. The author of the compilation typically chooses which facts to include, in what order to place them, and how to arrange the collected data so that they may be used effectively by readers. These choices as to selection and arrangement, if made independently by the compiler with a minimum degree of creativity, are sufficiently original to be copyrightable. Thus, even a directory that contains absolutely no copyrightable elements, only facts, meets the requirements for copyright protection if it features an original selection or arrangement.[5]

But although compilations of facts *can* be copyrightable, they are not copyrightable per se.[6] Something more than mere "collection and assembling" is required. The fact that someone has expended a great deal of time, effort, and money to create the compilation has no bearing on its copyrightability.[7] The "sweat of the brow" expended by the compiler in gathering and compiling data does not constitute the requisite originality necessary to qualify the compilation for copyright.[8]

In determining whether a fact-based work is copyrightable, courts focus on the manner in which the collected facts have been *selected, coordinated, and arranged*. Facts are never original, so the compilation author can claim originality, if at all, only in the way the facts are presented. Thus, the principal focus is on whether the selection, coordination, and arrangement are sufficiently original to merit protection.[9]

The originality requirement is not particularly stringent. It merely calls for independent creation, not novelty. Thus, a compilation of facts can qualify for copyright protection even though it is similar to a work previously produced by others, and hence is not novel.[10] (Originality is discussed in chapter 3, section 3.2).

A compiler may settle upon a selection or arrangement that others have used. Originality requires only that the author make the selection or arrangement independently (i.e., without copying that selection or arrangement from another work), and that it display some minimum level of creativity. The vast majority of compilations will pass this test, but not all will. There remains a narrow category of works in which the creative spark is utterly lacking or so trivial as to be virtually nonexistent.[11] The selection and arrangement of facts cannot be so mechanical or routine as to require no creativity whatsoever. The standard of originality is low, but it does exist.[12]

Thus, for example, the Supreme Court has held that there is nothing remotely creative about arranging names alphabetically in the white pages of a telephone directory. It is an age-old practice, firmly rooted in tradition and so commonplace that it has come to be expected as a matter of course.[13] In other words, it is a selection and arrangement of facts that is so mechanical or routine as to require no creativity.[14]

Even if a compilation of noncopyrightable data qualifies as a copyrightable compilation, it receives only limited protection. Copyright protects only the author's original contributions (i.e., the selection, coordination, and arrangement)—not the facts or information conveyed. The copyright in a compilation extends only to the material contributed by the author of such work, as distinguished from the preexisting material employed in the work, and does not imply any exclusive right in the preexisting material.[15]

In other words, the copyright in a factual compilation is thin. Notwithstanding a valid copyright, a subsequent compiler remains free to use the facts contained in another's publication to aid in preparing a competing work, so long as the competing work does not feature the same selection and arrangement.[16] No matter how much original authorship the work displays, the facts and ideas it exposes are free for the taking. The very same facts and ideas may be divorced from the context imposed by the author, and restated and reshuffled by others, even if the author was the first to discover the facts or to propose the ideas.[17] Thus, for example, in one case the defendant was free to copy the subscriber information in the Illinois Bell Telephone directory and rearrange the information into phone number or street order, notwithstanding that the telephone directory "as a whole" was copyrightable because it contained some copyrightable text and yellow pages advertisements.[18]

Accordingly, when licensing rights to a database of uncopyrighted facts, the only thing to be licensed is the right to the copyrightable selection, coordination, and arrangement of the original compiler of the database. The facts themselves can be freely copied without a license (so long as they are divorced from the copyrightable expression added by the person who created the database).

1.1.2 Databases of Copyrighted Works.   In contrast to a database of facts (where copyright protects only the selection and organization of the data), a database consisting of several copyrighted works (such as a database of articles from various publications) involves numerous copyrights, and taking anything from such a database without permission will most likely involve copyright infringement. The person compiling the database is required to obtain permission from the copyright owner of each of the component parts included within the database, and is normally presumed to have acquired only the right to reproduce and distribute the individual contributions as part of the entire database, but not independently.[19]

When licensing rights to a database consisting of multiple copyrighted contributions, you must consider the need to license both the copyright in the entire database itself, as well as the separate copyrights in the individual contributions. Thus, if you want to license the right to use one contribution to a database of copyrighted works, you will have to license that right from the owner of the copyright in the contribution itself. On the other hand, if you want to license the entire database, that right must be obtained from the owner of the copyright in the database itself. In addition, however, you will need to determine whether the owner of the copyright in the database has a license to each of the copyrightable components that authorizes the particular use that you propose to make. If not, you will also be required to obtain such a license from the owner of each copyrightable component as well.

If you intend to license anything less than the complete database, or intend to significantly alter or modify any of the copyrighted contributions to the database, it will undoubtedly be necessary to secure permission from the owner of the copyright in each of the copyrighted contributions involved.

1.2 Trademarks and Unfair Competition

Many databases incorporate trademarks from a variety of sources. For example, a database of articles from a variety of publications will typically include the name of the publication (i.e., the trademark) under which the material was published. Accordingly, trademark issues may arise in the context of licensing and using certain databases.

If you want to use the trademarks from a database in a manner that functions as a trademark (e.g., including a group of articles from the *New York Times* in your multimedia title under a category designated as the "*New York Times* Library"), you will need to obtain permission from the owner of the trademark to authorize your use. This requirement is in addition to the permission that is required to authorize your reproduction of copyrighted articles.

Unfair competition issues may also be a factor. As noted above, the facts contained in a database may be copied without fear of copyright infringement, so long as the copying is divorced from the selection, coordination, and arrangement used by the author of the database. However, the Supreme Court has specifically noted that there may be a cause of action for unfair competition in the event that such information is copied.[20] In addition, in one recent case involving the unauthorized distribution of copyrighted Sega computer games via a computer bulletin board, the court found that the fact that the games displayed a Sega trademark when used on a computer by persons who downloaded them from the bulletin board constituted a claim of unfair competition by false designation of origin.[21]

1.3 Right of Privacy

To the extent that a database contains private facts about individuals, you need to also consider whether your proposed use of the database constitutes an infringement of such individuals' right of privacy. A database containing payment and credit information, or a database of medical records, for example, may raise such an issue.

When dealing with a database that contains information on numerous individuals, the only practical approach (assuming the database does not appear to violate anyone's right of privacy) may be to obtain an appropriate warranty from the licensor that no violation of anyone's right of privacy has occurred, and further, to obtain indemnification in the event you are sued as a result of your use of the licensed database.

2. Identifying and Finding the Owners of the Rights

The publisher of the database is normally the best place to start in attempting to identify and locate the owner of the copyrights involved. If the publisher does not own the copyright in the database itself, it should be in a position to put you in touch with the copyright owner.

When dealing with databases of separately copyrightable works owned by third parties, you will have to go a step further. The owners of each of the copyrights compiled into the database will, in many cases, be identified in each of the component elements of the database itself. If not, however, the publisher or copyright owner of the database should be able to assist you in identifying the copyright owners of the component elements.

An alternative to contacting the publishers is to conduct your own search of the records of the Copyright Office in an attempt to locate the copyright registration for the database and/or its component copyrightable parts. Such registration will disclose the name and address of the applicable copyright owner. The process of performing a Copyright Office search is discussed in chapter 12, section 3.3.

One word of caution is in order. With databases of copyrighted works, there may be an issue as to whether the owners of the copyright in each of the individual component works have authorized electronic distribution of their works. In late 1993, Mead Data Central, *Time, The New York Times, Newsday,* and University Microfilms were sued by a group of authors who asserted that the licenses to reprint their articles originally granted to the newspapers and magazines in which they first appeared did not include any online and database rights.[22]

Endnotes

1   17 U.S.C. §§ 101 and 103(a).

2   *Feist Publications, Inc. v. Rural Tele. Serv. Co.*, 499 U.S. 340, 111 S. Ct. 1282, 1287, 1288, 1289, 1290, 1293 (1991).

3   17 U.S.C. § 103(a). A compilation is defined as "a work formed by the *collection and assembling* of preexisting materials or of data that are *selected, coordinated,* or *arranged* in such a way that the resulting work as a whole constitutes an original work of authorship." 17 U.S.C. § 101 (emphasis added).

4   *Feist Publications, Inc. v. Rural Tele. Serv. Co.*, 499 U.S. 340, 111 S. Ct. 1282, 1289 (1991).

5   *Feist Publications, Inc. v. Rural Tele. Serv. Co.*, 499 U.S. 340, 111 S. Ct. 1282, 1289 (1991).

6   *Feist Publications, Inc. v. Rural Tele. Serv. Co.*, 499 U.S. 340, 111 S. Ct. 1282, 1293 (1991).

7   *Feist Publications, Inc. v. Rural Tele. Serv. Co.*, 499 U.S. 340, 111 S. Ct. 1282, 1290-92 (1991).

8   See *Suid v. NewsWeek Magazine*, 503 F. Supp. 146, 147-48 (D.D.C. 1980) (research to discover quotations from unpublished letters does not justify copyright to the discoverer of those quotations). But "[p]rotection for the fruits of such research . . . may in certain circumstances be available under a theory of unfair competition." *Feist Publications, Inc. v. Rural Tele. Serv. Co.*, 499 U.S. 340, 111 S. Ct. 1282, 1292 (1991).

9   *Feist Publications, Inc. v. Rural Tele. Serv. Co.*, 111 S.Ct. 1282, 1294 (1991).

10 **Originality** means only that the work owes its origin to the author, that is, it is independently created, and not copied from other works. *Alfred Bell & Co. v. Catalda Fine Arts, Inc.*, 191 F.2d 99, 102 (2d Cir. 1951); *Wihtol v. Wells*, 231 F.2d 550, 553 (7th Cir. 1956).

11 *Feist Publications, Inc. v. Rural Tele. Serv. Co.* 499 U.S. 340, 111 S. Ct. 1282, 1294 (1991).

12 *Feist Publications, Inc. v. Rural Tele. Serv. Co.*, 499 U.S. 340, 111 S. Ct. 1282, 1296 (1991).

13 *Feist Publications, Inc. v. Rural Tele. Serv. Co.*, 449 U.S. 340, 111 S. Ct. 1282, 1297 (1991).

14 *Feist Publications, Inc. v. Rural Tele. Serv. Co.*, 499 U.S. 340, 111 S. Ct. 1282, 1296 (1991).

15 *Feist Publications, Inc. v. Rural Tele. Serv. Co.*, 499 U.S. 340, 111 S. Ct. 1282, 1294-95 (1991).

16 *Feist Publications, Inc. v. Rural Tele. Serv. Co.*, 499 U.S. 340, 111 S. Ct. 1282, 1289, 1295 (1991).

17 *Feist Publications, Inc. v. Rural Tele. Serv. Co.*, 499 U.S. 340, 111 S. Ct. 1282, 1289 (1991).

18 *Illinois Bell Tele. Co. v. Haines & Co.*, 932 F.2d 610 (7th Cir. 1991).

19 17 U.S.C. § 201(c).

20 *Feist Publications, Inc. v. Rural Tele. Serv. Co.*, 499 U.S. 340. 111 S. Ct. 1282, 1992 (1991).

21 *Sega Enters. Ltd. v. Maphia*, 1994 U.S. Dist. LEXIS 5266 (N.D. Cal. Mar. 28, 1994).

22 *Tasini, et al. v. New York Times Co.*, No. 93 Civ. 8678 (SS) (S.D.N.Y., filed in 1993).

Licensing Characters

Licensing Characters

Preexisting fictional characters frequently form the basis for a multimedia title. Examples include multimedia titles that are based on (or simply use in a limited way), the characters appearing in the *Star Trek* series, characters from children's television shows such as *Sesame Street* or *Barney & Friends*, or popular cartoon characters such as Mickey Mouse, Batman, and Superman.

Since such characters are frequently well recognized and very popular, using them in the context of a multimedia title, or basing a multimedia title around them, can significantly enhance the value and popularity of the resulting product. But preexisting characters are protected in a variety of ways, and before you use any of them, it is important that you clear all of the appropriate rights. Thus, if your multimedia work will use cartoon characters or other licensed characters, it will be necessary to obtain a license from the owners of the character. Accordingly, it is important to understand that characters can be protected in a variety of forms.

1. Rights to Be Cleared

Characters are protected primarily by the law of copyright, trademark, and unfair competition. Consequently, when beginning the process of clearing the rights, these are the primary areas to consider.

1.1 Copyright

Fictional characters can exist in a visual form (e.g., Mickey Mouse, Superman), in a literary form, such as in the text of a story (e.g., Sherlock Holmes, the Hardy Boys, or

James Bond), or as represented by actors in a motion picture or television program (e.g., E.T., Darth Vader, or Superman). In each of these cases they *can* be entitled to copyright protection.[1]

Characters are most readily protectable when they exist in some sort of pictorial or graphic form in both the original work and the work in which they are copied. Classic examples are cartoon characters such as Mickey Mouse, Donald Duck, Superman, and the characters in the "Peanuts" comic strip.[2]

Characters that exist only in the words of a book or play can also be protected by copyright, separate and apart from the text containing the story in which they appear. But whether or not they are protected by copyright depends upon the degree to which they are developed in the story. The less developed the characters, the less likely it is that they can be copyrighted.[3]

If a character is protected by copyright, you will need to obtain permission from the copyright owner for any use that you make of the character in a multimedia product. It makes no difference that your use of the character will be divorced from any story in which the character originally appeared. It is the character itself that is protected, and any use of the character (regardless of the setting) will require permission from the copyright owner.

1.2 Trademark

Characters may also be protected by trademark law and the law of unfair competition when the character functions as a trademark to indicate the source of a product.[4]

Dual protection under copyright and trademark laws is particularly appropriate for graphic representations of characters. A character deemed an artistic creation deserving copyright protection may also serve to identify the creator, thus meriting protection under theories of trademark or unfair competition. Indeed, because of their special value in distinguishing goods and services, names and pictorial representations of characters are often registered as trademarks.[5] Thus, for example, characters like Mickey Mouse, Bugs Bunny, and Superman are all registered trademarks.

Trademark protection may also be appropriate for characters that are not represented pictorially, but are merely described through the text of the stories in which they appear. For example, in one case involving the scripts for the *Amos 'n Andy* radio programs (which were in the public domain, and thus not protected by copyright), the court noted that one who makes free use of the characters, character names and physical embodiments, characterizations, and character relationships may incur liability because characters like Amos and Andy may be protected by the law of trademark or unfair competition.[6]

2. Identifying and Finding the Owners of the Rights

The rights to a cartoon character may be held by the cartoonists or animator, or animation house that developed the character. For other characters, such as those appearing in stories or otherwise not involving cartoon characters, your search will generally begin with the publisher of the work, who will either own the copyright or be able to direct you to the copyright owner. There are a number of approaches you can use to identify and locate the owner of these rights.

• **Review the Work Itself.** If you have a copy of the work in which the character appears (or can obtain a copy such as through a library), the credits will frequently identify the copyright owner or creator of the work. If not, it should at least identify the publisher, who may or may not own the copyright, but who can frequently put you in touch with the copyright owner.

• **Union Assistance.** When dealing with cartoon characters, you may obtain assistance in identifying the owner from the Screen Cartoonists, Local 839 of the International Alliance of Theatrical Stage Employees (IATSE), located in Los Angeles, California.

• **Copyright Office Search.** Another alternative is to perform a search of the records of the copyright office in an attempt to locate the copyright registration for the character involved. While characters are not typically registered separate and apart from the works in which they appear, it is possible that such a search will reveal a separate registration, or may find the registration for a work in which the character appears. Such a registration will disclose the name and address of the copyright owner. The process of performing a Copyright Office search is discussed in chapter 12, section 3.3.

• **Trademark Office Search.** With respect to characters that may be used as trademarks, another alternative is to perform a search of the records of the Trademark Office in an attempt to locate a registration for the trademark to the character involved. This registration will identify the name and address of the trademark owner (who may or may not also on the copyright), but from whom permission will be required in any event.

5. Professional Assistance. Finally, you may wish to consider getting professional assistance in the process. Several organizations provide a service of assisting in the clearance of rights to characters and other copyrighted and trademark works. You will, of course, have to pay a fee for their assistance, but they may be able to greatly facilitate the process of identifying the owners of the relevant rights and obtaining the appropriate permissions.

Endnotes

1   See *Walt Disney Prods. v. Air Pirates,* 581 F.2d 751 (9th Cir. 1978) (Mickey Mouse, Donald Duck, and several other Disney characters); *Detective Comics, Inc. v. Bruns Publications, Inc.,* 111 F.2d 432, 433-34 (2d Cir. 1940) (Superman character); *United Feature Syndicate, Inc. v. Sunrise Mold Co.,* 569 F. Supp. 1475, 1480 (S.D. Fla. 1983) ("Peanuts" characters); *Eden Toys, Inc. v. Florelee Undergarment Co.,* 697 F.2d 27 (2d Cir. 1982) (Paddington Bear, a character in a series of children's books); *Ideal Top Corp. v. Kenner Prods. Div. of General Mills Fun Group, Inc.,* 443 F. Supp. 291, 301 (S.D.N.Y. 1977).

2   See *Walt Disney Prods. v. Air Pirates,* 581 F.2d 751, 755 (9th Cir. 1978) ("while many literary characters may embody little more than an unprotected idea . . . , a comic book character, which has physical as well as conceptual qualities, is more likely to contain some unique elements of expression").

3   *Nichols v. Universal Pictures Corp.,* 45 F.2d 119, 121 (2d Cir. 1930), *cert. denied,* 282 U.S. 902 (1931).

4   Cases involving characters as trademarks include *MGM-Pathe Communications Co. v. Pink Panther Patrol,* 774 F. Supp. 869 (S.D.N.Y. 1991) (Pink Panther character); *In re Paramount Pictures,* 213 U.S.P.Q. 1111 (TTAB 1982) (Mork and Mindy characters); *Silverman v. Columbia Broadcasting Sys., Inc.,* 632 F. Supp. 1344, 1356 (S.D.N.Y. 1986) (*Amos 'n' Andy* characters), *cert. denied,* 492 U.S. 907 (1989); *Conan Properties, Inc. v. Conans Pizza, Inc.,* 752 F.2d 145, 150 (5th Cir. 1985) (Conan the Barbarian); *In re D.C. Comics, Inc.,* 689 F.2d 1042, 1044-45 (CCPA 1982); *United Feature Syndicate v. Sunrise Mold Co.,* 569 F. Supp. 1475, 1481 (S.D. Fla. 1983) ("Peanuts" characters); *Geisel v. Poynter Prods., Inc.,* 295 F. Supp. 331, 351-53 (S.D.N.Y. 1968) (Dr. Seuss figures); *D.C. Comics, Inc. v. Filmation Assocs.,* 486 F. Supp. 1273 (S.D.N.Y. 1980).

5   *Frederick Warne & Co. v. Book Sales, Inc.,* 481 F. Supp. 1191, 1196-97 (S.D.N.Y. 1979).

6   *Silverman v. Columbia Broadcasting Sys., Inc.,* 632 F. Supp. 1344 (S.D.N.Y. 1986), *cert. denied,* 492 U.S. 907 (1989). This case was subsequently reversed; however, the Court of Appeals ruled that any trademark rights in the characters had been abandoned, and thus were also in the public domain. *Silverman v. Columbia Broadcasting Sys., Inc.,* 870 F.2d 40 (2d Cir.), *cert. denied,* 492 U.S. 907 (1989).

Licensing Musical Works

Licensing Musical Works

Music has become an important component of multimedia titles. Whether the product is one that features the musical works of a particular artist, teaches the user how to play a musical instrument, or merely uses music as background, there is no doubt that music is an important part of multimedia.

1. Rights to Be Cleared

Obtaining the right to use a musical work is primarily a matter of clearing the copyright. This is true both for musical works that you will perform yourself and musical works that form part of a sound recording performed by someone else. Note, however, that musical works and sound recordings of musical works are different. This chapter discusses the licensing of musical works, but not the licensing of sound recordings of musical works, which represents a separate category of copyrightable works. The licensing of sound recordings is discussed in chapter 18. See section 1.2 of this chapter for a discussion of the distinction between the two.

1.1 Copyright

Musical works are protected by copyright.[1] Copyright protection for musical works extends to both the words and the music, and copying either or both of these elements will constitute copyright infringement if done without permission.[2] Even if the music alone or the lyrics alone are in the public domain or not sufficiently original and expressive to qualify for copyright, the combination may be original enough to qualify.[3]

A musical work can be embodied in any medium.[4] Thus, for example, a musical work can exist on paper (e.g., sheet music), on a piano roll, or on what the Copyright Act refers to as a *phonorecord*.[5] A *phonorecord* is any material object, such as a cassette tape, CD, CD-ROM disc, or long-playing record (LP), in which sounds (other than those accompanying a motion picture or other audiovisual work) are fixed, and from which the sounds can be perceived, reproduced, or otherwise communicated, either directly or with the aid of a machine.[6]

1.2 Distinguishing Musical Works from Sound Recordings

It is important to distinguish a musical work from a *sound recording* of a musical work. They represent two separate and distinct copyrights. In other words, copyright applies to two separate elements that make up what we know as "music": (1) the music that is written by the composer (and any lyrics written by a lyricist), and (2) a recording of a particular rendition of that music by a performer or performers. An easy way to remember these two elements is to think of them as "composed music" and "performed music." The first is the composition itself; the second is the individual rendition of the composition by a particular performer or performers.

For example, Irving Berlin wrote both the music and the lyrics to "White Christmas," and he obtained the copyright to the music and lyrics that he wrote. But every rendition of "White Christmas" by an individual recording artist is a separately copyrightable work.

Accordingly, if you want to license rights to a particular song, you may have to license multiple copyrights. The first is the copyright in the musical work itself—that is, the notes and the lyrics. If you want to use a sound recording of the musical work performed by a specific artist or a specific group of artists, a second copyright—the copyright in the sound recording—is also involved. Licensing sound recordings is discussed in chapter 18.

2. Music Industry Licenses

The music industry has developed several different types of licenses for the use of musical works, depending on how the licensee plans to use the musical work. The following discussion summarizes the types of licenses that are most likely to be relevant to the development of multimedia works.

2.1 Mechanical Licenses

The music industry refers to the right to record, reproduce, and distribute musical works in phonorecords (such as phonograph records, cassette tapes, and CDs) as a mechanical right, and licenses of that right are called **mechanical licenses.**[7] A mechanical license permits the reproduction of a musical work in a form that does not involve the use of still images or motion pictures, and that is primarily intended for distribution to the public for private (e.g., in-home).[8] Thus, a mechanical license grants permission to record a musical work on CD, cassette tape, and so forth. The most common form of mechanical reproduction at this time is the CD.

Because mechanical licenses are used only where the musical work will not be synchronized with any visual image or motion picture, they are normally not appropriate for multimedia titles. That is, because most multimedia titles involve the use of still images or motion pictures, the use of a musical work in a multimedia title normally requires rights beyond the audio-only rights included in a mechanical license. However, a mechanical license may be appropriate where a multimedia work includes a musical work accompanied by nothing but text on a computer screen, although this issue has not been decided.

Mechanical licenses, like most licenses, are typically obtained from the copyright owner of the musical work (or the owner's agent). However, mechanical licenses are unique in that once a phonorecord of a musical work has been distributed to the public with the authorization of the copyright owner (i.e., the composer has authorized at least one performer to record his or her song), the U.S. copyright law allows anyone else to obtain a *compulsory* mechanical license authorizing them to record and distribute phonorecords of the musical work. That is, you do not need to obtain permission from the copyright owner—the Copyright Act itself gives you the right to obtain a compulsory license to make and distribute phonorecords of a musical work.[9] Compulsory licenses are available under the following circumstances:

1. The copyright owner must have already authorized at least one recording and distribution to the public of that recording of the work;

2. The work must be a "nondramatic" musical work;[10]

3. The licensee must observe the requirements stated in the law for payment of royalties and the filing of accounting statements[11] ;

4. The licensee's primary purpose must be to distribute its phonorecords to the public for use by individuals in their own homes, not for commercial use; and

5. Although the licensee can adapt the musical work, the adaptation cannot vary a great deal from the original musical work.

Although compulsory mechanical licenses are available, the procedure is not heavily used. In most cases, licensees obtain mechanical licenses from the copyright owner of the musical work, or his or her agent, such as The Harry Fox Agency. See this chapter, section 4 for a discussion relating to obtaining mechanical licenses through the Harry Fox Agency.

In addition, it is important to note that the mechanical licenses authorized by the Copyright Act allow the licensee to make and distribute only phonorecords. By definition, however, phonorecords include media in which only sounds are fixed.[12] In other words, they do not include any media incorporating both sounds and images or motion pictures.[13]

Thus, the compulsory license does not apply to objects in which the sounds accompany an audiovisual work. The compulsory license will therefore not be available for most multimedia works because they are audiovisual works.

2.2 Synchronization Licenses

A **synchronization license** grants the right to record and perform a musical work in "timed-relation" to visual images; that is, to "synchronize" the music with an audiovisual work. In other words, it permits you to make a recording of the musical work that will then become part of an audiovisual work.

A synchronization license is normally obtained where a musical work is to be synchronized with images or motion pictures and used in connection with a public performance of the resulting work (e.g., showing the motion picture in a theater or on television, or otherwise in connection with a television broadcast). Where the musical work will be synchronized with images or motion pictures and distributed to the public for private performance (e.g., in-home use), such as on tape, CD, video cassette, optical laser disc, or other home video device (in contrast to public exposition in a theater or on television), the license is now known as a **videogram license.** (Videogram licenses are discussed below in section 2.3).

Thus, a synchronization license is used to obtain permission to record a musical composition for use in a television program, motion picture, or music video that will be performed publicly. The license is usually very specific about the kind of audiovisual work into which the music is licensed for synchronization, and the license is limited to that precise use.

Synchronization licenses are typically obtained by a producer of a movie or television program in which the musical work will be incorporated. The producer gets this kind of license in order to exhibit the movie or audiovisual work on television or in a theater in which movies are ordinarily exhibited. For that reason, synchronization licenses, like mechanical licenses, will generally not be appropriate for multimedia works distributed to the home market on CD-ROM. However, multimedia works that are produced for use in interactive television, public kiosks, or other applications involving a public performance may require a synchronization license.

2.3 Videogram Licenses

A videogram license permits one to record and reproduce a musical work in timed-relation to visual images, for distribution into the home market on tape, CD, video-cassette, optical laser disc, or other home video device. This license is used when music is synchronized with images and distributed to the public primarily for private use (e.g., in-home use), such as on a VCR or laser disc player.

Although synchronization licenses and videogram licenses both grant "sync" rights, there are a number of key differences between them. First, synchronization licenses typically include a license of the public performance rights (e.g., the right to perform the music publicly as part of a movie or exhibited in a theater or a show broadcast on television), whereas the videogram license is intended primarily for distribution to the public for private (e.g. in-home) use. Second, the medium itself is typically different. Synchronization licenses typically involve incorporation of a musical work on film or as part of a television broadcast. Videogram licenses, on the other hand, involve reproduction of the musical work in media such as disks, tape, CD-ROM, video discs, optical laser discs, and video cassette—media typically distributed to the general public for in-home use.

2.4 Public Performance Licenses

A public performance license grants permission to perform a musical composition publicly on a commercial basis. (The public performance right is explained in chapter 3, section 4.4). In the music world, there are essentially two types of performance rights: **dramatic performing rights** (sometimes referred to as "**grand rights**"), and **nondramatic performing rights** (sometimes referred to as "**small rights**").

A dramatic performance of a musical work is a performance that tells a story—that is, there is a plot depicted by action and the performance of the musical composition is woven into and carries forward a plot. Public performance of the music to an opera is a good example of a dramatic performance. A nondramatic performance of a musical work is a performance that is not part of a story or plot, such as merely singing a song or broadcasting a recording of a song on the radio. The public performance of most musical works will probably fall into the nondramatic category.

The copyright owners of musical works typically become a member of one of the **performing rights societies**—that is, ASCAP, BMI, or SESAC—and grant the performance rights society a license to sublicense others to publicly perform their musical works. Generally, the performing rights society is licensed to grant only nondramatic public performance licenses. Moreover, it is a nonexclusive license. Thus, you can obtain a public performance license to a musical composition either from the performing rights society to which the copyright owner is a member, or direct from the copyright owner. (The manner in which these organizations operate with respect to public performance licenses is discussed in more detail in this chapter, section 4).

Although the need for public performance licenses does not exist for multimedia works distributed for in-home private use, they will be necessary for multimedia works designed for public performances, such as kiosks or information centers intended for use by the public in museums, shopping centers, or anywhere else accessible to the public, or for distribution via interactive television.

2.5 Multimedia Licenses

Although the forms of music licenses discussed above can be related to one or more of the activities involved in creating a multimedia product, none of them completely addresses the bundle of rights typically required for the use of a musical composition in a multimedia product. This is due primarily to the fact that they were intended for more traditional uses of music, such as recording music on CD or using music in connection with a motion picture or television program.

As a consequence, the use of music in connection with a multimedia product may require the development of new forms of music industry licenses to deal with the new and different uses of musical works contemplated for multimedia. For example, when a musical work is recorded and stored digitally in the form of an MIDI file, what type of license applies? MIDI files are computer files that contain instructions controlling how and when devices like digital synthesizers produce sound. They can be stored in a digital form on computer-readable media such as disks and CD-ROM discs and later recalled to play back the musical work that is the subject of the MIDI recording. Does the distribution of MIDI files require a mechanical license, a synchronization license, and/or a public performance license? Perhaps a new form of license offers the best solution.

In December 1993 a class action lawsuit was filed on behalf of more than 140 owners of musical compositions against CompuServe alleging that the uploading to, storage by, and downloading from CompuServe of MIDI files constitutes an infringement of the right of public performance granted to the owners of the copyright in the underlying musical compositions.[14] The suit alleged that CompuServe, by allowing its users to upload and download MIDI files, had permitted, facilitated, and participated in the recording and distribution of performances of several copyrighted musical compositions. This is the first case to allege infringement of the public performance right in a musical composition by the transmission and storage of digital MIDI files.

The same problem is presented by many other aspects of the licensing of musical compositions for inclusion in a multimedia product. Thus, rather than adhering to the traditional forms of licensing used in the music industry, it is perhaps more appropriate to ensure that any license you obtain adequately grants you the rights to use the musical composition in the form and in the manner in which you intend to use it, and via the media through which you intend to distribute it. In fact, The Harry Fox Agency has already developed a special form of multimedia license. See also chapter 30 for a sample multimedia license for musical works.

Beware of being locked into standard industry licensing formats for your multimedia uses. Be sure that the license grants you the specific rights that you need.

3. Identifying and Finding the Owners of the Rights

The copyright in a musical work is owned initially by the creator of the work—that is, the composer (and lyricist, if any).[15] However, composers and lyricists frequently assign their rights to the musical works they have created to either music publishers or record companies in exchange for a percentage of royalties. All copyright rights to popular music, for example, are customarily assigned to music publishers.[16]

In most cases, a music publisher will both own and administer all of the copyright rights in a musical work. The publisher will then register the copyright, handle the negotiating and granting of mechanical licenses, synchronization licenses, and other forms of licenses, collect the appropriate license fees and royalties, and pay the agreed upon portion of those sums to the composer and lyricist.

Rights to reproduce the musical composition on phonorecords, for example, are then licensed to a record company. Rights of nondramatic public performance, as on television, radio, and in clubs and restaurants, are sublicensed by the music publisher to performing rights societies—ASCAP, BMI, and SESAC—on a nonexclusive basis. The composer then shares in the license fees received by the music publisher from licensing the mechanical rights, synchronization or reproduction of music on television and movie soundtracks (synchronization licenses), and the public performance rights.

Identifying and finding the publisher (or other person who owns the copyright) to a musical composition, can often be a difficult task. Nonetheless, there are number of approaches you can use to accomplish the task. They include the following:

• **Look at Media Containing the Musical Work**. If you know the correct name of the musical work, you can try to learn the name(s) of the copyright owner(s) by looking at the record album, CD, or videocassette in which the musical work originally appeared. Even if the information you are looking for is not listed (as is commonly the case), you may find the identity of other sources (such as the record company) that can direct you to the copyright owner.

• **Contact Agencies and Groups that Can Help You**. Another good source is The Harry Fox Agency.[17] Because The Harry Fox Agency represents most music publishers, there is a good chance that it will be able to help you identify the publisher of a particular song and, in many cases, facilitate obtaining a license as well.

The Songwriters Guild of America[18] can often provide assistance in locating songwriters and publishers. The Guild represents authors and composers worldwide.

Another source is to contact the performing rights society that represents the music publisher in the licensing of performance rights to the musical composition (i.e., ASCAP,[19] BMI,[20] or SESAC[21]). The name of the performance rights society that the music publisher is affiliated with is typically listed in the materials that come with the CD or record album containing the song. These performing rights societies maintain databases of information indexing songs and copyright owners, and may be able to provide you with the relevant information.

• **Copyright Office Search.** Another alternative is to perform a search of the records of the copyright office in an attempt to locate their copyright registration for the musical work involved. This registration will disclose the name and address of the copyright owner. The process of performing a copyright office search is discussed in chapter 12, section 3.3.

• **Music Clearinghouses**. Finally, you may wish to consider getting professional assistance in the process. Several organizations act as clearinghouses that will give you professional help clearing licenses to musical works. A list of some of these organizations is included in chapter 36. These clearinghouses have relationships with the major music publishers and may stand a better chance of succeeding at obtaining the clearances you need than you do. They will, however, charge you a fee for the assistance they provide.

4. Who Controls the License?

A license to use a musical composition is typically obtained from the music publisher or its agent, such as the Harry Fox Agency.

The following is a summary of the most likely sources of licenses of the relevant rights in a musical work:

• **Mechanical Licenses**. Although the Copyright Act allows anyone to obtain a "compulsory" mechanical license (once the publisher has permitted the release of any record embodying that musical work), a mechanical license is normally obtained from the owner of the copyright (usually the music publisher), or from a mechanical rights agency, such as The Harry Fox Agency, Inc. in New York City. Most major U.S. music publishers authorize The Harry Fox Agency to issue mechanical licenses on their behalf.

The Harry Fox Agency, Inc.[22] was created to act as agent trustee to administer mechanical licenses on behalf of publishers who wished to avail themselves of its services. The Harry Fox Agency is a wholly-owned subsidiary of the **National Music Publishers Association, Inc. (NMPA)**. In Canada a similar function is performed by the Canadian Music Reproduction Rights Agency, Ltd. (CMRRA).[23]

The Harry Fox Agency represents more than 12,000 music publishers. Its services include the issuance of mechanical and synchronization licenses and the supervision of collections from record companies.

Other organizations that license mechanical and synchronization rights for music publishers and songwriters include the American Mechanical Rights Association (AMRA),[24] Copyright Management, Inc.,[25] and Publishers Licensing Corp.[26]

● **Synchronization Licenses.** The Harry Fox agency also handles synchronization licenses, but in some cases you will have to license these rights directly from the music publisher and/or the author of the musical work.

● **Public Performance Licenses.** Nondramatic public performance licenses are usually obtained from the music publisher or its agent. Most U.S. music publishers use ASCAP, BMI or SESAC as their agent for licensing public performance rights. Dramatic performance rights are typically retained by the music publisher (or the author of the musical work), and thus, ASCAP, BMI, or SESAC may not be in a position to license grand performance rights.

The performing rights societies, primarily ASCAP and BMI, play an important role in the licensing of nondramatic public performance rights. With respect to "small" (i.e., nondramatic as compared to "grand" or dramatic) public performance rights, it is customary to allow ASCAP and BMI to handle the licensing thereof, irrespective of who owns the rights.[27] Performance fees are collected by the performing rights society from radio and television stations, and from other commercial users of music, such as nightclubs and hotels, for the right to perform copyrighted music. These organizations remit payments separately to the writer and the publisher of the musical composition.

ASCAP is an unincorporated membership association organized in 1914. Its members include more than 30,000 composers and authors and more than 12,000 music publishers, and it controls a repertoire of about 3 million musical works. BMI is a nonprofit corporation organized in 1939 to compete with ASCAP.[28] BMI represents about 65,000 writers and some 37,000 publishers, and has a repertoire of about 1.5 million works. The third performance licensing organization, SESAC, is the smallest of the three major performing-right organizations in the U.S. It is a private licensing company founded in 1930 and as of 1989 represented about 1,900 writers, as well as publishers who own approximately 850 catalogs.

ASCAP and BMI control about 95 percent of the market in the United States for performance rights to musical works,[29] and licensees (e.g., broadcasters) who regularly perform musical works must generally have licenses from both organizations. The two groups grant blanket licenses to numerous kinds of organizations, including traditional television and cable television systems, radio stations, and jukeboxes. Blanket licenses allow the licensee to perform any musical work in the group's repertoire without having to obtain an individual license for each work. The fee does not depend on the popularity or the number of works used; it is a single, negotiated fee, either a flat rate or a percentage of the licensee's gross revenue.[30]

Endnotes

1   17 U.S.C. § 102(a)(2).

2   See *Mills Music, Inc. v. Arizona*, 187 U.S.P.Q. 22, 31 (D. Ariz. 1975), *aff'd*, 591 F.2d 1278 (9th Cir. 1979).

3   *Plymouth Music Co. v. Magnus Organ Corp.*, 456 F. Supp. 676, 679 (S.D.N.Y. 1978).

4   17 U.S.C. § 102.

5   COPYRIGHT OFFICE CIR. 56A, COPYRIGHT REGISTRATION OF MUSICAL COMPOSITIONS AND SOUND RECORDINGS 1 (1989).

6   17 U.S.C. § 101.

7   See AL KOHN & BOB KOHN, THE ART OF MUSIC LICENSING, 305-38 (1992); SIDNEY SHEMEL & M. WILLIAM KRASILOVSKY, THIS BUSINESS OF MUSIC, 237-47 (6th Ed. 1990).

8   Licenses to record and reproduce musical works in a medium not accompanied by still pictures or motion pictures, but intended to facilitate radio broadcast, background music services, and other public performance purposes, are known as *electrical transcription licenses*.

9   See 17 U.S.C. § 115.

10   The Copyright Act does not define "dramatic" or "nondramatic" works. However, a dramatic work may generally be thought of as one that tells a story. A screen play, for example, is a dramatic work. The music to an opera, similarly, would seem to qualify as a dramatic work. Most musical works, however, neither fall into this category nor are incorporated into works that fall into this category, and they are therefore "nondramatic."

11   The royalty rates for compulsory mechanical licenses are established by the Copyright Office. As of January 1, 1992, the rate was the greater of 6.25¢ per unit or 1.2¢ per minute of playing time, or fraction thereof, per unit. The rate is adjusted every two years.

12   17 U.S.C. § 101.

13   But note that the same medium can be a phonorecord in one case and not qualify as a phonorecord in another case. For example, a CD-ROM disc will be considered a phonorecord if it includes only recorded sounds. On the other hand, a typical multimedia CD-ROM that incorporates both sounds and images is not a phonorecord for purposes of the Copyright Act.

14   *Frank Music Corp. v. CompuServe, Inc.*, No. 93 Civ. 8153 (S.D.N.Y. filed Dec. 1993).

15   Unless, of course, the musical work was created as a **work made for hire**, such as if it was written by an employee or pursuant to a work for hire contract for a specific project, such as a motion picture. The rules regarding works for hire are discussed in chapter 23, section 1.2.

16   SIDNEY SHEMEL & M. WILLIAM KRASILOVSKY, THIS BUSINESS OF MUSIC 176 (6th ed. 1990)

17   Harry Fox Agency, Inc., 205 E. 42nd Street, New York, New York 10017; phone: (212) 370-5330; fax: (212) 953-2384.

18   Songwriters Guild of America, 276 Fifth Avenue, New York, New York 10001; phone: (212) 686-6820, fax: (212) 486-3680.

19   American Society of Composers, Authors and Publishers, 1 Lincoln Plaza, New York, New York 10023; phone: (212) 595-3050; fax: (212) 724-9664.

20   Broadcast Music, Inc. 320 W. 57th Street, New York, New York 10019; phone: (212) 586-2000; fax: (212) 246-2163.

21   SESAC, Inc. 156 W. 56th Street, New York, New York 10019; phone: (212) 586-3450; fax: (212) 397-4682.

22   The Harry Fox Agency, Inc., 205 E. 42nd Street, New York, New York 10017; phone: (212) 370-5330; fax: (212) 953-2384.

23   Canadian Music Reproduction Rights Agency, Ltd., 198 Davenport Road, Toronto, Ontario M5R1J2, Canada.

24   The American Mechanical Rights Association, 2112 Broadway, New York, New York 10023.

25   Copyright Management, Inc., 1102 17th Avenue South, Nashville, Tennessee 37212.

26   Publishers Licensing Corp., 15 Engle Street, Englewood, New Jersey 07631.

27   Rights of nondramatic public performance, as on television, radio, and in clubs and restaurants are sublicensed by the songwriter and/or the music publisher to performing rights societies — ASCAP, BMI, and SESAC — on a nonexclusive basis.

28   Janet L. Avery, The Struggle Over Performing Rights to Music: *BMI and ASCAP v. Cable Television*, in 1992-93 Entertainment, Publishing and the Arts Handbook 212-14. David Vierta & Robert Thornee eds. 1992-93).

29   Janet L. Avery, *The Struggle Over Performing Rights to Music*: BMI and ASCAP v. Cable Television, *in* 1992-93 *Entertainment, Publishing and the Arts Handbook* 212-14 (John David Viera & Robert Thome eds. 1992-93).

30   Janet L. Avery, *The Struggle Over Performing Rights to Music: BMI and ASCAP v. Cable Television, in 1992-93 Entertainment, Publishing and the Arts Handbook* 212-14 (John David Viera & Robert Thome eds. 1992-93).

CHAPTER 18

Licensing Sound Recordings

Licensing Sound Recordings

Sound is an important part of virtually all multimedia applications. This includes not only performances of musical works, but also human speech, animal sounds, and a wide variety of special effects. Unless you make your own sound recordings, however, you will inevitably be required to license the use of a preexisting sound recording.

1. Rights to Be Cleared

Licensing sound recordings requires clearance of the copyright, publicity rights, and third-party contract rights that are frequently part of a sound recording.

1.1 Copyright

Sound recordings are copyrightable regardless of the nature of the sounds recorded.[1] Common examples of copyrightable sound recordings include a recording of a performance of a copyrighted or public domain musical work, a recording of spoken words, such as a drama or a speech (whether or not copyrighted), a recording of sounds of nature (e.g., birds chirping or waves crashing onto the shore), special sound effects (e.g., a door slamming or cars crashing together), or virtually any other sound that can be recorded.[2]

Sound recordings are "works that result from the recording of a series of musical, spoken, or other sounds, regardless of the nature of the physical medium, such as discs or tapes, in which they are embodied."[3] However, a sound recording does not include any sounds accompanying a motion picture or other audiovisual work.[4] In that case, the sound is treated as part of the motion picture or audiovisual work that it accompanies.[5]

The material object in which a sound recording is fixed, and from which it may be perceived, reproduced, or otherwise communicated, either directly or with the aid of a machine, is known as a phonorecord.[6] Thus, the term *phonorecord* includes LPs, CDs, magnetic tape (such as cassette tape), and CD-ROMs.[7] A computer chip within which sounds are fixed also constitutes a sound recording.[8] A sound recording copyright may be claimed in the series of sounds recorded on any such tangible media. However, the copyrightable work comprises the aggregation of sounds, not the physical object (e.g., CD, tape, or LP) in which the sound recording is fixed.[9]

1.1.1 What Is Copyrightable about a Sound Recording?   Copyright protection generally extends to two elements in a sound recording: (1) the contribution of the performers whose performance is captured, and (2) the contribution of the person or persons responsible for capturing and processing the sounds to make the final recording.[10] Thus, the authors of a sound recording of a musical work (and the original owners of the copyright) are both the performer(s) whose performance is recorded, and the record producer who produces the sounds and fixes them into a master recording.

A recording artist's rendition of a musical work written by another is itself a copyrightable work.[11] The copyrightable expression can be seen in the differences between the performance of the same song by two different performers. Where the "performer" is not a human being (e.g., recordings of bird calls or the sounds of racing cars), there will, of course, be no copyright in the "performance" element of the sound recording.

Copyrightable authorship may also be claimed by the record producer responsible for setting up the recording session, capturing and electronically processing the sounds, and compiling and editing them to make the final sound recording.[12] These acts are closely analogous to the acts of a photographer in capturing and photographically processing light images to create a copyrightable photograph. Sound recording firms provide the equipment and organize the diverse talents of arrangers, performers, and technicians. These activities satisfy the requirements of authorship required for copyright. Likewise, compiling and editing sounds supports a copyright claim.[13]

1.1.2 Distinguishing a Sound Recording from the Underlying Work. It is important to note that the copyright in a sound recording is distinct from the copyright in the literary, dramatic, or musical work being performed. Copyright in a sound recording is not the same as, or a substitute for, copyright in the underlying musical work.[14] Thus, the copyright in a recording artist's performance of a song is separate and distinct from the copyright in the musical work comprising the song. Similarly, the copyright in a performer's recitation of a poem is separate and distinct from the copyright in the poem itself. Moreover, each of these separate copyrights is likely to be owned by different persons.

As a consequence, if you want to create your own sound recording of a copyrighted song or poem, you need to get permission from the owner of the copyright of the song or the poem. Failure to get such permission not only constitutes copyright infringement, but will also invalidate the copyright in the sound recording you create.[15]

And if you want to copy a sound recording of a song or poem done by someone else, you need to get permission from *both* the owner of the copyright in the song or poem and the owner of the copyright in the sound recording. Using a sound recording without permission (either the entire recording or a sample) risks infringing upon both the copyright in the underlying work (such as the musical work) and the copyright in the sound recording of that work.

Thus, as the foregoing discussion illustrates, licensing the right to use a sound recording often involves licensing two or more copyrights—that is, the copyright in the sound recording and the copyright in the underlying work that has been recorded (such as a musical work or a dramatic reading).[16] Unless you obtain a license to use both copyrights (usually from separate copyright owners), your use of the sound recording will infringe at least one of the two copyrights.

1.1.3 When Was it Created? Sound recordings have not always enjoyed copyright protection.[17] Whether a particular sound recording is protected by copyright depends upon the date it was created and/or first published.

• **Sound Recordings Created Prior to February 15, 1972.** Copyright protection does not apply to sound recordings created prior to February 15, 1972.[18] However, that does not necessarily mean you can freely copy them without need of permission. If a sound recording created before this date constituted a performance or derivative work of an underlying copyrighted work, copying and distributing the sound recording will still constitute infringement of the underlying copyrighted work. In one case, for example, the court found that duplicating, remixing, and distributing tapes of *Lone Ranger* radio programs constituted an infringement of the underlying copyrighted scripts, even though the sound recordings themselves were not protected by copyright.[19] In addition, in some states, sound recordings created prior to 1972 may also be protected by common law and local state laws relating to record piracy, such as unfair competition law, common law copyright, and state statutes relating to record piracy.[20]

● **Sound Recordings Created After February 15, 1972.** Sound recordings that were created and first published (distributed to the public) on or after February 15, 1972, and before January 1, 1978, are protected by copyright as a result of the Sound Recording Act of 1972.[21] This was the first time that American copyright law recognized sound recordings as copyrightable works, but the law extended protection only against unauthorized duplication. Sound recordings created after January 1, 1978, are protected under the current Copyright Act,[22] regardless of whether they are published or unpublished.

1.1.4 Limits on Sound Recording Copyright.

Under the current law, copyright in a sound recording protects the particular series of sounds that are "fixed" (i.e., embodied) in the recording against unauthorized reproduction and revision and against the unauthorized distribution of phonorecords containing those sounds. However, the scope of copyright protection for sound recordings is not as broad as the rights granted to owners of other copyrightable works. (The rights generally granted to the owners of a copyrighted work are explained in chapter 3, section 4). Specifically, it is limited as follows:

● **Reproduction Right.** The right of the owner of the copyright in a sound recording to copy or reproduce the sound recording extends only to the particular sounds of which the recording consists, and does not prevent a separate recording of another performance in which the sounds are imitated. In other words, it is infringement only to recapture the actual sounds fixed in the copyrighted recording, such as by sampling. It is not copyright infringement to make another sound recording that imitates or simulates the copyrighted sound recording.[23]

Thus, while it would be an infringement if you were to copy a copyrighted sound recording of a barking dog without permission, there is nothing wrong with making another recording of the same dog doing the same barking, so long as you make a new recording (i.e., you do not copy the actual sounds directly from the original recording). Mere imitation of a sound recording of a performance does not constitute a copyright infringement even where you deliberately set out to simulate another's performance as exactly as possible.[24] However, such an imitation may violate another copyright (such as the copyright in the musical work being performed), or may infringe the first performer's right of publicity (such as in the soundalike cases). See chapter 5, section 2.1 regarding soundalike cases.

With respect to the copyright in the sound recording, however, it would not be infringement of a sound recording to hire the very same artists to perform the very same arrangement, even if the resultant second recording was indistinguishable from the copyrighted first recording, even to a trained ear. So long as there is no re-recording of the first recording—that is, no recapturing of the actual sounds from the first recording in the second recording—there is no infringement.[25] Thus, it has been said that the reproduction right afforded to owners of copyrights in sound recordings "is limited to a right against dubbing."[26] In other words, copyright protection extends only to the exact sounds the owner creates.

● **Adaptation Right.** The right of the copyright owner in a sound recording to prepare derivative works (i.e., to adapt or modify the sound recording) is limited to the right to prepare a derivative work in which the actual sounds fixed in the original copyrighted sound recording are rearranged, remixed, or otherwise altered in sequence or quality.[27]

● **Public Performance Right.** Copyright protection for sound recordings does *not* include a right of public performance.[28] Thus, public performance of a sound recording does not infringe the owner's copyright. A composer of a musical work, for example, has a performance right in the underlying composition, but those who produce a sound recording of the musical work do not have the exclusive right to authorize the public performance of the recording itself. Thus, publicly performing a copyrighted sound recording, such as by playing a tape of unique sound effects over the radio, is not an infringement of the sound recording copyright. Similarly, playing a phonorecord embodying a performance of a musical work in restaurants, nightclubs, or on the radio is not an infringement of the right of the owner of the sound recording. It will, however, infringe the public performance right of the owner of the copyright in any other copyrightable work incorporated in the sound recording (such as a musical work), if done without permission.

● **Educational Use.** There is also an exception for sound recordings that are included in educational television and radio programs distributed or transmitted by or through public broadcasting entities. They may use reproductions of copyrighted sound recordings without infringing on any copyrights.[29] Similarly, the two other exclusive rights of copyright owners—to prepare derivative works and to distribute copyrighted works—are also subject to this educational program exception.[30]

1.2 Right of Publicity

In addition to copyright protection available for sound recordings, the right of publicity provides additional protection for the commercial value of the identity or persona of each of the performers who participated in the creation of the sound recording. (See chapter 5 for a general explanation of the right of publicity.) This can have an important impact on your proposed use of a sound recording in two respects. First, if you want to license the right to use a sound recording that includes the voice of a relatively well-known personality, obtaining a license from the copyright owner in the sound recording that will not necessarily be sufficient. You will also need to obtain a release of the rights of publicity held by each of the performers to the sound recording.

Second, as noted above, the copyright protection for a sound recording protects only the actual sounds as recorded. It does not prohibit you from making another sound recording that imitates or simulates the copyrighted sound recording. However, any attempt to imitate or simulate a sound recording by a particular artist, although not copyright infringement, may nonetheless infringe their right of publicity. Thus, for example, in a well-known case involving a Ford Motor Company commercial, a court found that using someone to imitate Bette Midler's voice while singing a particular song represented an infringement of her right of publicity.[31]

1.3 Third-Party Contract Rights

Sound recordings of musical works created by union talent are subject to the payment of the reuse fees specified in the applicable union collective bargaining agreement with the original recording studio. In the case of sound recordings involving union recording artists, reuse fees are required by the AFTRA collective bargaining agreement if the sound recording is utilized in a different media than that for which it was originally created.

Similarly, to the extent any union musicians or instrumentalists were involved, the collective bargaining agreement with the AF of M requires the payment of reuse fees for the use of the performance in a new medium such as multimedia.

The AFTRA and AF of M agreements with the recording company typically require either that the recording company pay the applicable reuse fees, or contractually require its licensee to pay the applicable fees. (See discussion of AFTRA and AF of M reuse provisions in chapter 21, sections 5 and 6).

In addition to the reuse fees, sound recordings involving very well known and popular recording artists may be subject to contractual restrictions on the reuse of the recording that are contained in a contract between the recording artist and the record company. Such contracts may restrict the media for which the sound recording can be licensed, impose restrictions on the use that can be made of the sound recording, or require the recording artists' consent for a reuse of the sound recording.

This situation typically occurs with popular recording artists who have the bargaining power to negotiate a contract that includes the right to control the use of their performances. In addition, a superstar may be able to retain copyright ownership in the "master recording" or obtain a reversion of copyright ownership in the master recording after a certain period of time and under certain circumstances.

2. Identifying and Finding the Owners of the Rights

Determining who is the "author" of a sound recording (and thus the owner of the copyright in the sound recording) is sometimes a difficult task, as a sound recording frequently reflects the contributions of several persons working in different capacities. Typically, the copyrightable elements in a sound recording involve authorship by both the performers and by the producer of the sound recording (who is in charge of planning the recording session, recording and processing the sounds, and assembling and editing them into the final sound recording). In some cases the producer contributes very little (e.g., pushing a button to start the recorder), whereas in other situations (such as recording natural sounds such as crowd noises or animal sounds), the producer is the only one making a copyrightable contribution.

In cases involving copyrightable contributions by both performers and the producer of the sound recording (e.g., when recordings are made of musical works), the parties will typically determine by contract the ownership of the resulting copyright in the sound recording. In the absence of an agreement by contract (or a work for hire dictated by an employment relationship), the copyright in the resulting sound recording will be jointly owned by everyone who contributed copyrightable expression to the work (such as the performing artists and the record producer). (See chapter 23 for a discussion of copyright ownership.)

The copyright interest in a sound recording of a musical work is, however, typically owned by the record company. The record company usually obtains the rights in the sound recording from the "authors" of that work, such as the recording artists, composers, lyricists, or engineers. Where that is the case, you will need to get permission to use the sound recording from only one entity, the record company. However, if the sound recording embodies a performance of a copyrighted work (such as a musical work, poem, and so forth), you will still need to obtain permission from the copyright owner of the work being performed.

Nonetheless, it is possible that other persons may be owners of the rights in a sound recording. For example, as noted above, the performers themselves may have obtained some rights to the renditions they have created, or union contracts may reserve some rights to the performers involved.

Finding the owners of these rights to a sound recording may be an easier task than finding the owners of the rights to a musical work. Since most of the copyrights (at least to musical recordings) are owned by the record companies, contacting the appropriate record company is generally the appropriate place to start. Most record companies are set up to handle the granting of licenses to use their sound recordings, and to the extent you need to obtain releases from the performers, can presumably put you in touch with the relevant performers or their agents. To begin this process, contact the "special markets" division of the record company.

3. Licensing from Libraries of Music and Other Sound Recordings

An alternative to the sound recording clearance process is to obtain sound recordings of music, sound effects, and other sound recordings from businesses that maintain libraries of such sound recordings. Obtaining sound recordings from these stock libraries greatly simplifies the clearance process, as they generally own (or have the right to distribute) both the music and the sound recording of the music. Stock libraries do not have popular recordings by hit artists, but often have a wide selection of music that may be suitable for your project.

Music library licenses typically grant synchronization and mechanical reproduction rights, but often do not grant public performance rights.

Stock music libraries are often sensitive about using their music in the "clear" (unmixed with any other sounds, voice, music, or images). Thus, sound recordings of music from stock libraries are typically licensed on a nonexclusive basis for use only in synchronization with other audiovisual elements that you add. In some cases, additional consent must be obtained if the music is a feature part of the project rather than an incidental or background element.

In some cases you may not be able to obtain public performance rights to the music. If performance rights are granted, they are often conditioned upon the performance by broadcasters and transmitters who have valid performance rights licenses from the owner of the copyrights in the musical compositions. In other cases, public performance rights will be limited to cases in which the music is combined with other audiovisual elements and the music is not a featured part of the presentation, but rather is an incidental or background element.

The music library will typically warrant that it is the holder of the copyright to the music or has the right to license it to you. However, you may be required to indemnify the music library from any and all claims, suits, liability, losses, and damages that may be made or brought against it by reason of your use of the music.

Music is often licensed on the basis of a "needledrop." A *needledrop* is a segment of music of any length used in a production. Music is also licensed on a "production blanket" basis. This type of license is based on the actual length of your program, thus allowing you to use an unlimited number of needledrops within a particular production for a fixed price. The price for a music license depends upon your intended use and the market and/or medium of distribution.

Typically, the payment for a synchronization license to use the music is only made once. However, if there are any changes or revisions in the original production, an additional synchronization license must be obtained in order to reuse the music in the changed or revised version.

Endnotes

1   17 U.S.C. § 102(a)(7).

2   See, e.g., *Innovative Concepts in Entertainment, Inc. v. Entertainment Enters., Ltd.*, 576 F. Supp. 457, 461 (E.D.N.Y. 1983) (sound recording of crowd noises from an actual hockey game was copyrightable).

3   17 U.S.C. § 101.

4   17 U.S.C. § 101.

5   17 U.S.C. § 101.

6   17 U.S.C. § 101.

7   Copyright Office Cir. 56, Copyright for Sound Recordings 2 (1991). It does not, however, include a sound track that is integrated with a motion picture. Such a sound track is considered part of the motion picture and is protected as part of the motion picture copyright. See chapter 20.

8   *Innovative Concepts in Entertainment, Inc. v. Entertainment Enters., Ltd.*, 576 F. Supp. 457, 461 (E.D.N.Y. 1983).

9   See H.R. Rep. No. 1476, 94th Cong. 2d Sess. 56 (1976), *reprinted in* 1976 U.S.C.C.A.N. 5659, 5669; Copyright Office Cir. 56, Copyright For Sound Recordings 1 (1991).

10   Copyright Office Cir. 56, Copyright for Sound Recordings 2 (1991). No copyright may be claimed in "sounds [which] are fixed by some purely mechanical means without originality of any kind." However, the required originality may emanate from either "the performers whose performances is captured," or from "the record producer responsible for setting up the recording session, capturing and electronically processing the sounds, and compiling and editing them to make the final sound recording," or more generally, from both. H.R. Rep. No. 1476, 94th Cong., 2d Sess. 56 (1976), *reprinted in* 1976 U.S.C.C.A.N. 5659, 5669.

11   *Forward v. Thorogood*, 985 F.2d 604, 605 (1st Cir. 1993) ("The performer of a musical work is the author, as it were, of the performance.").

12   H.R. Rep. No. 1476, 94th Cong., 2d Sess. 56 (1976), *reprinted in* 1976 U.S.C.C.A.N. 5659, 5669.

13   See *Innovative Concepts in Entertainment, Inc. v. Entertainment Enters., Ltd.*, 576 F. Supp. 457, 462 (E.D.N.Y. 1983) (editing sounds of crowd noises from a hockey game into a short segment found to be copyrightable).

14   Copyright Office Cir. 56a, Copyright Registration of Musical Compositions and Sound Recordings 1 (1989).

15   17 U.S.C. § 103(a). See e.g., *Jarvis v. A & M Records*, 827 F. Supp. 282, 292 (D.N.J. 1993) ("copyright protection for a sound recording of musical compositions must be denied if the copyright claimant of the sound recording has not lawfully obtained the rights to utilize the musical compositions in the sound recordings").

16   This is not an issue, of course, if what is recorded is not itself copyrightable, such as birds chirping, crowd noises, sound effects, public domain musical works, and so forth.

17   See, e.g., *Lone Ranger Tele., Inc. v. Program Radio Corp.*, 740 F.2d 718, 720-21 (9th Cir. 1984); *Goldstein v. California*, 412 U.S. 546, 568, 93 S. Ct. 2303, 2315 (1973).

18   17 U.S.C. § 301(c).

19   *Lone Ranger Tele., Inc. v. Program Radio* Corp., 740 F.2d 718, 722 (9th Cir. 1984).

20   *Lone Ranger Tele., Inc. v. Program Radio* Corp., 740 F.2d 718, 725 (9th Cir. 1984); see also Cal. Civ. Code § 980(a)(2) (codifying ownership rights in sound recordings fixed before 1972); Cal. Penal Code § 653(h)(b) (enacted to punish record piracy); *U.S. Sporting Prods., Inc. v. Johnny Stewart Game Calls, Inc.*, 865 S.W.2d 214 (Tex. App. 1993) (tape recordings of animal sounds made prior to February 15, 1972 protected against copying by Texas State Law of Misappropriation).

21   Sound Recording Act of 1972, Pub. L. No. 92-140, 85 Stat. 391 (codified as amended in scattered sections of 17 U.S.C.).

22   17 U.S.C. § 102(a)(7).

23   17 U.S.C. § 114(b); H.R. Rep. No. 1476, 94th Cong., 2d Sess. 106 (1976), *reprinted in* 1976 U.S.-C.C.A.N. 5659, 5721; *United States v. Taxe*, 380 F. Supp. 1010, 1017 (C.D. Cal. 1974), *aff'd in part and vacated in part*, 540 F.2d 961, 965 (9th Cir. 1976), *cert. denied*, 429 U.S. 1040 (1977).

24   H.R. Rep. No. 1476, 94th Cong., 2d Sess. 106 (1976), *reprinted in* 1976 U.S.C.C.A.N. 5659, 5721.

25   *United States v. Taxe*, 380 F. Supp. 1010, 1017 (C.D. Cal. 1974), *aff'd in part and vacated in part*, 540 F.2d 961, 965 (9th Cir. 1976), *cert. denied*, 429 U.S. 1040 (1977).

26   Paul Goldstein, Copyright § 5.2.1.2.a (1989).

27   17 U.S.C. § 114(b).

28   17 U.S.C. §§ 114(a) and (b).

29   17 U.S.C. § 114(b).

30   17 U.S.C. § 114(b).

31   *Midler v. Ford Motor Co.*, 849 F.2d 460 (9th Cir. 1988).

CHAPTER 19

Licensing Photographs and Still Images

Visual images are a key component of virtually all multimedia works. Strictly speaking, they come in two forms. Still images, such as photographs, drawings, designs, patterns, blueprints, and the like, and moving pictures, such as film, video, and television broadcasts. This chapter will focus on the licensing of still images. Chapter 20 will focus on the licensing of motion pictures and other audiovisual works.

1. Rights to Be Cleared

Licensing photographs and other still images require the clearance of the copyright to the image. In addition, clearance may be required with respect to trademarks, rights of publicity and privacy, as well as defamation.

1.1 Copyright

Pictorial, graphic, and sculptural works are copyrightable.[1] They include two-dimensional and three-dimensional works of fine, graphic, and applied art, photographs, prints and art reproductions, maps, globes, charts, diagrams, and models.[2] Also included are illustrations, plans, and drawings, and works in any of the foregoing categories intended for use in advertising and commerce.[3] There is no implied criterion of artistic taste, aesthetic value, or intrinsic quality necessary for copyrightability.[4]

Examples of works that qualify for copyright protection as "pictorial, graphic and sculptural works" include advertisements, commercial prints, labels, cartoons, comic strips, drawings, paintings, murals, floor and wall covering designs, games, puzzles, greeting cards, holograms, computer and laser artwork, logo artwork, maps, cartographic works, masks, models, mosaics, patterns, photographs, photomontages, reproductions, technical drawings, architectural drawings or plans, blueprints, diagrams, and mechanical drawings.[5]

● **Photographs.** Photographs are copyrightable regardless of the form the photograph takes, such as print, negative, filmstrip, slide, or machine-readable digital form. In one recent case, for example, a court held that making digitized versions of copyrighted photographs available on a computer bulletin board infringes the copyright owner's rights of distribution and public display.[6]

If you want to use a preexisting photograph, it will be necessary to obtain a license from the copyright holder of the photograph. This is usually the photographer or the publisher for whom the photographer was employed. If you want to use graphic art, you must obtain an appropriate license from the graphic artist.

● **Ornamental Designs.** Patterns and designs are generally considered to be copyrightable.[7]

● **Reproductions of Works of Art.** A reproduction of an original work of art is copyrightable, even where the original is in the public domain,[8] so long as the reproduction contains some original contribution.

Using reproductions of fine art in a multimedia work requires that rights be obtained from two sources. First, you must obtain a license from the artist of the artwork (unless the work is in the public domain). Second, you must obtain a license from the copyright holder of the photograph or reproduction of the art work that will be used in the multimedia work.

● **Maps.** The Copyright Act specifically provides that maps are amenable to copyright if they evidence the requisite degree of originality,[9] and courts have long recognized maps as copyrightable subject matter.[10] However, because facts are not copyrightable, and because maps are usually drafted with the purpose of accurately presenting factual geographic information, there is a significant issue as to when, and to what extent, a map is copyrightable. As one court has noted, "In the case of maps . . . if each be faithful, identity is inevitable, because each seeks only to set down the same facts in precisely the same relations to each other. So far as each is successful, each will be exactly the same."[11]

1.2 Right of Publicity

Permission from the copyright owner of a photograph may not be sufficient. The use of photographs and other still images that include actual persons can result in an infringement of the right of publicity of the persons depicted, at least where the use amounts to a commercial exploitation of their image or likeness without their consent. This is particularly true if the photograph is of a well-known person. Use of the person's likeness may infringe his or her right of publicity if done without permission, even for many years after the person's death. (See discussion regarding right of publicity in chapter 5.) Thus, for example, courts have found that the use of photographs has resulted in an infringement of one's right of publicity where photographs of baseball players were used on chewing gum cards without permission,[12] and where a picture of the head of Cary Grant was combined with the body of a model, as part of a fashion article.[13]

Accordingly, you must think not only about who owns the copyright to the photograph, but also about any rights attached to the people or objects in the photo. Ideally, you should obtain releases from any of the recognizable persons (whether private persons or public figures) appearing in the picture.

1.3 Right of Privacy

The use of photographs can also constitute an infringement of an individual's right of privacy. This frequently occurs when a photograph is used in relation to other content in a manner that creates an improper negative impression about the person in the photo.

In one case, for example, a court found an invasion of privacy occurred through the use of a photograph of a woman to illustrate an article about a mother who abandoned her child.[14] In another case, a photograph of a couple kissing to illustrate an article on the shallowness of love at first sight was found to constitute an infringement of the right of privacy.[15] And in yet another case, a court found that using the photograph of a woman in conjunction with two newspaper articles on the subject of neighborhood prostitution, when in fact the woman had no connection with prostitution, could constitute an infringement of her right of privacy.[16]

Everyone has a privacy right that may be violated by your use of his or her photograph. Thus, you should be sure to get the necessary release from any person whose image appears in a photograph.

1.4 Defamation

A photograph can be defamatory if (1) it does not accurately reflect the image originally sought to be captured, or (2) it is displayed in a context (e.g., in conjunction with other photographs, caption or text) that suggests a defamatory "fact" about the person depicted.[17]

Obviously, multimedia technology creates the potential for liability through either of these avenues. Because digital alteration of photographs and images makes it impossible to distinguish the altered image from the original, it is easy to envision liability for inaccurately portraying the original image. Liability for contextual defamation is also a clear possibility given the ease with which text and images may be combined through multimedia technology to communicate defamatory "facts."

For example, alterations of photographs have been held to be defamatory. In one case, for example, a picture of a woman was altered to make it appear as though she were bald.[18] In another case, liability was imposed when a photograph of a female model was juxtaposed with a picture of a elderly male holding a "dirty book."[19]

2. Identifying and Finding the Owners of the Rights

Determining who owns the rights to a particular photograph can often be difficult and time-consuming. With respect to photographs appearing in books, magazines, and other publications, the publisher may have acquired ownership of the copyright in the photograph. However, more often than not, the copyright to the photograph is retained by the photographer. In fact, in many cases it is customary for the photographer who took the picture to retain the copyright, and sell to the publication only the right to use it in specific ways. If the agreement between the photographer and the publisher can be located, it may contain a variety of restrictions on use and reproduction of the photograph. This is especially likely if the photographer is well known. The agreement may, for example, limit reproduction of the photograph to a particular size, specified quality of resolution, format (e.g., black and white or color), medium (e.g., a particular magazine), time period, geographic area, or number of copies that can be reproduced.

Nonetheless, the publisher of the book or magazine in which the photograph appeared is often a good place to start in your search to identify and locate the owner of the copyright. If the publisher does not own the copyright, he or she can presumably put you in touch with the photographer or the agency representing the photographer.

Photographers are often represented by photo stock agencies. Many photo stock agencies belong to the Picture Agency Council of America (PACA).[20] It publishes the *PACA Directory*, which includes information about each member agency, with a description of their collections.

3. Licensing Images from Stock Photo Houses

As an alternative to clearing the rights to one or more individual photographs that you would like to use, consider obtaining photographs from stock photo houses. They are often a good source of images for use in your multimedia product.

Stock photo houses typically own the copyright in the photographs that they make available, or have licensing authorization from the copyright owner. Thus, by obtaining photographs from stock photo houses, you eliminate the problem of locating and negotiating with the owner of the copyright. In many cases, stock photograph houses will also have releases from persons depicted in the photos. However, this should always be verified before a photo of a person is used in a manner that would normally require a release.

Prices for stock photographs will typically be based on your intended use of the photograph.

Endnotes

1   17 U.S.C. § 102(a)(5). Copyright is explained in chapter 3.

2   17 U.S.C. § 101 (definition of "pictorial, graphic and sculptural works").

3   H.R. REP. NO. 1476, 94th Cong. 2d Sess. 54 (1976), *reprinted in* 1976 U.S.C.C.A.N. 5659, 5667.

4   H.R. REP. NO. 1476, 94th Cong. 2d Sess. 54 (1976), *reprinted in* 1976 U.S.C.C.A.N. 5659, 5667.

5   COPYRIGHT OFFICE CIR. 40, COPYRIGHT REGISTRATION FOR WORKS OF THE VISUAL ARTS 2 (1990).

6   *Playboy Enters., Inc. v. Frena*, 839 F.Supp. 1552 (M.D.Fla. 1993).

7   *Peter Pan Fabrics, Inc. v. Dan River Mills, Inc.*, 295 F. Supp. 1366, 1368 (S.D.N.Y. 1969) (ornamental designs on uncolored fabric); *Soptra Fabrics Corp. v. Stafford Knitting Mills, Inc.*, 490 F.2d 1092, (2d Cir. 1974); *Primcot Fabrics, Dep't of Prismatic Fabrics, Inc. v. Kleinfab Corp.*, 368 F. Supp. 482 (S.D.N.Y. 1974) (juxtaposition of colors in patch plaid design held sufficient originality).

8   See *Alfred Bell & Co. v. Catalda Fine Arts, Inc.*, 191 F.2d 99, 104-05 (2d Cir. 1951); *Home Art, Inc. v. Glensder Textile Corp.*, 81 F. Supp. 551, 552 (S.D.N.Y. 1948).

9   17 U.S.C. §§ 101, 102(2)(5).

10   See, e.g., *General Drafting Co. v. Andrews*, 37 F.2d 54 (2d Cir. 1930); *Kern River Gas Transmission Co. v. Coastal Corp.*, 899 F.2d 1458, 1463 (5th Cir.), *cert. denied*, 498 U.S. 952 (1990).

11   *Alfred Bell & Co. v. Catalda Fine Arts Inc.*, 191 F.2d 99, 104 n. 21 (2d Cir. 1951) (quoting *Fred Fisher, Inc. v. Dillingham*, 298 F. 145, 150-51 (S.D.N.Y. 1924) (Judge Learned Hand).

12   *Haelan Lab., Inc. v. Topps Chewing Gum, Inc.*, 202 F.2d 866, 868-69 (2d Cir.), *cert. denied*, 346 U.S. 816 (1953).

13   *Grant v. Esquire, Inc.*, 367 F. Supp. 876, 878-80 (S.D.N.Y. 1973) (remanded for review of First Amendment issues).

14   *Price-Prystash v. Best Medium Publishing Co.*, 157 Conn. 507, 254 A.2d 872 (1969); see also RESTATEMENT (SECOND) OF TORTS, § 652E, illustrations 6-9.

15   *Gill v. Curtis Publishing Co.*, 38 Cal.2d 273, 239 P.2d 630 (1952).

16   *Parnell v. Booth Newspapers, Inc.* 572 F. Supp. 909, 921-22 (W.D. Mich. 1983).

17   *Roskos v. New York News, Inc.*, 4 Media L. Rep. 2148 (N.Y. Sup. Ct. 1979).

18   *Carlson v. Hillman Periodicals, Inc.* 3 A.D.2d 987, 163 N.Y.S.2d 21 (N.Y. App. Div. 1957).

19   *Russell v. Marlboro Books*, 18 Misc.2d 166, 183 N.Y.S.2d 8 (N.Y. Sup. Ct. 1959).

20   Picture Agency Council of America, 1530 Westlake Ave., Seattle, Washington 98109.

Licensing Motion Pictures and Other Audiovisual Works

Licensing Motion Pictures and Other Audiovisual Works

Motion pictures, or video, can significantly enhance any multimedia product. Suppose, for example, that you want to use a clip from the film *Gone With The Wind* for a multimedia product dealing with the Civil War, or a portion of an old cigarette commercial for a multimedia product dealing with advertising, or perhaps some footage from an old World War II movie to enhance a multimedia product on warfare. How do you go about obtaining licenses to use this content? To understand the process, we need to begin with a review of the sometimes complex set of rights that may need to be cleared.

1. Rights to Be Cleared

Clearing the rights to use a portion of a motion picture, television broadcast, or other audiovisual work typically involves dealing with numerous and sometimes complex rights. These include copyright rights, rights of publicity, and third-party contract rights.

1.1 Copyright

The Copyright Act specifically states that motion pictures and other audiovisual works are copyrightable subject matter.[1]

Audiovisual works are works that consist of a series of related images that are intrinsically intended to be shown by the use of machines or devices such as projectors, viewers, VCRs, televisions, computers, or other electronic equipment, together with accompanying sounds, if any. It makes no difference whether the series of images is embodied on film, tape, disk, CD-ROM, or any other material object.[2] Thus, audiovisual works include a filmstrip, a set of slides, a film, a videotape, a videodisc, a television news broadcast[3], and a video game.[4]

Motion pictures are a subset of audiovisual works. Specifically, they are audiovisual works consisting of a series of related images that, when shown in succession, impart an impression of motion.[5] The impression of motion is the essence of a motion picture. A series of slides shown sequentially, although an audiovisual work, is not a motion picture, because it does not when shown impart an impression of motion.[6] Motion pictures, like other audiovisual works, can be embodied on film, videotape, videodisc, CD-ROM, CD-I, disk, or any other tangible form.

The copyright in a motion picture, by definition, includes the accompanying sounds, if any.[7] Thus, the soundtrack of a motion picture is also protected by the motion picture copyright. It is not considered a sound recording. (See chapter 18, section 1.1 regarding sound recording copyright.)

Because motion pictures and other audiovisual works are copyrightable, you will need to obtain permission from the copyright owner in order to incorporate clips from popular movies, television programs, newscasts or commercials into a multimedia product, unless they have entered the public domain. This is true even though you want to use only a short clip lasting a few seconds. "Borrowing" bits and pieces of a film or television clip is still copyright infringement.[8] Furthermore, electronically distorting the clip does not change the fact of infringement or make the manipulated clip yours.[9]

Obtaining this permission, however, can often be a difficult and complex task in large part because of the overlapping copyrights and separation of rights that occur with respect to a film clip or television broadcast. These issues are discussed in this chapter at section 3.

1.2 Right of Publicity

In addition to licensing the applicable copyright rights, it will be necessary to address the right of publicity of each of the performers that appears in the film or television clip. Performers have a proprietary right in their personas, that includes their names, visual images of their likenesses, and audio sounds of their voices. This right derives from the right of publicity. (The right of publicity is explained in chapter 5.)

Before using a film or video clip you have licensed from the copyright owner, you will also need to obtain a release of these rights—that is, the rights to use the name, likeness, and voice of each recognizable person who appears in the motion picture clip being licensed. Note that obtaining clearance of this right is independent of obtaining a license from the copyright owner to use the film clip. Moreover, it is necessary regardless of whether or not the copyright to the film clip is in the public domain. (For a discussion of the issues that arise with regard to motion picture and film clips that are in the public domain, see chapter 11, section 1.2).

1.3 Third-Party Contract Rights

In addition to the legal rights inherent in a movie or television clip, you also need to consider a variety of contract rights that may exist. These contract rights can be grouped into two general categories: contract rights that arise as a result of individually negotiated contracts between the producer and a performer or other creative person involved in the preparation of the work, and contract rights created by virtue of the various union collective bargaining agreements entered into by the producer of a film or television program that uses union talent.

Union collective bargaining agreements not only establish minimum terms upon which their members may be employed in the production of a film or television program, but they also secure other rights and benefits for their members. Most significant among those additional rights and benefits, when you want to license the use of the film or television program, is that most union agreements require that their members be compensated for any reuse or new use of film or television program in any medium or market other than that for which it was originally created. Thus, if you want to use a clip from a movie or television program created with union talent, then, in addition to the license fees that must be paid to the copyright owner, and any fees that must be paid to the performers for releases of their rights of publicity, you will be obligated to pay certain additional fees specified in the applicable union collective bargaining agreements.

Pursuant to union collective bargaining agreements, fees may be due to the WGA, the DGA, the AF of M (if musicians were involved in the production), AFTRA (if it was a television program), SAG (if it was a film), and perhaps other unions as well. The details regarding the reuse fees payable to the various unions are set forth in chapter 21.

The producer of the film (as owner of the copyright) is contractually obligated to pay the unions (and/or the performers) in the event that it licenses someone else to use the film or television program in a different medium, or in the alternative, is obligated to obtain a commitment from the licensee to make the payment directly to the union (and/or the performer).

In addition, because union collective bargaining agreements specify only the "minimum" terms of employment between the union member and the production company, it is frequently the case that many celebrities or stars will negotiate contracts containing many additional terms and conditions (as well as substantially higher rates of compensation). Sometimes these contracts with individual performers or artists include significant provisions governing control over the subsequent use or alteration of the resulting work.

There are a variety of ways in which artists may want to control the use of their work. These may include limitations or prohibitions on any adaptations or alterations of the work, a requirement that the author's name be displayed in a certain manner in connection with the use of the work, limitations or prohibitions on the use of less than the entire work, and issues relating to the modification or destruction of the work. As one court has noted: "It is the writer or performer . . . who suffers the consequences of the mutilation, for the public will have only the final product by which to evaluate the work."[10]

Contractual restrictions on the use of copyrighted content imposed by the author of the work can also have a significant impact on the ability of the licensor to grant you the rights necessary for your proposed use of the content. In one case, for example, actor/director Warren Beatty successfully prohibited a network television broadcast of the movie *Reds*, based on contract provisions governing final cut for television broadcast. Specifically, his contract with Paramount Pictures had given him final cutting rights on the movie, which extended to use for television. Consequently, even though ABC had licensed the movie from Paramount, they were unable to show the movie in the manner intended.[11]

In addition to the reuse fees and other control provisions noted above, it is also important to understand that the Writers Guild of America Basic Agreement includes provisions relating to the concept of separation of rights—i.e., allowing writers to retain certain rights in the works they create, even though they will not retain ownership of the copyright in the works themselves. Under these provisions, the writer may retain one or more of a variety of rights, including sequel rights (the right to use the leading character for a substantially different story), merchandising rights (the right to manufacture and sell any unique and original object or thing first described in the material or written by the writer), and reacquisition rights (the right to reacquire unproduced original material from the producer). The provisions are discussed in chapter 21, section 2.2.

Accordingly, when licensing film or television clips, in addition to paying the applicable reuse fees you will need to determine whether the writer has retained any such rights, and, to the extent that impacts your proposed use of the film or television clip, it may be necessary to separately negotiate with the writer to obtain permission to use the clip.

2. Difficulties in Licensing Motion Picture Rights

When it comes to obtaining permission to use motion pictures and other audiovisual works, perhaps the least organized and most difficult to deal with is the world of moving images. This situation exists for several reasons.

First, film and television programs often involve a complicated bundle of rights—such as (1) copyrights to the underlying story, screenplay, preexisting music, preexisting characters, etc.; (2) the publicity or reuse rights of the performers; and (3) obligations to make payments to unions and perhaps others. The content owner has to be certain that its contracts allow it to grant the multimedia use rights you require, and that there is enough money in the deal to satisfy all parties.

Second, the custom and practice in the movie industry do not always support adequately documented contracts clearly setting forth the rights of each party to a motion picture.[12]

Third, film studios and television producers often have large investments in their productions, and frequently believe that there is some kind of integrity in the whole. Consequently, they often feel that licensing clips somehow cheapens the product, and damages the market for the entire production.

Fourth, most film and television companies are not set up to locate, provide, and license the material you want on any kind of regular basis. Each transaction requires the involvement of business affairs executives, lawyers, laboratory research personnel, and others. It is not their primary business and they often view it as a nuisance.

Finally, many studios and program producers are getting into multimedia production themselves, or have formed alliances with developers, and are saving their properties for their own projects. So, unless you are prepared to spend a substantial amount of money for a license, don't even think of incorporating a few seconds of a major motion picture into your next multimedia production.

As a consequence, getting such permission can be a daunting task. The basic steps in the process can be summarized as follows:

1. identify each of the component rights in the motion picture or television clip to be used;

2. identify and locate the owners of each of those rights or their agents;

3. obtain a license from the owners of all the copyrightable component rights in the motion picture or television clip;

4. obtain a license or release from every recognizable performer appearing in the clip, whether living or dead; and

5. pay applicable union/guild reuse fees for the clip.

3. Elements to Be Licensed

Motion pictures and television programs embody the creative contributions of writers, producers, directors, performers and many others, and typically constitute an amalgam of numerous component artistic works and rights, including a variety of copyrights, publicity rights, and contract rights.

The copyrights that are typically part of a motion picture or other audiovisual work (in addition to the copyright in the complete motion picture itself) may include:

- the script, i.e., the screenplay or teleplay (a *screenplay* refers to the script upon which a motion picture is based; a *teleplay* refers to the script upon which a television program is based);

- any preexisting literary work upon which the script is based;

- the performers' performances;

- the music or soundtrack and its performance;

- animation, special effects, and other works created for the production; and
- preexisting works of art embedded in the production, for example, other film clips, stills, animation, and artwork.

See chapter 23 for a discussion of the distinction between the copyright that applies to a complete work, such as a multimedia product or a motion picture, and the copyrights in each of the individual component parts that comprise the completed product.

Thus, not only is the motion picture or television program itself a copyrightable work, but many of its component parts may also be separately copyrightable works. (See discussion of this problem of overlapping copyrights in chapter 3, section 7.) Consequently, the "bundle" of copyright rights—the reproduction right, adaptation right, distribution right, performance right and display right—may exist for several component works as well as for the motion picture or television program as whole. (These copyright rights are explained in chapter 3, section 4.)

This means that getting permission to use a clip may require that you obtain permission from others besides the owner of the copyright in the motion picture or television program itself. This also means that some of the rights in the copyright rights bundle may be owned by one person or entity while other rights in the bundle may be owned by another person or entity.

In addition to the copyrights, there are a number of other rights that may be present. First, every performer possesses a right of publicity in his or her identity or persona (for example, name, image, likeness, and voice), as it is used in the motion picture. (See chapter 5 for a discussion of the right of publicity.) Second, the unions or guilds representing the artistic talent that created and/or performed in the audiovisual work may have reserved a contractual right to certain payments, such as reuse fees. Third, the stars and other well recognized individuals who created and/or performed in the audiovisual work may have also contractually obtained the right to royalties and/or residual payments for the use of the work (in addition to the fees they received for their work, and separate from their rights of publicity).

Generally, to identify the component works requires a careful eye and ear. Besides identifying the performers appearing in the scene, you should look for such "invisible" components such as special effects, narration or voiceovers, and artwork or other film clips appearing in the background.

However, it does not necessarily mean that you must get permission from everyone who had anything to do with any part of the motion picture or television program. The task of obtaining permission can be narrowed by focusing on the specific clip you want to use, and determining who contributed to the clip as opposed to the entire motion picture or television program. For example, you would not need the permission of performers or owners of the rights to music or special effects that are not part of the specific clip you propose to license.

When licensing film or video clips, it is important to understand the distinction between the intrinsic and extrinsic properties that make up the motion picture. **Extrinsic properties** are (1) the copyrightable works created independently of the motion picture or television program—that is, preexisting works or works created for use in the motion picture by independent contractors who have retained ownership of the copyright, and (2) the right of each of the performers in his or her identity or persona (e.g., name, image, likeness, and voice)—that is, their right of publicity. (See chapter 5 for a discussion of the right of publicity.)

Examples of extrinsic properties include the book on which a movie is based, the animated cartoon character depicted in a movie, preexisting music incorporated within the motion picture, preexisting film clips included in the motion picture, preexisting works of art (such as paintings and photographs) included in the film clip, and reuse rights involving the actors persona or commercial image. Frequently, many of these will be listed in the credits. Separate licenses are required with regard to the rights in the extrinsic properties.

Intrinsic properties, on the other hand typically include any creations made for the production under a work made for hire contract. (Work made for hire contracts are discussed in chapter 23, section 1.2.) Generally no separate license is required for intrinsic properties—that is, they are included in the license of rights you obtain from the owner of the copyright in the complete motion picture. However, this is true only if the creator of these elements did not contractually reserve some of the rights in what he or she created via a separation of rights arrangement. (Separation of rights is explained in chapter 3, section 6.) In such a case, the producer of the motion picture will not obtain all rights to the work, and thus may still be necessary to obtain a license from the creator.

3.1 The Script

Normally, the script for a film or television production is considered as an intrinsic element. As such, you will normally not have to be concerned about it when licensing rights to the clip. However, in certain cases the writer of the script may have retained certain rights to it pursuant to a separation of rights clause in his or her contract with the producer. If this is the case, then, depending upon your proposed use of the clip and the accompanying script, and depending upon the rights reserved by the writer, you may have to obtain a license from the writer or his or her agent.

It is common, for example, for writers who are members of the Writers Guild of America (WGA) to use a separation of rights clause in their contract with the producer to retain one or more rights to the script, such as print publication rights, sequel rights, and merchandising rights. (This subject is discussed in more detail in chapter 3, section 6, and chapter 21, section 2.)

3.2 Preexisting Literary Works

In those cases where a motion picture is based on a preexisting literary work, such as a book, it is likely that the author of the book only granted the production company limited rights to make the motion picture based on the book, and reserved all other rights in the book, including rights in the title, plot, characters and story line, and particularly the right to adapt the literary work to new forms such as multimedia. In these circumstances, you will need to secure permission from the author.[13]

3.3 Performers' Performances

One of the copyrightable aspects of a motion picture or television program is the performance of the actors and actresses,[14] although that copyright is usually assigned to the producer or originally owned by the producer pursuant to a work-for-hire arrangement. Accordingly, the copyright in the performance will normally be an intrinsic part of the motion picture that is obtained as part of the license from the copyright owner. However, the stars who performed in the motion picture may have also contractually obtained the right to royalties and/or residual payments for the use of the work (in addition to the fees they received for their performance). In such a case, it will be necessary to contract with them (or their agents) as well.

3.4 Music or Soundtrack

Music or a soundtrack that is created for and integrated into a motion picture or television program is protectible as part of the motion picture.[15] If, however, preexisting music is used in the motion picture with permission of the copyright owner, then the music will be considered as an extrinsic property, and it will be necessary to license the right to use the music from the copyright owner. Similarly, if the music was created especially for the motion picture or television program, but the composer retained the copyright or certain limited aspects of it, it may also be necessary to license appropriate rights from the composer or his or her agent. In addition, if the music or soundtrack of the motion picture is recorded separately, for example, as in a separate CD to be sold in retail music outlets, the music is a "sound recording" and is itself copyrightable separate from the motion picture or television program.

An example is the lip sync of the rock classic "Bohemian Rhapsody" by Wayne and Garth, and others in the motion picture *Wayne's World*. To use this clip, you would need, at a minimum, the permission of both the owner of the copyright in *Wayne's World*, the owner of the copyright in the musical work, and the owner of the copyright in the performance of that musical work by the rock group Queen that was incorporated into the film.

3.5 Animation and Special Effects

The creators of animation and special effects may also have reserved rights to their works, or if the work is based on preexisting material, may hold rights to the material from which the production was adapted. This is particularly true of cartoon characters that have an existence independent of the motion picture (for example, a newspaper comic strip such as "Peanuts", or a cartoon character such as Mickey Mouse). In such a case, it will be necessary to obtain a license from the cartoonist, animator, or other person holding the rights to such material.

3.6 Embedded Works of Art, Film Clips, and Stills

Often a motion picture or television clip will itself contain a film clip, a still photograph, or artwork. For example, a scene from one movie may be playing on a television in the background of a scene in the movie you want to license. If your multimedia product will highlight such an item by making it the focus of the clip, for example, by bringing into the foreground a famous painting that is otherwise part of the background of the clip, then you should get permission from the owner of the copyright in the embedded work (e.g., from the owner of the copyright in the painting).

4. Identifying and Finding the Owners of the Rights

4.1 Owners of the Copyrights

While identifying the component parts takes careful attention, the more difficult task is identifying the copyright holder to each of the component works you have identified.

When searching for the owner of the copyright to a particular film clip, it is often a good idea to begin with the film distributor. While the distributor may not have the right to authorize your use of the film clip in a multimedia work, the distributor should be in a position to help you find the party that does own the appropriate rights, such as the production company.

As a general rule, the production company financing the motion picture or television program owns the copyright in the motion picture or television program itself.[16] Thus, the production company is likely to own the copyright in those component works created specifically for the motion picture or television program; that is, the intrinsic properties. The production company acquires ownership of the intrinsic properties by contracting with the writers, producers, directors, and performers on a "work for hire" basis. The Copyright Act provides that a "work for hire" relationship will be deemed to exist both in a typical employment situation and in a situation where a work is commissioned for inclusion in certain audiovisual works, such as in motion pictures and television programs, and the parties agree in a written document that it will be a work for hire.[17] (Work for hire is explained section 23-1.2). The practical result of employing the writers, producers, directors, and performers on a work-for-hire basis is that the production company is the owner of the copyright in the intrinsic properties these artists produce. Therefore, the place to start to identify holders of rights is with the production company. The production company should know which rights in the intrinsic properties of the motion picture or television program it owns, and which rights have been reserved by the various contributors.

Provided that the production company owns the copyright to the motion picture or television program, to all of the intrinsic properties as well as the whole bundle of rights that comprise each copyright, a single license from the production company to use the clip itself will necessarily include permission to use these intrinsic properties. In such a case, the task of obtaining the necessary permission is greatly simplified. The only other permission you would then have to obtain would be with respect to the extrinsic properties discussed above.

There are, however, exceptions to this general rule that a production company will own all the copyright rights to the motion picture or television program as well as to the intrinsic properties. For example, producers who finance their motion pictures independently of production companies are likely to retain copyright ownership of the motion picture as well as of its intrinsic properties.[18] It is also possible that the producer has reserved rights under his or her contract with the production company such as literary rights, character rights, or a right of first or last refusal to sequel material. Star performers and sought-after directors and producers may be able to retain certain rights as well.

The question of who owns which components of a work and who owns which rights in the "bundle" of copyright rights in each component works is a matter of the respective bargaining power of the parties, that is, a matter of contract. Consequently, if possible, you should consult the contracts of these respective contributors to the motion picture or television program to determine whether they have reserved any rights. If they have, you must obtain a separate license to such rights if these rights are necessary to the multimedia product.

The production company will also frequently be in a position to help you identify and locate the owners of the various extrinsic properties incorporated within the motion picture clip you would like to license.

Another way to go about identifying the holders of the rights to the various component works is to review credits of the motion picture or television program, to examine any copyright registrations and assignments on file with the Copyright Office and to contact any owners of any rights uncovered through such a search. (For a discussion of the procedure for obtaining a copyright search, see chapter 12, section 3.3.)

Writers. Screenwriters and television writers may be located through the WGA. The WGA represents screenwriters and television and radio writers. (See chapter 21, section 2.)

Producers. A producer or the producer's agent can usually be located by contacting the Producers Guild of America (PGA). The PGA represents executive producers, producers, associate producers and coproducers, supervising producers, segment producers, and coordinating producers.

Directors. A director or the director's agent can usually be located through the DGA. The DGA represents directors and their supporting personnel including assistant directors, unit production managers, associate directors, stage managers, and production associates. (See chapter 21, section 3.)

Music/Soundtrack. Composers and performers can usually be located through the AF of M. (See chapter 21, section 6.)

4.2 Owners of the Reuse Rights

The process of locating and contacting performers to obtain a release of their rights of publicity and permission to reuse their performance in another market can be difficult and time-consuming. However, both television and motion picture performers or their agents can often be located through the applicable union. Television performers or their agents can usually be located through AFTRA. (See chapter 21, section 5.) AFTRA represents actors and actresses, singers, narrators and other performers. Actors and actresses who perform in motion pictures that originate on film can usually be located through the SAG. (See chapter 21, section 4.) Once you have obtained the name of the performer's agent, you can contact the agent who will negotiate on behalf of the performer with respect to the permission you require.

It should be noted that there are no general rules governing the reuse fee charged by actors or actresses. That is, they are free to require payment of any amount they so desire, whether reasonable or not.

If the performer is a member of the applicable union, then, in addition to the reuse fee paid to the performer, you will also have to pay an additional 12-½ percent of the total amount of the fee to the union for its pension and welfare fund.

5. Summary of the Licensing Process

As the foregoing discussion indicates, licensing the right to use a motion picture or a television clip can be a rather involved process, requiring the execution of numerous copyright licenses, releases from performers regarding their right of publicity, and payment of several union fees.

In addition to obtaining a license from the copyright owner of the motion picture or television program as a whole, additional copyright licenses will be required from the owner of the copyright in each of the extrinsic properties appearing in the film clip you want to use, as well as the owner of any intrinsic properties that has reserved rights that impact your proposed use.

In addition to the copyright license, you must obtain a license or release from every recognizable performer appearing in the clip whether living or dead. This must be done in all cases regardless of the ownership of the motion picture or television program itself or of the various intrinsic and extrinsic properties that comprise the motion picture or television program. (A sample release of a performer's rights to name, likeness, and publicity can be found in chapter 31).

Finally, applicable reuse fees and health and pension plan fees may be due to a variety of unions involved in the preparation of the motion picture or television program, including the WGA, DGA, AF of M, AFTRA, and SAG (see chapter 21).

6. Stock Footage—A Possible Alternative

Another source of material for multimedia products is stock footage. There are commercial suppliers of stock footage, sometimes called stock footage houses, that have assembled and archived holdings of movie and television footage. Some stock footage houses furnish general footage, others specialize in a particular area, such as historical or sports footage.

These stock footage houses greatly simplify the process of obtaining permission to use this material in that they generally own the copyright or have a license to distribute the footage. Another plus is that the stock footage house will usually be able to grant worldwide rights in the footage.

Stock film and video is typically licensed on a nonexclusive basis for use only in a single specified production. It cannot be reused in any other production without the payment of an additional license fee.

License fees are based on the length of the clip, usually measured in minutes or seconds, and the market in which the clip will be used (e.g., broadcast television, cable television, internal corporate use, home video, CD-ROM, and so forth). Market definitions vary from company to company.

Stock houses generally make no warranties with respect to the material they provide, other than, perhaps, a warranty that they own the copyright in the material they have provided, or that they have the right to license it to you. Thus, it is important to understand that using stock video and film clips does not necessarily solve all of your rights clearance problems. Most stock video and film clips are provided without any clearances of the rights of applicable unions or persons appearing in the clips. In other words, you get a license to the copyright, but you are responsible for obtaining and paying for any and all necessary clearances or releases from performers, stunt performers, guilds, and unions. Moreover, in many cases they require that you indemnify them from any damages they may suffer arising out of your use of the stock footage.

Restrictions on your use of the clip may also apply. For example, some stock houses prohibit the use of any narration, sound, or voice-over that may accompany the footage. Others prohibit any use of the image or voice of any principal actor/actress, correspondent, or reporter that may be contained in the footage.

Fees for stock film and video clips typically involve a combination of research fees, duplication fees, and license fees, as follows:

• **Research Fees.** Most stock houses charge research fees to cover the time they spend and the costs they incur in finding, screening, and selecting footage based on criteria that you supply. Often they will prepare a demo tape of the film or video clips they locate that meet your criteria, which you can use to select the clips you want.[19] In some cases, additional fees are charged for the creation of these demo tapes.

• **Duplication Fees.** Stock houses typically charge for duplication costs, that is, making a copy from the master in their collection. Sales tax, shipping, and handling charges are also typically added.

• **License Fees.** License fees are typically based on the intended market in which the film or video will be used, and the amount of footage actually used (typically based on the number of seconds used). Such fees are often not refundable even if the film or video clip is not used, and in many cases must be paid in advance of shipment of the clip. Some stock houses also have a minimum charge (for example, 10 seconds).

License fees for stock video and film footage are typically charged by the second, and may range from $15 to $150 per second, depending upon the market in which the film or video will be used.

Endnotes

1   17 U.S.C. § 102(a)(6).

2   17 U.S.C. § 101.

3   See *WGN Continental Broadcasting Co. v. United Video, Inc.*, 693 F.2d 622, 626 (7th Cir. 1982).

4   See *Midway Mfg. Co. v. Artic Int'l, Inc.*, 704 F.2d 1009, 1011 (7th Cir.), *cert. denied*, 464 U.S. 823 (1983).

5   17 U.S.C. § 101.

6   See H.R. REP. No. 1476, 94th Cong. 2d Sess. 56 (1976), *reprinted in* 1976 U.S.C.C.A.N. 5659, 5669.

7   17 U.S.C. § 101.

8   "To constitute an invasion of copyright it is not necessary that the whole of a work should be copied, nor even a large portion it in form or substance, but that, if so much is taken that the value of the original is sensibly diminished or the labors of the original author are substantially, to an injurious extent, appropriated by another, that is sufficient to constitute an infringement. The test of infringement is whether the work is recognizable by an ordinary observer as having been taken from the copyrighted source." *Bradbury v. Columbia Broadcasting Sys., Inc.*, 287 F.2d 478, 485 (9th Cir.), *cert. dismissed*, 368 U.S. 801 (1961). See *Roy Export Co. Establishment, etc. v. Columbia Broadcasting Sys., Inc.*, 503 F. Supp. 1137, 1145 (S.D.N.Y. 1980), *aff'd*, 672 F.2d 1095 (2d Cir.), *cert. denied*, 459 U.S. 826 (1982) (use of less than one minute of a Charlie Chaplin film held to be an infringement, and not a "fair use" because the taking, though "quantitatively small," was "qualitatively great"); *Universal Pictures Co. v. Harold Lloyd Corp.*, 162 F.2d 354, 360 (9th Cir. 1947) (taking approximately 20 percent of a film was qualitatively substantial). See further discussion of this issue in chapter 11, section 3.

9   See *National Geographic Soc'y. v. Classified Geographic, Inc.*, 27 F. Supp. 655, 660 (D. Mass. 1939) (defendant's production of books that it had assembled by cutting up, rearranging, and rebinding original articles cut from copies of plaintiff's magazine infringed plaintiff's right to adapt its copyrighted work); see also *Mirage Editions, Inc. v. Albuquerque A.R.T. Co.*, 856 F.2d 1341, 1342-43 (9th Cir. 1988) (process whereby defendant purchased books containing copyrighted works of art, glued individual page prints onto a rectangular sheet of black plastic material exposing a narrow black margin on the print, glued the black sheet with print onto a major surface of a rectangular white ceramic tile, applied a transparent plastic film over the print, black sheet and ceramic tile surface, and offered the tile with artwork mounted thereon for sale on the retail market constitutes the unauthorized preparation of a derivative work that infringed the copyright in the original work of art), *cert denied*, 489 U.S. 1018 (1989).

10   *Gilliam v. American Broadcasting Cos.*, 538 F.2d 14, 24 (2d. Cir. 1976); See also *Preminger v. Columbia Pictures Corp.*, 49 Misc. 2d 363, 267 N.Y.S.2d. 594 (N.Y. Sup. Ct.), *aff'd*, 25 A.D. 2d 830, 269 N.Y.S. 2d 913 (N.Y. App. Div.), *aff'd*, 18 N.Y.2d 659, 219 N.E.2d 431, 273 N.Y.S.2d 80 (N.Y. 1966) (director sued to enjoin cuts in his film *Anatomy of a Murder* for television viewing asserting that such cuts were "mutilation" that would both destroy the film's commercial value and damage his own reputation).

11   See *In re Arbitration between Directors Guild of America, Inc., Warren Beatty, JRS Prods., Inc., Paramount Pictures Corp., American Broadcasting Cos., Inc.*, 6 Ent. L. Rep. No. 12, at 8 (May 1985).

12   See, e.g., *Effects Assocs., Inc. v. Cohen*, 908 F.2d 555 (9th Cir. 1990) (finding unenforceable a purported transfer of copyright without a written agreement as required by 17 U.S.C. § 204(a), but noting that such an arrangement is "apparently not uncommon in the motion picture industry" and characterizing plaintiff's argument in favor of the validity of an oral transfer as "movie makers do lunch, not contracts"); *Subafilms, Ltd. v. MGM-Pathe Communications Co.*, 1993 U.S. App. LEXIS 4068, at *4 (9th Cir. Feb. 17, 1993) (characterizing distribution agreements for the animated Beatles film *Yellow Submarine* as "verbose, redundant, misleading and ambiguous.").

13   See, e.g., *Russell v. Price*, 448 F. Supp. 303, 304-05 (C.D. Cal. 1977), *aff'd*, 612 F.2d 1123 (9th Cir. 1979). In that case, the defendant distributed and performed copies of a motion picture that was in the public domain. However, because the movie was based on a book that was still protected by copyright, the court held that distribution and exhibition of the motion picture was copyright infringement because the matter contained in the movie was a derivative of a book still covered by copyright.

14   1 Melville B. Nimmer & David Nimmer, Nimmer on Copyright, § 2.10[A][2][a] (1993); *Baltimore Orioles, Inc. v. Major League Baseball Players Ass'n*, 805 F.2d 663, 670 (7th Cir. 1986), *cert. denied*, 480 U.S. 941 (1987).

15   17 U.S.C. § 101 provides that audiovisual works include "accompanying sounds, if any." *Cf.* 17 U.S.C. § 101 (defining "sound recording" to exclude "the sounds accompanying a motion picture or other audio visual work").

16   4 Melville B. Nimmer & David Nimmer, Nimmer on Copyright, § 23.01, at 23-2.1 (1993). See also 2 Alexander Lindey, Lindey on Entertainment, Publishing & the Arts, § 5.04[10][11], at 5-273, § 6.07[3][oo], at 6-189 (1993).

17   Note, however, that these presumptions regarding works made for hire do not necessarily hold true for foreign films. "Unlike in the United States, where directors and writers typically render services on a work-for-hire basis and the production company is the owner of the entire copyright, in Europe, screenwriters and directors often grant a producer only a 'one picture license' to exploit a single motion picture incorporating their work." 4 Melville B. Nimmer & David Nimmer, Nimmer on Copyright, § 23.04[D], at 23-130.1 (1993). Foreign films also raise the potential for moral rights claims by performers. Many foreign countries treat moral rights as inalienable, and may consider any contractual waiver to be voidable. *Id.*

18   4 Melville B. Nimmer & David Nimmer, Nimmer on Copyright, § 23.01, at 23-3, § 23.08, at 23-68 (1993).

19   Demo tapes are typically furnished in either 3/4-inch or VHS formats, and usually have a visual time code superimposed over the picture. This code is used to identify the specific segment of the film or video to be licensed.

The Impact of Entertainment Industry Unions

The Impact of Entertainment Industry Unions

Unions are a powerful force in the U.S. entertainment industry.[1] Virtually every level of employment is unionized, from stage hands and extras to writers, directors, musicians, recording artists, and performers. As a consequence, unions have a significant impact both on the development of multimedia content and on the licensing of preexisting content that was originally created with union talent.

If you want to use union talent to develop content (or the entire multimedia product), you will normally have to sign the collective bargaining agreement of the union that represents the category of talent you want to employ (e.g., writers, directors, performers, recording artists, musicians), and thereby become subject to all of its terms and conditions. But you can't necessarily avoid dealing with the various unions simply by using nonunion talent to develop your multimedia product. If any of the preexisting content you want to incorporate in your product was created by union talent, then, in addition to paying a license fee to the copyright owner, it may be necessary to pay additional fees to one or more of the unions that were involved.

From the perspective of multimedia development and licensing, the most important entertainment unions include the following: the Writers Guild of America (WGA), the Directors Guild of America (DGA), the American Federation of Musicians (AF of M), the American Federation of Television and Radio Artists (AFTRA), and the Screen Actors Guild (SAG). This chapter will begin with a general explanation of the role that these unions play in both the development of multimedia content and licensing of preexisting content created using union talent. Then it will discuss each union individually.

1. Overview of Union Impact on Multimedia Production

Entertainment industry unions are typically divided along the lines of the functions their members perform. Thus, for example, there are separate unions for writers (WGA), directors (DGA), film actors (SAG), recording artists and radio and television performers (AFTRA), and musicians (AF of M). In addition, there are varying classifications of the functions performed by the members within each union. For example, DGA represents directors, unit production managers, first assistant directors, second assistant directors, and technical coordinators. Similarly, AFTRA divides members into a number of categories based on their role in a particular production, such as principal performers, off-camera announcers, groups and choruses, performers who speak five lines or less, sportscasters, walk-ons and extras, and so forth.

Like all unions, the entertainment industry unions bargain collectively to establish the terms and conditions of employment for their members. However, unlike other unions (with the possible exception of sports-related unions), the collective bargaining agreements between the entertainment industry unions and the employers who utilize the services of their members establish only the *minimum* terms and conditions under which their members may be employed. In essence, they lay the groundwork for the negotiation of private contracts between the employer and the union member by setting forth required contract provisions, prohibited provisions, and minimum terms. Depending upon the stature of the artist (e.g., whether he or she is a star), the individual agreement between employer and artist may include other terms more favorable than those provided by the union collective bargaining agreement. Thus, individual agreements may provide for compensation over and above the minimum compensation set forth in the union agreement, a reservation of royalties or other residual payment rights, and a reservation of certain rights to control the production and use of the ultimate work being created.

In other words, the union agreement is, in many cases, nothing more than the floor, or point from which negotiations on the terms of individual contracts for each production begin. An example of this approach is set forth in the AFTRA 1994 Interactive Media Agreement, which provides:

> A. Producer will not enter into any Agreement with or employ any performer for the production of material for Interactive Media upon terms and conditions less favorable to the performer than those set forth in this Agreement.
>
> B. . . .
>
> C. Nothing in this Agreement shall be deemed to prevent any performer from negotiating for and/or obtaining from Producer better terms than the minimum terms provided for herein.[2]

As one court has pointed out (referring to the DGA Basic Agreement): "The very purpose of the Basic Agreement was to put a floor under directors' compensation and to prevent producers, with their obvious leverage, from requiring directors who, for one reason or another lacked individual leverage, to agree to work for less money in order to obtain employment."[3]

In addition to the unions that engage in collective bargaining for their members, there are several other organizations that can play an important role. For example, the National Writers Union (NWU) represents all types of writers, including poets, novelists, technical writers, and screenwriters. The NWU is a labor union, but does not have bargaining power comparable to that enjoyed by other unions such as the DGA or the SAG. Nonetheless, the NWU has a number of recommended contracts that can play an important role in using NWU members, although these are not enforced industrywide as are the collective bargaining agreements of the other unions. In the area of multimedia, however, it has established no standards. While the NWU is considering the issues raised by multimedia, it has not currently drafted any standard contractual provisions for use by its members. A multimedia developer who seeks to incorporate written material is left to negotiate on a clean slate with the individual writer or the writer's agent.

1.1 Using Union Talent To Create Content

As a general rule, to hire union talent you must sign the collective bargaining agreement for the applicable union (frequently referred to as its "Basic Agreement").

Union members are normally prohibited from working for a nonunion employer (unless they get a waiver). Otherwise they can face substantial penalties.

Generally, if you do not sign a union's collective bargaining agreement, you will be unable to hire members of the union to help develop your product. However, some unions allow multimedia producers to enter into a single production agreement that authorizes the hiring of union members for one project without requiring that you become a signatory to their Basic Agreement. These are frequently referred to as "one-production-only" or "OPO" agreements. In effect, they allow you to become a signatory to the union agreement for one production only.

Otherwise, once you sign a union's basic agreement, you are required to abide by all of its provisions for the term of the agreement, which usually runs for several years. This usually means that you can hire only union members (or persons who agree to join the union) for the category of talent the union represents (e.g., performers, musicians, and so forth). But although signing an agreement with one union may obligate you to use members of that union for particular artistic or creative positions (e.g., actors and actresses), it does not mean that you have to use members of other unions for other work not covered by the agreement (e.g., writers, directors, or musicians).

The terms and conditions of employment typically covered by a union agreement include minimum pay scales, restrictions on working conditions, a requirement that additional fees be paid for use of the work in supplemental markets, a requirement of contributions to union health and pension plan funds, arbitration provisions, and the like. The terms of the union agreement will become part of each individual agreement that you negotiate with the union talent that you hire, unless the individual agreement provides for more favorable terms.

Two key financial provisions incorporated in union collective bargain agreements are minimum payment scales guaranteed to each union member for his or her work on the original production, along with a right to the payment of what are called reuse fees in connection with the rerelease of the work or use of the work in markets other than the one for which it was originally developed. These provisions are designed to allow the talent to share in the profits made as a result of a subsequent new use of the original work.

1.2 Using Preexisting Content Created by Union Members

Union collective bargaining agreements not only establish minimum terms upon which their members may be employed, but they also secure other rights and benefits for their members. Most significant among these additional rights and benefits, from your perspective, is that most union agreements provide that their members have a right to receive additional compensation when the works they created are released in markets or media other than those for which they were produced (often called "supplemental markets"), or are used in other works. These rights are spelled out in what are commonly called "reuse" or "repurposing" provisions of union contracts. For example, the SAG Basic Agreement states:

> No part of the photography or sound track of a performer shall be used other than in the picture for which he was employed, without separately bargaining with the performer and reaching an agreement regarding such use. The foregoing requirement of separate bargaining hereafter applies to reuse of photography or sound track in other pictures, television, theatrical or other, or the use in any other field or medium. Bargaining shall occur prior to the time such reuse is made, but performer may not agree to such reuse at the time of original employment. The foregoing shall apply only if the performer is recognizable and, as to stunts, only if the stunt is identifiable.[4]

Similarly, the DGA agreement that covers production of television programs authorizes a single broadcast of the show in each city in the United States. If the production company wants to broadcast the television show more often, it is required to pay additional compensation for the reruns.[5] And if the production company intends to release the program in a media other than television, it is obligated to pay the director additional compensation in an amount to be negotiated with the Directors Guild.[6] If the production company wants to use excerpts from television programs to produce compilation programs (such as "25 years of Lucy on Television," "NBC's 50th Anniversary," "Johnny Carson Anniversary Program"), it must pay the director a fee based on the length of the television program on which such excerpts are used.[7] Finally, if the production company wants to release a television program in a supplemental market such as videocassettes or discs intended for replay through a television receiver, or via pay television, it must pay additional compensation to the director calculated as a percentage of its gross receipts.[8]

The same rules come into play when motion pictures and television programs are used in multimedia. Consequently, even if you do not use any union talent when producing your multimedia product, you must deal with these unions whenever you want to incorporate into your multimedia product a preexisting work that was made under a union agreement using union talent.[9]

With DGA, WGA and AF of M agreements, the amount of these fees is established in the collective bargaining agreement, and they are typically paid to the union for distribution to the applicable union members. With other unions (such as the AFTRA Agreement and the SAG Agreement cited above), the producer is obligated to bargain directly with the performer (or the performer's agent) and reach an agreement regarding such use. In such cases, the performer is free to demand whatever fee he or she desires, or to refuse to grant his or her consent at all. In some cases, the union agreement also requires a payment to the union's health and pension funds.

As a multimedia developer who has not signed onto such an agreement, how can you be required to pay reuse fees when you license the right to use a preexisting work from the copyright owner? The union agreements have ensured payment of such fees through provisions in their collective bargaining agreements that obligate the original production company to pay the fees unless they get their licensee to contractually assume the obligation.

For example, the AFTRA National Code of Fair Practice for Network Television Broadcasting provides that upon the license or distribution of the right to exhibit a television program in supplemental markets, the producer will not be responsible to AFTRA or any of the performers for the payment of the applicable reuse fees only if the producer has the licensee execute an "assumption agreement" whereby the licensee expressly agrees to make the required reuse payments and applicable contributions to the AFTRA health and retirement funds.[10]

Thus, even though you may not be a signatory to the union agreement, the original producer (who is a signatory), will remain liable for such payment, and thus will condition its permission to use the excerpt of the copyrighted work on your payment of the applicable union fees.

It is important to understand that the payment of reuse fees (and corresponding contributions to union health and pension funds) are separate from, and in addition to, the license fees paid to the owner of the copyright in the content being licensed. The reuse fees are additional payments contractually required by union collective bargaining agreements in order to provide additional compensation to the artist for the further use of his or her work.

Most of the unions have not yet established standard procedures or fee schedules to address the use of preexisting works in multimedia. However, all are beginning to consider the issues raised by multimedia. In the meantime, some are relying upon fee schedules established for the use of preexisting works in other media, primarily in television. Because the unions appreciate the uniqueness of multimedia, it is a good idea to contact each union, first, to verify that it has jurisdiction over the content that you want to incorporate, and second, to verify what the fee will be for the contemplated use. If your use is unusual, the union may be willing to specially negotiate with you even if it is relying on some established fee structure.

2. Writers Guild of America (WGA)

The Writers Guild of America (WGA) represents writers for movies and television productions.[11] The WGA is divided between the WGA East and the WGA West. The Writers Guild of America–East is located in New York[12] and represents 3,500 writers located east of the Mississippi River. The Writers Guild of America–West is located in Los Angeles[13] and represents 6,500 writers located west of the Mississippi River.

2.1 Using Members to Develop Content

If you want to use WGA members for a multimedia development project, you have three choices. First, you can sign the WGA's collective bargaining agreement, pursuant to which you will become subject to all of its terms and conditions. This agreement is called the WGA 1988 Theatrical and Television Basic Agreement, and by virtue of a 1992 Extension Agreement, is effective through May 1, 1995. This agreement consists of a 423-page document that governs numerous aspects of the employment relationship between producers and writers, such as credits to be given to the writers, minimum compensation levels, reuse fees for use of movies and television programs in supplemental markets and reruns, pension plan and health fund contributions, and a variety of other provisions.

Second, the writer whom you would like to employ can obtain a waiver from the WGA. However, this has some adverse consequences for the individual union member that may make it an unattractive option, such as foregoing contributions to the WGA pension plan and health funds contributions in connection with the proposed employment.

Third, the WGA has created what it calls its Interactive Program Contract (also known as a Letter of Adherence), to cover interactive, digital multimedia projects. Under the Interactive Program Contract, WGA members may enter into agreements with non-union multimedia producers for a single production. It is an OPO agreement that allows you to use union writers for a single, named production only.

The contract itself is a very simple one-page agreement. It does not set fees, and, with one exception, does not impose on you any of the terms of the WGA Basic Agreement. The exception is that you agree to make contributions to the Producer-Writers Guild of America Pension Plan and the Writers Guild-Industry Health Fund as set forth in Article 17 of the WGA 1988 Theatrical and Television Basic Agreement and the 1992 Extension Agreement. These contributions currently amount to a total of 12.5 percent of the compensation paid to the writer. In addition, you will be bound to the terms and conditions of the Pension Plan Agreement and the Health Fund Trust Agreement. However, no other terms of the WGA 1988 Theatrical and Television Basic Agreement or the 1992 Extension Agreement apply to your employment of such writers.

In summary, if you execute an Interactive Program Contract you agree to nothing more than to make standard contributions to the Writers Pension Plan and Health Fund. The contract applies only to a single, specific project, and ends with completion of the project. All other issues between you and the writer you hire are subject to negotiation directly between the two of you. For further information, contact the WGA at (310) 205-2511.

To assist you in locating WGA members, the WGA publishes an *Informational and Interactive Program Writers Directory* that is available from the WGA at no charge. This directory lists writers by specialty and by geographic area. Specialty categories include interactive, media presentations, design, and programming. To obtain copies of this directory and the Interactive Program Contract, contact the WGA directly.

2.2 Licensing Content Created by Members

When licensing content that involves a script or other element created by WGA members, there are two key issues that you need to consider. The first is the reuse payments that are required by the WGA Basic Agreement. The second is the rights in the work that are retained by WGA members pursuant to the "Separation of Rights" provisions of the WGA Basic Agreement.

The WGA Basic Agreement requires that signatory companies pay a reuse fee in cases where a work or part of it is used in a different market or medium.

The Writers Guild–East does not have a fee structure that specifically addresses the use of motion picture and television clips in multimedia works. Instead, the Writers Guild–East charges the same rates for the use of motion picture and television clips in CD-ROM as it does for the use of such clips in television programs. The fees (for the period ending May 1, 1995) are $293 for ten seconds or less, and $878 for uses that are greater than ten seconds but do not exceed two minutes.[14]

Although these are standard set fees, the Writers Guild–East may negotiate with you if your use is unique. Special rates apply to the use of a collection of clips. More specific information can be obtained by contacting the Writers Guild–East directly.[15] There is no additional fee for pension or health and welfare benefits. Payments are made directly to the Writers Guild–East.

Likewise, the Writers Guild–West does not have an established fee structure that specifically addresses the use of motion picture and film clips in multimedia works. At this time, the Writers Guild–West evaluates each use on a case-by-case basis. If the clip is less than ten minutes in length, the fee structure for television and videocassettes is used for multimedia works.

If the multimedia work includes a collection of television or video clips, then the fee is based on the length of the clips as well as a subjective evaluation of the compilation of clips in relation to the entire work. You may contact the Writers Guild–West to negotiate the fee in such a situation. The Writers Guild–West is generally able to negotiate a fee before the multimedia project is begun so long as you are able to give the guild a close approximation of the length of the clips and their place in the overall concept of the multimedia work.

There is no additional fee for pension or health and welfare benefits. Payments are made directly to the Writers Guild–West. More specific information can be obtained by contacting the Writers Guild–West directly.[16]

In addition to the reuse fees noted above, it is also important to understand that the WGA Basic Agreement includes provisions reserving to writers certain rights in the screenplay, teleplay, characters, or other elements of a movie or television production that they create, even though they will not retain ownership of the copyright in the work itself. These are known as separation of rights provisions.[17] Under these provisions, writers can retain a variety of rights in certain situations. These rights include the following:

- **Merchandising Rights**—the right to manufacture and sell any object or thing first described in the literary material written by the writer;[18]

- **Publication Rights**—the right to publish the writer's work in book, magazine, or periodical form, including serial publication;[19]

- **Reacquisition Rights**—the right to reacquire literary material from the producer;[20] and

- **Sequel Rights**—the right to use one or more leading characters from a work in a substantially different story, such as a spinoff television program, or a new motion picture in which the characters from the first motion picture participate in an entirely new and different story.[21]

The WGA Basic Agreement specifies the circumstances under which writers may retain or acquire such rights.

As a consequence of these separation of rights provisions, it is very possible that the writer of the script for a television or movie clip that you want to use may have retained rights that you will need to produce and market your multimedia work. Accordingly, when licensing film or television clips, in addition to paying the applicable reuse fees you will need to determine whether the writer has retained any such rights. To the extent they impact your proposed use of the film or television clip, it may be necessary to negotiate separately with the writer to obtain permission to use the clip.

3. Directors Guild of America (DGA)

The DGA[22] represents directors, assistant directors, associate directors, unit production managers, stage managers, and technical coordinators in the television and motion picture industries. It has 9,700 members.

3.1 Using Members to Develop Content

The DGA has three basic collective bargaining agreements: The Directors Guild of America 1990 Basic Agreement, a 253-page agreement that governs the production of motion pictures; the Directors Guild of America 1990 Freelance Live and Tape

Television Agreement, a 222-page agreement that governs the production of television programs; and the Directors Guild of America Commercial Agreement of 1991, a 68-page agreement that governs the production of television commercials.

The DGA does not have a form agreement for use with multimedia projects. Generally, the DGA works with multimedia developers on a case-by-case basis.

If you want to use a DGA member for the production of a multimedia product, you will probably be required to sign one of the DGA collective bargaining agreements. The only alternative is for a DGA member to get a waiver from the union that requires the DGA member to sacrifice some of the benefits to which members are entitled.

It is the practice in the industry for directors to negotiate with producers for individual contracts on a production-by-production basis. In these negotiations the director is generally represented by a talent agency.[23] The three DGA agreements specify minimum salary levels, required contributions to pension, health, and welfare plans, the credit to be given to the directors, and various rights that the director has with respect to the preparation of the work (e.g., participation in decisions with respect to script revision, casting, location, selection, set design, and so forth).

3.2 Licensing Content Created by Members

The DGA collective bargaining agreements require that reuse fees be paid to the union for reuse of television clips and motion pictures in supplemental markets. The DGA uses the same fee structure for the use of clips in multimedia as it does for the use of clips on television. Currently, DGA fees for reuse of television clips in multimedia works are $310 for ten seconds or less, $930 for eleven seconds to one minute, and for clips in excess of one minute, the fee is $930 plus $150 for each additional minute or portion thereof. For uses that run longer than ten minutes, the applicable rerun fee is charged.

These fees are fixed, nonnegotiable, one-time-only payments. There are additional fees for pension, health, and welfare contributions in the amount of 12.5 percent of the total clip fee. The fees are payable directly to the DGA and are due no later than thirty days after the initial airing of the work in which the clip is used.[24] The DGA also requires that all payments be accompanied by a statement or letter detailing each clip used, its length, the director of each, and the name of the work in which the clip is used.

4. Screen Actors Guild (SAG)

The Screen Actors Guild (SAG)[25] represents film actors and actresses, narrators, dancers, and extras. It is affiliated with the American Federation of Labor (AFL-CIO) and has a national membership of approximately 78,000 members. Another union, the American Federation of Television and Radio Artists (AFTRA) (discussed in section 5 below) also represents actors and actresses, narrators, dancers, and extras, as well as recording artists, announcers, and news anchors. Thus, there is a fair amount of overlap between the jurisdiction of SAG and AFTRA, and many performers are members of both unions. As a general rule, SAG represents performers in productions that originated on film, while AFTRA represents performers in productions that originated on videotape,[26] as well as sound recording artists.

4.1 Using Members to Develop Content

In June 1993, SAG developed a collective bargaining agreement for multimedia developers known as the Standard Interactive Media Agreement. This is not an OPO agreement. By signing this agreement you recognize SAG as the exclusive bargaining agent for all principal performers and extra performers in the production of audiovisual material for interactive use that may be played on home-type television or computer screens, subject to certain exceptions.[27]

The Interactive Media Agreement is a five-page document that incorporates all of the terms and conditions of its 163-page 1992 Television Agreement for Independent Producers.[28] It expires on June 30, 1995. This agreement provides for a $504 minimum pay rate for day performers and voiceover artists and a $99 per day rate for extras. In addition, you will be required to make a contribution of 12.65 percent of the wages paid to SAG's pension and health plan.[29]

Because of the uncertainty over multimedia, this agreement is somewhat experimental in nature. Moreover, it is currently in the process of being rewritten. Thus, if you want to use SAG talent you should obtain and carefully review this agreement to determine whether it fits your needs, or whether an OPO agreement would be more appropriate. However, SAG stresses that it is very willing to work with multimedia developers, and is open to addressing the unique issues raised by multimedia. For further information, contact Michael Prohaska at (213) 549-6847.

4.2 Licensing Content Created by Members

If you want to use a preexisting film involving SAG members, you should contact SAG to initiate the process of obtaining the necessary consents and negotiating appropriate reuse fees. Reuse fees are not set by SAG, however, but must be negotiated with each individual performer or the performer's agent. SAG can assist you in identifying the agents of the various performers, or the executors of their estates if they are deceased. However, you will have to contact the performers or their agents directly to negotiate the appropriate permission and reuse fee.

Publicity rights are usually negotiated with each individual performer and the performer's agent in tandem with negotiations for the reuse rights. SAG does not set fees or participate in negotiations as to publicity rights.

Because use of preexisting material in multimedia is considered a reuse, the performers are paid according to the same fee schedule that applies to the original performance. The fees differ depending upon whether the performer is an actor or actress, dancer, singer, or extra. The fees also vary depending upon whether the performer is on-screen or off-screen. The amount of the fees may be prorated in relation to the length of the clip used. However, these fees are recommended minimums; individual performers may negotiate higher per day fees. Moreover, any individual performer can arbitrarily set the fee charged for any reuse of his or her image (and voice) in the film clip or may refuse to negotiate either with regard to reuse or publicity rights and thereby prevent you from using a particular clip.

Contributions to the union's pension and health and welfare plans in the amount of 12.65 percent of the total paid all performers are also required.

5. American Federation of Television and Radio Artists (AFTRA)

The American Federation of Television and Radio Artists (AFTRA)[30] represents actors and actresses, narrators, dancers, extras, recording artists, announcers and news anchors. It currently has 75,000 members. AFTRA represents four major groups: television entertainment, commercials (television and radio), broadcast and news, and sound recording.

As noted above in section 4, SAG represents many of the same categories of performers. Thus, there is some confusion and potential overlap in a given situation with respect to the appropriate union to be contacted. As a general rule, SAG represents performers in productions that originated on film, while AFTRA represents performers in productions that originated on videotape, as well as artists who perform on sound recordings.[31]

5.1 Using Members to Develop Content

In early 1994, AFTRA released its Interactive Media Agreement that governs the use of AFTRA performers in the development of interactive multimedia products.[32] The Interactive Media Agreement allows you to use the results of the services of AFTRA performers in the program for which they were employed in all interactive media. Interactive media includes any media on which an interactive product operates including, but not limited to, PCs, games, machines, arcade games, all CD-interactive machines and all similar machines, and the digitized, electronic, or any other formats now known or that may be invented.

Like the SAG Agreement, the AFTRA Interactive Media Agreement is not an OPO agreement. Rather, you are required to recognize AFTRA as the exclusive bargaining agent for all performers in the production of audiovisual material for interactive media recorded on video tape or by any other means or method except recordation by motion picture film photography.[33] The agreement runs until June 30, 1995, at which point it will be renegotiated.

In obtaining the services of AFTRA performers, the Interactive Media Agreement provides for a $504 minimum pay rate for day performers and voiceover artists, and a $103 per day pay rate for extras.[34] In addition, you will be required to make a contribution of 12.65 percent of the wages paid to the performers to AFTRA's Pension and Health Plan.[35]

It is important to note, however, that while payment of the foregoing minimum rates (or such higher rates as the performers may negotiate with you) entitles you to use the results of their services in a particular multimedia product, there are a number of restrictions. First, you cannot reuse the result of their performance in any linear program product without separately bargaining with the individual performer and reaching an agreement as to additional fees. The minimum payable to a performer for the reuse of any portion of an interactive program in a linear program is the AFTRA minimum pay scale for the field in which the interactive material is to be reused (e.g., broadcast television or cable).[36] *Linear programs* are media that do not possess interactive qualities, such as videotape, film, and photography.

Second, if you want to make your multimedia product accessible to users via remote delivery you will have to pay a reuse fee to each of the performers at a minimum rate of 100 percent of the total applicable salary that they were paid for their performance in the original multimedia work.[37] *Remote delivery* includes any system under which your multimedia work can be accessed for use from a location that is remote from the CPU on which the product is primarily used or stored, such as an online service, a delivery service over cable television lines, telephone lines, microwave signals, radio waves, satellite or wireless cable.

Third, if you want to include a performer's performance in an interactive multimedia product for which they were not previously employed to render services, you will also have to pay a reuse fee that, at a minimum, is 100 percent of the total salary they were paid for their original performance.[38]

Like the SAG Interactive Media Agreement, the AFTRA agreement is somewhat experimental in nature. If you want to use AFTRA talent you should obtain and carefully review this agreement to determine whether it fits your needs, or whether an OPO agreement would be more appropriate. However, AFTRA stresses that it is very willing to work with multimedia developers, and is open to addressing the unique issues raised by multimedia. For further information, contact Karen Stuart at (213) 461-8111 x-400.

5.2 Licensing Content Created by Members

If you want to use a video clip or sound recording originally created with AFTRA performers, you should contact AFTRA to initiate negotiations over appropriate reuse fees. Fees are not set by the AFTRA, however, but must be negotiated with each individual performer. AFTRA can assist you in identifying the agents of the various performer or the executors of their estates. However, you will have to contact them directly and negotiate the appropriate permission and fee with each performer or the performer's agent.

Because use of preexisting material in multimedia is considered a reuse, the performers are paid according to the same pay scale that applies to the original performance. The fees differ depending upon whether the performer is an actor or actress, dancer, singer, or extra. The fees also vary depending upon whether the performer is on-screen or off-screen. The amount of the fees may be prorated in relation to the length of the clip used. However, these fees are recommended minimums and a starting point in that individual performers may negotiate higher per day fees.

Moreover, any individual performer can arbitrarily set the fee charged for any reuse of his or her image (and voice) in the video clip or may refuse to negotiate either with regard to reuse or publicity rights and prevent you from using a particular clip or recording.

Contributions to the union's pension and health and welfare plans in the amount of 12.65 percent of the total paid all performers is also required.

6. American Federation of Musicians (AF of M)

The American Federation of Musicians (AF of M)[39] represents musicians, but not composers or lyricists.[40] It is a union of instrumentalists. It currently has 175,000 members.

The federation has established agreements addressing, for example, the employment of studio musicians to record a composition or the reuse of a recorded composition, and corresponding fee schedules for various markets, but does not currently have uniform contractual provisions or fees schedules dealing with the use of pre-existing musical works in multimedia.[41]

6.1 Using Members to Develop Content

Currently, the AF of M does not have a formal agreement in place for the interactive/multimedia field. While it is in the process of establishing such an agreement, at the present time each project is being negotiated on an individual and experimental basis.

The AF of M Phonograph Record Labor Agreement governs the terms and conditions under which AF of M Union Musicians may be employed in the recording of phonograph records. While the AF of M advises that this agreement is not necessarily appropriate for the interactive/multimedia field, it will give you a general idea of the approach taken by the AF of M in its collective bargaining relationships.

The agreement covers union members who perform (as employees) services as instrumental musicians or as leaders, contractors, copyists, orchestrators, and arrangers of instrumental music in the recording of phonograph records.[42] The agreement obligates the recording company to pay at least the minimum union scale set forth in the agreement.

Signatories to the AF of M Phonograph Record Labor Agreement are also obligated to become signatories to the Phonograph Record Manufacturer's Special Payments Fund Agreement and the Phonograph Trust Agreement. These agreements obligate the record manufacturer to make certain additional payments, based on record sales. Sums collected by the administrator under the Special Payments Trust Agreement are ultimately distributed to members of the AF of M who participated in the recordings. Sums paid pursuant to the Phonograph Record Trust Agreement are used by the trustee "for the purposes and objectives of arranging and organizing the presentation of personal performances by instrumental musicians in the areas throughout the United States . . . on such occasions and at such times and places as in the judgment of the trustee will contribute to the public knowledge and appreciation of music."[43] The trustee is obligated to organize performances for live audiences upon occasions where no admissions fees are charged, in connection with activities of patriotic, charitable, educational, civic, and general public nature.

The schedule of payments to the administrator of the Special Payments Fund requires payments ranging from .51 to .54 percent of the suggested retail price of the phonograph record, depending upon the price range involved. Payments to the trustee of the Phonograph Record Trust are .23625 percent of the manufacturer's suggested retail price (up to a maximum suggested retail price of $8.98 for records and $10.98 for CDs), effective August 1, 1995. Prior to that, the rate is .25200 percent.

The AF of M agreement prohibits dubbing, rerecording, or retranscribing any recordings containing performances by persons covered by any AF of M union agreements since January 1954. However, dubbing is allowed if the record company notifies the union of its intention to do so and pays the union scale and applicable fringe benefits for the new use as if it were an original performance.

6.2 Licensing Content Created by Members

If you want to use a sound recording, motion picture, or television clip containing the performance of a musical work that involves union musicians, you will have to pay reuse fees to the AF of M. This process normally begins by contacting the AF of M, which can help you determine whether union musicians were involved in the recording. Reuse fees for multimedia projects are normally negotiated on a project-by-project basis.

The AF of M agreement also requires payments to the Special Payments Fund and Phonograph Record Trust in the event the record company licenses use of any master record created using union talent for the purpose of allowing such other person to manufacture phonograph records for sale. In the case of such a license, the recording company is obligated to require that you agree to become a signatory to the Special Payments Fund Agreement, and make all applicable payments due to the Special Payment Fund and pursuant to the Trust Agreement.

Accordingly, if you want to license any sound recording recorded using AF of M musicians, you would have to become a signatory to the Special Payments Fund Agreement and make payments both pursuant to that agreement and the Record Trust Agreement in addition to paying the applicable license fee for the sound recording to the copyright owner.

Endnotes

1   For a general discussion of labor unions in the entertainment industry, see Jan Wilson, *Special Effects of Unions in Hollywood*, 12 Loy. L.A. Ent. L.J. 403 (1992).

2   1994 AFTRA Interactive Media Agreement, Article I, § 9. See also SAG Codified Basic Agreement of 1989 for Independent Producers § 12 ("Nothing contained in this Agreement shall prevent any individual from negotiating and obtaining from Producer better conditions and terms of employment that those herein contained. This Agreement shall not effect any of the terms or conditions of employment contained in any individual personal service contract that are better than those herein contained").

3   That Way Prod. Co. v. Directors Guild of America, Inc., 96 Cal. App. 3d 960, 967 (1979).

4   SAG Codified Basic Agreement of 1989 for Independent Producers, General Provisions § 21.A.

5   DGA 1990 Freelance Live and Tape Television Agreement, Article 7.

6   DGA 1990 Freelance Live and Tape Television Agreement, Article 23.

7   DGA 1990 Freelance Live and Tape Television Agreement, Article 23, Section B.

8   DGA 1990 Freelance Live and Tape Television Agreement, Article 23, Section D.

9   You can determine whether a work was made using union talent by examining the credits, if possible, or by contacting the appropriate unions.

10   AFTRA National Code of Fair Practice for National Television Broadcasting, Exhibit

11   See comment regarding the NWU in chapter 21, section 1.

12   Writers Guild of America–East, 555 W. 57th Street, New York, New York 10019; phone: (212) 767-7800; fax: (212) 582-1909.

13   Writers Guild of America–West, 8955 Beverly Boulevard, West Hollywood, California 90048; phone: (310) 550-1000; fax: (310) 550-8185.

14   See WGA 1988 Theatrical and Television Basic Agreement, Article 15.B.10(dd).

15   The Writers Guild–East of America can be contacted at 555 West 57th Street, New York, New York 10019; phone: 212-767-7800; fax: (212) 582-1909.

16   The Writers Guild–West can be contacted at 8955 Beverly Boulevard, West Hollywood, California 90048-2455; phone: (310) 550-1000; fax: (310) 550-8185.

17   See WGA 1988 Theatrical and Television Basic Agreement, Articles 16A (Theatrical) and 16B (Television).

18   WGA 1988 Theatrical and Television Basic Agreement, Articles 1.B.8 and 1.C.14.

19   WGA 1988 Theatrical and Television Basic Agreement, Articles 1.C.7 and 16.A.1.B.

20   WGA 1988 Theatrical and Television Basic Agreement, Articles 16.A.8 and 16.B.2.

21   WGA 1988 Theatrical and Television Basic Agreement, Articles 16.A.8 and 16.B.2.

22   Directors Guild of America, 7920 Sunset Boulevard, Los Angeles, California 90046; phone: (310) 289-2000; fax: (310) 289-2029. New York office: 110 W. 57th Street, New York, New York 10019; phone: (212) 581-0370; fax: (212) 581-1441.

23   *That Way Prod. Co. v. Directors Guild of America, Inc.*, 96 Cal. App. 3d 960, 962 (1979).

24   Because the DGA uses its fee schedule for the use of clips in television programs, it is unclear what "airing" means in the context of a multimedia product.

25   Screen Actors Guild, 5757 Wilshire Boulevard, Los Angeles, California 90036-3600; phone: (213) 549-6847; fax: (213) 549-5801. New York office: 1515 Broadway, 44th Floor, New York, New York 10036; phone: (212) 944-1030.

26   This division of SAG's and AFTRA's respective jurisdictions based on the film versus videotape rule sometimes breaks down. For example, *Moonlighting* was produced on film, and although a television series, is under the jurisdiction of SAG. SAG and AFTRA should be able to assist you in identifying which of them has jurisdiction over a particular work. Beware, however, in certain areas, such as works produced on videotape or multimedia works that fall into the industrial/educational production category, SAG and AFTRA each claim jurisdiction. Consequently, it is advisable to contact both in an attempt to clarify jurisdiction over any particular work.

27   SAG Standard Interactive Media Agreement §§ 1, 2.

28   SAG Standard Interactive Media Agreement § 3.

29   SAG Standard Interactive Media Agreement § 10.

30   American Federation of Television and Radio Artists (AFTRA), 6922 Hollywood Boulevard, Hollywood, California 90028; phone: (213) 461-8111. New York office: 260 Madison Avenue, New York, New York 10016; phone: (212) 532-0800.

31   This division of SAG's and AFTRA's respective jurisdictions based on the film versus videotape rule sometimes breaks down. For example, *Moonlighting* was produced on film, and although a television series, is under the jurisdiction of SAG. SAG and AFTRA should be able to assist you in identifying which of them has jurisdiction over a particular work. Beware, however, that in certain areas, SAG and AFTRA each claim jurisdiction. Consequently, it is advisable to contact both in any attempt to clarify jurisdiction over any particular work.

32   See 1994 AFTRA Interactive Media Agreement.

33   1994 AFTRA Interactive Media Agreement, Article I, § 2. *Interactive Media* is defined as "any media on which interactive product operates and through which the user may interact with such product including but not limited to personal computers, games, machines, arcade games, all CD-interactive machines, and any and all analogous, similar or dissimilar microprocessor based units." *Id.* Article I, § 4C.

34   See 1994 AFTRA Interactive Media Agreement, Article I, § 17.

35   See 1994 AFTRA Interactive Media Agreement, Article I, § 32.

36   See 1994 AFTRA Interactive Media Agreement, Article I, §15.1.8.

37   See 1994 AFTRA Interactive Media Agreement, Article I, §§ 14.A, 17.C.

38   1994 AFTRA Interactive Media Agreement, Article I, § 15.2.

39   American Federation of Musicians, 1501 Broadway, Suite 600, New York, New York 10036; phone: (212) 869-1330.

40   It is necessary to obtain separate permission from the holder(s) of the copyrights in the musical score and lyrics in addition to paying the musicians through the AF of M. If the copyrights are held by the composer and lyricist you must individually locate and negotiate with these artists or their agents because, unlike musicians, composers and lyricists are not represented by any labor union. Consequently, there are no guild or union fees to be paid to composers and lyricists. While a composer or lyricist may hold these copyrights, it is more likely that a music publisher or recording company will hold them. See chapter 17.

41   The AF of M is currently working to address the issues raised by multimedia, and it is anticipated that the AF of M will soon have standard contract provisions in place that will govern the use of union musicians to create original musical recordings and the use of preexisting musical recording by union musicians for multimedia works.

42   *Phonograph records* are defined as including photograph records, wire or tape recordings, or other devices reproducing sound.

43   Phonograph Record Trust Agreement § 3(a).

CHAPTER 22

Using an Independent Developer to Put It All Together

1. Allocation of Responsibilities
2. Specifications
3. Deliverables
4. Acceptance
5. Warranties
6. Support
7. Charges
8. Ownership
9. Confidentiality
10. Indemnification
11. Default
12. Source Code Access

Using an Independent
Developer to Put
It All Together

Instead of producing and developing a multimedia product in-house, you may want to contract with an outside vendor to do the work. Such a transaction is normally governed by a multimedia product development agreement. The purpose of such an agreement is to specify exactly what work will be done by the developer, the price to be paid, and the scope of each party's rights in the resulting product.

The very nature of the project, however, makes the contract very difficult to draft, and even more difficult to implement and enforce. This is a reflection of the basic problem with the task at hand: it is hard to define. Thus whether the developer agrees to develop your multimedia product (1) pursuant to previously defined specifications, (2) pursuant to specifications to be developed during the course of the contract, or (3) merely to meet a general goal with undefined specifications, it will frequently be difficult to determine whether the goal has been achieved.

Although it is easier said than done, the key to structuring a successful multimedia product development agreement is to sufficiently define the product to be developed so that, by reference to the contract, both parties will be provided with an objective standard to determine whether and when the contract has been completed. As long as such an objective standard exists, future disputes between the parties will be minimized. Consequently, until all parties have agreed on the detailed multimedia product specifications, it may be unwise to attempt to proceed to a finished product. The contract must also accommodate the changes that will inevitably occur during performance, and provide a mechanism to identify and correct problems as soon as they arise.

The multimedia product development agreement must also address the difficult question of ownership. Ideally, you should acquire ownership of all rights in the resulting multimedia product, and in all component parts specifically developed for the project. To do so, however, requires an appropriately drafted written agreement that reflects a transfer of ownership to you, and specifies what rights, if any, the developer will retain. In many cases, however, obtaining ownership rights may not be feasible. If the developer is to retain ownership rights, it becomes important that you obtain a license to the resulting multimedia product that adequately covers your anticipated needs.

1. Allocation of Responsibilities

Developing a multimedia product requires content, software, and the technical and creative talents necessary to put it all together. When retaining an independent contractor to produce a multimedia product, the first issue to be addressed is which of these elements you will provide to the developer and which of these elements will be provided by the developer.

The content that goes into the product may be acquired from third-parties, may be in the public domain, or may be developed specifically for your multimedia product. Who will have the responsibility of creating and/or licensing the content that goes into the product? Similarly, the software used to develop the multimedia product and the software incorporated within the final product is a major component of the project. Such software can be licensed from third-parties or independently developed specifically for this project. Who is to be responsible for obtaining and/or developing the necessary software?

2. Specifications

When you contract for the development of a multimedia product, one of the most important parts of the contract is the one that defines the work to be performed by the developer. In fact, the key to structuring a successful agreement lies in defining the product to be developed well enough so that, by reference to the contract, both parties will be able to determine whether and how well the contract has been completed. As long as such an objective standard exists, future disputes between the parties will be minimized.

Not surprisingly, it is also one of the most difficult sections to draft. In many cases, you may not know exactly what you want, and the developer may be unfamiliar with the subject you want to cover. Adding to this confusion is the fact that both parties' perception of a project will frequently change during its lifetime, often with disastrous effects on the original timetable and cost estimates.

To handle this problem, you may want to consider dividing your development project into two or more distinct phases. The first one or two phases could be limited to the process of defining the nature of the product to be developed, its specifications, the content it will contain, its overall design and user interface, and so forth. Only after these specifications and other details have been worked out and agreed upon should any development work actually begin. This will allow you to learn enough about the available options to make critical choices in advance, before development work begins. Then, having a detailed mutual understanding of the task at hand, the financial arrangements for the actual product development work can be made and the multimedia product developed. Until both parties are agreed on the specifications and product definition, however, it is often unwise to proceed with the balance of the project.

The goal is to define the work to be performed so clearly that a neutral third-party (such as a judge) could easily decide whether the developer had completed the job and is entitled to full payment. This is not always an easy task, but careful negotiations and drafting at the beginning of a project will pay substantial dividends in time and money by minimizing the chances of a dispute at the end. When the scope of the work is thoroughly defined, each party can more easily enforce its rights and meet its obligations than would otherwise be the case. An ambiguous or otherwise poorly drafted development agreement is, in other words, an "accident just waiting to happen."

Once you have adequately defined the product to be developed, you must also face another issue, namely, how to deal with changes that arise during the course of performance. Just as with the construction of a family residence, your needs and desires may evolve as the project takes shape, and new and better ways of doing things may occur to you or the developer. It is important that your agreement contain the flexibility to accommodate such changes. By the same token, the agreement should contain a mechanism for ensuring that you are protected from unfair surprises. For example, you need to know, in advance, the cost and the delay that will be associated with any requested change. Accordingly, the contract should specify a procedure for handling requests for changes.

3. Deliverables

When is the developer obligated to deliver the multimedia product called for in the contract? The developer may be unable or unwilling to commit to a definite delivery date. This is especially true where the project is large and where it is not well defined. In such a case it is important to work out some sort of arrangement that will provide you with some assurance of getting the multimedia product within a reasonable timetable.

It is also important to specify each of the deliverables that the developer is obligated to provide. Delivery of a multimedia product may typically take the form of a CD-ROM write-once disc for your review and acceptance. However, there are a number of other items to be considered. They include, for example, documentation in the use, operation, maintenance, and support of the multimedia product, a copy of the source code for any software used in the multimedia product, copies of applicable license agreements for content or software licensed by the developer (or perhaps assignments of those agreements to you), as well as, where relevant, commitments by the developer to provide support and/or training. You may also want the contract to specify a remedy in the event that delivery is late, such as a right to cancel and to obtain a refund of all amounts previously paid, or a provision for "liquidated damages" set at a certain amount for each day, week, or month that the delivery is late.

4. Acceptance

A multimedia product development agreement should provide you with an opportunity to review and evaluate the multimedia product before accepting it and making the final payment, in order to ensure that it meets the contract specifications. Such a review and evaluation typically takes the form of an acceptance test. The purpose of such a test is to give you an opportunity to operate, use, and evaluate the multimedia product in order to determine whether it conforms to the contract and is otherwise acceptable for your needs.

Ideally, such a determination would be made on a subjective basis, that is, you decide whether or not you like it without reference to more objective contract criteria or specifications. However, in most cases, an acceptance test should be designed so that both parties know in advance what requirements must be met by the multimedia product, so that they can objectively determine whether the multimedia product has in fact met those requirements. If properly done, an acceptance test will allow you to satisfy yourself that the multimedia product performs properly and meets your requirements, while at the same time assuring the developer that acceptance will be based upon objective criteria and that it will receive payment within a relatively short period of time.

In designing such a test, it is important to determine in advance the requirements and specifications that the multimedia product must meet. It is important that the specifications be clearly set forth so that both parties know whether or not the product has passed the test.

Finally, you should also specify what happens if the test fails. A number of options are available. For example, the contract could require that, upon failure, the developer will make all necessary repairs and that the test will be redone at that time. Alternatively, you may want the option of canceling the project and getting a refund of what you have paid to date.

5. Warranties

What does the developer warrant to you with respect to your multimedia product? You should consider obtaining warranties relating to the performance of the product, warranties relating to original development and clear title, warranties relating to the scope of authority and authorization with respect to licensed content and licensed software used in the multimedia title, and warranties of noninfringement of third-party rights. See discussions of warranty issues in chapter 13, section 9 and chapter 28, section 5.

6. Support

In any multimedia product development contract you should consider the issue of support. Depending upon the nature of your relationship, the issue of support can cover a variety of topics. The end users who want to use your product may require support in the nature of documentation or someone who will answer questions by phone on how to install and/or use the multimedia product. You may be able to provide this type of support yourself, with some training from the developer, or alternatively, you may want the vendor to undertake this responsibility.

If the software or other technology embodied in the multimedia product contains bugs or other problems, or simply does not operate properly, this raises yet another question with respect to the issue of support. If the developer is the one responsible for developing and/or providing the software and technology, the developer may be the only one in the position to deal with these types of problems. On the other hand, the implications can be significant. If you have already manufactured 10,000 CD-ROM discs, finding that they contain a major error basically renders them worthless. Who bears the cost of this and what responsibility, if any, does the developer have to remedy the problem?

Finally, there is the issue of support with respect to future enhancements or modifications to the CD-ROM product that you might want to make on your own or through the use of another multimedia product developer. In such a case, some level of support from the original developer may be necessary to deal with the technical issues presented by modifying a previously developed product.

7. Charges

The cost of the multimedia product development effort is one of your primary concerns. Consequently, the payment terms, whatever they are, must be spelled out clearly and completely so that there are no disputes or disagreements between the parties.

Three questions should be considered: what type of fee structure will be used, what products and services are included in the agreed-upon fee, and when is payment due?

The types of fees or charges used in a multimedia product development contract are usually a fixed fee or an hourly rate for the cost of the labor plus any out-of-pocket expenses, an arrangement commonly referred to as "time and materials." In some cases, a developer may also be willing to accept all or a portion of its compensation in the form of royalties from future sales of the product.

In addition to the "cost" of the development project, you may also need to factor in the cost of any license fees or royalties due in connection with the use of content or software that you or the developer have licensed from third-parties. For example, if the developer licenses a search and retrieval software engine for use in your multimedia product, you need to ensure that the developer has paid all of the fees required for your intended use of the multimedia product (such as reproduction and distribution). Alternatively, you need to make arrangements to pay any additional fees or royalties (such as per copy charges) that will be required as a result of your intended use of the multimedia product.

Regardless of the fee arrangements, the contract should specify what is covered by the fee. That is, what do you get for your money? For example, in addition to the multimedia product itself, does the price cover access to or ownership of any content and/or computer programs created by the developer, a license to third-party content or software incorporated within the multimedia title (or will you be required to pay additional license fees for each copy you manufacture and distribute), support for the use and operation of the multimedia product, or technical support for further maintenance and/or enhancement of the multimedia product? To the extent that any of these items are included or excluded from the fee paid, they should be clearly set forth in the contract so that there can be no disagreements over what was and was not covered by the contract.

The third critical issue with respect to cost is the question of when payment is due. Generally, payment can be required on a specified date (such as March 15), at specified periodic intervals (such as monthly or quarterly), or upon the occurrence of specified events. Events that are often used to trigger payment obligations include the execution of the contract, the delivery of a beta version of the multimedia product for your review, upon your acceptance of the multimedia product following a predefined acceptance test, or a specified number of days after any one of the above events.

Where payments are to be made in installments, it is important to specify the relevant installment dates. You may want to tie them to the completion of certain tasks defined in the contract, or to some other factor. It may also be appropriate to hold back a certain percentage of the payment (for example, the percentage that represents the developer's profit) until the project is completed and accepted.

8. Ownership

Ownership of the intellectual property rights in the newly developed multimedia product is an important subject that should be dealt with in every development agreement.

The question of who owns the rights to the multimedia product (and each of its components) is one that should be resolved through negotiation between the parties before the contract is signed. If the matter is not resolved by the terms of the contract, however, the law may hold that the developer is the owner of the multimedia product. (For a discussion of who owns the copyright in multimedia works developed by independent consultants, see chapter 23, section 1.2.)

The question of ownership is more than just the issue of who owns the proprietary rights to the multimedia product. It also addresses the issues relating to ownership of the various component parts incorporated into the product, such as the content and the software that, when combined together, form the multimedia product. As discussed in chapter 23, ownership of a completed multimedia product can be separate from ownership of the individual components incorporated within it. However, to the extent that you do not own those components, or have adequate license rights to them, your right to market the complete multimedia product (even if you own the rights in the complete product) could be significantly limited.

As a general rule, the multimedia developer will retain ownership of the rights to your multimedia product and any component parts (content or software) developed for it, unless those rights are assigned to you in an appropriate assignment agreement, or alternatively the project is done pursuant to an appropriate work-for-hire agreement.

In addition to ownership of what the developer creates, you also need to address issues relating to the licenses of content and software developed by third-parties but incorporated within your multimedia product. Who has the responsibility for obtaining those licenses? Is the scope of those licenses adequate to meet your particular needs? (See discussion in chapter 13.)

Finally, you need to address the issue of the rights of privacy and publicity, and the question of defamation, with respect to the content incorporated within the multimedia work. (These rights are discussed in chapters 5 through 7.) To the extent that the content makes reference to actual persons, it is important to take care that the material does not infringe their rights of privacy or otherwise constitute defamation. And finally, with respect to their rights of publicity, someone will have to take the responsibility for obtaining the appropriate releases from the individuals appearing or referenced in any of the content included in the multimedia title.

9. Confidentiality

The development of a multimedia product may involve the creation of new and proprietary technology and/or may involve the use of proprietary information owned by others. In addition, until the product is publicly released, you may have reasons for desiring that the nature of the product or other information relating to it be kept confidential until such public release. To the extent that any of these confidentiality issues are important, your relationship with the multimedia developer should include an appropriate provision protecting the confidentiality of that information that you desire to keep secret. (See additional discussion in chapter 26.)

10. Indemnification

As with any project that involves the development of intellectual property, there is a risk that the developer will use preexisting content or software without permission of the rightful owner. This could result in an infringement of owner's copyright or patent rights, or a misappropriation of the owner's trade secret rights. In addition, even where the content is rightfully used, if the developer has neglected to obtain appropriate permissions from the persons involved (e.g., waiving their rights of publicity and privacy), or has otherwise made references to persons that result in defamation, you run the risk of additional liability. Accordingly, your contract with the developer should take steps to ensure that all content, software, and the multimedia title itself constitute an original development (except where appropriate materials are used with appropriate permissions), and that all appropriate releases have been obtained. In addition, however, you should attempt to obtain an indemnification from the developer in the event you are sued by anyone claiming that his or her rights have been infringed or misappropriated.

A typical form of an indemnification clause provides that the developer will pay any expenses you incur or damages you suffer in the event that you are sued under a certain enumerated list of theories, provided that you meet certain requirements set forth in the clause.

The following is an example of a short indemnification clause:

> In the event Client is sued on a claim that the Multimedia Product infringes any patent, copyright, or trade secret of any third-party, violates any rights of publicity or privacy, or is in any way defamatory, Developer will defend such suit at its own expense, and will pay any judgment entered against Client, provided that Client promptly notifies Developer of such suit and allows Developer complete control of its defense.

One word of caution is in order: The protection provided by an indemnification clause is only as good as the financial strength of the indemnifier.

11. Default

A default section is often included in development contracts in order to specify what type of breach will constitute a default, and to define the procedures by which the injured party can terminate the agreement or pursue its other remedies. Specifying what constitutes a breach of the agreement is normally not necessary, since any act contrary to the terms of the contract or any failure to do what is required by the contract will be a breach of the agreement. Some breaches are more serious than others, however, and you may want to specify those that will give rise to the right to terminate the agreement or to invoke other specific types of remedies. Moreover, the parties will frequently wish to identify acts that, on their face do not violate any terms of the contract, but which will nonetheless be deemed to constitute a breach of the agreement. For example, the default section might state that if either party becomes insolvent, that party will be deemed to be in default. This gives the other party the option of acting on the default without waiting for a failure to pay or other similar violation of the agreement.

The main purpose of a contract section dealing with default, however, is to specify the procedures that must be followed in the event of a default. Normally, the contract will provide that in the event of a breach of the agreement the injured party must give the breaching party written notice of the breach, whereupon the party in default will have a specified number of days to cure the breach. If the breach has not been cured at the expiration of that time period, the injured party may terminate the agreement and pursue its other remedies. However, if the breach is cured during that time period the contract continues in full force.

12. Source Code Access

A potentially key issue that arises when you use a third-party to develop a multimedia product is the question of your right to have access to the source code for the software ultimately incorporated in your multimedia product. If the developer has written new software specifically for your product (but retains the copyright), or if the developer uses software owned by a third party (pursuant to a license), you may need to obtain access to the source code so that you can maintain the product if necessary, and/or further enhance or update the product for future releases. In addition, there is always a concern that the developer will be unable or unwilling to devote the necessary resources to perform future support or other work that you require, or that the developer will cease doing business or otherwise be unable to provide the help that you need.

Ideally, the contract should require the developer to provide you with a copy of the source code to any software incorporated within the product. If, however, due to the nature of the relationship or otherwise, this is not possible, you should consider insisting upon a source code escrow arrangement. Under such an arrangement, the developer will deliver a copy of the source code to a third-party escrow agent to hold it in escrow and release it to you only upon the occurrence of certain predefined events, such as the developer's failure to provide appropriate support services or the developer's cessation of business.

When setting up a source code escrow, you should first determine what materials will be included. Simply depositing a copy of the source code may be insufficient, since you will presumably need other information if you are to maintain the multimedia product. This may include technical documentation, file layouts, record layouts, flowcharts, coding annotations, and any other information that would help you understand how the system works. Ideally, the source code escrow should contain all of the materials that would be necessary to maintain or enhance the program without the help of any other person or the need to refer to any other materials. Indeed, this is what you will require if it ever becomes necessary to obtain the materials from the source code escrow.

You also need to agree on some method of verifying that the developer has deposited of all of the required materials. This may require the assistance of a third-party in analyzing the materials deposited and comparing those to the software actually used in your multimedia product.

One of the most critical aspects of any source code escrow agreement is a definition of the events that will trigger release of the source code to you and the procedure by which that release will be accomplished. Events that have typically been used to trigger release of the source code include the following:

- the filing of bankruptcy by the developer;
- the dissolution or liquidation of the developer's business;
- in the case of a sole proprietorship, the death of the vendor; or
- the developer's failure to support the product according to the agreement.

The procedure to be used to inform the escrow agent that one of these events has occurred, and to instruct him or her to release the multimedia product to you, is also an area that causes significant problems for both parties. Ideally, you would like the right to obtain the source code merely upon notice to the escrow agent that one of the triggering events has occurred. However, this requirement may be resisted by the developer on the ground that it gives you too much discretion.

If the developer objects to your request for a release of the source code, however, the whole intent of the escrow agreement can be frustrated. Unless the parties can resolve their differences, it will be up to a court (or an arbitrator if the agreement so provides) to determine whether the escrowed materials should be released. The escrow agent, who is concerned about his or her liability to either party if he or she acts improperly, will almost certainly refuse to release the escrow materials if there is a dispute between the parties. If you have an immediate need for the source code because of an imminent maintenance problem that the developer has failed to resolve, or because of a pending vendor bankruptcy, the option of resorting to the courts, as well as the cost, may effectively leave you without a remedy.

Finally, the source code escrow agreement should specify what rights you have to use the source code following its release.

PART 3

Protecting Multimedia Products

Who Owns the Copyright to Your Multimedia Product?

Who Owns the Copyright to Your Multimedia Product?

You may be surprised to learn that you may not own the copyright to the multimedia product (or content, or software) that you paid a significant sum to develop. And if you do own the copyright, you may not be totally free to use or distribute it in any way you want. Spending a lot of money to develop a multimedia product is no guarantee that you will own the work when it is done, or that you will have total freedom with respect to its distribution.

Who owns the copyright to the multimedia work you developed and what rights does the owner have? In many cases these can be rather complex questions. Answering them usually requires consideration of two issues: Who is the author of the multimedia work, and what type of work is it?

1. Who Is the Author?

By law, the copyright in your multimedia product, and any separable content or software you develop is initially owned by the *author*.[1] But who is the author? The answer to that question depends on the circumstances.

As a general rule, the author (and thus, the owner of the copyright) is the person who actually creates the work; that is, the person who translates an idea into a fixed, tangible expression entitled to copyright protection.[2] Thus, it is the person who wrote the text, the photographer who took the picture, the recording artists who performed the musical work, the sound engineer who performed the task of capturing and electronically processing the sounds, the person who actually compiled and edited recorded sounds or visual images, and so forth.

But this is not always true. In some cases, the copyright law considers the author to be the person who commissioned the work and who paid for the time and materials necessary to create it, rather than the person who actually did the creative work. In other cases, however, the person who paid for the work to be created has no rights in the resulting product, regardless of the price paid. And in either case, it is also important to understand that there may be multiple authors.

The identity of the author(s) is determined by the nature of your relationship with the person(s) who created the work.

1.1 Works Created by an Individual

When someone creates a multimedia work individually, with no assistance from anyone else, and outside the scope of any employment obligations, there is no question that he or she is the author of the multimedia work, and consequently the owner of the copyright.[3] Thus, if you personally created the work on your own behalf, you will be the individual owner of the copyright. This is the easiest case to deal with.

1.2 The Work-for-Hire Doctrine

Multimedia works (as well as many other copyrighted works) are frequently developed by businesses through their employees, or by one person or business for another. In these circumstances, it is important to consider whether the work is a **work made for hire,** as that term is defined in the Copyright Act. If it is a work for hire, then the person for whom the work was prepared is considered the author, and hence the owner of the copyright.[4] The person(s) who actually created the work will have no rights in the copyright. However, if it is not a work made for hire, then the person(s) who actually created the work will own the copyright.

The Copyright Act provides two mutually exclusive ways for works to acquire work-for-hire status: one for cases where the work is created by *employees* and the other for cases where the work is created by *independent contractors.*[5] Consequently, in order to determine whether you have a work-for-hire relationship with the persons developing your multimedia product (or some of the content that will form a part of it), you need to first ascertain whether they are performing the work as employees or independent contractors.[6]

1.2.1 Employee or Independent Contractor. Unfortunately, it is not always easy to determine whether an individual is an "employee" for purposes of the work-for-hire doctrine, or an "independent contractor" (in which case a different set of work-for-hire rules apply—see section 1.2.2). The Copyright Act does not define the terms "employee" or "independent contractor." Thus, whether someone is your employee or an independent contractor is determined using principles of the general common law of agency.[7] This requires consideration of your right to control the manner and means by which the product is created.

According to the Supreme Court, to make this determination you need to consider the following factors:[8]

1. your right to control the manner and means by which the resulting product is accomplished—you will generally have a greater right to control the work of employees;

2. the source of the instrumentalities and tools used by the individual to perform the work—employees are more likely to get their tools from their employer, independent contractors are more likely to have their own tools;

3. the location of the work—employees are more likely to work at their employer's premises, independent contractors are more likely to work at their own office;

4. the duration of the relationship between the parties—the longer the relationship the more likely it is to be an employment relationship;

5. whether you have the right to assign additional projects to the hired party—this right is more likely to be present in employment relationships than independent contractor relationships;

6. the extent of the hired party's discretion over when and how long to work—independent contractors are more likely to be able to set their own hours;

7. the method of payment—employees are more likely to be paid via a regular payroll arrangement, whereas independent contractors typically invoice for services;

8. the role of the hired party in hiring and paying assistants—independent contractors normally have the right to hire their own assistants; employees normally do not;

9. whether the work is part of your regular business—for example, if the production of sound recordings is not normally something you do as part of your business, it is more likely that you will use an independent contractor (rather than an employee) on the rare occasion when you do produce a sound recording;

10. whether you provide employee benefits—employee benefits are typically provided to employees, but not to independent contractors; and

11. how you treated the hired party for tax purposes—that is, withholding of income tax and FICA payments is typically done for employees, but not for independent contractors.

No one of these factors is determinative. However, certain of these factors, such as your right to control the manner in which the work is created, whether or not employee benefits are provided or social security taxes are withhold from the compensation paid, and your right to assign other projects to the persons performing the services, are considered to be some of the most important.[9]

1.2.2 Works Created by Employees.   If the persons you have hired are considered as "employees" under this test, any multimedia product (or content) prepared by them within the scope of their employment is considered to be a work made for hire.[10] As a consequence, you as the employer (rather than the employees who actually created the work) are considered to be the "author" of the work, and will own all of the rights comprised in the copyright.[11] The employee who created the work will not have any rights in the copyright whatsoever, unless you expressly grant rights to the employee in a written document signed by both of you.[12]

But note that only works created by employees within the scope of their employment will be governed by the "work made for hire" doctrine. Work done outside the normal scope of employment will not normally be covered. Generalizations in this area can be misleading, however, and in case a dispute arises over ownership, you should seek the advice of competent legal counsel.

1.2.3 Works Created by Independent Contractors. The reality of the multimedia development process is that very frequently the persons you commission to develop the work are not your employees (in the literal employee/employer sense). Independent contractors and freelance talent abound in the computer and entertainment industries, and companies both large and small frequently use independent contractors to develop multimedia products and content for them. This raises the troublesome question of who owns the copyright to the resulting work—an issue that is frequently not even discussed between the parties.[13]

When a multimedia work or a portion of a multimedia work is created for you by an independent contractor, the issue of copyright ownership of the resulting product can become complex. Generally, because independent contractors are not employees, their work is not considered as "work for hire," and consequently they will own the copyright in any multimedia works that they develop for you.

If you want to own the copyright in works created for you by independent contractors, you have two options. First, you can obtain a written assignment of the copyright from the independent contractor. Assignments are discussed in chapter 3, section 5, and sample assignments are included in chapters 29 and 33. Second, you can enter into a written work-for-hire agreement, provided that the nature of the project is one that the copyright law considers to be eligible for work-for-hire treatment.[14]

Under the Copyright Act, two criteria must be satisfied before the work of an independent contractor will be considered a work made for hire:[15]

1. the work must be specially ordered or commissioned for use as one of the following: (a) a contribution to a collective work,[16] (b) part of a motion picture or other audiovisual work,[17] (c) a translation, (d) a supplementary work,[18] (e) a compilation,[19] (f) an instructional text, (g) a test, (h) answer material for a test, or (i) an atlas; and

2. the parties must expressly agree in a written instrument signed by both of them that the work will be considered a work made for hire.

It is important to note that unless both of these requirements are fulfilled, the work will not be considered a "work made for hire" and you will not own the copyright in the work created by the independent contractor you hired. Thus, merely signing a contract with an independent contractor specifying that a multimedia work is to be deemed a "work made for hire" (the second of the two requirements) will not necessarily deprive the independent contractor of his or her copyright. The work must also fulfill the first requirement by falling within one of the nine categories listed above.

Although a number of the nine categories may not necessarily relate to a particular multimedia product you are developing (e.g., a translation, a test, or answer material for a test, or an atlas), it is entirely possible that several of the categories will be applicable to a great deal of the work you would like to have created by independent contractors. For example, to the extent that your multimedia product qualifies as an audiovisual work, using an independent contractor to create content would presumably meet the requirement that it is specially ordered or commissioned for use as "part of a motion picture or other audiovisual work." Similarly, to the extent that the content being created by the independent contractor consists of a work prepared as a secondary adjunct to your multimedia product for the purpose of introducing, concluding, illustrating, explaining, revising, commenting upon, or assisting in the use of your multimedia product, such as pictorial illustrations, maps, charts, tables, musical arrangements, bibliographies, appendices, and indexes, it may qualify as a work specially ordered or commissioned for use as "a supplementary work." In addition, educational multimedia products may qualify as instructional texts, and translating content from one language to another may qualify as a translation.

In any event, if you want to structure a work-for-hire relationship with an independent contractor, you must be sure that the work you have commissioned falls into one of these nine categories. Otherwise, it will not qualify as a work for hire, even though the contract includes the "work for hire" language.

Even if the work performed by a consultant meets the first part of the two-part test, it is important to remember that the Copyright Act also requires a written agreement between the parties specifically stating that the work to be created by the consultant is a "work made for hire." And the agreement must be signed by both parties.[20]

If work performed by an independent contractor cannot be fitted within the "work made for hire" doctrine, but you nonetheless want to obtain the copyright ownership in the resulting product, the only alternative is to have the independent contractor execute a written assignment of his or her copyright to you. Assignments are discussed in chapter 3, section 5, and sample assignments are included in chapters 29 and 33.

2. What Is the Nature of the Work?

In many cases, the question of copyright ownership in your multimedia product will involve more than simply obtaining the copyright to the works created by your employees and independent contractors. Many multimedia products, for example, are developed using preexisting content and software. You will obtain a license to use the content and software, but not ownership of the copyright to it. Similarly, many multimedia products may be developed as joint ventures between two or more entities, both of whom may want to share in the copyright ownership. And in yet other cases, the independent contractors that you hire may not be willing to part with copyright ownership of the content they develop.

The net result is that the multimedia product you develop may include content owned by others. In addition, your multimedia product itself may be jointly developed with others who have a claim on the rights in the completed product.

These multiple copyright ownership interests in your multimedia product, and/or the content and software it contains, have an important impact on the scope of the rights that you have in the product, and your ability to exercise the reproduction, adaptation, distribution, public performance, and public display rights normally provided to the copyright owner. Depending upon the intentions of each author at the time his, her or its contribution is created, the resulting multimedia work will be classified as a **joint work**, a **compilation**, and/or a **derivative work**. This classification can be extremely important in determining the respective rights of each of the contributing authors.

In this context, it is important to distinguish between the copyright in a completed multimedia product and the copyright in each of the several preexisting segments of content and software incorporated within the completed product. They represent two separate and distinct categories of copyrights. That is, there is a copyright in your multimedia product as a whole that is separate and distinct from the copyrights in each of the preexisting component parts that may have been incorporated within the multimedia product. The discussion in the following sections focuses on the nature of the copyright in the multimedia product as a whole, but in doing so must of necessity relate to the copyrights in the individual preexisting components of content and software incorporated within the multimedia product.

2.1. Joint Works

2.1.1 Definition of a Joint Work.

If multiple authors are involved in the creation of a multimedia work, and each of the authors intends that their separate contributions be merged into inseparable or interdependent parts of the final product, the resulting multimedia work will be considered a joint work,[21] and all of the coauthors will be co-owners of the copyright in the resulting product.[22]

There are two types of situations in which a joint copyright can be created. The first occurs where the creative expression contributed by each author is *inseparable*— that is, it is not separately identifiable. For example, if two authors jointly create a novel, where each contributes both text and editing to each chapter in the book, their respective contributions are inseparable, they clearly intended to create a single product, and the resulting novel will be considered a joint work.

Alternatively, a joint work can be created where the contributions of each of the authors are *interdependent*. This occurs in situations where the two contributions, although separately identifiable, are intended to go together. Examples include musical works where the words were written by one author and the music composed by another; computer programs where the copyrightable user interface is designed by one author and the computer code that creates the interface is designed by another; and motion pictures where the screenplay is written by one author and the musical score written by another.

In either case, the key to a joint work is the intention of the parties at the time they each create their respective copyrightable contributions.[23] So long as the parties are in agreement, prior to the creation of their individual contributions, that the objective is to create a single work, the requisite intention is present for the creation of a joint work. It is not necessary that they work together or that their contributions be equal.[24] In fact, it is not even necessary that they create their respective portions of the work at the same time, or even that they be acquainted with each other.[25]

In order for a participant in a multimedia development project to be considered a joint author, the copyright law requires that the contribution made by the party to the work is, by itself, copyrightable. Thus, a contribution that does not involve the creation of copyrightable expression, such as describing to the developer how the multimedia work should function, what content it should include, and how the user interface should look, does not make a participant (including the hiring party) a "joint author" sufficient to give it copyright ownership rights.[26]

In one case, for example, the hiring party claimed that software developed by an independent consultant was a joint work because he had explained the operation of his business to the consultant and defined the information that he wanted to be able to obtain from the computer. But the court held that the information and advice that the hiring party provided was little more than one would expect from the operator of any business who seeks to have a computer system designed for him. It is similar to an owner explaining to an architect the type and functions of a building the architect is to design for the owner. The architectural drawings are not coauthored by the owner, no matter how detailed the ideas and limitations expressed by the owner. Thus, such general assistance and contributions to the fund of knowledge of the programmer did not make the hiring party a creator of any original work, nor a coauthor of the work created by the consultant.[27]

In another case, two individuals decided to collaborate on the development of a new spreadsheet program. They met and brainstormed ideas and concepts for the new system. During this process the first person gave the second person a handwritten list of user commands he felt the spreadsheet should contain. However, all of the source code containing the ideas that the two programmers had "brainstormed" together was drafted by the second person when the two were separated. The first person then claimed that a portion of the resulting product was a joint work because the handwritten list of user commands that he provided was utilized to develop the final list of user commands for the software product.

The court disagreed, however, finding that the list was "only a list of labels for user commands, many of which were common commands that were already available in other software programs." In the court's view, there was nothing about the list which was "innovative or novel" and it did not contain any source code implementing the suggested commands. The first person merely told the second person what tasks he believed the interface should allow the user to perform. Since the court found the list to be only an idea unprotectable under the copyright law, it concluded that the program at issue was not a joint work.[28]

Finally, in a third case, a company retained an independent contractor to develop a payroll package, but did nothing more than describe the sort of programs it wanted the contractor to write, what tasks the software was to perform, and how it was to sort data. Consequently, the court rejected its claim of joint authorship, noting that

> a person who merely describes to an author what the commissioned work should do or look like is not a joint author for

purposes of the Copyright Act. . . . To be a joint author, one must supply more than mere direction or ideas: one must 'translate[] an idea into a fixed, tangible expression entitled to copyright protection.' . . . The supplier of an idea is no more an 'author' of a program than is the supplier of the disk on which the program is stored.[29]

2.1.2 Your Rights in a Joint Work.   If your multimedia work is considered a joint work, then each coauthor shares equally in ownership of the work, and has the right to use the entire multimedia work (including all the contributions of the other authors). This includes the right to license others to use the product on a nonexclusive basis, without obtaining the consent of the other joint owners.[30] This is true even if their respective contributions are not equal.[31] However, each joint owner is accountable to the others for a ratable share of any profits he or she may realize on licensing the work, unless they specifically agree otherwise.[32]

2.2. Compilations and Collective Works

When a multimedia work is created by the combination of *preexisting* textual, visual, and audio content (such as prerecorded hit songs, clips from movies and television broadcasts, or preexisting still pictures, the author of any of those preexisting works is not considered a joint author in the resulting multimedia product. In such a case, the multimedia product is either a compilation or a derivative work.

2.2.1 Definition of Compilation and Collective Work.   A **compilation** is a work formed by the collection and assembling of preexisting materials or of data that are selected, coordinated, or arranged in such a way that the resulting work as a whole constitutes an original work of authorship.[33]

A compilation results from a process of selecting, bringing together, organizing, and arranging previously existing material of all kinds, regardless of whether the individual items in the material have been or ever could have been subject to copyright. Examples of compilations include catalogs, databases, maps, and collective works. The preexisting materials incorporated within a compilation do not have to be copyrightable. Thus, a database of uncopyrightable facts may constitute a copyrightable compilation.[34] Similarly, a multimedia product composed entirely of public domain content could constitute a copyrightable compilation.

Where the preexisting works incorporated into a compilation are all copyrightable works, the compilation is referred to as a collective work. A **collective work** is a work in which a number of contributions, each constituting a separate and independent copyrightable work in themselves, are assembled into a collective whole.[35] Examples of collective works ordinarily include periodical issues, encyclopedias, anthologies, symposia, and collections of the discrete writings of the same author. However, works where relatively few separate elements have been brought together, such as a composition consisting of words and music, a work published with illustrations or frontmatter, or three one-act plays, are not considered compilations.[36]

2.2.2 Your Rights in a Compilation.   If you create a multimedia work by assembling previously existing content created by a variety of authors (e.g., a multimedia encyclopedia), the result would be a form of compilation known as a collective work. The copyright in the individual content would remain the property of the authors who created it,[37] while at the same time you would have a separate and distinct copyright in the collective multimedia work as a whole (i.e., the compilation of the content).[38] In other words, there is a separate copyright in the collective work as a whole, that is owned by the person who, with the permission of the copyright owners of the individual content, prepared the compilation.[39] However, as owner of the copyright in the collective work, you acquire only the right to reproduce and distribute the individual content as part of the entire multimedia work.[40] You cannot split up your multimedia work into its individual components, and use each of the components for other purposes (such as in a new multimedia product) without obtaining additional permission from the owner of the copyright in the components involved.

The rights you obtain as the owner of the copyright in a collective work extend to the elements of compilation and editing that went into the collective work as a whole, as well as the contributions that were written for hire by your employees, and those copyrighted contributions that have been transferred in writing to you by their authors. However, unless there has been an express transfer of more, you acquire only the privilege of reproducing and distributing the contributions as part of that particular collective work, any revision of that collective work, and any later collective work in the same series.[41] You do not acquire any rights to the underlying contributions included within the collective work merely by virtue of owning the copyright in the collective work itself.

As the owner of the copyright in a collective work (such as a multimedia encyclopedia) you could use a contribution from the first edition of the encyclopedia in a later revision of it.[42] But you cannot revise the contribution itself or include it in a new anthology or an entirely different multimedia product.[43]

Remember, however, that your rights to your multimedia work can also be significantly restricted by the nature and extent of the scope of the permission to use the preexisting copyrighted content granted by the owner of such content. For example, if the owner of preexisting content that you incorporate in your multimedia work restricts his consent to use the content to a given medium (such as CD-ROM), you may not publish your multimedia work in a different medium (such as interactive television), so long as it continues to incorporate the content subject to the restrictive license.[44] And if the term of your license to use the content expires, you will not be able to publish your multimedia work at all, if it continues to incorporate the content that is subject to the expired license.

However, if the copyright in the underlying work is terminated (such as because the term of the copyright has expired or the work has been intentionally or unintentionally put into the public domain), then all restrictions on use that are imposed by the copyright owner of the content are no longer effective.[45] Note, however, that the converse is not necessarily true. That is, if a collective work enters the public domain, that does not affect the copyright status of any content incorporated within the work with permission. That content will remain protected by copyright, and copying of that content (even by virtue of copying the public domain collective work) will constitute copyright infringement.[46]

2.3. Derivative Works

2.3.1 Definition of a Derivative Work.

A *derivative work* is a work based on one or more preexisting copyrightable works, such as a translation, fictionalization, motion picture version, sound recording, art reproduction, abridgement, condensation, or any other form in which a work may be recast, transformed, or adapted. A work consisting of editorial revisions, annotations, elaborations, or other modifications that, as a whole, represent an original work of authorship, is a derivative work.[47] Examples of derivative works include the translation of a book from English to French, a movie based on a book, a new version of a computer program, and a sound recording that is based on a copyrighted musical composition. Even a new version of a work in the public domain can constitute a derivative work.[48]

Like a collective work, a derivative work is separately copyrightable from the work on which it was based (so long as the work upon which it is based is used with permission). Thus, for example, a movie that is based on a copyrighted book is entitled to copyright protection in its own right, notwithstanding the fact that it is a derivative work of another copyrighted work.

To qualify as a derivative work, two elements must be present. First the work must be based on a preexisting work; that is, a derivative work must incorporate copyrightable expression from the prior work.[49]

Merely using ideas or uncopyrightable facts from a prior work does not make the second work a derivative work. As some courts have stated it, a new work is considered a derivative work of a preexisting work only if it would infringe the copyright in the preexisting work had the material taken from the preexisting work been taken without consent of the copyright owner.[50]

Second, the original work must be recast, transformed, or adapted,[51] not merely copied. The author must contribute his or her own original material to a preexisting work so as to recast, transform, or adapt the preexisting work.[52] Thus, for example, incorporating musical works, sound recordings, or photographs into your multimedia product will not likely create a derivative work. However, if the musical work is revised or modified, the sound recording is sampled and adapted, or the photograph is edited, morphed, or otherwise changed, the result will most likely be a derivative work.

2.3.2 Your Rights in a Derivative Work. The Copyright Act makes clear that the copyright in a derivative work extends only to the matter contributed by the author of such work, as distinguished from the preexisting material employed in the work, and does not imply any exclusive right in the preexisting material.[53] Thus, to the extent that your multimedia product constitutes a derivative work of the content on which it is based, your copyright in the complete multimedia product covers only those elements that are original to you.[54]

Because, by definition, a derivative work incorporates copyrightable content from a preexisting work, it is, of course, necessary to obtain permission to use and adapt the preexisting work. As a consequence, however, your ability to exercise your rights of ownership with respect to the resulting multimedia product will be limited by the scope of the permission you received to use the underlying work.

Thus, your rights to your multimedia work can be significantly restricted by the nature and extent of the scope of the permission to use the preexisting copyrighted content granted to you by the owner of such content. For example, if the owner of preexisting content that you incorporate in your multimedia work restricts his consent to use the content to a given medium (such as CD-ROM), you may not publish your multimedia work in a different medium (such as interactive television), so long as it continues to constitute a derivative work of the content subject to the restrictive license.[55]

Similarly, if your license to use content incorporated within a work is limited in time, then you may not publish your multimedia work (if it continues to include that content) after the time limit has expired.

However, if the copyright in the underlying work is terminated (such as because the term of the copyright has expired or the work has been intentionally or unintentionally put into the public domain), then all restrictions on use that are imposed by the copyright owner of the content are no longer effective.[56] Note, however, that the converse is not necessarily true. That is, if a derivative work enters the public domain, that does not affect the copyright status of any content incorporated within the work with permission. That content will remain protected by copyright, and copying of that content (even by virtue of copying the public domain collective or derivative work) will constitute copyright infringement.[57]

2.4. Comparison of All Three

It is important to distinguish a joint work from a collective work and a derivative work. That is because the rights that you can exercise are different, depending on the characterization of your multimedia work.

In the case of a joint work, the authors intend at the time of the creation of the work that their separate contributions will be merged into a single work. In the case of a collective work, the preexisting works of one or more authors are merely collected and assembled. In the case of a derivative work, the preexisting materials are recast, transformed, or adapted.

There is one copyright in a joint work that is co-owned by all of the joint authors. There are multiple copyrights involved with collective works and derivative works. Each individual author retains his or her copyright in that author's original contribution to a collective work and a derivative work, and in addition, there is a copyright in the entire collective work and derivative work itself. The author of a component module in a collective work (e.g., the author of one short story in an anthology), and the author of an underlying work on which a derivative work is based (e.g., the author of a book that is used as the basis for a movie) is free to use his or her contribution in any way that he or she desires. Such authors are not, however, free to use the complete collective work or derivative work without the permission of its copyright owner.

The implications for multimedia works are obvious. When the works of many independent developers[58] are combined to create a single multimedia work, two possible results can occur, depending on their intentions at the time. If they intend that their separate contributions be merged into inseparable or interdependent parts of the final product, the multimedia work will be considered a joint work, in which case all of the developers will jointly own the single copyright in the resulting multimedia work. Alternatively, if their separate contributions were originally created as individual works (e.g., unrelated recordings of popular songs, photographs, and so forth), the resulting multimedia work will be considered as a collective work if the separate contributions were merely assembled together, or will be considered as a derivative work if one or more contributions were recast, transformed, or adapted, in which case each author of the original contributions will own the separate copyright in his or her contribution, but not the copyright in the entire multimedia work. The copyright in the complete multimedia work (i.e., the compilation or derivative work) is owned by the person who assembled it, with the permission of the individual contributors.

In other words, with derivative works and collective works, the authors of content incorporated within those works own only their own contributions and do not have an interest in the copyright in the resulting multimedia product itself. In the case of a joint work, on the other hand, each contributing author owns an undivided interest in the resulting multimedia work, which interest includes the right to use all separately contributed component parts. Note that a multimedia work can, in some cases, constitute both a joint work on one hand and a collective or derivative work on the other hand, at the same time. For example, a motion picture is a joint work consisting of a number of contributions by different authors, such as the writer of the screenplay, the director, the photographer, the actors, and possibly others, such as the set and costume designers.[59] At the same time, it may be a derivative work of the book on which it is based.

3. Works that Contain Unauthorized Material

If you incorporate preexisting copyrighted content in your multimedia products without appropriate permission from the copyright owners, you run two significant legal risks. First, you may be sued for copyrighted infringement by the copyright owner of the content that you used without permission. Second, you risk invalidating the copyright to the work you have created. This is because of the copyright rules with respect to compilations and derivative works, which state that copyright protection does not extend to any part of a work in which preexisting copyrighted material has been used unlawfully.[60]

Thus, even if you are not "caught" by the content copyright owner, or the copyright owner does not object, your product may be worthless when it comes time to sell your business or sell all rights in the product, because the copyright may be invalidated.

Endnotes

1 17 U.S.C. § 201(a). The author can, of course, always assign ownership of the copyright to someone else. See chapter 3, section 5.

2 *Community for Creative Non-Violence v. Reid*, 490 U.S. 730, 109 S. Ct. 2166, 2171 (1989).

3 17 U.S.C. § 201(a).

4 17 U.S.C. § 201(b).

5 17 U.S.C. § 101 (definition of "work made for hire"); *Community for Creative Non-Violence v. Reid*, 490 U.S. 730, 109 S. Ct. 2166, 2176 (1989).

6 *Community for Creative Non-Violence v. Reid*, 490 U.S. 730, 109 S. Ct. 2166, 2178 (1989).

7 *Community for Creative Non-Violence v. Reid*, 490 U.S. 730, 109 S. Ct. 2166, 2172-73, 2178 (1989).

8 *Community for Creative Non-Violence v. Reid*, 490 U.S. 730, 109 S. Ct. 2166, 2178-79 (1989).

9 *Aymes v. Bonelli*, 980 F.2d 857 (2d Cir. 1992).

10 17 U.S.C. § 101 (definition of "work made for hire").

11 17 U.S.C. § 201(b).

12 17 U.S.C. §201(b).

13 In some cases, you may not particularly care about ownership at the time you enter into an agreement with an independent contractor. For example, if you need a multimedia product for use as part of your internal employee training program, you may not particularly care whether you own the intellectual property rights or not, as long as the product meets your needs and operates properly. However, it often becomes very important at a later date. For example, you may decide that the product is so good that you would like to re-market the product to others, or, alternatively, that you may want to use portions of the

product in the development of a second product. You may then be surprised to find yourself in a situation in which you do not own the rights to what you believe to be your multimedia product. See, e.g., *Whelan Assocs., Inc. v. Jaslow Dental Lab., Inc.*, 609 F. Supp. 1307 1318-19 (E.D. Pa. 1985), *aff'd on other issues*, 797 F.2d 1222 (3d Cir. 1986), where the plaintiff, an independent contractor who had no prior knowledge of defendant's business, conferred extensively with defendant in order to learn the operation of its business and to identify the features, capabilities, and functions that the defendant sought to implement in its business, and then designed and wrote software to meet the defendant's requirements, all at the defendant's expense. However, the plaintiff retained title to the copyright. When the defendant wanted to write a similar program for another computer, the plaintiff argued (quite successfully) that it was an infringement.

14   Note that, by contrast, all work performed by employees for their employers within the scope of their employment are considered works for hire. With independent contractors, however, only nine specially enumerated categories of work can qualify for work-for-hire treatment. 17 U.S.C. § 101 (definition of "work made for hire").

15   17 U.S.C. § 101 (definition of "work made for hire").

16   Collective works are discussed in chapter 23, section 2.2.

17   *Audiovisual works* "are works that consist of a series of related images which are intrinsically intended to be shown by the use of machines or devices such as projectors, viewers, or electronic equipment, together with accompanying sounds, if any." 17 U.S.C. § 101 (definition of "audiovisual works").

18   A *supplementary work* "is a work prepared for publication as a secondary adjunct to a work by another author for the purpose of introducing, concluding, illustrating, explaining, revising, commenting upon, or assisting in the use of the other work, such as forewords, afterwords, pictorial illustrations, maps, charts, tables, editorial notes, musical arrangements, answer material for tests, bibliographies, appendices, and indexes." 17 U.S.C. § 101 (definition of "work made for hire").

19   Compilations are discussed in chapter 23, section 2.2.

20   *Schiller & Schmidt, Inc. v. Nordisco Corp.*, 969 F.2d 410, 412 (7th Cir. 1992) (Statutory language requires that writing be signed "by both parties, and it means what it says." Moreover, the execution of the contract must occur before creation of the subject work.).

21   17 U.S.C. § 101 (definition of "joint work").

22   17 U.S.C. § 201(a).

23   See H.R. Rep. No. 94th Cong., 2d Sess. 120 (1976), *reprinted in* 1976 U.S.C.C.A.N. 5659, 5736; *Eckert v. Hurley Chicago Co.*, 638 F. Supp. 699, 702 (N.D. Ill.).

24   *Edward B. Marks Music Corp. v. Jerry Vogel Music Co.*, 47 F. Supp. 490, 491 (S.D.N.Y. 1942) *aff'd*, 140 F.2d 266, 267 (2d Cir. 1944); *Sweet Music, Inc. v. Melrose Music Corp.*, 189 F. Supp. 655, 659 (S.D. Cal. 1960).

25   See *Edward B. Marks Music Corp. v. Jerry Vogel Music Co.*, 47 F. Supp. 490, 491 (S.D.N.Y. 1942), *aff'd*, 140 F.2d 266, 267 (2d Cir. 1944).

26   *Ashton-Tate Corp. v. Ross*, 728 F. Supp. 597, 601-02 (N.D. Cal. 1989), *aff'd*, 916 F.2d 516, 520-21 (9th Cir. 1990); *S.O.S., Inc. v. Payday, Inc.*, 886 F.2d 1081, 1086-87 (9th Cir. 1989); *Erickson v. Trinity Theatre, Inc.*, 13 F.3d 1061, 1069 (7th Cir. 1994).

27   *Whelan Assocs., Inc. v. Jaslow Dental Lab., Inc.*, 609 F. Supp. 1307, 1318-19 (E.D. Pa. 1985), *aff'd on other issues*, 797 F.2d 1222 (3d Cir. 1986).

28   *Ashton-Tate Corp. v. Ross*, 728 F. Supp. 597, 601-02 (N.D. Cal. 1989), *aff'd,* 916 F.2d, 516, 520-21 (9th Cir. 1990).

29   *S.O.S., Inc. v. Payday, Inc.*, 886 F.2d 1081, 1087 (9th Cir. 1989).

30   See H.R. REP. No. 1476, 94th Cong., 2d Sess. 121 (1976), *reprinted in* 1976 U.S.C.C.A.N. 5659, 5736-37; *Oddo v. Ries*, 743 F.2d 630, 633 (9th Cir. 1984); *Pye v. Mitchell*, 574 F.2d 476, 480 (9th Cir. 1978); *Weinstein v. University of Illinois*, 811 F.2d 1091, 1095 (7th Cir. 1987) (joint owner may prepare and publish derivative work); *Meredith v. Smith*, 145 F.2d 620, 621 (9th Cir. 1994); *Words & Data, Inc. v. GTE Communications Servs., Inc.*, 765 F. Supp. 570, 574 (W.D. Mo. 1991); *Geshwind v. Garrick*, 734 F. Supp. 644, 651 (S.D.N.Y. 1990).

31   *Community for Creative Non-Violence v. Reid*, 846 F.2d 1485, 1498 (D.C. Cir. 1988), *aff'd*, 490 U.S. 730, 109 S. Ct. 2166 (1989); *Sweet Music, Inc. v. Melrose Music Corp.*, 189 F. Supp. 655, 659 (S.D. Cal. 1960).

32   *Oddo v. Ries*, 743 F.2d 630, 633 (9th Cir. 1984); H.R. REP. No. 1476, 94th Cong., 2d Sess. 121 (1976) *reprinted in* 1976 U.S.C.C.A.N. 5659, 5736-37 (co-owners of a copyright are "treated generally as tenants in common, with each co-owner having an independent right to use or license the use of a work, subject to a duty of accounting to the other co-owners for any profits"); *Shapiro, Bernstein & Co. v. Jerry Vogel Music Co.*, 221 F.2d 569, 571 (2d Cir.), *adhered to on reh'g*, 223 F.2d 252 (2d Cir. 1955).

33   17 U.S.C. § 101 (definition of "compilation").

34   *Feist Publications, Inc. v. Rural Tele. Serv. Co.*, 499 U.S. 340, 111 S. Ct. 1282, 1287 (1991); See also *Pic Design Corp. v. Sterling Precision Corp.*, 231 F.Supp. 106, 109 (S.D.N.Y. 1964) (trade catalogs are copyrightable even though the subject matter contained in the catalog is within the public domain).

35   17 U.S.C. § 101.

36   H.R. REP. No. 1476, 94th Cong., 2d Sess. 122 (1976), *reprinted in* 1976 U.S.C.C.A.N. 5659, 5737-38.

37   Each separate contribution to a collective work is distinct from the copyright in the collective work as a whole, and vests initially in the author of the contribution. 17 U.S.C. § 201(c).

38   However, the copyright that you have in the collective work extends only to the original elements you have added to it - that is, the process of selecting, bringing together, organizing, and arranging previously existing material of all kinds. H.R. Rep. No. 1476, 94th Cong., 2d Sess. 57 (1976), *reprinted in* 1976 U.S.C.C.A.N. 5659, 5670-71.

39   17 U.S.C. § 201(c); See also 17 U.S.C. § 103(b).

40   17 U.S.C. § 201(c).

41   17 U.S.C. § 201(c); H.R. REP. No. 1476, 94th Cong., 2d Sess. 122 (1976), *reprinted in* 1976 U.S.C.C.A.N. 5659, 5737-38.

42   This assumes, of course, that the license by which you obtained the right to use the contribution in the first place does not contractually prohibit such subsequent use.

43   H. R. REP. No. 1476, 94th Cong., 2d Sess. 122-23 (1976) *reprinted in* 1976 U.S.C.C.A.N. 5659, 57.

44   *Gilliam v. American Broadcasting Co.*, 538 F.2d 14, 20 (2d Cir. 1976); *G. Ricordi & Co. v. Paramount Pictures, Inc.*, 189 F.2d 469, 471-72 (2d Cir.), *cert. denied*, 342 U.S. 849 (1951).

45   *G. Ricordi & Co. v. Paramount Pictures, Inc.*, 189 F.2d 469, 471-72 (2d Cir.), *cert. denied*, 342 U.S. 849 (1951).

46   See *Russell v. Price*, 612 F.2d 1123, 1128 (9th Cir. 1979).

47   17 U.S.C. § 101 (definition of "derivative work").

48   See e.g., *SAS Institute, Inc. v. S&H Computer Sys., Inc.*, 605 F. Supp. 816 (M.D. Tenn. 1985); *Alfred Bell & Co. v. Catalda Fine Arts, Inc.*, 191 F.2d 99 (2d Cir. 1951).

49   17 U.S.C. § 101; *Litchfield v. Spielberg*, 736 F.2d 1352, 1357 (9th Cir. 1984).

50   *Oddo v. Ries*, 743 F.2d 630, 634 (9th Cir. 1984); *Mirage Editions, Inc. v. Albuquerque A.R.T. Co.*, 856 F.2d 1341, 1343 (9th Cir. 1988), *cert. denied*, 489 U.S. 1018 (1989).

51   17 U.S.C. § 101.

52   *Paramount Pictures Corp. v. Video Broadcasting Sys., Inc.*, 724 F. Supp. 808, 821 (D. Kan. 1989).

53   17 U.S.C. § 103(b).

54   See, e.g., *Durham Indus., Inc. v. Tomy Corp.*, 630 F.2d 905, 909 (2d Cir. 1980).

55   *Gilliam v. American Broadcasting Cos.*, 538 F.2d 14, 20 (2d Cir. 1976); *G. Ricordi & Co. v. Paramount Pictures, Inc.*, 189 F.2d 469, 471-72 (2d Cir.), *cert. denied*, 342 U.S. 849 (1951).

56   *G. Ricordi & Co. v. Paramount Pictures, Inc.* 189 F.2d 469, 471-72 (2d Cir.), *cert. denied*, 342 U.S. 849 (1951).

57   See *Russell v. Price*, 612 F.2d 1123, 1128 (9th Cir. 1979).

58   This assumes that they are not working as employees. The rules for employees are different. See section 23-1.2.2.

59   See, e.g., *Easter Seal Soc'y for Crippled Children & Adults, Inc., v. Playboy Enters., Inc.*, 815 F.2d 323, 337 (5th Cir. 1987), *cert. denied*, 485 U.S. 981 (1988).

60   17 U.S.C. § 103(a).

Perfecting Your Copyright— Notice and Registration

Perfecting Your Copyright— Notice and Registration

Multimedia works are automatically protected by federal copyright law as soon as they are created. Nothing else is required to obtain a copyright. (Determining who owns this automatically obtained copyright, however, is another issue. This is discussed in chapter 23. This chapter assumes that you are the owner of the copyright.)

As a copyright owner, there are two other things you should do in order to obtain the full benefit of the protection provided by the copyright law. First, you should include a proper copyright notice on your multimedia work in order to put users on notice of your claim. Second, you should register the copyright to your multimedia work with the U.S. Copyright Office to facilitate enforcement of your copyright.

1. Copyright Notice

A copyright notice is not required in order to obtain copyright protection in most countries, including the United States.[1] However, it is strongly recommended that you use a copyright notice. It is the best way to advise others of your copyright claim. In addition, if a proper copyright notice is used, infringers will not be able to reduce their liability for damages by arguing that their infringement was "innocent."

1.1 Format of the Notice

The copyright notice to be included on multimedia works must contain three basic elements:[2]

1. the symbol © (the letter "c" in a circle), or the word "Copyright," or the abbreviation "Copr."
2. the year of first publication of your multimedia work[3]
3. the name of the owner of the copyright in the work, or an abbreviation by which the name can be recognized, or a generally known alternative designation of the owner.

Thus, for a multimedia work first published in 1995, any of the following would constitute a proper copyright notice:

- Copyright 1995 [name of owner of copyright]
- Copr. 1995 [name of owner of copyright]
- © 1995 [name of owner of copyright]
- Copyright © 1995 [name of owner of copyright]

With respect to the year in the copyright notice, remember that it should be the year in which your multimedia work was first published, which may not necessarily be the year in which it was created.

1.2 What Is Publication?

Publication is a term of art under the Copyright Act. Generally, publication occurs when you distribute copies of your multimedia work to the public by sale or other transfer of ownership, or by rental, lease, or lending. Publication also occurs when you offer to distribute copies of your multimedia work to a group of persons for purposes of further distribution. Note that the year in which publication of your multimedia work first occurs, which may not be the same as the year that the work was completed, is the year to be used on the copyright notice.

1.3 Location of the Notice

The copyright notice should be applied to your multimedia work in such a manner and location so as to give reasonable notice of the claim of copyright.[4] The acceptability of the notice depends upon its being permanently legible to an ordinary user of the multimedia work under normal conditions of use and otherwise not concealed from view upon reasonable examination.[5] Ideally, the notice should appear on the screen during the use of the product and on any physical media in which the work is stored, sold, licensed, or transported, such as CD-ROM discs.

During use, the copyright notice should be displayed on the computer screen, either continuously or as part of an initial sign-on or boot screen display.[6] With respect to the medium on which copies of the multimedia work are distributed, such as CD-ROM or magnetic disk, the notice should be printed on the medium or reproduced durably, so as to withstand normal use, on a label securely attached to the copy itself, or to the box, jewel case, cartridge, cassette, or other container used as the permanent receptacle for the multimedia product.[7]

The notice on documentation, user manuals, and other literature should be treated the same as a notice on a book. It should appear on the first, last, or title page.

As a general rule, the more places the notice appears, the better the protection will be.

2. Copyright Registration in General

Copyright registration is a formal procedure that makes a public record of your copyright with the U.S. Copyright Office, enables you to sue infringers of your copyright, helps you to prove that you are the owner of a valid copyright, and allows for the recovery of certain damages and attorneys fees in the event of litigation against infringers. Both published and unpublished multimedia works can be registered, although it is not necessary to register either. But even though registration of your multimedia work is not a condition of copyright protection,[8] the copyright law is designed to encourage registration.

2.1 Advantages of Registration

There are several advantages to registering multimedia works. They can be summarized as follows:

1. Registration establishes a public record of your copyright claim.

2. Registration is necessary before you can file an infringement suit.[9]

3. If your multimedia work is registered within five years of publication (defined in chapter 24, section 1.2), registration will establish **prima facie** evidence in court of the validity of your copyright and of the facts stated in the certificate of registration (e.g., name of copyright owner, date of first publication, and so forth).[10] This is important because it makes your burden of proof in a lawsuit easier and because it increases the likelihood of obtaining a preliminary injunction against an infringer.

4. If your multimedia work is registered prior to an infringement (or within three months of publication if such infringement occurs after publication), statutory damages and attorneys' fees will be available to you in court actions for relating to such infringement. Otherwise, only actual damages may be recovered.[11] (Damages are discussed in chapter 3, section 9.4).

2.2 What Does Registration Cover?

Registration of the copyright to your multimedia work covers all copyrightable aspects of the work that you have contributed, including the copyright in any content or software that you developed, the copyright in your selection, organization, or arrangement of preexisting content, the copyright in the changes or adaptations that you have made to preexisting content, and the copyright in your screen displays. However, it does not cover the copyright to any preexisting content or software that you have used with permission.

2.3 When Should Your Multimedia Work Be Registered?

It is advisable to register the copyright of your multimedia work as soon as possible after it has been completed, and no later than three months after publication. If your multimedia work is registered more than three months after the date of first publication, you will lose the right to obtain statutory damages and to recover attorneys' fees for any infringement that occurs before the effective date of registration. If your multimedia work is not registered until more than five years after the date of first publication, then you will lose the benefit of the presumption of validity that comes with registration—that is, in the event of a lawsuit, a court is not required to presume that you are the lawful owner of a valid copyright.[12] However, a multimedia work can be registered at any time before the copyright expires, either before or after it has been published.[13] But remember that late registration results in a waiver of the right to obtain statutory damages or attorney's fees with respect to any infringement occurring before the registration. (See section 2.1).

2.4 How Long Does the Registration Last?

Copyright registration lasts for the duration of the copyright. Once your multimedia work has been registered, there is no need to renew that registration. In general, the term of the copyright for a multimedia work lasts for the life of the author plus fifty years after the author's death. If the multimedia work was a work made for hire (such as software written by an employee for his or her employer), the term of the copyright is seventy-five years from the year of its first publication, or one hundred years from the year of its creation, whichever expires first.

3. Registration Procedure

All copyrightable elements of the multimedia work may generally be registered with a single application, provided: (1) they are not published, or are published together as a single unit; and (2) the copyright claimant is the same for each element. Separate registrations for individual elements may be made by submitting a separate application and filing fee for each. A separate registration is required, however, for any element of your multimedia work that you publish separately, or for any element for which someone else claims to be the copyright owner.[14]

3.1 What Is Required for Registration?

When registering your multimedia work, the following three items must be sent to the Copyright Office in the same envelope or package:

1. a properly completed application form,
2. the filing fee, and
3. a deposit of the multimedia product being registered.

The address is: Register of Copyrights, Library of Congress, Washington, D.C. 20559. Each of these items is further explained in the following sections.

3.2 Application Form

The Copyright Office uses a variety of different application forms, depending on the copyrighted item being registered. The appropriate form for registration depends on what elements make up the multimedia work. According to the Copyright Office, you should select the application form on the following basis:[15]

- Use Form PA if the work contains an audiovisual element (i.e., a series of related images), such as photographs, film clips, or video clips, regardless of whether there are any sounds.

- Use Form SR if the work does not contain an audiovisual element, but contains an audio tape or disk in which sound recording authorship is claimed.

- Use Form TX if the work contains only text, such a manual and computer program that produces a textual screen display.[16]

Note that regardless of the form used, the application may include a claim in all accompanying authorship.

To order forms and circulars, call the Copyright Office forms and circulars hotline at (202) 707-9100, or write to U.S. Copyright Office, Publications Section, LM-455, Library of Congress, Washington D.C. 20559.

A copy of Form PA (the form generally used to register multimedia works), as well as instructions for filling out the form, can be found in section 4.

3.3 Filing Fee

The filing fee is currently $20.[17] The fee should be paid by check or money order payable to the Register of Copyrights.

3.4 Deposit

A deposit of the multimedia work being registered must accompany each application for registration. The deposit requirement varies according to the type of work being registered, and whether the work has been published.

If your multimedia work was first published in the United States on CD-ROM, deposit one "complete copy" of the **best published edition**—that is, in the same form as packaged and distributed to customers. A "complete copy" includes all elements in the unit of publication.[18] Thus, if your multimedia product is marketed on a CD-ROM disc that is distributed in a jewel case with a user manual and other supporting literature, all of which is packaged in a printed box, the entire product should be submitted.

If you are also claiming copyright in the software included in your multimedia product, it will also be necessary to deposit source code.[19] The deposit rules are based on whether it is a new program or a revised version of a preexisting program, and whether or not it contains trade secrets.

● **Entirely New Computer Programs.** If you are registering a new program that does *not* contain trade secrets, send the first and last twenty-five pages of source code, together with the page containing the copyright notice, if any. If the program is fifty pages or less in length, send the entire source code.

If the program contains trade secrets, then as an alternative you may send the page containing the copyright notice, if any, plus one of the following:

1. The first and last twenty-five pages of source code with portions containing trade secrets blocked out; or

2. The first and last ten pages of source code alone with no block-out portions; or

3. The first and last twenty-five pages of object code plus any ten or more consecutive pages of source code with no blocked-out portions; or

4. If the program is fifty pages or less in length, entire source code with trade secret portions blocked out.

● **Revised Computer Programs.** If you are registering a revised version of a program that has been previously published, previously registered, or that is in the public domain, and does not contain trade secrets, send the page containing the copyright notice, if any, plus the first and last twenty-five pages, if the revisions occur throughout the entire program. If the revisions do not appear in the first and last twenty-five pages, send any fifty pages of the source code representative of the revised material in the new program.

If you are registering a revised version of a program that does contain trade secrets, send the page containing the copyright notice, if any. If the revisions are present in the first and last twenty-five pages, also send any one of the following:

1. the first and last twenty-five pages of source code with portions containing trade secrets blocked out; or

2. the first and last ten pages of source code alone with no blocked-out portions; or

3. the first and last twenty-five pages of object code plus any ten or more consecutive pages of source code with no blocked-out portions; or

4. if the program is fifty pages or less in length, entire source code with trade secret portions blocked out.

If the revisions are not present in the first and last twenty-five pages, send the page containing the copyright notice, as well as

1. twenty pages of source code containing the revisions with no blocked out portions, or

2. any fifty pages of source code containing the revisions with some portions blocked out.

Note: Whenever portions of code are blocked out, the blocked-out portions must be proportionately less than the material remaining, and the visible portion must represent an appreciable amount of original computer code.[20]

The source code in all cases must be reproduced in a form visually perceptible without the aid of a machine or device, either on paper or in microform.

If a published user's manual (or other printed documentation) accompanies the computer program, deposit one copy of the user's manual along with one copy of the source code.

For HyperCard computer programs created in scripted language, the script is considered the equivalent of source code. Thus the same number of pages of script would be required as is required for source code. Reproductions of on-screen text, buttons, and commands are not an appropriate substitute for this source code deposit. Where a HyperCard program contains trade secrets, deposit script pages meeting the requirements for computer programs containing trade secrets as discussed above.[21]

3.5 When Is My Registration Effective?

Your registration will be effective as of the date that the application form, filing fee, and deposit are received by the Copyright Office, regardless of how long it then takes to process the application and mail the certificate of registration.[22]

3.6 What Does the Copyright Office Do with My Application?

When the application form, filing fee, and deposit are received by the Copyright Office, it examines the registration form and deposited materials to ensure that they constitute copyrightable subject matter, that there is a sufficient amount of authorship present in the deposited materials, and that all of the formalities have been complied with. If there are any problems, the Copyright Office will contact you. Otherwise, it will issue a certificate of registration.

You will not receive an acknowledgment that your application has been received (as the office receives more than 650,000 applications annually), but you can expect:

- a letter or telephone call from a copyright examiner or other staff member if further information is needed;
- a certificate of registration to indicate that the work has been registered;
- if registration cannot be made, a letter explaining why it has been refused.

If you want to know when the Copyright Office received your material, you should send it by registered or certified mail and request a return receipt from the U.S. Postal Service, or enclose a stamped, self-addressed postcard identifying the multimedia work being registered, which the Copyright Office will date and time stamp and return to you.

3.7 How Long Does It Take to Get a Certificate of Registration?

The registration process typically takes approximately four to six weeks. This is dependent upon the workload of the Copyright Office at the time the application is filed, and in many cases it may be shorter or longer.

4. Instructions for Completing Copyright Registration Form PA

The following are instructions for completing copyright registration form PA, the most commonly used form for registration of multimedia products.

4.1. Filling Out Section 1

- **Title of This Work.** Enter the name of the multimedia product being registered. Every work submitted for copyright registration must be given a title to identify it. The Copyright Office indexing of the registration and future identification of the work will depend on the information you provide here. Remember, however, that the copyright law does not protect your title[23] (see chapter 3, section 3.2) although the title may be protectable under trademark or unfair competition law.[24] (See chapters 4 and 25.)

- **Previous or Alternate Titles.** Complete this space if there are any additional titles for your multimedia work under which someone searching for the registration might be likely to look, or under which a document pertaining to the multimedia work might be recorded.

- **Nature of this Work.** In this space you should briefly describe the general nature or character of the work being registered for copyright. "Audiovisual work" is probably most appropriate for most multimedia works.

4.2 Filling Out Section 2

Section 2 asks for information about every "author" who contributed any appreciable amount of copyrightable material to this version of the multimedia product. Note that the form provides space for information about three authors (in sections "a," "b," and "c"). If there are more than three authors, list additional authors on Form

FORM PA
For a Work of the Performing Arts
UNITED STATES COPYRIGHT OFFICE

REGISTRATION NUMBER

PA   PAU

EFFECTIVE DATE OF REGISTRATION

Month   Day   Year

DO NOT WRITE ABOVE THIS LINE. IF YOU NEED MORE SPACE, USE A SEPARATE CONTINUATION SHEET.

1

TITLE OF THIS WORK ▼

PREVIOUS OR ALTERNATIVE TITLES ▼

NATURE OF THIS WORK ▼ See instructions

---

2 **a**

NAME OF AUTHOR ▼

DATES OF BIRTH AND DEATH
Year Born ▼ Year Died ▼

Was this contribution to the work a "work made for hire"?
☐ Yes
☐ No

AUTHOR'S NATIONALITY OR DOMICILE
Name of Country
OR { Citizen of ▶
Domiciled in ▶

WAS THIS AUTHOR'S CONTRIBUTION TO THE WORK
Anonymous? ☐ Yes ☐ No
Pseudonymous? ☐ Yes ☐ No
If the answer to either of these questions is "Yes," see detailed instructions.

NATURE OF AUTHORSHIP Briefly describe nature of material created by this author in which copyright is claimed. ▼

NOTE

Under the law the "author" of a "work made for hire" is generally the employer, not the employee (see instructions). For any part of this work that was "made for hire" check "Yes" in the space provided, give the employer (or other person for whom the work was prepared) as "Author" of that part, and leave the space for dates of birth and death blank.

b

NAME OF AUTHOR ▼

DATES OF BIRTH AND DEATH
Year Born ▼ Year Died ▼

Was this contribution to the work a "work made for hire"?
☐ Yes
☐ No

AUTHOR'S NATIONALITY OR DOMICILE
Name of Country
OR { Citizen of ▶
Domiciled in ▶

WAS THIS AUTHOR'S CONTRIBUTION TO THE WORK
Anonymous? ☐ Yes ☐ No
Pseudonymous? ☐ Yes ☐ No
If the answer to either of these questions is "Yes," see detailed instructions.

NATURE OF AUTHORSHIP Briefly describe nature of material created by this author in which copyright is claimed. ▼

c

NAME OF AUTHOR ▼

DATES OF BIRTH AND DEATH
Year Born ▼ Year Died ▼

Was this contribution to the work a "work made for hire"?
☐ Yes
☐ No

AUTHOR'S NATIONALITY OR DOMICILE
Name of Country
OR { Citizen of ▶
Domiciled in ▶

WAS THIS AUTHOR'S CONTRIBUTION TO THE WORK
Anonymous? ☐ Yes ☐ No
Pseudonymous? ☐ Yes ☐ No
If the answer to either of these questions is "Yes," see detailed instructions.

NATURE OF AUTHORSHIP Briefly describe nature of material created by this author in which copyright is claimed. ▼

---

3 **a**

YEAR IN WHICH CREATION OF THIS WORK WAS COMPLETED This information must be given ◀ Year in all cases.

b **DATE AND NATION OF FIRST PUBLICATION OF THIS PARTICULAR WORK**
Complete this information ONLY if this work has been published.
Month ▶ Day ▶ Year ▶
◀ Nation

4

See instructions before completing this space.

COPYRIGHT CLAIMANT(S) Name and address must be given even if the claimant is the same as the author given in space 2. ▼

TRANSFER If the claimant(s) named here in space 4 is (are) different from the author(s) named in space 2, give a brief statement of how the claimant(s) obtained ownership of the copyright. ▼

APPLICATION RECEIVED

ONE DEPOSIT RECEIVED

TWO DEPOSITS RECEIVED

FUNDS RECEIVED

DO NOT WRITE HERE
OFFICE USE ONLY

MORE ON BACK ▶
• Complete all applicable spaces (numbers 5-9) on the reverse side of this page.
• See detailed instructions.
• Sign the form at line 8.

DO NOT WRITE HERE
Page 1 of _____ pages

EXAMINED BY	FORM PA
CHECKED BY	
☐ CORRESPONDENCE Yes	FOR COPYRIGHT OFFICE USE ONLY

DO NOT WRITE ABOVE THIS LINE. IF YOU NEED MORE SPACE, USE A SEPARATE CONTINUATION SHEET.

PREVIOUS REGISTRATION Has registration for this work, or for an earlier version of this work, already been made in the Copyright Office?

☐ **Yes** ☐ **No** If your answer is "Yes," why is another registration being sought? (Check appropriate box) ▼

a. ☐ This is the first published edition of a work previously registered in unpublished form.

b. ☐ This is the first application submitted by this author as copyright claimant.

c. ☐ This is a changed version of the work, as shown by space 6 on this application.

If your answer is "Yes," give: **Previous Registration Number** ▼   **Year of Registration** ▼

5

DERIVATIVE WORK OR COMPILATION Complete both space 6a and 6b for a derivative work; complete only 6b for a compilation.

a. **Preexisting Material** Identify any preexisting work or works that this work is based on or incorporates. ▼

b. **Material Added to This Work** Give a brief, general statement of the material that has been added to this work and in which copyright is claimed. ▼

6

See instructions before completing this space.

DEPOSIT ACCOUNT If the registration fee is to be charged to a Deposit Account established in the Copyright Office, give name and number of Account.

Name ▼   **Account Number** ▼

7

CORRESPONDENCE Give name and address to which correspondence about this application should be sent.   Name/Address/Apt/City/State/ZIP ▼

Area Code and Telephone Number ▶

Be sure to give your daytime phone ◀ number

CERTIFICATION* I, the undersigned, hereby certify that I am the

Check only one ▼

☐ author

☐ other copyright claimant

☐ owner of exclusive right(s)

☐ authorized agent of _____
Name of author or other copyright claimant, or owner of exclusive right(s) ▲

8

of the work identified in this application and that the statements made by me in this application are correct to the best of my knowledge.

Typed or printed name and date ▼ If this application gives a date of publication in space 3, do not sign and submit it before that date.

_____ date ▶

☞ **Handwritten signature (X)** ▼

MAIL CERTIFI- CATE TO	Name ▼	**YOU MUST:** • Complete all necessary spaces • Sign your application in space 8	**9**
	Number/Street/Apartment Number ▼	**SEND ALL 3 ELEMENTS IN THE SAME PACKAGE:** 1. Application form 2. Nonrefundable $20 filing fee in check or money order payable to *Register of Copyrights* 3. Deposit material	The Copyright Office has the authority to ad- just fees at 5-year inter- vals, based on changes in the Consumer Price Index. The next adjust- ment is due in 1996.
Certificate will be mailed in window envelope	City/State/ZIP ▼	**MAIL TO:** Register of Copyrights Library of Congress Washington, D.C. 20559-6000	Please contact the Copyright Office after July 1995 to determine the actual fee schedule.

*17 U.S.C. § 506(e): Any person who knowingly makes a false representation of a material fact in the application for copyright registration provided for by section 409, or in any written statement filed in connection with the application, shall be fined not more than $2,500.

July 1993—400,000   ♻ PRINTED ON RECYCLED PAPER

☆U.S. GOVERNMENT PRINTING OFFICE: 1993-342-582/80,018

PA/CON. You should provide the requested information about every author who contributed any appreciable amount of copyrightable matter to the multimedia work being registered. But remember that you are registering the copyright to the completed multimedia product, not the copyright to any individual preexisting content that you may have used in the multimedia product with permission. Accordingly, section 2 asks for the identity of the author of the multimedia product, not any of its content or software components.

- **Name of Author.** Insert the name of the author(s) of the multimedia product in this space. You need to take care, however, to ensure that you have properly identified the author(s): in many cases, the person(s) who created the work is/are not the author(s).

  As a general rule, the author is the person who actually created the multimedia product. However, if the multimedia product is a work made for hire, then the employer or other person for whom the work was prepared is considered the author. To determine the identity of the author, review the work-for-hire discussion in chapter 23, section 1.

  If the multimedia product was developed by an employee in the scope of his or her employment, then the employer is the author under work-for-hire rules, and you should insert the full legal name of the employer as the author, and check the box marked "Yes" in response to the question, "Was this contribution to the work a work made for hire?" Remember that independent contractors are not employees.

  If the multimedia product was developed by an independent contractor and the two requirements for a work made for hire set forth in chapter 23, section 1.2.3 were satisfied, then the person or business for whom the multimedia product was developed is the author under "work for hire" rules, and you should insert the full legal name of the person or business for whom the work was done as the author, and check the box marked "Yes" in response to the question, "Was this contribution to the work a work made for hire?"

  If the multimedia product was developed by an independent contractor in a situation that does not meet the requirements for a work made for hire, then the independent contractor retains ownership of the copyright in the multimedia product, and only the independent contractor can register the copyright. However, if the independent contractor has assigned its copyright to you via a written agreement, you should list the independent contractor who actually created the multimedia product as the author, and you should check the box marked "No" in response to the question, "Was this contribution to the work a work made for hire?" In such a case, you will also need to complete the part of section 4 titled "Transfer," to show how title was transferred. (See section 4.4.)

- **Dates of Birth and Death.** If the author is an individual, enter the year of birth and death (if relevant) for each individual author. The author's date of birth is optional, but is useful for identification. If the author is dead, include the year of death unless the work was anonymous or pseudonymous. If the author is a business (i.e., the multimedia work is a work made for hire), leave this space blank.

- **Author's Nationality or Domicile.** If the author is an individual, enter either the country in which the author is a citizen or in which the author lives. If the author is a business, enter the country in which it is incorporated or maintains its principal place of business.

- **This Author's Contribution to the Work.** If the author is an individual, check the appropriate box. An author's contribution to a work is considered "anonymous" if that author is not identified on the copies of the multimedia work. An author's contribution to the multimedia work is "pseudonymous" if that author is identified on the copies under a fictitious name. If the author is a business (i.e., the multimedia work is a work made for hire), leave this section blank.

- **Nature of Authorship.** This section is very important. It provides the Copyright Office with a brief general statement of the nature of the author's contribution to the multimedia product, and helps the Copyright Office decide whether it qualifies for registration. No special language is required, but the description must refer to copyrightable subject matter. If you are registering an entirely new multimedia work and are claiming ownership of the copyright in all copyrightable aspects of the work, the nature of authorship can be described as "entire work" or "entire multimedia work."

    On the other hand, if you are claiming authorship of only certain portions of the multimedia work, a description that identifies those elements in which you are claiming a copyright will be more appropriate. In other words, if your product incorporates content or software licensed from a third party, then you are not the author of the entire work. Instead, your authorship might be described in terms such as the following: "created and/or collected, compiled, and coordinated text, images, and sound recordings to form a new multimedia work."

4.3 Filling Out Section 3

- **Year in Which Creation of Work Was Completed.** When you fill out section 3, it is important to remember the difference between **creation** and **publication.** In this part of section 3, specify the year in which creation of this version of the multimedia product was completed. This may be earlier than the year in which the multimedia product was first published. Under the Copyright Act, a work is created when it is fixed in a copy (e.g., on paper, disk, tape, or CD-ROM) for the first time. Use the year in which the author completed the version that you are registering, even if other versions exist or if further changes or additions are planned.

- **Date and Nation of First Publication of This Particular Work.** This section should be filled out only if the multimedia product has been published. Publication occurs when copies have been distributed to the public or offered to a group of persons for purposes of further distribution. If you have merely displayed or demonstrated the multimedia product without distributing copies, or licensed it to a select group with restrictions on its use and disclosure, this would not necessarily be a "publication."[25]

  If your multimedia product has been published, you should include the full date (month, day, and year) of first publication. The year you enter here must be the same as the year that appears in the copyright notice. You must also enter the name of the country where publication first occurred. If first publication took place simultaneously in the United States and other countries, it is sufficient to state "U.S.A."

4.4 Filling Out Section 4

- **Copyright Claimants.** Enter the full name and address of the person(s) or entity(ies) claiming to be the owner of the copyright. The owner is the author identified in section 2 of the form unless the author has transferred the copyright to someone else.

■ **Transfer**. If the copyright has been transferred to you from someone else, briefly state how ownership of the copyright was transferred. For example, if the copyright was transferred to you by a written agreement, then it is appropriate to say that the copyright was transferred "by contract" or "by assignment." If the copyright was transferred by inheritance, you should state that. It is not necessary to attach copies of any transfer or inheritance documents.

4.5 Filling Out Section 5

Section 5 is intended to help the Copyright Office determine whether a previous version of this multimedia product has been registered, and, if so, whether there is any basis for a new registration. If there has been no previous registration, simply check the "No" box. Otherwise, check "Yes" and fill out the rest of section 5.

If you have checked the box marked "Yes," you must supply the previous registration number and the year of the previous registration. You must also indicate (by checking the appropriate box) why you are seeking another registration. If this version of the multimedia product is substantially the same as the previously registered version, you cannot get a second registration unless (1) the multimedia product was previously registered in unpublished form and you are now seeking a second registration to cover the first published edition; or (2) the copyright was previously registered to another claimant, and you are now seeking registration in your own name. If either of these two exceptions applies, check the appropriate box and enter the earlier registration number and the date.

If the multimedia product has been substantially changed, and you are now seeking registration to cover the additions or revisions, check the last box in space 5, give the earlier registration number and date, and complete both parts of space 6, following the instructions below.

4.6 Filling Out Section 6

You should only fill out section 6 if this work is a derivative work, or compilation, and if it incorporates one or more earlier works that have already been published or registered, or that have fallen into the public domain. If your multimedia product is a derivative work, you should complete both sections 6(a) and 6(b). If your multimedia product is a compilation, you should complete only section 6(b). (Derivative works and compilations are explained in chapter 23, sections 2.2 and 2.3).

If your multimedia product is a derivative work, you must identify the previous works on which it is based. That is, you should identify the preexisting work that has been recast, transformed, or adapted. You do not have to identify each individual preexisting work. Instead, you can refer to them by category, such as by stating, for example, "previously published photographs, musical works, text, and video clips." If the multimedia work you are registering is a compilation, leave this section blank.

For both derivative works and compilations, you must limit the copyright claim to the copyrightable new material by completing section 6(b) entitled "Material Added to This Work." You should give a brief, general statement of the new material covered by the copyright claim for which registration is sought. For a multimedia product comprising a derivative work, an example of such a statement might be "compiled, edited, and coordinated preexisting material, and added original text, images, and sound recordings." If the multimedia product being registered is a compilation, you should describe both the compilation itself and the material that has been compiled. For example, "compilation of photographs, text, and sound recordings relating to NFL football playoffs." The multimedia product being registered may be both a derivative work and a compilation, in which case a sample statement might be: "compilation and additional new material." If the preexisting material has never been registered or published, or if the amount of preexisting material is not substantial, you do not need to complete the "Material Added" section.

4.7 Filling Out Section 7

- **Deposit Account**. If you file a large number of copyright applications, you may set up a deposit account with the Copyright Office. This permits the Office to automatically deduct the application fees from your account. If you have such an account, enter the account name and number. If not, skip this section and send the fee of $20 with your application and deposit.

- **Correspondence**. Enter the name, address, and daytime telephone number of the person whom the Copyright Office should contact if there are any questions about the application for registration.

4.8 Filling Out Section 8

The application must be manually signed by the author, the copyright claimant, the owner of the exclusive rights to the copyright, or an authorized agent of the copyright owner (usually an attorney). The name of this person must be printed or typewritten in section 8 above the signature.

4.9 Filling Out Section 9

Insert the name and address of the person to whom the copyright registration certificate should be mailed. It is not necessary that this be the same person who signs the certification in section 8.

Endnotes

1   17 U.S.C. § 401(a). This provision is effective for works first published after March 1, 1989.

2   17 U.S.C. § 401(b).

3   In the case of modified versions of previously published multimedia works, the year of first publication of the modified version is sufficient. 17 U.S.C. § 401(b)(2). In the case of compilations or derivative works incorporating previously published material, the year date of first publication of the compilation or derivative work is sufficient.

4   17 U.S.C. § 401(c).

5   37 C.F.R. § 201.20(c)(1)

6   37 C.F.R. § 201.20(g).

7   37 C.F.R. § 201.20(g).

8   17 U.S.C. § 408(a).

9   17 U.S.C. § 411.

10   17 U.S.C. § 410(c).

11   17 U.S.C. § 412.

12   17 U.S.C. § 410(c).

13   17 U.S.C. § 408(a).

14   COPYRIGHT OFFICE CIR. 55, COPYRIGHT REGISTRATION FOR MULTIMEDIA WORKS 2 (1992).

15   COPYRIGHT OFFICE CIR. 55, COPYRIGHT REGISTRATION FOR MULTIMEDIA WORKS 3 (1992).

16   See COPYRIGHT OFFICE CIR. 61, COPYRIGHT REGISTRATION FOR COMPUTER PROGRAMS (1993), for further information.

17   Copyright registration fees are adjusted at five-year intervals, based on changes in the Consumer Price Index. The next adjustment is due in 1995. Contact the Copyright Office in January 1995 for the new fee schedule. See COPYRIGHT OFFICE CIR. 55, COPYRIGHT REGISTRATION FOR MULTMEDIA WORKS (1992).

18   COPYRIGHT OFFICE CIR. 55, COPYRIGHT REGISTRATION FOR MULTIMEDIA WORKS 3 (1992).

19   COPYRIGHT OFFICE CIR. 55, COPYRIGHT REGISTRATION FOR MULTIMEDIA WORKS 3 (1992). See COPYRIGHT OFFICE CIR. 61, COPYRIGHT REGISTRATION FOR COMPUTER PROGRAMS) (1993) for further information.

This applies only when you are claiming a copyright in the software. If your multimedia product includes software you have licensed from someone else, it is not necessary to deposit source code.

20   COPYRIGHT OFFICE CIR. 61, COPYRIGHT REGISTRATION FOR COMPUTER PROGRAMS 3 (1993).

21   COPYRIGHT OFFICE CIR. 61, COPYRIGHT REGISTRATION FOR COMPUTER PROGRAMS 3 (1993).

22   17 U.S.C. § 410(d).

23   Words and short phrases such as names, titles, and slogans are not subject to copyright protection.

24   A trademark can be any word, name, symbol, or slogan used by a vendor to identify its products and to distinguish them from similar products marketed by someone else. 1-2-3, Apple, Microsoft, IBM, dBASEIV, WordPerfect, DEC, and Windows are all examples of trademarks. However, not all words, names, or symbols will qualify as trademarks. Trademarks are governed by a separate registration process.

25   *Publication* is a term of art under the Copyright Act. Publication occurs when copies of a work are distributed "to the public by sale or other transfer of ownership, or by rental, lease, or lending," or when the work is offered "to a group of persons for purposes of further distribution." 17 U.S.C. § 101. However, such a distribution or offering for distribution does not constitute a publication if it is made to a select group for a limited purpose in a way that prohibits "disclosure" and transfer of the contents of the program. Thus, for example, if your multimedia work is displayed publicly, but does not change hands, it is not a publication no matter how many people are exposed to it. 17 U.S.C. § 101.

Protecting Your Trademark

Protecting Your Trademark

If you plan to market your multimedia products, you may want to consider selecting a trademark to identify them and distinguish them from the competition. Even if you market your products under your company name, that name can itself be a trademark. Basic trademark law principles relevant to both your own trademarks and your use of other people's trademarks are set forth in chapter 4. This chapter discusses practical steps you can take to protect your own trademarks.

1. Selecting a Trademark

1.1 Trademark Distinctiveness or Strength

When selecting a trademark, it is best to choose a mark that will provide the strongest level of protection possible under the circumstances. Trademarks may be strong or weak, depending on their degree of distinctiveness. The stronger the mark, the greater its scope of protection. The intrinsic *strength* of a mark may be rated (from strongest to weakest), as follows: fanciful or coined, arbitrary, suggestive, descriptive, and generic. The differences between these categories of marks are discussed in detail in chapter 4.

When choosing a name, you should consider adopting as strong and distinctive a mark as you can. Many marketing-oriented professionals are tempted to use descriptive terms as trademarks, and business considerations may support this. However, you should recognize that descriptive marks will be harder to register and protect. Of course, an intrinsically weak mark may become stronger as it achieves public recognition, and an intrinsically strong mark may be weakened by the existence of other similar marks.

1.2 Trademark Search

Before adopting or using a trademark in connection with any of your multimedia products (or spending any money marketing with such a mark), you should conduct a trademark search to make sure the mark is not already taken. This will help to avoid a possible infringement action in the future, and to ensure that your mark can be protected. Similarly, before using a trademark in the content of a multimedia product, a trademark search can help determine whether the mark has been registered, and if so, the identity of the owner of the mark, and the nature of the goods and services on which the mark is used.

There are a number of professional trademark search firms that provide these services (several are listed in chapter 36) and trademark searches are also routinely done by attorneys. Many libraries also provide basic trademark search services. Because of the complexity of this area, however, you should always have a trademark attorney interpret any search.

A trademark search of federal and state registrations will not guarantee that a particular mark is available. It will only show whether someone else has registered or applied for registration of the same or a similar mark.[1] If someone else is already using the mark, even without a registration, they still may have priority over you. Nonetheless, a trademark search will provide a reasonable degree of certainty as to the mark's availability.

In choosing a name and running a search, it is important to remember the tests for trademark infringement discussed in chapter 4, section 3.1. Your trademark can still be infringing, even if it is not identical to an existing mark. The test is whether your mark, when used on your goods or services, would tend to cause confusion as to source or sponsorship of goods or services when compared to the other mark and its goods and services. This is why you should have a trademark attorney review the search.

2. Federal Registration of Trademarks

Trademarks can be registered with the U.S. Patent and Trademark Office. Registration is not required, but can give you many benefits. A trademark registration is effective for ten years,[2] and may be renewed for additional ten-year terms.[3]

2.1 Advantages of Registration

Federal trademark registration confers certain advantages that, in many cases, make it highly recommended. Registration can also have great practical value when it comes to protecting trademark rights.

The most valuable advantages that flow from federal registration of a trademark are as follows:[4]

• The certificate of registration is prima facie evidence of the validity of the registration, your ownership of the trademark, and your exclusive right to use the mark in commerce in connection with the specified goods or services.[5] This means that the mere fact of registration is sufficient to prove these elements, unless the contrary is established.

• Registration constitutes constructive notice to everyone else of your claim of ownership of the trademark.[6] This means that no one can claim that they did not know that the trademark rights were owned by someone else. (This is one reason why it is advisable to conduct a federal trademark search prior to adopting a mark.)

• After five consecutive years of use, you obtain "incontestable" rights in the mark. This means that, with certain exceptions, no one can challenge the validity of the trademark or your exclusive rights in it.[7]

• You can have the U.S. Customs stop imports of infringing goods at the border.[8]

• Any attempt by another person to register a conflicting mark will be blocked where there is a likelihood of confusion.[9]

• In certain cases, treble damages and attorneys' fees are available to you if you have been injured by an infringer.[10]

• Finally, federal registration on the Principal Register will serve to expand your exclusive rights to include the entire United States, even if actual use has only taken place in a portion of the country.[11]

2.2 Qualification for Registration

With certain exceptions, any mark may be federally registered, provided that it is distinctive of your goods or services and has been used in interstate commerce.[12] As discussed below, an application for registration can be filed prior to actual use, under a special provision of the Lanham Act.

Certain types of marks do not qualify for registration. For example, a mark that is descriptive or is a person's surname may not be registered on the Principal Register, unless it has acquired secondary meaning.[13] Other exceptions to registration include marks that are immoral, deceptive, or scandalous, marks consisting of a government flag or other insignia, and marks that consist of a person's name, portrait, or signature used without his or her consent.[14]

Finally, an otherwise eligible mark cannot be registered if there is a likelihood that it will be confused with an existing trademark.[15] The Trademark Office will therefore review an application for registration and compare it with existing registrations, using the same factors described in chapter 4, section 3.1.

Once an application is approved by the Trademark Office, it will be published for opposition in the Official Gazette. Interested parties will then have thirty days to oppose the registration. If an opposition is filed, the matter will be referred to the Trademark Trial and Appeal Board, and will proceed like a regular litigation, with pleadings, discovery, and a trial. If no opposition is filed, you will be issued a registration.

Under 1989 revisions of the Lanham Act, you can also file an application for trademark registration *prior* to using a mark, if you have a bona fide intent to use the mark in interstate commerce.[16] These applications are handled in a similar manner to actual use applications, and are examined and published for opposition. Then, when you actually use the mark, the registration will issue with an effective date retroactive to the filing date. This system permits you to obtain priority over others based on the filing date rather than actual date of first use, which can be a valuable tool for trademark-intensive businesses. To qualify, you must use the mark within six months after the application is allowed, although six-month extensions of time (up to a total of two years) may be granted at extra cost.

2.3 Trademark Notices

If federal registration is granted, you may use any one of the following three notices with the mark:[17]

1. "Registered in U.S. Patent and Trademark Office"
2. "Reg. U.S. Pat. & TM. Off."
3. "®"

Such a notice is not required by the law, but its use gives you certain benefits. Without the notice, you may not be able to recover damages for an infringement.[18] Therefore, it is advisable to use the notice with all federally registered trademarks.

It is important to note that these trademark notices may *not* be used prior to the issuance of a federal trademark registration. If you are using an unregistered trademark, you should give notice of your claim of trademark ownership by use of the term "TM" for trademarks and "SM" for service marks. Neither of these designations confers any special legal status, but by serving as some notice of a claim of trademark ownership, they may deter a potential infringer.

3. State Registration of Trademarks

In addition to the federal Lanham Act, each of the fifty states also has its own trademark laws. If a trademark is federally registered, however, there is usually no need for state registration. The benefits of state registration apply only to the state in which registration is made, and are not nearly as extensive as the benefits of federal registration. State registration can usually be accomplished more quickly than federal registration, however, and is thus often utilized while a federal application is pending. In addition, if the mark is only used in one state, and thus does not yet qualify for federal registration, you may wish to obtain a state registration.

4. Protecting Your Trademark

In order to maintain the valuable property rights acquired in a trademark, it is important that steps be taken to ensure that the mark does not become weakened or generic, and that others are not permitted to infringe it. If your mark becomes generic, in essence it becomes public property. If others are permitted to infringe without objection, the value of the mark may be diminished.

First and foremost, to retain a mark's strength and prevent it from becoming generic, you should use the trademark in a proper and consistent manner. The mark should be printed in initial or all capital letters; in correspondence, the use of quotation marks is suggested. If the mark is registered, it should always be used in the form registered and the symbol "®" should immediately follow the mark. Prior to registration, it is a common practice to use the symbol "TM" after the mark; while this does not confer any special legal status to the mark, it will demonstrate that you consider it to be a trademark.

The mark should always be used as an adjective followed by a common name for the product. It should never be used as a noun or verb. For example, Xerox Corp. is careful to phrase its advertisements to refer to a "XEROX brand plain paper copier" or a "XEROX computer", rather than to "making a xerox" or "xeroxing a copy."

Second, you should take steps to prevent generic or improper use of the trademark by others. This can involve monitoring use by dealers, distributors, licensees, media, and outsiders and objecting to any misuses that occur. Such misuses could include improper format, lack of trademark notice, or generic use, as well as any infringing use.

In developing an approach to misuse by outsiders, you should assess the value of the trademark, the need to prevent loss of distinctiveness, and your financial ability to maintain a lawsuit to protect the trademark. Protecting against misuses by outsiders may involve monitoring trade and other print media, publishing advertisements informing the general public of the proper way to use the trademark, and following up on misuses by letters, personal contacts, and, if necessary, lawsuits. Trademark watch services are also available to monitor new federal and state trademark applications or registrations. You should recognize that a trademark infringement suit can be quite costly, but depending on the type of misuse and the value of the mark, a suit may be the advisable course, not only to prevent the current misuse, but to demonstrate a willingness to protect the mark and thus deter future misuses.

5. Loss of Trademark—Abandonment

Trademark rights can be lost through abandonment. Once the trademark is abandoned, anyone else is free to adopt it.

Abandonment can occur when use of the trademark is discontinued with an intent not to resume use. Under the Lanham Act, nonuse of a trademark for two consecutive years is considered prima facie evidence of abandonment.[19]

Abandonment can also occur when a trademark becomes generic. A trademark can become generic when the public begins to use the trademark to identify the particular type of product itself, rather than to identify the brand of the product produced by the trademark owner. This has happened to "aspirin," "thermos," "escalator," "formica," and "cellophane," as well as many other marks, all of which were at one time trademarks identifying specific product brands. Fears of "genericide" are what cause certain corporations to advertise their products using the trademark followed by the word "brand" and the generic name for the product. There are a number of steps that you can take to police the use of your mark to insure that your trademark does not become generic. These are described in detail in section 4.

Finally, abandonment can occur when you assign or license the trademark to others without proper protection. When assigning a trademark, it is important that the assignment include all of the good will associated with the trademark. Otherwise, the assignment can be deemed an abandonment.[20] When licensing others to use a trademark, it is important to include provisions allowing you to control the quality of goods or services produced under the trademark. A "naked license" without adequate quality controls can be deemed an abandonment.[21]

6. Foreign Trademark Issues

The above sections discuss trademark law as it is applied in the United States. Unlike copyright laws, which by various international treaties can be used to protect copyrights internationally, trademark rights must be protected in each country under that country's laws.[22] Under the Paris Convention, an international treaty to which the United States is a party, a U.S. trademark owner can get a priority foreign registration date if it files for trademark registration in a member country within six months of filing for U.S. registration.[23]

In certain foreign countries, trademark rights are only available by registration, and there is no protection for unregistered marks. In many countries, the first to file for trademark protection is granted priority, rather than the first to use the mark. This has resulted in unfortunate situations where the manufacturer of a famous product is unable to protect its mark from infringement in a foreign country, because someone else filed for registration there first. Thus, if there is an international market for your multimedia product, you should review the need for trademark registrations in other countries.

7. Trademark Licensing and Merchandising

The increased importance and value of brand identity has resulted in a growth of trademark licensing. Under a trademark license, the trademark owner gives someone else permission to use its trademark on goods or services manufactured, sold, or offered by the licensee. This can be as simple as a manufacturing agreement where the licensee contracts to manufacture the licensor's goods in accordance with the licensor's specifications and standards or can be as complex as a national franchise where each franchisee is permitted to use the trademark owner's marks on its goods and services, such as restaurants, service stations and the like.

Another growth area for licensing is the extension of a brand identity beyond the trademark owner's original product line, such as use of a clothing designer's name for other products such as perfumes and luggage, or the use of a cartoon or film character in connection with collateral merchandise such as clothing and games.

Trademark licenses usually require the payment of royalties based on sales, and will always carry with them requirements that the licensor's specifications or quality standards be met. Quality control is an essential element of any trademark license, and no licensor should permit unfettered use of its mark without control or supervision over the quality of the goods and services. A license without adequate quality control can result in abandonment of the mark. (See chapter 4, section 5).

Endnotes

1   Note that the owner of a pending application may have priority over you, even if they have not yet used the mark. Under the 1989 amendments to the Lanham Act, discussed in section 25-2.2, the owner of a federal intent-to-use application may obtain priority based on its application filing date, which may be earlier than the date of first use. This new system of priority makes trademark searches even more important, since one can no longer rely merely on one's knowledge of the marks used in an industry.

2   Trademark registrations issued or renewed before November 16, 1989, were effective for twenty-year terms.

3   In addition, certain procedural requirements must be met to keep a trademark registration in force, including filing an affidavit during the sixth year after registration stating that the mark is still in use. A registration may be canceled, and cannot be renewed, if the mark has been abandoned. See this chapter, section 5 for a discussion of abandonment.

4   Most of these advantages only apply to registrations on the Principal Register. There is also a Supplemental Register for descriptive or surname marks, which has fewer benefits, but does permit use of the ® symbol.

5   15 U.S.C. § 1057(b).

6   15 U.S.C. § 1072.

7   15 U.S.C. §§ 1065, 1115. However, if an innocent party has used the mark prior to the registrant's registration, the innocent party may continue to use the mark in its geographic area of prior use. *Burger King v. Hoots*, 403 F.2d 904 (7th Cir. 1968).

8   15 U.S.C. § 1124, 19 U.S.C. § 1526.

9   15 U.S.C. § 1052(d).

10   15 U.S.C. § 1117.

11   *John R. Thompson Co. v. Holloway*, 366 F.2d 108, 115 (5th Cir. 1966). Technically, the trademark owner cannot actually proceed against an infringer until the infringer is in the same market (or the market is within the owner's impending area of expansion). However, once the owner is in the infringer's area, the owner will have priority based on its registration. *Dawn Donut Co. v. Hart's Food Stores, Inc.*, 267 F.2d 358 (2d Cir. 1959).

12   "Use in interstate commerce" means the mark must be used on goods or in connection with services sold across state lines. Merely advertising in interstate commerce does not constitute "use" sufficient to qualify for trademark registration. Advertising will, however, constitute sufficient use to qualify for registration of a service mark, as long as the services are sold in interstate commerce.

13   15 U.S.C. §§ 1052(e), (f). However, a descriptive or surname mark which has not acquired secondary meaning may be registered on the SUPPLEMENTAL REGISTER. For a discussion of secondary meaning, see chapter 4, section 1.2, under the discussion of descriptive marks.

14   15 U.S.C. § 1052.

15   15 U.S.C. § 1052(d).

16   15 U.S.C. 1051(d).

17   15 U.S.C. § 1111.

18   15 U.S.C. § 1111. Lack of a notice will not deprive the owner of profits or damages if the infringer had actual notice of the registration.

19   15 U.S.C. § 1127.

20   RESTATEMENT (THIRD) OF UNFAIR COMPETITION § 34, comment (f) (tentative draft No. 3, 1991).

21   *Heaton Enters. of Nevada, Inc. v. Lang*, 7 U.S.P.Q.2d 1842 (TTAB 1988).

22   An overview of foreign trademark laws is beyond the scope of this book. For a quick discussion of international trademark issues, See J. THOMAS MCCARTHY, MCCARTHY ON TRADEMARKS AND UNFAIR COMPETITION, Chapter 29 (1994), and references cited therein.

23   See generally LADAS, PATENTS, TRADEMARKS AND RELATED RIGHTS: NATIONAL AND INTERNATIONAL PROTECTION (1975).

Protecting Your Trade Secrets

Protecting Your Trade Secrets

Trade secret law offers an important vehicle for protection of new technology that you develop and incorporate in your multimedia product. It can also be used to provide protection for the identity and content of your multimedia product prior to its public release.

The major risk of relying on the trade secret laws to protect proprietary technology or product information is that once the secret is out, the protection is gone. Thus, protecting your trade secrets begins with an understanding of how you might lose your trade secrets.

1. How Trade Secret Protection Can Be Lost

Although trade secret protection is broader than that offered by copyright, it is also very fragile. It is automatically lost whenever it is disclosed or becomes generally known within the industry. There are three ways this can happen—independent discovery, unrestricted disclosure, and failure to keep it secret.

1.1 Independent Discovery

Your trade secrets are protected only as long as competitors fail to duplicate them by legitimate independent research.[1] Once someone independently discovers your trade secret, that person is free to use or disclose it. It will remain a trade secret, however, even though known to two persons instead of one, if you both keep it secret. But if either discloses it to the industry, the secret is lost to both.

Independent discovery can occur in two ways. First, another person can seren-dipitously happen on to the same idea or solution, or can do the work and spend the money necessary to independently develop it. Second, another person can purchase your product, take it apart, study it, and figure out how it works. This latter process is known as *reverse engineering* and is perfectly legal once a product is sold on the market.[2] The mere fact that your product is on the market and available for reverse engineering, however, will not permit others to steal its trade secret by improper means. The law requires all trade secrets to be obtained honestly if at all.[3] If it will require an extensive period of time, and/or a large expenditure of money in order to reverse-engineer your product, even after it is out in the market, then the trade secret can be protected to the extent of this time and cost advantage.

1.2 Unrestricted Disclosure

Disclosure of your trade secrets in the context of a confidential relationship will not result in the loss of trade secret protection. For example, you are free to disclose trade secrets to your employees, because by law, employees are legally bound to keep all of their employer's trade secrets confidential. Similarly, you can disclose your trade secrets to anyone who will sign a contract specifically agreeing to keep the trade secrets confidential.

On the other hand, unrestricted disclosure of a trade secret will forfeit its pro-tected status. An unrestricted disclosure of a trade secret is a disclosure to anyone who is not legally obligated to keep it confidential. This frequently occurs through simple carelessness on the part of the trade secret owner. In one case, for example, trade secret protection was lost when a company allowed one of its employees to publish an article explaining its system to other experts in the field. The court found that the information in the article was sufficient to enable an experienced engineer to duplicate the product without too much difficulty.[4] Disclosures like this should never be allowed to occur.

Another way that unrestricted disclosure can occur is through marketing. Any product that has been sold on the market is generally open to duplication by skilled engineers.[5] If the product is sold outright instead of being licensed, and if the trade secret can be determined by an inspection of the product itself, the trade secret will be lost when that occurs. If the product (such as software or other technology) is licensed, however, and the licensee is contractually bound to keep it confidential, this will constitute a protected disclosure and trade secret protection will not be waived. In other words, the party to a confidentiality agreement will not be permitted to obtain rights in the trade secret even by reverse engineering.

1.3 Failure to Keep It Secret

In addition to the requirement that your information be secret within the industry, the law also imposes a burden on you to take steps to maintain its secrecy. In essence, the law says that the information must not only be secret, but also that you must act as if it is a valuable secret and guard it accordingly. Otherwise, the protection provided by the trade secret laws may be lost, even though the information is not otherwise known in the industry. In one case, for example, a court held that software used in the design and manufacture of class rings was not a trade secret because, among other things, the plaintiff never proved that it intended to keep the relevant information secret.[6] This conclusion was based in part on the fact that when the software was installed, no policy was established to keep it secret, and that the plaintiff had allowed one of its employees to write an article explaining the system to other experts in the field.

Simply put, to maintain protection for your trade secrets, the information must be treated as a trade secret. If you freely distribute "trade secret" information within your own firm, you may find that the courts will deny you protection. Courts will generally not enforce trade secret protection unless there is evidence that you have taken clear action to protect its secrecy. If you do not treat it like a valuable secret and try to protect it, why should the courts?

Depending on the circumstances, fulfilling this obligation to maintain secrecy may require the establishment of an affirmative course of action reasonably designed to ensure that the information will remain secret.[7] Steps that can be taken to ensure protection of software are described in the next section.

2. Protecting Trade Secrets

While there is no way to prevent independent discovery, it is possible to guard against loss of your trade secret through theft and careless or inadvertent disclosure. As noted above, the failure to take steps to prevent inadvertent disclosure may, itself, result in waiver of the protection. The ease with which your proprietary information can be obtained may furnish a valid defense to a charge of trade secret misappropriation.

Thus, whether you have taken adequate steps to protect the secrecy of your proprietary information is frequently one of the key issues in trade secret litigation.

Standard measures that you take to protect your trade secrets involve both the use of contractual safeguards for customer relationships and the establishment of internal controls within your organization. The level of effort and expense required to protect a trade secret varies widely, and thus a decision as to whether to implement any particular procedure should be based on (1) an analysis of the value of the information and (2) the likelihood that it will be subject to misappropriation. There is no requirement that any specific procedures be implemented; the test is simply whether or not you treated the information as one would treat a valuable secret. The following sections discuss the most widely used and commonly recognized techniques for protecting a trade secret.

2.1 Restrict Access to the Information

Perhaps the primary method available for protecting your trade secrets is to restrict the number of individuals who have access to them to the absolute minimum. No one who is not directly working with the information, and authorized to do so, should have access to it.

Online access can be restricted through the use of passwords that should be changed periodically, restricted libraries, or other similar procedures. Access to the physical computer-readable media, such as CD-ROMs, disks, and diskettes containing the information should be carefully controlled by keeping such media in a secure and locked area. Access to printed source code and other sensitive documentation should be similarly restricted. Only authorized personnel should be allowed access to this media, and control procedures should be instituted where appropriate.

Allowing persons with no need to know to have access to the information can lead to the loss of a trade secret and should be carefully controlled, if allowed at all. Furthermore, all source code and documentation relating to the information should be marked with legends such as "Secret," "Confidential," "For Use by Authorized Personnel Only," or "Not for Publication." And if information is disclosed to third persons such as customers or technicians, a written record of such disclosure should be kept and the third party should execute a written commitment not to reveal the information to anyone else. Like all methods of protecting trade secrets, carefully restricting access both makes disclosure less likely and puts a thief at a distinct disadvantage in the eyes of a court.

The extent to which these procedures are implemented depends, of course, on the nature of your business, the value of the trade secrets, and the likelihood of misappropriation. Large corporations with extremely valuable products may go to the extent of installing closed circuit cameras, keeping certain information in safes, and having guards patrol the premises. A one-person operation, on the other hand, might just simply refrain from allowing anyone else to see the information or have access to the place in which it is kept.

2.2 Establish an Obligation of Confidentiality

While it is important to restrict access to your trade secrets, there are some persons who must have access. This includes employees and independent contractors employed to develop products that require the use of your trade secrets, potential business partners who may want to evaluate your technology before entering into a relationship, and in many cases, customers. You can disclose your trade secrets to these persons without losing your trade secret protection only if such persons are bound by an obligation of confidentiality. Thus, before making any disclosures of your trade secret information, it is important that you establish the existence of an obligation of confidentiality binding upon the recipient. The rules for doing this vary, depending upon whether or not the recipient is an employee or not.

2.2.1 Confidentiality and Employees.   The law implies the existence of a confidential relationship between every employer and employee.[8] In other words, the law implies an agreement that prohibits employees from disclosing any trade secrets revealed to them in the course of their employment, and from using those trade secrets for their own or someone else's benefit.[9] But an employee is entitled to fair notice of the confidential nature of the relationship and what material is to be kept confidential.[10] Consequently, the implied obligation of confidentiality may only apply to trade secrets of which (1) your employees have been expressly made aware, such as through specific designation; or (2) your employees can be said to have "constructive knowledge," such as from the context in which the information was disclosed, the measures you take to protect the secret, or from the knowledge that an employee can reasonably be expected to possess as to what provides your business with an advantage over your competitors.[11]

Consequently, it is often wise to have your employees sign **confidentiality agreements** in which they expressly acknowledge that the software and other confidential information with which they will be working is considered to be your trade secret, and that they will not improperly use or disclose it. An employee confidentiality agreement serves to demonstrate that you consider your developments to be secret and valuable. It is also the most persuasive possible evidence that employees were informed from the outset that they would not be permitted to use your software and other trade secrets except in your business.

If your employee leaves to work for a competitor, a confidentiality agreement gives you a sound legal basis for preventing the employee from taking or using your secret information in his or her new job. The existence of a confidentiality agreement, if made known to the new employer, may also help to reduce the employer's enthusiasm for exploiting the employee's confidential knowledge.

A sample employee agreement that contains a confidentiality provision is set out in chapter 33.

Finally, when an employee announces his or her intention to leave, it is also appropriate to conduct an exit interview. The purpose of such an interview is to remind the employee of his or her obligations with respect to trade secrets and to ensure that the employee has returned all software, documentation, and any other materials that belong to you.

2.2.2 Confidentiality and Others.

There are, of course, many good reasons for disclosing trade secrets to persons other than employees. The most obvious example is the disclosure of trade secrets to an independent contractor that you have retained to assist in your development efforts. Similarly, trade secrets may be disclosed to others for evaluation, as a precursor to entering into a joint venture relationship, or as "advertising." In all of these cases, it is extremely important that those to whom the information is to be disclosed execute a confidentiality agreement in which they agree (1) to limit their use of the information as specified in the contract, and (2) not to disclose the information to any other party without the express permission of the owner. The necessary element of secrecy is not lost if the holder of the trade secret reveals it to another "in confidence," and under an obligation not to disclose it. A sample third party confidentiality agreement is included in chapter 33.

2.3 Provide Notice of Your Trade Secret Claim

With respect to those who must have access (such as employees and independent contractors bound by an obligation of confidentiality) it is important to notify them that you consider it to be a valuable trade secret. One who is truly unaware that particular information constitutes a trade secret will be more difficult to prosecute for misappropriation.

Providing notice that information is considered to be a valuable trade secret is easy to do. For example, confidentiality notices such as the following can be included on all copies of the information:

> Warning—This information is a trade secret of ABC Corp., and is
> to be kept confidential at all times. Anyone who wrongfully uses
> or discloses this information may be subject to civil and/or crim-
> inal penalties.

Trade secret notices can also be ink-stamped on the top of any sensitive documents or applied by gummed label to binders containing information as well as to CD-ROMs, disks, tapes, manuals, or diskettes containing machine-readable copies of the information. Appropriate notices should also be inserted in any sensitive documentation.

It is also advisable to inform employees, customers, and anyone else to whom sensitive material is to be disclosed, both verbally and by written contract, of the fact that you consider it to be a valuable trade secret, and that they must keep it confidential.

The primary goal is to be sure that everyone who comes into contact with the information is aware of the fact that you consider it to be a valuable trade secret. This will encourage individuals to whom it has been disclosed in confidence to treat it as a trade secret, and will make it easier for a court to punish anyone who discloses what he or she knows to be a trade secret.

3. Detecting Misappropriation

Trade secret protection is of little value if you are unable to detect and prosecute those who are misappropriating your trade secrets. Unfortunately, detecting misappropriation is often a difficult task in which luck plays a large role.

Nonetheless, there are some steps that can be taken. The first is to watch the situations with the greatest potential for misappropriation. The factual settings in which most trade secret cases arise can be categorized as follows:

1. an employee changes jobs or leaves to form a competing company, and takes your trade secrets with him or her;

2. an independent contractor misuses your proprietary information disclosed to it for purposes of evaluating or developing a product for you;

3. a licensee of your trade secret product information develops a competing product using trade secrets disclosed to it in confidence pursuant to the license agreement;

4. a competitor gains access to your trade secrets through merger or acquisition of one of your licensees.

If a trade secret is misappropriated, the result of that misappropriation is frequently a product that is similar to and competitive with the misappropriated product. Thus, another important technique for detecting misappropriation is to analyze all new competing products. Announcements and advertisements in trade journals, as well as information obtained from customers and potential customers, are all excellent sources of leads.

Obviously, the mere appearance of a new competing product does not, by itself, suggest that there has been a misappropriation of trade secrets. Suspicions should be raised, however, if (1) the source of the new product appears to be someone who has had access to the trade secret; or (2) information indicates that the competing product was developed in a very short time or that the expense of its development was very low. Under these circumstances, further investigation is warranted.

You should contact a qualified attorney before initiating an in-depth investigation. It is important that no unfounded accusations be made that might lead to charges of libel, tortious interference with business relations, or antitrust violations.

The investigation should attempt to obtain as much information as possible about the company marketing the suspect product, and about the product itself. If possible, a copy of the competing product should be legitimately obtained for further examination.

Endnotes

1 *University Computing Co. v. Lykes-Youngstown Corp.*, 504 F.2d 518, 534 (5th Cir. 1974).

2 Cal. Civ. Code § 3426.1(c); 765 ILCS 1065/2(a). See *Atari Games Corp. v. Nintendo of America, Inc.*, 24 U.S.P.Q.2d 1015 (Fed. Cir. 1992)("Reverse engineering object code to discern the unprotectable ideas in a computer program is a fair use."); *Sega Enters., Ltd. v. Accolade, Inc.*, 977 F.2d 1510 (9th Cir. 1992)("where disassembly is the only way to gain access to the ideas and functional elements embodied in a copyrighted computer program and where there is a legitimate reason for seeking such access, disassembly is a fair use of the copyrighted work, as a matter of law").

3 See, e.g., *Digital Dev. Corp. v. International Memory Sys.*, 185 U.S.P.Q. 136, 141 (S.D. Cal. 1973); *Thermotics, Inc. v. Bat-Jac Tool Co.*, 541 S.W.2d 255, 260-61 (Tex. Civ. App. 1976); *Colony Corp. v. Crown Glass Corp.*, 430 N.E.2d 225, 227 (Ill. App. 1981).

4 *Jostens, Inc. v. National Computer Sys., Inc.*, 318 N.W.2d 691, 700 (Minn. 1982).

5 *Analogic Corp. v. Data Translation, Inc.*, 358 N.E.2d 804, 807 (Mass. 1976).

6 *Jostens, Inc. v. National Computer Sys. Inc.*, 318 N.W.2d 691, 700 (Minn. l982).

7 *Amoco Prod. Co. v. Lindley,* 609 P.2d 733, 743 (Okla. l980).

8 See, e.g., *Integrated Cash Management Servs., Inc. v. Digital Transactions, Inc.*, 732 F. Supp 370 (S.D.N.Y. 1989); *Engineered Mechanical Servs., Inc. v. Langlois*, 464 So. 2d 329 (La. Ct. App. 1984), *cert. denied*, 467 So. 2d 531 (La. 1985).

9 *Jostens, Inc. v. National Computer Sys., Inc.*, 318 N.W.2d 691, 701 (Minn. 1982).

10 *Jostens, Inc. v. National Computer Sys., Inc.*, 318 N.W.2d 691, 702 (Minn. 1982).

11 *Jostens, Inc. v. National Computer Sys., Inc.*, 318 N.W.2d 691, 702 (Minn. 1982).

Protecting Your Patent Rights

Protecting Your Patent Rights

The importance of the patent law for multimedia became evident to the entire industry with the November 1993 announcement by Comptons of its multimedia search patent. See chapter 9, section 2. But many other aspects of multimedia are, or can be, protected by patent. The data compression standard known as MPEG-1, for example, is governed by several patents. To the extent you develop any new patentable inventions, you should carefully consider whether obtaining patent protection is appropriate. This chapter will summarize the basics behind the patenting process.

1. Who Owns the Patent Rights to Your Inventions?

Under the patent law, the inventor or discoverer of patentable subject matter owns the patent.[1] Thus, as a general rule, the patent rights in any patentable invention will be owned by your employees or the independent contractors who developed the invention. This is true even if the invention was made within the scope of the inventor's employment. There are, however, two exceptions: (1) if you hire or retain someone for the specific purpose of making a particular invention or solving a particular problem, the invention will belong to you as the employer,[2] and (2) if you enter into a contract with your employee or independent contractor that expressly calls for the assignment to you of inventions made by them within the scope of their employment.

Normally, an assignment from the inventor to you cannot be implied and must be in writing.[3] However, there are certain situations where the law may imply the existence of such an assignment. This could occur in the case of inventions made by officers or directors of a corporation,[4] and in the case of employment specifically for the purpose of inventing patentable subject matter.[5] However, even under these circumstances, it is still possible that patent rights will remain with the inventor in the absence of an express written assignment.

Thus, if you wish to own all patent rights to the multimedia technology invented by any of your employees or independent contractors, you should enter into an appropriate written assignment agreement with the individuals involved. Such agreements are valid if required as a condition of employment, but may require additional consideration if entered into after the employment has commenced. Moreover, the laws in some states impose restrictions on the scope of such assignment agreements. Thus, it is important to consult with legal counsel when developing such agreements.

Even if an employee or independent contractor does not assign his or her patent rights to you, in most cases you will still have the right to use the patentable invention under what is known as the "shop rights" doctrine. This doctrine provides that the employer has a perpetual, royalty-free license to use in its business any patented invention created by an employee in the course of his employment.[6] This right, however, is not exclusive, and the employee or independent contractor is still free to go out and market the patented invention. On the other hand, the employer may use the patented invention only in the course of its business and may not sell or license it to anyone else.

Thus, to fully exploit a patentable invention you should be sure to obtain an assignment of the patent rights from any employees and/or independent contractors who create the invention. Such an assignment should be entered into prior to the time the invention is created (ideally, as a condition of employment), as it will be presumably much harder to obtain (and perhaps costly) if the assignment is sought only after the invention has been created.

2. Time Limits for Patent Applications

Regardless of who owns the patent rights, the right to obtain a patent in a given invention can be lost forever if the patent application is not filed within a certain time. The Patent Act requires the inventor to file his or her application within one year of the date in which the invention is first (1) in public use, (2) on sale in this country, (3) described in a printed publication in this or a foreign country, or (4) patented in a foreign country.[7] Private use of the invention will not trigger the one-year limitation period. However, any nonsecret use of the invention (other than for experimental purposes) either by the inventor or by another person with the inventor's permission, is considered a "public use." The experimental use exception is a treacherous area in which there has been much recent change in the law. Consequently, no field testing or other experiment outside of the inventor's workplace or home should be done without first consulting a qualified patent attorney.

To preserve foreign patent rights in most of the commercially significant countries, no delay between commercial or public use or publication is permitted. The safest practice is to file a U.S. Patent Application (which preserves for one year the right to file in most foreign countries) before any field testing or attempt to sell is made.

3. Process of Obtaining a Patent

Patent rights in the United States are obtained only by grant from the federal government. Following the creation of an invention (such as software), the process of obtaining a patent begins with the patent application. It is a time-consuming process and may be expensive. The time between first submission of the application and issuance of the patent may often span several years, and the cost can easily exceed $15,000. However, the payments are typically spread out over a period of time and should be compared with the cost of other types of protection, such as the cost of providing the security necessary to protect trade secrets, and the enhancement of market value potentially resulting from being able to exclude all infringers from the marketplace. Also, the nature of the patent application process is a stepwise one. Hence, there are a number of points in the process at which the application may be dropped if you decide that it is no longer economical.

Although the use of a patent attorney is not required by law, it is a practical necessity in order to ensure that a patent application is properly drafted and prosecuted before the Patent and Trademark Office. The following sections describe the patent application process in general, but do not attempt to provide the detailed information necessary to apply for a patent. That is best done in consultation with a competent patent attorney.

3.1. Who May Apply for a Patent

As a general rule, the only person who may apply for a patent for software or any other type of invention is the inventor.[8] When two or more persons are involved in the creation of the invention to be patented, all of them must join in the patent application and sign the required oath or declaration.[9]

Where patentable software or other patentable inventions are created by employees in the scope of their employment, you should require them to sign a patent assignment agreement, whereby they agree that any and all inventions that they make are assigned to you, their employer. Such an agreement is normally effective to assign all rights in the patent to you as the employer, but such an assignment will normally not allow you the employer to apply for the patent yourself. The employee(s) who created the software must execute the patent application, except in very limited situations.[10]

3.2 Form and Content of the Patent Application

A patent application can be a lengthy and complex document. Moreover, much care must be taken in drafting the patent application, since the way in which it is framed will determine the scope of the patent rights to be granted, and in some cases may even determine whether a patent will be granted at all.

A complete patent application must include the following elements:[11]

1. a specification describing the invention and the manner and process of making and using it, including one or more "claims";

2. an oath or declaration by the applicant that he or she believes himself or herself to be the original and first inventor[12] ;

3. drawings, when necessary for an understanding of the subject matter to be patented[13] ; and

4. the prescribed filing fee, which is at least $355 for "small entities" and $710 for everyone else.[14] Additional fees are charged for applications that contain many claims, and/or certain categories of claims.

The heart of the patent application is found in the specification section. Basically, this section of the patent application must do two things. First, it must disclose the operation of the invention with enough detail so that someone familiar with the particular art (such as computer programming) could reproduce the invention.[15] Second, it must set forth the claims that are to be the subject of the patent, that is, the specific claims for which you wish to be granted a limited monopoly.[16] The claims define what it is that has been invented, and delimit the extent of the monopoly granted by the patent. Consequently, it is very important that the claims be properly drafted. If they are too broad, the patent will not be issued; if too narrow, the protection provided by the patent will be reduced accordingly.

3.3. Examination by the Patent Office

Once a patent application is filed with the Patent and Trademark Office, it is assigned for examination to an examiner for the appropriate class of invention to which the application relates.[17] Applications are taken up for examination by the examiner to whom they have been assigned in the order in which they have been filed.[18] The patent examiner reviews the application to determine whether it complies with applicable statutes and rules and also to determine the patentability of the claimed invention. This examination requires a thorough study and investigation of the available prior art relating to the subject matter of the claimed invention.[19]

At the conclusion of this examination, if the patent examiner determines that the invention is not patentable, you will be notified of the examiner's rejection of the application.[20] You then have the right to require reconsideration of the patent application by the Patent and Trademark Office.[21] The reconsideration process also permits you to modify (amend) your claims in an effort to meet the examiner's objections. In practice, most patent applications have most or all of their claims initially rejected.

The application process is such that you can, in effect, negotiate the language of allowable claims with the examiner. If you and the examiner are unable to reach agreement on allowable claims, the Patent and Trademark Office issues a Final Rejection.[22] You may appeal the Final Rejection within the Patent and Trademark Office or to federal court if you so desire.[23]

If a patent application is approved, you will be so notified, and upon payment of the patent issue fees,[24] the patent will be granted. The grant of a patent is evidenced by a printed document called Letters Patent.

While a patent application is pending, secrecy is maintained by the Patent Office. Thus no trade secrets that may be embodied in the invention are compromised before the patent has actually been issued, at which time the contents of the application become public knowledge.

It takes approximately two years for the Patent and Trademark Office to process a patent application. The cost for the preparation of the patent application, an initial patent search, prosecution of the patent application before the Patent and Trademark Office, and the necessary fees can easily run in excess of $15,000. Thus, even with respect to an invention that qualifies for patent protection, it may not be worth obtaining the patent unless the useful life of the invention, and its value, justifies the time and expense required. However, for an invention that does have a sufficient useful life and a substantial potential market, the advantages of patent protection are such that patent protection ought to be seriously considered with the assistance of a qualified patent lawyer.

3.4 Patent Notice

A patent notice consists merely of the word "patent" or the abbreviation "pat." followed by the number of the patent.[25] In the case of a patent application that is pending but not granted, the notice may be simply the phrase "patent pending." A penalty may be imposed for an improper notice,[26] so one should not be used unless appropriate.

There is no requirement that a patented invention be marked with a patent notice. However, if the notice has not been used, and someone infringes your patent, you will be allowed to recover money damages only for the period subsequent to the date on which the infringer received actual notice that the invention was patented.[27]

Endnotes

1   35 U.S.C. § 101.

2   *United States v. Dubilier Condenser Corp.*, 289 U.S. 178, 187, 53 S. Ct. 554, 557 (1933).

3   35 U.S.C. § 261.

4   *Dowse v. Federal Rubber Co.*, 254 F. 308 (D. Ill. 1918).

5   *Lyon Mfg. Corp. v. Chicago Flexible Shaft Co.*, 106 F.2d 930, 933-934 (7th Cir. 1939); *Dinwiddie v. St. Louis & O'Fallon Coal Co.*, 64 F.2d 303, 306 (4th Cir. 1933).

6   C.T. DRECHSLER, ANNOTATION, APPLICATION AND EFFECT OF "SHOP RIGHT RULE" OR LICENSE GIVING EMPLOYER LIMITED RIGHTS IN EMPLOYEES' INVENTIONS AND DISCOVERIES, 61 A.L.R.2d 356 (1958); *United States v. Dubilier Condensor Corp.*, 289 U.S. 178, 188-89, 53 S. Ct. 554, 557-58 (1933).

7   35 U.S.C. § 102(b).

8   35 U.S.C. § 111; 37 C.F.R. § 1.41.

9   35 U.S.C. § 116; 37 C.F.R. § 1.45.

10   35 U.S.C. § 118.

11   35 U.S.C. §§ 111, 112, 113, 115; 37 C.F.R. § 1.51.

12   35 U.S.C. § 115; 37 C.F.R. § 1.63.

13   35 U.S.C. § 113; 37 C.F.R. §§ 1.81-1.88.

14   37 C.F.R. § 1.16. A "small entity" is defined as "an independent inventor, a small business concern or a non-profit organization." A "small business" concern is one with fewer than 500 employees. 37 C.F.R. § 1.9.

15   35 U.S.C. § 112; 37 C.F.R. § 1.71.

16   37 C.F.R. § 1.75.

17   37 C.F.R. § 1.101(a).

18   37 C.F.R. § 1.101(a).

19   37 C.F.R. § 1.104(a).

20   37 C.F.R. § 1.104(b).

21   37 C.F.R. § 1.111.

22   37 C.F.R. § 1.113.

23   37 C.F.R. § 1.113.

24   37 C.F.R. § 1.18.

25   35 U.S.C. § 287.

26   35 U.S.C. § 292.

27   35 U.S.C. § 287.

PART 4

Marketing Multimedia Products

28 Licensing Your Multimedia Product for Distribution

Licensing Your Multimedia Product for Distribution

Licensing Your Multimedia Product for Distribution

Distribution of multimedia works can take a variety of forms. At present, perhaps the most common is distribution via CD-ROM. In the future distribution via online network and interactive television may become more common.

This chapter looks at some of the issues you need to consider when entering into a relationship with another entity for the distribution of your multimedia product.

1. Goals of the Distribution Process

To begin the analysis, it is important to keep in mind the various goals that you will typically seek to achieve through distribution of your multimedia product.

The first, and perhaps the most obvious, goal is simply to achieve as widespread of a distribution for your product as possible, so as to maximize the income generated by the sale or licensing of your product. This assumes, of course, that you are compensated for each copy that is distributed, another key goal of the distribution process. In other words, while you want to maximize distribution, you want to minimize piracy.

Relatedly, a key goal of the distribution process is to ensure that all of your proprietary rights in the multimedia work are adequately protected and respected. This includes your copyright in the multimedia product, the trademark that you use in connection with marketing the product, and any trade secret and patent rights that may relate to the technology incorporated within the product. You need to ensure that these rights are properly respected by any distributor that you license, and that the distributor distributes your multimedia products in a manner that will protect these rights and minimize infringement by other third parties. At the same time, it is important to ensure that your distribution does not infringe the rights of anyone else, or exceed the scope of any content or software license agreements that you have entered into.

Next is the issue of liability. Normally you have no control over the way in which your products are used, and the potential liabilities to which you may be exposed if, as is certainly very possible, there is a problem with the product. Accordingly, you need to take appropriate steps to limit your liability both to the distributor and any end users who ultimately acquire your product.

Finally, you need flexibility with respect to the distribution relationship itself. That is, to the extent you were unhappy with the relationship, feel that the distributor is not doing an adequate job, or have opportunities for other more lucrative distribution relationships, you need the flexibility to terminate the relationship. On the other hand, of course, the distributor may want some guaranteed time frame for which the distribution rights will apply in order to make the necessary investment to market and promote the product.

With these goals as background, the following sections will consider some of the key issues arising in the context of a distribution license relationship.

2. Scope of Rights Granted

When entering into a distribution arrangement, you, as the owner of the copyright to your multimedia product, grant to a publisher or distributor selected rights to your multimedia product, and impose restrictions on the exercise of those rights. Thus, you must consider both the activities that you will authorize the distributor to engage in, and the limitations you want to impose on the distributor's right to engage in those activities.

The activities that you may authorize distributors to engage in derive from the rights you have as copyright owner to copy, adapt, distribute, perform, and display copies of your multimedia product. The activities that you authorize distributors to engage in, and the limits you place on their right to conduct those activities, are typically determined by considering both your marketing goals and objectives, and the limitations imposed on your ability to market your multimedia product by the terms of the content licenses you have negotiated with respect to the content incorporated within your multimedia product.

If the rights you grant to your distributors exceed the scope of the rights granted to you, you run the risk of being liable for copyright infringement and the issuance of an injunction prohibiting the further distribution of your multimedia product, as well as liability for damages.[1]

2.1. What Activities Are Authorized?

As the owner of the copyright in your multimedia product, you possess the exclusive right to engage in five basic activities: to copy the product, to adapt the product (i.e., prepare derivative works based on it), to distribute the product, to display the product publicly, and to perform the product publicly. (These rights are explained in chapter 3, section 4). Thus, the first issue you should consider is which of the foregoing rights you will authorize your distributors to exercise.

Generally, the process of distributing your multimedia product will require, at a minimum, that you grant distribution rights. In addition, however, it may be appropriate to grant licenses to exercise a number of the other rights that you possess in order to facilitate the distribution process.

● **Reproduction Right.** When your multimedia product is manufactured for distribution (such as on a CD-ROM disc), this constitutes copying. In some distribution arrangements, you may want to take care of the copying yourself, (such as by making your own arrangements with a CD-ROM replicator), and merely ship manufactured copies to a distributor for resale. On the other hand, in some publishing and distribution arrangements, it may be preferable to grant the distributor the right to do this copying.

When you authorize distributors to reproduce your multimedia product, quality control becomes an important issue. You need to ensure, for example, that the distributor takes care not to allow the introduction of any virus onto the media in which the product is duplicated. You may also want to review and/or specify the quality standards for the materials incorporated in the product, such as the CD-ROM discs, the paper and binding for manuals and other inserts, and the packaging itself.

Typically, you should also specify all of the content that goes into the product packaging, including the manner and location of the display of your trademarks, logos, trade names, and copyright notices.

• **Adaptation Right.** Most distribution licenses do not include a license of the adaptation right. Normally, you are attempting to market a complete product, and do not want further modification of that product throughout the distribution channel. However, in some situations, such as a publishing arrangement, it may be appropriate to license the adaption right to the publisher, who may make its own arrangements for further enhancement and modification of your multimedia title before distributing it to the public.

• **Distribution Right.** The right to distribute your multimedia product is, of course, the key and fundamental right included in every distribution agreement. However, you should note that the distribution right is separate and distinct from the reproduction right. The right to reproduce your multimedia title does not, by itself, include the right to distribute it. Similarly, the right to distribute your multimedia title does not, by itself, include the right to reproduce it.

Your ability to grant distribution rights to distributors is limited, of course, by any restrictions imposed upon your use of content licensed from third parties and incorporated in your multimedia product. For example, if you obtained a film clip pursuant to a license that authorized distribution in the United States only, you will not be able to authorize anyone else to distribute your multimedia product (if it incorporates the restricted film clip) outside of the United States.

In addition to limitations imposed by content licenses, you should also be aware of the prohibitions against rental of sound recordings and computer programs that appear in the Copyright Act.[2] Unless you obtain specific permission from the owner of any sound recordings or computer software that is incorporated in your multimedia title, you will not be authorized to rent the completed title to anyone else. Accordingly, in such cases your distribution agreements should similarly prohibit rental.

2.2. What Limitations Are Imposed on the Rights Granted?

In addition to the activities that you authorize your distributors to engage in (such as copy, adapt, distribute, and so forth), a key issue is the limitations you may want to impose on the rights you have granted to engage in each of the activities. As owner of the copyright, you can impose whatever conditions or restrictions you desire on the grant of rights that you make.[3] As one court has noted, "A copyright proprietor must be allowed substantial freedom to limit licenses to perform his work in public to defined periods and areas or audiences"[4] Moreover, to the extent your multimedia title includes content that is licensed from others pursuant to limited rights or restricted licenses, you need to ensure that you impose similar limitations on your distributors, so that you do not inadvertently find yourself liable for copyright infringement by exceeding the scope of the licenses granted to you.

As the copyright owner, you can impose an almost unlimited number of different types of limitations on the distribution of your multimedia product. Some of the more common restrictions are discussed below.

- **Media.** If you authorize replication of your multimedia product, you may want to specify a particular medium and/or format, such as CD-ROM, CD-i, diskette, and so forth.

- **Distribution Channels.** In addition to covering the media on which the multimedia title will be embodied, you may also want to ensure that the scope of the rights granted is limited to the appropriate distribution channel. These may include, for example, distribution of media via retail outlets, bundling with hardware products, and so forth.

- **Territories.** Distribution licenses frequently limit distribution to a specific geographical area, such as the United States and/or selected other countries. You should at least ensure that the scope of rights granted does not exceed your rights in any licensed content.

- **Exclusive or Nonexclusive.** Most multimedia product distribution licenses are nonexclusive, thereby leaving you free to distribute your product through others as well. However, in certain situations it may be appropriate to grant an exclusive license. Because this will deprive you of the right to distribute your product through anyone else, however, you may want to charge a higher license fee and require additional protection. Such protection may include larger royalty payments, specified marketing commitments, guaranteed minimum royalties, and automatic conversion to a nonexclusive license if certain royalty projections are not met.

3. Term of the Agreement

In any distribution agreement, it is wise to specify the length of time for which those rights are granted. The term of the contract is an issue often overlooked, but one that can be of critical importance. In an exclusive distributorship agreement, for example, you may subsequently decide that a different distributor can generate more revenue, or that an alternative marketing scheme would be better. Absent a fixed term or the ability to terminate the contract, your flexibility is severely limited.

4. Fees, Payments, and Bookkeeping

The payment terms, whatever they are, must be spelled out clearly and completely so that there are no disputes or disagreements between the parties. Three questions should be considered: what type of fee structure will be used; when is payment due, and, in cases where you authorize the distributor to duplicate your multimedia product, what provisions are to be made for verifying the number of copies of the multimedia product distributed?

If you deliver prepackaged copies of the multimedia product (such as on CD-ROM) to the distributor, it is common to charge for each copy pursuant to a price list, or discount from a standard list price. On the other hand, if you authorize the distributor to replicate the product, two types of payment structures are generally utilized. The first is an arrangement under which the distributor pays a percentage of the income it receives from the licensing or sale of the multimedia product. Under this arrangement, your income will depend on both the price charged by the distributor to its customers and on its success in the sale or license of the multimedia product. Under the second type of arrangement, the distributor pays a fixed fee for each copy of the multimedia sold or licensed to a customer. In this case, you are assured of receiving a set fee for each copy of the multimedia product that is sold or licensed, regardless of the price charged by the distributor.

The second critical issue is the question of when payment is due. This involves establishing payment terms for copies of products ordered by the distributor, and accounting and reporting provisions with respect to copies of products replicated by the distributor. Where the distributor replicates the multimedia product (such as on a CD-ROM), you should consider what conduct will trigger the obligation to make a payment. For example, are fees due when the copies are replicated, when the copies are shipped, or on some other basis?

Finally, for distributors who are granted the right to replicate the product, you should require them to keep complete records of all of their replication and distribution activities, and to make those records available for audit upon request to verify royalty reports submitted.

5. Multimedia Product Warranties

An issue that typically arises in a distribution relationship is that of warranties. Specifically, the distributor will want to know what warranties you are willing to make regarding issues such as your ownership or right to distribute your multimedia product, and the performance of the product itself. Generally the distributor will be interested in both the warranty that you make to the distributor and the warranty, if any, that the distributor is authorized to pass along to the retail and/or end-user customer on your behalf.

Warranty law is primarily governed by Article 2 of the Uniform Commercial Code. This is a state law that has been enacted in forty-nine of the fifty states and is designed primarily to govern the sale of goods. It is not entirely clear that this statute will govern the sale or license of multimedia products. However, as virtually all courts addressing the issue have concluded that Article 2 of the UCC governs licenses of computer software,[5] it is likely that courts will also conclude that it covers multimedia product transactions, be they licenses or sales.

A warranty can be created by any statement that a certain fact with respect to your multimedia product is true, or will be true at the appropriate time. For example, a statement by you that your multimedia product will run on any MPC-compliant computer is a warranty, as is a statement that your product is free from defects in material and workmanship. Whenever your multimedia product fails to perform as warranted, you may be liable for breach of warranty.

There are two types of warranties: express warranties and warranties implied by law. Express warranties do not come into existence unless you make a statement or representation of fact. Implied warranties, on the other hand, come into existence automatically and can become part of your contract with the distributor unless they are expressly disclaimed.

5.1. Express Warranties

An *express warranty* can be created by any explicit statement or affirmative action on your part. Words such as "warranty" or "guarantee" are not necessary in order to create an express warranty.[6] In fact, you do not even need to have an intention to make a warranty, since any statement of fact relating to your multimedia product, as opposed to a statement of opinion, may be considered a warranty. An express warranty can be created in one of three ways.

The first way to create an express warranty is by an "affirmation of fact or promise" that relates to your multimedia product and becomes part of the basis of the transaction.[7] Warranties arising in this manner can result from representations made orally by sales personnel, written representations in letters and other documents sent to the distributor, by claims made in advertisements, in sales literature, on packaging, and in instruction manuals, or in virtually any other form to which the distributor or user is exposed prior to entering into the contract, and which actually induces them to enter into the contract.[8]

The second method by which an express warranty can arise is through your description of your multimedia product,[9] such as through technical specifications, tables, and users' manuals.

The third type of express warranty can result from your demonstration of the product.[10] Under the law, you are deemed to warrant that the products you sell will perform as well as the product you demonstrate.

In short, any representation made by word or deed better be true, because it is likely to constitute a warranty. There is, however, no legal requirement that you make any express warranties at all.

5.2. Implied Warranties

Implied warranties are warranties that become part of the transaction even though they are not expressly included in the written contract, and even though they were never discussed by the parties. They are warranties implied by the law and automatically become part of the contract unless they are specifically excluded.[11]

There are two basic warranties that can be implied by law. They are the warranty of merchantability and the warranty of *fitness for a particular purpose.*

• **Implied Warranty of Merchantability.** This is a warranty that what is being offered for sale is fit for the ordinary purpose for which it is used, and of a quality that is commercially acceptable for products of that type.[12] It is not entirely clear how such a warranty would apply to a multimedia product. However, it is possible, for example, that if your product is distributed on CD-ROM in a manner that implies it will operate on a PC, there may be an implied warranty that it will operate on an average PC (assuming such a thing exists) in the absence of any notice indicating any special memory, hardware, or software requirements.

  • **Implied Warranty of Fitness for a Particular Purpose.** This is a warranty that a product will fulfill the specific needs of the purchaser.[13] Thus, even though your multimedia product runs properly for most users, if it proves inadequate to meet the needs of a given customer, that customer may have a claim for breach of the implied warranty of fitness for a particular purpose. The circumstances that will give rise to this particular warranty are as follows:

1. you must have had reason to know of the particular purpose for which the multimedia product was being acquired;

2. you must also have had reason to know that the user was relying on your skill or judgment to select or furnish a suitable product; and

3. the user must actually have relied on your judgment in selecting your multimedia product to meet its special needs.[14]

When these three requirements are fulfilled, the warranty of fitness for a particular purpose will be implied in the contract.

5.3. Consumer Product Warranties

The concept of express and implied warranties applies to all multimedia product transactions. Additional rules apply to both of these types of warranties, however, when your multimedia product is considered a "consumer product" and sold as part of a "consumer transaction." The federal government and a number of the states have enacted consumer warranty statutes designed to expand the scope of warranty protection provided to consumers.[15] Generally, what these statutes do is regulate the content of express warranties and limit or prohibit any disclaimer of the implied warranties. The following discussion will focus on the most important of these statutes, the Magnuson-Moss Warranty Act.

The Magnuson-Moss Warranty Act is a federal statute that prescribes comprehensive standards for warranties on consumer products. The requirements of the act are rather strict, and the penalties for failure to comply could result in serious consequences. Accordingly, compliance with its requirements is advised in any transaction that could conceivably fall within its terms.

The Act only applies to written warranties given to an end-user consumer in connection with the "sale" of "consumer products." It does not apply to license transactions or distribution agreements. If it applies to your multimedia product at all, it only applies when multimedia product is sold, and only in situations where the multimedia product is a "consumer product."

The Act defines "consumer product" as "any tangible personal property that is distributed in commerce and that is normally used for personal, family, or household purposes."[16] Although it is clear that a multimedia product will not be covered unless it is of a type used for personal, family, or household purposes, it need not be used exclusively for these purposes in order to qualify. As long as it is "not uncommon" for a particular multimedia product to be used for personal, family, or household purposes, it may be deemed a "consumer product" under the act.[17] For example, products such as automobiles and typewriters that are used for both personal and commercial purposes come within the definition of "consumer product." Moreover, where it is unclear whether a particular product falls within the definition of consumer product, any ambiguity will be resolved in favor of coverage.[18] Consequently, it is reasonable to assume that a multimedia product purchased for home computer use would be covered by the Act.

If it is determined that a multimedia product qualifies as a consumer product, then the act will govern certain written warranties made in connection with its sale to a consumer. The act does not cover oral warranties, nor does the act require that you make any warranties at all. It merely governs the terms of written warranties in the event they are made.

Three general types of written warranties are covered by the act. These are warranties that the product is free of defects, warranties that it will meet a specified level of performance over a specified period of time, and warranties undertaking to refund, repair, replace, or to take other remedial action in the event that the product fails to meet the specifications set forth in the undertaking.[19]

If a multimedia product warranty is covered by the Act, it must comply with the warranty disclosure rules contained in the regulations issued by the Federal Trade Commission.[20] Those rules are detailed and require that any written warranty for a consumer product must fully and conspicuously disclose a specified number of items in simple and readily understood language. In addition, the written warranty must also be clearly and conspicuously designated as either "full (statement of duration) warranty" or "limited warranty," as those terms are defined in the statute.[21]

The Act also prohibits you from disclaiming or modifying any implied warranties arising under state law,[22] and any attempt to disclaim or modify implied warranties in a written warranty will be deemed ineffective.[23]

In the event that you fail to comply with the terms of the Magnuson-Moss Warranty Act, you will be liable to the user for all damages suffered, including costs and attorneys' fees. Thus, if you are contemplating the marketing of a multimedia product that could be considered a consumer product you would be well-advised to consult legal counsel before making any of the warranties covered by the act.

6. Limiting Liability for Breach of Warranty

Notwithstanding your best efforts, your multimedia product may contain defects that will, at some time, cause problems. While most of these problems are relatively minor and will cause nothing more than inconvenience, some can have extremely serious consequences. If, as a result of an error in your multimedia encyclopedia, a high school student makes a mistake in a homework assignment, the damages are probably rather trivial. On the other hand, if your multimedia flight simulation training program contains an error that causes an airline pilot to improperly respond in a real-life situation, the consequences can be disastrous.

The risk of such significant liabilities arising from the failure of a product to perform as warranted has led virtually all vendors to draft their contracts so as to limit their exposure to the extent possible. There are several contractual provisions that can be used to limit your liability. Each, if properly drafted, is usually enforceable, although there are always exceptions, particularly in cases involving personal injuries.

6.1 Limiting the Number and Types of Warranties Made

As discussed in section 5.1, virtually any statement or representation you make can be construed as an express warranty that will become part of the contract. Moreover, the law often adds a number of implied warranties to the contract. The more warranties that become part of the deal, the greater the obligations you undertake, and the greater your potential liability.

The first step in limiting that liability is to restrict your warranties to those that you specifically agree to undertake. To do this, the written agreement between you and your distributor and/or end-user should specifically set forth all express warranties (if any), to which you have expressly agreed to be bound, followed by a provision excluding from the agreement all other statements and representations that could be construed as express warranties. In other words, you want to exclude any other express warranty that may have arisen as a result of your advertising, representations, or other conduct prior to entering into the transaction.

In addition, you should normally consider disclaiming all implied warranties. Although implied warranties arise automatically, you have the right to disclaim them[24] unless the multimedia product is sold as part of a consumer transaction governed by the Magnuson-Moss Act,[25] or by the law of one of the few states that limit the right of a vendor to disclaim implied warranties in consumer transactions. Included in this group are the states of Alabama, California, Kansas, Maine, Maryland, Massachusetts, Minnesota, Mississippi, Vermont, Washington, and West Virginia.

Any disclaimer of express or implied warranties must also be "conspicuous."[26] That is, it must be so obvious that the user is likely to read it before entering into the transaction. To meet this requirement, disclaimers are typically printed in all capital letters and boldfaced type, often in type larger than the type used for the rest of the agreement, and captioned with a heading such as "DISCLAIMER OF WARRANTIES," which is designed to attract the customer's attention.

In addition, certain "magic words" are required to disclaim the implied warranty of merchantability. To be effective, the contractual language must specifically mention the word "merchantability."[27] No similar requirement exists when disclaiming the implied warranty of fitness for a particular purpose, but to be safe it should be specifically mentioned as well. An example of language that will disclaim both the implied warranty of merchantability and the implied warranty of fitness for a particular purpose, as well as all express warranties not included in the contract, is the following:

> **VENDOR MAKES NO WARRANTIES EXCEPT FOR THE WARRANTIES SPECIFIED IN THIS CONTRACT. VENDOR DISCLAIMS ALL OTHER EXPRESS WARRANTIES AND ALL IMPLIED WARRANTIES, INCLUDING, BUT NOT LIMITED TO, THE IMPLIED WARRANTIES OF MERCHANTABILITY AND FITNESS FOR A PARTICULAR PURPOSE.**

Note that this language (1) is conspicuous by its capital letters and boldfaced type, and (2) specifically mentions both implied warranties to be excluded.

In addition to the foregoing, there are other ways to disclaim express and implied warranties. If, for example, the contract contains language such as "AS IS," or "WITH ALL FAULTS," or other similar language that calls the user's attention to the fact that no warranties are being made, then the implied warranties will be disclaimed.[28] Whether this approach is practical from a marketing standpoint depends upon the circumstances of the transaction involved, but if a customer is willing to accept a multimedia product with no warranties whatsoever, a "no-warranty" contract can certainly be enforceable. To ensure that it is enforceable, however, it should contain an appropriate disclaimer such as:

> **THIS MULTIMEDIA PRODUCT IS LICENSED "AS IS".
> VENDOR MAKES NO WARRANTIES WHATSOEVER,
> EITHER EXPRESS OR IMPLIED.**

It should also be noted that if a user has had an opportunity to examine the multimedia product in detail prior to its sale or license, no implied warranty will exist as to any defects that would have been discovered pursuant to such an inspection.

To be effective, however, a disclaimer of any implied warranty must be part of a contract between the parties entered into prior to delivery of the multimedia product. A disclaimer will have no effect if made after the contract is signed and the multimedia product delivered, such as by inserting it in the documentation. This can be a practical problem in the event that you seek to disclaim express and implied warranties through the use of a shrinkwrap license or bootscreen contract. Because these contracts are frequently not seen by the customer until after the transaction has been completed, two courts have held that warranty disclaimers in such contracts are not effective.[29]

6.2 Limiting the Scope of Warranties

Once you have reduced your warranty obligations to a specified set of written warranties, you can further limit your potential liability by imposing reasonable limitations on their scope.

The most frequently used warranty limitation is a limitation on the time period during which the warranty will be effective. This can range anywhere from a few days to several years, but the important point is to set an end to the warranty obligation.

6.3 Exclusive Remedy in Case of Breach

Notwithstanding your efforts to limit the number and scope of your warranties, it is still possible that your multimedia product will not live up to the warranties actually made. Because such an occurrence is possible, at least with a newly released multimedia product, you should consider how you can limit your potential liability for any losses the user may suffer.

One commonly used method of dealing with this problem is to limit the types of remedies available to the user in case of breach. To avoid the prospect of having to pay damages or to refund the license fees, while at the same time insuring that the user gets what it paid for, the parties can agree to a "limited remedy."[30] The "limited remedy" that is usually used is the promise to repair or replace the product in the event that it fails to perform as warranted. However, this approach will operate as a limitation on the remedies available to the user only if it specifies that it will be deemed to be the user's "sole and exclusive remedy." Otherwise, it will be considered only an optional remedy for the user, who will be free to pursue any other remedies he or she may have under the law, including an action for damages or, in the proper situation, an action to rescind the contract.[31]

The primary purpose of such a limited remedy is to give you an opportunity to make your multimedia product conform to its warranties, while limiting your exposure to the risk of paying any damages that might otherwise be due. The user may also benefit from your incentive to provide a multimedia product that conforms to the contract within a reasonable time.

A problem can arise with the "repair only" limitation when you are unable or unwilling to correct the problem, or unreasonably delay in doing so. In that case, the exclusive remedy is said to "fail of its essential purpose," and will become null and void.[32] Otherwise, the user would be left with no remedy whatsoever.

When an exclusive remedy fails of its essential purpose the user is allowed to pursue all of the remedies it would have otherwise had under the contract.

6.4 Maximum Dollar Limitation on Damages

If the contract does not provide for an exclusive remedy, or if the exclusive remedy fails of its essential purpose, you will be liable for damages suffered by the user. But except in the case of personal injury, the amount of your liability for those damages may be limited to a dollar amount specified in the contract,[33] provided that the dollar limitation is not so low that the user is left without a realistic remedy in the event you breach the contract.[34]

Damage limitations are frequently tied to the license fee paid for the multimedia product. If the amount chosen is reasonable, the worst that can happen is that you will have to refund the user's money. A typical limitation of liability provision of this type is written as follows:

> Vendor's liability, if any, for loss or damages relating to or arising out of the license of the multimedia product shall not exceed the charges paid by customer for such products

6.5 Exclusion of Consequential Damages

In addition to limiting the dollar *amount* of your potential liability, you may also limit the *type* of damages for which you can be held liable. Specifically, it is usually advisable to disclaim so-called consequential damages, such as lost profits.

So-called *consequential damages* generally refer to losses that are not directly caused by the failure of a product to perform as warranted, but rather as a consequence thereof. For example, if a multimedia product fails to perform properly, a user's direct damages might be the cost of obtaining an alternate product. But if, as a consequence of the failure, distributor's business is damaged, and it suffers significant lost profits, those lost profits are considered as consequential damages. This typically represents your largest potential exposure.

Under the law you are not liable for consequential damages unless you had reason to know of their potential at the time you entered into the contract,[35] but this protection is often more theoretical than real. Given the fact that many distributors and users rely on your expertise in selecting your multimedia product, exposure to such damages is often part of such transactions. Thus it is prudent to include a conspicuous clause in your contract that excludes liability for all consequential damages.[36] A clause excluding such liability can be phrased as follows:

> IN NO EVENT WILL VENDOR BE LIABLE FOR CONSEQUEN-
> TIAL DAMAGES EVEN IF VENDOR HAS BEEN ADVISED OF
> THE POSSIBILITY OF SUCH DAMAGES.

It should be noted, however, that this exclusion of consequential damages will only apply to economic losses, not to personal injuries.[37]

6.6 "No Liability" Clauses

If you can reduce your liability through the use of appropriate contract language, why not contractually eliminate all of your liability by the inclusion of a clause that completely excludes all liability for any cause whatsoever?

Normally, the law says that each party must be left with some remedy in the event of a breach by the other. When two parties enter into a contract, they must accept the fact that there be at least a fair quantum of remedy for breach of the obligations or duties set forth in the contract. Consequently, any clause purporting to eliminate all liability runs the risk of being unenforceable on the ground of unconscionability.[38]

As a general proposition, you cannot represent that your product will do certain things and at the same time immunize itself from all liability if it does not. However, in those situations where a multimedia product has been sold or licensed "as is," "with all faults," or otherwise with no promise that it will perform for the buyer, a court will probably enforce a clause eliminating all of your liability for product defects and malfunctions. As long as it is clear to the user that you are making no representations whatsoever about the product, and providing there is no great disparity in bargaining power between the parties, it is proper for you to exclude all of your liability.

Where a transaction is between two businesspeople dealing at arms' length, such total exclusions of liability have been upheld in certain cases.[39] But since this type of a clause may be held to be unenforceable in many situations, it should be very sparingly used.

How do you limit your liability for defects in your multimedia product? A well-drafted license agreement has always been considered an effective first line of defense. And there is no doubt that putting the right words in a contract is important. But you can never be sure they will be enforceable in all situations. In the final analysis, there is no substitute for a quality product honestly and accurately represented.

7. Termination

When two parties enter into a distribution relationship, they both usually look forward to a mutually profitable and beneficial relationship, and thus focus their contract efforts on issues relating to product, price, performance, and the like. The question of when either party may terminate the relationship is often never discussed. It is, however, one of the most important issues to be addressed.

Termination rights are a two-edged sword. Each party to the contract must ensure that it has sufficient flexibility to terminate the relationship in the event that it is no longer profitable or desirable to continue the relationship. On the other hand, each party must also be concerned about termination by the other party in situations where it would view such termination as undesirable.

Some simple examples will put the issue in proper perspective. If you enter into an exclusive distribution agreement with a distributor, you need to ensure that you can terminate the relationship (in order to find an alternative distributor) in the event that the original exclusive distributor is not exerting sufficient efforts to market the product. The distributor, on the other hand, wants protection from termination. Especially in situations where the distributor may be required to invest significant time and resources in developing a market for the product, it must ensure that the contract will remain in force for a period long enough to enjoy the fruits of that labor.

In analyzing the termination issue, two basic questions are presented: when can either party terminate? and, what happens upon such termination? Both issues should be carefully thought through in order to ensure that maximum protection is obtained in the event that the agreement becomes undesirable for any reason.

Thus, a termination clause should normally be included in all distribution agreements to describe the manner in which the contract may be ended by either party and to specify the consequences of termination.

If the contract is for a specified term (such as one year, five years, and so forth), termination will automatically occur at the end of that term. However, the parties may wish to provide for the right to terminate the contract earlier. Similarly, if the contract has no specified ending date, the parties should decide when and under what circumstances it may be brought to a close.

After defining the circumstances under which the agreement may be terminated, it is also necessary to specify what will happen upon termination. In distribution agreements, there are two major considerations: (1) what happens to the materials supplied to the distributor, such as golden master discs, other product materials, and the like; and (2) what obligations imposed on the parties by the contract will survive its termination.

For your protection, the termination clause should provide that the distributor will stop replicating your multimedia product upon termination and will either destroy all copies of the multimedia product in its possession or return them to the vendor. In such a case, using or marketing the multimedia product after termination will constitute an independent breach of the agreement.[40]

The termination clause should also specify which obligations imposed on the parties will survive termination. If there are any license fees, royalties, unpaid taxes, or other similar amounts due and owing from the distributor, the termination of the agreement should not relieve the distributor of its obligation to pay what it owes. Also, where the distributor has granted sublicenses to its customers, termination of the distribution agreement should not affect the validity of the sublicenses between the distributor and its customers.

Endnotes

1   See, e.g., *Gilliam v. American Broadcasting Cos.*, 538 F.2d 14 (2d Cir. 1976).

2   17 U.S.C. § 109(b).

3   "One who obtains permission to use a copyrighted script in the production of a derivative work, however, may not exceed the specific purpose for which permission was granted." *Gilliam v. American Broadcasting Cos.*, 538 F.2d 14, 20 (2d Cir. 1976).

4   *United Artists Tele., Inc. v. Fortnightly Corp.*, 377 F.2d 872, 882 (2d Cir. 1967), *rev'd on other grounds*, 392 U.S. 390 (1968).

5   Prepackaged software licensed separately is generally considered a "good" and subject to Article 2 of the Uniform Commercial Code. Cases addressing software-only transactions include *Colonial Life Ins. Co. v. Electronic Data Sys. Corp.*, 817 F. Supp. 235, 238-39 (D.N.H. 1993) (contract for license to use software is predominately a contract for the sale of goods despite servicing aspect of agreement because thrust of services was to support the software product); *Systems Design & Management Info., Inc. v. Kansas City Post Office Employees Credit Union*, 14 Kan. App. 2d 266, 788 P.2d 878 (1990) (court held that software was goods under the UCC and concluded that the transaction was subject to the UCC); *Communications Groups, Inc. v. Warner Communications, Inc.*, 138 Misc. 2d 80, 527 N.Y.S.2d 341, 344 (N.Y. Civ. Ct. 1988) (courts generally consider software to be a tangible, movable item and therefore a "good" within the scope of Article 2. Software is not solely intangible ideas and services. Article 2 applies to lease of software even if lessor retains title to the goods because the transaction is analogous to a sale and therefore within the scope of Article 2); *Schroders, Inc. v. Hogan Sys., Inc.*, 137 Misc. 2d 738, 522 N.Y.S. 2d 404, 406 (N.Y. Sup. Ct. 1987) (although

the parties' agreement did not involve sale of computer hardware, but simply a license of software, the arrangement should nevertheless be construed to fall within the provisions of UCC Article 2); *RRX Indus., Inc. v. Lab-Con, Inc.,* 772 F.2d 543, 546 (9th Cir. 1985) (Article 2 applies to software agreement because sales aspect of the transaction predominates. Employee training, repair services, and system upgrading were incidental to sale of the software package and did not defeat characterization of the system as a good).

6   U.C.C. § 2-313(2).

7   U.C.C. § 2-313(1)(a).

8   See, e.g., *Chatlos Sys., Inc. v. National Cash Register Corp.,* 479 F. Supp 738, 743 (D.N.J. 1979) (applying New Jersey law), *aff'd,* 635 F.2d 1081 (3d Cir. 1980).

9   U.C.C. § 2-313(1)(b).

10   U.C.C. § 2-313(1)(c).

11   See, e.g., *Office Supply Co. v. Basic/Four Corp.,* 538 F. Supp. 776, 782 (E.D. Wis. 1982) (applying California law).

12   U.C.C. § 2-314.

13   U.C.C. § 2-315.

14   See U.C.C. § 2-315.

15   See, e.g., *15 U.S.C. § 2301; Cal. Civ. Code §§ 1790-1794.2; Kan. Stat. Ann. §§ 50-623 to -644; Minn. Stat. Ann. §§ 3256.17-.20; W. Va. Code §§ 46A-6-101 to -108.*

16   15 U.S.C. § 2301(1).

17   16 C.F.R. § 700.1(a).

18   16 C.F.R. § 700.1(a).

19   15 U.S.C. § 2301(6).

20   16 C.F.R. § 701.3(a).

21   15 U.S.C. §§ 2303, 2304, 2308.

22   15 U.S.C. § 2308(a).

23   15 U.S.C. § 2308(c); *Federal Trade Comm'n v. Virginia Homes Mfg. Corp.* 509 F. Supp. 51, 57 (D. Md. 1981).

24   U.C.C. § 2-316; *Office Supply Co. v. Basic/Four Corp.,* 538 F. Supp. 776, 783 (E.D. Wis. 1982) (applying California law); *Aplications, Inc. v. Hewlett-Packard Co.,* 501 F. Supp. 129, 133 (S.D.N.Y. 1980) (applying California law); *Badger Bearing Co. v. Burroughs Corp.,* 444 F. Supp. 919, 922-23 (E.D. Wis. 1977) (applying Wisconsin law).

25   15 U.S.C. § 2301(7).

26   U.C.C. § 2-316(2).

27   U.C.C. § 2-316(2).

28   U.C.C. § 2-316(3).

29   See *Arizona Retail Sys. Inc. v. Software-Link, Inc.,* 831 F. Supp. 759 (D. Ariz. 1993); *Step-Saver Data Sys., Inc. v. Wyse Technology,* 939 F.2d 91 (3d Cir. 1991).

30   U.C.C. § 2-719(1)(a).

31   U.C.C. § 2-719(1)(b).

32   U.C.C. § 2-719(2); *Office Supply Co. v. Basic/Four Corp.*, 538 F. Supp. 776, 787, 789-91 (E.D. Wis. 1982) (applying California law); *Chatlos Sys., Inc. v. National Cash Register Corp.*, 635 F.2d 1081, 1085 (3d Cir. 1980) (applying New Jersey law).

33   See U.C.C. § 2-719(1)(a); *Farris Eng'g. Corp. v. Service Bureau Corp.*, 276 F.Supp. 643, 645 (D.N.J. 1967), *aff'd,*406 F.2d 519 (3d Cir. 1969).

34   See U.C.C. § 2-719 comment 1.

35   U.C.C. § 2-715(2).

36   U.C.C. § 2-719.

37   U.C.C. § 2-719(3).

38   U.C.C. § 2-719 comment 1. See, e.g., *Chesapeake Petroleum & Supply Co. v. Burroughs Corp.*, 6 Computer L. Serv. Rep. 768, 769 (Md. Cir. Ct. 1977), *aff'd,* 6 Computer L. Serv. Rep. 782 (Md. 1978).

39   See *R. N. Weaver Co. v. Burroughs Corp.*, 580 S.W.2d 76 (Tex. Civ. App. 1979).

40   *S & H Computer Sys., Inc. v. SAS Inst., Inc.*, 568 F. Supp. 416, 421 (M.D. Tenn. 1983).

PART 5

Checklists and
Sample Agreements

Assignments of Rights

1. Checklist of Issues
2. Sample Assignment

Assignments of Rights

CHECKLIST OF ISSUES

1. **What is the Subject Matter of the Assignment?**
    a. Identify the content to be assigned to you
2. **Scope of Rights Assigned**
    a. What rights are assigned to you?
        (1) All of the copyright rights?
        (2) Reproduction right—that is, the right to copy the content?
        (3) Adaptation right—that is, the right to adapt, modify, or enhance the content, incorporate the content into another work, translate the content into a foreign language, and so forth?
        (4) Distribution right—that is, the right to distribute copies of the content?
        (5) Public performance right—that is, the right to publicly perform the content?
        (6) Public display right—that is, the right to display the content publicly?
    b. Are any limits imposed on your exercise of the rights assigned to you? For example, are your rights limited to a specific:
        (1) Media?
        (2) Distribution channel?
        (3) Territory?
        (4) Hardware platform?
        (5) Software (operating system) platform?
        (6) Language?
        (7) Market?

3. **Delivery**
   a. What deliverables has the seller agreed to provide?—for example, master copy of content in a specified form or media?
   b. When will the content be delivered?
4. **Purchase Price**
   a. What type of payment will be required?
      (1) Lump sum?
      (2) Royalty?
      (3) Other?
   b. What is the amount of the payment?
   c. If payment is in the form of royalties, what is the basis of the payment calculations?
      (1) Per title in which the content is used?
      (2) Per copy sold?
      (3) Gross income generated?
      (4) Other?
   d. If payment is in the form of royalties:
      (1) Does the seller get an advance payment? If so, is the advance credited against future royalties due?
      (2) Are there any guaranteed or minimum payment amounts?
      (3) When is each payment due?
5. **Bookkeeping Requirements and Audit Rights (For Royalty Payments)**
   a. What record-keeping requirements are imposed on you in order to keep track of all sales or licenses of the content, to ensure that the seller is paid all sums owed?
   b. How often must you send reports to the seller, and what information must be contained in each report?
   c. What rights does the seller have to audit your books?
6. **Warranties**
   a. Is the content assigned "AS IS" or does the seller make any warranties?
   b. What warranties (if any) are included?
      (1) Does the seller warrant that it owns all rights to the content and that it has power and authority to assign all of those rights to you free and clear of all liens, encumbrances, and other claims by third parties?

      (2)   Does the seller warrant that the content does not infringe the copyrights, trademarks, publicity rights, and privacy rights of any third party?

      (3)   Does the seller warrant that it has obtained consents from all relevant third parties, such as unions, actors, recording artists, musicians, persons appearing in the work, and so forth?

7. **Indemnification**
   a. Will the seller agree to defend you and to pay any damages or expenses you incur in the event you are sued by someone challenging the seller's rights to the content or right to assign those rights to you?
   b. If so, what are the terms and conditions for indemnification?
      (1) Timely notice of claims?
      (2) Cooperation in defense?
   c. Are there any limits on the seller's indemnification liability?

SAMPLE
ASSIGNMENT[1]

THIS ASSIGNMENT is made and delivered by _____ ,
[a _____ corporation/an   individual]
located at _____ (the "Seller").

For good and valuable consideration, the receipt of which is hereby acknowledged, Seller does hereby grant, sell, transfer, assign, and deliver to_____
_____ , a _____ corporation, its successors and assigns,
(the "Buyer"), all right, title, and interest of every kind and character throughout the
world (including but not limited to all copyrights, moral rights, trade secret rights,
patent rights, and other proprietary rights) in the following work
(the "Work").

Seller represents and warrants to Buyer that Seller has full right, power and
authority to make this Assignment of the Work to Buyer in the manner set forth
above, and that Seller is transferring to Buyer good and marketable title to the Work,
free and clear of all liens, security interests, claims, interests, options, encumbrances,
or indebtedness of any kind.

Seller agrees to indemnify, defend and hold Buyer harmless against any and all
actions, suits, losses, liabilities, damages, deficiencies, claims, demands, costs and
expenses (including attorney's fees and costs of investigation) that may arise out of
any breach of the foregoing warranty or any or nonfulfillment of this Assignment by
Seller.

IN WITNESS WHEREOF, Seller has executed this Assignment as of the day of
_____ , 19___ .

[NAME OF SELLER] _____

By:_____
Its:_____

Endnote

1   See also the assignment sections contained in the employee and work-for-hire contracts in
chapter 33.

CHAPTER 30

Licenses to Use Content

Licenses to Use Content

CHECKLIST OF ISSUES

1. **What is the Subject Matter of the License?**
   a. Identify the content that you are licensing
2. **Scope of Rights Granted**
   a. What rights to use the content are granted to you?
      (1) Reproduction right—that is, the right to copy the content?
      (2) Adaptation right—that is, the right to adapt, modify, or enhance the content, incorporate the content into another work, translate the content into a foreign language, and so forth?
      (3) Distribution right—that is, the right to distribute copies of the content?
      (4) Public performance right—that is, the right to publicly perform the content?
      (5) Public display right—that is, the right to publicly display the content?
   b. Are any limits imposed on your exercise of the rights granted? For example, is your use of the content limited to a specific:
      (1) Multimedia product?
      (2) Media?
      (3) Hardware platform?
      (4) Software (operating system) platform?
      (5) Language?
      (6) Distribution channel?
      (7) Territory?
      (8) Market?

    c.   Does the license obligate you to use the content?

    d.   Is the license exclusive or non-exclusive?

3. Term

    a.   What is the term of the license? When does your right to use the content end?

    b.   Do you have the right to renew the license when it expires?

    c.   Does the copyright owner have the right to terminate the license before it would otherwise end? If so, under what circumstances?

4. Credits

    a.   Do you have an obligation to include the copyright owner's copyright notice, or otherwise give credit to the owner or artist?

5. Ownership of Content

    a.   Does the copyright owner represent that it owns the content or that it has the right to license it?

6. Third Party Consents

    a.   In addition to getting permission from the copyright owner, what other persons must consent to your use of the content?

        (1)   Original author/artist?

        (2)   Unions?

        (3)   Performers?

        (4)   Persons depicted in the content?

        (5)   Owners of other copyrighted works included in the content?

        (6)   Others?

    b.   Who will secure the required third-party consents?

        (1)   You?

        (2)   Copyright owner?

    c.   Who will pay any applicable fees to such third parties?

        (1)   You?

        (2)   Copyright owner?

7. Delivery

    a.   What deliverables has the copyright owner agreed to provide to you?—for example, master copy of content in a specified form or media?

    b.   In what format will the content be delivered—for example, camera ready, gold master disk, CD-write once (CD-WO) disc, and so forth?

    c.   When will the content be delivered?

8. **License Fees and Royalties**
    a. What type of payment will be required?
        (1) Lump sum (paid-up license)?
        (2) Percentage royalty?
        (3) Fixed fee royalty?
        (4) Other (for example, yearly fee plus per-copy fee)?
    b. What is the basis of payment calculations?
        (1) Per copy of the multimedia work incorporating the content that is purchased, sold, or licensed?
        (2) Percentage of the income you receive?
        (3) Other?
    c. What is the amount of the payment?
    d. If payments will be made in the form of royalties:
        (1) Does the copyright owner get an advance payment? If so, is the advance credited against future royalties due?
        (2) Are there any guaranteed or minimum payment amounts?
        (3) When is each payment due?
9. **Bookkeeping Requirements and Audit Rights (For Royalty Payments)**
    a. What record-keeping requirements are imposed on you in order to keep track of all sales or licenses of the content, to ensure that the content owner is paid all sums owed?
    b. What information must you record with respect to each sale or license?
    c. How often must you send reports to the content owner, and what information must be contained in each report?
    d. What rights does the content owner have to audit your books?
10. **Warranties**
    a. Is the content licensed "AS IS" or does the copyright owner make any warranties?
    b. What warranties (if any) are included?
        (1) Does the copyright owner warrant that it owns the rights in the content that are being licensed to you, or that it has power and authority to grant the license (if the owner does not own the right to the content it is licensing to you)?
        (2) Does the copyright owner warrant that the content does not infringe any copyrights or other rights of third parties?

(3)   Does the copyright owner warrant that the content is not defamatory and that it does not infringe anyone's rights of privacy or publicity?

(4)   Does the copyright owner warrant that the copyright owner has obtained consents from all relevant third parties, such as actors, other recording artists, musicians, persons performing or appearing in the work, and so forth?

11.   **Limitations of Liability**

a.   Is there a limit on the dollar amount of damages either party can recover from the other in the event of any breach of the agreement?

b.   Is there a limit on the type of damages either party can recover from the other in the event of any breach of the agreement? (e.g., has either party excluded liability for consequential damages, such as lost profits, or claims by customers and other third parties?)

12.   **Indemnification**

a.   Will the copyright owner agree to defend you and to pay any damages or expenses you incur in the event you are sued by someone challenging your right to use the content or alleging that it is defamatory, and so forth?

b.   If so, what are the terms and conditions for such indemnification?

(1)   Timely notice of claims?

(2)   Cooperation in defense?

c.   Are there any limits on the copyright owner's indemnification liability?

13.   **Default**

a.   What are each party's rights in the event of a breach of the agreement by the other party?

(1)   Terminate contract?

(2)   Liquidated damages?

(3)   Injunction?

(4)   Other?

b.   Does the breaching party have a right to receive notice and an opportunity to cure its breach before the other party can terminate the agreement?

14.   **Assignment Rights**

a.   Does the copyright owner have the right to assign the license agreement?

b.   Do you have the right to assign the license agreement?

SAMPLE

TEXT LICENSE[1]

This Agreement is made and entered into on _____ , 199__ , by and between _____ a _____ corporation located at _____ , ("Multimedia Developer") and _____ , a _____corporation located at _____ ("Book Publisher").

BACKGROUND

A. Book Publisher is the owner of the copyright to the excerpt from the book identified on Exhibit A of this Agreement ("Text").

B. Multimedia Developer is developing a digital, machine-readable, interactive, multimedia work tentatively titled "_____" (the "Multimedia Product").

C. Multimedia Developer desires to incorporate the Text as part of the Multimedia Product, and to reproduce and distribute the Text as so incorporated, on a worldwide basis.

D. Book Publisher is willing to grant such rights to Multimedia Developer, subject to the terms and conditions of this Agreement.

NOW THEREFORE, the parties hereby agree as follows:

1. GRANT OF LICENSE

(a) Rights Granted to Multimedia Developer. Book Publisher grants Multimedia Developer a nonexclusive license and right to (1) convert the Text into digital machine-readable form and incorporate all or any part of the Text within the Multimedia Product; (2) reproduce the Text, as incorporated in the Multimedia Product, in the Media described in Exhibit A; and (3) manufacture, package, market, promote, sell, license and otherwise distribute copies of all or any part of the Text, as incorporated in the Multimedia Product, both directly to end users and indirectly through distributors, dealers, resellers, agents, and other third parties within the Territory specified in Exhibit A.

(b) Restricted Use. Use of the Text is restricted to the uses described in paragraph (a) above. Multimedia Developer shall have no right to alter, modify, or distort the Text, nor to create derivative works thereof except to the extent specifically authorized in this Agreement.

(c) Ancillary Uses. Notwithstanding the foregoing, Multimedia Developer may use the Text or any portion thereof in printed materials that accompany the

Multimedia Product for delivery to end users, and in connection with advertising, publicizing, or distributing the Multimedia Product.

(d) **Derogatory Uses.** Multimedia Developer shall not use the Text in any manner or context that will be in any way derogatory to the book from which it came, the author, or any person connected with the creation thereof or depicted therein. Furthermore, the Text will not be used in any way so as to constitute an express or implied endorsement of any product or service by anyone associated with Book Publisher or the author.

(e) **Rights Reserved to Book Publisher.** Multimedia Developer acknowledges that it has no rights to use the Text except those expressly granted by this Agreement. Book publisher retains all rights not expressly granted herein.

(f) **No Obligation to Use Content.** Book Publisher acknowledges that Multimedia Developer is not obligated or required to use or incorporate the Text in the Multimedia Product.

2. **COPYRIGHT NOTICE AND CREDITS**

In every copy of the Multimedia Product that includes the Text, Multimedia Developer agrees to include Book Publisher's copyright notice, and to give credit to Book Publisher and the author of the book, in the form specified on Exhibit A, in the same manner as it accords credit to all other artists and copyright owners whose works are included in the Multimedia Product.

3. **BOOK PUBLISHER'S WARRANTIES**

(a) **Authority**. Book Publisher represents and warrants that it has the right and authority to enter into this Agreement and to grant to Multimedia Developer the rights to the Text that are granted in this Agreement.

(b) **Noninfringement.** Book Publisher warrants to Multimedia Developer that incorporation of the Text in the Multimedia Product, and the reproduction and distribution of the Text as so incorporated, will not infringe upon or misappropriate the proprietary rights of any third party, and in addition, that the Text does not contain any matter that is defamatory or that otherwise violates the privacy rights of any person.

(c) **DISCLAIMER.** THE FOREGOING ARE THE ONLY WARRANTIES MADE BY BOOK PUBLISHER. BOOK PUBLISHER SPECIFICALLY DISCLAIMS ALL OTHER WARRANTIES, EXPRESS OR IMPLIED, INCLUDING, BUT NOT LIMITED TO, THE IMPLIED WARRANTIES OF MERCHANTABILITY AND FITNESS FOR A PARTICULAR PURPOSE.

4. INDEMNIFICATION

Each party will defend, at its expense, any claim, suit or proceeding brought against the other insofar it is based on a claim that arises out of its breach of any warranty, representation, undertaking, or obligation in this agreement, and will pay all damages, costs, and expenses finally awarded against the other party in connection with such claim. To qualify for such defense and payment, the party sued must (1) give the indemnifying party prompt written notice of such claim, and (2) allow the indemnifying party to control the defense and/or settlement of such claim.

5. PAYMENT TO BOOK PUBLISHER

In full and final consideration of the rights granted to Multimedia Developer in this Agreement, Multimedia Developer will pay Book Publisher the License Fee specified in Exhibit A within _____ days of the date of this Agreement.

6. TERMINATION OF LICENSE

(a) Termination. This Agreement may be terminated by written notice if: (1) Multimedia Developer does not publish the Multimedia Product containing the Text within _____ years after the date of this Agreement; (2) the Multimedia Product goes "out of print," in that it is not commercially available for a period of _____ months after its initial publication; or (3) Multimedia Developer commits a material breach of this Agreement and fails to remedy such breach within thirty (30) days of written notice from Book Publisher.

(b) Effect of Termination. Upon termination of this Agreement for any reason, Multimedia Developer will immediately cease duplication of the Text and production of copies of the Multimedia Product containing the Text. However, Multimedia Developer shall have the right to distribute all copies of the Multimedia Product in Multimedia Developer's inventory as of the date of termination.

7. MISCELLANEOUS

(a) Governing Law. This Agreement shall be construed in accordance with the law of the State of _____ .

(b) Entire Agreement. This Agreement constitutes the entire agreement between the parties pertaining to the subject matter contains herein, and supersedes all prior agreements related thereto.

IN WITNESS WHEREOF, the parties have executed this Agreement as of the date set forth above.

[MULTIMEDIA DEVELOPER]   [BOOK PUBLISHER]

By:_____   By:_____
Its:_____   Its:_____

EXHIBIT A

1. **Text**: Pages _____ through _____ of the book titled "_____"
by _____ .
2. **Term**: Perpetuity.
3. **License Fee**: $_____ .
4. **Territory**: Worldwide.
5. **Credit**: "The Text from [*name of book in which Text appeared, and name of author*] made available courtesy of [*Name of Book Publisher*]."
6. **Media**: All electronic or computer readable media now known or hereafter developed, including but not limited to magnetic disk and optical disc (such as CD-ROM and CD-i).

SAMPLE
MUSIC LICENSE[2]

This Agreement is made and entered into on _____ , 199__ , by and between _____ , a _____ corporation located at _____ , ("Multimedia Developer") and _____ , a _____ corporation located at _____ , ("Music Publisher").

BACKGROUND

A. Music Publisher is owner of all rights to the Musical Composition identified on Exhibit A.

B. Multimedia Developer intends to develop, manufacture, and distribute to the general public a digital, machine-readable, interactive multimedia product designed for use in conjunction with computer monitor visual displays tentatively titled "_____" on the subject of "_____" ("Multimedia Product").

C. In connection therewith, Multimedia Developer desires to record a performance of all or a part of the Musical Composition in digital machine-readable form, to incorporate such recorded performance in synchronization with certain visual images or under user control within the Multimedia Product, and to reproduce and distribute such recordings of the Musical Composition, as so incorporated, worldwide.

D. Music Publisher is willing to grant such rights to Multimedia Developer subject to the terms and conditions of this Agreement.

NOW THEREFORE, the parties hereby agree as follows:

1. GRANT OF LICENSE

(a) Rights Granted to Multimedia Developer. Music Publisher grants to Multimedia Developer a nonexclusive, world-wide, paid-up license and right to:

(1) record and rerecord the Musical Composition (including the music and/or lyrics thereof in any arrangement, orchestration or language), in digital machine-readable form;

(2) incorporate all or any portion of such recordings into the Multimedia Product, whether or not in synchronization or timed relation with any visual images;

(3) reproduce any number of copies of the Multimedia Product incorporating these recordings, in any manner, medium, or form, whether now known or hereafter devised; and

(4) market, promote, sell, license, rent, distribute, and subdistribute, copies of the Multimedia Product that include such recordings from and into any country.

(b) **Performance Rights Excluded.** This license does not include a grant of any public performance rights.

(c) **Rights Reserved to Music Publisher.** Multimedia Developer acknowledges that it has no rights in the Musical Corporation except those expressly granted by this Agreement. Nothing herein shall be construed as restricting Music Publisher's right to sell, lease, license, modify, publish, or otherwise distribute the Musical Composition in whole or in part, to any other person.

2.   RESTRICTIONS AND EXCLUSIONS

(a) **Duration.** The recording of the Musical Composition embodied in the Multimedia Product shall not exceed _____ minutes and _____ seconds.

(b) **Exclusions.** This license does not include the rights to: (1) distribute the Musical Composition in any way separate and apart from the Multimedia Product; (2) make any change in the original lyrics or in the fundamental character of the Musical Composition; (3) publicly perform the Musical Composition; (4) use the title of the Musical Composition in the title of the Multimedia Product; or (5) make any other use of the Musical Composition not expressly authorized in this license.

3.   MUSIC PUBLISHER'S WARRANTIES

(a) **Authority**. Music Publisher represents and warrants that it has the right and authority to enter into this Agreement and to grant to Multimedia Developer the rights to the Musical Composition that are granted in this Agreement.

(b) **Noninfringement.** Music Publisher represents and warrants to Multimedia Developer that recording the Musical Corporation, incorporating the Musical Composition in the Multimedia Product, and reproducing and distributing the Musical Composition as so incorporated, will not infringe upon or misappropriate the proprietary rights of any third party, or otherwise violate any rights of any kind or nature whatsoever of any person, firm, corporation, association or society.

(c) **DISCLAIMER. THE FOREGOING ARE THE ONLY WARRANTIES MADE BY MUSIC PUBLISHER. MUSIC PUBLISHER SPECIFICALLY DISCLAIMS ALL OTHER WARRANTIES, EXPRESS OR IMPLIED, INCLUDING, BUT NOT LIMITED TO, THE IMPLIED WARRANTIES OF MERCHANTABILITY AND FITNESS FOR A PARTICULAR PURPOSE.**

4.   PAYMENT

In full and final consideration of the rights granted to Multimedia Developer in this Agreement, Multimedia Developer will pay Music Publisher the sum of

$ _____ . The foregoing fee shall be payable only if Multimedia Developer shall actually include a recording of any part of the Musical Composition in the Multimedia Product. The fee shall be payable in full within thirty (30) days after first publication of the Multimedia Product.

5. **CREDIT AND COPYRIGHT NOTICE**

Multimedia Developer shall include, in every copy of the Multimedia Product that includes a recording of any part of the Musical Composition, a conspicuous notice to clearly read as follows:

> [*Name of Musical Composition*] by [*Names of Writers*].
> Copyright © 19 ___ [name of Music Publisher].
> All rights reserved.

The size, prominence, and placement of such notice shall be in Multimedia Developer's sole discretion, provided that it shall be identical to the size, prominence, and placement of similar notices for other similarly utilized musical compositions.

6. **INDEMNIFICATION**

Music Publisher will defend, indemnify and hold Multimedia Developer harmless from and against any and all liabilities, losses, damages, costs and expenses (including legal fees) associated with any claim or action brought against Multimedia Developer for infringement of any U.S. copyright, trademark, or other property right based upon the duplication, sale, license or use of the Musical Composition in accordance with this Agreement, provided that Multimedia Developer promptly notifies Music Publisher in writing of the claim and allows Music Publisher to control, and fully cooperates with Music Publisher in, the defense and all related settlement negotiations. Music Publisher shall have no liability for any settlement or compromise made without its consent.

7. **LIMITATION OF LIABILITY**

Music Publisher's liability to Multimedia Developer shall be limited to direct damages and, except as provided in the section titled "indemnification," shall not exceed the amount of the fees paid by Multimedia Developer to Music Publisher hereunder. In no event will Music Publisher be liable for incidental, special, or consequential damages (including lost profits) suffered by Multimedia Developer, even if it has previously been advised of the possibility of such damages.

8. **TERM AND TERMINATION**

(a) **Term.** This license shall remain in full force and effect for the Term set forth on Exhibit A.

(b) Termination for Breach. Music Publisher may terminate this Agreement only in the event of a material breach of the terms or conditions of this Agreement by Multimedia Developer which breach is not cured within thirty (30) days of written notice from Music Publisher.

(c) Effect of Termination. Upon expiration or termination of this Agreement for any reason, Multimedia Developer's right to make copies of the Multimedia Product that incorporate a recording of any part of the Musical Composition shall terminate. However, Multimedia Developer shall have the right to distribute all copies of the Multimedia Product in Multimedia Developer's inventory as of the date of termination.

IN WITNESS WHEREOF, the parties have executed this Agreement as of the date set forth above.

[MULTIMEDIA DEVELOPER]   [MUSIC PUBLISHER]

By:_____   By:_____

Its: _____   Its:_____

EXHIBIT A
MUSICAL COMPOSITION

1. Musical Composition:
   a. Title: _____
   b. Composer: _____
   c. Lyricist: _____
2. Term: _____

SAMPLE
SOUND RECORDING LICENSE [3]

This Agreement is made and entered into on _____ , 19___ , by and between _____ , an _____ corporation located at _____ , ("Multimedia Developer"), and _____ an _____ corporation located at _____ ("Record Company").

BACKGROUND

A. Record Company is the owner of all rights throughout the world to the master sound recording identified on Exhibit A ("Sound Recording").

B. Multimedia Developer intends to develop, manufacture and distribute a digital, machine-readable, interactive multimedia product tentatively titled "_____" ("Multimedia Product"), and in connection therewith desires to use, adapt, and incorporate the Sound Recording within such Multimedia Product.

C. Record Company is willing to grant such rights to Multimedia Developer, subject to the terms and conditions of this Agreement.

NOW THEREFORE, the parties hereby agree as follows:

1. GRANT OF LICENSE

(a) Rights Granted to Multimedia Developer. Subject to Multimedia Developer obtaining the music publishing and union clearances referred to in this Agreement, Record Company grants Multimedia Developer a perpetual, nonexclusive, worldwide, paid-up license and right to:

(1) adapt, modify, revise and enhance the Sound Recording and otherwise prepare derivative works thereof;

(2) incorporate all or any part of the Sound Recording as so adapted within the Multimedia Product and synchronize it in timed-relation with the visual images contained in such Multimedia Product;

(3) reproduce such version of the Sound Recording, as part of the Multimedia Product, in any media now known or hereafter developed, including but not limited to CD-ROM, videocassette, videodisc, computer network, broadcast television, cable television, and all other broadcasts or transmissions for public or private use;

(4) manufacture, market, promote, sell, license and distribute copies of all or any part of such version of the Sound Recording as part of the Multimedia Product, both directly to end users and indirectly through distributors, dealers, resellers, agents, and other third parties; and

(5) use the name, likeness, biography, and other identification of the Artist identified on Exhibit A whose performance is captured in the Sound Recording, for the Multimedia Product and the distribution, exhibition, advertising, and exploitation of the Multimedia Product.

(b) Rights Reserved to Record Company. Multimedia Developer acknowledges that it has no rights in the Sound Recording except those expressly granted by this Agreement. Nothing herein shall be construed as restricting Record Company's right to sell, lease on a nonexclusive basis, license, modify, publish or otherwise distribute the Sound Recording, in whole or in part, to any other person.

(c) Exclusions. This license does not include rights to: (1) distribute the Sound Recording in any way separate and apart from the Multimedia Product; (2) make, sell or distribute audio phonorecords that reproduce the Sound Recording; (3) use the title of the Sound Recording as part of the title of the Multimedia Product; or (4) make any other use of the Sound Recording not expressly authorized herein.

(d) No License to Musical Composition. This license does not include any grant of rights with respect to the musical composition performed in the Sound Recording. Prior to exercising any of the rights granted in this Agreement, Multimedia Developer shall obtain, from the owners of the copyrights in the musical work performed in the Sound Recording, all licenses that may be required for the use of that musical work in the Multimedia Product. Multimedia Developer will pay all copyright fees to the music publisher of such musical work and shall indemnify and hold Record Company harmless with respect to all such fees.

(e) No Obligation to Use Content. Nothing herein shall obligate or require Multimedia Developer to use or incorporate the Sound Recording in the Multimedia Product. Record Company acknowledges and agrees that the use of the Sound Recording by Multimedia Developer in the Multimedia Product is at the sole discretion of Multimedia Developer.

2. **CREDITS**

If the Sound Recording is used in the Multimedia Product, Multimedia Developer will provide a credit and copyright notice in the Multimedia Product in substantially the following form: "[*Sound Recording*] performed by _____ , courtesy of _____ . Copyright © 19____ , [*Record Company*]" The placement, size, prominence, and duration of such credit shall be in the same manner as the credit given to all other artists and record companies whose works are included in the Multimedia Product.

3.   RECORD COMPANY'S DELIVERY OBLIGATIONS

Immediately following execution of this Agreement, Record Company will provide Multimedia Developer with a master copy of the Sound Recording in a mutually agreeable computer-readable form that can be reproduced by Multimedia Developer.

4.   QUALITY REVIEW

Multimedia Developer will submit a final copy of the Multimedia Product incorporating the Sound Recording in CD-ROM or CD-WO format as soon as possible following its completion, but in no event later than ____ days prior to publication, for review and approval by Record Company. If Record Company determines that the quality of the Multimedia Product is below Record Company's comparable product standards, Record Company shall so advise Multimedia Developer of the manner in which the use of the Sound Recording is unacceptable within ____ days of receipt thereof. Record Company will not unreasonably withhold its approval. Upon receipt of a notice of quality deficiency, Multimedia Developer shall take appropriate steps to improve the quality of its Multimedia Product so that it meets Record Company's normal commercial standards.

5.   RECORD COMPANY'S WARRANTIES

(a) Authority. Record Company represents and warrants that it has the right and authority to enter into this Agreement and to grant to Multimedia Developer the rights to the Sound Recording that are granted in this Agreement.

(b) Noninfringement. Record Company warrants to Multimedia Developer that the adaptation and incorporation of the Sound Recording in the Multimedia Product, and the reproduction and distribution of the Sound Recording as so incorporated, will not infringe upon or misappropriate the proprietary rights of any third party.

(c) Recording Artist and Producer Rights. Record Company warrants and represents that it has obtained approval from all persons or entities whose approval is required for the license and grant of rights made herein, other than the owners of the copyright in the musical works performed in the Sound Recording, and that it shall be solely responsible for (and shall indemnify and hold Multimedia Developer harmless from) any payments to the artists and/or producers of the Sound Recording with regard to Multimedia Developer's use of the Sound Recording.

(d) **DISCLAIMER.** THE FOREGOING ARE THE ONLY WARRANTIES MADE BY RECORD COMPANY. RECORD COMPANY SPECIFICALLY DISCLAIMS ALL OTHER WARRANTIES, EXPRESS OR IMPLIED, INCLUDING, BUT NOT LIMITED TO, THE IMPLIED WARRANTIES OF MERCHANTABILITY AND FITNESS FOR A PARTICULAR PURPOSE.

6. INDEMNIFICATION

Record Company will defend, indemnify and hold Multimedia Developer harmless from and against any and all liabilities, losses, damages, costs and expenses (including legal fees) associated with any claim or action brought against Multimedia Developer for infringement of any copyright, trademark, or other property right based upon the duplication, sale, license or use of the Sound Recording in accordance with this Agreement, provided that Multimedia Developer promptly notifies Record Company in writing of the claim and allows Record Company to control, and fully cooperates with Record Company in, the defense and all related settlement negotiations. Record Company shall have no liability for any settlement or compromise made without its consent.

7. PAYMENT TO RECORD COMPANY

In full and final consideration of the rights granted to Multimedia Developer in this Agreement, Multimedia Developer will pay Record Company the License Fee specified on Exhibit A within _____ days of delivery of a copy of the Sound Recording.

8. THIRD-PARTY CONSENTS AND PAYMENTS

Multimedia Developer shall make the following payments to third parties required in connection with the manufacture, sale, licensing, or distribution of the Sound recording as part of the Multimedia Product:

(a) **Owners of Musical Work.** Multimedia Developer will obtain a license from the owners of the copyright in the musical work performed in the Sound Recording sufficient to authorize the use contemplated by Multimedia Developer, and shall pay all applicable royalties and/or license fees required by the owner of the copyright in such musical work.

(b) **Union Payments.** Multimedia Developer will pay all sums, if any, payable to the AF of M Music Performance Trust Fund and Special Payments Trust Fund, the AFTRA Pension and Welfare Fund, or any similar funds, and re-use fees, if any, that may be required by applicable unions as a result of Multimedia Developer's use of the Sound Recording in the Multimedia Product, immediately after receipt of notice from Record Company as to the amount of such fees.

(c) **Indemnification**. Multimedia Developer will indemnify and hold Record Company harmless from any and all claims, liabilities, costs, losses, damages or expenses, including attorneys' fees, arising out of or in any way connected with Multimedia Developer's use of the Sound Recording hereunder, to the extent they are based on any breach of its obligations in paragraphs (a) and (b) above.

9.   LIMITATION OF LIABILITY

Record Company's liability to Multimedia Developer shall be limited to direct damages and, except as provided in the section titled "indemnification," shall not exceed the amount of the fees paid by Multimedia Developer to Record Company hereunder. In no event will Record Company be liable for incidental, special, or consequential damages (including lost profits) suffered by Multimedia Developer, even if it has previously been advised of the possibility of such damages.

10.   TERM AND TERMINATION

(a) **Termination for Breach.** Record Company may terminate this Agreement only in the event of a material breach of the terms or conditions of this Agreement by Multimedia Developer which breach is not cured within thirty (30) days of written notice from Record Company.

(b) **Effect of Termination.** Upon termination of this Agreement for any reason, Multimedia Developer will immediately cease duplication of the Sound Recording and production of Multimedia Products containing the Sound Recording, and will return to Record Company, at Multimedia Developer's expense, the master versions of Sound Recording. However, Multimedia Developer shall have the right to distribute all copies of Multimedia Products in Multimedia Developer's inventory as of the date of termination, unless termination is due to a material breach by Multimedia Developer.

IN WITNESS WHEREOF, the parties have executed this Agreement as of the date set forth above.

[MULTIMEDIA DEVELOPER]   [RECORD COMPANY]

By: _____   By:_____
Its:_____   Its:_____

EXHIBIT A
SOUND RECORDING

1. Sound Recording:
   a. Title: _____
   b. Writer(s): _____
   c. Artist(s): _____
   d. Phonorecord No.: _____
2. License Fee: _____

SAMPLE
PHOTOGRAPH LICENSE[4]

This Agreement is made and entered into on _____ , 199___ , by and between _____ , a _____ corporation located at _____ , ("Multimedia Developer") and _____ , a _____ corporation located at _____ , ("Photographer").

BACKGROUND

A. Photographer is owner of all rights to the following photograph: _____ ("Photograph").

B. Multimedia Developer intends to develop, manufacture, and distribute to the general public, a digital, computer-readable, interactive multimedia product tentatively titled "_____" on the subject of "_____" ("Multimedia Product").

C. In connection therewith, Multimedia Developer desires to use and incorporate a copy of all or a portion of the Photograph in the Multimedia Product.

D. Photographer is willing to grant Multimedia Developer the right to incorporate the Photograph, in whole or in part, within the Multimedia Product, and distribute the Photograph as so incorporated, worldwide.

NOW THEREFORE, the parties hereby agree as follows:

1. GRANT OF LICENSE

(a) Rights Granted to Multimedia Developer. Photographer grants to Multimedia Developer a perpetual, nonexclusive, worldwide, paid-up license and right to:

(1) incorporate the Photograph, in whole or in part, within the Multimedia Product and in doing so, to crop and otherwise alter and edit the Photograph, as the Multimedia Developer deems appropriate, to fit space or to enhance the function or effectiveness of use of the Photograph;

(2) reproduce the Photograph, as incorporated in the Multimedia Product, in any manner, medium, or form, whether now known or hereafter devised;

(3) sell, license, and distribute copies of the Photograph, as incorporated in the Multimedia Product, worldwide;

(4) display the Photograph publicly, as incorporated in the Multimedia Product, subject to the terms set forth below.

(5) use the Photograph together with photographer's name and pertinent biographical data, in advertising and promotion of the Multimedia Product.

(b) Conditions of Use. The foregoing license is subject to the requirement that Multimedia Developer first obtain the consent of the identifiable persons (if any) appearing in the Photograph.

(c) Rights Reserved to Photographer. Multimedia Developer acknowledges that it has no rights in the Photograph except those expressly granted by this Agreement. Nothing herein shall be construed as restricting Photographer's right to sell, lease on a nonexclusive basis, license, modify, publish or otherwise distribute the Photograph in whole or in part, to any other person.

2. **DELIVERY**

Upon execution of this Agreement, Photographer will deliver a copy of the Photograph to Developer in the form of a color slide [or digital file on computer-readable medium] suitable for reproduction. Such material shall remain the property of Photographer, and shall be returned to Photographer after it has been reproduced by Multimedia Developer.

3. **PHOTOGRAPHER'S WARRANTIES**

(a) Authority. Photographer represents and warrants that the Photograph is original and created by Photographer, and that Photographer has the right and authority to enter into this Agreement and to grant to Multimedia Developer the rights to the Photograph that are granted in this Agreement.

(b) Noninfringement. Photographer represents and warrants to Multimedia Developer that adaption and incorporation of the Photograph in the Multimedia Product, and the reproduction and distribution of the Photograph as so incorporated, will not infringe upon or misappropriate the proprietary rights of any third party.

4. **PAYMENT**

In full and final consideration of the rights granted to Multimedia Developer in this Agreement, Multimedia Developer will pay Photographer the sum of $_____ upon execution of this Agreement.

5. **CREDIT AND COPYRIGHT NOTICE**

Multimedia Developer will give the Photographer credit in the following form: "Courtesy of [*Photographer*]". In addition, the following copyright notice must appear in connection with Multimedia Developer's use of the photograph: "Copyright © 19___ [*Photographer*] All Rights Reserved."

6.   INDEMNIFICATION

Photographer will defend, indemnify and hold Multimedia Developer harmless from and against any and all liabilities, losses, damages, costs and expenses (including legal fees) associated with any claim or action brought against Multimedia Developer for infringement of any U.S. copyright, trademark, or other property right based upon the duplication, sale, license or use of the Photograph in accordance with this Agreement, provided that Multimedia Developer promptly notifies Photographer in writing of the claim and allows Photographer to control, and fully cooperates with Photographer in, the defense and all related settlement negotiations. Photographer shall have no liability for any settlement or compromise made without its consent.

7.   LIMITATION OF LIABILITY

Photographer's liability to multimedia developer shall be limited to direct damages and, except as provided in the section titled "Indemnification," shall not exceed the amount of the fees paid by multimedia developer to photographer hereunder. In no event will photographer be liable for incidental, special, or consequential damages (including lost profits) suffered by multimedia developer, even if it has previously been advised of the possibility of such damages.

8.   TERM AND TERMINATION

(a) Term. This license shall remain in full force and effect for the duration of all copyrights in the Photograph, including any renewals and extensions thereof.

(b) Termination for Breach. Photographer may terminate this Agreement only in the event of a material breach of the terms or conditions of this Agreement by Multimedia Developer which breach is not cured within thirty (30) days of written notice from Photographer.

(c) Effect of Termination. Upon termination of this Agreement for any reason, Multimedia Developer will immediately cease duplication of the Photograph and production of copies of the Multimedia Product containing the Photograph. However, Multimedia Developer shall have the right to distribute all copies of Multimedia Product in Multimedia Developer's inventory as of the date of termination, unless termination is due to material breach by Multimedia Developer.

IN WITNESS WHEREOF, the parties have executed this Agreement as of the date set forth above.

[MULTIMEDIA DEVELOPER]   [PHOTOGRAPHER]
By:_____   By:_____
Its: _____   Its:_____

SAMPLE
FILM CLIP LICENSE AGREEMENT[5]

This Agreement is made and entered into on _____ , 19___ , by and between _____ , a _____ corporation located at _____ , ("Multimedia Developer") and _____ , a _____ corporation located at _____ , ("Movie Studio").

BACKGROUND

A.   Movie Studio is the owner of the copyright to the motion picture identified on Exhibit A of this Agreement. "Film Clip" means the excerpt of the motion picture (including the soundtrack) identified on Exhibit A.

B.   Multimedia Developer is developing a digital, machine-readable, interactive multimedia work tentatively titled "_____ " (the "Multimedia Product").

C.   Multimedia Developer desires to reproduce, incorporate, and distribute the Film Clip as part of such Multimedia Product.

D.   Movie Studio is willing to grant such rights to Multimedia Developer subject to the terms and conditions of this Agreement.

NOW THEREFORE, the parties hereby agree as follows:

1.   LICENSE

(a) Rights Granted to Multimedia Developer. Movie Studio grants Multimedia Developer a nonexclusive, nontransferable license and right for the Term, Territory, and Fee described on Exhibit A to:

(1) incorporate all or any part of the Film Clip within the Multimedia Product;

(2) reproduce all or any part of the Film Clip, as incorporated in the Multimedia Product, in any media now known or hereafter developed, including, but not limited to, CD-ROM, CD-i, and videodisc;

(3) manufacture, package, market, promote, sell, license, and distribute copies of all or any part of the Film Clip, as part of the Multimedia Product, both directly to end users and indirectly through distributors, dealers, resellers, agents, and other third parties.

(b) Restrictions on Use.

(1) The Film Clip is restricted to the uses described in paragraph (a). The Film Clip may not be used for any other purpose or purposes whatsoever.

(2) Multimedia Developer will not reproduce the Film Clip except for use in and as part of the Multimedia Product.

(3) While Multimedia Developer may use the Film Clip in advertising the Multimedia Product, Multimedia Developer shall not use the name of Movie Studio for any purposes in connection with the advertising, publicizing or distribution of the Multimedia Work without the prior written consent of Movie Studio.

(4) Multimedia Developer shall not use the Film Clip in a manner or context that will be in any way derogatory to the Motion Picture from which the Film Clip was taken, any person connected with the production thereof or depicted therein, or the Movie Studio and/or the literary material upon which the Film Clip is based. Furthermore, the Film Clip will not be used in any way so as to constitute an express or implied endorsement of any product or service by anyone associated with the Motion Picture from which the Film Clip was derived.

(c) **Rights Reserved to Movie Studio**. Multimedia Developer acknowledges that it has no rights in the Film Clip except those expressly granted by this Agreement. Movie Studio shall at all times have the right to use, or authorize others to use on a nonexclusive basis the Film Clip in any way Movie Studio may desire.

(d) **No Obligation to Use Film Clip.** Movie Studio acknowledges that Multimedia Developer is not obligated or required to use or incorporate the Film Clip in the Multimedia Product.

2.   CREDITS

Multimedia Developer agrees to give Movie Studio appropriate credit on copies of the Multimedia Product that include the Film Clip in the form specified on Exhibit A, which credit shall be displayed in the same manner as credits to all other artists and copyright owners whose works are included in the Multimedia Products.

3.   THIRD-PARTY CONSENTS

(a) **Releases.** Multimedia Developer shall not have the right to use the Film Clip until it obtains all required individual authorizations, consents, licenses, and releases that may be necessary for the use of the Film Clip under this Agreement including, without limitation:

(1) consents from those who appear recognizably in the Film Clip and from all stunt persons appearing in any stunt identifiable in the Film Clip;

(2) consents from unions and guilds to the extent required under applicable collective bargaining agreements; and

(3) if any preexisting copyrighted works (such as music) are included in the Film Clip, licenses from the copyright owners of such works.

(b) Copies. At Movie Studio's request, Multimedia Developer shall deliver to Movie Studio copies of all authorizations, consents, releases, and licenses required to be obtained under the foregoing paragraph.

(c) Payments to Third Parties. Multimedia Developer shall pay, or cause to be paid, to the extent that the Multimedia Developer may be additionally liable therefore as a result of sales of copies of such Multimedia Products embodying the Film Clip, all payments to applicable union pension and welfare funds, as applicable.

4. **MOVIE STUDIO'S DELIVERY OBLIGATIONS**

Immediately following execution of this Agreement, Movie Studio will provide Multimedia Developer with the copy of the Film Clip on a mutually agreeable medium that can be reproduced by Multimedia Developer.

5. **MOVIE STUDIO'S WARRANTIES**

(a) Authority. Movie Studio represents and warrants that it has the right and authority to enter into this Agreement and to grant to Multimedia Developer the rights to the Film Clip that are granted in this Agreement.

(b) Noninfringement. Movie Studio warrants to Multimedia Developer that the inclusion of the Film Clip in the Multimedia Work, and reproduction and distribution of the Film Clip as part of the Multimedia Work, if done pursuant to the terms of this Agreement, will not infringe upon or misappropriate the proprietary rights of any third party.

6. **INDEMNIFICATIONS**

Each party will indemnify, save, and hold the other (and its respective parent, affiliates, subsidiaries, agents, directors, officers, employees successors, licensees, and assignees) harmless from and against any and all damages, costs, liabilities, losses, and expenses (including reasonable attorney's fees) arising out of or connected with any third-party claim, demand, or action inconsistent with any of the warranties, representations, undertakings, or covenants made by the indemnitor in this Agreement which results in a final adverse judgment, arbitration award or settlement with the consent of the indemnitor (not to be unreasonably withheld). The indemnified party agrees to give indemnitor notice of any action to which the foregoing indemnity applies, and the indemnitor may participate in the defense of same, at its expense, through counsel of its own choosing.

7. **PAYMENT TO MOVIES STUDIO**

(a) License Fee. In full and final consideration of the rights granted to Multimedia Developer in this Agreement, Multimedia Developer will pay Movie Studio the Fee specified in Exhibit A within _____ days of delivery of a copy of the Film Clip.

(b) Materials Fee. In addition, Multimedia Developer agrees to pay Movie Studio a fee of $ _____ for reproducing and delivering the master copy of the Film Clip to be used by Multimedia Developer.

8.   **TERMINATION OF LICENSE**

(a) **Termination for Breach.** Movie Studio may terminate this Agreement only in the event of a material breach of the terms or conditions of this Agreement by Multimedia Developer which breach is not cured within thirty (30) days of written notice from Movie Studio. In addition to these rights of termination, each party will have the right, in the event of an uncured breach by the other party, to avail itself of all remedies or causes of action, in law or equity, for damages as a result of such breach.

(b) **Effect of Termination.** Upon termination of this Agreement for any reason, Multimedia Developer will immediately cease duplication of the Film Clip and production of the Multimedia Product containing the Film Clip, and will return to Movie Studio, at Multimedia Developer's expense, the master version of the Film Clip. However, Multimedia Developer shall have the right to distribute all copies of the Multimedia Product in Multimedia Developer's inventory as of the date of termination.

IN WITNESS WHEREOF, the parties have executed this Agreement as of the date set forth above.

[MULTIMEDIA DEVELOPER]   [MOVIE STUDIO]
By:_____   By:_____
Its:_____   Its:_____

EXHIBIT A

1. **Motion Picture**: _____ .
2. **Film Clip:** [Designate specific portion of Motion Picture to be licensed].
3. **Term:** Perpetuity.
4. **Fee:** _____ .
5. **Territory:** Worldwide.
6. **Credit:** "The Film Clip from [*name of motion picture* in which Film Clip appeared] made available courtesy of [*Name of Movie Studio*]."

Endnotes

1   This contract is an example of the way that a license to use textual material in a multimedia product might be structured. It is designed to help you identify the issues that may need to be considered and the corresponding provisions that might be included, and to suggest a possible structure for such an agreement. However, it is not necessarily representative of an agreement that a copyright owner would be willing to agree to. Moreover, it is not intended to be used as a form, since each agreement should be tailored to meet the needs of the situation in which it is to be used, and the law of the governing jurisdiction.

2   This contract is an example of the way that a license to use a musical composition in a multimedia product might be structured. It is designed to help you identify the issues that may need to be considered and the corresponding provisions that might be included, and to suggest a possible structure for such an agreement. However, it is not necessarily representative of an agreement that the copyright owner of a musical composition would be willing to agree to. Moreover, it is not intended to be used as a form, since each agreement should be tailored to meet the needs of the situation in which it is to be used, and the law of the governing jurisdiction.

3   This contract is an example of the way that a license to use a sound recording in a multimedia product might be structured. It is designed to help you identify the issues that may need to be considered and the corresponding provisions that might be included, and to suggest a possible structure for such an agreement. However, it is not necessarily representative of an agreement that the owner of copyright in a sound recording would be willing to agree to. Moreover, it is not intended to be used as a form, since each agreement should be tailored to meet the needs of the situation in which it is to be used, and the law of the governing jurisdiction.

4   This contract is an example of the way that a license to use a photograph in a multimedia product might be structured. It is designed to help you identify the issues that may need to be considered and the corresponding provisions that might be included, and to suggest a possible structure for such an agreement. However, it is not necessarily representative of an agreement that a copyright owner of a photograph would be willing to agree to. Moreover, it is not intended to be used as a form, since each agreement should be tailored to meet the needs of the situation in which it is to be used, and the law of the governing jurisdiction.

5   This contract is an example of the way that a license to use a film clip in a multimedia product might be structured. It is designed to help you identify the issues that may need to be considered and the corresponding provisions that might be included, and to suggest a possible structure for such an agreement. However, it is not necessarily representative of an agreement that a film clip copyright owner would be willing to agree to. Moreover, it is not intended to be used as a form, since each agreement should be tailored to meet the needs of the situation in which it is to be used, and the law of the governing jurisdiction.

Releases

Releases

CHECKLIST OF ISSUES

1. **Subject Matter of the Release**
    a. Identify type of subject matter covered by the Release
        (1) Name
        (2) Visual likeness (photographs, video, film, and so forth)
        (3) Voice
        (4) Sound recording
        (5) Quotes
        (6) Photograph
        (7) Graphics or other artwork
        (8) Music
        (9) Motion picture, video, or other audiovisual material
    b. Provide specific description of subject matter of the release
2. **Scope of the Release**
    a. What uses of the subject matter are authorized by the release?
        (1) Right to copy the subject matter of the release?
        (2) Right to adapt, modify, or enhance the subject matter of the release?
        (3) Right to incorporate the subject matter of the release into a multimedia work?
        (4) Right to distribute the subject matter of the release?
        (5) Right to publicly perform or display the subject matter of the release?
    b. Does the consent contain any restrictions limiting the use to a specific:
        (1) Multimedia title?
        (2) Media?

      (3)   Distribution channel?

      (4)   Territory?

      (5)   Hardware platform?

      (6)   Software (operating system) platform?

      (7)   Language?

      (8)   Market?

3. Ownership of Content

   a.   Does the person granting the release acknowledge that you will be the exclusive owner of all right, title, and interest, including copyright, in any and all authorized uses made of the released materials?

4. What Rights Are Released?

   a.   All claims arising out of or relating to authorized use?

   b.   Specific rights?

      (1)   Invasion of privacy

      (2)   Right of publicity

      (3)   Defamation

      (4)   Copyright infringement

      (5)   Moral rights

      (6)   Any other personal or property rights

5. Consideration

   a.   Does the release recite that the person granting the release has received some consideration or value?

6. Warranties

   a.   Does the person granting the release warrant that he or she has the authority to grant the permissions and release the rights set forth in the agreement?

**SAMPLE
RELEASE**

To: _____

Subject: _____

    For value received, I hereby give you the absolute and irrevocable right and permission to use, adapt, modify, reproduce, distribute, publicly perform and display the [*state subject of release*] in whole or in part, individually or in conjunction with other materials, in any medium now known or later developed, and for any purpose whatsoever, including but not limited to _____ .

    I hereby release, waive, and discharge you, your heirs, executors, successors, and assigns, from any and all demands or claims that I have or may have arising out of or in connection with the foregoing use of the [*subject of release*], including but not limited to any claims for invasion of privacy, defamation, infringement of my right of publicity, copyright infringement, or any other causes of action arising out of the use, adaptation, reproduction, distribution, broadcast, or exhibition of the [*subject of release*].

    I warrant and represent that I have the authority to grant the foregoing permission and release.

    I understand, acknowledge, and agree that you shall have the sole and exclusive right to all works that use, are based on, or otherwise incorporate the [*subject of release*], including but not limited to all copyrights.

           Name: _____

           Signature: _____

           Date: _____

Multimedia Product Development Agreements

1. Checklist of Issues
2. Sample Multimedia Product Development Agreement

CHAPTER 32

Multimedia Product Development Agreements

CHECKLIST OF ISSUES

1. **Subject Matter of the Contract**
   a. Identify and describe the multimedia product to be developed.
      (1) What content should it include?
      (2) How should the user interface look?
      (3) What functions must it be capable of performing?
      (4) What user search capabilities should it have?
      (5) How should the overall product be designed?
   b. Identify and describe any associated documentation to be developed.
      (1) User documentation
      (2) Technical documentation
      (3) Documentation standards, level of detail, and so forth.
   c. Identify any other relevant deliverables.
2. **Work to Be Performed by Developer**
   a. What has the developer agreed to do?
      (1) Develop functional specifications?
      (2) Develop design specifications?
      (3) Develop the user interface?
      (4) Design the multimedia product?
      (5) Test the multimedia product?
   b. Will the work be done in separate phases? If so, how will each phase be defined?

    c.   What specifications govern the developer's work in each phase of the project?

    d.   How will the parties handle changes you request in the work being done by the developer during the life of the project?

3. **Delivery and Deliverables**
    a.   What deliverables have you agreed to provide to the developer?
        (1) Specifications?
        (2) Content?
        (3) Software?
    b.   What deliverables has the developer agreed to provide?
        (1) Specifications?
        (2) Content?
        (3) Software?
        (4) Completed multimedia product?
        (5) Documentation?
    c.   When will the completed multimedia product be delivered?
    d.   What is your remedy for late delivery?
    e.   What happens to the delivery schedule if you request any changes in the specifications during the life of the project?

4. **Acceptance of Multimedia Product**
    a.   What rights do you have to review and test the multimedia product before you accept it?
    b.   If there is an acceptance test:
        (1) What requirements must the multimedia product meet?
        (2) What happens if the test fails?
        (3) Who decides when the test is passed?
    c.   What is the standard to be met for acceptance?
        (1) Your subjective "satisfaction"?
        (2) Compliance with written specifications and warranties?
        (3) Compliance with other predefined test criteria?
    d.   When will you be deemed to have "accepted" the multimedia product?

5. **Warranties**
    a.   What express warranties (if any) are provided by the developer?
        (1) Warranty that the multimedia product was originally developed?

(2) Warranty that all preexisting components are properly licensed (if developer is not the developer of all components of the multimedia product that it provides to you)?

(3) Warranty that multimedia product conforms to specifications?

(4) Warranty of performance?

(5) Warranty of adequacy of documentation?

(6) Warranty of noninfringement of patents, copyrights, and trade secrets?

(7) Warranty as to the minimum equipment required to support the multimedia product?

(8) Warranty as to the operating system and any other software required to support the multimedia product?

(9) Free from defects in material and workmanship?

(10) Free from date bombs, viruses, and so forth?

b. How long do the warranties last?

c. If the multimedia product fails to work as warranted, what is your remedy?

6. **Support**

a. What support (if any) will the developer provide to you?

(1) Telephone assistance?

(2) Error corrections?

(3) Updates and enhancements?

b. What support (if any) will the developer provide for your customers?

7. **Payment**

a. What type of fee is charged?

(1) Fixed lump sum?

(2) Hourly rate plus out-of-pocket expenses?

b. What is the amount of the fixed fee or the hourly rate?

c. When is payment due?

8. **Ownership of Multimedia Product**

a. Who owns the multimedia product developed?

(1) The developer?

(2) You?

(3) Both parties (i.e., joint ownership)?

b. Does the developer represent that it will not use any content that is owned by others, or that it will not do so without first obtaining your permission?

    c.   If the developer owns the multimedia product, what rights are granted to you?

        (1)   What is the scope of your right to copy the multimedia product?

        (2)   What is the scope of your right to adopt or modify the multimedia product?

        (3)   What is the scope of your right to distribute the multimedia product?

9. Confidentiality

    a.   Is either party obligated to keep any information confidential?

    b.   Does each party agree that it will not use or disclose any confidential information that it learns about the business or products of the other?

    c.   What is the term of the confidentiality obligation?

10. Indemnification

    a.   Will the developer defend you and pay any damages or expenses incurred if you are sued by someone claiming the multimedia product (or any part of it) infringes on the rights of any other parties?

    b.   What are the conditions for indemnification?

        (1)   Timely notice of claims?

        (2)   Cooperation in defense?

        (3)   Developer right to control or participate in the defense?

    c.   Are there any limits on the developer's indemnification liability?

11. Limitations of liability

    a.   Is there a limit on the dollar amount of damages you can recover from the developer in the event the multimedia product fails to work properly or it otherwise breaches the agreement?

    b.   Is there a limit on the type of damages you can recover from the developer in the event the multimedia product fails to work properly or it otherwise breaches the agreement? (for example, has the developer excluded liability for consequential damages, such as lost profits, or claims by third parties?)

12. Default

    a.   What are each party's rights in the event of a breach of the agreement by the other party?

        (1)   Suspend performance?

        (2)   Terminate contract?

        (3)   Liquidated damages?

        (4)   Injunction?

        (5)   Other?

  b. Is the nonbreaching party required to give notice of the breach to the other party?

  c. Does the breaching party have an opportunity to cure its breach before the other party can terminate the agreement?

13. **Term and termination**

  a. When does the developer begin work?

  b. When is the project scheduled to be completed?

  c. Does either party have the right to terminate the project before it is finished? If so, when?

    (1) On default of other party?

    (2) On a specified number of days notice?

    (3) At the terminating party's discretion?

    (4) On bankruptcy or insolvency of the other party?

  d. What happens on termination?

    (1) Discontinue development?

    (2) All work to date turned over to you or retained by developer?

    (3) All past due payments must be made?

  e. Do any obligations survive termination?

    (1) Confidentiality?

    (2) Indemnification?

    (3) Payments due and owing (fees, expenses, taxes, and so forth)?

SAMPLE
MULTIMEDIA PRODUCT DEVELOPMENT AGREEMENT[1]

THIS AGREEMENT is made and entered into on _____ , 199__ , by and between _____ , a _____ corporation ("Developer") and _____ , a _____ corporation, ("Client").

1.   BACKGROUND

(a) Client is the owner or licensee of certain Content that it would like to embody in a digital, machine-readable, interactive Multimedia Product on CD-ROM;

(b) Client and Developer desire to enter into a relationship whereby Developer will provide the software and services necessary to develop a Multimedia Product using Client Content, in accordance with specifications attached.

2.   DEFINITIONS

(a) **Functional Specifications** means the specifications attached as Exhibit A that define the tasks and functions that must be performed by the Multimedia Product to be produced by Developer, as well as its operating system and environment requirements, language specifications, data content and format requirements, functional capabilities, and performance characteristics.

(b) **User Interface Specifications** means the specifications that define the screens, windows, menus, online help, and so forth, displayed to the user of the Multimedia Product to convey information and/or accept data or instructions from the user, including but not limited to their design, format, layout, and color, and their flow or sequencing.

(c) **Technical Design Specifications** means the specifications that define the way the Multimedia Product must be organized and programmed, and the manner in which the Content is to be sewn together, in order to accomplish the tasks and functions identified in the Functional Specifications and User Interface Specifications.

(d) **Content** means the text, data, musical works, sound recordings, still pictures, illustrations, graphics, motion pictures, other audiovisual materials, and other information provided by Client for inclusion in the Multimedia Product and to be made available to End-Users for access, viewing, and other use through interaction with the Search and Retrieval Software.

(e) **Search and Retrieval Software** means the executable software and any associated indexes, tables, pointers, and other data or information provided by

Developer, that allows End-Users of the Multimedia Product to access, use, search, retrieve, and interact with the Content component of the Multimedia Product.

(f) **User Interface** means the software layer provided by Developer that is displayed to End Users upon loading the Multimedia Product and is the primary means by which End Users interact with the Search and Retrieval Software and the Content, and includes any on-line help or tutorials provided by Developer.

(g) **Multimedia Product** means the Content owned or licensed by Client, embodied on a CD-ROM disc, and enhanced with the addition of the Search and Retrieval Software and the User Interface, to produce a complete and interactive CD-ROM product for use by End-User customers, in accordance with the Functional Specifications, the User Interface Specifications, and the Technical Design Specifications, tentatively titled, _____ , created pursuant to this Agreement.

(h) **Documentation** means the instruction/user manual booklet designed for insertion into the jewel case with the CD-ROM disc containing the Multimedia Product for delivery to End-User customers.

(i) **End-User** means a person who acquires a copy of a Multimedia Product from any source primarily for his or her own personal use, and not for resale -- that is, an ultimate user of a Multimedia Product.

3.   **OVERVIEW.** Developer will provide the services and software necessary to develop the Multimedia Product in accordance with the Functional Specifications, User Interface Specifications, and Technical Design Specifications, using Content provided by Client, along with a User Interface and Search and Retrieval Software provided by Developer, in order to produce a gold master CD-ROM disc for the Multimedia Product, as further described in this Agreement. Developer agrees to perform all Services necessary to develop the Multimedia Product for Client in two (2) phases, as set forth below.

4.   **PHASE 1—DEVELOPMENT OF SPECIFICATIONS**. In consultation with Client, Developer will prepare Technical Design Specifications and User Interface Specifications for the development of the Multimedia Product capable of performing in accordance with the Functional Specifications and the requirements of Client.

5.   **ACCEPTANCE OF PHASE 1 SPECIFICATIONS.** Upon completion and delivery of the User Interface Specifications and the Technical Design Specifications to be developed in Phase 1 of this Agreement, Client shall have ten (10) business days to examine same in order to determine whether or not they conform to the Functional Specifications and otherwise meet Client's requirements. If they satisfy

such requirements, Client shall notify Developer in writing of its acceptance and Developer will promptly begin work on Phase2. If they fail to satisfy Client's requirements, Client shall notify Developer, specifying the desired changes, and Developer shall correct, modify, or improve the User Interface Specifications and the Technical Design Specifications to meet all of Client's requirements. Thereafter, the foregoing acceptance process shall be repeated.

6. **PHASE 2—PRODUCTION OF MULTIMEDIA PRODUCT.** Upon completion of Phase 1, and Client's acceptance of the Technical Design Specifications and User Interface Specifications, Developer will create, test, and debug the Multimedia Product pursuant to the Functional Specifications, Technical Design Specifications, and User Interface Specifications, and prepare the Documentation.

7. **CONTENT—EDITORIAL CREATION.** Client shall be responsible for creating and/or licensing the Content for the Multimedia Product, and in connection therewith, shall provide all Content for the Multimedia Product to Developer in digital machine-readable form as mutually agreed by the parties.

8. **SEARCH AND RETRIEVAL SOFTWARE.** Developer will obtain from a third party or independently develop, appropriate Search and Retrieval Software that complies with all of the Specifications, and will test same to ensure proper operation with the Content for the Multimedia Product. If the Search and Retrieval Software is licensed from a third party, the terms of such license must be approved by Client.

9. **USER INTERFACE.** Developer will obtain from a third party or independently develop a User Interface that complies with the Specifications and that is otherwise mutually agreeable to the parties. If the User Interface is licensed from a third party, the terms and conditions of such license must be approved by Client.

10. **DOCUMENTATION.** The Documentation for the Multimedia Product shall be created by Developer, and approved by Client in writing. Client will be responsible for providing the camera-ready art work for the cover of the instruction/user manual and jewel case insert.

11. **PRE-MASTERING.** For the Multimedia Product, Developer will perform all tasks, including the creation of new computer programming, necessary to convert, coordinate, modify, and index the Content as necessary for incorporation on a CD-ROM disc, and to manage and merge the Content, the Search and Retrieval Software and the User Interface for the Multimedia Product. Developer will create six CD-ROM write-once discs containing the Multimedia Product ("CD-WO Discs")

and test the operation of the Multimedia Product pursuant to all of the Specifications. Five of these CD-WO Discs will be sent to Client for its review and approval.

12.   MODIFICATIONS TO SPECIFICATIONS. Developer shall develop the Multimedia Product in Phase 2 pursuant to the Functional Specifications, the User Interface Specifications, and Technical Design Specifications as accepted by Client, which specifications shall be deemed to be part of this Agreement. No changes in or deviations from the specifications will be permitted unless the following procedure is followed:

(a) Client must submit a written request detailing the changes that it desires.

(b) Within ten (10) days of the receipt of the request, Developer will inform Client, in writing, of any problems posed by the proposed change, and of any change in price or schedule that will be caused by the proposed change in specifications.

(c) Unless Client accepts the change, in writing, within ten (10) business days thereafter, the change will not be made. If the change is accepted the written request for change, and Developer's response thereto, will be deemed to constitute an amendment to this Agreement.

If the parties agree to any change in the Specifications and such change results in increasing or decreasing Developer's cost of performing the work, the prices shall be adjusted in order to fairly reflect such increase or decrease in cost.

13.   ACCEPTANCE OF PHASE 2 MULTIMEDIA PRODUCT. Client shall review the CD-WO Discs and Documentation prepared by Developer and, no more than thirty (30) business days after receiving same from Developer, approve them or specify in writing the manner in which they fail to conform to any of the Specifications (whereupon Developer will promptly make all required corrections and resubmit the revised CD-WO Discs and/or Documentation for Client's approval). Requested departures from the Specifications for the functionality or User Interface of the CD-WO Disc will be considered chargeable enhancements. Following approval by Client of the CD-WO Discs and Documentation, Developer will create and deliver to Client a final gold master CD-ROM to be used for replication.

If the Multimedia Product fails to conform to the Specifications, Client shall notify Developer of such failure in writing and Developer shall have _____ days after receipt of such notice to correct, modify, or improve the Multimedia Product so that it conforms to the Specifications. Thereafter, Client shall reconduct the Acceptance Test specified above. This process shall be repeated as may be necessary until the Multimedia Product is deemed to be accepted hereunder; provided, however, that if the Multimedia Product is not accepted hereunder within 180 days after the beginning of the acceptance process, Client shall have the right and option to declare Developer to be in default, terminate this Agreement, and receive a refund of all sums paid to Developer.

14.   SUPPORT. For a period of six (6) months after acceptance of the Multimedia Product, Developer agrees to provide Client, at no charge, all telephone and on-site support reasonably required to assist Client in the use and operation of the Multimedia Product, and all analysis and programming services necessary to correct and resolve any errors or problems that appear in the Multimedia Product as a result of its use by Client and its End User customers. Developer's obligation to provide such Multimedia Product Support is contingent upon the accurate and timely reporting of any errors or problems in the Multimedia Product by Client, and upon Client providing Developer with sufficient information concerning the nature, frequency and other documentation necessary to Developer's diagnosis and correction of the errors or problems.

15.   PAYMENT TO DEVELOPER. Client shall pay Developer for the work performed hereunder as follows:

(a) **Phase 1.** The Specifications to be provided under Phase 1 shall be developed on a fixed-fee basis, for $ _____ . Payment of this amount shall be made within twenty (20) days of acceptance of the Phase 1 Specifications.

(b) **Phase 2.** The Multimedia Product to be provided under Phase 2 shall be developed on a time and expense basis. Client shall pay Developer at the hourly rate set forth on Exhibit B for all time expended, plus reimbursement of all reasonable out-of-pocket expenses incurred by Developer. Developer will submit invoices monthly. Client will pay 90 percent of the amount invoiced within thirty (30) days of receipt, with the balance to be paid within twenty (20) days of the acceptance of the Phase 2 Multimedia Product.

(c) **Taxes.** Developer's price for its Services under this Agreement does not include any taxes that may be levied upon the services or Multimedia Product provided under this Agreement. If, during the term of this Agreement, or thereafter, taxes on the services or Multimedia Product should be imposed, Client agrees that it will pay all such taxes and that it will hold Developer harmless for the payment of any and all such taxes.

16.   WARRANTIES

(a) **Warranty of Expertise.** Developer represents and warrants that it is highly skilled and experienced in producing multimedia products, and that it also possesses the additional expertise needed to develop and provide the particular Multimedia Product required by this Agreement. Developer acknowledges that Client is relying upon the skill and expertise of Developer for the performance of this Agreement.

(b) **Warranty of Original Development.** Developer represents and warrants that, except for the Content provided by Client, and the Search and Retrieval Software and/or User Interface licensed from third parties in accordance with license agreements approved by Client, the Multimedia Product developed by Developer pursuant to this Agreement (including all components, data, software, and other materials provided by Developer), will be of original development by Developer and will not infringe upon or violate any patent, copyright, trade secret, or other property right of any third party. Developer will indemnify and hold Client harmless from and against any loss, cost, liability, or expense (including reasonable attorneys' fees) arising out of any breach or claimed breach of this warranty.

(c) **Warranty of Multimedia Product Functions.** Developer represents and warrants that the Multimedia Product and Documentation delivered hereunder will conform to the Functional Specifications, the User Interface Specifications, the Technical Design Specifications, and the other requirements described or incorporated in this Agreement. Developer will, without additional charge to Client, make such additions, modifications, or adjustments to the Multimedia Product as may be necessary to correct any problems or defects discovered in the Multimedia Product or Documentation and reported to Developer by Client for a period of six (6) months after acceptance date, excluding defects or problems arising from misuse or modification by Client.

(d) **Developer Performance.** Developer warrants that it will perform the services described herein in a good and workmanlike manner and in accordance with the Specifications.

(e) **DISCLAIMER. THE FOREGOING ARE THE ONLY WARRANTIES MADE BY EITHER PARTY. BOTH PARTIES SPECIFICALLY DISCLAIM ALL OTHER WARRANTIES, EXPRESS OR IMPLIED, INCLUDING, BUT NOT LIMITED TO, THE IMPLIED WARRANTIES OF MERCHANTABILITY AND FITNESS FOR A PARTICULAR PURPOSE.**

17.   OWNERSHIP AND PROPRIETARY RIGHTS

(a) **Rights Reserved to Client.** Developer acknowledges that the Content provided by Client for the Multimedia Product is the property of Client or its licensors and that Developer has no rights in the foregoing except those expressly granted by this Agreement.

(b) Rights Reserved to Developer. Client acknowledges that the Search and Retrieval Software, and User Interface provided by Developer are the property of Developer or its licensors, and that Client has no rights in the foregoing except those expressly granted by this Agreement and any applicable license agreements.

(c) Ownership of Multimedia Product. The Multimedia Product developed pursuant to this Agreement, and all corresponding copyrights, trade secret rights, and patent rights, shall be the sole and exclusive property of Client, subject to the rights of Developer (or its licensor) in the Search and Retrieval Software and User Interface. Developer hereby assigns to Client all right, title and interest in and to all rights to the Multimedia Product, Documentation, and all copies thereof in whatever form, without additional consideration, and agrees to assist Client to register and enforce all patents, copyrights and other rights and protection relating to the Multimedia Product in any and all countries. Developer agrees to execute and deliver all additional documents reasonably requested by Client in order to perfect, register, and/or enforce any such rights in Client. Developer hereby grants Client a perpetual, worldwide, royalty-free nonexclusive license to use, copy, adapt, distribute, perform, and display the Search and Retrieval Software and User Interface provided by Developer and incorporated within the Multimedia Product.

(d) Copyright Notices. Developer will affix the following copyright notice to the Multimedia Product and Documentation: "Copyright © 19___ by [*Client name*]." Said notice will be affixed on all tangible versions of the Multimedia Product and Documentation, and also will be programmed into all versions of the Multimedia Product so that it will appear at the beginning of all visual displays of the Multimedia Product.

(e) Confidentiality. Developer acknowledges that, during the course of this Agreement it will be entrusted with, and further develop, confidential information relating to the business and Multimedia Product of Client. Developer agrees that it will not use such confidential information for any purpose except the performance of this Agreement, and that it will not disclose any such confidential information to any person unless such disclosure is authorized by the other party in writing. At no time, without the prior written consent of Client, will Developer use, copy, disclose to any third party, license, transfer or otherwise exploit the Multimedia Product, the Documentation, or any of the Specifications for the Multimedia Product unless and until they become public knowledge through no fault of Developer. Further, Developer will maintain the confidentiality of the Multimedia Product and of the fact that Client is pursuing development of the Multimedia Product. Developer will use and maintain appropriate security measures to honor all of its obligations under this Agreement.

The foregoing obligation of confidentiality will not apply to information that: (i) is or becomes generally known or available by publication, commercial use, sale of copies of Multimedia Product, or otherwise through no fault of the receiving party; (ii) is known by Developer prior to the time of disclosure and is not subject to restriction; (iii) is independently developed or learned by Developer other than pursuant to this Agreement; (iv) is lawfully obtained from a third party, including end-user customers, who has the right to make such disclosure without restriction; or (v) is released for publication by Client in writing.

18.   INDEMNIFICATION. Developer will defend, indemnify and hold Client harmless from and against any and all liabilities, losses, damages, costs and expenses (including legal fees and expenses) associated with any claim or action brought against Client for actual or alleged infringement of any patent, copyright, trademark, service mark, trade secret or other property right based upon the duplication, sale, license or use of the User Interface, Search and Retrieval Software, Documentation, other computer programming, and/or other data or material, provided by Developer as part of the Multimedia Product, provided that Developer is promptly notified in writing of the claim by Client. Developer will have the sole right to conduct the defense of any such claim or action and all negotiations for its settlement or compromise unless otherwise agreed to in writing. However, if Developer, after receiving notice of any such proceeding, fails to immediately begin the defense of such claim or action, Client may (without further notice to Developer) retain counsel and undertake the defense, compromise, or settlement of such claim or action at the expense of Developer.

19.   LIMITATION OF LIABILITY. The liability of Developer to Client shall be limited to direct damages and, except for Developer's "Indemnification" obligation under this Agreement, shall not exceed the amount of the fees paid by Client to Developer during the term of this Agreement. Developer will not be liable for incidental, special, or consequential damages (including lost profits or lost business suffered by Client), even if it has previously been advised of the possibility of such damages.

20.   TERMINATION

(a) **Early Termination.** Client may, for any reason, terminate this Agreement at any time effective upon Developer's receipt of written notice thereof. In the event of termination, Developer will deliver to Client copies of its work product completed to that date. Upon receipt of such work product, Client will pay all sums due to Developer for work completed as of the date of such notice, including prorated fees and expenses for items partially complete at time of termination.

(b) **Default.** Either party may terminate this Agreement prior to the expiration of any Term in the event (i) the other party is in material breach of the terms or conditions of this Agreement and such breach is not cured within thirty (30) days of written notice from the party not in breach, or (ii) the other party becomes insolvent or unable to pay its debts as they become due, a voluntary or involuntary bankruptcy proceeding is filed by or against the other party, or a receiver or assignee for the benefit of the other party's creditors is appointed.

21.   ASSIGNABILITY. This Agreement and the rights and obligations hereunder may not be assigned in whole or in part by either party without the prior written consent of the other party, and any purported assignment without such written consent shall be void and of no effect.

22.   GENERAL PROVISIONS

(a) **Relationship of the Parties.** Nothing stated in this Agreement shall be deemed to create the relationship of partners, joint venturers, employer-employee, master-servant, or franchisor-franchisee between the parties hereto.

(b) **Force Majeure.** Neither party shall be responsible for delays or failure of performance resulting from acts beyond the reasonable control of such party. Such acts shall include, but not be limited to, acts of God, strikes, walkouts, riots, acts of war, epidemics, failure of suppliers to perform, governmental regulations, power failure(s), earthquakes, or other disasters.

(c) **Survival of Certain Provisions.** The warranties, indemnification obligations, and confidentiality requirements set forth in the Agreement shall survive the termination of the Agreement by either party for any reason.

(d) **Notices.** All notices and demands of any kind or nature that either party to this Agreement may be required or may desire to serve upon the other in connection with this Agreement shall be in writing and may be served personally or by prepaid registered or certified United States mail or by private mail service (such as Federal Express or DHL), in either case to the addresses set forth at the beginning of this Agreement.

Either party may from time to time, by notice in writing served upon the other party as aforesaid, designate a different mailing address or a different person to which following such service all further notices or demands are thereafter to be addressed.

(e) Headings. The titles and headings of the various sections and paragraphs hereof are intended solely for convenience of reference and are not intended for any other purpose whatsoever, or to explain, modify or place any construction upon or on any of the provisions of this Agreement.

(f) Governing Law. This Agreement shall be construed in accordance with, and governed by, the laws of the State of _____ .

(g) Severability. Should any provision or part of any provision of this Agreement be void or unenforceable, such provision, or part thereof, shall be deemed omitted, and the Agreement, with such provision or part thereof omitted, shall remain in full force and effect.

(h) Entire Agreement. This Agreement constitutes the entire agreement between the parties pertaining to the subject matter contained herein and supersedes all prior agreements. No provisions in either party's purchase orders, or in any other business forms employed by either party will supersede the terms and conditions of this Agreement, and no supplement, modification, or amendment of this Agreement shall be binding, unless executed in writing by both parties to this Agreement.

[DEVELOPER]   [CLIENT]

By: _____   By:_____

Its: _____   Its:_____

EXHIBIT A
FUNCTIONAL SPECIFICATIONS

Endnote

1   This contract is an example of the way a Multimedia Product Development Agreement might be structured, and the types of provisions that might be included in such an agreement. It is not intended to be used as a form, however, since the structure and content of each contract must be tailored to meet the needs of the situation in which it is to be used, and the law of the jurisdiction that will govern the transaction.

CHAPTER 33

Confidentiality and Rights Assignment Agreements

Confidentiality and Rights Assignment Agreements

SAMPLE

EMPLOYEE AGREEMENT [1]

(To be signed by all employees on the first day of employment)

As an employee of _____
(the Company) I understand and agree that I have a responsibility to protect and
avoid the unauthorized use or disclosure of Confidential Information of the Company, and to assign to the Company my rights in the inventions and other work
product I create on behalf of the Company as follows:

1. **PROTECTION OF CONFIDENTIAL INFORMATION**

   (a) Confidential Information. For purposes of this Agreement, the term
"Confidential Information" means all information that is not generally known and
that: (i) I obtain from the Company, or learn, discover, develop, conceive, or create
during the term of my employment with the Company, and (ii) relates directly to the
business or assets of the Company. The term "Confidential Information" shall
include, but shall not be limited to: inventions, discoveries, know-how, ideas, computer programs, designs, algorithms, processes and structures; product information;
research and development information; lists of clients and other information relating thereto; financial data and information; business plans and processes; and any
other information of the Company that the Company informs me, or that I should
know by virtue of my position or the circumstances in which I learned it, is to be kept
confidential. Confidential Information also includes information obtained by the

Company in confidence from its vendors or clients. Confidential Information may or may not be labeled as "confidential." I shall use common sense and good judgment when determining whether unlabeled information is confidential, and I will ask for help if I am uncertain.

Confidential Information does **not** include any information that has been made generally available to the public, nor does it include any general technical skills or general experience gained by me during my employment with the Company, and I understand that the Company has no objection to my using these skills and experience in any new business venture or employment following termination of my employment with the Company.

(b) Obligation to Protect Confidential Information. I agree that I will not disclose to others, use for my own benefit or for the benefit of anyone other than the Company, or otherwise appropriate or copy, any Confidential Information, whether or not developed by me, except as required in the lawful performance of my employment duties to the Company. I will also take all reasonable measures, in accordance with the Company policy, and instructions from my manager, to protect Confidential Information from any accidental, unauthorized, or premature use, disclosure, or destruction.

(c) Term. My obligation to protect Confidential Information as defined above shall continue throughout my employment with Company, and shall survive termination of my employment for a period of three (3) years, or if such responsibilities concern a trade secret, for as long as such trade secret remains a trade secret if that is a longer time.

2.   ASSIGNMENT OF RIGHTS IN WORK PRODUCT

(a) Original Development. I represent and warrant to the Company that all work that I perform for the Company, and all work product that I produce, including but not limited to literary works, software, documentation, memoranda, musical works, photographs, artwork, sound recordings, audiovisual works, ideas, designs, inventions, processes, algorithms, and so forth ("Work Product"), will not knowingly infringe upon or violate any patent, copyright, trade secret, or other property right of any of my former employers or of any other third party. I will not disclose to the Company, or use in any of my Work Product, any confidential or proprietary information belonging to others, unless both the owner thereof and the Company have consented.

(b) Disclosure. I will promptly disclose to the Company all Work Products developed by me within the scope of my employment with the Company.

(c) Copyright Ownership. I acknowledge and agree that all copyrightable Work Products prepared by me within the scope of my employment with the Company are "works made for hire" and, consequently, that the Company owns all copyrights thereto.

(d) Assignment. I hereby assign to the Company all of my other rights, title, and interest (including but not limited to all patent, copyright, and trade secret rights) in and to all Work Products prepared by me, whether patentable or not, made or conceived in whole or in part by me within the scope of my employment by the Company, or that relate directly to, or involve the use of Confidential Information.

Pursuant to the provisions of the Illinois Employee Patent Act, I acknowledge receipt of notice that this assignment does not apply to an invention for which no equipment, supplies, facility, or trade secret of the Company was used and which was developed entirely on my own time, unless (a) the invention relates (i) to the business of the Company, or (ii) to the Company's actual or demonstrably anticipated research or development, or (b) the invention results from any work performed by me for the Company.[2]

(e) Documents. I will execute all documents reasonably requested by the Company to further evidence the foregoing assignment and to provide all reasonable assistance to the Company (at the Company's expense) in perfecting or protecting any or all of the Company's rights in my Work Product.

(f) Preexisting Work Product Not Assigned. I have indicated on the signature page of this Agreement all work product possibly related to the Company's business and created prior to my employment by the Company in which I have any right, title, or interest that I do not assign to the Company. If I do not have any such work product to indicate, I will write "none" on the signature page.

3. **TERMINATION**

Upon termination of my employment with the Company for any reason, or at any time upon request of the Company, I agree to deliver to the Company all materials of any nature that are in my possession or control and that constitute or contain Confidential Information or Work Product, or that are otherwise the property of the Company including, but not limited to: writings, designs, documents, records, data, memoranda, photographs, sound recordings, tapes and disks containing software, computer source code listings, routines, file layouts, record layouts, system design information, models, manuals, documentation, and notes.

4.   GENERAL

By signing this document I understand that I have a legal commitment to abide by the above obligations.

I certify that I have read and understand the statement above. I fully understand my responsibility to comply with the guidelines as stated herein. I recognize that any violation of these guidelines may be cause for disciplinary action including, but not limited to, dismissal and legal action, as appropriate.

_____   _____
Employee's Signature   Date

_____   _____
Witness's Signature   Date

Preexisting Work Product Not Assigned

I have rights in the following work products that were created prior to my employment by the Company that I do not assign to the Company. If none, please write "None."

> (NOTE: It is in your interest to establish that any such work products were made before employment by the Company. You should not disclose such inventions or software products in detail, but should identify them only by the titles and dates of documents describing them.)

_____   _____
Employee's Signature   Date

SAMPLE
WORK-FOR-HIRE CONSULTANT AGREEMENT[3]
(Individual Consultant)

This Agreement is made _____ , 19 ____ , between
_____ , a _____ corporation located at
_____ ("Multimedia Company"), and
_____ , an individual residing at
_____ ("Consultant").

In consideration of the mutual covenants herein contained, the parties hereby agree as follows:

1. Services. Consultant agrees to provide the services specified in any Project Schedule that shall, from time to time, be defined and executed by the parties and attached to this Agreement as Exhibit A. Such services are hereinafter referred to as "Services."

2. Term and Termination. This Agreement shall continue until terminated by either party upon ____ days' written notice, provided that termination by Consultant shall not be effective until completion of any specifically defined work set forth on any Project Schedule applicable at the time of such notice, unless otherwise agreed.

3. Payment For Services

(a) Charges. As full compensation for the Services to be provided by Consultant pursuant to any Project Schedule, Multimedia Company agrees to pay Consultant the charges set forth in such Project Schedule.

(b) Reimbursement for Expenses. Multimedia Company shall reimburse Consultant for reasonable out-of-pocket expenses incurred by Consultant in the performance of Services only if specifically included on the applicable Project Schedule. In the event of such agreement, Consultant agrees to maintain appropriate records and to submit copies of all receipts necessary to support such expenses at the intervals and the manner prescribed by Multimedia Company.

4. Independent Contractor. It is understood and agreed that Consultant shall perform the Services as an independent contractor and consultant. Consultant shall not be deemed to be an employee of Multimedia Company. Consultant shall not be entitled to any benefits provided by Multimedia Company to its employees, and Multimedia Company will make no deductions from any of the payments due to Consultant hereunder for state or federal tax purposes. Consultant agrees that he shall be personally responsible for any and all taxes and other payments due on payments consultant receives by him from Multimedia Company hereunder.

5. **Warranty**

(a) **Original Development.** Consultant represents and warrants that all work performed by him for or on behalf of Multimedia Company, and all work products produced thereby, will not knowingly infringe upon or violate any patent, copyright, trade secret, or other property right of any former employer, client, or other third party.

(b) **Warranty of Expertise.** Consultant represents and warrants that he is highly skilled and experienced in providing the Services required under each Project Schedule that Consultant enters into hereunder. Consultant acknowledges that Multimedia Company is relying on his skill and expertise in the foregoing for the performance of this Agreement, and agrees to notify Multimedia Company whenever he does not have the necessary skill and experience to fully perform hereunder.

(c) **Other Agreements.** Consultant represents and warrants that his signing of this Agreement and the performance of his consulting Services hereunder is not and will not be in violation of any other contract, agreement or understanding to which he is a party.

6. **Indemnification.** Consultant shall indemnify Multimedia Company from all claims, losses, and damages that may arise from the breach of any of his obligations under this Agreement.

7. **Protection of Confidential Information**

(a) **Confidential Information.** For purposes of this Agreement, the term "Confidential Information" means all information that is not generally known and that: (i) is obtained by Consultant from Multimedia Company, or that is learned, discovered, developed, conceived, originated, or prepared by Consultant during the process of providing Services to Multimedia Company, and (ii) relates directly to the business or assets of Multimedia Company. The term "Confidential Information" shall include, but shall not be limited to: inventions, discoveries, trade secrets, and know-how; computer software code, designs, routines, algorithms, and structures; product information; research and development information; lists of clients and other information relating thereto; financial data and information; business plans and processes; and any other information of Multimedia Company that Multimedia Company informs Consultant, or that Consultant should know by virtue of his position, is to be kept confidential.

(b) Obligation of Confidentiality. During the term of this Agreement with Multimedia Company, and at all times thereafter, Consultant agrees that he will not disclose to others, use for his own benefit or for the benefit of anyone other than Multimedia Company, or otherwise appropriate or copy, any Confidential Information, whether or not developed by Consultant, except as required in the lawful performance of his obligations to Multimedia Company hereunder. The obligations of Consultant under this paragraph shall not apply to any information that becomes public knowledge through no fault of Consultant.

8.   **Rights to Work Product.**

(a) Disclosure. Consultant agrees to promptly disclose to Multimedia Company all work products developed in whole or in part by Consultant within the scope of this Agreement with Multimedia Company ("Work Product") including but not limited to: any literary works, musical works, sound recordings, audiovisual works, artwork, graphics, software, or any concept, idea, or design relating thereto; and all flow charts, systems design, documentation, manuals, letters, pamphlets, drafts, memoranda, and other documents, writings, or tangible things of any kind relating thereto.

(b) Ownership and Assignment of Rights. All Work Product created by Consultant shall belong exclusively to Multimedia Company and shall, to the extent possible, be considered a work made for hire for Multimedia Company within the meaning of Title 17 of the United States Code. To the extent Multimedia Company does not own such Work Product as a work made for hire, Consultant hereby assigns to Multimedia Company all rights to such Work Products, including but not limited to all other patent rights, copyrights, and trade secret rights. Consultant agrees to execute all documents reasonably requested by Multimedia Company to further evidence the foregoing assignment and to provide all reasonable assistance to Multimedia Company in perfecting or protecting Multimedia Company's rights in such Work Product.

9.   **Duty Upon Termination of Services.** Upon termination of his relationship with Multimedia Company for any reason, or at any time upon request of Multimedia Company, Consultant agrees to deliver to Multimedia Company all materials of any nature that are in his possession or control and that are or contain Confidential Information, or Work Product, or that are otherwise the property of Multimedia Company or of any Multimedia Company customer, including, but not limited to: writings, designs, documents, records, data, memoranda, tapes and disks containing

software, computer source code listings, routines, file layouts, record layouts, system design information, models, manuals, documentation, and notes.

10.   **Subcontracting and Assignment.** This Agreement and the rights and obligations of Consultant hereunder may not be subcontracted, assigned or transferred by Consultant, in whole or in part, without the written consent of Multimedia Company.

11.   **Governing Law.** This contract will be governed by and construed in accordance with the laws of the State of _____ .

12.   **Consent to Breach Not Waiver.** No term or provision hereof shall be deemed waived and no breach excused, unless such waiver or consent be in writing and signed by the party claimed to have waived or consented. No consent by any party to, or waiver of, a breach by the other party shall constitute a consent to, waiver of, or excuse of any other different or subsequent breach.

13.   **Gender.** Whenever the content of this Agreement requires, the masculine gender shall be deemed to include the feminine.

14.   **Entire Agreement.** This Agreement constitutes the complete and exclusive statement of the agreement between the parties with regard to the matters set forth herein, and it supersedes all other agreements, proposals, and representations, oral or written, express or implied, with regard thereto.

IN WITNESS WHEREOF, the parties have executed this Agreement as of the day and year set forth above.

CONSULTANT   MULTIMEDIA COMPANY

By: _____   By:_____

Its:_____   Its:_____

EXHIBIT A
PROJECT SCHEDULE

Attached to and made a part of the Work-for-Hire Consultant Agreement between Multimedia Company and Consultant dated _____ .

1.   Services to Be Provided

2.   Charges

3.   Deliverables

4.   Term

CONSULTANT   MULTIMEDIA COMPANY

By: _____   By:_____

Its: _____   Its:_____

SAMPLE

THIRD-PARTY CONFIDENTIALITY AGREEMENT[4]

The undersigned requests that it be given access to certain Confidential Information that constitutes the proprietary property of _____Corporation ("XYZ"), solely for the limited purpose of evaluating same, and in order to induce XYZ to disclose such Confidential Information, agrees that it will be bound by the following terms and conditions:

1. **CONFIDENTIAL INFORMATION**

   The term "Confidential Information" means all information relating to _____that is disclosed to the undersigned by XYZ (either orally or in a tangible form), including but not limited to inventions, discoveries, processes, and know-how; computer software code, designs, routines, algorithms, and structures; product information; research and development information; information relating to actual and potential customers; financial data and information; business plans; marketing materials and strategies; and any other information regarding the foregoing that XYZ discloses to the undersigned hereunder. Failure to include a confidentiality notice on any materials disclosed to the undersigned shall not give rise to an inference that the information disclosed is not confidential.

   Confidential Information shall not include information that the undersigned can establish (i) is generally known to the public (other than as a result of a breach of this Agreement); (ii) is independently developed by the undersigned; (iii) was lawfully obtained from a third party; or (iv) is later published or generally disclosed to the public by XYZ.

2. **PROTECTION AND USE OF CONFIDENTIAL INFORMATION**

   (a) Limited Use. The undersigned agrees to use the Confidential Information only for the limited time specified herein and solely for the purpose of evaluating XYZ's _____ in order to determine whether to _____ . The undersigned shall have no right to use the Confidential Information for production or commercial purposes without obtaining a license therefore from XYZ.

   (b) Protection. The undersigned hereby agrees to take all steps reasonably necessary to maintain and protect the Confidential Information in the strictest confidence for the benefit of XYZ, and will not, at any time without the express written permission of XYZ, disclose the Confidential Information directly or indirectly to any third person, excepting employees of the undersigned who have expressly agreed in writing to be bound by the terms of this Agreement.

(c) Term of Obligation. The undersigned's obligations with respect to the Confidential Information shall continue for the shorter of _____ (__) years from the date of its receipt of the Confidential Information, or until such information is subject to one of the exclusions set forth above.

3. **RETURN OF CONFIDENTIAL INFORMATION**

The undersigned acknowledges that its limited right to evaluate the Confidential Information shall expire _____ , and agrees that all Confidential Information in a tangible form, including all copies thereof, will be returned to XYZ at that time, or at such earlier time as XYZ may request. At such time, the undersigned also agrees to completely erase and destroy all copies of all portions of any software comprising the Confidential Information in its possession or under its responsibility which may have been loaded onto the undersigned's computers.

4. **DISCLAIMERS**

This Agreement does not require XYZ to disclose any Confidential Information. All Confidential Information disclosed by XYZ is disclosed on an "AS IS" basis. XYZ will not be liable for any damages arising out of use of the Confidential Information, and the use of such Information is at the undersigned's own risk. Neither this Agreement nor the disclosure of any Confidential Information grants the undersigned any license under any patents, copyrights, or trade secrets.

5. **GOVERNING LAW**

This Agreement shall be governed by and construed in accordance with the laws of the State of _____ covering agreements made and to be performed in that State.

Firm Name	Authorized Signature
Address	Type or Print Name
City State Zip	Title
Telephone Number	Date

Endnotes

1   This contract is an example of the way an Employee Agreement might be structured, and the types of provisions that might be included in such an agreement. It is not intended to be used as a form, however, since the structure and content of each contract must be tailored to meet the needs of the situation in which it is to be used, and the law of the jurisdiction that will govern the transaction. Note that this agreement only addresses issues relating to confidentiality and ownership of work product.

2   A provision such as this is used to comply with the Employee Patent Act in Illinois and several other states. Please consult with your attorney regarding the need for such a provision in your state.

3   This contract is an example of the way a Work-for-Hire Consultant Agreement might be structured, and the types of provisions that might be included in such an agreement. It is not intended to be used as a form, however, since the structure and content of each contract must be tailored to meet the needs of the situation in which it is to be used, and the law of the jurisdiction that will govern the transaction.

4   This contract is an example of the way a Confidentiality Agreement might be structured, and the types of provisions that might be included in such an agreement. It is not intended to be used as a form, however, since the structure and content of each contract must be tailored to meet the needs of the situation in which it is to be used, and the law of the jurisdiction that will govern the transaction.

CHAPTER 34

Distribution Agreements

1. Checklist of Issues
2. Sample Multimedia Product Replication and Distribution Agreement
3. Sample Multimedia CD-ROM Product License Agreement

Distribution Agreements

CHECKLIST OF ISSUES

(For Distribution of a Multimedia Product on CD-ROM)

1. **What Is the Subject Matter of the Contract?**
   a. Identify the multimedia product to be provided.
      (1) Which version?
      (2) Are subsequent versions included?
   b. Identify the documentation to be provided.
   c. Identify any other relevant deliverables.
2. **Scope of Rights Granted to Distributor**
   a. What is the form of the license?
      (1) Exclusive or nonexclusive?
      (2) Transferable or nontransferable?
      (3) Worldwide or restricted to a specific territory or market?
   b. What rights do you grant to the distributor?
      (1) Right to purchase and distribute prepackaged copies of the multimedia product?
      (2) Right to copy, package, and distribute the multimedia product?
      (3) Right to use your trademarks?
   c. What is the scope of Distributor's right to purchase and distribute prepackaged copies of the multimedia product?
      (1) What is the procedure for ordering copies of multimedia product
      (2) Is Distributor required to order any minimum quantities?
      (3) Is there a maximum quantity Distributor can order?
      (4) Is Distributor required to commit in advance to specific quantities?
      (5) Does the Distributor have the right to change or cancel orders, and if so, under what terms and conditions?
   d. What is the scope of Distributor's right to copy the multimedia product?

       (1)   Can the Distributor use third parties to replicate the multimedia product and documentation, and if so, must such third parties be preauthorized by you?

       (2)   Are there any restrictions imposed on the replication process?

       (3)   Can the Distributor modify or enhance the multimedia product?

       (4)   How is the multimedia product to be labeled?

   e.   What is the scope of Distributor's right to distribute the multimedia product?

       (1)   How is the multimedia product to be marketed?

          (i)   As a stand-alone product?

          (ii)   Bundled with other hardware or multimedia products?

       (2)   What other restrictions are imposed on the Distributor's marketing activities?

          (a)   Restricted to a specific territory?

          (b)   Restricted to a particular market (for example, the medical services market)?

          (c)   Restricted to a particular class of customers (for example, government agencies)?

3. **Delivery and Returns**

   a.   What deliverables have you agreed to provide to the Distributor?

       (1)   Master copy of multimedia product and documentation?

       (2)   Prepackaged copies of the multimedia product and documentation?

       (3)   Subsequent updates and enhancements?

   b.   What services do you provide to the Distributor?

       (1)   Training?

       (2)   Support?

   c.   If Distributor orders prepackaged copies from you, then:

       (1)   How soon after the Distributor places an order will you deliver the multimedia product to the Distributor?

       (2)   Who pays freight?

       (3)   What about insurance?

       (4)   When does risk of loss pass to Distributor?

       (5)   Does Distributor have right to cancel orders? On what terms?

       (6)   Does Distributor have the right to return copies of product purchased, and if so, under what terms and conditions?

(7)   What are Distributor's rights to return defective products, outdated versions, and so forth?

4. **Distributor's Marketing Obligations**
    a.   What are the Distributor's obligations to market the multimedia product?
        (1)   Is the Distributor required to make any specified marketing efforts (e.g., devote a set dollar amount to advertising, employ a specified number of salespersons devoted full time to marketing the multimedia product, and so forth)?
        (2)   Is the Distributor required to use its "best efforts" to market the multimedia product?
        (3)   Is the Distributor required to meet any sales quotas?
    b.   What marketing assistance will you provide to Distributor?

5. **Multimedia Product Support**
    a.   What support, if any, do you provide for the Distributor?
    b.   Who provides support for the Distributor's customers (you or Distributor)?
    c.   What is the scope of the Distributor's obligations to provide support to its customers?

6. **Price and Payment [where you provide copies]**
    a.   What is the price for each multimedia product ordered by Distributor?
    b.   When is each payment due?
    c.   Are any discounts allowed for volume?
    d.   Do you have the right to change the price during the term of the agreement? If so, does the Distributor get any price protection for outstanding orders?
    e.   Does the Distributor get a credit for returns?

7. **License Fees and Royalties [where Distributor makes copies]**
    a.   Payments by Distributor to you
        (1)   What type of payment will be required?
            (a)   Lump sum (paid-up license)?
            (b)   Percentage royalty per copy?
            (c)   Set dollar royalty per copy?
            (d)   Other (e.g., yearly fee plus per copy fee)?
        (2)   What is the basis of payment calculations?
        (3)   What is the amount of the payment?
        (4)   Do you get an advance payment?
        (5)   Are there any guaranteed or minimum payment amounts?

  (6) When is each payment due?

  (7) Are any discounts allowed for volume?

  (8) Do you have the right to change the price during the term of the agreement? If so, does the Distributor get any price protection?

  (9) Does the Distributor get a credit for returns from end users?

 b. Distributor bookkeeping requirements

  (1) What record-keeping requirements are imposed on the Distributor in order to keep track of all sales or licenses of the multimedia product to ensure that you are paid all sums owed?

  (2) What information must the Distributor record with respect to each sale or license?

  (3) How often must the Distributor send you reports, and what information must be contained in each report?

  (4) What rights do you have to audit the Distributor's books?

8. Taxes

 a. Who pays for any federal, state, or local taxes imposed on the sale or license of the multimedia product by the Distributor?

9. Confidentiality

 a. Is either party obligated to keep confidential any information relating to the other party's products or business?

 b. Does this confidentiality obligation continue after the license agreement ends?

10. Warranties

 a. Is your multimedia product licensed "AS IS" or do you make any warranties?

 b. What express warranties (if any) do you make to the distributor?

  (1) Warranty that you have the right to enter into the agreement?

  (2) Warranty of performance of the multimedia product?

  (3) Warranty of noninfringement of patents, copyrights, and trade secrets?

  (4) Warranty as to minimum equipment required to support the multimedia product?

  (5) Warranty as to the operating system and any other multimedia product required to support the multimedia product?

 c. Do you make any of these warranties direct to the end user, or is the Distributor authorized to pass on any warranties to the end user customer?

    d. How long does the warranty last?

    e. Have you disclaimed all express warranties not specifically included in the contract?

    f. Have you disclaimed the warranties of merchantability and fitness for particular purpose implied by law?

    g. If the multimedia product fails to work as warranted, have you limited the Distributor's remedy to repair or some other specified remedy (e.g., refund)?

    h. If the multimedia product fails to work as warranted, have you limited the end user's remedy to repair or some other specified remedy (e.g., refund)?

    i. Are there any conditions that will void the warranty?

11. **Limitations of Liability**

    a. Is there a limit on the dollar amount of damages to which you are exposed in the event the multimedia product fails to work properly?

    b. Is there a limit on the *type* of damages to which you are exposed in the event the multimedia product fails to work properly (e.g., have you excluded liability for consequential damages, such as lost profits, or claims by customers and other third parties)?

12. **Indemnification**

    a. Will you agree to pay any damages or expenses suffered by the Distributor and/or its customers if your ownership rights to the multimedia product are challenged by anyone? If so, under what terms and conditions?

    b. Will the Distributor pay all damages suffered by you if the Distributor makes any misrepresentations to its customers?

    c. Does the indemnifying party have the right to control or participate in the defense?

    d. What are the conditions for indemnification?

       (1) Timely notice of claims?

       (2) Cooperation in defense?

       (3) Exception for claims caused by indemnitee's misconduct or gross negligence

    e. Are there any limits on indemnification liability?

13. **Default**

    a. What are each party's rights in the event of a breach of the agreement by the other party?

       (1) Suspend performance?

      (2)   Terminate contract?

      (3)   Liquidated damages?

      (4)   Injunction?

      (5)   Other?

   b.   Is the nonbreaching party required to give notice of the breach to the other party?

   c.   Does the breaching party have an opportunity to cure its breach before the other party can terminate the agreement?

14.   Term and Termination

   a.   What is the term of the distributor's right to distribute your multimedia product?

   b.   Does the Distributor have the right to renew the agreement when it expires?

   c.   Is the right to renew conditioned upon the Distributor's performance or some other criteria?

   d.   Does either party have the right to terminate the agreement before it would otherwise end? If so, under what circumstances?

   e.   What happens on termination?

      (1)   Distributor must discontinue marketing and distribution of multimedia product

      (2)   Distributor must destroy or return all copies of multimedia product and documentation

      (3)   Distributor must certify destruction and/or return of all materials.

   f.   If the Distributor was supporting the multimedia product for its customers, who will provide such support after the license ends?

   g.   Do any obligations survive termination?

      (1)   Confidentiality?

      (2)   Indemnification?

      (3)   Payments due and owing (fees, taxes, royalties, and so forth)?

   h.   Does Distributor have the right to return inventory for refund upon termination of the Agreement?

15.   Assignment Rights

   a.   Do you have the right to assign the distribution agreement?

   b.   Does the Distributor have the right to assign the distribution agreement?

16. **Export Regulations**
    a. Does the Distributor have the right to export the multimedia product to other countries?
    b. If so, has the Distributor agreed to comply with federal export regulations?
17. **Miscellaneous**
    a. **Governing Law.** What state's law will govern any disputes?
    b. **Notices.** Is there a provision outlining how notices are to be given and when they are effective?
    c. **Waiver.** Is there a provision that a waiver of rights on one occasion shall not be deemed a waiver on future occasions?
    d. **Severability.** Is there a provision that permits the contract to continue in force even if certain provisions are deemed unenforceable (severability clause)?
    e. **Entire Agreement.** Is this contract the entire agreement of the parties?

SAMPLE
MULTIMEDIA PRODUCT REPLICATION AND
DISTRIBUTION AGREEMENT[1]
(U.S. Distribution)

This Agreement is made and entered into on ＿＿＿＿＿＿ , 199 ＿ , by and
between ＿＿＿＿＿＿＿＿＿＿＿＿＿＿＿＿＿ , a ＿＿＿＿＿ corporation located
at ＿＿＿＿＿＿＿＿＿＿＿ , ("Distributor") and ＿＿＿＿＿＿＿＿＿＿＿ ,
a ＿＿＿＿ corporation located at ＿＿＿＿＿＿＿＿＿ , ("Vendor").

BACKGROUND

A. Vendor is the developer and owner of all rights to the Multimedia Title
identified on Exhibit A.

B. Vendor desires to enter into a distribution agreement with Distributor
whereby Distributor will be responsible for replicating and packaging Vendor's
Multimedia Title and associated Documentation, and distributing such packaged
Multimedia Title to Retail Dealers and directly to End User customers in accordance
with the terms and conditions of this Agreement.

C. Distributor desires to obtain the right to replicate and package Vendor's
Multimedia Title and Documentation, and to distribute same in accordance with the
terms of this Agreement.

NOW THEREFORE, the parties hereby agree as follows:

1. DEFINITIONS.

(a) Multimedia Title means Vendor's multimedia product identified on
Exhibit A, including all subsequent versions thereof provided to Distributor pursuant to this Agreement.

(b) Documentation means the printed collateral materials to be provided to
End Users for use of the Multimedia Title (such as instruction/user manuals, tem-
plates, overlays, quick reference guides, brochures, data sheets, and registration
cards), that are identified on Exhibit A, and all subsequent versions thereof provided
to Distributor pursuant to this Agreement.

(c) End-User Agreement means the written license agreement attached
hereto as Exhibit B that governs the use of the Multimedia Title by End Users, and
which is to be included with each copy of the Multimedia Title packaged by Distributor hereunder.

(d) Product means a copy of the Multimedia Title, Documentation, and End-
User Agreement, packaged together in accordance with this Agreement.

(e) **End User** means a person or entity that acquires a copy of the Product for use rather than resale or distribution.

(f) **Retail Dealer** means a third party who acquires a copy of the Product from Distributor pursuant to a Retail Dealer Agreement that complies with the requirements of this Agreement, and that grants such party the right to distribute copies of the Product to End User customers, but without the right to license any other dealers or distributors.

(g) **Vendor Trademarks** means the trademarks, trade names, and logos used by Vendor and identified on Exhibit A.

(h) **Territory** means the United States of America.

2.   **LICENSE**

(a) **Rights Granted to Distributor.** Vendor grants Distributor a nonexclusive license and right to:

(1) reproduce the Multimedia Title, Documentation, and the End-User Agreement on CD-ROM discs in accordance with Vendor's specifications;

(2) package the Multimedia Title, Documentation, and the End-User Agreement in the manner specified by Vendor;

(3) utilize the Vendor Trademarks in connection with the replication of the Multimedia Title, printing of the Documentation, and packaging and distribution of the Product, in the manner specified by Vendor; and

(4) distribute copies of the Product to Retail Dealers in the Territory for further distribution to End Users in the Territory, and direct to End Users in the Territory, subject to the restrictions set forth in this Agreement.

(b) **Rights Reserved to Vendor.** Distributor acknowledges that the Multimedia Title and Documentation are the property of Vendor or its licensors and that Distributor has no rights in thefore going except those expressly granted by this Agreement. Nothing herein shall be construed as restricting Vendor's right to sell, lease, license, modify, publish, or otherwise distribute the Multimedia Title or Documentation, in whole or in part, to any other person.

3.   **REPRODUCTION BY DISTRIBUTOR**

(a) **Reproduction and Packaging.** Distributor agrees to accurately replicate the Multimedia Title and print the Documentation provided by Vendor, to apply labels to the CD-ROM discs containing the Multimedia Title in the form specified by Vendor, and to package these items as specified by Vendor.

(b) **Vendor Trademarks and Legends.** Distributor shall include copies of the Vendor Trademarks, copyright notices and other proprietary rights legends, on all copies of the Documentation and CD-ROM discs containing the Multimedia Title that it manufactures, in the manner specified by Vendor.

(c) **Materials.** Unless otherwise provided, Distributor will supply the materials for the Product (CD-ROM discs, jewel cases, paper, binding materials, packaging materials, and so forth) in accordance with Vendor's specifications. If Distributor is unable to obtain such materials or other equivalents in necessary quantities, the parties will select mutually agreeable substitute materials.

(d) **Samples.** Vendor may request samples of Products or any components thereof at any time for review to assure Vendor's quality standards are being satisfied.

(e) **Subcontracting.** Distributor may subcontract to third parties such portions of the reproduction, printing, and packaging of the Multimedia Title, Documentation, and End User Agreements, as Distributor may, in its discretion, determine; provided, however, that Distributor remains primarily liable for the performance of any such subcontractor and that any replication of the Multimedia Title may be subcontracted only to parties who have been previously approved by Vendor and who agree in writing to be bound by the confidentiality provisions of this Agreement.

4.   DISTRIBUTION BY DISTRIBUTOR

(a) **Inventory.** Distributor will maintain an inventory of Products sufficient to serve adequately the needs of its Retail Dealers and End User customers.

(b) **Packaging.** Distributor will distribute the Products only as packaged in accordance with this Agreement, with all packaging, warranties, disclaimers and End User Agreements intact. Distributor will make copies of the current End User Agreement available to its Retail Dealers and End User customers.

(c) **Product Returns.** Distributor agrees to honor any refund requests received from its Retail Dealers or End User customers pursuant to the terms of the End User Agreement relating to Products distributed by Distributor.

(d) **Cost of Distribution.** All costs relating to replication, packaging, and distribution of the Multimedia Title and Documentation shall be borne by Distributor.

(e) **Prices.** Distributor is free to determine its own prices for the Products to its Retail Dealers and End User customers.

(f) **Retail Dealer Agreements.** Distributor may establish Retail Dealers for the Products, and sell Products to such Retail Dealers for resale to End Users in the

Territory, on such terms and conditions as may be determined by Distributor, provided, however, that each Retail Dealer shall execute a Retail Dealer Agreement that includes the Retail Dealer Terms attached hereto as Exhibit D.

5. DISTRIBUTOR MARKETING OBLIGATIONS

Distributor agrees to use its best efforts to market, promote, sublicense, and distribute the Multimedia Title. Distributor agrees to advertise the Multimedia Title in appropriate commercial media, to identify and contact potential End Users using direct mailings and other reasonable means, and to accurately advise potential End Users on the specifications, selection, use, and functionality of the Multimedia Title in accordance with the Documentation.

6. VENDOR'S DELIVERY OBLIGATIONS

Vendor will deliver the current version of the Multimedia Title and Documentation to Distributor immediately following execution of this Agreement. Vendor will provide Distributor with a gold master of the Multimedia Title or another mutually agreeable computer-readable form that can be reproduced by Distributor, and one copy of the Documentation in either camera-ready copy or computer-readable form. Vendor will also provide Distributor with the format for the labels to be applied to or imprinted on the CD-ROM discs containing the Multimedia Title, and the packaging to be used for the Multimedia Title.

7. VENDOR'S SUPPORT OBLIGATIONS

(a) Support for End Users. Vendor will provide support to End Users of the Multimedia Title to be distributed hereunder, in accordance with its then-current published Multimedia Title Support Policy, if any.

(b) Support for Distributor. Vendor will provide Distributor, without charge, such technical information, current maintenance documentation, and telephone assistance as is necessary to enable Distributor to effectively reproduce, package, and distribute the Multimedia Title.

8. VENDOR'S WARRANTIES

(a) Authority. Vendor represents that it has the right and authority to enter into this Agreement and to grant to Distributor the rights to the Multimedia Title and Documentation granted in this Agreement.

(b) Noninfringement. Vendor warrants to Distributor that the reproduction and distribution of the Multimedia Title and Documentation by Distributor, the marketing and distribution thereof by its Retail Dealers, and the use of the Vendor

Trademarks in connection therewith, in accordance with the provisions of this Agreement, will not infringe upon or misappropriate the proprietary rights of any third party.

(c) **End User Warranties.** Vendor will provide a warranty for the End Users of the Multimedia Title as set forth in the End User Agreement attached as Exhibit B. Distributor is not authorized to make any warranties on Vendor's behalf.

(d) **DISCLAIMER. THE FOREGOING ARE THE ONLY WARRANTIES MADE BY VENDOR. VENDOR SPECIFICALLY DISCLAIMS ALL OTHER WARRANTIES, EXPRESS OR IMPLIED, INCLUDING, BUT NOT LIMITED TO, THE IMPLIED WARRANTIES OF MERCHANTABILITY AND FITNESS FOR A PARTICULAR PURPOSE.**

9. DISTRIBUTOR WARRANTIES

(a) **Authority.** Distributor represents that it has the right and authority to enter into this Agreement.

(b) **Replication.** Distributor represents and warrants that it will accurately replicate the Multimedia Title and Documentation, and that all CD-ROM discs containing any portion of the Multimedia Title that are distributed by Distributor will not contain any viruses, worms, date bombs, time bombs, or other code that is specifically designed to cause the Multimedia Title to cease operating or to damage, interrupt, or interfere with any End User's software or data.

(c) **Returns and replacement warranty**. Distributor will provide CD-ROM replacement warranty service for all End User customers who have received damaged or defective copies of the CD-ROM Title replicated by Distributor. Distributor will pay the costs involved in replacing copies of the CD-ROM Title where the defect was due to the fault of Distributor. For copies of the CD-ROM Title returned to Distributor for reasons other than manufacturing defects caused by Distributor, the parties will agree, on a case-by-case basis, as to who should pay the cost of the refund or replacement copy.

10. ROYALTIES

(a) **Amount.** Distributor will pay Vendor a Royalty in accordance with the Royalty Schedule attached hereto as Exhibit C, for each copy of the Product delivered to a Retail Dealer or an End User by Distributor, provided, however, that no Royalty shall be due for copies of Products returned to Distributor for refund in accordance with the End-User Agreement, or because of defects or errors, regardless of source.

(b) Taxes. Distributor will pay, or require its Retail Dealers or End-User customers to pay, all federal, state, and local taxes designated, levied, or based upon the sale of Products by Distributor.

(c) Payment and Reports. Within twenty (20) days after the end of each month, Distributor will remit to Vendor the Royalty due on copies of Products delivered by Distributor to Retail Dealers and to End User customers during the immediately preceding month, and provide Vendor with a written report, specifying the number of copies of Products that Distributor has shipped during the immediately prior month and the calculation of the amounts due to Vendor in connection therewith.

(d) Book and Records. Distributor agrees to maintain adequate books and records relating to the production, packaging and shipping of Products to Retail Dealers and End User customers. Such books and records shall be available at their place of keeping for inspection by Vendor or its representative, for the purpose of determining whether the correct Royalties have been paid to Vendor in accordance with the terms of this Agreement, and whether Distributor has otherwise complied with the terms of this Agreement. Vendor shall have the right to conduct such an audit upon ten (10) days' advance notice twice each year. In the event such an audit discloses an underpayment of more than five percent (5%), then Distributor shall pay the costs of such audit.

(e) Failure to Pay. Any Royalty payment or part of a payment that is not paid when due shall bear interest at the rate of 1.5 percent per month, or at the highest contract rate allowed by law, whichever is less, from its due date until paid. Failure of Distributor to pay any Royalties or other charges when due shall constitute sufficient cause for Vendor to immediately suspend its performance hereunder and/or to terminate this Agreement.

11. CONFIDENTIALITY.

Distributor acknowledges that, from time to time, it may be exposed to certain information concerning the Multimedia Title and proposed new versions of the Multimedia Title that is Vendor's confidential and proprietary information and not generally known to the public ("Confidential Information"). Distributor agrees that it will take appropriate steps to protect such Confidential Information from unauthorized disclosure, that it will not disclose such Information to any third party, and that it will not use any Confidential Information (other than as authorized by this Agreement) without the prior written consent of Vendor. Distributor's obligations with respect to Confidential Information shall continue for the shorter of three (3) years from the date of termination of this Agreement, or until such information becomes publicly known other than by breach of this Agreement by Distributor.

12. VENDOR TRADEMARKS

(a) **Use.** Distributor acknowledges that the Vendor Trademarks are trademarks owned solely and exclusively by Vendor, and agrees to use the Vendor Trademarks only in the form and manner and with appropriate legends as prescribed by Vendor. Distributor agrees not to use any other trademark or service mark in connection with any of the Vendor Trademarks without prior written approval of Vendor. Distributor agrees to mark all advertising and other uses of the Vendor Trademarks with a legend indicating the Vendor Trademarks are the property of Vendor and that they are being used under license from Vendor, together with any other legends or markings which may be required by law. All use of the Vendor Trademarks shall inure to the benefit of Vendor.

(b) **Vendor Review.** From time to time as Vendor shall reasonably request, Distributor shall furnish to Vendor for its examination samples of CD-ROM discs containing the Multimedia Title, all Product packaging and Documentation, as well as advertising, brochures, and other materials used in connection with the marketing of the Multimedia Title.

(c) **Notices.** Distributor shall not remove, alter, cover or obfuscate any copyright notice or other proprietary rights notice placed in or on the Multimedia Title or Documentation by Vendor, whether in machine language or human-readable form.

13. INDEMNIFICATION

(a) **By Vendor.** Vendor will defend, indemnify, and hold Distributor harmless from and against any and all liabilities, losses, damages, costs, and expenses (including legal fees and expenses) associated with any claim or action brought against Distributor for actual or alleged infringement of any U.S. patent, copyright, trademark, service mark, trade secret, or other property right based upon the duplication, sale, license or use of the Multimedia Title or Documentation by Distributor in accordance with this Agreement, provided that Distributor promptly notifies Vendor in writing of the claim and allows Vendor to control, and fully cooperates with Vendor in, the defense and all related settlement negotiations. Vendor shall have no liability for any settlement or compromise made without its consent. Upon notice of an alleged infringement, or if in the Vendor's opinion such a claim is likely, Vendor shall have the right, at its option, to obtain the right for Distributor to continue to exercise the rights granted under this Agreement, or modify the Multimedia

Title so that it is no longer infringing. In the event that neither of the above options are reasonably available, in Vendor's sole opinion, Vendor may terminate this Agreement.

(b) By Distributor. Distributor shall indemnify and hold Vendor harmless from and against any and all liabilities, losses, damages, costs, and expenses (including legal fees and expenses) associated with any claim or action brought against Vendor that may arise from the improper or unauthorized replication, packaging, marketing, distribution, or support of the Multimedia Title by Distributor or its Retail Dealers, including claims based on representations, warranties, or misrepresentations made by Distributor, inadequate installation, support, or assistance by Distributor or its Retail Dealers, or any other improper or unauthorized act or failure to act on the part of Distributor.

14. LIMITATION OF LIABILITY

Vendor's liability to distributor shall be limited to direct damages and, except as provided in the section titled "indemnification," shall not exceed the amount of the royalties paid by distributor to vendor hereunder. In no event will vendor be liable for incidental, special, or consequential damages (including lost profits) suffered by distributor, even if it has previously been advised of the possibility of such damages.

15. TERM AND TERMINATION

(a) Term. This Agreement will continue in effect for _____ (__) years from the date hereof ("Initial Term"). Upon expiration of the Initial Term and each Renewal Term thereafter, this Agreement will be automatically renewed for an additional one (1) year term ("Renewal Term") unless terminated by either party upon ninety (90) days' notice prior to the expiration of the Initial Term or any Renewal Term.

(b) Termination for Breach. Either party may terminate this Agreement prior to the expiration of any Term in the event of a material breach of the terms or conditions of this Agreement by the other party which breach is not cured within thirty (30) days of written notice from the party not in breach. In addition to these rights of termination, each party will have the right, in the event of an uncured breach by the other party, to avail itself of all remedies or causes of action, in law or equity, for damages as a result of such breach.

(c) Effect of Termination. Upon termination of this Agreement for any reason, Distributor will immediately cease duplication of the Multimedia Title and Documentation, and will return to Vendor, at Distributor's expense, the master versions of all Multimedia Title, Documentation, and Confidential Information of Vendor. Distributor shall remit all Royalties and other fees due to Vendor within ten (10) days of such termination.

(d) **Effect on End Users.** Termination by either party will not affect the rights of any End User under the terms of the End User Agreement.

16.   GENERAL PROVISIONS

(a) **Assignment.** This Agreement may not be assigned by Distributor or by operation of law to any other person, persons, firms, or corporation without the express written approval of Vendor.

(b) **Notices.** All notices and demands hereunder shall be in writing and shall be served by personal service or by mail at the address of the receiving party set forth in this Agreement (or at such different address as may be designated by such party by written notice to the other party). All notices or demands by mail shall be by certified or registered mail, return receipt requested, or by nationally recognized private express courier, and shall be deemed complete upon receipt.

(c) **Governing Law.** This Agreement shall be governed by and construed in accordance with the substantive laws of the State of _____ .

(d) **Relationship of the Parties.** Each party is acting as an independent contractor and not as an agent, partner, or joint venturer with the other party for any purpose. Except as provided in this Agreement, neither party shall have any right, power, or authority to act or to create any obligation, express or implied, on behalf of the other.

(e) **Force Majeure.** Neither party shall be responsible for delays or failure of performance resulting from acts beyond the reasonable control of such party. Such acts shall include, but not be limited to, acts of God, strikes, walkouts, riots, acts of war, epidemics, failure of suppliers to perform, governmental regulations, power failure(s), earthquakes, or other disasters.

(f) **Survival of Certain Provisions.** The indemnification and confidentiality obligations set forth in the Agreement shall survive the termination of the Agreement by either party for any reason.

(g) **Headings.** The titles and headings of the various sections and paragraphs in this Agreement are intended solely for convenience of reference and are not intended for any other purpose whatsoever, or to explain, modify, or place any construction upon or on any of the provisions of this Agreement.

(h) **All Amendments in Writing.** No provisions in either party's purchase orders, or in any other business forms employed by either party, will supersede the terms and conditions of this Agreement, and no supplement, modification, or amendment of this Agreement shall be binding, unless executed in writing by a duly authorized representative of each party to this Agreement.

(i) Entire Agreement. The parties have read this Agreement and agree to be bound by its terms, and further agree that it constitutes the complete and entire agreement of the parties and supersedes all previous communications, oral or written, and all other communications between them relating to the license and to the subject matter hereof. No representations or statements of any kind made by either party, which are not expressly stated herein, shall be binding on such party.

IN WITNESS WHEREOF, the parties have executed this Agreement as of the date set forth above.

[DISTRIBUTOR]   [VENDOR]

By:_____   By:_____

Its: _____   Its:_____

EXHIBIT A

I.   MULTIMEDIA TITLE

II. DOCUMENTATION

III. VENDOR TRADEMARKS

EXHIBIT B
END-USER AGREEMENT

EXHIBIT C
ROYALTY SCHEDULE

EXHIBIT D
RETAIL DEALER TERMS

Each Retail Dealer Agreement between Distributor and a Retail Dealer shall contain terms substantially similar in intent and legal effect to the following:

1. DISTRIBUTION BY RETAIL DEALER

(1) Territory. Retailer Dealer will distribute Products solely to End Users located in the United States of America.

(2) Inventory. Retail Dealer will maintain an inventory of Products sufficient to serve adequately the needs of its End-User customers.

(3) Packaging. Retail Dealer will distribute the Products only as packaged when received from Distributor, with all packaging, warranties, disclaimers and End-User Agreements intact. Retail Dealer will make copies of the current End-User Agreement available to its End-User customers.

(4) Product Returns. Retail Dealer agrees to honor any refund requests received from its End-User customers pursuant to the terms of the End-User Agreement relating to Products distributed by Retail Dealer.

(5) Prices. Retail Dealer is free to determine the prices at which it will make the Products available to its End-User customers.

2. OTHER ISSUES

a. Support for Retail Dealer. Retail Dealer understands and acknowledges that Vendor will not provide any support direct to Retail Dealer, and that any support required by Retail Dealer should be obtained from Distributor.

b. End-User Warranties. Vendor will provide a warranty for the End Users of the Multimedia Title as set forth in the End-User Agreement. Retail Dealer is not authorized to make any warranties on Vendor's behalf.

c. DISCLAIMER. THE FOREGOING ARE THE ONLY WARRANTIES MADE BY VENDOR. VENDOR MAKES NO WARRANTIES TO RETAIL DEALER AND SPECIFICALLY DISCLAIMS ALL WARRANTIES, EXPRESS OR IMPLIED, INCLUDING, BUT NOT LIMITED TO, THE IMPLIED WARRANTIES OF MERCHANTABILITY AND FITNESS FOR A PARTICULAR PURPOSE.

SAMPLE
MULTIMEDIA CD-ROM[2]
PRODUCT LICENSE AGREEMENT

**1. NOTICE. WE ARE WILLING TO LICENSE THE MULTIMEDIA CD-
ROM PRODUCT TITLED "_____" ("MULTIMEDIA PRODUCT")
TO YOU ONLY ON THE CONDITION THAT YOU ACCEPT ALL OF THE
TERMS CONTAINED IN THIS LICENSE AGREEMENT. PLEASE READ THIS
LICENSE AGREEMENT CAREFULLY BEFORE OPENING THE SEALED DISC
PACKAGE. BY OPENING THIS PACKAGE YOU AGREE TO BE BOUND BY
THE TERMS OF THIS AGREEMENT. IF YOU DO NOT AGREE TO THESE
TERMS WE ARE UNWILLING TO LICENSE THE MULTIMEDIA PRODUCT
TO YOU, AND YOU SHOULD NOT OPEN THE DISC PACKAGE. IN SUCH
CASE, PROMPTLY RETURN THE UNOPENED DISC PACKAGE AND ALL
OTHER MATERIAL IN THIS PACKAGE ALONG WITH PROOF OF PAY-
MENT, TO THE AUTHORIZED DEALER FROM WHOM YOU OBTAINED IT
FOR A FULL REFUND OF THE PRICE YOU PAID.**

2.   Ownership and License. This is a license agreement and NOT an agreement
for sale. It permits you to use one copy of the Multimedia Product on a single computer. The Multimedia Product, including any text, data, music, sound recordings,
images, photographs, animations, motion pictures, and other video incorporated in
the Multimedia Product, is owned by us or our licensors, and is protected by U.S.
and international copyright laws. Your rights to use the Multimedia Product are
specified in this Agreement, and we retain all rights not expressly granted to you in
this Agreement.

3.   Grant of License. You may use one copy of the Multimedia Product on a single computer. After you have run that portion of the Multimedia Product called
"installation" on your computer, you may use the Multimedia Product on a different
computer only if you first delete the files installed by the installation program from
the first computer. Other than the foregoing, you may not copy any portion of the
Multimedia Product to your computer hard disk or any other media. You may not
copy any of the documentation or other printed materials accompanying the Multimedia Product.

4.   Transfer and Other Restrictions. You may not rent, lend, or lease this Multimedia Product. However, you may transfer this license to use the Multimedia

Product to another party on a permanent basis by transferring this copy of the License Agreement, the Multimedia Product, and all documentation.

Such transfer of possession terminates your license from us. Such other party shall be licensed under the terms of this Agreement upon its acceptance of this Agreement by its initial use of the Multimedia Product. If you transfer the Multimedia Product, you must remove the installation files from your hard disk and you may not retain any copies of those files for your own use.

5. **Limited Warranty.** We make the following limited warranties, for a period of _____ (____) days from the date you acquired the Multimedia Product from us or our authorized dealer:

(a) **Media.** The disc containing the Multimedia Product will be free from defects in materials and workmanship under normal use. If the disc fails to conform to this warranty, you may, as your sole and exclusive remedy, obtain a replacement free of charge if you return the defective disc to us with a dated proof of purchase.

(b) **Multimedia Product.** The Multimedia Product in this package will materially conform to the documentation that accompanies it. If the Multimedia Product fails to operate in accordance with this warranty, you may, as your sole and exclusive remedy, return the Multimedia Product and the documentation to the authorized dealer from whom you acquired it, along with a dated proof of purchase, specifying the problem, and we will provide you with a new disc containing the Multimedia Product or a full refund at our election.

(c) **WARRANTY DISCLAIMER. WE DO NOT WARRANT THAT THE MULTIMEDIA PRODUCT WILL MEET YOUR REQUIREMENTS OR THAT ITS OPERATION WILL BE UNINTERRUPTED OR ERROR-FREE. WE EXCLUDE AND EXPRESSLY DISCLAIM ALL EXPRESS AND IMPLIED WARRANTIES NOT STATED HEREIN, INCLUDING THE IMPLIED WARRANTIES OF MERCHANTABILITY AND FITNESS FOR A PARTICULAR PURPOSE.**

Some states do not allow the exclusion of implied warranties, so the above exclusion may not apply to you. This limited warranty gives you specific legal rights, and you may also have other legal rights, which vary from state to state.

6. **LIMITATION OF LIABILITY. OUR LIABILITY TO YOU FOR ANY LOSSES SHALL BE LIMITED TO DIRECT DAMAGES, AND SHALL NOT EXCEED THE AMOUNT YOU ORIGINALLY PAID FOR THE MULTIMEDIA PRODUCT. IN NO EVENT WILL WE BE LIABLE TO YOU FOR ANY INDIRECT, SPECIAL, INCIDENTAL, OR CONSEQUENTIAL DAMAGES (INCLUDING LOSS OF PROFITS) EVEN IF WE HAVE BEEN ADVISED OF THE POSSIBILITY OF SUCH DAMAGES.**

Some jurisdictions do not allow these limitations or exclusions, so they may not apply to you.

7.   United States Government Restricted Rights. The Multimedia Product and documentation are provided with Restricted Rights. Use, duplication or disclosure by the U.S. Government or any agency or instrumentality thereof is subject to restrictions as set forth in subdivision (c)(1)(ii) of the Rights in Technical Data and Computer Multimedia Product clause at 48 C. F.R. 252.227-7013, or in subdivision (c)(1) and (2) of the Commercial Computer Multimedia Product—Restricted Rights Clause at 48 C.F.R. 52.227-19, as applicable. Manufacturer is [insert name and address of licensor].

8.   Termination. This license and your right to use this Multimedia Product automatically terminate if you fail to comply with any provisions of this Agreement, destroy the copy of the Multimedia Product in your possession, or voluntarily return the Multimedia Product to us. Upon termination you will destroy all copy of the Multimedia Product and documentation.

9.   Miscellaneous Provisions. This Agreement will be governed by and construed in accordance with the substantive laws of [State]. This is the entire agreement between us relating to the Multimedia Product, and supersedes any prior purchase order, communications, advertising or representations concerning the contents of this package. No change or modification of this Agreement will be valid unless it is in writing, and is signed by us.

If you have any questions about this Agreement, write to us at [_____ _____] or call us at (800) _____ - _____ .

Endnote

1   This contract is an example of the way a Multimedia Product Replication and Distribution Agreement might be structured, and the types of provisions that might be included in such an agreement. It is not intended to be used as a form, however, since the structure and content of each contract must be tailored to meet the needs of the situation in which it is to be used, and the law of the governing jurisdiction.

2   This contract is an example of the way a multimedia CD-ROM Product License Agreement (sometimes referred to as a Shrinkwrap License) might be structured, and the types of provisions that might be included in such an agreement. It is designed as an End-User Agreement to be packaged with a Multimedia Product marketed on a CD-ROM disc. However, it is important to understand that the use of an unsigned Shrinkwrap License Agreement packaged with the product presents a significant risk that the contract will be found to be unenforceable in the event of a dispute.

PART 6

Appendices

Selected Unions and Professional Associations

1. Writers
2. Producers
3. Directors
4. Musicians
5. Performers
6. Cartoonists/Graphic Artists
7. Songwriters
8. Photographers

Selected Unions and Professional Associations

1. Writers

American Society of Journalists & Authors
1501 Broadway
Suite 302
New York, NY 10036
Phone: (212) 997-0947
Fax: (212) 768-7414

Author's Guild
330 West 42nd Street
29th Floor
New York, NY 10036
Phone: (212) 563-5904
Fax: (212) 564-5363

National Writer's Union
873 Broadway
Suite 203
New York, NY 10036
Phone: (212) 254-0279
Fax: (212) 254-0673

Writers Guild of America, East, Inc. (WGA East)
555 West 57th Street
New York, NY 10019
Phone: (212) 767-7800
Fax: (212) 582-1909

Writers Guild of America, West, Inc. (WGA West)
8955 Beverly Boulevard
West Hollywood, CA 90048
Phone: (310) 550-1000
Fax: (310) 205-2594

2. Producers

Producers Guild of America, Inc.
400 South Beverly Drive
Suite 211
Beverly Hills, CA 90212
Phone: (310) 557-0807
Fax: (310) 557-0436

3. Directors

Directors Guild of America (DGA)
Chicago Office:
400 North Michigan Avenue
Suite 307
Chicago, IL 60611
Phone: (312) 644-5050
Fax: (312) 644-5776

Los Angeles Office:
7920 Sunset Boulevard
Los Angeles, CA 90046
Phone: (310) 289-2000
Fax: (310) 289-2029

New York Office:
110 West 57th Street
New York, NY 10019
Phone: (212) 581-0370
Fax: (212) 581-1441

4. Musicians

American Federation of Musicians (AF of M)
1777 North Vine Street
Suite 500
Hollywood, CA 90028
Phone: (213) 461-3441 Fax: (213) 462-8340

5. Performers

American Federation of Television and
Radio Artists (AFTRA)

Chicago Office:
75 East Wacker Drive
14th Floor
Chicago, IL 60601
Phone: (312) 372-8081
Fax: (312) 372-5025

Hollywood Office:
6922 Hollywood Blvd.
Suite 800
Hollywood, CA 90028
Phone: (213) 461-8111
Fax: (213) 463-9040
Contact: Karen Stuart, Ext. 400

Nashville Office:
1108 17th Avenue South
Box 121087
Nashville, TN 37212
Phone: (615) 327-2944
Fax: (615) 329-2803

New York Office:
260 Madison Avenue
New York, NY 10016
Phone: (212) 532-0800
Fax: (212) 545-1238

Screen Actors Guild (SAG)

Chicago Office:
75 East Wacker Drive
14th Floor
Chicago, IL 60601
Phone: (312) 372-8081
Fax: (312) 372-5025

Dallas Office:
6060 N. Central Expressway
Suite 302
Dallas, TX 75206
Phone: (214) 363-8300
Fax: (214) 365-5386

Los Angeles Office:
5757 Wilshire Blvd.
Los Angeles, CA 90036
Phone: (213) 954-1600
Fax: (213) 549-6801
Contact: Mike Prohaska
213-549-6847

New York Office:
1515 Broadway
44th Floor
New York, NY 10036
Phone: (212) 944-1030
Fax: (212) 944-6774

Nashville Office:
P.O. Box 121087
Nashville, TN 37212
Phone: (615) 327-2958
Fax: (615) 329-2803

San Francisco Office:
235 Pine Street
Suite 1100
San Francisco, CA 94104
Phone: (415) 391-7510
Fax: (415) 391-1108

6. Cartoonists/Graphic Artists

Graphic Artists Guild
11 West 20th Street
8th Floor
New York, NY 10011
Phone: (212) 463-7730
Fax: (212) 463-8779

International Alliance of Theatrical and Stage Employees
(IATSE) Motion Picture Screen Cartoonists,
Local 839
4729 Lankershim Blvd.,
North Hollywood, CA 91602-1864
Phone: (818) 766-7151
Fax: (818) 506-4805

7. Songwriters

Songwriters Guild of America (SGA)

Hollywood Office:
6430 Sunset Blvd.
Hollywood, CA 90028
Phone: (213) 462-1108
Fax: (213) 462-5430

Nashville Office:
1222 Sixteenth Avenue S.
Nashville, TN 37212
Phone: (615) 329-1782
Fax: (615) 329-2623

New York Office:
1500 Harbor Road
Weehawken, NJ 07087-6732
Phone: (201) 867-7603
Fax: (201) 867-7535

8. Photographers

American Society of Media Photographers
14 Washington Road
Suite 502
Princeton Junction, NJ 08550
Phone: (609) 799-8300
Fax: (609) 799-2233

IATSE International Photographers
(Cinematographers)
Local 659
7715 Sunset Blvd., Suite 300
Hollywood, CA 90046
Phone: (213) 876-0160
Fax: (213) 876-6383

Clearance Assistance

1. Rights Clearance Agencies
2. Copyright Search Firms
3. Trademark Search Firms
4. Music Licensing Organizations

CHAPTER 36

Clearance Assistance

1. Rights Clearance Agencies

BZ/Rights & Permissions, Inc.
(Barbara Zimmerman)
125 West 72nd Street
New York, NY 10023
Phone: (212) 580-0615
Fax: (212) 769-9224

Clearing House Ltd.
6605 Hollywood Blvd.
Suite 200
Hollywood, CA 90028
Phone: (213) 469-3186
Fax: (213) 895-4699

The Content Company
171 East 74th Street
2nd Floor
New York, NY 10021
Phone: (212) 772-7363
Fax: (212) 772-7393

Vicki Grimsland
4038-A Lincoln Avenue
Culver City, CA 90232
Phone: (310) 559-2921

Total Clearance
(Jill Arofs)
P.O. Box 836
Mill Valley, CA 94942
Phone: (415) 445-5800

2. Copyright Search Firms

Government Liaison Services
3030 Clarendon Blvd., Suite 209
Arlington, VA 22201
Phone: (800) 642-6564
Fax: (703) 524-8200

Prentice Hall Legal & Financial Services
500 Central Avenue
Albany, NY 12206-2290
Phone: (800) 833-9848
       (518) 458-8111
Fax: (518) 459-2559

Thomson & Thomson Copyright Research Group
1750 K. Street N.W., Suite 200
Washington, DC 20006
Phone: (202) 835-0240
       (800) 356-8630
Fax: (202) 728-0744
     (800) 822-8823

U.S. Copyright Office
Library of Congress
Washington, DC 20559
Phone: (202) 287-8700

XL Corporate Services
ATTN: Mark Moel, Esq.
62 White Street
New York, NY 10013
Phone: (800) 221-2972
Phone: (212) 431-1441

3. Trademark Search Firms

Coresearch
16 West 22nd Street
8th Floor
New York, NY 10010
Phone: (800) 732-7241
　　　　(212) 627-0330
Fax: (800) 233-2986

Government Liaison Services
3030 Clarendon Blvd., Suite 209
Arlington, VA 22201
Phone: (800) 642-6564
　　　　(703) 524-8200
Fax: (703) 525-8451

NuPatco, Ltd.
44 Abbett Avunue
Morristown, NJ 07960
Phone: (800) 221-6275
　　　　(201) 326-1962
Fax: (201) 326-1908

Prentice Hall Legal & Financial Services
500 Central Avenue
Albany, NY 12206-2290
Phone: (800) 833-9848
　　　　(518) 458-8111
Fax: (518)459-2959

Thomson & Thomson
500 Victory Road
North Quincy, MA 02171
Phone: (800) 692-8833
　　　　(617) 479-1600
Fax: (617) 786-8273

4. Music Licensing Organizations

American Society of Composers, Authors
& Publishers (ASCAP)

Chicago Office:
Phone: (312) 527-9775
Fax: (312) 527-9774

Los Angeles Office:
Phone: (213) 466-7681
Fax: (213) 466-6677

Nashville Office:
Phone: (615) 742-5000
Fax: (615) 327-0314

New York Office:
1 Lincoln Plaza
New York, NY 10023
Phone: (212) 595-3050
　　　　　(212) 724-9024

The American Mechanical Rights Association
333 S. Tamiami Trail
Suite 295
Venice, FL 34285
Phone: (813) 488-9695
Fax: (813) 488-7259

Broadcast Music, Inc. (BMI)
Hollywood Office:
(Song indexing)
Phone: (213) 659-9109

New York Office:
(Headquarters and eastern U.S. licensing)
320 W. 57th Street
New York, NY 10019
Phone: (212) 586-2000
       (800) 326-4264

Phoenix Office:
(Western U.S. licensing)
410 North 44th Street
New York, NY 10019
Phone: (800) 326-4264

Society of European Stage Authors &
Composers (SESAC)
Nashville Office:
Phone:(615) 320-0055

New York Office:
421 West 54th Street
New York, NY 10019
Phone:(212) 586-3450
Fax:(212) 397-4682

Copyright Management, Inc.
1102 17th Avenue South
Suite 400
Nashville, TN 37212
Phone: (615) 327-1517
Fax: (615) 321-0652

National Music Publishers Association, Inc.
The Harry Fox Agency, Inc.
711 Third Avenue
8th Floor
New York, NY 10017
Phone: (212) 370-5330

Publishers Licensing Corp.
P.O. Box 5807
Englewood, NJ 07631
Phone: (212) 319-4000
Fax: (212) 753-4530

CHAPTER 37

Glossary

Adaptation Right. The adaptation right refers to the exclusive right granted to the owner of a copyright to prepare derivative works of the work in which he or she owns the copyright. 17 U.S.C. § 106(2). (See chapter 3, section 4.2.) See also Derivative Works.

AF of M. See American Federation of Musicians.

AFTRA. See American Federation of Television and Radio Artists.

AGAC. See American Guild of Authors and Composers.

American Federation of Musicians (AF of M). This is a union for musicians, leaders, contractors, copyists, orchestrators, and arrangers of instrumental music. (See chapter 21, section 6.)

American Federation of Television and Radio Artists (AFTRA). This is a union that represents actors and actresses, narrators, dancers, extras, recording artists, announcers, and news anchors. It currently has about 75,000 members and represents four major groups: television entertainment, commercials (television and radio), broadcast and news, and sound recording. (See chapter 21, section 5.)

American Guild of Authors and Composers. This is an organization of composers of music and lyrics, but is not a union for collective bargaining purposes.

American Society of Composers, Authors and Publishers (ASCAP). This is a performing rights society representing numerous composers, lyricists, and music publishers in the licensing of small performing rights on a nonexclusive basis. (See chapter 17, section 4.)

Assign, Assignment. An assignment is the transfer or sale of property or of rights granted by a contract. For example, if a user licenses the right to use content from the copyright owner, and then transfers his or her right to use the content (granted in the license agreement) to another person, he or she will have "assigned" the license agreement.

Audiovisual Works. Audiovisual works are works that consist of a series of related images that are intrinsically intended to be shown by the use of machines or devices such as projectors, viewers, or electronic equipment, together with accompanying sounds, if any, regardless of the nature of the material objects, such as films or tapes, in which the works are embodied. 17 U.S.C. § 101.

Best Published Edition. The best edition of a work is the edition, published in the United States at any time before the date of deposit, that the Library of Congress determines to be the most suitable for its purposes. 17 U.S.C. § 101.

BMI. See Broadcast Music, Inc.

Broadcast Music, Inc. (BMI). This is a performing rights society similar to ASCAP. It represents numerous composers, lyricists, and music publishers in the licensing of small performing rights to musical works on a nonexclusive basis. (See chapter 17, section 4.)

Buyout. A buyout license is simply a "paid-up" license, under which you are granted the right to use content for a fixed fee, usually paid up front. A buyout license is to be distinguished from a license for royalties to be paid based on sales of a product incorporating the content.

CD-ROM. Acronym for "Compact Disc Read-Only Memory."

C.F.R. See Code of Federal Regulations.

Cir. This is an abbreviation for "Circuit" and refers to the United States Circuit Courts of Appeal. At present there are twelve federal appeals courts. Eleven of them cover geographical areas and the twelfth, the Federal Circuit, hears appeals in patent, trademark, and certain other subject matter areas.

Code of Federal Regulations. This is a compilation of all of the regulations issued by the administrative agencies of the federal government.

Collective Work. A collective work is a work, such as a periodical issue, anthology, or encyclopedia, in which a number of contributions, constituting separate and interdependent works in themselves, are assembled into a collective whole. 17 U.S.C. § 101. (See chapter 23, section 2.2.)

Commission on New Technological Uses of Copyrighted Works. This is a commission that was established by Congress on December 31, 1974, to analyze the impact of the computer on copyrighted works. This commission, which is generally referred to as "CONTU," collected data and held hearings over a period of three years. On July 31, 1978, it issued its final report titled, "Final report of the National Commission on New Technological Uses of Copyrighted Works, 1978." In this report CONTU recommended amendments to the Copyright Act designed to deal with the issues raised by software. CONTU's recommendations were enacted with minor modifications in the Computer Software Copyright Act of 1980.

Common Law. Common law is the law established through the decisions of our courts. It is to be distinguished from statutory laws enacted by the Congress or state legislatures.

Compendium II. See Compendium of Copyright Office Practices.

Compendium of Copyright Office Practices. The Compendium of Copyright Office Practices is a manual intended primarily for use by the staff of the Copyright Office as a general guide to its examining practices and operations. It is amended from time to time by the Copyright Office to reflect changes in practice. The compendium currently in effect was released in early 1985 and is known as *Compendium II.*

Compilation. A compilation is a work formed by the collection and assembling of preexisting materials or of data that are selected, coordinated, or arranged in such a way that the resulting work as a whole constitutes an original work of authorship. The term "compilation" includes collective works. 17 U.S.C. § 101. (See chapter 23, section 2.2.)

Compulsory License. A compulsory license is a license to make and distribute phonorecords of nondramatic musical works that anyone is entitled to, as a matter of right under the Copyright Act when phonorecords of the nondramatic musical work have been distributed to the public in the United States under the authority of the copyright owner. 17 U.S.C. § 115.

Computer Program. Under the Copyright Act a computer program is defined as "a set of statements or instructions to be used directly or indirectly in a computer in order to bring about a certain result." 17 U.S.C. § 101.

Confidentiality Agreement. This is an agreement that secret information disclosed by its owner to an individual or organization will be kept confidential and not disclosed to anyone else. This agreement is a binding contract that places the person to whom the information has been disclosed under a legal obligation not to use the information in a manner not authorized by its owner, and not to disclose the information to anyone else.

Consequential Damages. Consequential damages are losses that do not flow directly and immediately from the breach of contract or tortious act of another party, but only from the consequences of the act. They are also referred to as indirect damages. The loss of an expectancy of income, such as a loss of potential future profits, is usually considered to be consequential damages.

Content. The term "content" is used to refer to the various types of data that can be displayed by a computer, such as text, sound, images, photographs, and motion pictures. Content should be contrasted with software, which is the set of computer programs used to make the content available to the user.

CONTU. See Commission on New Technological Uses of Copyrighted Works.

Copy. A copy, as that term is used in the Copyright Act, is any material object, other than phonorecords, in which a work is fixed by any method now known or later developed, and from which the work can be perceived, reproduced, or otherwise communicated, either directly or with the aid of a machine or device. 17 U.S.C. § 101. See also Phonorecord.

Copyright. Copyright is the exclusive right granted "to authors" under the U.S. Copyright Act to copy, adapt, distribute, publicly perform, and publicly display their works of authorship, such as literary works, databases, musical works, sound recordings, photographs, and other still images, and motion pictures and other audiovisual works. Copyright is further explained in chapter 3.

Copyright Act of 1909. The Copyright Act of 1909 was the statute that governed copyright protection for works created between 1909 and December 31, 1977. On January 1, 1978, the Copyright Act of 1909 was superseded by the provisions of the current Copyright Act, known as the Copyright Act of 1976.

Copyright Act of 1976. The Copyright Act of 1976 is the current statute governing copyright protection for works of authorship. It became effective on January 1, 1978, and can be found at 17 U.S.C. § 101 et seq.

Creation. A copyrightable work is "created" when it is fixed in a copy or phonorecord for the first time; where a work is prepared over a period of time, the portion of it that has been fixed at any particular time constitutes the work as of that time, and where the work has been prepared in different versions, each version constitutes a separate work. 17 U.S.C. § 101.

D. This is an abbreviation for "District" in the citation of a federal court case. It is used to identify the federal trial court in a particular state in which the decision was rendered. If there is more than one federal district court in the state, each district is identified separately, such as Northern District (N.D.), Southern District (S.D.), Central District (C.D.), and so forth. For example, the federal trial court in Chicago is known as the United States District Court for the Northern District of Illinois, abbreviated "N.D. Ill."

Damages. Damages are any loss suffered by a person as the result of a breach of contract or tortious act committed by another person. Such losses can include out-of-pocket expenses, lost profits, lost time, injury to goodwill, and a host of other types of injuries that individuals and business entities may suffer.

Defamation. Any communication that is false and injurious to the reputation of another. Defamation can take two forms: (1) libel, which is written and visual defamation, and (2) slander, which is oral and aural defamation. (See chapter 7.)

Defendant. The defendant is the individual or business entity being sued in a lawsuit.

Derivative Work. As defined in the Copyright Act, "a derivative work is a work based upon one or more preexisting works, such as a translation, musical arrangement, dramatization, fictionalization, motion picture version, sound recording, art reproduction, abridgment, condensation, or any other form in which a work may be recast, transformed, or adapted. A work consisting of editorial revisions, annotations, elaborations, or other modifications which, as a whole, represent an original work of authorship is a derivative work." 17 U.S.C. § 101. For example, a movie based on a book is a derivative work of the book, a french translation of an English novel is a derivative work, and a sound recording of a copyrightable musical work is a derivative work. (See chapter 3, section 4.2.)

Direct Damages. Direct damages are the damages that arise naturally or ordinarily (that is, as a direct result) of a breach of contract or tortious act of another person. Direct damages should be distinguished from consequential (or indirect) damages, which refer to losses that do not flow directly from the act of another, but only from the consequences of such an act, such as the more speculative loss of business, and from punitive damages that are not a measure of any damages, but more in the nature of a penalty intended to punish the wrongdoer.

Directors Guild of America (DGA). This is a union representing movie and television directors and related persons for collective bargaining purposes. (See chapter 21, section 21-3.)

Display. To "display" a work means to show a copy of it, either directly or by means of a film, slide, television image, or any other device or process or, in the case of a motion picture or audiovisual work, to show individual images nonsequentially. 17 U.S.C. § 101.

Distribution Right. The term "distribution right" refers to the exclusive right granted to the owner of a copyright to distribute copies of his or her copyrighted work publicly by sale, rental, lease, or lending. 17 U.S.C. § 106(3). (See chapter 3, section 4.3.)

Extrinsic Properties. Extrinsic properties are elements of a motion picture or television program that are independently copyrightable because they were created independently of the motion picture or television program, such as a book on which a movie is based, an animated cartoon character depicted in a movie, preexisting music incorporated within a motion picture, preexisting film clips included in a motion picture, and so forth. (See chapter 20, section 3.)

F. This is an abbreviation for *Federal Reporter*, a series of books containing copies of the decisions of the Federal Courts of Appeals from the years 1800 to 1924. The *Federal Reporter* series consists of three hundred volumes and is published by West Publishing Company.

F.2d. This is an abbreviation for *"Federal Reporter 2d Series,"* which is a continuation of the *Federal Reporter*. It contains decisions from all of the Federal Courts of Appeals from 1924 through 1993. The F.2d. series of *Federal Reporters* consists of 1,000 volumes and is published by West Publishing Company.

F.3d. This is the abbreviation for *"Federal Reporter 3d Series,"* which is a continuation of the *Federal Reporter 2d Series*. It contains decisions from all of the Federal Courts of Appeals from 1993 through the present. It is also published by West Publishing Company.

F. Supp. This is an abbreviation for *"Federal Supplement,"* a series of books containing the decisions of the Federal District Courts (that is, the trial courts) from 1932 through the present. The F. Supp. series of *Federal Reporters* consists of over 800 volumes.

Federal Register. The *Federal Register* is a daily government publication that includes information regarding new and proposed regulations of the various federal agencies. It is used to solicit comments on any proposed regulations and to announce newly adopted regulations. Newly adopted regulations are subsequently printed in the Code of Federal Regulations.

First Serial Rights. These are rights granted in connection with books; it refers to the right to print an extract from a book in a newspaper or magazine prior to its initial publication in book form.

Fixed. A work is "fixed" in a tangible medium of expression when its embodiment in a copy or phonorecord, by or under the authority of the author, is sufficiently permanent or stable to permit it to be perceived, reproduced, or otherwise communicated for a period of more than transitory duration. A work consisting of sounds, images, or both, that are being transmitted, is "fixed" for purposes of the Copyright Act title if a fixation of the work is being made simultaneously with its transmission. 17 U.S.C. § 101.

The Harry Fox Agency. The Harry Fox Agency represents music publishers in the licensing of mechanical reproduction rights. It also grants licenses for the use of music in films on behalf of many music publishers. In addition to issuing mechanical licenses, it also grants licenses for the synchronization of music with motion pictures, television programs, and other audiovisual works, licenses for the creation of electrical transcriptions, and licenses for the use of music and commercial advertising. It also engages in the auditing of books and records of the licensees, such as record companies, using music under licenses issued by the agency. The Harry Fox Agency is a wholly owned subsidiary of the National Music Publishers Association. (See chapter 17, section 4.)

Grand (or Dramatic) Performing Rights. Grand rights (with respect to music) are rights to perform a musical composition in connection with telling a story (that is, in connection with a dramatic work).

H.R. Rep. No. 94-1476. This refers to the U.S. House of Representative's *Report on the Copyright Act of 1976*, dated September 3, 1976. This document is, in essence, the legislative history of the current Copyright Act, and is frequently referred to by courts seeking to interpret the various provisions of the Copyright Act.

Indemnification. An indemnification agreement is an undertaking by one party to reimburse a second party for payments the second party is required to make to a third party. An insurance policy is a classic example of an indemnity agreement. The indemnity clause typically found in a license agreement obligates the copyright owner to indemnify the licensee for any loss or expense incurred by the licensee as a result of a lawsuit filed by a third party against the licensee over ownership of the content.

Indirect Damages. See Consequential Damages.

Infringement. The concept of infringement arises in patent, copyright, or trademark law. When someone copies software without permission of the copyright or patent owner, or uses a trademark without the permission of the trademark owner, he or she has committed an act of infringement, that is, he or she has infringed the rights of the copyright, patent, and/or trademark owner.

Injunction. An injunction is a court order directing a party to a lawsuit to do or refrain from doing something.

Intangible Asset. An intangible asset is a property right having no physical substance such as patent rights, copyrights, trademark rights, and trade secret rights.

Intrinsic Properties. Intrinsic properties are elements that make up a motion picture or television program that were created specifically for the production of the movie or television program under a work-for-hire contract. There is typically no separate copyright in the intrinsic properties of a movie or television program—they are included within the scope of the copyright in the movie or television program itself. (See chapter 20, section 3.)

Joint Work. A "joint work" is a work prepared by two or more authors with the intention that their contributions be merged into inseparable or interdependent parts of a unitary whole. 17 U.S.C. § 101. (See chapter 23, section 2.1.)

Libel. See Defamation.

Licensee. The licensee is the party who receives the right to use the content, subject to the terms and conditions imposed by the licensor, in the license agreement. A licensee obtains no ownership rights in the copy of the content that he or she receives.

Licensor. The licensor is the party who grants to another the right to possess and use the content.

Limited Rights. A license for the use of copyrightable content that grants "limited rights" typically restricts use of the content to a particular multimedia product, media, distribution channel, territory, market, term, and so forth. (See chapter 13, section 2.2.)

Literary Works. "Literary works" are works, other than audiovisual works, expressed in words, numbers, or other verbal or numerical symbols or indicia, regardless of the nature of the material objects, such as books, periodicals, manuscripts, phonorecords, film, tapes, disks, or cards, in which they are embodied. 17 U.S.C. § 101.

Mechanical License. A mechanical license is the form of permission that authorizes one to make mechanical reproductions of a musical composition, that are not accompanied by a motion picture or other audiovisual work, and that are made for the purpose of distributing them to the public for private use. (See chapter 17, section 2.1.)

Merchandise Rights. Merchandise rights refer to the rights to exploit the title and/or character of a work in other forms, such as toys, games, T-shirts, posters, and so forth.

Misappropriation. Misappropriation refers to the theft or other improper use or disclosure of the trade secrets of one party by another.

Moral Rights. Moral rights are a form of copyright rights granted to the author. These generally include the right to prevent distortion, mutilation or destruction of the work (right of integrity); the right to attribution and the right against misattribution, and to prevent others from using the work or the author's name in a way as to prejudice the author's professional standing (right of attribution); the right to control the work's publication (right of disclosure); and the right to withdraw, modify, or disavow a work after it has been published (right of withdrawal). (See section 3-4.6.)

Morphing. Morphing (short for metamorphosis) is a process that involves a transition of two documents (such as pictures) into a third; a dynamic blending of two still images creating a sequence of in-between images that, when played back rapidly, metamorphosis the first image into the last.

Musical Works. Musical works are copyrightable works of authorship that typically consists of a musical composition (that is, the notes) and, in some cases, corresponding lyrics.

National Commission on New Technological Uses of Copyrighted Works. See Commission on New Technological Uses of Copyrighted Works.

National Music Publishers Association, Inc. (NMPA). The NMPA is a trade association that represents over 400 of the leading U.S. music publishers. The Harry Fox Agency is a wholly owned subsidiary of NMPA.

NMPA. See National Music Publishers Association, Inc.

Nondisclosure Agreement. See Confidentiality Agreement.

Patent. A patent is a grant of exclusive rights issued by the U.S. Patent Office that gives an inventor a seventeen-year monopoly on the right to "practice" or make, use, and sell his or her invention.

Performing Rights Society. This is an association or corporation that licenses the public performance of nondramatic musical works on behalf of the copyright owners, such as the American Society of Composers, Authors and Publishers, Broadcast Music, Inc., and SESAC, Inc. 17 U.S.C. §116(e)(3).

Permanent Injunction. An injunction issued by the court at the conclusion of a lawsuit. See Injunction and Preliminary Injunction.

Phonorecord. Phonorecords are material objects in which sounds, other than those accompanying a motion picture or other audiovisual work, are fixed by any method now known or later developed, and from which the sounds can be perceived, reproduced, or otherwise communicated, either directly or with the aid of a machine or device. 17 U.S.C. § 101. Thus, a CD is a phonorecord.

Plaintiff. The plaintiff is the person who brings suit against someone, the defendant, whom the plaintiff believes is responsible for doing him or her harm.

Preliminary Injunction. A preliminary injunction is a temporary injunction entered at the beginning or during the course of a lawsuit that lasts only until a trial is held and a decision reached. Its purpose is to preserve the status quo pending the conclusion of the lawsuit. The preliminary injunction will either be terminated or converted into a permanent injunction after the trial is over.

Prima Facie. Evidence introduced during the trial of a lawsuit that, if unrebutted, would entitle the person having the burden of proof to the relief he or she is seeking. Stated another way, it is enough evidence to require the opponent to introduce evidence in his or her defense or risk losing the case.

Proprietary Rights. The term "proprietary rights," as used in this book, refers to the rights that the owner of content or a multimedia title has in the content or a multimedia title, such as the copyright, trade secret, and patent rights (if applicable) and so forth. These are rights (such as the right to copy or the right to license) that no one else possesses unless they are granted by the owner of the original proprietary rights.

Public Display Right. The term "public display right" refers to the exclusive right granted to the owner of a copyright to display (and to authorize others to display) his or her work publicly. 17 U.S.C. § 106(5).

Public Performance Right. The term "public performance right" refers to the exclusive right granted to the owner of a copyright to perform (and to authorize others to perform) his or her work publicly. 17 U.S.C. § 106(4).

Published (Publication). Publication, under the Copyright Act, is the distribution of copies of software to the public by sale or other transfer of ownership, or by rental, lease, or lending. The offering to distribute copies to a group of persons for purposes of further distribution, public performance, or public display also constitutes publication. A public performance or display of a work does not of itself constitute publication. 17 U.S.C. § 101.

Reproduction Right. The term "reproduction right" refers to the exclusive right granted to the owner of a copyright to make (and authorize others to make) copies of his or her work. 17 U.S.C. § 106(1).

Residuals. See "Reuse Fees."

Reuse Fees. Reuse fees are additional payments owed to creative contributors to a work (such as a motion picture) when the work is released in a market other than the market for which it was originally created. Reuse fees are often required pursuant to the terms of the contracts between the parties involved. For example, pursuant to the Writers Guild of America Basic Agreement, writers may be entitled to reuse fees when motion pictures are broadcast on television or made available in other markets, such as by videocassette or cable television. Similarly, the Directors Guild of America Basic Agreement includes provisions for the payment of reuse fees to directors for reruns and foreign broadcast of television films, and to directors of motion pictures produced mainly for pay television and the videocassette market. These fees are also referred to as "new use fees," "supplemental market fees," or "residuals."

SAG. See Screen Actors Guild.

Sampling. Sampling is the conversion of analog sound waves into a digital code. The digital code that describes the sampled music can then be reused, manipulated, or combined with other digitized or recorded sounds using a machine with digital dataprocessing capabilities, such as a computerized synthesizer. Sampling also refers to the process of copying a portion of a sound recording in a digital form for subsequent editing and/or incorporation in a new work.

Scan. Scanning is the process by which an image (such as a photograph, drawing, or text) is digitized—that is, converted into a digital form. The resulting digital image is also called a scan.

Screen Actors Guild (SAG). This is a union representing performers in movie and television productions for collective bargaining purposes. (See chapter 21, section 4.)

Screenplay. A screenplay refers to the script upon which a motion picture is based. See also Teleplay.

Second Serial Rights. This refers to the right to print a portion of a book in a newspaper or magazine after the book has been published in hardcover or softcover form.

Secondary Meaning. This is a trademark term that refers to a mark that is initially merely descriptive but that over time acquires a meaning over and above the meaning ordinarily ascribed to it. See chapter 4, section 4-12.

Sequel Rights. A grant of the right to make sequels or of sequel rights is the right to make "subsequent stories employing the same characters in different plots or sequences." *Landon v. Twentieth Century-Fox Film Corp.*, 384 F. Supp. 450, 456 (S.D.N.Y. 1974).

SESAC. This is a performing rights society that represents several composers, lyricists, and music publishers in the licensing of small performing rights on a non-exclusive basis.

Slander. See Defamation.

Software. See Computer Program.

Sound Recordings. Sound recordings are works that result from the fixation of a series of musical, spoken, or other sounds, regardless of the nature of the physical medium, such as disks or tapes, in which they are embodied. 17 U.S.C. § 101. However, the soundtrack of a motion picture is not considered a sound recording, but is rather considered to be part of the copyright in the motion picture.

Special Damages. See Consequential Damages.

Statutory Damages. In situations where the plaintiff is unable to prove the actual damages that he or she sustained as a result of the wrongful acts of the defendant, some statutes allow a court to award damages in any event. One such statute is the Copyright Act, which provides that the plaintiff may recover between $500 and $100,000 for each copyrighted work infringed by the defendant, regardless of whether he or she is able to prove in court that he or she has actually been damaged. 17 U.S.C. § 504.

Synchronization License. A synchronization license is the form of permission that authorizes one to make mechanical reproductions of a musical composition, that are accompanied by a motion picture or other audiovisual work, for use in connection with a motion picture, theatrical performance, or television broadcast. (See chapter 17, section 2.2.)

Teleplay. A teleplay refers to the script upon which a television program is based. See also Screenplay.

Temporary Restraining Order. A temporary restraining order is an injunction issued by the court for a very short period of time (usually no more than ten days) in order to prevent some immediate harm from occurring before the court can have a hearing on a motion for a preliminary injunction. For example, if a defendant in a lawsuit is about to destroy the only copy of the source code for software over which the ownership was in dispute, a court might issue a temporary order prohibiting such destruction for ten (10) days until it had time to hold a hearing into the dispute.

Tort. A tort is a wrong for which the injured person has a right to recover damages under the common law. Examples include negligence, fraud, theft, and defamation.

Trademark. Any word, name, symbol, or device or any combination thereof adopted and used by a manufacturer or merchant to identify his or her goods and distinguish them from those manufactured or sold by others. 15 U.S.C. § 1127. (See chapter 4.)

Trade Secret. Any secret formula, pattern, device, or compilation of information which is used in one's business and which gives an advantage over competitors who do not know or use it is considered to be a trade secret. (See chapter 8.)

TRO. See Temporary Restraining Order.

U.C.C. See Uniform Commercial Code.

Uniform Commercial Code. The Uniform Commercial Code is a body of law governing the sale of goods, banking transactions, and security interests, among other things, which has been adopted (with minor variations) in all states except Louisiana. All sales of goods, such as the sale of computer hardware, are governed by the Uniform Commercial Code. It is unclear whether a content license agreement is also covered by the Uniform Commercial Code, since it is not clear that such a license involves a sale of goods.

Unlimited Rights. An unlimited rights license to use copyrightable content imposes no limits on the scope of the rights granted to the multimedia developer — that is, the multimedia developer can use the content so licensed without any restrictions as to media, distribution, territory, hardware or software platform, and so forth. (See chapter 13, section 2.2.)

U.S.C. This is an abbreviation for United States Code. This is a codification of all laws passed by the federal government. References to these laws are usually expressed in the format as x U.S.C. y, where "x" refers to the "title" or chapter of the statute and "y" refers to the section of the statute. The Copyright Act, for example, begins at 17 U.S.C. § 101.

Unpublished. This is a copyright term that indicates that a work (such as content or a multimedia title) has not yet been "published" as that term is defined in the copyright law.

U.S.P.Q. This is an abbreviation for *United States Patent Quarterly*, a series of volumes of a reporter that contains copies of all patent cases decided by the U.S. courts.

Videogram License. A videogram license is the form of permission that authorizes one to make mechanical reproductions of a musical composition, that are accompanied by a motion picture or other audiovisual work, and that may be distributed on videocassette, optical laser disk, or other home video device for distribution into the home video market. (See chapter 17, section 2.3.)

WGA. See Writers Guild of America.

Work-for-Hire. A work-for-hire is a copyrightable work of authorship that is either (1) a work prepared by an employee within the scope of his or her employment; or (2) a work specially ordered or commissioned for use as a contribution to a collective work, as part of a motion picture or other audiovisual work, as a translation, as a supplementary work, as a compilation, as an instructional text, as a test, as answer material for a test, or as an atlas, if the parties expressly agree in a written instrument signed by them that the work shall be considered a work-for-hire. See 17 U.S.C. § 101. (See chapter 23, section 1.2.)

Writers Guild of America (WGA). This is a union representing writers of screenplays and teleplays for collective bargaining purposes. (See chapter 21, section 2.)

INDEX

A

Access technology. *See* Software

Accounting, 152, 153

Adaptation right, 52-53, 234-236, 605

AF of M. *See* American Federation of Musicians

AFTRA. *See* American Federation of Television and Radio Artists

AGAC (American Guild of Authors and Composers), 605

Agreement samples
  assignment, 488
  employee, 547-551
  film clip license, 513-517
  multimedia CD-ROM product license, 584-586
  multimedia product development, 532-542
  multimedia product replication and distribution, 570-583
  music license, 499-503
  photograph license, 510-512
  release, 523
  sound recording license, 504-509
  text license, 495-498
  third-party confidentiality, 557-558
  work-for-hire consultant, 552-556

American Federation of Musicians
  address of, 593
  AF of M Phonograph Record Labor Agreement, 358-359
  licensing content created by members of, 359-360

membership of, 358
  using members to develop content, 358-359

American Federation of Television and Radio Artists
  1994 Interactive Media Agreement, 345
  addresses of
    Chicago office, 593
    Hollywood office, 593
    Nashville office, 593
    New York office, 594
  licensing content created by members of, 357-358
  membership, 355-356
  National Code of Fair Practice for Network Television Broadcasting, 348
  using members to develop content, 356-357

American Graffiti, 242-243

American Guild of Authors and Composers, 605

American Mechanical Rights Association, 602

American Society of Composers, Authors, and Publishers, 602

American Society of Journalists & Authors, 591

American Society of Media Photographers, 596

ASCAP (American Society of Composers, Authors, and Publishers), 602

Assignments
  agreement checklist, 485-487

619